AMERICA IN THE FRENCH IMAGINARY, 1789–1914

Music in Society and Culture

ISSN 2047-2773

Series Editors
VANESSA AGNEW, KATHARINE ELLIS,
JONATHAN GLIXON & DAVID GRAMIT

Consulting Editor
TIM BLANNING

This series brings history and musicology together in ways that will embed social and cultural questions into the very fabric of music-history writing. *Music in Society and Culture* approaches music not as a discipline, but as a subject that can be discussed in myriad ways. Those ways are cross-disciplinary, requiring a mastery of more than one mode of enquiry. This series therefore invites research on art and popular music in the Western tradition and in cross-cultural encounters involving Western music, from the early modern period to the twenty-first century. Books in the series will demonstrate how music operates within a particular historical, social, political or institutional context; how and why society and its constituent groups choose their music; how historical, cultural and musical change interrelate; and how, for whom and why music's value undergoes critical reassessment.

Proposals or queries should be sent in the first instance to the series editors or Boydell & Brewer at the addresses shown below.

Professor Vanessa Agnew, University of Duisburg-Essen,
Department of Anglophone Studies, R12 S04 H,
Universitätsstr. 12, 45141 Essen, Germany
email: vanessa.agnew@uni-due.de

Professor Katharine Ellis, Faculty of Music, University of Cambridge,
11 West Road, Cambridge, CB3 9DP, UK
email: kje32@cam.ac.uk

Professor Jonathan Glixon, School of Music, 105 Fine Arts Building,
University of Kentucky, Lexington, KY 40506-0022, USA
email: jonathan.glixon@uky.edu

Professor David Gramit, Department of Music, University of Alberta,
3–82 Fine Arts Building, Edmonton, Alberta, T6G 2C9, Canada
email: dgramit@ualberta.ca

Boydell & Brewer, PO Box 9, Woodbridge, Suffolk, IP12 3DF, UK
email: editorial@boydell.co.uk

Previously published titles in the series are listed at the back of this volume.

AMERICA IN THE FRENCH IMAGINARY, 1789–1914

MUSIC, REVOLUTION AND RACE

Edited by
*Diana R. Hallman and
César A. Leal*

THE BOYDELL PRESS

© Contributors 2022

All Rights Reserved. Except as permitted under current legislation
no part of this work may be photocopied, stored in a retrieval system,
published, performed in public, adapted, broadcast,
transmitted, recorded or reproduced in any form or by any means,
without the prior permission of the copyright owner

First published 2022
The Boydell Press, Woodbridge

ISBN 978-1-78327-700-1

The Boydell Press is an imprint of Boydell & Brewer Ltd
PO Box 9, Woodbridge, Suffolk IP12 3DF, UK
and of Boydell & Brewer Inc.
668 Mt. Hope Avenue, Rochester NY 14620-2731, USA
website: www.boydellandbrewer.com

The publisher has no responsibility for the continued existence or accuracy of
URLs for external or third-party internet websites referred to in this book, and
does not guarantee that any content on such websites is, or will remain, accurate
or appropriate

A CIP record for this title is available
from the British Library

This publication is printed on acid-free paper

In memory of
William Stewart Hallman
and
Alfonso Leal

Contents

List of Illustrations	ix
List of Music Examples	xiii
List of Abbreviations	xv
Editorial Notes	xvii
List of Contributors	xix
Acknowledgements	xxiii
Preface	xxv
Introduction	1

PART I. AMERICAN *LIBERTÉ, SAUVAGERIE* AND *ESCLAVAGE*

1 Between Amérique and Colonial France: Revolutionary Tales of *liberté* and *esclavage*   15

   Diana R. Hallman

2 Justamant's *Le Bossu* and Depictions of Indigenous Americans in Nineteenth-Century French Ballet   50

   Marian Smith, Sarah Gutsche-Miller and Helena Kopchick Spencer

3 Louisiana Imagined: Gender, Race and Slavery in *Le Planteur* (1839)   100

   Helena Kopchick Spencer

PART II. MYTHS OF AMERICA AND INTERSECTING IDENTITIES

4 'Brise du Sud': American Identity and War in the Popular Sheet Music of Francophone New Orleans   149

   Charlotte Bentley

viii   *Contents*

5 'The Most Seductive Creole Indolence': Louis Moreau Gottschalk in
   the French Press   172

   Laura Moore Pruett

6 Symphonies from the New World: The Myths and Realities of
   American Orchestral Music in France   196

   Douglas W. Shadle

PART III. SOUNDSCAPES AND SONIC FANTASIES

7 Historical Acoustemology in the French Romantic Travelogue:
   Chateaubriand's Sonic Imagining of the New World   217

   Ruth E. Rosenberg

8 *La Liberté éclairant le monde*: Transatlantic Soundscapes for the
   Statue of Liberty   233

   Annegret Fauser

PART IV. AMERICA, COMMODIFICATION AND RACE AT THE
FIN DE SIÈCLE

9 Buffalo Bill and the Sound of America during the 1889 World's Fair   265

   Mark A. Pottinger

10 Cakewalking in Paris: New Representations and Contexts of African
   American Culture   296

   César A. Leal

Bibliography   329

Index   359

Illustrations

Figures

1.1 Georges Biassou. Dubroca and Juan López Cancelada, *Vida de J.J. Dessalines, Gefe de los negroes de Santo Domingo* (Mexico City: M. de Zúñiga y Ontiveros, 1806).   26

1.2 Unidentified artist, *Toussaint Louverture, Chef des noirs insurgés de Saint Domingue* ('Commander of the Black Insurgents of Saint-Domingue'), 1796–9.   27

1.3 Virginie giving a drink of water to the slave Zabi, in Kreutzer, *Paul et Virginie* (opéra comique), Act I Scene 2, costume of Mlle Alexandrine Saint-Aubin: 'Drink, *bon Noir*, drink. If that doesn't quench your thirst enough, I'll make a second trip.' Paris: Martinet, 1810.   43

2.1 Henri Justamant, 'Divertissements de *Juagarita* [sic], réglés par Mr H. Justamant, représentés pour la première fois à Lyon sur le Grand Théâtre 1856 à 1857, direction de Mr Halanzier', in Henri Justamant, *Divertissements d'opéras comiques avec coryphées et dames du corps de ballet*, p. 15.   61

2.2 Paul Lormier, costume design for an 'Américaine' in *Ozaï* (1847).   64

2.3 Paul Lormier, costume design for a 'femme sauvage' in *Les Mohicans* (1837).   65

2.4 Auguste Trichon, engraving of the principal tableaux from *Le Tour du monde en 80 jours* (1874).   70

2.5 'Dame du corps de ballet / et secondes danseuses / sauvage / Jupe et corsage en tarlatanne blanche / Suissesse argent, garnie au bas de plumes / Coiffure tombante de chaque côté en plumes/ (Les plumes sont rouges et blanches) / Collier en perles de couleur / Maillot et soulier couleur chair'. Publicity photograph and costume description in Justamant, 'Ballet du *Bossu*', in *Divertissements de La Tour de Nesle et du Bossu* (1867), p. 65.   84

x   *Illustrations*

2.6   'Mademoiselle Rozé – sauvage / Jupe et corsage en satin blanc / Cinture et garnitures en broderie argent / Coiffure tombante de chaque côté en plumes blanches / Collier et bracelets en perles blanches / Maillot et soulier couleur chair'. Publicity photograph and costume description in Justamant, 'Ballet du *Bossu*', in *Divertissements de La Tour de Nesle et du Bossu* (1867), p. 66.   85

2.7   'Monsieur Bertoto. Maillot et pentalon [*sic*] couleur bronze et tatoués / pentalon ringrave l'arge couleur maron / garniture en plumes de toutes couleurs'. Publicity photograph and costume description in Justamant, 'Ballet du *Bossu*', in *Divertissements de La Tour de Nesle et du Bossu* (1867), p. 68.   87

2.8   Unidentified artist, French school, *Allegory of America* (early nineteenth century).   92

2.9   Henri Justamant, 'Pas de Diane, musique de Mr Calandini [sic], réglé par Justamant, dansé par Mlle Déléchaux, Girod, Wesmaël, quatre coryphées et huit dames du corps de ballet à Bruxelles (1862)', in *Grands pas composés par Mr H. Justamant representés à Marseille et Bruxelles*, p. 45.   93

2.10   Henri Justamant, 'Ballet du *Bossu*', in *Divertissements de La Tour de Nesle et du Bossu* (1867), p. 17, 'Entrée des Chasseresses', opening.   94

2.11   Paul Lormier, costume design for Carlotta Grisi as Diane *chasseresse* in *La Jolie Fille de Gand* (1842).   96

2.12   'Dame du corps de Ballet / et Coryphées / Chasseresses / Maillot couleur chair; jupe et écharpe en satin couleur cerise; Sainte Cécile argent ou or; cinture [*sic*] et galon au bas de la jupe or; coiffure plumes blanches et rouges montées sur diadème; collier et garnitures en dents d'animeaux'. Publicity photograph and costume description in Justamant, 'Ballet du *Bossu*', in *Divertissements de La Tour de Nesle et du Bossu* (1867), p. 67.   97

3.1   Jenny-Marguerite Colon. Lithograph portrait by Léon Noël. Paris: Lemercier, Benard & Co., 1837. Printed in *L'Artiste*, 14 (1837), 284.   123

3.2   Ad. Brebant, illustration used for the title page of the song 'La Créole. Chantée par Mr L^{id} Amat. Paroles de A. Bonsergent. Musique d'H^{re} Colin'. Paris: Guérin, [1840]. Estampes Scènes CréoleColin (1).   140

4.1   Cover of 'Le Réveil: Chanson patriotique' by Hubert Rolling and E. Berté-St-Ange. New Orleans: F. Charpaux, 1877.   168

4.2	Cover of 'Les Gardes Lafayette de la Nouvelle-Orléans!' by Jules Cartier and Fernand d'Héramberg. New Orleans: Henri Wehrmann, n.d. [1877].	169
5.1	L[ouis] M[oreau] Gottschalk, *Bamboula: Danse des Nègres, fantaisie pour piano*, cover and p. 1.	182
6.1	Louis Antoine Jullien, *The Fireman's Quadrille* (1854).	203
8.1	Albert Fénique, head of the Statue of Liberty, Exposition Universelle, Paris, 1878. Black-and-white photograph.	249
8.2	'Versailles. – Grande Cavalcade des cinq parties du monde, le dimanche, 17 mai', *L'Univers illustré*, 22 (1879), 312.	252
9.1	'Mammoth Edison Lamp', in *The Universal Exhibition of Paris: The United States of America, 1889*, p. 130. New York, London, and Paris: American Commission, 1889.	271
9.2	Cover page of the Wild West Company's French-language souvenir booklet *L'Ouest Sauvage de Buffalo Bill*. Paris: Parrot et Cie, 1889.	276
9.3	Buffalo Bill's Wild West Cowboy Band, 1887.	279
9.4	Front cover of 'My Gal is a High-Born Lady' by Barney Fagan. New York: M. Witmark & Sons, 1896.	281
9.5	Programme of the Wild West Show in Paris, inset, in Buffalo Bill (Col. W.-F. Cody), *L'Ouest Sauvage de Buffalo Bill: Récits américains, description illustrée et aperçus de faits historiques*. Paris: Parrot et Cie, 1889.	284
9.6	É. Ouvrard. 'Ainsi soit-il, Buffalo Bill!', p. 1. Paris: E. Benoit, 1889.	289
9.7	É. Ouvrard, 'Ainsi soit-il, Buffalo Bill!', cover page. Paris: E. Benoit, 1889.	294
10.1	*Nouveau Cirque: Le Cake-Walk* (1903), poster by Maurice Mahul (1879–1929).	301
10.2	Poster of *La Noce de Chocolat* (1900).	310
10.3	F. Volpatti, *Black and White: Américan Cake Walk*. Paris: E. Gaudet, 1903.	311
10.4	Louis Balleron, *Les Nègres blancs: Veritable Cakewalk*. Paris: Fatout & Girard, 1903.	313
10.5	Kerry Mills, *Whistling Rufus*. New York: F. A. Mills, 1899.	319
10.6	Kerry Mills, *Le Nègre siffleur/Whistling Rufus*. Paris: Enoch & Cie, 1899.	320

xii   *Illustrations*

10.7   Kerry Mills, *Rufus das Pfeifgigerl*. Berlin: C. M. Roehr, *c*.1900.   321

10.8   Roger de Beaumercy, *Cake Walk de salon*, cover, 'Introduction',
       and 'Promenade'. Paris: E. Gallet, 1903.   323

Tables

6.1   Programme of All-American Composer Concert, Trocadéro,
       Exposition Universelle, Paris, 12 July 1889, Frank Van der
       Stucken (conductor).   208

8.1   Programme, *Grande Solennité Musicale*, Palais Garnier, 25 April
       1876.   240

8.2   Programme, dedication ceremony of the Statue of Liberty,
       Bedloe Island, 28 October 1886.   261

9.1   Text and translation of 'Ainsi soit-il, Buffalo Bill!' by Éloi Ouvrard.   291

Full credit details are provided in the captions to the images in the text. The editors, contributors, and publisher are grateful to all the institutions and persons for permission to reproduce the materials in which they hold copyright. Every effort has been made to trace the copyright holders; apologies are offered for any omission, and the publisher will be pleased to add any necessary acknowledgement in subsequent editions.

Music Examples

1.1   Rodolphe Kreutzer, *Paul et Virginie* [orchestral score], Act I, Trio (Zabi, Paul, Virginie), pt I, bb. 46–61. Paris: auteur, n.d.   36

1.2   Rodolphe Kreutzer, *Paul et Virginie* [orchestral score], Act I, Trio (Zabi, Paul, Virginie), pt II, bb. 56–72. Paris: auteur, n.d.   38

3.1   Hippolyte Monpou, *Le Planteur*, Act I, No. 5: Finale, bb. 164–89 [piano-vocal score]. Paris: Richault, n.d. [1839].   117

3.2   Hippolyte Monpou, *Le Planteur*, Act I, No. 5: Finale, bb. 371–90 [piano-vocal score]. Paris: Richault, n.d. [1839].   120

3.3   Hippolyte Monpou, *Le Planteur*, Act I, No. 1: Introduction, bb. 1–35 [piano-vocal score]. Paris: Richault, n.d. [1839].   127

3.4   Hippolyte Monpou, *Le Planteur*, Act I, No. 1: Introduction, bb. 161–88 [piano-vocal score]. Paris: Richault, n.d. [1839].   136

3.5   Hippolyte Monpou, *Le Planteur*, Act II, No. 6: Chansonnette, Chœur des Femmes, bb. 98–112 [piano-vocal score]. Paris: Richault, n.d. [1839].   142

4.1   Excerpt from *The Hero of New Orleans: The Battle of the Memorable 8th of January 1815* by Philippe Laroque, p. 6. Philadelphia: G. Willig [1818].   155

4.2   Four-bar coda alluding to the *Marseillaise* in 'Brise du Sud' by Eugène Chassaignac. New Orleans: The Bronze Pen Press, 1864.   162

5.1   L[ouis] M[oreau] Gottschalk, *Bamboula: Danse des Nègres, fantaisie pour piano*, bb. 16–26. Paris: Bureau Central de Musique, n.d. [1849].   186

8.1   Charles Gounod, *La Liberté éclairant le monde*, text by Emile Guiard, bb. 51-64. Paris: Imp. Arouy, Fouquet, 1876.   242

9.1   Melody of 'My Gal is a High-Born Lady' by Barney Fagan, bb. 1–17. New York: M. Witmark & Sons, 1896.   282

9.2   Melody and basic harmonic movement of 'Ainsi soit-il, Buffalo Bill!' by Éloi Ouvrard, bb. 1–16. Paris: E. Benoit, 1889.   295

Abbreviations

c.	circa
ed. and eds	editor(s)
edn	edition
e.g.	*exempli gratia*; for example
et al.	*et alia*; and others
etc.	*et cetera*; and the rest
ex.	example
fig.	figure
fol. and fols.	folio(s)
i.e.	*id est*; that is
n. and nn.	note/s
n.d.	no date
No.	number
p. and pp.	page(s)
pt	part
repr.	reprinted
rev.	revised
[*sic*]	intentionally so written
St	saint
trans.	translated
vol. and vols	volume(s)

Editorial Notes

The editors of this volume have chosen to capitalise the racial labels and concepts of 'Black', 'White', 'Blackness', 'Whiteness', 'African American', 'Indigenous American', 'Native American', 'Indian', and 'Creole' to call attention to their usage as contested social-racial constructions, as well as to reflect current orthographical practices. (Exceptions will include their appearance in quotations without capitalisation.) In response to common French practice, racial terms such as 'nègre' or négresse' will not be capitalised unless they begin with upper-case letters in original texts or titles, or unless they refer to recognised archetypes. Most often, racialised French terms will be kept in the original language to avoid suggesting an equivalency between English and French terms and to avoid translations that are typically understood to be intensely offensive to English-speaking readers and communities of colour.

Contributors

Charlotte Bentley (Cambridge University, PhD, 2017) is Lecturer in Music at Newcastle University, having previously held fellowships at Emmanuel College, Cambridge and The Reid School of Music, University of Edinburgh. Her publications have appeared in *Cambridge Opera Journal* and *Journal of the Royal Musical Association*, as well as in the collections *Operatic Geographies: The Place of Opera and the Opera House* (2018), *Carmen Abroad: Bizet's Opera on the Global Stage* (2020), and *Italian Opera in Global and Transnational Perspective: Reimagining Italianità in the Long Nineteenth Century* (2022). Her monograph, *New Orleans and the Creation of Transatlantic Opera, 1819-1859*, will be published in 2022.

Annegret Fauser is the Cary C. Boshamer Distinguished Professor of Music, Harold J. Glass USAF Faculty Mentor/Graduate Fellow Distinguished Term Professor (2017–20), and Adjunct Professor of Women's and Gender Studies at the University of North Carolina at Chapel Hill. She is author of *Der Orchestergesang in Frankreich zwischen 1870 und 1920* (1994), *Musical Encounters at the 1889 Paris World's Fair* (2005), *Sounds of War: Music in the United States during World War II* (2013) – for which she received both the Music in American Culture Award of the American Musicological Society and an American Society of Composers, Authors and Publishers Deems Taylor Award – *The Politics of Musical Identity: Selected Writings* (2015), and *Aaron Copland's Appalachian Spring* (2017). Fauser was awarded the 2011 Edward J. Dent Medal of the Royal Musical Association and served as Editor-in-Chief of the *Journal of the American Musicological Society*, 2011–13.

Sarah Gutsche-Miller is Assistant Professor of Musicology at the University of Toronto in the Faculty of Music and Centre for Drama, Theatre, and Performance Studies. Her research on late nineteenth- and early twentieth-century dance, dance music, nationalism, and women in the performing arts has appeared in the journals *Dance Research, Dance Research Journal*, and *Journal of Musicology* and in several edited collections. She has published a monograph about ballet in French popular venues titled *Parisian Music-Hall Ballet, 1871–1913* (2015). Her research on nineteenth-century French ballet is supported by the Social Sciences and Humanities Research Council of Canada.

Diana R. Hallman, Professor, University Research Professor, and Coordinator of the Opera Research Alliance at the University Kentucky, is author of *Opera, Liberalism, and Antisemitism in Nineteenth-Century France: The Politics of Halévy's La Juive* (2002) and articles in *The Cambridge Companion to*

xx *Contributors*

Grand Opera (2003), *Music, Theater, and Cultural Transfer: Paris, 1830–1914* (2009), *Le Concours du Prix de Rome de la musique* (2011), *Sephardism: Spanish Jewish History in the Modern Literary Imagination* (2012), *Meyerbeer and Grand Opéra from the July Monarchy to the Present* (2016), *The Oxford Handbook of Music and Medievalism* (2020), and *Histoire de l'opéra français* (2020). Current projects include a monograph on opéra comique in the July Monarchy.

César A. Leal is Assistant Professor and Director of Orchestral Activities at Gettysburg College (Sunderman Conservatory), having served as artistic director of the Sewanee Symphony Orchestra and associate of the Sewanee Summer Music Festival. Building on his PhD research on the French impresario, writer, and editor Gabriel Astruc (1864–1938), Leal has published on cultural life in *fin de siècle* Paris and has presented papers at meetings of the American Musicological Society, the International Musicological Society, and the Biennial Conference of Nineteenth-century Music.

Mark A. Pottinger is Professor of Music and Chair of the Music and Theater Department at Manhattan College, where he recently founded the undergraduate Sound Studies program. Winner of the Berlin Prize in 2017, Dr Pottinger has published on the music and cultural life of the nineteenth century and the contemporary listening environment, including an essay in *The Cambridge History of Music Criticism* (2019) and articles in *Nineteenth-Century Music Review, Change Over Time: An International Journal of Conservation and the Built Environment*, and *The Germanic Review: Literature, Culture, Theory*. His current book project, 'Science and the Romantic Vision in Early Nineteenth-Century Opera', examines the sciences in the early nineteenth century and their relationship to the sound of nature in early romantic opera. Presently serving as co-chief editor of *Sound Studies Review*, Dr Pottinger regularly lectures for the Metropolitan Opera and its HD Live in the Schools educational programming.

Laura Moore Pruett is Associate Professor of Music in the Department of Visual and Performing Arts at Merrimack College. She focuses her research on nineteenth-century American music and culture and has published articles on the works and career of Louis Moreau Gottschalk, including articles in *19th-Century Music* and the *Journal for the Society of American Music*. She is currently preparing Gottschalk's two symphonies for a new edition to be published in the series Music of the United States of America, as well as a study of the Bostonian music critic John Sullivan Dwight.

Ruth E. Rosenberg is Associate Professor at the University of Illinois at Chicago (UIC) and recipient of a Mellon postdoctoral fellowship at Columbia University and a faculty fellowship from the Institute of the Humanities at UIC. She is author of the book *Music, Travel, and Imperial Encounter in Nineteenth-Century France: Musical Apprehensions* (2014), along with articles in *Current Musicology, The Musical Quarterly*, and *Nineteenth-Century French Studies*. She has presented at meetings of the Society for Ethnomusicology,

Contributors xxi

the American Anthropological Association, and the American Musicological Society.

Douglas W. Shadle is Associate Professor of Musicology at the Vanderbilt University Blair School of Music. He is author of the award-winning *Orchestrating the Nation: The Nineteenth-Century American Symphonic Enterprise* (2016) and *Antonín Dvořák's New World Symphony* (2021); he also served as co-editor of *A Portrait in Four Movements: The Chicago Symphony Orchestra under Barenboim, Boulez, Haitink, and Muti* (2019).

Marian Smith is Professor Emerita of Musicology at the University of Oregon, where she was awarded the Thomas A. Herman Award for Distinguished Teaching. Her book *Ballet in Opera in the Age of Giselle* (2000) won the de la Torre Bueno Award in dance history writing in 2000. She has edited the volume *La Sylphide: Paris 1832 and Beyond* (2012) and has contributed articles to dance and musicology journals as well as chapters to *Rethinking the Sylph* (1997), *Reading Critics Reading* (2001), *The Cambridge Companion to Grand Opera* (2003), *Music, Theater, and Cultural Transfer: Paris, 1830–1914* (2009), and *The Cambridge Companion to Ballet* (2011). With Doug Fullington, she is completing the book *Five Ballets from Paris and St Petersburg*.

Helena Kopchick Spencer is Associate Professor of Music History and Affiliated Faculty in Women's & Gender Studies at the University of North Carolina at Wilmington. She has published essays in the volumes *La Sylphide: Paris 1832 and Beyond* (2012) and *Meyerbeer and Grand Opéra from the July Monarchy to the Present* (2016). She is currently preparing a book on nineteenth- and twentieth-century re-imaginings of the Romantic ballet *Giselle*.

Acknowledgements

In the development and support of the volume we have many to thank, first and foremost our contributors, whose collaboration and willingness to rethink old and new ground fostered an environment of invigorating synergy and warm collegiality. We are also grateful to Michael Middeke, Boydell & Brewer's Editorial Director of Modern History and Music, whose enthusiasm and continued patience, generosity, and sound advice have buoyed and sustained our efforts; to Elizabeth Howard, Assistant Editor, whose thoughtfulness and care with stylistic and practical details have helped carry us to publication; and to Vanessa Agnew, Katharine Ellis, Jonathan Glixon, and David Gramit, editors of the Boydell & Brewer series Music in Society and Culture, who approved the project. We thank the two readers for their informed insights and critiques that helped to strengthen our work, and all others who inspired and offered suggestions to the volume's editors and contributors along the way, some of whom are acknowledged within individual essays. For assistance in preparing and refining music examples, we are grateful for the promptness and professionalism of Daniel Arnold and Juan Carlos Marulanda. We also heartily thank Fiona Little for her assiduous copy-editing refinements and Erin Fulton for the careful compiling of the index.

For research and financial support, we are truly appreciative of the fellowships and grants awarded by our respective institutions, present and past: the University of Kentucky (College of Fine Arts, School of Music), the University of the South, and Gettysburg College (Sunderman Conservatory of Music). We also thank the American Musicological Society's Publications Committee and James R. Anthony Fund for granting this volume a publication subvention award aided by the National Endowment for the Humanities and the Andrew W. Mellon Foundation.

In the face of the destabilising political conflicts and brutal years of global pandemic that overshadowed this project, we are forever indebted to all those who kept us safe, including many selfless, courageous frontline workers and medical professionals, to our colleagues and students who kept us connected to our musical and educational missions, and to friends Keith Walters (an accomplished sociolinguist who inspired our use of 'imaginary' in the title), Whit Whitaker, Vickie Steele, Elisa Moskovitz, Eric Stogner, Barb Phillips, Madison Moore, and Troy Johnson, who surrounded us with care and support, even when virtually delivered. For their never-ending love and attentive ears, we especially thank Janice E. Hallman (Diana's sister), Janeth Jaramillo and Eduardo Leal (César's parents), and those we lost to cancer and Covid: our beloved brother and uncle, to whom this volume is dedicated.

Diana Hallman and César Leal
Lexington, KY, and Gettysburg, PA
1 October 2021

Preface

The seeds of this project took root in long, unbounded conversations in Paris and other locales, enriched by our shared love of France and the United States, our curiosity about cultural interconnections between them and within the Atlantic world, and our deep interest in interrogations of race, gender, and 'silent' areas of music historiography. This volume has also emerged out of a collective interest in the ways in which early encounters between France and America continue to resonate in today's geopolitical alliances, national commemorations, and distinct but correlating ideas about transatlantic history. Events in the public spotlight in 2021, such as France's precipitous cancellation of its commemoration of French assistance in the American Revolutionary War over the AUKUS agreement in September, its decision to place the remains of African American singer-dancer Josephine Baker in the hallowed space of the Panthéon, or the puzzling responses to Haitian political, economic, and refugee crises by the United States and Europe, represent only a few examples that seem to echo the dynamics of past relations and perceptions. In this volume of collected essays, we have opted to interrogate French views of America, not only of the young United States, but also the wider 'Amérique' (or Amérique septentrionale') that France knew in earlier centuries, encompassing parts of the North American continent as well as its own colonial islands of the West Indies.

As editors of this collection of essays, we quickly came to realise that our study of French representations of 'America' or 'Amérique' in music, theatre, dance, and spectacle could not escape revisiting the themes of revolution and race that played such prominent roles in transatlantic exchanges within our chosen time frame of the long nineteenth century. In light of present-day revolutions of thought and civic action that have begun to shine more powerful light on obscured subjects in the writing and teaching of history and culture – in particular, the history and legacy of transatlantic slavery – we have approached this project with a sense of urgency to contribute to the expansion of musicological enquiry about race beyond the more established studies of jazz-era Paris or the exoticism of Josephine Baker.

This volume is bookended by several essays that examine theatrical portrayals of slavery, negotiations of Blackness and Whiteness, and the creation of coded images and sounds linked to Black and Indigenous Americans in performances and spectacles of music and dance. Several essays explore repertoire seldom considered in musicological literature, such as the melodrama *Adonis, ou Le Bon Nègre* (1798), situated in France's former colony of Saint-Domingue, the opéra comique *Le Planteur* (1839), set in Louisiana, a locale evocative of empire as well as desecration, and the 'Indian' ballets of *Le Bossu* (1862/1867),

xxvi   *Preface*

while other studies recontextualise and remediate familiar subjects and icons such as Louis Moreau Gottschalk, Buffalo Bill, the Statue of Liberty, and the cakewalk in Paris.

Recurring themes and tropes interwoven throughout many chapters disclose – in varied artistic contexts – the permeation of racial and cultural oppositions in French conceptions of the colonial and post-colonial world of Amérique: the presentation of exoticism and Otherness and the binaries of 'civilisation' and 'barbarism', the vanishing, primeval 'noble savage' and blood-thirsty 'Indian', the 'mauvais' and 'bon nègre', or the uncivilised and 'whitened' Noir. Historical figures such as the American Revolution's Washington and Lafayette and the Black Haitian revolutionaries Biassou and Toussaint Louverture, the musical symbols of the *Marseillaise* and 'The Star-Spangled Banner', and the imagined spaces of Louisiana, Saint-Domingue, and the American South appear centrally or peripherally as recurring signifiers within divergent narratives. Merging with or functioning outside such racialised discourse, the sounds (and noise) of America – from the sonic visions of Chateaubriand and Francophone or Creole American expressions to the 'vanished soundscapes' of the Statue of Liberty's transatlantic ceremonies, along with American symphonies, the 'Wild West' at the 1889 World's Fair, and the cakewalk 'invasion' in Paris – are 'reheard' within these pages, further revealing a multiplicity of Americas in the French imaginary of the long nineteenth century.

Introduction

Diana R. Hallman and César A. Leal

Within the long nineteenth century that frames the first hundred years of the American republic, French writers, artists, and musicians became increasingly enthralled by the young nation's political experiments, vast landscapes, and diverse culture. Following the American Revolution that upended the rule of British colonial masters (with strategic aid by General Lafayette and his compatriots), French observers often viewed the United States as a laboratory for the forging of new practices of *liberté* and *égalité*, in affinity with and as models for France's own revolutionary ideals and experiences. Tributes to American freedom, resiliency, and power and the natural beauty of the New World appeared in many forms, while competing with anti-American depictions of an inferior environment of fetid swamps, sterile deserts, and degenerated animals that had emerged in the influential naturalist writings of Georges Louis Leclerc, Comte de Buffon, and Cornelius De Pauw; these authors' imagined terrains reverberated with the anti-colonialist views of Enlightenment thinkers such as Voltaire, Denis Diderot, and Guillaume Thomas Raynal.[1] Although acclamations of America as an inspiration of revolution and freedom would peak in the early years of the French Revolution, French encomiums to George Washington and Benjamin Franklin and other symbols of Revolutionary America would continue to appear well into the nineteenth century, as Alexis de Tocqueville's *De la démocratie en Amérique* (1835) would reinforce the American republic's status as an icon of democracy. The Franco-American bond forged through revolutionary battles and the 'exchange of revolutionary culture' would also foster a political and moral rivalry, as proposed by Suzanne Desan.[2] As political tensions rose between the two nations and the

---

1 Philippe Roger, *The American Enemy: The History of French Anti-Americanism*, trans. Sharon Bowman (Chicago: University of Chicago Press, 2005), pp. 1–27, argues that the 'dispute of the New World' beginning *c.*1750, which formed the basis of later strains of anti-Americanism, originated in such writings as Buffon's *Variétés dans l'espèce humaine* (1749), *Animaux de l'ancien continent, Animaux du nouveau monde, Animaux communs aux deux continents* (1761), *De la dégénération des animaux* (1766); De Pauw's *Récherches philosophiques sur les Américains ou mémoires intéressans pour server à l'histoire de l'espèce humaine* (1768), and Raynal's *Histoire philosophique et politique des établissements et du commerce des Européens dans les deux Indes* (1775).

2 Suzanne Desan, 'Transatlantic Spaces of Revolution: The French Revolution, *Sciotomanie*, and American Lands', *Journal of Early Modern History*, 12 (2008), 467–505, at p. 467.

French landscape shifted between republican, monarchical, and imperial forms of government, the rivalry could be seen through the reshaping of anti-American tropes of backwardness, savagery, and degeneration in new cultural guises, including those of uncouth frontiersmen, uncultured businessmen, and aesthetically inferior artists and musicians. By the mid- to late nineteenth century, as the American capitalist economy expanded, condescension or revilement of the young country, captured in Baudelaire's condemnations of America's 'greedy' materialism,[3] jostled against the promotion of renewed Franco-American alliances. One such coalition, the Union Franco-Amérique, helped to finance France's gift of the Statue of Liberty, erected in 1886 to celebrate, belatedly, the centenary of American independence, to commemorate cultural ties, and perhaps to resurrect shared ideologies between the two nations.

From revolutionary times to the *fin de siècle*, the presence of non-European natives, slaves, immigrants, and Creoles within American shores and island colonies of Amérique proved particularly fascinating to French observers. In contrast to Buffon's portrayals of atrophied humans and De Pauw's descriptions of 'coarse', 'vegetating' Indigenous populations,[4] certain Enlightenment-inspired authors and artists portrayed American Indians, or Native Americans, as embodiments of Jean-Jacques Rousseau's idealised 'noble savage' or 'natural man', but also as honourable 'warrior elites',[5] who would, paradoxically, be sacrificed to the desires and fears of the expanding immigrant population in the United States. In the early nineteenth century, the French Romantic author François-René de Chateaubriand created beloved, sentimentalised portraits of North American 'Indians', while contemporaneous theatrical depictions sometimes reverted to those of violent and grotesque *sauvagerie*.[6] Not too dissimilarly, contrasting French views of Africans and Black Creoles of Amérique co-existed and vacillated over time – with some writers labelling African Americans as barbarous and uncivilised, but others creating empathetic portrayals as they disdained the practice of slavery, not only within the United States, but beyond to France's own territories and colonies in the New World. One French traveller, Edouard de Montulé, after reporting on 'many savages at New Orleans', condemned American beliefs of racial superiority and the 'wretched fate of the poor negro'.[7]

---

3 Roger, *The American Enemy* speaks of Baudelaire's analogies between the 'commercial smell' of America and Belgium and his fears of a materialistic, artistically devoid 'Americanised' world in *Fusées; Mon Coeur mis à nu*, begun in 1855 (pp. 59–63).

4 Roger, *The American Enemy*, pp. 12–19.

5 C. W. Thompson, *French Romantic Travel Writing: Chateaubriand to Nerval* (Oxford: Oxford University Press, 2012), p. 330.

6 Joellen A. Meglin, '*Sauvages*, Sex Roles, and Semiotics: Representations of Native Americans in the French Ballet 1736–1837, Part Two: The Nineteenth Century', *Dance Chronicle*, 23:3 (2000), 275–320, at p. 276.

7 Edouard de Montulé, *A Voyage to North America and the West Indies in 1817* (London:

Introduction   3

Late eighteenth-century French discourses on slavery, particularly by abolitionist authors, were often infused with revolutionary rhetoric as they were impacted by revolutionary events themselves. Moreover, the practice of slavery would expose the ambiguous vacillations between republic and empire that would continue to haunt France and the United States throughout the long nineteenth century: as abolitionists would recognise, the trading and holding of slaves signalled the stamp of empire, rather than actions of a republic of free individuals as promised by Revolutionary idealists. Beyond the American and French Revolutions of 1776 and 1789, two other political conflicts served as clear turning points in France's responses to and relationship with transatlantic slave practices: the first, the so-called Haitian Revolution of 1791–1804, which occurred within the wider scope of Amérique in France's West Indies or Caribbean colonies, triggered the first abolition of slavery under the République in 1794; the second, the Revolution of 1848, led to the final abolition in French colonies in the early months of the Deuxième République. The cataclysmic Haitian Revolution, that is, the slave revolution of Saint-Domingue (the French colony that would become independent Haiti in 1804), openly thrust the racial hierarchies and slavery systems dominating the Atlantic world against the philosophical-political ideals of *liberté* and *égalité* that had fuelled the American and French Revolutions and united the two young republics.[8] By the time of the Civil War in the United States, France's own slavery practices – before the 1848 abolition – would cast only a dim shadow over its sharp critiques of American enslavement, while certain periodicals such as the *Revue contemporaine* and authors such as Edwin De Leon would favour the Confederacy (as did Napoléon III reputedly) and promote the idea that the Union's central goal in fighting the war was not to suppress slavery practices but to overtake the property and prosperity of the South.[9]

Across the long nineteenth century, cultural commentaries and imaginings of America appeared in wide-ranging genres that embraced fascination with and wariness of the New World as they revealed tensions between French ideals of an egalitarian republic, desires of imperial, colonialist power, and unease over its shared dealings in slavery – often tempered by a belief in the beneficent power of French culture and 'civilisation'. Among frequently cited genres are French travel writings, from Jacques Pierre Brissot's *Nouveau Voyage dans les États-Unis de l'Amérique septentrionale*, published in 1791, to Chateaubriand's *Les Natchez* and *Voyage en Amérique* of 1826 and 1827 and,

---

Sir Richard Phillips & Co., 1821), pp. 55, 58–9. See also the pointed commentary on American slavery by Gustave de Beaumont, Alexis de Tocqueville's aristocratic friend and New World travelling companion, in *Marie, ou L'Esclavage aux États-Unis* (Paris: Librairie de Charles Gosselin, 1835).

8   Jeremy D. Popkin, *Facing Racial Revolution: Eyewitness Accounts of the Haitian Insurrection* (Chicago: University of Chicago Press, 2007), p. 1.

9   Roger, *The American Enemy*, pp. 80–4.

as mentioned above, de Tocqueville's *De la démocratie en Amérique*, written after his 1831–2 visit. Whereas Brissot's *Nouveau Voyage* depicted Americans, particularly Quakers and American farmers, as exemplars of *liberté* to be emulated,[10] the writings of Chateaubriand and others in the early nineteenth century presented colonialist narratives evoking the 'civilising' forces of the French as well as nostalgically recalling a lost 'Nouveau Monde', particularly after a large swath of French territory was sold to the United States government in the Louisiana Purchase of 1803. As Ruth Rosenberg notes, 'memories of empire' appeared in literary and artistic genres centred on the North American territory that was once 'la Nouvelle France'.[11] Novels that imagined America include Chateaubriand's early novella *Atala, ou Les Amours de deux sauvages dans le désert* (1801), a story of doomed love set in Louisiana through which the French author reconsiders the 'noble savagery' of the Natchez and warring tribes as he portrays the benevolent effects of European Christianity on the Native American Chactas and bi-racial Atala. (Anne-Louis Girodet's painting *The Entombment of Atala* of 1808 intensified France's captivation with Chateaubriand's exotic story.) In the more politically overt novel *Bug-Jargal* (1818, rev. 1826), Victor Hugo creates a historical fiction of the slave revolution of Saint-Domingue that confronts cultural-political-racial realities played out on Franco-American soil.[12] By the early 1850s, translations and staged renderings of Harriet Beecher Stowe's anti-slavery novel *Uncle Tom's Cabin* set off a 'Tom mania' in France, which allowed readers and audiences to maintain a certain distance from their nation's own slave-owning past while 'negotiat[ing] between evoking U.S. particularity and drawing analogies to the French context'.[13] At the *fin de siècle*, France's racial apprehensions, contradictions, and common conflations of African American and African imagery emerged in diverse publications, including Gaston Bergeret's *Journal d'un nègre à l'Exposition de 1900*, an account of colonialist exhibitions written in the guise of a Black author.[14]

10 J. P. Brissot (Warville), *Nouveau Voyage dans les États-Unis de l'Amérique septentrionale, fait en 1788* (Paris: Buisson, 1791), vol. i, pp. xxi–xxv. On French views of the Quaker, see, e.g., the early study by Edith Philips, *The Good Quaker in French Legend* (Philadelphia: University of Pennsylvania Press, 1932).

11 Ruth E. Rosenberg, *Music, Travel, and Imperial Encounter in 19th-Century France: Musical Apprehensions* (New York: Routledge, 2014), pp. 74–5.

12 Christopher L. Miller, *Blank Darkness: Africanist Discourse in French* (Chicago: University of Chicago Press, 1985), p. 109.

13 Emily Sahakian, 'Eliza's French Fathers: Race, Gender, and Transatlantic Paternalism in French Stage Adaptations of *Uncle Tom's Cabin*, 1853', in *Uncle Tom's Cabins: The Transnational History of America's Most Mutable Book*, ed. Tracy C. Davis and Stefka Mihavlova (Ann Arbor: University of Michigan Press, 2018), pp. 81–115, at pp. 81, 94.

14 Gaston Bergeret, *Journal d'un nègre à l'Exposition de 1900* (Paris, 1901), cited in James Smalls, '"Race" as Spectacle in Late-Nineteenth-Century French Art and Popular Culture', *French Historical Studies*, 26:2 (Spring 2003), 351–82, at p. 351.

Introduction 5

Throughout the long century multiple visions of America co-existed in the French mind, and to search for a single, coherent conception would be an elusive task. Instead, this volume will explore multiple Americas, multiple myths of America, and multiple sounds, images, and symbols of America. 'America' will not only encompass the United States, but 'Amérique' as understood and recalled by the French, which embraced the present and former French colonies of the Antilles or West Indies as well as 'la Nouvelle France', including Louisiana.[15] In dialogue with French literary and historical discourses, the imagining of America appeared in diverse forms of French music, dance, theatre, and art. Sonic, visual, theatrical, and literary representations – which potentially offer windows into cultural systems and attitudes that may be obscured in historical accounts and documentation – will serve as the principal focus of the present group of essays.

Written by musicologists, an ethnomusicologist, and cultural historians with research expertise in French and/or American studies, these essays will individually and collectively interrogate fluctuating, multivalent ideas of America, or Amérique. The case studies will highlight new or rarely treated subjects or works in musicological studies as well as historical, hermeneutical, and semiotic reinterpretations or reapplications of well-studied themes such as exoticism and savagery, with the intent of enriching our present understanding of France's competing visions of America through music/sound, theatre, dance, and related literary and visual media, c.1789–c.1914. Against the backdrop of ambiguous and pro- and anti-American strains of thought, contributors will examine music and music-related genres, including opéra comique, melodrama, vaudeville, ballet, the cakewalk, songs, symphonic and piano works, and soundscapes, to illumine ways in which particular repertoire, performances, sounds, characters, and movements helped to construct and perpetuate concepts, images, and tropes that connected, or at times disconnected, France, New World colonies, and the American republic politically, philosophically, and culturally. They will assess varied cultural narratives, critical modes, and representational techniques as they consider depictions and imaginings of the colonial and post-colonial New World as the site and source of revolutionary, democratic, and aesthetic inspiration, kinship, or rivalry, as well as the locus of noble and ignoble savagery, exotic or uncivilised Otherness, and myth-creating or myth-shattering racialised, racist, classist, gendered, and colonialist systems that entangled French, American, and Francophone Americans and left indelible marks on both France and the United States.

Considerations of revolution, often in coordination with concepts of freedom or *liberté*, will relate not only to the transnational, transatlantic political revolutions linking France and America, but also to social, cultural, or musical

---

15 The term 'Amérique septentrionale' was still being used in the late eighteenth century as a designation for northern America above present-day Mexico and Central America and including Canada; see the title of Brissot's travel writing cited in n. 10 above.

revolutions that French creators and critics associated with certain American figures, archetypes, and genres. Moreover, themes of revolution and race will be treated separately and together: intersections will extend from French representations of slavery in Amérique from the Revolutionary period to the July Monarchy, to the 'revolutionary' breaking of racial and social boundaries in varied depictions of cross-racial relations, and the subversive appropriations of Black/non-White forms of American musical expression and dance movement during the *fin de siècle*. As noted above, discussions of race will also contend with the pervasive tropes of barbarism or savagery, in opposition to concepts of 'civilisation', with the aim of revealing their persistence in French interpretations of America as well as their malleable, multi-layered meanings. Ideas of American 'savagery', in echoes of Buffonian constructs of degeneration, appeared most obviously in the recurring associations with Indigenous Americans and African slaves, but they also underpin French descriptions of America's youth and naïveté, ignorant, uncultivated Anglo-Saxon residents, or the aesthetic mediocrity of its art-less (or opera-less) world, as Stendhal would bemoan.

In the volume, topical threads and inter-dialogues will link the diverse studies of musical, artistic, and literary representations that helped to shape and reshape French visions and myths of America. For example, French views of the United States as an enlightened font of *liberté* will be considered in several essays: in Diana Hallman's opening treatment of staged encomiums to the American Revolution and Republic; Charlotte Bentley's examination of late nineteenth-century Francophone songs of New Orleans that nostalgically echoed the revolutionary past as they revealed a longing for a Franco-American Republic (Chapter 4); Ruth Rosenberg's binding of Chateaubriand's entangled thoughts on revolution and empire with his imagined sounds of the New World (Chapter 7); and Annegret Fauser's recreation of the Statue of Liberty's sonic celebrations of political freedom (Chapter 8). Moreover, implicit connections between aural vestiges of 'la Nouvelle France' and musical tributes to a rising Creole nationalism in Franco-American communities in Bentley's essay and melded sentiments of *créolité* and Frenchness in Laura Pruett's essay (Chapter 5) will underscore the tenacity of France's colonial American bonds and the commingling of French, American, Louisianian, or Creole identities.

In tandem with the broadening scholarship of racialised discourses and practices in Western Europe and the United States, several essays will centre their interrogations of race in French interpretations of American music and identity,[16] with an emphasis on French constructions of Blacks, African Amer-

---

16 An important example of new musicological scholarship on race, including concepts and effects of 'Blackness', is the special issue on 'Music, Race, and Ethnicity' of the *Journal of the American Musicological Society*, 72:3 (Fall 2019), which contains articles such as Arne Spohr's '"Mohr und Trompeter": Blackness and Social Status in Early Modern Germany' (pp. 613–64) and Matthew D. Morrison's 'Race, Blacksound, and the (Re)Making of Musicological Discourse' (pp. 781–823).

icans, or Native Americans within the United States, on the French colonial islands of Amérique, or within Paris itself. Selected chapters will examine coded images, sounds, characters, language, and movements as signifiers of exoticism or racial, class, and gender difference, political symbols of colonial domination and patriarchy, tools for abolitionist arguments, or means for renegotiating cultural identity through cultural appropriation. The chapter co-authored by Marian Smith, Sarah Gutsche-Miller, and Helena Spencer explores danced representations of Indigenous Americans seen on nineteenth-century Parisian stages (Chapter 2), and Spencer, in a separate chapter, highlights the 'Tragic Mulatta' as a racialised, sexualised figure in the opéra comique *Le Planteur* (1839) and a central archetype in nineteenth-century literary and theatrical representations (Chapter 3). In other fictionalised treatments of slavery, Hallman examines the recurring figure of the *bon nègre*, or faithful Black servant (Chapter 1). César Leal, in his study of the cakewalk in *fin de siècle* Paris, along with Spencer and other authors, considers distinctions in French and American uses of certain tropes, caricatures, and commodifications of race while examining diverse venues for French representation, appropriation, and 'whitening' or 'civilising' of Blackness (Chapter 10). Ambiguous meanings of 'Creole', with fluctuating links to Blackness and Whiteness, are addressed in several chapters: for example, Pruett re-examines the metaphorical racial mixing in the music and Creole identity of Louis Moreau Gottschalk, looking further into the composer's musical encodings of race that Parisians heard as reminiscences of colonial Saint-Domingue and Louisiana (Chapter 5).

The study of French theatrical and literary works on slavery during this period reveals distinct patterns and language in the confronting of race, with American settings offering a physically remote site for contemplation. Similar tensions and contradictions become evident as anti-slavery allegories vie with pro-slavery justifications in works of the Revolutionary years as well as those of the Restoration and July Monarchy, as reflected in plays, novels, and operas considered by Hallman and Spencer. Even close in time to the first and second abolitions of slavery, in 1794 and 1848, French representations of race continued to bear the imprint of long-standing categories found in amendments to the *Code noir*, first imposed in France's slave colonies in 1685 under Louis XIV: adult Black slaves, or 'esclaves', came to be designated 'nègres' and 'négresses', children up to twelve years old as 'négrillons', and men and women of mixed race as 'mulâtres' and 'mulâtresses'. In Chapter 10, Leal finds these terms, in particular 'négrillon', in use as late as the early twentieth century in Parisian materials related to the cakewalk. Some portrayals and references also retain the obsessive colour coding of the slave-owning lawyer and writer Moreau de Saint-Méry in his 1789 *Description topographique, physique, civile, politique et historique de la partie française de l'isle Saint-Domingue*, which defines nine main interracial categories containing 128 racialised specifications.[17]

---

17 Médéric-Louis-Élie Moreau de Saint-Méry, *Description topographique, physique,*

Performances of race in musical-theatrical-visual genres inevitably tap into the problematic arena of 'blackface' or 'redface' enactments or parodies that had been a part of French pre-1789 court entertainment and mid- to late eighteenth-century theatre long before the creation and importation of American Black minstrelsy. Costume sketches of operas and ballets of the 1830s suggest that colour-changing makeup may have been applied, though Smith, Gutsche-Miller, and Spencer (Chapter 2) find that, in French ballet performances of the 1860s, the simulation of Native American skin tone was achieved through the use of tights. In later appropriations or reinterpretations of African American music, dance, and imagery in French theatrical spaces and on artistic canvases of the *fin de siècle*, 'playing Black' (even without alterations of pigmentation) reveals an attraction to the expressive freedom, and even subversiveness or transgressiveness, of these 'foreign' forms of music and dance, as well as an aversion or condescension towards Black alterity and corporeality.

Some essays will focus their attention on French critiques of American music and musicians, including Douglas Shadle's study (Chapter 6) of the reception of Americanised adaptations of European symphonic traditions and Pruett's previously mentioned chapter on Gottschalk's Parisian concerts, *c.*1849–52. Diverse impressions and images of America will extend to reconsiderations of two well-known Franco-American spectacles at the *fin de siècle*: Annegret Fauser's examination of the Statue of Liberty commemorations of 1875–86 (Chapter 8) and Mark Pottinger's study of Buffalo Bill's Wild West Show at the World's Fair of 1889 (Chapter 9). Rather than concentrating on the iconic sculpture exclusively, Fauser looks to soundscapes for the semiotic and aesthetic transmission of Franco-American ideas of freedom, partnership, and commemoration, contrasting the 'immutability of the monument and the ephemerality of its sonic vernaculars' (p. 236). Pottinger places the Wild West's multi-cultural production in the liminal space between the history and myth of America, but particularly as a display of Americanised showmanship and marketing within an increasingly commercial Parisian entertainment world.

These studies will intersect with and build upon burgeoning literature within a range of fields, including Francophone Atlantic, Black Atlantic, Caribbean, transatlantic revolutionary, and slavery studies.[18] In addition to intriguing publications emerging from Liverpool University Press,[19] Barbara T. Cooper

---

civile, politique et historique de la partie française de l'isle Saint-Domingue [...] à l'époque du 18 octobre 1789 et d'une nouvelle carte (Paris: Dupont, 1797).

18 A number of publications from these fields, such as Sean X. Goudie, *Creole America: The West Indies and the Formation of Literature and Culture in the New Republic* (Philadelphia: University of Pennsylvania Press, 2006), were consulted by authors in this volume (see Bibliography).

19 See, e.g., Marlene L. Daut, *Tropics of Haiti: Race and the Literary History of the Haitian Revolution in the Atlantic World, 1789–1865* (Liverpool: Liverpool University Press, 2015).

Introduction 9

has brought forward a series of L'Harmattan editions of plays and operas that centre on race and slavery in eighteenth- and nineteenth-century French theatre and that feature carefully researched introductions, including two used in this volume: Prosper (Lepoitevin de L'Égreville) and Anicet-Bourgeois's *Les Massacres de Saint-Domingue* and Hippolyte Monpou's *Le Planteur* (see Chapters 1 and 3). Among studies beginning to give a clearer picture of music, theatre, and dance in the former French Caribbean colonies are David M. Powers's *From Plantation to Paradise: Cultural Politics and Musical Theatre in French Slave Colonies, 1764–1789* (2014) and Julia T. Prest's research projects and articles on theatre and dance of Saint-Domingue, which offer potential links to theatrical practices in France and the United States.[20]

Although several essays in this volume, such as Pruett's and Leal's, touch on subjects that have been explored in musicological studies on Franco-American musical exchanges or Americans and African Americans in Paris, they offer differently nuanced and more in-depth discussions of race than previous publications; moreover, they do not overlap with the abundantly studied subject of Josephine Baker or the highly popular 'jazz era' in Paris.[21] Among complemen-

---

20 See Julia T. Prest, 'The Familiar Other: Blackface Performance in Creole Works from 1780s Saint-Domingue', in *Colonialism and Slavery in Performance: Theatre and the Eighteenth-Century French Caribbean*, ed. J. Leichman and K. Bénac-Girous (Liverpool: Liverpool University Press, 2021), pp. 41–63; Julia T. Prest, 'Pale Imitations: White Performances of Slave Dance in the Public Theatres of Pre-Revolutionary Saint-Domingue', *Atlantic Studies*, 16:4 (2019), 502–20 <https://doi.org/10.1080/14788810. 2018.1469352>. Among Prest's projects is the Network for the Study of Colonial-Era Caribbean Theatre and Opera.

21 Jody Blake, *Le Tumulte noir: Modernist Art and Popular Entertainment in Jazz-Age Paris, 1900–1930* (University Park, PA: Pennsylvania State University Press, 1999) was one of the first studies to trace connections between African American music and dance, including the grizzly bear, cakewalk, and foxtrot, and the approaches and subjects of Modernist art in Paris. In a more recent provocative study, *Second Skin: Josephine Baker and the Modern Surface* (Oxford: Oxford University Press, 2011), Anne Anlin Cheng also relates the development of Modernist art and African American performance, particularly through the figure of Josephine Baker as 'dynamic fulcrum' of Modernist currents. Andy Fry's *Paris Blues: African American Music and French Popular Culture, 1920–1960* (Chicago: University of Chicago Press, 2014) contextualises Baker and other African American musicians in his historical reconsiderations of race and jazz during the core years of the 'jazz era' in France. Among recent scholarship on other types of Franco-American exchanges, see, e.g., the 2015 international conference held at the Université de Montréal and sponsored by the Canadian research organisation Observatoire Interdisciplinaire de Création et de Recherche en Musique (OICRM), 'Les Musiques Franco-Européennes en Amérique du Nord (1900–1950): Étude des transferts culturels', which had as its goal 'comprendre l'influence qu'ont exercée les musiques franco-européennes sur le développement de la vie musicale en Amérique du Nord et, inversement, la fascination que l'Amérique suscite chez de nombreux artistes franco-européens'. In 2017, Steven Huebner and Federico Laz-

tary musicological studies that have considered concepts, subjects, and images of America in music and theatre of earlier periods, Pierpaolo Polzonetti, in *Italian Opera in the Age of the American Revolution*, has examined the Rousseauian *bon sauvage* in Niccolo Piccinni's *L'americano* (1772), the Quaker in Italian opera, and, more philosophically, the role played by operatic culture 'in the dissemination of ideas inspired by the American Revolution', including their impact on Beaumarchais and Mozart.[22] Axel Körner's *America in Italy: The United States in the Political Thought and Imagination of the Risorgimento, 1763–1865* has deepened the understanding of America's philosophical and political influence on Italy, offering a new look into the roots of the Risorgimento, the nineteenth-century independence movement often associated with Verdi and other Italian composers.[23]

Relevant publications on American or Black imagery in French literature and theatre – though without concentrations on music or dance – range from early studies such as Edith Lucas's *La Littérature anti-esclavagiste au dix-neuvième siècle: Étude sur Madame Beecher Stowe et son influence en France* (Boccard, 1930) and Léon-François Hoffmann, *Le Nègre romantique* (Payot, 1973)[24] to more recent studies on French travel writing on America, including Thompson's *French Romantic Travel Writing* (see n. 5) and publications on French literature and theatrical works with subjects and settings in the New World. These latter include Sarah Meer, *Uncle Tom Mania: Slavery, Minstrelsy, and Transatlantic Culture in the 1850s* (University of Georgia Press, 2005), Tracy C. Davis and Stefka Mihaylova (eds), *Uncle Tom's Cabins* (see n. 13), Christopher L. Miller's *Blank Darkness* (see n. 12), his later book, *The French Atlantic Triangle: Literature and Culture of the Slave Trade* (Duke University Press, 2008), and Doris Y. Kadish's *Fathers, Daughters, and Slaves: Women Writers and French Colonial Slavery* (Liverpool University Press, 2013).

---

zaro organised another interdisciplinary OICRM conference with a Franco-American focus, 'Artistic Migration and Identity: Paris, 1870–1940', at McGill University, Montréal, and then edited the conference's papers, which explore 'the formation of national imaginaries, the place occupied by foreigners in the artistic tradition of a territory, and the relationship among nationalism, internationalism, xenophobia, and aesthetic judgment' during the Third Republic (Peter Lang, peterlang.com, 2020).

22 Pierpaolo Polzonetti, *Italian Opera in the Age of the American Revolution* (Cambridge: Cambridge University Press, 2011), pp. 17, 317–30. On his extensive discussion of Quakers, see chapter 7, 'The Good Quaker and his Slaves' (pp. 228–68) and chapter 8, 'Quakers with Guns' (pp. 269–307).

23 Axel Körner's *America in Italy: The United States in the Political Thought and Imagination of the Risorgimento, 1763–1865* (Princeton: Princeton University Press, 2017).

24 Also see, e.g., René Rémond's *Les États-Unis devant l'opinion française (1852–1952)* (2 vols, Paris: Armand Colin, 1962) and Simon Jeune's *De F. T. Graindorge à A. O. Barnabooth: Les Types américains dans le roman et le théâtre français (1861–1917)* (Paris: Librairie Marcel Didier, 1963).

Introduction   11

Among the many critical race and exoticism studies (particularly those related to French and transatlantic depictions of race) that have stimulated important lines of enquiry are Pratima Prasad's *Colonialism, Race, and the French Romantic Imagination* (Routledge, 2009), Robin Mitchell's *Vénus Noire: Black Women and Colonial Fantasies in Nineteenth-Century France* (University of Georgia Press, 2020), and Kimberly Snyder Manganelli's *Transatlantic Spectacles of Race: The Tragic Mulatta and the Tragic Muse* (Rutgers University Press, 2012). Ralph Locke's studies of musical exoticism have inspired many authors in this volume, and Naomi André's new evaluations of Blackness in opera, including suggested connections between opera (particularly American opera) and minstrelsy practices, correspond with the implications of blackface performance found in French theatrical works of America examined in several essays.[25]

This volume's juxtaposition of views, myths, tropes, images, and sounds of America in the long nineteenth century aims to demonstrate the complexity and multiplicity of 'Americas' in the French imaginary and to highlight intersecting patterns of thought and representation for future explorations. One galvanising objective is the questioning of the manner in which French authors and creators may have used American representations as prisms through which they viewed their own culture as they attempted to navigate or even transform conflicting or problematic elements of French national or cultural identity through deflection, refraction, projection, or contrast. The studies of American-centred theatrical works, for example, interpret French lyrical and non-lyrical dramas set in colonies of the New World (or dislocated New World) as allegorical conduits for obscuring, overcoming, justifying, or contradicting the harsh realities of France's own slave practices. In interrelated ways, the volume reflects on the cultural implications of shifting discourses, such as those suggested by James Smalls, who links 'commodified modes of spectacle' featuring African American performers and signifiers to social transformation of 'racial difference and class distinctiveness' and even to the 'modernization process' in *fin de siècle* France.[26] It also offers openings for considering the impact of French thinking on America's view of itself, assessing how French observations of and intersections with American music, revolution, race, and culture may have affected, conflicted with, or reflected back on broader discourses, histories, and home-grown practices of American musical culture.

25   See, e.g., Ralph P. Locke, *Musical Exoticism: Images and Reflections* (Cambridge: Cambridge University Press, 2009; Naomi André, *Black Opera: History, Power, Engagement* (Urbana, Illinois: University of Illinois Press, 2018); Naomi André, Karen M. Bryan, and Eric Saylor (eds), *Blackness in Opera* (Urbana, Illinois: University of Illinois Press, 2012).

26   Smalls, '"Race" as Spectacle', p. 355.

PART I

AMERICAN *LIBERTÉ, SAUVAGERIE* AND *ESCLAVAGE*

1

Between Amérique and Colonial France: Revolutionary Tales of *liberté* and *esclavage*

Diana R. Hallman

In French operas, dramas, and novels of the Revolutionary era and early decades of the nineteenth century, stories and images of America centred on themes inextricably linked in the history of both nations: those of *liberté* and *esclavage*. Representations of the American colonists' struggle for freedom and portrayals of beloved American patriots and French soldiers who aided them mirrored France's own turbulent quest to construct a republic and transform its subjects into *citoyens*. As counterpoint to staged encomiums to American independence and democracy, French dramas that touched on the controversial subject of slavery cast light on practices that undermined fundamental principles of America's Declaration of Independence and France's *Déclaration des droits de l'homme et du citoyen* as they prolonged colonialist systems enabled by the monarchies that the Revolutions of 1776 and 1789 had overthrown. Theatrical as well as literary works joined in Revolutionary and post-Revolutionary abolitionist critiques that intimated comparisons between French and North American slavery practices, while simultaneously mitigating or validating them in France's American colonies. Theatrical slave narratives in island settings alluded to France's colonies of the West and East Indies as they highlighted the overcoming of slavery's harsh realities with utopian ideals of racial *égalité* and promises of *liberté*. Of particular interest to ideas of revolution are those whose plots and characters centre on a cataclysmic event of Caribbean Amérique: the slave insurrections of 1791–1804 in the French colony of Saint-Domingue, commonly known as the Haitian Revolution today.

In contrast to the American and French Revolutions, as the historian Jeremy Popkin underscores, the Saint-Domingue/Haitian Revolution 'directly challenged the system of racial hierarchy' that dominated the Atlantic world and starkly exposed the 'incompatibility' of slavery with the Franco-American ideals of *liberté* and *égalité*.[1] Led by Toussaint Louverture (*c.*1743–1803) and other island leaders, who 'deploy[ed] the language of Republican rights and the

---

1 Jeremy D. Popkin, *Facing Racial Revolution: Eyewitness Accounts of the Haitian Insurrection* (Chicago: University of Chicago Press, 2007), p. 1.

promise of individual liberty', the Saint-Domingue Revolution 'emerged symbiotically [with the French Revolution] as news, ideologies, and people crisscrossed the Atlantic', as Laurent Dubois writes.[2] The symbiosis encompassed the United States, with its shared ideological values and republican model, reinforced by the appearance of Franco-Caribbean news in metropolitan periodicals and Francophone communities.[3] Although France sent troops to battle the colonial insurgents and attempted to reinstate French rule in 1801–3 under Napoléon, the Saint-Domingue insurrection would help to initiate the first abolition of slavery by the French National Convention in February 1794 and would ultimately result in the establishment of Haiti, the first Black-led republic, in 1804, twelve years after the formation of France's First Republic. In French responses to Saint-Domingue events, revolutionary, republican, and abolitionist ideals would compete with imperial, colonialist anger at the forfeiture of France's lucrative sugar-producing colony and the loss of slave labour: this island revolution would become a controversial touchstone of conflicting French views on slavery, race, and colonial power, one that would lead to periodic suppression or controlled interpretation of the subject in published histories and official discourses.[4] As Michel-Rolph Trouillot argues in his oft-cited book *Silencing the Past*, such publications failed 'to understand the revolution on its own terms', but instead interpreted it within 'ready-made categories [...] that were incompatible with the idea of a slave revolution'.[5] Nonetheless, various types of narratives of the Revolution abounded in a 'transatlantic print culture', as Marlene Daut and other authors have noted; Ada Ferrer writes that, 'as news of the slaves' actions erupted onto the world stage, everyone seemed to be talking and thinking about the events in Saint-Domingue'.[6]

---

2 Laurent Dubois, *A Colony of Citizens: Revolution & Slave Emancipation in the French Caribbean, 1787–1804* (Chapel Hill: University of North Carolina Press, 2004), pp. 3, 7. 'Louverture' is also spelled 'L'Ouverture' in some texts.

3 Jeremy D. Popkin, *You Are All Free: The Haitian Revolution and the Abolition of Slavery* (Cambridge: Cambridge University Press, 2010), p. 5, notes that, by the summer of 1793, Haitian refugee stories frequently appeared in American newspapers and filtered through the French ministry of Edmond Charles Genêt and French consulates in Norfolk, Baltimore, Philadelphia, Charleston, and New York.

4 Popkin, *Facing Racial Revolution*, p. 2. As Popkin states, 'this humiliating defeat' had long been excluded from French histories, although well treated by Haitian authors such as Thomas Madiou, *Histoire d'Haiti* (1847) and Beaubrun Ardoin, *Études sur l'histoire d'Haiti* (1853).

5 Michel-Rolph Trouillot, *Silencing the Past: Power and the Production of History* (Boston: Beacon, 1995), p. 73, as cited in Marlene L. Daut, *Tropics of Haiti: Race and the Literary History of the Haitian Revolution in the Atlantic World, 1789–1865* (Liverpool: Liverpool University Press, 2015), pp. 2–3. Trouillot's publication, as well as the 1994 bicentennial of France's first abolition of slavery, helped to stimulate the growth of Haitian and Black Atlantic studies.

6 Daut, *Tropics of Haiti*, p. 3, n. 3, explains that this 'transatlantic print culture' entails the

Revolutionary Tales of liberté and esclavage   17

From the vantage point of the French stage and its intersections with 'print culture', this chapter interrogates the transatlantic nexus of revolution, republic, and race in a broader contemporaneous understanding of Amérique – encompassing the United States and France's New World colonies. After briefly exploring theatrical representations of the American Revolution that depicted the young American republic as a close ideological ally and inspirational beacon of *liberté* – primarily Edme Billardon de Sauvigny's tragedy, *Vashington, ou La Liberté du Nouveau Monde* (1791) – I will focus my discussion on revolutionary tales of *esclavage* set on French colonial islands that probe the lack of, or the promise of, *liberté*. In these counter-narratives of Amérique, I will consider divergent strands of revolutionary or republican ideology, abolitionist critique, and colonialist apologia that run through them, with emphasis on interconnecting approaches to the dramatisation of *esclavage*. Assessments of text and music will focus on the characterisation of Black slaves as reflections of France's complex notions of race that built upon categories of the pre-Revolutionary *Code noir*; these will hinge on depictions of master-slave relations and starkly etched stereotypes of the loyal *bon nègre*, who paid homage to the protections and cultural gifts of *bon maîtres*, along with the fearsome Black savage, the beautiful *négresse*, the devoted nanny, and the entertaining/dancing slave.[7] In these narratives, sympathetic, sentimental portrayals of Black characters and empathy for slave conditions vie with references to the killing of Whites, destruction of plantations, and toppling of the colonialist racial hierarchy. Benevolent masters and mistresses appear prominently, in opposition to cruel, slave-chasing masters, and as protectors of freedom-seeking slaves as they confront, often without challenging, the racial power structure.

The exploration of theatrical *esclavage* related to the history and symbolism of the Saint-Domingue/Haitian Revolution will begin with a focus on Louis-François-Guillaume Béraud's and Joseph de Rosny's melodrama *Adonis, ou Le Bon Nègre*, inspired by J. B. Picquenard's 'anecdote colonial' of 1798 and performed at the Théâtre de l'Ambigu-Comique the same year.[8] In addition

---

'adapting, modifying, reprinting, translating, and circulating texts' that appeared during the Haitian Revolution and throughout the approximately sixty years after it. Ada Ferrer, 'Talk about Haiti: The Archive and the Atlantic's Haitian Revolution', in *Tree of Liberty: Cultural Legacies of the Haitian Revolution*, ed. Doris L. Garraway (Charlottesville: University of Virginia Press, 2008), pp. 21–40, at p. 22, as cited in Daut, *Tropics of Haiti*, p. 2. Also see Popkin, *Facing Racial Revolution*, pp. 2–4; Popkin, *You Are All Free*, p. 5; Philippe R. Girard, 'The Haitian Revolution, History's New Frontier: State of the Scholarship and Archival Sources', *Slavery & Abolition* 34:3 (Sept. 2013), 485–507.

7   The French terms 'nègre' (Negro) and 'négresse' (Negress) will be retained untranslated in this article because of their problematic use in English today; moreover, as Dubois points out in *Slave Revolution*, p. 51, n. 2, 'no English term precisely captures [their] connotations'; he also cites 'noir' (Black) as a 'more respectful' term than 'nègre'.

8   J. B. Picquenard, *Adonis, ou Le Bon Nègre, anecdote colonial* (Paris: Didot jeune, 1798). Joseph de Rosny *et al.* labelled Picquenard's novel 'the counterpart of the immortal novel

to the use of stereotyped figures, likely performed in blackface, this and other Saint-Domingue-related narratives reinforced tropes of American and African savagery and exoticism already present in eighteenth-century French theatre – featuring sounds and instruments, spoken and sung dialect, and unfamiliar names to connote Otherness – as they allegorised the Saint-Domingue insurrection, at times echoing first-hand accounts of White colonists. The depictions of slavery and slave characters in *Adonis* will, secondarily, be compared with the utopian representations in Rodolphe Kreutzer's operatic adaptation of Jacques-Bernardin de Saint-Pierre's novel *Paul et Virginie* (1788), which first appeared on 15 January 1791 at the Théâtre de l'Opéra-Comique, close in time to François Le Sueur's opéra comique of the same title and subject.[9] Although *Paul et Virginie* adaptations, like the novel itself, take place on the 'Isle de France', the French colony known as Mauritius today, I am metaphorically viewing this island under the colonial concept of the 'deux Indes' – in essence, seeing it as a 'displaced' surrogate for France's New World island colonies.

To reveal the continuing resonance and racial-political symbolism of the Saint-Domingue/Haitian Revolution in France, I will also consider early nineteenth-century theatrical and literary interpretations of the Revolution that adopted similar tropes and characters, particularly Victor Hugo's early historical novel *Bug-Jargal* (1818, rev. 1826) and Prosper and Anicet-Bourgeois's melodrama *Les Massacres de Saint-Domingue, ou L'Expédition du general Leclerc* (1837). Hugo would recognise the racially charged import of Saint-Domingue, the 1791 insurrection, and the Revolutionary years that followed: in his preface for *Bug-Jargal*'s 1832 edition, he likened the 'immense subject' of his novel to an inter-continental 'struggle of giants' as the 'three worlds' of Europe, Africa, and America collided on the American racial 'battlefield'.[10]

As I will argue, such narratives of *esclavage* complicate French imaginings of Amérique as a land and New World of *liberté*. Some would indeed endorse the emancipation of slaves, with allusions to anti-slavery views asserted in influential publications such as Guillaume Thomas Raynal's *L'Histoire philosophique et politique des établissements et du commerce des Européens dans les deux Indes*, to which other Enlightenment authors contributed, or those promoted by the abolitionist group the Société des Amis des Noirs. Yet stories such as *Adonis*, despite abolitionist leanings, would ambiguously function as colonialist ration-

---

    Paul et Virginie' ('le pendant de l'immortel roman de *Paul et Virginie*') in *Le Tribunal d'Apollon, ou Jugement en dernier resort de tous les auteurs vivans*, vol. 2 (Paris: Marchand, 1799), p. 160. For other French theatrical works written between 1789 and 1799 that addressed colonial slavery, see n. 27 below. Translations are mine unless otherwise noted.

9 Jacques-Bernardin-Henri de Saint-Pierre, *Paul et Virginie* (Lausanne: Chez J. Mourer, 1788). Le Sueur's opera premiered at the Théâtre de l'Opéra-Comique on 13 January 1794.

10 'un si immense sujet, la révolte des noirs de Saint-Domingue en 1791, lutte de géants, trois mondes intéressés dans la question, l'Europe et l'Afrique pour combattants, l'Amérique pour champ de bataille': Victor Hugo, 'Préface de 1832', in *Bug-Jargal*, ed. Roger Borderie (Paris: Gallimard, 1970), p. 18.

alisation while they masked the harsh realities of slavery through sentimental master–slave portrayals – perhaps to distinguish French practices from those in continental America in reflection of a developing 'moral rivalry' between the two republics.[11] Through the downplaying of slaves' desires for emancipation and depicting of the Saint-Domingue uprisings as more vengeful rebellion than revolution – unlike the noble battles for freedom of the American and French Revolutions – these narratives confront the *liberté–esclavage* paradox by subverting the 'beacon of liberty' myths that would come to dominate official images of the United States, the broader idea of Amérique in France, and even France itself.

The Revolutionary Rhetoric of *liberté* and *esclavage*

As is commonly known, the word 'liberté' resonates throughout Revolutionary rhetoric, often paired with 'esclavage' – at times without allusion to actual corporeal slavery. A central meaning of 'esclavage' denoted bondage to tyrannical rulers or governments, with 'liberté' evoking the overthrowing of oppressive governments: for example, the *Revolutionary Catechism* of 1793–4 starkly defines 'revolution' as 'a violent passage from a state of slavery to a state of liberty'.[12] A number of Enlightenment writers, however, did evoke corporeal slavery and the figure of the slave in their concepts of social freedom.[13] In *Du Contrat social; ou Principes du droit politique* (*The Social Contract or Principles of Political Rights*) of 1762, for example, Rousseau used the images of 'master' and 'slave' and the opposition of freedom and slavery in discussing the governance of individuals in a society. In one of his most well-known pronouncements, Rousseau begins with imagery of corporeal slavery: 'Man is born free, but is everywhere in chains.'[14] With a strong emphasis on an individual's humanity (or manhood), he states: 'Every man having been born free and master of himself,

---

11   Suzanne Desan, 'Transatlantic Spaces of Revolution: The French Revolution, *Sciotomanie*, and American Lands', *Journal of Early Modern History*, 12 (2008), 467–505, at p. 467. Descriptions of violent treatment in the United States appear in French travel accounts: see commentary from Edouard de Montulé's *A Voyage to North America and the West Indies in 1817* (London: Sir Richard Phillips & Co., 1821) in the Introduction, n. 7.

12   *Catéchisme révolutionnaire, ou L'Histoire de la Révolution française, par demandes et par réponses: à l'usage de la jeunesse républicaine, et de tous les peuples qui veulent devenir libres* (Paris: Debarle, 1793–4), p. 3, as cited and translated in Malick W. Ghachem, *The Old Regime and the Haitian Revolution* (Cambridge: Cambridge University Press, 2012), p. 1.

13   Dubois, *A Colony of Citizens*, pp. 62–3. Among *philosophe* writings that critique slavery, Dubois cites Montesquieu's *Persian Letters* (1721), Rousseau's *Social Contract* (1762), and Voltaire's *L'A,B,C* (1768) and novella *Candide* (1759).

14   'L'Homme est né libre, & par-tout il est dans le fers': Jean-Jacques Rousseau, *Du Contrat social; ou Principes du droit politique* (Amsterdam: Chez Marc Michel Rey, 1762), p. 2.

no one else may under any pretext whatever subject him without his consent. To determine that the son of a slave is born a slave is to determine that he is not born a man.'[15] Though his meaning of 'esclavage' encompassed varied types of social and political bondage, not specifically that of Black slavery, others directly applied his ideas to anti-slavery efforts and writings, including Jacques-Pierre Brissot, the revolutionary Girondin, author of *Nouveau Voyage dans les États-Unis*, and founder of the Société des Amis des Noirs in 1788.

Revolutionary rhetoric that centred on freedom from tyrannical governments pervades the four-act historical tragedy *Washington ou La Liberté du Nouveau Monde*, which first appeared at the Théâtre de la Nation on 13 July 1791, a year before the founding of the French Republic.[16] According to François Moreau, it and other plays by Billardon de Sauvigny helped to create the French 'myth of America' and to convey 'the influence of the American dream on French theater of the Enlightenment'.[17] First set in the camp of the iconic American leader and the halls of Congress, the play contains scenes filled with the words 'liberté' and 'esclavage' in the dialogue of Washington and his compatriots Lincol, Laurens fils, and Laurens père, who serve as mouthpieces for the dramatist's philosophical ideals. At the play's opening, Lincol expresses dejection after the American loss to the British in Charleston, before exclaiming to the lieutenant Macdal that his fighters would prefer 'death' to 'slavery'. In Act I Scene 5, when the envoy of the British king (the unnamed George III) offers the king's pardon and promise to re-establish American 'rights' ('droits'), Washington heatedly reminds him that seven years of 'devastation' ('ravages') by the British cannot be so easily forgotten; Washington's righteous anger builds as he warns the British envoy that man has woken up from the oppression of 'a dual slavery' ('un double esclavage') by thrones and altars, and, with the help of reason, is finding 'the love of justice and freedom' ('l'amour de la justice et de la liberté'). The *esclavage–liberté* binary also dominates an exchange between the 'Président' of the American Congress, Laurens *père*, and its 'Sécretaire' in Act III Scene 1. In this passage, Laurens *père* echoes Rousseau when he speaks of 'liberty' emerging in the heart of man who has been 'born into the prejudices

---

15 'Tout homme étant né libre & maître de lui-même, nul ne peut, sous quelque prétexte que ce puisse être, l'assujettir sans son aveu. Décider que le fils d'une esclave naît esclave, c'est decider qu'il ne naît pas homme': Rousseau, *Du Contrat social*, p. 159.

16 Edme-Louis Billardon de Sauvigny, *Washington, ou La Liberté du Nouveau Monde, tragédie en quatre actes, par M. de Sauvigny, représentée pour la première fois le 13 juillet 1791, sur le Théâtre de la Nation* (Paris, Chez Maillard d'Orivelle, 1791).

17 'L'influence du rêve américain sur le théâtre français des Lumières': François Moreau, 'Des Guerres d'Amérique à la Révolution française: Le Théâtre de Billardon de Sauvigny', *Revue de la Société d'histoire du théâtre*, 41:3 (June 1989), 271–84, at pp. 273, 275. Describing Billardon as a 'monarchiste' before 1789 and a 'patriote' and 'protégé' of Rousseau after 1789, Moreau emphasises that the author's love of the American people originated in part from his hatred of England (pp. 271–2). Along with *Vashington*, Billardon's American dramas include *Hirza ou les Illinois* (1767).

Revolutionary Tales of liberté *and* esclavage   21

of shameful slavery' and concludes, 'The slave becomes man in becoming its master' – that is, he becomes the master of 'liberté'.[18]

At key moments, Billardon emphasises that freedom-loving Americans serve as models for, and even teachers of, the French, while highlighting the heroism of French soldiers and their alliances with American patriots. In Act I Scene 2, Washington commends the French for their courage and 'noble apprenticeship' ('le noble aprentissage') to freedom – ideas underscored by Billardon in an addendum to the 1791 edition that resonate with those of Brissot. In *Nouveau Voyage dans les États-Unis*, Brissot explicitly calls upon the French to study and emulate Americans, who, as upholders of 'liberté', understand it and know how to conserve it; moreover, their 'liberty can dispose them to universal brotherhood' ('liberté peut [...] les disposer à la fraternité universelle').[19]

Real-life figures of the American Revolution and American settings that symbolised Franco-American alliances create an aura of encomium and *actualité*. Both Washington and Laurens praise the actions of French heroes: in Act I Scene 7, Laurens responds to Washington with references to Rochambeau (Jean Baptiste Donatien de Vimeur, comte de Rochambeau, 1725–1807), the commander of French forces in the American War, and General La Fayette (Gilbert du Motier, Marquis de La Fayette, 1757–1834), who camped with the real-life Washington at Valley Forge in December 1777 and led American soldiers in the Siege of Yorktown in 1781. In Act IV Scene 1, set on 'the shores of the Delaware' for the signing of a treaty with the French, Laurens again extols the Franco-American alliance, calling on France, 'Generous ally, avenger of America', to 'breathe with us the air of freedom!'[20]

The drama's homage to Washington as a humane, nearly divine warrior and sage teacher correlates with portrayals in contemporary French writings.[21] Its passing reference to Benjamin Franklin, prominent member of the Continental Congress who served as the United States minister to France from 1778 to 1785, also resonates with tributes to Franklin that recur in French publications: among them, an ode to Franklin as a wise, daring breaker of the chains

---

18   'Né dans les préjugés d'un honteux esclavage / [...] L'esclave deviant homme en devenant son maître': Billardon, *Vashington*, Act III Scene 1.

19   J. P. Brissot (Warville), *Nouveau Voyage dans les États-Unis de l'Amérique septentrionale, fait en 1788* (Paris: Buisson, 1791), vol. 1, p. xxi. Brissot also describes Quakers as models of independence and morality (p. xxv). Dubois, *A Colony of Citizens*, clarifies that Dénis Diderot and other Enlightenment or abolitionist writers 'took inspiration from the actions of the Quakers in North America' (p. 62).

20   'Généreux allié, vengeur de l'Amérique, / [...] Respirer avec nous l'air de la liberté!': Billardon, *Vashington*, Act IV Scene 1.

21   One passage lauding Washington's wisdom in Billardon's *Vashington* occurs in Act IV Scene 4, when Lincol says: 'The wise Washington possesses a supreme art, / It is to teach man to esteem himself' ('Le sage Washington possède un art supreme, C'est d'enseigner à l'homme, à s'estimer lui-même').

22   *Diana R. Hallman*

of 'esclavage', in *Mercure de France*.[22] In *Nouveau Voyage*, Brissot ranks Franklin, with Washington, among the 'principled men' ('hommes à principes') and 'heroes of humanity' ('vrais héros de l'humanité').[23]

Close in time to *Vashington*, another theatrical reference to Franklin appeared with more overt linkage to France's own realisation of *liberté* in the one-act *divertissement lyrique Le Triomphe de la République ou Le Camp de Grand Pré* by François-Joseph Gossec, with libretto by Marie-Joseph Chénier and ballets by Maximilien Gardel (Opéra, 27 January 1793).[24] In the final scene of this divertissement, which Mark Darlow describes as a work in which the 'Revolution celebrates itself',[25] the allegorical figure of La Liberté, accompanied by the 'Génies des Arts et de l'Abondence', descends as *deus ex machina* to recount her birth in Greece, entombment in Rome, revival in Helvétie, and – after Guillaume Tell had brought her to new life – her transplantation by Franklin to 'another Universe'. She then concludes that, even more than in Greece, Rome, Switzerland, or America, France has fulfilled her ideals: 'The French nation has understood her rights the best; / She knows how to proclaim, in banishing her kings, the unity of the Republic'.[26] Continental America, led by Franklin, is thus portrayed as an important nexus of freedom between Greece and its ultimate destination, France. After the goddess's declarations, a triumphant, brass-filled D major chorus, 'Vive la liberté', resounds; it leads to an *entrée des nations* (a convention inherited from *tragédie lyrique*; see Chapter 2, n. 44) including an *entrée des nègres*, with dancing and the playing of drums. Here, the revival of 'La Liberté', first in Franklin-led

---

22   *Mercure de France*, 130:23 (10 June 1786), 49. Other Franklin references in this periodical include his portrait (12 Feb. 1791) and a review of his *Mémoires* (25 June 1791). On the Franklin 'cult' in France, see James A. Leith, 'Le Culte de Franklin en France avant et pendant la Revolution Française', *Annales historiques de la Révolution française*, 48:226 (1976), 543–71.

23   Brissot (Warville), *Nouveau Voyage*, vol. 1, p. xxv.

24   François Gossec, *Le Triomphe de la République ou Le Camp de Grand Pré, divertissement lyrique en un acte, représenté à L'Opéra le 27 Janvier l'an 2ème de la République Française une et indivisible, paroles du Citoyen Chenier, la musique du Citoyen Gossec, les ballets du Citoyen Gardel* (Paris: Mozin, H. Naderman, n.d.). ('Grand Pré' probably refers to the 1747 Battle of Grandpré, when French Acadians and 'Indian' fighters surprised British forces during the War of the Austrian Succession.) The revolutionary one-act comédie by Nicolas Dalayrac and B. J. Marsollier des Vivetières *Arnill, ou Le Prisonnier américain* (Théâtre de l'Opéra-Comique, 1795) features the young, imprisoned American Arnill as a 'warm partisan of liberty' and lover of (French) painting and music.

25   Mark Darlow, *Staging the French Revolution: Cultural Politics and the Paris Opéra, 1789–1794* (New York: Oxford University Press, 2012), p. 332. On revolutionary rhetoric at the Opéra, see also M. Elizabeth C. Bartlet, 'The New Repertory at the Opéra during the Reign of Terror: Revolutionary Rhetoric and Operatic Consequences', in *Music and the French Revolution*, ed. Malcolm Boyd (Cambridge: Cambridge University Press, 1992), pp. 107–56.

26   'La Nation Française a mieux connu ses droits;/ Elle a su proclaimer, en banissant ses Rois,/ L'unité de la République': Gossec, *Le Triomphe de la République*.

Revolutionary Tales of liberté *and* esclavage   23

America and then in France, merges with an emblem of their shared power as enslavers of Africans. Save for this *entrée*, actual *esclavage* remains distant or subliminal in these enactments.

Counternarratives of Amérique:
Slavery and the Saint-Domingue/Haitian Revolution

In French Revolutionary theatre, a number of works written between 1789 and 1799 directly confronted the subject of colonial slavery, including those set in Amérique.[27] Among dramas overtly critical of the institution is *L'Esclavage des noirs, ou L'Heureux Naufrage*, a play of 1789 by Olympe de Gouges (1748–93), the feminist and abolitionist who would become victim of the *Terreur*'s guillotine. At its premiere at the Comédie Française on 28 December 1789, the play risked the ire of anti-abolitionists, colonialists, Club Massiac members,[28] and even certain American visitors to Paris: according to *Le Moniteur universel*, an animated audience, who came prepared to comment on 'the great cause of the liberty of *nègres*', responded raucously at its first performance.[29] The 'tumultuous' reaction helped to pull the work after only three performances, although de Gouges herself claimed in the preface to the play's 1792 edition that 'the colonists, who spare no expense to satisfy their cruel ambitions, bought off the actors'.[30]

By comparison, *Adonis, ou Le Bon Nègre*, first performed at the Théâtre de l'Ambigu-Comique in 1798, appears a somewhat less seditious piece, with

27 Jean-Claude Halpern's overview of French slavery works in 'L'Esclavage sur la scène révolutionnaire', *Annales historiques de la Révolution française*, 293–4 (1993), 409–20, includes (along with those mentioned in my text) the anonymous opera *Les Sauvages civilisés ou Le Roi bienfaisant* (Académie Royale de Musique, 1789), Charles-Jacob Guillemain's *Le Nègre aubergiste* (Théâtre du Vaudeville, 1793), J. M. Gassier's *La Liberté des nègres* (Variétés Amusante de Lazzari, 1794), Larivallière's comédie *Les Africains, ou La Triomphe de l'humanité* (Théâtre de la République, ?1795), and Favières's opéra-comique *Elisca ou L'Amour maternel* (Théâtre de l'Opéra-Comique, 1799). Moreover, 'sub-Saharan elements' appear in pre-1789 works performed in Paris and French colonies; see the listing of sixty-five French operas, seven divertissements/ballets, and twenty-nine plays in David M. Powers, *From Plantation to Paradise: Cultural Politics and Musical Theatre in French Slave Colonies, 1764–1789* (East Lansing, MI: Michigan State University Press, 2014), appendix 7, pp. 165–92.

28 The Club Massiac was a pro-slavery club of colonial planters located in Paris, with chapters in the provinces.

29 'la grande cause de la liberté des nègres': *Le Moniteur universel*, cited in Halpern, 'L'Esclavage sur la scène révolutionnaire', p. 410.

30 Halpern, 'L'Esclavage sur la scène révolutionnaire', p. 410; Olympe de Gouges, 'Preface to *The Slavery of the Blacks*, 1792', trans. in Laurent Dubois and John D. Garrigus (eds), *Slave Revolution in the Caribbean, 1789–1804: A Brief History with Documents* (Boston: Bedford/St Martin's, 2016), pp. 108–10, at p. 109.

24   *Diana R. Hallman*

its marked condemnations of rebellious slaves intertwined with sentimental, exotic slave portrayals.[31] Its Saint-Domingue backdrop placed it in the midst of a still-heated discourse, in proximity to the 1791 slave uprisings, the island's continuing conflicts, and France's first abolition of slavery in 1794. Underscoring the melodrama's topicality is the casting of the historical figure Georges Biassou (1741–1801), a general of the Black insurrection (fig. 1.1) who serves as dramatic foil to characters identified as *bons nègres*, particularly the trusted commander Adonis. While the naming of this title character after the Greek god connotes an idealised, even sexualised figure, the name Adonis may allude to the more collaborative revolutionary hero of Saint-Domingue, Toussaint Louverture (*c.*1743–1803), who, as French ally after the 1794 abolition, was made commander of French forces by 1796; as the island's governor (1797–1802), he worked to free it from colonial rule before his 1802 arrest and return to France at Napoléon's command (fig. 1.2).[32]

Another contemporary French play set in Saint-Domingue, Pigault-Lebrun's *Le Blanc et le noir* (1795), joined *Adonis* in engaging the Enlightenment-inspired discourse on slavery, with blatant references to Raynal and Rousseau: on the title page, Pigault-Lebrun includes an epigraph by Raynal, 'Anyone who tries to justify the system of slavery deserves deep contempt from the philosopher and a strike of the sword from the *nègre*'; and in his preface he acknowledges the author's inspiration, stating, 'I have read Raynal and I have written this work'; within the play itself, the master's son, Beauval *fils*, reads Raynal and Rousseau.[33]

While *Adonis* culminates with a clear abolitionist action in the freeing of slaves by White slave-owning planters, the d'Hérouvilles, the melodrama does

---

31   With reference to Picquenard's novel, my descriptions of *Adonis* are primarily based on the melodrama's published text: Louis-François-Guillaume Béraud and Joseph de Rosny, *Adonis, ou Le Bon Nègre, mélodrame, en quatre actes, avec danses, chansons, décors et costumes Créoles, par les Citoyens Béraud de la Rochelle et Joseph Rosny, ballets du Cit. Milon, artiste du Théâtre des Arts, représentée, pour la première fois, sur le théâtre de l'Ambigu-Comique, en fructidor de l'an 6e de la République* (Paris: Chez Glisau, Pigoreau, Pan, 1798). To date, I have not found original music, dance, or *mise en scène* sources.

32   The character may also have recalled Jean-Baptiste Belley (1747–1805), the Saint-Domingue *député* who helped sway the French Assemblée to abolish slavery. A 1797 painting by Anne-Louis Giroudet depicts Belley leaning against a bust of Raynal; with tricolours in scarf and hat, his portrayal symbolises the intersection of Enlightenment ideals, Republican principles, and freedom of French colonial slaves. See Pap Ndiaye and Louise Madinier, *Le Modèle noir de Géricault à Matisse: La Chronologie* (Paris, Musée d'Orsay: Flammarion, 2019), pp. 12–13.

33   'Quiconque s'efforce de justifier le système du l'esclavage, mérite du philosophe un profonde mépris et du nègre un coup de poignard'; 'J'ai lu Raynal & j'ai écrit cet ouvrage': Pigault-Lebrun, *Le Blanc et le noir, drame en quatre actes et en prose, représenté et tombé sur le Théâtre de la Cité le 14 Brumaire de l'an IV* (Paris: Mayeur, Libraire et Commissionnaire; Barba, Libraire, 1795), p. v. See also Halpern, 'L'Esclavage sur la scène révolutionnaire', p. 417.

not fully veer from a White colonialist perspective.[34] Its plot downplays slavery's cruelty by highlighting the serenity of faithful servants and the goodness of White masters. Moreover, in correspondence with the novel and with circulating accounts of slave uprisings by Saint-Domingue *colons*, it emphasises the violence of Biassou and his Black followers and their upending of racial hierarchy, while obscuring the abusive, dehumanising conditions of their *esclavage*. In an inversion of colonial reality, Biassou, described as 'the most formidable and ferocious of all the Africans' in Picquenard's novel,[35] becomes the brutal master who imprisons and enslaves Monsieur d'Hérouville. Set in opposition to Biassou, Adonis does not break the paternalistic code of French *colons*, but instead collaborates with and defends the White planters. In this allegory of slavery as a benevolent, paternalistic system, other Black characters demonstrate their contentment through music and dance, along with homages to their kind masters.

The music-making, dance, and even romance of island slaves in the opening sun-filled scenes of *Adonis* set a tone of levity and jollity. In the impersonation of slave characters, performers at the Ambigu-Comique appeared in 'costumes Créoles' and possibly in blackface;[36] some of them danced and played instruments linked to Black island culture, and spoke and sang in a dialect distinct from the language of White characters. In Scene 1, the young slave Lindor speaks of the old slave and drummer Simon before he says, in Creole dialect, that he wants to dance with the *négresse* Marinette but knows that she prefers being wooed; he then breaks into a serenade to Marinette, accompanied by his *banza*, or banjo.[37] Although Lindor adopts the European convention of serenading under his beloved's window, his African instrument and 'unrefined' dialect convey his racial difference and lower class status. His exotically coded (though 'authentic') banjo and use of the Creole pronoun 'li', 'z' fricatives, and

---

34 The melodrama's perspective reflects that of Picquenard's 'anecdote colonial', in which the author 'declares' that his story comes 'directly from the same family whose misfortunes I report, and from the *bon Nègre* who ended them' ('directement de la famille même dont je rapporte les malheurs, et du *bon Nègre* qui les terminés') and from his own Saint-Domingue experiences; Picquenard, *Adonis*, pp. vij, x–xj.

35 'le plus redoutable et le plus féroce de tous les africains': Picquenard, *Adonis*, p. 18.

36 Béraud and de Rosny, *Adonis*, title page. In *Réflexions sur les hommes nègres*, in *Oeuvres* (Paris: Cailleau, 1788), vol. 3, p. 97, Olympe de Gouges advises French actors 'to adopt the colour and the costume *nègre*' ('d'adopter la couleur et le costume nègre'), which she claims had not previously been done; cited in Léon-François Hoffmann, *Le Nègre romantique: Personnage littéraire et obsession collective* (Paris: Payot, 1973), p. 108.

37 Béraud and Joseph de Rosny, *Adonis*, Act I Scene 2, pp. 4–5. (Hereafter, references to text and staging of *Adonis* are drawn from this 1798 playscript.) Whether an actual banjo was heard cannot be confirmed without an available score and detailed press descriptions. Conceivably, the instrument may have been used only as an on-stage prop, while another string instrument in the orchestra imitated its sounds. The practice of orchestral instruments simulating the sounds of a lyre or guitar was common in operatic serenade scenes.

Figure 1.1. Georges Biassou. Dubroca and Juan López Cancelada, 1806. *Vida de J.J. Dessalines, Gefe de los negroes de Santo Domingo* (Mexico City: M. de Zúñiga y Ontiveros, 1806). Wikipedia Commons.

other language markers – as in the first *couplet* of his serenade, 'Zami bay moi p'tit baiser [...] Bouch! Toi li trop joliette' – helped audiences to imagine slave life in Saint-Domingue, perhaps even triggering memories in a portion of the French audience made up of exiled or visiting *colons*. Although not the first French theatrical work to use a type of 'petit-nègre', once a common French term for literary adaptations and often pseudo-versions of Black dialect, *Adonis* incorporates an early 'transcription' of Haitian *créole* by authors who appear to have some knowledge of the language, according to Léon-François Hoffmann.[38]

---

38 Hoffmann, *Le Nègre romantique*, pp. 106, 111.

Figure 1.2. Unidentified artist, *Toussaint Louverture, chef des noirs insurgés de Saint Domingue* ('commander of the Black insurgents of Saint-Domingue'), 1796–9. Bibliothèque Nationale de France.

28   Diana R. Hallman

Scenes 2 and 3 further enhance the *couleur locale* of Saint-Domingue with the inclusion of instruments familiar to the West Indies – perhaps an early attempt to convey a 'sonic color line'.[39] As Lindor playfully interacts with Marinette in Scene 2, they hear Simon calling fellow slaves to dance by playing his bamboula – the name for a single-headed drum of the French Caribbean and also a drum-accompanied dance of Saint-Domingue.[40] In Scene 3, to greet Adonis and the slaves' returning master, Simon beats his drum with *nègres* and *négresses* playing *calebasses*, possibly gourd shakers, to accompany singing and dancing. Without the availability of original scores or sources for the choreography by Louis Milon (1766?–1849?), we can only speculate about the dance styles that he created. As a product of the Paris Opéra ballet school who had performed as a Saracen as a teenager in *La Jérusalem délivrée* and as diverse pantomime characters in Parisian theatres by 1797, Milon would probably have employed generic codes common to late eighteenth-century French ballet and opera for other races, cultures, or nationalities.

Problematising the racial codes suggested through music, dance, and spoken or sung language, explicit statements and actions that contrast benign slavery and Black violence are woven into these entertaining scenes. In Scene 2, Marinette speaks of her master's suffering since 'le mauvais nègre' Biassou had begun 'to burn refineries and kill whites' ('brûler sucreries, et tuyer blancs'), triggering Lindor to promise that he, along with his slave brothers, will defend their master 'to the death' ('Jusqu'à la mort') against Biassou. In Scene 3, as slaves dance around her, Marinette sings *couplets* that describe her 'bonne maitresse' as a joyful, tender-hearted mother 'who takes care of her [slave] children' ('Qui gagner soin de ses enfans') and clearly depicts, in the *second couplet*, a cheerful picture of slavery that is 'bearable' ('supportable') when masters and mistresses are kind:

> Slavery is bearable.
> Oh! oh! oh!
> When it's like that
> Master is not less to us.
> Oh! oh! oh!
> That's true.
> Kindness is the model
> You must love him tenderly.
> Oh! oh! oh!

---

39   Jennifer Lynn Stoever, *The Sonic Color Line: Race and the Cultural Politics of Listening* (New York: New York University Press, 2016), cited in Matthew D. Morrison, 'Race, Blacksound, and the (Re)Making of Musicological Discourse', *Journal of the American Musicological Society*, 72:3 (Fall 2019), 781–823; he relates Stoever's term, defining the 'black/white hierarchical division of sound', to the 'construction of racialised scripts' within American popular music (p. 793).

40   This dance was also known in New Orleans and performed in Congo Square (see Chapter 5).

Revolutionary Tales of liberté *and* esclavage   29

Nègre is sensitive, *nègre* is faithful
When master is not mean to him.
Oh! oh! oh![41]

Further tributes to the kind Madame d'Hérouville follow in Scene 5 as the slaves celebrate her birthday, offering bouquets of flowers to the accompaniment of 'sweet music' ('une musique douce'). Deeply moved by their affectionate gestures, Madame d'Hérouville then announces that she and her husband are planning to return to France, free their slaves, and leave them their plantation. Rather than respond with joyful surprise, Simon, Marinette, and Lindor refuse, saying they would rather go with the d'Hérouvilles – signifying that devotion to their owners outweighs their desire for freedom.

This fantasy of happy harmony between mistress and slaves re-emerges in later scenes in Act III, which portray Azaca and Marinette playing 'nanny', or 'mammy', roles in caring for the d'Hérouville child: in Scene 1, Marinette sings a lullaby ('Dors, dors, bell' bell' petit fanfan') as she swings him in a hammock; in Scene 2, she and Azaca speak of their protectiveness of the 'petit maître', as Marinette addresses him. In thinking of the abandoned child's distress (as well as his mother's), with the kidnapping of Monsieur d'Hérouville, Adonis, and other slaves, Azaca echoes Lindor's earlier oath, declaring, 'Azaca would give her blood, her life to dry tears.'[42] Music accompanies sentimental gestures of the slaves' maternal affection, as indicated by stage directions: 'Marinette takes the child in her arms, sits down, and puts him on her knees and caresses him. Azaca, standing beside Marinette, also caresses him.'[43] As he waits for his mother, the young child responds to their affection, though he balks at their gentle admonishments; his use of dialect further reveals his close relationship to them and perhaps his juvenile use of language, or his own identity as an island-born White Creole.[44]

Adonis's personification of the *bon nègre*, 'the faithful and grateful servant' who would become a conventional type in French literature after 1789,[45]

---

41 'Esclavage être supportable. / Oh! oh! oh! / Quand c'est comm' ça /Maître à nous n'est pas moins / Oh! oh! oh! / C'est vrai cela. / De la bonté c'est le modèle, / Faut aimer li bien tendrement. / Oh! oh! oh! / Nègre est sensibl', nègre est fidèle, / Quand maître à il n'es pas méchant': Béraud and de Rosny, *Adonis*, Act I Scene 3.

42 'Azaca donneroit son sang, sa vie pour sécher larmes': Béraud and de Rosny, *Adonis*, Act III Scene 2.

43 'Musique. Marinette prend l'enfant dans ses bras, va s'asseoir, le met sur ses genoux et le caresse. Azaca, debout à côté de Marinette, le caresse aussi': Béraud and de Rosny, *Adonis*, Act III Scene 2.

44 Béraud and de Rosny, *Adonis*, Act III Scene 2.

45 Hoffmann, *Le Nègre romantique*, p. 138. Servais Étienne traces this type, which he labels 'le nègre généreux', to pre-Revolutionary literature, citing as examples Oroonoko in Madame Aphra Behn's English novel *Oroonoko or the Royal Slave* (1688) and Ziméo in Jean-François de Saint Lambert's short story *Ziméo* (1769); see Servais Éti-

deepens the portrayal of a harmonious, hierarchical world of master and slave. Shown as exceptionally close with the d'Hérouvilles, Adonis defends his owners against the imminent attack of Biassou and his band of Black soldiers, having declared in Act I Scene 6, 'Before they touch you, the earth must drink all the blood of Adonis.'[46] Despite the efforts of this loyal servant and other d'Hérouville slaves to stave off revolters in the battle of Act I Scene 8, Biassou kidnaps both Monsieur d'Hérouville and Adonis. (Previously Biassou has also taken Adonis's beloved Zerbine, whom he has made his concubine.) At the beginning of Act II in Biassou's palace, surrounded by soldiers, Adonis comforts his exhausted, beaten master, who speaks of the burned land, the 'smoking blood', bones, and ashes of victims, and his fear of a similar fate. Adonis attempts to reassure him, prays for freedom, and appeals to the soldiers to save his master; when d'Hérouville faints, Adonis holds him and wipes his face with a handkerchief. The sharp contrast between Biassou's cruelty and Adonis's devotion, shown through his caring gestures and willingness to die to protect his master, is blatantly conveyed in later scenes. In Act III Scene 6, after the French colonial forces of the *dragons rouges* have captured Adonis during his one-day release by Biassou, the slave falls at the feet of Madame d'Hérouville, who has come to the French camp to save him from a false accusation. He cries out, 'Mistress! Mistress! save Adonis! ... me not bandit, [...], me *bon nègre* who loves Whites always.'[47] To the astonishment of the soldiers, she momentarily breaks the code of race and class and tells Adonis that he should have thrown himself in her arms rather than at her feet. She then addresses the French officer, pleading for the innocent Adonis, whose integrity and defence of her husband distinguish him from Biassou. The officer immediately relents, reassuring Adonis that he should not fear and saying, 'all Whites will be your friends and your brothers', while ordering him to return to Biassou's palace to act as informant.[48]

Beyond the transparent plot and characterisation, philosophical exchanges between Biassou and Monsieur d'Hérouville give voice to Béraud and de Rosny's distinction of a 'humane' type of slavery with charitable slave-owners while acknowledging dual perspectives of master and slave. In Act I Scene 8, the White slave-owner and Black revolutionary leader argue their divergent views of humanity and social hierarchy, with Biassou insinuating that all 'barbares Européens' of Saint-Domingue have shamed and oppressed Blacks, before d'Hérouville retorts that it is Biassou who is both unlawfully brutal and unthankful of French graciousness: 'You call the French barbarians, you

---

enne, *Les Sources de 'Bug-Jargal'* (Brussels: L'Académie Royale de Langue et de Littérature Françaises, 1923), pp. 12, 17, 22, 28.

46 'Avant que li toucher vous, il faut que terre boive tout sang d'Adonis': Béraud and de Rosny, *Adonis*, Act I Scene 6.

47 'Maitresse! Maitresse! Sauvez Adonis! ... moi pas brigand, [...] moi bon nègre, qui aimer toujours blancs': Béraud and de Rosny, *Adonis*, Act III Scene 6.

48 'tous les blancs seront tes amis et tes frères': Béraud and de Rosny, *Adonis*, Act III Scene 6.

who were once well received in their homeland. ... You are ungrateful! ... who gave you the right to exercise violence?'[49] In a chastising diatribe that follows, d'Hérouville articulates a view that would become common in justifications of slavery: that only cruel slave-owners were guilty of oppression, but White women and children, and others who were kind and humane, were 'innocent' and thus undeserving of Biassou's ruthless attacks:

> I will not seek here to justify the cruelties that some Whites have committed, but should we punish the innocent for the guilty? What have these loving mothers done, these faithful wives, these nursing children, whom you mercilessly slaughter? [...] Who heals your wounds, who consoles you in your infirmities, if not these same White ones in whose blood you bathed? You who do not foresee anything beyond the day that enlightens you, what will be your fate, when you have looted, devastated, set everything on fire? Assuming that no White man escapes your fury, do you mean to extinguish the race? And these millions of inhabitants, who inhabit the Old World, will they not come to avenge the death of their massacred brothers! [...] abandon those who use your arm to appease their hatred, their passions; become a man again, and you will find your reward in the good you have done.[50]

Suggesting that Biassou has become 'sub-human' in his viciousness, D'Hérouville echoes ideas found in first-hand accounts and published propaganda during the years of the insurrection, which 'cast the violence in Saint-Domingue as a stark, racialised confrontation between civilised whites and barbaric enemies', as Popkin writes.[51] Visual depictions, such as 'Revolte des Négres à St. Domingue', reinforced the image of the Black insurrectionists as cut-throat and merciless.[52]

49 'Tu traits les Français de barbares, toi qui jadis fus bien reçu dans leur patrie! .... Tu es un ingrat! ... qui t'a donné le droit d'exercer la violence?': Béraud and de Rosny, *Adonis*, Act I Scene 8.

50 'Je ne chercherai point ici à justifier les cruautés que quelques blancs ont commises, mais doit-on punir l'innocent pour le coupable? Qu'ont fait ces mères tendres, ces épouses fidelles, ces enfans à la mamelle, que vous égorgez impitoyablement? [...] qui pansoit vos blessures, qui vous consoloit dans vos infirmités, si ce n'est ces mêmes blanches dans le sang desquelles vous vous baigués? Vous qui ne prévoyez rien au'delà du jour qui vous éclaire, quel sera votre sort, lorsque vous aurez tout pillé, dévasté, incendié? En supposant qu'aucun blanc n'échappe à votre fureur, pensez-vous pour cela en éteindre la race? et ces millions d'habitans, qui peuplent l'ancien monde, ne viendront-ils pas venger la mort de leurs frères massacrés! [...] abandonne ceux qui se servent de ton bras pour assouvir leur haine, leurs passions, redeviens homme, et tu trouveras ta récompense dans le bien que tu auras fait': Béraud and de Rosny, *Adonis*, Act I Scene 8.

51 Popkin, *Facing Racial Revolution*, pp. 9, 16. Popkin cites, for example, a 1793 letter written by Tarin, a White colonist, that describes the massacre of 800 Whites and his escape to survival existence in the woods.

52 Popkin, *Facing Racial Revolution*, pp. 9–10, fig. 1.

The upending of the White–Black hierarchy reaches a dramatic focal point in Act II, set in the palatial 'court' of Biassou. Following the above-mentioned scenes that highlight the 'esclavage' of d'Hérouville, Biassou speaks of the rich jewellery he has given Zerbine, and a group of slaves celebrate his power in a 'danse de caractère'. Biassou's dialogue heightens the role reversal, of slave now master, as he tells the plantation owner that he has saved his life because his 'talent' can serve him. (This theatrical directive corresponds to an account by an anonymous White author who reported that Boukman (Dutty), an early insurrectionist leader, restrained his soldiers from killing him because of his practical knowledge.[53]) Biassou later negotiates that 'when all the Whites recognise me as founder of the "liberté des noirs"' – that is, as both 'liberator' and 'master' – he will allow the couple to retire to their plantation or 'patrie'.[54] Further accentuating the inversion of the master–slave order, Madame d'Hérouville sings of sharing her husband's 'esclavage', and the slave Azaca greets Adonis as the 'master's liberator': in freeing his master, Adonis has counteracted Biassou's subversion and helped to re-establish the White–Black hierarchy.

The rebalancing of the racial power structure comes most strongly through the d'Hérouvilles' paternalistic displays of humanity and the liberation of Adonis and other slaves: actions that reinforce their 'proper' authority as granters of freedom. In Act III Scene 5, when Madame d'Hérouville hears that Adonis's life is at stake, she quickly expresses concern for his fate and affirms her morality in wanting to save him: 'let us extend our hand to virtue and serve humanité'.[55] As the melodrama ends, after the penultimate battle against Biassou, the abolitionist message prevails: Madame d'Hérouville takes the hand of Adonis, saying that his 'courage' and 'valour' have won him the title of 'saviour of the Colony' ('sauveur de la Colonie'), and Monsieur d'Hérouville pronounces that his slaves are free; he then directs Adonis, 'our friend, our brother' ('notre ami, notre frère'), to tell all the slaves that 'this earth, on which they have laboured for so long, is now their patrimonie'.[56]

Along with the denouement of liberation, the melodrama's picture of slave–master amity corresponds to accounts of Saint-Domingue colonists that obscure the maltreatment of slaves and extol loyal slaves during the insurrection; yet its portrayals – if set against descriptions of slavery, racial inequality, and anti-Black disdain in the United States by French travel writers of the late eighteenth century

---

53 Anonymous, 'La Révolution de Saint Domingue, contenant tout ce qui s'est passé dans la colonie française depuis le commencement de la Révolution jusqu'au départ de l'auteur pour la France le 8 septembre 1792', in Popkin, *Facing Racial Revolution*, p. 51.

54 'lorsque tous les blancs m'auront reconnu pour le fondateur de la liberté des noirs': Béraud and de Rosny, *Adonis*, Act IV Scene 5.

55 'allons tendre la main à la vertu, et servir l'humanité': Béraud and de Rosny, *Adonis*, Act III Scene 5.

56 'cette terre, qu'ils ont si long-tems labourée, est maintenant leur patrimoine': Béraud and de Rosny, *Adonis*, Act IV Scene 9.

Revolutionary Tales of liberté and esclavage   33

– indirectly diverge from seemingly less progressive and benevolent practices of the United States. In *Journal de voyage en Amérique*, the exiled Frédéric-Alexandre de la Rochefoucauld, duc de Liancourt, bemoaned the lack of concern for the problem of slavery in the United States, along with a lack of respect for republican laws and values. As Doina Pasca Harsanti explains, Liancourt writes that 'most Americans talked of equality without being bothered either by slavery and the horrific legislation designed for Blacks, or by the displacement of the Indians'.[57] In Liancourt's own words, written shortly after France's 1794 abolition of slavery, the treatment of Blacks and 'Indians' in the United States represented "'two stains, two big stains on the freedom of the Americans'".[58] Another French noble of Liancourt's circle, Médéric-Louis-Élie Moreau de Saint-Méry, known for his voluminous study of the French West Indies, *Loiz et constitutions des colonies françaises de l'Amérique sous le vent* (1784–90), reinforced his friend's assessments of racial problems in the United States, pointing out the nation's 'most universal prejudice against non-white people' and its coercion of even free Blacks to lives of poverty and degradation.[59] As a member of France's pro-slavery, pro-*colon* Club Massiac and designer of a detailed scheme of racial categorisation in French colonies, Moreau made one-sided condemnations which ring hollow. Harsanti speculates that the author may 'have had the ulterior motive of showing that ending slavery did not bring about the benefits abolitionists sought';[60] equally likely, he may have intended to accentuate France's comparative moral superiority, or simply projected onto the United States similar abuses that French colonists had committed and that France had long supported.

Though *Adonis* enjoyed 'the most brilliant success' ('le succès le plus brilliant') according to one theatre almanac,[61] a more enduring Revolutionary tale of French colonial slavery emerged in the theatrical adaptations of Bernardin de Saint-Pierre's novel, including Kreutzer's opéra comique of 1791 and the ballet adapted from it in 1806.[62] In these portrayals, the young lovers Paul and

---

57 Doina Pasca Harsanti, *Lessons from America: Liberal French Nobles in Exile, 1793–1798* (University Park, Pennsylvania: Pennsylvania State University Press, 2010), p. 73.

58 Frédéric-Alexandre de la Rochefoucauld, duc de Liancourt, *Journal de voyage en Amérique et d'un séjour à Philadelphie, 1 octobre 1794–18 avril 1795, avec des lettres et des notes sur la conspiration de Pichegru* (Baltimore: Johns Hopkins University Press, 1940), as cited and translated in Harsanti, *Lessons from America*, p. 73.

59 Médéric-Louis-Élie Moreau de Saint-Méry, *Voyage aux États-Unis d'Amérique, 1793–1798*, ed. Stewart L. Mims (New Haven: Yale University Press, 1913), as cited in Harsanti, *Lessons from America*, p. 74.

60 Harsanti, *Lessons from America*, p. 74.

61 Fabien Pillet, *Indicateur dramatique ou Almanach des théâtres* (Paris: chez Lefort; Malherbes, 1798), p. 194.

62 Rodolphe Kreutzer, *Paul et Virginie, comédie en prose et en trois actes, paroles de M **** [Edmond de Favières], *representée pour la 1re fois par les comédiens italiens le samedy [sic] 15 janvier 1791* [orchestral score] (Paris, Auteur, n.d.); Edmond de Favières, *Paul et Virginie, comédie en trois actes, en prose melée d'ariettes, représenté par les comédiens italiens*

Virginie live happily, along with their mothers, on a French colonial island, symbolically a space of freedom and exile; Kathrine Bonin describes this 'literary island' story as a 'timeless pastoral' merging the 'ideal and real'.[63] Although sentimental, pastoral ideas and cross-racial interchange play a greater role in this narrative, similar racialised tropes can be found. The title characters are kind, 'egalitarian' masters. The *bon nègre* Domingue, whose name cryptically links to the colony of Saint-Domingue, appears as a protective, fatherly figure who tills the soil beside his young master Paul and who, in Kreutzer's version, saves the lost, hungry pair from the treacherous island terrain.[64] The two masters and servant display mutual affection as their lives and identities intertwine: Virginie appropriates Domingue's song – to a beloved figure named 'Zoe' – in the first music heard in Act I; in this *chansonette* (*Allegretto*, 2/4), she sings syllabically, predominantly on quavers, in short folkish phrases in F major without overt exotic touches, and is joined by Paul in unison in the last phrase of her *couplets*. Domingue also addresses Paul with a 'Z' nickname that typically connotes a Black character – 'ma Zizi' – perhaps to signify intimacy as well as Paul's Creole status.[65] Moreover, Black characters again speak or sing in dialect. Slaves who help to rescue the lost Paul and Virginie sing in lilting folk-like rhythms and grace notes in the 'Choeur de nègres' of Act I, in C major and 6/8, addressing them

---

[libretto] (Paris: J. L. de Boubers, 1794); Rodolphe Kreutzer, *Paul et Virginie. Ballet-pantomime en 3 actes. Musique de Kreutzer. Représenté pour la première fois le jeudi 12 juin 1806* [*Musique manuscrite*]; Pierre-Gabriel Gardel, *Paul et Virginie, ballet-pantomime en trois actes par M. Gardel, maître des ballets de sa majesté, chef de la danse de L'Académie royale de musique, et membre de la Société philotechnique. musique de M. Kreutzer, premier violon de la Chapelle de Sa Majesté. représenté sur le théâtre de L'Académie de musique le mardi 24 du mois de juin 1806* [ballet libretto] (Paris: Chez Roullet, 1815). Also see François Le Sueur, *Paul et Virginie (ou Le Triomphe et la vertu), drame lyrique en trois actes représentée sur le Théâtre Faydeau [sic], paroles de l'auteur d'Iphigénie en Tauride de Piccinni* [Alphonse Dubreuil], *musique de Lesueur* [orchestral score] (Paris: J. H. Naderman, n.d.).

63 Kathrine M. Bonin, 'Reading the Literary Island: Colonial Narratives of France 1762–1832' (unpublished PhD dissertation, University of California, Berkeley, 2003), pp. 34, 69.

64 In Act I Scene 2 of Kreutzer's ballet-pantomime of 1806, Domingo (Domingue) and his wife Marie dance the *bamboula* at Paul and Virginie's request, enhancing perceptual links to Saint-Domingue.

65 'Z' names are commonly assigned to Black characters in late eighteenth- and early nineteenth-century French plays, operas, and novels. Along with 'Zoe' of Virginie's (Domingue's) *chansonette* and 'Zabi' in *Paul et Virginie*, 'Zerbine' appears in *Adonis* and 'Zoflora' in J. B. Picquenard's novel *Zoflora ou La Bonne Négresse* (Paris: Didot, 1800). In addition to uses in literary works, as Hoffmann notes (*Le Nègre romantique*, p. 63), 'Z' names became popular for court servants in eighteenth-century Paris, influenced by colonial examples as well as 'la mode orientale'; he cites 'Zambo, Zingha, Ziméo, Zulmé, Zoflora, Zizi, Zéphir' as well as 'Zamor', the Benghali servant of Madame du Barry who would become a Jacobin informant who helped seal her fate at the guillotine.

affectionately as 'Petits blancs, bien doux' ('Very sweet little Whites').[66] In the Act II storm scene, enacted in pantomime with lightning flashes and swirling string patterns and tremolos, an unnamed slave character strikes a protective pose as he gazes at the helpless Virginie on a storm-tossed ship, as the score describes: 'a Nègre, on his knees, who appears to want to tear her from the stern to save her'.[67]

Despite Paul and Virginie's benevolence and compassion for the plight of slaves and their defiance of the menacing *colon* Dorval, they are nonetheless enmeshed in the patriarchal system: signifying her higher status, Virginie addresses the older Domingue as 'tu', and Paul speaks of buying a slave's children to save them from more brutal masters. As in *Adonis*, a blissful accord exists among *bons maîtres* and *bons nègres*. When the *noir* Zabi, the pitilessly treated slave of Dorval, arrives in Act I Scene 2, suffering and weary after being pursued by slave-hunters, Virginie wipes the sweat from his forehead, and Paul wraps palm leaves around his bloody feet. In the Act I trio that follows, Paul encourages Zabi to tell him and his 'humane' sister Virginie of the pain he has suffered; as the music shifts from the pastoral F major to F minor in 2/4, Zabi, begins to sing syllabically and 'roughly', with semiquaver triplets in the second violins and violas projecting his agitation as he tells of the ruthless master who has sold him to a 'François', forcing him to flee and abandon his children (ex. 1.1). He wants to drown himself, but Paul responds empathetically, in dialogue preceding the trio's final section, inviting him (and his children) to live with them and work alongside Domingue. In the final phrases, now in B flat major and 6/8, the young masters sing joyfully of offering the fruit of their orchards to the 'bon Noir' as Zabi sings, 'no longer will he have to fear slavery' (ex. 1.2).[68] Then, in dialogue, after asking Zabi if he is thirsty, Virginie offers him water from her hands. This gesture, depicted in an illustration for the 1810 production of Kreutzer's opera at the Théâtre de l'Opéra-Comique (Feydeau), encapsulates the message that slavery can exist 'humanely' with the protection of sympathetic Whites, in the colonial Indies of Amérique and the East (fig. 1.3).

As in *Adonis*, the theatrical critique of slavery and promise of freedom in Kreutzer's *Paul et Virginie* adaptations appears overshadowed by the portrayal of 'benign' bondage. Despite the allusions to an egalitarian sharing of Creole culture, the central message remains: if White masters and mistresses are kind and good, and slaves, or Blacks, remain faithful, they can perhaps earn their freedom and co-exist in a blissful paradise. This moral underpins the dramas, clearly making the stories more palatable to French audiences than de Gouges's 'seditious' play. As Halpern speculates, the French public 'better accepts a freedom granted by generous Whites than the character of the vengeful Black who emancipates him-

---

66 Kreutzer, *Paul et Virginie* [orchestral score], p. 179.

67 'Un Nègre est à ses genoux qui paroit vouloir l'arracher de la poupe pour la sauver': Kreutzer, *Paul et Virginie* [orchestral score], p. 179.

68 'plus n'aurais peur de l'esclavage': Kreutzer, *Paul et Virginie* [orchestral score], pp. 45–6. This latter phrase sung by Zabi does not appear in Favières's libretto, *Paul et Virginie*, p. 8.

Example 1.1. Rodolphe Kreutzer, *Paul et Virginie* [orchestral score], Act I, Trio (Zabi, Paul, Virginie), pt I, bb. 46–61. Paris: auteur, n.d.

—(continued)

Example 1.1—*concluded*

Example 1.2. Rodolphe Kreutzer, *Paul et Virginie* [orchestral score], Act I, Trio (Zabi, Paul, Virginie), pt II, bb. 56–72. Paris: auteur, n.d.

—*(continued)*

self and does not respect the values of the White world.'[69] In lieu of the novel's tragic ending of Virginie's death through shipwreck, as poignantly depicted in Augustin Legrand's late eighteenth-century painting, Kreutzer's opera concludes with Paul and Zabi saving Virginie, the governor La Bourdonnais granting the '*bon Noir*' his freedom, and Zabi joining in a final chorus to a 'more beautiful day' ('plus beau jour').

69 'accepte mieux une liberté octroyée par des Blancs généreux que le personage du Vengeur noir qui s'émancipe par lui-même et ne respecte pas les valeurs du monde des Blancs': Halpern, 'L'Esclavage sur la scène révolutionnaire', p. 420.

Example 1.2—*continued*

—(*continued*)

Liberté, Esclavage, and Saint-Domingue in Early Nineteenth-Century Narratives

French theatrical works of the early nineteenth century would look again to the New World to portray the revolutionary rhetoric of *liberté*, with the American War of Independence enduring as subject and setting during the Restoration and July Monarchy. Examples include Leon Halévy's play *L'Espion* (Théâtre de l'Odéon, 1828), which depicts George Washington under the alias Harper in a tale of espionage during the American Revolution, and Paul Foucher's and Alboize's drama *La Guerre de l'independence ou L'Amérique en 1780* (Théâtre de la Gaîté, 1840), which brings back Washington as noble leader, with opening calls of 'Vive l'Amérique!' and references to Rochambeau and Lafayette as fight-

Example 1.2—continued

—(continued)

ers for American freedom. The lauded figure of Benjamin Franklin also reappears in Francis Cornu and Frédéric de Courcy's 1832 *vaudeville anecdotique Franklin à Passy ou le Bonhomme Richard*, given at the Théâtre du Palais Royal.

Against the grain of these and other allegories of liberty-loving America, French theatrical works and novels continued to depict stories of slavery set in the United States as well as French colonies of Amérique, although the Saint-Domingue massacres and Napoléon's reinstatement of slavery in 1802 had diminished the power of abolitionist ideology. *Paul et Virginie* adaptations, including Kreutzer's 1806 ballet-pantomine, would linger in the thea-

Example 1.2—*continued*

—(*continued*)

tre.[70] By the July Monarchy, some works with American settings incorporated secondary slavery-related plot elements and characters: Halévy's and Scribe's ballet-pantomime *Manon Lescaut* (Opéra, 1830), set in the time of Louis XV, moves to scenes in New Orleans in Act III (see Chapter 2).[71] The physical

70 Along with reprises, new staged versions include August Boulé and Eugène Cormon's 1841 drama (see Hoffmann, *Le Nègre romantique*, p. 92), and Victor Massé's opera (Théâtre Lyrique, 1876). Moreover, the widespread dissemination of Bernardin de Saint-Pierre's novel is evidenced by over 500 editions and translations indexed in Paul Toinet's *Paul et Virginie: Répertoire bibliographique et iconographique* (Paris: G.-P. Maisonneuve et Larose, 1963).

71 Fromental Halévy and Eugène Scribe, *Manon Lescaut, ballet-pantomime en trois actes,*

Example 1.2—concluded

beating of slaves is enacted, leading to Manon and the slave character Niuka becoming each other's protector as each suffers losses of freedom. With a more peripheral treatment of slavery, Halévy's and Saint-Georges's opéra-comique *L'Éclair* (Théâtre de l'Opéra-Comique, 1835), set in Boston, alludes to Henriette's owning of plantations and her cousin George's disparaging encounter with a *négrillon*, or young Black slave (also see pp. 102; 135–8).[72] As Helena

---

par M. Scribe. Musique composée par M. Halévy. décors de M. Cicéri. représenté pour la première fois, sur le Théâtre de l'Académie Royale de Musique, le 30 Avril 1830 [libretto] (Paris: Bezou, 1830).

72 See the libretto by Eugène de Planard and Henri de Saint-Georges, *L'Éclair* (Paris:

Figure 1.3. Virginie giving a drink of water to the slave Zabi in Kreutzer, *Paul et Virginie* (opéra comique), Act I Scene 2, costume of Mlle Alexandrine Saint-Aubin: 'Drink, *bon Noir*, drink. If that doesn't quench your thirst enough, I'll make a second trip.' Paris: Martinet, 1810. Bibliothèque Nationale de France

Spencer discusses in Chapter 3, Monpou's *Le Planteur* (Opéra, 1839) focuses on race and slavery in Louisiana more centrally and thornily.

Among theatrical and literary works of the post-Revolutionary period, Saint-Domingue would periodically return as an iconic, contested site reflective of conflicting views of race, slavery, and emancipation. Novels inspired by the insurrection, after Picquenard's *Adonis*, include the same author's companion novel *Zoflora ou La Bonne Négresse* (1800), which features both Biassou and fellow revolutionary Boukman, and J.-B.C. Berthier's *Félix et Éléonore, ou Les Colons malheureux* (1801), which elaborates on the massacre of Whites, with particular emphasis on the violence of *mulâtres*.[73] According to Hoffmann, René Périn's *L'Incendie du Cap* (1802) was one of many novels that attacked revolutionary leaders, perhaps manifesting Napoleonic views as it maligned Toussaint Louverture, '"this serpent that France has warmed in her bosom, [...] this incredible assemblage of villainy, ingratitude, stupidity, self-love and baseness, [...] who has forgotten the kindnesses of which France deigned to fill him".[74] Hugo's *Bug-Jargal* echoes the ambivalence of *Adonis* in depicting slavery and freedom in Saint-Domingue; although Susan Castillo Street surmises that the novel 'arguably sets the template for much subsequent writing about race and slavery in the nineteenth-century Atlantic world', its tropes and contradictions have many precedents.[75] While referring to several historical figures, Hugo, as in *Adonis*, concentrates on Biassou as a cruel, barbaric slave leader cast in sharp contrast with the *bon nègre* Bug-Jargal. Though portrayed as a noble son of an African king and fierce fighter, Bug-Jargal (also called Pierrot) emerges as the protecting slave who not only loves but saves the White colonial heroine Marie, as well as her husband, the French-born captain Léopold d'Auverney.

Hugo tells his story through the reminiscences of d'Auverney, who had been raised on the island plantations of his wealthy slave-owning uncle. As this character recalls the events of Saint-Domingue that he experienced as a twenty-year-old officer, he holds the ambiguous position as inheritor and critic of the colonial system, but also conveyor of contradictory views and images. While revealing his 'feeling of benevolent pity' ('sentiment de pitié bienvaillante') for maltreated, barely clothed slaves, his concern for 'a long habit of absolute despotism' of many

---

Dubuisson, [1835]). Close in time to *L'Éclair*, Gustave de Beaumont published his 'tableau' of American racial prejudice and slavery *Marie, ou L'Esclavage aux États-Unis: Tableau de moeurs américaines*, 2nd edn (2 vols, Paris: Gosselin, 1835), emphasising in its preface the American conundrum of 'so much servitude in the middle of so much liberty'.

73 Hoffmann, *La Nègre romantique*, pp. 134–6.

74 '"ce serpent que la France a réchauffé dans son sein, [...] cet assemblage inouïe de scélératesse, d'ingratitude de sottise, d'amour-propre et de basses, [...] qui a oublié les bontés dont la France a daigné le combler"': cited in Hoffmann, *Le Nègre romantique*, p. 135.

75 Susan Castillo Street, 'Writing Race and Slavery in the Francophone Atlantic: Transatlantic Connections and Contradictions in Claire de Duras's *Ourika* and Victor Hugo's *Bug-Jargal*', in *The Edinburgh Companion to Atlantic Literary Studies*, ed. Leslie Elizabeth Eckel and Clare Frances Elliott (Edinburgh: Edinburgh University Press, 2016), pp. 119–30, at p. 119.

Revolutionary Tales of liberté and esclavage 45

planters, and a recognition of his having been born with 'all the privileges of rank in a country where colour was enough to give it', d'Auverney nonetheless does not throw off his heritage entirely.[76] For example, he denounces 'the disastrous decree' ('ce désastreux décret') of 15 May 1791 of France's National Assembly that 'granted to free men of colour the equal sharing of political rights with Whites' before recalling his own shunning of a rich 'sang mêlé' ('mixed blood').[77] In Hoffmann's evaluation of d'Auverney's equivocal views, he wonders if Hugo 'had wanted to neutralise certain judgements [...] which risked appearing too progressive and tolerant'.[78] Through the narrator's voice, Hugo further reveals a *colon*'s perspective when he describes the burning destruction and reports that 'rebellious slaves were, they say, already masters' of several plantations.[79] In heated quarrels of government officials overheard by d'Auverney, the island's governor more intensely paints scenes of horror; after announcing the massacre of *colons* and – corresponding to the brutal imagery in late eighteenth-century accounts and d'Hérouville's descriptions – he claims that the standard ('étendard') of rebelling slaves 'is the body of a child carried at the end of a spike'.[80] Among those expressing divergent reactions at the gathering, including members of the colonial and provincial assemblies and leading *colons*, the old general Rouvray mutters to d'Auverney that Enlightenment-fuelled ideas of 'philanthropists' and 'négrophiles' – ideas that 'are poison in the tropics' ('sont un poison sous les tropiques') – are to blame for the insurrection, which he sees as a 'consequence' ('contrecoup') of the fall of the Bastille.[81] While implying that the Club Massiac's promoting of a stringent version of slavery had fomented the insurrection's 'horrors', Rouvray's anti-revolutionary views resonate with the paternalistic magnanimity depicted in *Adonis* and *Paul et Virginie* when he says, 'it was necessary to treat the *nègres* with gentleness, not to call them to sudden emancipation'.[82]

In this complex novel, variously interpreted as both pro-abolitionist and pro-colonial,[83] Hugo plays with assumed racial prejudices and inherited racial

---

76 'une longue habitude de despotism absolu'; 'de tous les privileges du rang dans un pays où la couleur suffisait pour le donner': Hugo, *Bug-Jargal*, pp. 31, 34, 36–8.

77 Hugo, *Bug-Jargal*, p. 37.

78 Léon-François Hoffmann, 'Victor Hugo, les Noirs et l'esclavage', *Francofonia*, 31 (Autumn 1996), pp. 47–60, at p. 48.

79 'les esclaves rebelles étaient, disait-on, déjà maîtres': Hugo, *Bug-Jargal*, p. 73.

80 'Leur étendard est le corps d'un enfant porté au bout d'une pique': Hugo, *Bug-Jargal*, pp. 73–5.

81 Hugo, *Bug-Jargal*, p. 80. On the term 'négrophile', see this volume's Chapter 3, n. 37.

82 'Il fallait traiter les nègres avec douceur non les appeler à un affranchissement subit': Hugo, *Bug-Jargal*, p. 80.

83 See Kathrine M. Bonin, 'Signs of Origin: Victor Hugo's *Bug-Jargal*', *Nineteenth-Century French Studies*, 36:3–4 (Spring–Summer 2008), 193–204; Pascale Gaitet, 'Hybrid Creatures, Hybrid Politics, in Hugo's "Bug-Jargal" and "Le Dernier Jour d'un condamné"', *Nineteenth-Century French Studies*, 25:3–4 (Spring–Summer 1997), 251–65.

codes. When d'Auverney comes to know Bug-Jargal, his rival, saviour, and friend who is fluent in French and Spanish, he is surprised to discover that the hidden voice who serenades Marie is that of this slave hero; when he sees him carrying her off in the mayhem, he imagines that Bug-Jargal will rape, not protect her. As Street explains, while Hugo portrays the island hero as a 'noble embodiment of natural man', he also shows him, at least temporarily, as 'the incarnation of illicit, interracial desire'.[84] With further racist overtones, Hugo borrows Moreauian classifications, identifying, for example, Biassou as a *sacatra*, another insurrection leader, Ogé, as a *mulâtre*, and Habibrah, the *bouffon*-like slave favoured by d'Auverney's uncle but who eventually murders him, as a *griffe* – perhaps implying the dangers of miscegenation.[85] Hugo also reflects on island distinctions between 'les noirs *créoles*' and 'les nègres *congos*', or non-native-born Blacks.[86]

Striking parallels with *Adonis* can be found in d'Auverney's imprisonment by Biassou and his observations of a disordered world in which the Black general confuses French traditions and signifiers: he speaks French poorly, enslaves two White children, flies the Republican *tricolore* alongside the *ancien régime's* white *fleurdelysé*, wears a strangely concocted uniform, and orders his *obi* to perform a Catholic mass, which d'Auverney sees as a 'parody' for inspiring violence and revenge.[87] Biassou implies that Whites are barbarous, though less explicitly than in *Adonis*, but then refers repeatedly to 'revenge' and 'liberty' as dual inspirations for his followers. He blends the Creole dialect of the phrase 'Touyé papa moé, ma touyé quena toué!' ('Kill my father, I will kill yours') with French: 'Vengeance, gens du roi! Liberté à tous les hommes!' ('Vengeance, people of the king! Liberty to all men!').[88] D'Auverney's interpretations of Biassou's invocation for revolutionary freedom, which he mockingly categorises as a 'soldiery sermon' ('sermon soldatesque') and 'extraordinary pantomime' ('la pantomime extraordinaire'), call to mind early French historical accounts that refrained from viewing the slave insurrections as truly revolutionary or part of transatlantic revolutionary culture (see p. 16).[89]

---

84 Street, 'Writing Race and Slavery', p. 127.

85 Hugo, *Bug-Jargal*, pp. 33, 114–115. Citing Servais Étienne and Georges Debien, Hoffmann claims that Hugo drew from Bryan Edwards's *Histoire de St.-Domingue*, Garran Coulon's *Rapport sur les troubles de Saint-Domingue*, and Pamphile de Lacroix's *Mémoires*: see *Le Nègre romantique*, p. 171. He does not mention a direct use of Moreau's *Description topographique* (see p. 8, n. 17).

86 Hugo, *Bug-Jargal*, p. 58.

87 Hugo, *Bug-Jargal*, pp. 118–20.

88 Hugo, *Bug-Jargal*, pp. 122–3. Heather Turo discusses Hugo's enrichment of his 1826 edition with Haitian Creole and nuanced linguistic uses in '"Bug-Jargal" and Victor Hugo's Linguistic Commentary on Haitian Creole', *The Journal of the Midwest Modern Language Association*, 43:2 (Fall 2010), 169–85, at p. 171.

89 Hugo, *Bug-Jargal*, p. 124.

Revolutionary Tales of liberté and esclavage   47

In d'Auverney's imprisonment by Biassou, music and dance play important roles in depicting his anxiety as prisoner and dread of Black 'savagery', while signalling Hugo's application of 'local colour' to the Saint-Domingue setting. Instruments played by Biassou's followers include the African marimba, the *balafo* (*balafon*), drums (*tam-tams* and *tambours*), and guitars. Hugo also describes d'Auverney's recognition of *griots*, West African singing poets and story-tellers, whom he likens to minnesingers and *trouvères* before describing, in racialised, erotic language, their 'barbarous songs' ('les chansons barbares') that accompany 'lewd dances' ('des danses lubriques') of women, including the *chica*.[90] Rather than *Adonis*'s scenes of light-hearted entertainment, Hugo presents these, in d'Auverney's mind, as a frightening, grotesque, demonic *danse macabre* performed as preliminary rite for his execution: 'the ballet of the drama in whose dénouement I am to be covered in blood'.[91] He of course is saved from his imagined fate by Bug-Jargal.

In 1826, at the time of Hugo's revised *Bug-Jargal*, Henri-Montan Berton's opéra comique or 'drame lyrique' *Les Créoles* appeared at the Théâtre de l'Opéra-Comique on 14 October; according to *Le Figaro*, censors had changed its original setting of Saint-Domingue to Madagascar to avoid political sensitivities.[92] In the following decade, however, the Théâtre du Cirque Olympique would bring the still-controversial subject before the public in an intensely visceral treatment of the Saint-Domingue/Haitian Revolution, when Napoléon, as Consul, sent an expedition of over 3,000 soldiers in 1801–2 to restore France's direct rule and to arrest Louverture, after becoming increasingly fearful that he, as governor and army commander, had been acting to secure independence from France.[93] Spectacles of violence that encircled this expedition, which was headed by Napoléon's brother-in-law General Charles Leclerc, served as focal points in the staging of the melodrama *Les Massacres de Saint-Domingue, ou L'Expédition du général Leclerc* by Prosper and Anicet-Bourgeois, which premiered at the Cirque on 25 April 1837.[94] Extended enactments of fighting and

---

90 Hugo, *Bug-Jargal*, pp. 105–108, 112, 125. Julia Prest identifies the *chica* as a slave dance described by Moreau (Médéric-Louis-Élie Moreau de Saint-Méry, *De la danse* (Parma: Bodoni, 1801), pp. 43–5) as 'lascivious' and 'magical', imitated by Whites in Saint-Domingue theatres in the 1770s–80s, and banned from ballrooms: see Julia Prest, 'Pale Imitations: White Performances of Slave Dance in the Public Theatres of Pre-Revolutionary Saint-Domingue', *Atlantic Studies*, 16:4 (2019), 502–20, at pp. 4–6.

91 'le ballet du drame dont je devais ensanglanter le dénouement': Hugo, *Bug-Jargal*, pp. 106–8.

92 'Opéra-Comique', *Le Figaro*, 16 Oct. 1826, p. 2.

93 Philippe R. Girard, *The Slaves Who Defeated Napoléon: Toussaint Louverture and the Haitian War of Independence, 1801–1804* (Tuscaloosa: University of Alabama Press, 2011), pp. 40–8.

94 My discussion draws upon Barbara Cooper's edition or 'présentation', based on censors' manuscripts available in the Archives Nationales de France (F/18/1325). See Prosper (Auguste Lepoitevin de L'Égreville) and (Auguste) Anicet-Bourgeois, *Les Massacres*

death permeate the seven tableaux and three acts, as the critic Edouard Monnais summarised: 'Combats, dances, decorations, massacres, fires, nothing is lacking in the effect of mimodrama.'[95] The melodrama's emphasis on 'massacres' in title and staging resonated in many critics' responses: Frédéric Soulié of *La Presse* called the spectacle a 'hideous' one about 'this bacchanalia of assassinations and crimes' ('cette bacchanale d'assassinats et de crimes') while a writer for *L'Europe* understood its elemental appeal, predicting that 'All Paris will shudder' ('Tout Paris ira frémir').[96] Jules Janin demanded in racist language: 'Why illustrate [...] this horrible revolution of Saint-Domingue? What interest can we have in these ferocious animals who, under pretext that they have Black skin, bring iron, fire, rape, all the ravages to this miserable island?'[97] No longer the revolutionary hero, here Toussaint Louverture takes the place of Biassou: portrayed as rapacious and traitorous, he organises a civic banquet to celebrate racial goodwill that becomes a site for killing Whites and also murders the *bon nègre* Orféo, a character corresponding to Bug-Jargal, as Cooper notes.[98] Janin viewed 'cet horrible Toussaint-Louverture' as being as tyrannical as Caligula and Nero and made clear that he had not led a noble fight for independence, but a series of ignoble massacres, nothing like the battles of Napoléon and the Grande Armée enacted the previous evening in which French soldiers and Prussians, English, and Russians 'killed each other nobly, courageously, heroically.'[99]

Bringing the revolutionary tale of Saint-Domingue to a theatre then devoted to military history, not as a story of independence gallantly fought for and won, but as that of a bloody revolt of slaves versus masters, again exposed France's fluctuating, contradictory views of *liberté* in the face of still-existing *esclavage* in the New World. This and other slave narratives, particularly those centred

---

de Saint-Domingue, ou L'Expédition du Général Leclerc, pièce inédite, présentation de Barbara T. Cooper (Paris: L'Harmattan, 2019).

95 'Combats, décorations, danses, incendies, rien ne manque à l'effet du mimodrame': Ed. M. [Édouard Monnais], *Le Courrier français*, 17 April 1837, p. 2; cited in Prosper and Anicet-Bourgeois, *Les Massacres*, pp. xxxvi, 133.

96 Frédéric Soulié, *La Presse*, 17 April 1837, p. 2; ZZZ., *L'Europe*, 17 April 1837, p. 2; cited in Prosper and Anicet-Bourgeois, *Les Massacres*, p. 136.

97 'Pourquoi illustrer [...] cette horrible revolution de Saint-Domingue? Quel intérêt pouvons-nous porter à ces bêtes féroces qui, sous prétexte qu'elles ont la peau noire, portent dans cette île malheureuse le fer, le feu, le viol, tous les ravages?': J.J. [Jules Janin], *Journal des débats*, 17 April 1837, p. 2; cited in Prosper and Anicet-Bourgeois, *Les Massacres*, p. 137.

98 Barbara Cooper, 'Introduction', in Prosper and Auguste Anicet-Bourgeois, *Les Massacres*, points out many parallels between the melodrama and *Bug-Jargal*, including the shared use of the name Marie for the love interests of Bug-Jargal and Oréo, also an African prince, and the similar naming of the *colon* Dauvernay and Hugo's d'Auverney (p. xx).

99 J.J. [Jules Janin], *Journal des débats*, 17 April 1837, p. 2; cited in Prosper and Anicet-Bourgeois, *Les Massacres*, p. 137.

on Saint-Domingue and the 'grands malheurs en Amérique', as Hugo writes,[100] further reveal that, despite the ideals of Rousseau, Raynal, Brissot, and other Enlightenment and abolitionist authors, the Black struggle for *liberté* and *égalité* remained problematic for the French, particularly when hierarchical, colonial codes were broken. As *Adonis* and *Paul et Virginie* adaptations underscore in their attempts to persuade and appease audiences through contrived stereotypes of the *bon nègre* and *bon maître*, the belief that the *liberté* of Black slaves came most nobly when earned through fidelity, when granted by White masters or officials, or when slaves could live amicably within White power structures, overshadows the works' abolitionist tinges. Moreover, the representations of Biassou's and Louverture's fights for freedom, even though inspired by the same Enlightenment/republican ideals shared by France and the United States, would remain distinct from those of the revolutionary French-American heroes Washington, Rochambeau, or Lafayette. Hindered by alluring tropes of exoticism and barbarism and fears of uncontrolled difference, the Black subjects featured in these tales of *esclavage* and the Saint-Domingue/Haitian Revolution would be kept to the outer edges of transatlantic revolutionary history and culture, while casting a long shadow on France's myths and imaginings of *liberté* in Amérique and within its own shores.

---

100 Hugo, *Bug-Jargal*, p. 27.

2

Justamant's *Le Bossu* and Depictions of Indigenous Americans in Nineteenth-Century French Ballet

Marian Smith, Sarah Gutsche-Miller and Helena Kopchick Spencer[1]

On Saturday evening 19 January 1867, a revival of the play *Le Bossu* opened at the Théâtre de la Porte-Saint-Martin with new ballet divertissements choreographed by Henri Justamant starring the dancer Mlle Mariquita.[2] *Le Bossu*, an adaptation of Paul Féval's popular novel, was already well known to Parisian audiences, and the actors Mélingue, Vannoy, and Laurent all reprised their roles from the original 1862 production. The novelty of Justamant's ballets was therefore a key attraction: as Louis Ulbach wrote in *Le Temps*, 'the new ballet will bring the crowds back, even those that already applauded *Le Bossu*'.[3] Justamant created two new divertissements for the reprise: a series of lively 'gypsy' dances in the fourth tableau and an elaborate 'Grand Ballet Indien' in the eighth tableau, the latter of which featured Native American 'prairie girls' and 'huntresses' frolicking by the Mississippi River flowing pure gold.[4] Ulbach's review proved prophetic: Mariquita's fiery performance of Justamant's choreography, especially in the exotic 'Grand Ballet Indien', came to be one of the most celebrated elements of the show, and Justamant's 'Indian' ballet entered

---

1   We would like to acknowledge important contributions from Doug Fullington and Lisa Arkin in the writing of this chapter. We would also like to thank Dr Hedwig Müller (Universität zu Köln, Theaterwissenschaftliche Sammlung, Schloss Wahn) and the library staff at the New York Public Library and Bibliothèque Nationale de France who have assisted us in our archival study of Justamant's staging manuals.

2   Reviews alternated between referring to Mariquita as Mlle and Mme.

3   'Un ballet neuf va ramener la foule, même celle qui a déjà applaud le Bossu': Louis Ulbach, 'Revue théatrale', *Le Temps*, 28 Jan. 1867, p. 1.

4   Here and throughout the chapter we use the words 'gypsy' and 'Indian' when referring to, respectively, Romani people and Indigenous Americans as perceived and represented by Europeans in the nineteenth century. We use the term 'Native American' to refer to Indigenous communities in what is now the United States.

the popular imagination, becoming one of the most significant portrayals of Indigenous Americans in nineteenth-century Parisian ballet.

This essay examines representations of Indigenous Americans in nineteenth-century French ballet, focusing on the 'Grand Ballet Indien' of *Le Bossu* as a case study. Although several scholars have written about depictions of Indigenous peoples in European music and dance, most have focused on written texts (libretti, press reviews), iconography (costume designs), and sound (musical scores).[5] Few have studied movement. After all, any discussion of actual movement is difficult, if not impossible, given the ephemeral nature of dance as an embodied oral tradition. For *Le Bossu*, however, we have Justamant's manuscript staging manual with choreographic notations of his version of the 'Grand Ballet Indien' divertissement from the 1867 Porte-Saint-Martin revival. The notations have allowed us to reconstruct what these so-called 'Indian' dances would have looked like in late nineteenth-century Parisian ballet – or, at least, how they were envisioned by one of the leading choreographers of the day.[6]

---

5 Scholarship on French theatrical depictions of Indigenous Americans has given significant attention to Rameau's *Les Indes galantes* and its fourth *entrée*, *Les Sauvages*. See, for example, Roger Savage, 'Rameau's American Dancers', *Early Music*, 11:4 (1983), 441–52; Thomas Betzwieser, *Exotismus und 'Türkenoper' in der französischen Musik des Ancien Régime: Studien zu einem ästhetischen Phänomen* (Laaber: Laaber, 1993), pp. 177–9; Joellen A. Meglin, '*Sauvages*, Sex Roles, and Semiotics: Representations of Native Americans in the French Ballet 1736–1837, Part One: The Eighteenth Century', *Dance Chronicle*, 23:2 (2000), 87–132, at pp. 97–115; Reinhard Strohm, '*Les Sauvages*, Music in Utopia, and the Decline of the Courtly Pastoral', *Il saggiatore musicale* 11:1 (2004), 21–50; Michael V. Pisani, *Imagining Native America in Music* (New Haven: Yale University Press, 2005), pp. 37–43; Olivia Bloechl, *Native American Song at the Frontiers of Early Modern Music* (Cambridge: Cambridge University Press, 2008), pp. 177–215; Ralph P. Locke, *Music and the Exotic from the Renaissance to Mozart* (Cambridge: Cambridge University Press, 2015), pp. 235–8; and Devin Burke, 'Reinventing Colonialism: Staging Jean-Philippe Rameau's *Les Indes galantes* in the 21st Century', unpublished manuscript currently under review. The authors would like to thank Prof. Burke for generously sharing a draft of this article and other materials. Meglin's two-part survey of eighteenth- and nineteenth-century representations of Indigenous Americans in French ballet ends with *Les Mohicans* (Opéra, 1837). See Joellen A. Meglin, '*Sauvages*, Sex Roles, and Semiotics: Representations of Native Americans in the French Ballet 1736–1837, Part Two: The Nineteenth Century', *Dance Chronicle*, 23:3 (2000), 275–320. Pisani has also identified several early nineteenth-century musico-dramatic works featuring Indigenous American characters and has highlighted the significance of European-composed 'war dances' in constructing the 'pagan savage' trope. See Pisani, *Imagining Native America*, pp. 84–5 and 116–25.

6 Justamant's manuscript staging manuals are held principally by three archives: the Theaterwissenschaftliche Sammlung at the University of Cologne, the New York Public Library, and the Bibliothèque Nationale in Paris (the Parisian holdings have also been digitised on Gallica). Important foundational scholarship on Justamant includes Jane Pritchard, 'Divertissement Only: The Establishment, Development and Decline

Justamant's distinctive notation system is remarkably clear and explicit, and can be read by any dance scholar well versed in the gestural language of nineteenth-century ballet, making his staging manuals a valuable – if still largely untapped – resource. Choreography is illustrated using a combination of prose descriptions and stick-figure drawings of dancers (dancers are depicted as triangular torsos and bell-shaped skirts or, in shorthand, as small circles), with dotted lines tracing the dancers' directional path across the stage and prose commentary below each illustration explaining the specific steps and stage actions.[7] The right margin indicates musical cues, including changes of key, time signature, and/or tempo, as well as how many bars are used to execute each figure or combination. The staging manual for the 'Indian' ballet of *Le Bossu* also includes personnel lists and photographs of dancers in costume, offering an intriguing and unusually detailed glimpse into danced representations of Native Americans on the nineteenth-century French stage.

As Justamant's choreographic notations make clear, what constituted exotic 'Indigenous' dance was more complex and varied than one might expect from reading descriptions in libretti and reviews of various other nineteenth-century stage works featuring Indigenous American characters. While the notations for *Le Bossu* provide evidence of certain gestural markers associated with exoticism and *sauvagerie*, they also reveal how, even on a popular stage like the Porte-Saint-Martin, dances for characters labelled 'sauvages' did not exhibit as many visual stereotypes as one might assume. Rather, Justamant's choreography was highly stylised and mediated, relying primarily on the steps and poses of classical ballet. Furthermore, Justamant's pastoral images of Native Americans as gentle maidens and brave huntresses at one with their idyllic landscape drew on a long history of stereotypes associated with the myth of

---

of the Music Hall Ballet in London' (unpublished manuscript, 2005); Claudia Jeschke and Robert Atwood, 'Expanding Horizons: Techniques of Choreo-Graphy in Nineteenth-Century Dance', *Dance Chronicle*, 29:2 (2006), 195–214; Gabi Vettermann, 'In Search of Dance Creators' Biographies: The Life and Work of Henri Justamant', in *Les Choses Espagnoles: Research into the Hispanomania of Nineteenth-Century Dance*, ed. Claudia Jeschke, Gabi Vettermann, and Nicole Haitzinger (Munich: E-Podium, 2009), pp. 124–32. See also Sarah Gutsche-Miller, 'Liberated Women and Travesty Fetishes: Conflicting Representations of Gender in Parisian Fin-de-Siècle Music-Hall Ballet', *Dance Research*, 35:2 (2017), 187–208; Sarah Gutsche-Miller, *Parisian Music-Hall Ballet, 1871–1913* (Rochester: University of Rochester Press, 2015), pp. 70–1 and p. 307, n. 65. Gutsche-Miller adjusts Justamant's year of death to 1890, previously given as 1886 by Vettermann based on an incorrect death record. Justamant's notations for *Giselle*, *Paquita*, and *Le Corsaire* are analysed in Marian Smith and Doug Fullington, *Five Ballets from Paris and St Petersburg: Giselle, Paquita, Le Corsaire, La Bayadère, and Raymonda* (Oxford: Oxford University Press, forthcoming).

7 Gender is differentiated not by the shape of the figure but rather by the colour of ink: male characters and their stage directions are drawn in black ink, and female characters and their stage directions are in red.

Justamant's Le Bossu *and Depictions of Indigenous Americans*   53

the *bon sauvage* or 'noble savage'; this imagery contrasts sharply with the many nineteenth-century productions that portrayed Indigenous peoples as bloodthirsty and barbaric. Although no less problematic, Justamant's 'Grand Ballet Indien' adds nuance to our understanding of how stereotypes of Indigenous peoples were disseminated on the French stage into the late 1800s.

We begin our study by recalling some of the seminal artistic works and cultural encounters that shaped French perceptions of Indigenous Americans in the nineteenth century, in order to establish a context for understanding theatre-going Parisians' expectations of and assumptions about 'Indians'. We then provide a broad overview of the different kinds of danced representations of Indigenous Americans that French audiences might have seen presented on the Parisian stage throughout the nineteenth century in both state and commercial venues. While comparatively few nineteenth-century ballets depicted Indigenous Americans, those created at the Parisian boulevard theatres in particular were performed frequently, leaving a lasting impression that belies their relatively small number. Our study then moves into the specific case of *Le Bossu*, focusing on Justamant's choreography for the 1867 revival to explore what an 'Indian' ballet would have looked like.[8]

Indigenous Americans in the French Imagination

For much of the nineteenth century, no one was more influential in shaping French perceptions of America and its peoples than the Vicomte François-René de Chateaubriand, who through his novels and travelogues sparked the imagination of French readers, travellers, and creative artists with florid, highly romanticised depictions of America as a new Eden.[9] (On Chateaubriand's evoc-

---

8   Justamant's manuscript credits the music for this ballet to Artus and Calendini, but regrettably, their scores do not survive. The only extant trace of the music is Amédée Artus's 'Quadrille pour *Le Bossu*' for solo piano, published by Colombier. The sheet music is held by the Bibliothèque Nationale de France, VM12 E-346. The 1893 auction catalogue of Justamant's ballet manuscripts lists a musical score for 'Les Chasseresses' in lot 10 ('Ballets divers et Partitions musicales'): *Vente du 15 mai 1893 (Hôtel Drouot), Catalogue de livres anciens et modernes et des manuscrits originaux de M. Henri Justamant* (Paris: Paul, Huard et Guillemin, 1893), The New York Public Library, Performing Arts Research Collection, *MGP 86-49, pp. 19–20. Unfortunately, all of the volumes from lot 10 are now considered lost.

9   On *Atala* and *René* as reflections of France's contemporary colonial ambitions in America, see Colin Smethurst, *Chateaubriand: Atala and René* (London: Grant and Cutler, 1995), pp. 59–63. See also Laurence M. Porter, 'Consciousness of the Exotic and Exotic Consciousness in Chateaubriand', *Nineteenth-Century French Studies*, 38:3/4 (Spring–Summer 2010), 159–71; Pratima Prasad, *Colonialism, Race, and the French Romantic Imagination* (New York: Routledge, 2009), pp. 72–98; Jennifer Yee, *Exotic Subversions in Nineteenth-Century French Fiction* (New York: Routledge, 2008), pp. 25–44; and Ter

ative – if fantastical – American soundscapes, see Chapter 7.).[10] Chateaubriand's *Atala, ou Les Amours de deux sauvages dans le désert* (1801), a tale of doomed love between Chactas, a Natchez man, and Atala, a Christianised woman of mixed Seminole Indian and Spanish parentage, was especially influential, attracting a devoted popular following with its portrayals of tragic passion between exoticised Indigenous characters. The prose poem likewise made a powerful impression on French artists, inspiring paintings such as Anne-Louis Girodet's *Atala au tombeau* (1808) and Eugène Delacroix's *Les Natchez* (1835), as well as several Parisian stage adaptations.[11] Chateaubriand's American writings also indirectly generated character types and scenes in other theatrical works: for example, his account of a certain Monsieur Violet playing the pocket violin for the Iroquois – an allegory for the 'civilising' power of music and dance – inspired the comic figure of Jonathas the dancing-master in the ballet *Les Mohicans* (1837) and the flute-playing Frenchman in the drama *Bas-de-Cuir* (1866), both discussed below.[12] Though Chateaubriand's work has been rightfully criticised for contributing to the mythic trope of the 'vanishing Indian', his images of marginalised Indigenous peoples wandering amid the ruins of their 'lost empire' have also been read as a projection of Chateaubriand's own feelings of exile, alienation, and mourning for the fallen French empire.[13]

From the 1820s on, French readers also thrilled to images of Native Americans in the historical fiction of American author James Fenimore Cooper (1789–1851). Cooper's 'Leatherstocking Tales' featuring the woodsman Natty Bumppo and his Native American allies combined frontier adventure with an elegiac tone, thematising the conflict between colonial 'civilisation' and the 'vanishing wilderness' of Native America during the second half of the eight-

---

Ellingson, *The Myth of the Noble Savage* (Los Angeles and Berkeley: University of California Press, 2001), pp. 196–209.

10 On the songs and soundscapes of nature in Chateaubriand's *Atala*, see also Fabienne Moore, *Prose Poems of the French Enlightenment: Delimiting Genre* (Burlington, VT: Ashgate, 2009), pp. 223–37.

11 See David Wakefield, 'Chateaubriand's *Atala* as a Source of Inspiration in Nineteenth-Century Art', *The Burlington Magazine*, 120:898 (1978), 13–24. Stage adaptations included Thomas Thollé's two-act opera *Atala* (Théâtre Jeunes Artistes, 1802), the choreographer Louis Henry's ballet *Les Sauvages de la Floride* (Porte-Saint-Martin, 1807), Eugène Scribe and Jean-Henri Dupin's parody 'drame en 4 actes en style mêlé' *Chactas et Atala* (Théâtre des Variétés, 1818), and the 'drame lyrique' *Atala* by Alexandre Dumas *fils* with music by Alphonse Varney (Théâtre Historique, 1848). On *Les Sauvages de la Floride*, see Meglin, '*Sauvages*, Sex Roles, and Semiotics, Part Two', pp. 276–88.

12 Meglin, '*Sauvages*, Sex Roles, and Semiotics, Part Two', pp. 296–8. On the three versions of this story in Chateaubriand's writings, and the significance of Violet's 'savage ball' as 'a parable of an idealised French colonisation of North America', see Ruth E. Rosenberg, *Music, Travel, and Imperial Encounter in 19th-Century France: Musical Apprehensions* (New York: Routledge, 2014), pp. 81–9.

13 Rosenberg, *Music, Travel, and Imperial Encounter*, pp. 92–3.

eenth century.[14] Stage adaptations of Cooper's novels tended to take great liberties, sometimes using only the names of characters as a departure point for grossly stereotypical depictions, as in the ballet *Les Mohicans* and drama *Bas-de-Cuir*. Cooper's characters occasionally appeared in other works as a way of adding (imagined) verisimilitude: for example, the five-act drama *La Guerre de l'indépendance, ou L'Amérique en 1780* (Théâtre de la Gaîté, 1840) included the roles of 'Natty, dit Bas-de-Cuir' and 'Uncas, chef de sauvages' as quasi-historical figures alongside George Washington, Alexander Hamilton, and Benedict Arnold.[15] (On this and other stage works that invoked 'the revolutionary rhetoric of *liberté*', see Chapter 1.)

Beyond these literary encounters (and their theatrical adaptations), French citizens had opportunities to encounter Indigenous Americans in person – albeit in highly exoticised, usually exploitative presentations that denied these individuals' agency and commodified their bodies as objects of curiosity. (On the 'Indians' in Buffalo Bill's Wild West Company at the 1889 World's Fair, see Chapter 9.) Since the early colonial period, Indigenous peoples of the New World had been transported to France and displayed as public spectacles, often as a part of 'living museums' or 'human zoos'.[16] In keeping with this tradition, in 1827 the French-born American con artist David Delaunay persuaded four men and two women of the Osage tribe to travel from Missouri to France for financial gain.[17] Initially, the Osage visitors attracted vast crowds and were met with breathless coverage in the press, which listed their public appearances under 'Spectacles' alongside other entertainments. Their attendance at Parisian theatres ensured a spike in ticket sales, with audience members fascinated more by the sight of these

---

14 All five 'Leatherstocking' novels appeared in translations by Auguste Jean-Baptiste Defauconpret (1767–1843) within months of their publication in English. See Joseph Sabin, *A Dictionary of Books Relating to America, from its Discovery to the Present Time*, vol. 4 (New York: Sabin, 1871), pp. 490–510. Cooper's most popular 'Leatherstocking' novel, *The Last of the Mohicans*, was reissued in new editions and translations until the end of the century. See Ministère de l'Instruction Publique et des Beaux-Arts, *Catalogue général des livres imprimés de la Bibliothèque nationale: Auteurs*, vol. 31, Colombi–Corbiot (Paris: Imprimerie Nationale, 1907), pp. 1002–5. Jennifer Yee suggests that Cooper's wide readership in France may have consisted mostly of children. Jennifer Yee, *The Colonial Comedy: Imperialism in the French Realist Novel* (Oxford: Oxford University Press, 2016), p. 16, n. 65.

15 We would like to thank Diana R. Hallman for bringing this work to our attention.

16 On the earliest sixteenth- and seventeenth-century examples of this practice, see Olive Patricia Dickason, *The Myth of the Savage and the Beginnings of French Colonialism in the Americas* (Edmonton: University of Alberta Press, 1997), pp. 209–17.

17 See William Least Heat-Moon and James K. Wallace (eds), *An Osage Journey to Europe, 1827–1830: Three French Accounts* (Norman: University of Oklahoma Press, 2013). See also the first chapter on the Osage woman Sacred Sun in Margot Ford McMillen and Heather Robeson, *Into the Spotlight: Four Missouri Women* (Columbia: University of Missouri Press, 2004), pp. 1–34.

'sauvages' in their box than by the action on stage.[18] When public interest lagged, Delaunay generated a fresh sensation by arranging a *fête extraordinaire* in which the Osages performed 'savage dances of the Missouri' followed by one of their group, Kihegashugah ('Little Chief'), ascending in a hot-air balloon.[19]

In the same tradition of trafficking Indigenous peoples as marvels, the American lawyer-turned-artist George Catlin teamed up with his notorious fellow showman P. T. Barnum in the 1840s to take a troupe of Ojibwe and Iowa people – including children – to Europe as featured performers in Catlin's 'Indian Gallery'.[20] Then, in 1845, Catlin's Musée de l'Indien opened in Paris at the spacious Salle Valentino on Rue Saint-Honoré. The exhibition included Catlin's paintings (portraits of Native Americans and scenes of their customs), various artefacts, and twelve members of the Iowa tribe who performed war dances, hunting rituals, and ball games.[21] Attendees included such luminaries as Victor Hugo, Eugène Delacroix, Charles Baudelaire, Théophile Gautier, and George Sand, the latter two of whom revealed in written accounts their delight in the frisson of racialised fear.[22] In his review of 'Les Ioways Indiens' for *La Presse*, for instance, Gautier noted that 'nothing is more fantastic and more frightening than these dances'.[23] Gautier went on to describe the Iowas' apparently belligerent gestures – 'they wave their tomahawks [and] brandish their spears while screaming and rolling their eyes' – and expressed a momentary fear of being scalped.[24] Similarly lurid descriptions appeared in Sand's 'Relation d'un voyage chez les sauvages de Paris', first published in *Le Diable à Paris* in

18 Tracy N. Leavelle, 'The Osage in Europe: Romanticism, the Vanishing Indian, and French Civilization during the Restoration', in *National Stereotypes in Perspective: Americans in France, Frenchmen in America*, ed. William L. Chew, III, Studia Imagologica (Amsterdam: Rodopi, 2001), pp. 89–112, at pp. 102–4.

19 Pisani, *Imagining Native America*, p. 117.

20 Joseph B. Herring, 'Selling the "Noble Savage" Myth: George Catlin and the Iowa Indians in Europe, 1843–1845', *Kansas History*, 29 (2006–7), 226–45, at p. 231.

21 Jane M. Roos, 'Courbet, Catlin, and the Exploitation of Native Americans', in 'Call and Answer: Dialoguing the American West', *Transatlantica* (2017), no. 2, paragraph 7.

22 Sand's descriptions fit squarely within the 'vanishing Indian' trope and, as Joseph Herring reminds us, 'contained the two prevailing but contradictory premises of the day: first, the Indians were innocent, honest, and upright children of the wilderness; second, they were wild, inhuman, bloodthirsty savages': Herring, 'Selling the "Noble Savage" Myth', p. 240. See also Sharon L. Fairchild, 'George Sand and George Catlin – Masking Indian Realities', *Nineteenth-Century French Studies*, 22:3–4 (Spring–Summer 1994), 439–49.

23 'Rien n'est plus fantastique et plus effrayant que ces danses': Théophile Gautier, 'Théâtres. Les Indiens Ioways', *La Presse*, 19 May 1845, p. 2.

24 'Ils se trémoussent, ils sautent, ils agitent leurs tomahawks, brandissent leurs lances en poussant des cris, en roulant les yeux: on peut craindre qu'il ne leur prenne la fantaisie de vous arracher la peau de la tête pour enrichir leur collection': Gautier, 'Les Indiens Ioways', *La Presse*, 19 May 1845, p. 2.

Justamant's Le Bossu *and Depictions of Indigenous Americans*   57

1845. Sand admitted to initially feeling 'the most violent and most painful emotion' at the 'bizarre spectacle', even breaking out in 'a cold sweat' upon believing she would witness a real-life scalping.[25] Though her essay criticised the American government's exploitation of its Indigenous peoples, Sand herself reinforced dehumanising stereotypes: in their performances, Native Americans were terrifying 'demons of the desert, more dangerous and more implacable than wolves and bears' whose war-cries produced an 'infernal concert'; at the same time, she frequently compared the Iowas to ancient Greek gods, heroes, statues, and vases – as if they were silent otherworldly figures frozen in time.[26] These same stereotypes of diabolical warriors and stoic ancient deities shaped French audiences' expectations when they encountered theatrical representations of Indigenous Americans in opera, ballet, and other stage works.

Representations of Indigenous Americans in French Opera and Ballet

Though nineteenth-century French theatrical culture catered to a strong appetite for exotic locales – especially in the Middle East and North Africa – the most exclusive national lyric theatres, the Paris Opéra and Opéra-Comique, staged very few works representing North and South America's Indigenous peoples and their dancing. Given that operas and ballets staged at the Opéra tended to take place in Western Europe and its colonies (with French colonies as the most frequent exotic settings), perhaps the loss of France's American colonial territories was too great a source of humiliation to bear celebrating on stage.[27] The writings of Théophile Gautier offer another perspective on how representations of Indigenous Americans were considered 'inappropriate' for classical ballet. In his review of *Les Mohicans* (1837), the Opéra's notoriously disastrous adaptation of Cooper's *The Last of the Mohicans* – composed by Adolphe Adam to a libretto by Léon Halévy and choreographed by Antonio Guerra – Gautier opined that 'Indians' were a poor subject because such 'uncivilised' characters did not provide opportunities for the Opéra to display the kind of 'noble' dances, luxurious décor, and elegant apparel for which its productions were known.[28] Eight years later,

25 George Sand, 'Les Sauvages de Paris', in *Les Maîtres Mosaïstes* (Paris: Hetzel, 1856), pp. 41–8, at p. 44.

26 Sand, 'Les Sauvages de Paris', pp. 43–4. On Sand's numerous comparisons of the Iowas to figures from Classical antiquity, see Fairchild, 'George Sand and George Catlin', p. 443, and Herring, 'Selling the "Noble Savage" Myth', p. 241.

27 On the typical settings of operas and ballets at the Opéra, see Marian Smith, *Opera and Ballet in the Age of* Giselle (Princeton: Princeton University Press, 2000), pp. 22–5.

28 'The choice of subject is most unfortunate. Soldiers and savages have little to offer choreography. Naked redskins and other characters in buffalo skins provide nothing for the eyes to feast upon. A ballet demands brilliant scenery, sumptuous festivities

58   *Marian Smith, Sarah Gutsche-Miller and Helena Kopchick Spencer*

when Gautier attended Catlin's Musée de l'Indien, he noted that the 'mysterious' dances depicted in Catlin's paintings of Indigenous American life 'have a choreography difficult to appreciate at the Opéra' but 'nonetheless offer keen interest to the observer.'[29] In other words, while images of supposedly 'authentic' 'Indian' dances were fascinating in the context of Catlin's 'museum', these dances would not be well received if re-created on the stage of the Opéra.[30]

Of the few works to present Indigenous Americans, the most prominent example was Étienne de Jouy and Gaspare Spontini's *Fernand Cortez, ou La Conquête du Mexique* (1809, rev. 1817), which imagined a romance between the Spanish conquistador Hernán Cortés and the fictional Aztec princess Amazily, niece of the emperor Moctezuma II.[31] A fixture of the Opéra reper-

---

and magnificent courtly costumes': Gautier, 'Académie Royale de Musique' [review of *Les Mohicans*], *La Presse*, 11 July 1837, translated in *Gautier on Dance*, ed. and trans. Ivor Guest (London: Dance Books, 1986), p. 9. Quoted in Smith, *Ballet and Opera in the Age of Giselle*, p. 264. Another critic, Jules Janin, more overtly derided the comical movements performed by one of the male dancers in *Les Mohicans* and, like Gautier, found this kind of 'grotesque' style inappropriate for the Opéra. Jules Janin, *Journal des débats*, 10 July 1837; cited and translated in John V. Chapman, 'Jules Janin: Romantic Critic', in *Rethinking the Sylph: New Perspectives on the Romantic Ballet*, ed. Lynn Garafola (Hanover, NH: Wesleyan University Press, 1997), p. 228. See also Meglin, 'Sauvages, Sex Roles, and Semiotics, Part Two', p. 299. However, Janin's comments could be interpreted not as evidence of actual awkward or 'primitive' movements but rather as a product of the binaristic gendered discourse of nineteenth-century dance criticism, particularly his own disdain for the *danseur* and radical advocacy for the new 'ethereal' style of female dancing first made famous by Marie Taglioni. See Marian Smith, 'The Disappearing Danseur', *Cambridge Opera Journal*, 19:1 (2007), 33–57.

29   'La danse de l'ours, où les exécutants sont affublés de la peau du susdit animal; celle de l'écureuil, où ils portent adaptée à l'échine une grande queue de plumes ou de poils qui se recourbe au dessus de leur tête, pour être d'une chorégraphie difficilement appréciable à l'Opéra, n'en offrent pas moins un vif intérêt pour l'observateur': Gautier, 'Les Indiens Ioways', *La Presse*, 19 May 1845, p. 1.

30   Annegret Fauser has argued that the primitivism of *Le Sacre du printemps* was consistent with spectators' expectations of 'authentic' Indigenous music and dance at Expositions Universelles and the 'human zoos' of Paris's Jardin d'Acclimatation, but not at the elegant Théâtre des Champs-Elysées. See Annegret Fauser, '*Le Sacre du printemps*: A Ballet for Paris', in The Rite of Spring *at 100*, ed. Severine Neff, Maureen Carr, and Gretchen Horlacher, with John Reef (Bloomington: Indiana University Press, 2017), pp. 83–97, at pp. 87–8 and 90–2. See also, in the same volume, Tamara Levitz, 'Racism at *The Rite*', pp. 146–78, at p. 154.

31   Amazily was inspired by the enslaved Nahua woman baptised as 'Marina', Cortés's interpreter and the mother of his son Martín. See 'Avant-Propos historique', in Gaspare Spontini, *Fernand Cortez, ou La Conquête du Mexique, opéra en trois actes* (Paris: Roulet, 1817), p. 5. On *Fernand Cortez* as a typical 'Age of Discovery' opera, see James Parakilas, 'The Soldier and the Exotic: Operatic Variations on a Theme of Racial Encounter, Part I', *The Opera Quarterly*, 10:2 (1993), 36–7.

toire until the early 1840s,[32] *Fernand Cortez* included a large ensemble of characters who exemplify common exotic stereotypes, especially through dance: Aztec warriors perform 'barbaric dances' accompanied by a chorus of bloodthirsty priests, and young Indigenous Mexican women perform 'voluptuous dances' to seduce the Spaniard colonisers.[33]

A decade later, two opéras-comiques staged at the Opéra-National (later renamed the Théâtre Lyrique) similarly featured the archetype of the European explorer drawn to the charms of an Indigenous queen. *La Perle du Brésil* (1851) recycled the trope of a war-hungry Indigenous tribe placated by their Christianised queen, ending with the interracial lovers – the Portuguese naval officer Lorenz and the Brazilian princess Zora – happily united.[34] Though Félicien David's score showcased Zora's vocal beauty and virtuosity, the opera did not include any dances for the Indigenous Brazilians: the featured ballet in Act II was a comical fandango and tarantella performed by drunken sailors aboard their ship. Fromental Halévy's *Jaguarita l'Indienne* (1855), set in Dutch Guiana amid late eighteenth-century conflicts between Dutch settlers and the Indigenous peoples, ends with the Dutch captain Maurice marrying Jaguarita, the valiant queen of the fictitious 'Anakotaws', after she rescues him and other colonisers from her fearsome tribe by intoxicating her fellow 'Indians' with rum.[35] The opera included two representations of Indigenous dance: in Act II, the captive Jaguarita and her warrior-maiden companions of the chorus and ballet re-enact the dramatic scene of a nocturnal military march, attack of the enemy, and victory celebration – all to the delight of the ogling Dutch soldiers. In Act III, young 'Indian' girls dance around an idol of the god Bambouzi while throwing flowers as the chorus hails their powerful pagan deity.[36] According to a critic of *Le Ménestrel*, the 'piquant

32 Performance statistics retrieved from the Chronopera database <chronopera.free.fr>.

33 *Fernand Cortez*, p. 36. See Pisani, *Imagining Native America*, p. 120.

34 Parakilas identifies this as another 'Age of Discovery' opera: Parakilas, 'The Soldier and the Exotic, Part I', p. 36.

35 In this opera, the 'civilising mission' of European colonisers is blatantly stated by Maurice: 'But after all we are ordered to civilise those savages [...] and to make an ally of their charming queen becomes my duty as a soldier'. Quoted in Parakilas, 'The Soldier and the Exotic, Part I', pp. 37–8. However, as Ruth Jordan argues, for all of its stereotypes (including the Indigenous woman who happily abandons her own culture to marry a White man), *Jaguarita* makes colonialism a subject of satirical critique: the Dutch major Hector Van Trump is cowardly, and the mixed-race trapper Mama-Jumbo is a 'true freedom fighter'. Ruth Jordan, *Fromental Halévy: His Life and Music, 1799–1862* (New York: Limelight, 1996), p. 172.

36 The three main sections of this number may have been modelled after the three-part structure of the Iowas' dance rituals, as described by Catlin in the second volume of his *Notes of Eight Years' Travels and Residence in Europe with his North American Indian Collection*, originally published in 1848. According to Catlin's account, the Iowas' performance began with a 'Discovery Dance', followed by an 'Eagle Dance' and a final display of games and dancing: see Roos, 'Courbet, Catlin, and the Exploitation

divertissement guerrier' of Act II – along with the *mise-en-scène* and rich décor – contributed in no small part to *Jaguarita*'s 'brilliant success'.[37]

While the specific details of the choreographer Clair Bénie's divertissements for the original Parisian production of *Jaguarita* do not survive, the choreographer Henri Justamant notated the divertissements he created for a production during the 1856–7 season at the Grand Théâtre de Lyon, then under the direction of Olivier Halanzier.[38] Justamant's choreography for the Act II divertissement is of particular interest since some of the techniques used here would later appear in his 1867 choreography for the 'Grand Ballet Indien' of *Le Bossu* at the Théâtre de la Porte-Saint-Martin, discussed in greater detail below as our principal case study. In this divertissement from *Jaguarita* – labelled 'entrée des guerrières sauvages' in Justamant's notation – sixteen women of the *corps de ballet* enter carrying hunting bows to connote their role as 'savage' warrior women.[39] Justamant frequently choreographed 'prop' dances, using accessories such as scarves and garlands as expressive devices; in his *Jaguarita* divertissement, bows are also essential in generating choreographic exoticism since his *guerrières sauvages* perform predominantly classical ballet steps.[40] Throughout the divertissement, the *guerrières sauvages* wield their bows in a variety of positions to generate visual interest: they brandish them high above their heads (at times while others hold their bows low to the ground, thus creating multiple levels); they hold their bows to their shoulders and mime shooting; they switch their bows from hand to hand as part of a military march; they form semi-circles and extend their bows into the centre to create 'corbeille' (basket) shapes; and they hold their bows vertically to the ground and dance around them, or lean on them as support for arabesques and turns (fig. 2.1).[41]

Aside from the exotic Indigenous queen who captivates a European explorer, Indigenous American characters made only fleeting appearances on opera stages, and in most cases, their only purpose was to provide *couleur locale*. Eugène Scribe, for instance, cast 'Indiens' and 'Indiennes' along with 'Créoles',

---

of Native Americans', paragraph 13.

37 J. Lovy, 'Théâtre Lyrique', *Le Ménestrel*, 22:25 (20 May 1855), 1–2, at p. 2.

38 Henri Justamant, 'Divertissements de *Juagarita* [sic], réglés par Mr H. Justamant, représentés pour la première fois à Lyon sur le Grand Théâtre 1856 à 1857, direction de Mr Halanzier', in Henri Justamant, *Divertissements d'opéras comiques avec coryphées et dames du corps de ballet*, pp. 3–21, Bibliothèque Nationale de France, B.217 (19). On the significance of Halanzier's career and legacy, especially later in the century as director of the Paris Opéra, see Katharine Ellis, 'Olivier Halanzier and the Operatic Museum in Late Nineteenth-Century France', *Music and Letters*, 96:3 (2015), 390–417.

39 Justamant, 'Divertissements de *Juagarita*', p. 5.

40 On the 'full-context' paradigm of musical exoticism, see Ralph Locke, *Musical Exoticism: Images and Reflections* (Cambridge: Cambridge University Press, 2009), pp. 59–64.

41 Justamant, '*Divertissements de Juagarita*', pp. 5–15.

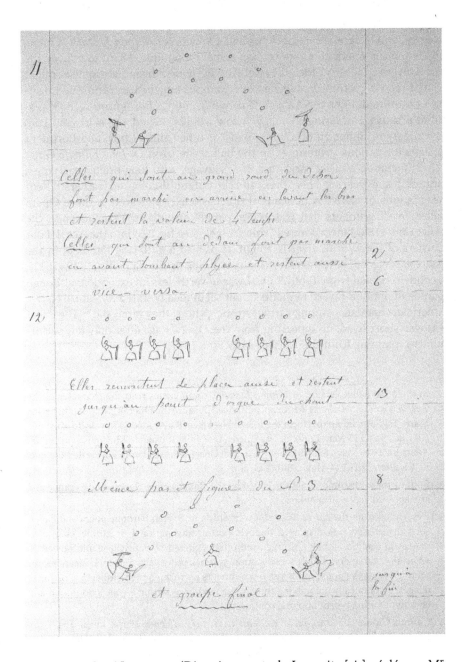

Figure 2.1. Henri Justamant, 'Divertissements de *Juagarita* [sic], réglés par Mr H. Justamant, représentés pour la première fois à Lyon sur le Grand Théâtre 1856 à 1857, direction de Mr Halanzier', in Henri Justamant, *Divertissements d'opéras comiques avec coryphées et dames du corps de ballet*, p. 15. Bibliothèque Nationale de France.

'Nègres', and 'Négresses' in both his ballet version of *Manon Lescaut* (Opéra, 1830) and his opéra comique version (Opéra-Comique, 1856) to convey the racial diversity of New Orleans in Act III.[42] Pseudo-Indigenous disguises might also be seen in costume ball scenes. For example, Eugène Lami and Paul Lormier's costume designs for Auber's *Gustave III, ou Le Bal masqué* (1833) featured a 'sauvage' wearing a shaggy yellow woollen headdress, skirt, and trim (seemingly in imitation of a lion's mane or other animal fur), and Lormier's designs for various 'grotesques' in the ball scene from *La Jolie Fille de Gand* (1842) included a racist caricature of a 'sauvage' with long braids, carrying a large club and wearing a headdress and skirt of multi-coloured feathers.[43] Representations of Native Americans also occasionally appeared in those Opéra ballet divertissements that featured a 'parade of nations'.[44] For instance, the ballet *Ozaï* (1847) incorporated 'Américaines' (see fig. 2.2) into the Act II 'Four Corners of the World' divertissement as part of a glittering fête held in the estate gardens of French explorer Louis-Antoine de Bougainville (1729–1811), recently returned from Tahiti.[45] *Ozaï* was nevertheless an exception: although 'parade of nations' divertissements might seem ideally suited to feature Native American characters among various exotic Others, they rarely did.[46] The ballet was also short-lived, disappearing from the Opéra stage after only ten performances spanning from late April to early June 1847.[47]

---

42 In the 1830 ballet version of *Manon Lescaut*, some critics read the character of the enslaved woman Niuka as 'Mexican' or 'Indian' because the Opéra's rising star ballerina Marie Taglioni did not perform the role in blackface. R., 'Académie Royale de Musique', *Gil Blas*, 5:245 (5 May 1830), 3; Unsigned, 'Académie Royale de Musique', *Journal des Artistes* 4:19 (9 May 1830), 557–60, at p. 558; Unsigned, 'Académie Royale de Musique', *La Vigilante*, 2:107 (4 May 1830), 2–3, at p. 3.

43 Both of these costume designs are held by the Bibliothèque Nationale de France and are digitised on <gallica.bnf.fr>.

44 Descended from the *entrée des nations* tradition in French Baroque opera and ballet, such divertissements displayed dancers performing national or ethnic 'character' dances in traditional folk costumes and often signified class privilege and power: to entertain characters of high social station, a series of (usually female) dancers representing various regions, countries, or continents performed their respective 'national' dances, symbolically embodying the diverse territories within a ruler's dominion and commemorating recent imperial conquests.

45 Casimir Gide *et al.*, *Ozaï, ballet en deux actes et six tableaux* (Paris: Jonas, 1847), pp. 12–13. This divertissement functioned as a kind of *mise en abyme* that celebrates the explorer's acquisition of sexualised biological treasures from around the world.

46 *La Jolie Fille de Gand* also included a 'Four Corners of the World' divertissement in the published libretto, with the dancer Mme Saulnier personifying 'L'Amérique': Adolphe Adam, *et al.*, *La Jolie Fille de Gand, ballet-pantomime en trois actes et neuf tableaux*, 2nd edn (Paris: Jonas, 1842), p. 5. However, this divertissement seems to have been scrapped before production.

47 Performance statistics retrieved from the Chronopera database <chronopera.free.fr>.

Fleeting appearances of exotic characters aside, efforts to bring America and its Indigenous peoples to the Opéra stage were notoriously unsuccessful. In the late 1830s, the Opéra ventured several failed attempts at full-length 'story' ballets set in the Americas, two of which centred on Indigenous characters.[48] *Brézila, ou La Tribu des femmes* (1835), set in a remote American forest surrounded by a rocky mountain rampart, was staged as a benefit for Marie Taglioni, choreographed by her father Filippo Taglioni to music by W. Robert (comte de) Gallenberg and 'laboriously' rehearsed, but it ultimately received only five performances.[49] Two years later, *Les Mohicans* (1837), a clumsy adaptation of Cooper's novel, as noted above, suffered a torrent of ridicule in the press and closed after only three performances.[50] The ballet ascribed familiar racist tropes to the Native Americans (see fig. 2.3), including a devotion to a 'primitive' pagan religion, irrational rage and vengeance, uncontrolled sensual appetites, sexual imperilment of a White woman, and barbaric practices of human sacrifice and cannibalism.[51] In the opening scene, the heads of 'Indiens sauvages' appear above the crest of the rocks, then 'disappear furtively' as they plot an unprovoked attack on the sleeping English soldiers below.[52] When the Mohicans attack the English camp at the end of Act I, they capture the two most vulnerable characters: Jonathas, the effete dancing-master, and Alice, the beautiful young daughter of Colonel Munro. Act II takes place in the Mohicans' camp,

---

48 We have omitted mention of the ballet *La Volière* from our overview above because its characters are 'Créoles' and 'Négresses', not 'Indiennes' or Indigenous 'Américaines'.

49 Théodore LaJarte, *Bibliothèque musicale du Théâtre de l'Opéra: Catalogue historique, chronologique, anecdotique* (2 vols, Paris: Librairie des Bibliophiles, 1876), vol. 2, p. 151. On this poorly received work, see Ivor Guest, *The Romantic Ballet in Paris* (Alton, Hampshire: Dance Books, 2008), pp. 247–51.

50 For a detailed discussion of *Les Mohicans*, see Meglin, 'Sauvages, Sex Roles, and Semiotics, Part Two', pp. 294–315; and Guest, *The Romantic Ballet in Paris*, pp. 287–8. *Les Mohicans* reused the sets from *Brézila* for its North American terrain of forested wilderness surrounded by treacherous mountains and escarpments, a 'hazardous' landscape symbolically associated with 'threatening events and characters': Debra Hickenlooper Sowell, 'Romantic Landscapes for Dance: Ballet Narratives and Edmund Burke's Theory of the Sublime', *Dance Chronicle*, 34:2 (2011), 183–216, at p. 200. Gautier noted disapprovingly that the setting of *Les Mohicans*, a 'picturesque site in North America', had already been presented in *Brézila* as a 'virgin forest in South America'. Quoted in Meglin, 'Sauvages, Sex Roles, and Semiotics, Part Two', p. 298. Gautier's review originally appeared in *La Presse*, 11 July 1837, and is translated in *Gautier on Dance*, ed. and trans. Guest, pp. 9–14.

51 Meglin views the crude stereotypical caricatures of *Les Mohicans* as the nadir in balletic representations of Indigenous Americans, 'with the erstwhile Noble Savage now entirely and ridiculously Ignoble': Meglin, 'Sauvages, Sex Roles, and Semiotics, Part Two', p. 315.

52 Adolphe Adam *et al.*, *Les Mohicans, ballet-pantomime en deux actes* (Paris: Thomassin, 1837), p. 5.

Figure 2.2. Paul Lormier, costume design for an 'Américaine' in *Ozaï* (1847). Bibliothèque Nationale de France.

Figure 2.3. Paul Lormier, costume design for a 'femme sauvage' in *Les Mohicans* (1837). Bibliothèque Nationale de France.

with its 'temple of the Fetish' bedecked with 'coarse images of idols', where the priests decree the will of the Fetish: Alice must 'belong' to the chief, and Jonathas must be cooked and eaten.[53] When Alice's fiancé Major Arwed arrives to rescue her, the lascivious Mohican chief in his 'anger and jealousy' demands that Arwed be burned at the stake.[54] In the end, Jonathas becomes an unlikely hero: in the spirit of Chateaubriand's Monsieur Violet, he compels the Mohicans to dance with his violin playing accompanying Alice's 'vivacious and graceful' dancing.[55] Caught up in their 'furious' dancing, the Mohicans lay down their daggers and 'head-bashing' clubs (*casse-têtes*) and are soon overwhelmed by the English soldiers and sailors who have come to rescue the captives.[56]

Representations of Indigenous Americans in the Parisian Boulevard Theatres

The Opéra, Opéra-Comique, and Opéra-National/Théâtre Lyrique were by no means the only venues in Paris to stage works that included representations of Indigenous Americans. Depictions of dancing 'Indians' or American 'sauvages' also made their appearance in several spectacles staged by popular theatres such as the Théâtre de la Porte-Saint-Martin, the Théâtre de la Gaîté, the Théâtre du Châtelet, and the Théâtre des Variétés. These venues, collectively dubbed 'boulevard theatres' because of their setting on Paris's stylish *grands boulevards*, specialised in staging evening-length comedies, dramas, comic operas, and *féeries* on a massive scale with extravagant staging and décors. One of the draws of these shows was ballet, and almost all boulevard-theatre productions with the designation 'à grand spectacle' included at least one extended ballet divertissement of fifteen to twenty minutes, and sometimes two or three, often interrupting the dramatic action with extravagant visual enchantments. Divertissements typically featured a mix of classical *danse d'école* and conventional character dances, but they could take any form a choreographer chose, with the result that boulevard-theatre ballets were often trendier or more innovative than divertissements in state theatres, and often vied with the Opéra's divertissements in popularity.

Boulevard-theatre spectacles ranged widely in what they presented. Literary adaptations enjoyed enduring success throughout the nineteenth century, as did fairy tales, but so too did any comedic or dramatic works that lent themselves to extravagant visual displays. Unlike the Opéra and Opéra-Comique, boulevard theatres did not receive government subsidies and had to appeal to

---

53 Adam *et al.*, *Les Mohicans*, pp. 10–11.

54 Adam *et al.*, *Les Mohicans*, p. 14.

55 Adam *et al.*, *Les Mohicans*, p. 14.

56 Adam *et al.*, *Les Mohicans*, p. 15.

as vast and varied a public as possible – and ideally one that would return to see the same spectacle more than once. Shows were therefore created to allow for many scene and costume changes, special effects, or dazzling visual tableaux, and authors and producers were always on the lookout for anything that could add colour and excitement. Exoticism, whether chronological or geographical, offered myriad opportunities for such scenes and so remained one of the most prevalent means for enlivening a show throughout the nineteenth century. It was common for a ballet divertissement to be set in picturesque eighteenth-century European villages or in distant lands such as Russia, Spain, Scotland, or the Middle East. Choreographers tended to favour opportunities for devising sensuous dances in revealing costumes, but any situation that allowed for rousing, high-spirited dancing could serve their purposes.

Visions of America seem as if they should have been a good fit: they were certainly exotic, they evoked many mythologised places and peoples, and they provided *couleur locale*. However, relatively few boulevard-theatre productions included dances depicting Indigenous Americans, especially in the first half of the nineteenth century, and when productions did include 'Indian' dances, these dances typically appeared outside formal divertissements.[57] As at the Opéra and Opéra-Comique, Indigenous Americans generally were not seen as appropriate characters for classical ballet. An 1850 vaudeville at the Théâtre des Variétés titled *L'Alchimiste, ou Le Train de plaisir pour la Californie*, for instance, began with a genie conjuring up a panorama of Missouri and the Kansas River, treating audiences to a view of 'Indians' chasing buffalos with a distant vision of a prairie on fire. In the second act, the genie took the protagonist, an alchemist, on a tour of America where he met beautiful Indigenous women – 'Iroquois, Missourian, Mexican, Sioux-Indian, Canadian and Peruvian' – who sang to him then offered themselves up for him to choose from.[58] More conventionally, in 1851, the Théâtre National (Ancien Cirque) featured a four-continent tour in the *féerie Les Quatre Parties du monde*,[59] and in 1853, the Théâtre de l'Ambigu-Comique staged the drama *La Prière des naufragés*, in which a young French castaway girl is raised by Native Americans and reunited with her family fifteen years later.[60] In 1857, the Ambigu-Comique also staged a short *folie-vaudeville* about lovers duped and then united that included a scene for characters who dress up as American 'sauvages' to scare their friends and

---

57 One exception is *Les Sauvages de la Floride* (Porte-Saint-Martin, 1807); see n. 11.

58 Clairville and Jules Cordier, *L'Alchimiste, ou Le Train de plaisir pour la Californie* (Paris: Tress, 1850).

59 Anicet-Bourgeois, Clairville, and Laurent, *Les Quatre Parties du monde* (Paris: Michel Lévy frères, 1851). See also Tommaso Sabbatini, 'Music, the Market, and the Marvelous: Parisian Féerie and the Emergence of Mass Culture, 1864–1900' (unpublished PhD dissertation, University of Chicago, 2020), p. 143.

60 *La Prière des naufragés*, written by Adolphe d'Ennery and published by Michel Lévy frères (Paris, 1853), was set in the early eighteenth century.

family. The show ended with great hilarity as all danced and sang in a 'Bal du sauvage', complete with a wild *galop final*.[61]

Choreographed portrayals of Indigenous Americans remained comparatively rare in boulevard-theatre productions in the second half of the century in relation to the vast number of shows created for commercial theatres, but the few that appeared had a far greater impact on public perceptions of American 'Indians' than did earlier popular representations: almost all were incorporated into grand spectacles staged by the most prominent and popular of the boulevard theatres. Frequent reprises and long performance runs also meant that these productions were seen by large audiences, and often several times by the same audiences, ingraining stereotyped movements and gestures associated with Indigenous Americans into the French popular imagination well into the early twentieth century. As we discuss below, the 'Grand Ballet Indien' in the Porte-Saint-Martin's acclaimed 1862 dramatisation of Féval's novel *Le Bossu*, for instance, reached vast audiences not only during its initial two hundred performances but also during its many reprises in Paris and the provinces.

While mid- to late nineteenth-century depictions of Indigenous Americans on the popular stage varied in tone, with authors casting their 'Indians' in a more or less sympathetic light, the vast majority perpetuated the racist caricatures of earlier literary conceptions. *Bas-de-Cuir*, a drama staged at the Théâtre de la Gaîté in 1866, was one of the most chauvinistic of the *fin de siècle* 'Indian' dramas: set in 1765, it narrated the story of 'civilised' Christian French settlers soon to return to the 'paradise' that is Paris to escape the 'eternal dangers' of North American forests teeming with 'miserable', bloodthirsty 'pagan savages'.[62] An already married Huron chief, Serpent-le-Feu, who has fallen in love with Marthe, the young daughter of a settler, offers himself as the family's escort through the forest in hopes of winning the girl's hand in marriage. Although she spurns him, stating that God has created an 'unbridgeable chasm' between 'her sovereign race and his [race] of slave', he vows to take her forcibly. Marthe is eventually saved by the naïve but steadfast Rayon-du-Soir – Serpent-le-Feu's faithful wife and a 'beautiful creature of nature' who knows how to talk about herself only in the third person – and Marthe's family escapes the clutches of the Huron warriors.

Bas-de-Cuir was probably inspired by Cooper's *Leatherstocking Tales* from the 1820s. At the very least, it capitalised on the familiarity of the name 'Bas-de-Cuir' or 'Leatherstocking'. *Bas-de-Cuir* came on the heels of several reprints of Cooper's novels issued throughout the 1850s and 1860s and no doubt traded on nostalgia for these stories of peril and adventure: French audiences of the 1860s would have grown up with the Leatherstocking tales in the 1830s and 1840s and may have been drawn to stage plays that recalled the swash-

---

61 Édouard Montagne and Alfred Reneaume, *Dans une île déserte* (Paris: Charlieu, 1857). Our thanks to Tommaso Sabbatini for bringing this work to our attention.
62 Xavier de Montépin and Jules Dornay, *Bas-de-Cuir* (Paris: Lacour, 1866).

buckling heroes of the adventure stories they had enjoyed in their youth.[63] The production featured scene after scene of violent clashes and chases, all of them painting the local Huron warriors as bloodthirsty primitives whose only interest was in collecting scalps. The Hurons were also depicted as overly fond of liquor, prone to falling victim to its soporific effects, and childlike in their inability to resist the flute music of one of the French travellers, dancing for as long as he is willing to play.[64] In the end, the French reign victorious, with jingoistic shouts of 'Vive la France' closing the show. The ballet in *Bas-de-Cuir*, in contrast, was comparatively bland, and followed the conventions of a nineteenth-century opera or ballet divertissement: the ruler – here the Huron chief Serpent-le-Feu – gathers his people for a grand celebration. First a cortège parades before him, with groups of 'Indian' musicians making 'miserable sounds' on 'strange instruments', then elders enter, followed by priests, chiefs, women, children, and more warriors. Serpent-le-Feu speaks to his people and orders the celebrations to begin, calling in the 'Filles des Ottawas' to begin their ballet of war dances.

Not all visions of Indigenous Americans were as relentlessly bigoted as the Gaîté's *Bas-de-Cuir*, but even the less abhorrent ones perpetuated racist stereotypes. In Jules Verne and d'Ennery's *Le Tour du monde en 80 jours*, first staged by the Porte-Saint-Martin in 1874, audiences were treated to an extended tableau depicting 'Indians' on snow-covered plains in Kearny, Nebraska, fifty miles from Omaha. Although occasionally called a ballet in reviews, this tableau consisted of a series of scenes that mixed pantomime and choreographed battles with dialogue.[65] First, Pawnee warriors and their chief stealthily detach a railway carriage from the engine and capture two women, then they are seen in a clearing plotting the women's death along with that of the hero Phineas Fogg, and finally, soldiers summoned by Fogg's valet arrive and open fire on the Pawnee (see fig. 2.4). Although the production continued in the vein of earlier representations in its depiction of Indigenous men as dangerous warriors out to destroy Europeans,

---

63 Henri Moréno quipped in his announcement of an upcoming production of *Bas-de-Cuir* at the Théâtre de la Gaîté in 1866 that it 'smells of America' and Fenimore Cooper ('Cela sent l'Amérique, les mocassins et les romans de Fenimore Cooper'): H. Moreno, 'Semaine théâtrale', *Le Ménestrel*, 33:18 (1 April 1866), 139–40, at p. 140. Émile de la Bédollière's new translations of the Leatherstocking tales were published by Barba in the 1850s and 1860s; in addition, Defauconpret's translations from the 1820s were reissued in the 1860s–1880s by Furne. See Ministère de l'Instruction Publique et des Beaux-Arts, *Catalogue général*, vol. 31, pp. 988–91, 996–8, 1003, 1011, 1015, 1017.

64 This trope is probably inspired by Chateaubriand's 'Monsieur Violet' anecdote, mentioned above.

65 The 'Indian' scenes took place at the end of Act III, in the ninth and tenth tableaux. Although reviews occasionally referred to the 'Indian' scene as a ballet, it was a ballet only in the sense of having been a choreographed battle – a common scene type in popular ballets. Reviews of later Porte-Saint-Martin productions also speak of a 'pas nègre' or a 'pas sauvage' danced by Mariquita, perhaps as part of a Nubian dance or Malaysian ballet.

Figure 2.4. Auguste Trichon, engraving of the principal tableaux from *Le Tour du monde en 80 jours* (1874). Bibliothèque Nationale de France.

arousing the usual titillating frisson of fear, the scenes in *Le Tour du monde* were notable on one front: before the warriors stormed the train, the Pawnee chief explains to the audience that their intent is not to pillage but to avenge their families murdered by White settlers: the 'Indians' are not portrayed as inherently bloodthirsty or barbarous but as victims. This slightly more nuanced view of Native Americans would have tempered the impression left by *Bas-de-Cuir*. Verne's drama was one of the most frequently restaged spectacles of the period and was seen by thousands. The Porte-Saint-Martin reprised its production in 1878, and the Châtelet staged one in 1876, 1884, 1886, 1889, 1891, 1896, and 1898. All of them played nightly for two to three months.[66]

Two later boulevard-theatre spectacles returned to the trope of American 'Indians' as dangerous primitives. In *Le Pays de l'or*, a *pièce à grand spectacle* premiered at the Théâtre de la Gaîté in 1892, Madame Mariquita created a 'divertissement sauvage' titled 'L'Orgie de l'eau de feu' ('The Liquor Orgy') danced by the Price sisters and a large ballet corps.[67] The divertissement, which included a 'Chœur des peaux rouges' and a 'Danse des sauvages', may have recalled aspects of the divertissement in *Le Bossu*, described below.[68] One review described the ballet as having taken place in California, with 'savage tribes' gathered near a river flowing with gold. Another, however, described it as an 'orgie' following the pillaging of a caravan with the 'Indians' donning stolen European clothing the wrong way around. In *Robinson Crusoé*, staged by the Châtelet in 1899, M. Van Hamme devised a 'Danse du triomphe' that included sacred dances of South American cannibals who celebrate their victory over an enemy people, complete with an 'introduction of the human sacrifice' and a 'final submission'.[69]

But what did these 'Indian' dances actually look like? What gestures and movements did choreographers – and audiences – associate with Indigenous Americans? Although one can perhaps visualise the sacrifice scenes in *Bas-de-Cuir* or *Robinson Crusoé* from descriptions in libretti and reviews, it is more difficult to imagine what French choreographers presented to their audiences as formal 'Indian' ballets. Reviews for these provide a few clues, but critics' descriptions are as brief as they are vague and offer only fleeting impressions of the choreography. Most of the ballets described above will thus forever remain elusive. However, thanks to Justamant, we are able to visualise in specific detail the 'Grand Ballet Indien' from *Le Bossu*. We now turn to *Le Bossu*

---

66 Each of the Porte-Saint-Martin productions had new ballets by different choreographers: Grédelue, Mariquita, and Balbiani. *Le Tour du monde* was also restaged by the Châtelet, smaller Parisian theatres, and French provincial theatres.

67 The production also had a ballet of sailors and another of jockeys. Henri Fouquier, 'Les Théâtres', *Le Figaro*, 27 Jan. 1892, pp. 5–6.

68 The piano-vocal score lists No. 23: 'Chœur des Peaux Rouges' and No. 24: Couplets et 'Danse des sauvages'.

69 *Robinson Crusoé*, programme, Théâtre du Châtelet, Oct. 1899, Bibliothèque Nationale de France, WNA-25.

and to Justamant's choreographic notations for the 1867 Porte-Saint-Martin revival to shed light on how Native Americans were represented in one popular boulevard-theatre drama in late nineteenth-century France.

Le Bossu

Le Bossu was a five-act, twelve-tableaux cloak-and-dagger drama by Auguste Anicet-Bourgeois and Paul Féval with music by Amédée Artus.[70] Written and premiered in 1862, the play was based on Féval's popular adventure novel set during the French Regency period (1715–23), first published serially in *Le Siècle* in the summer of 1857. The dramatised version follows the novel's basic outline. In the prologue, the evil Prince de Gonzague assassinates his cousin, Duke Philippe de Nevers, in order to steal his inheritance, but the swashbuckling hero Henri de Lagardère rescues Nevers's heir, his infant daughter Blanche. Vowing to protect her and avenge Nevers's death, he issues his iconic warning to Gonzague: 'If you do not come to Lagardère, Lagardère will come to you!' The five acts that follow take place fifteen years later: Nevers's widow, Blanche de Caylus, has been forced to marry Gonzague but continues to mourn Nevers and their daughter, whom she believes is also dead. In truth, Lagardère has been hiding the young Blanche de Nevers among a troupe of Spanish *gitani* performers in Segovia. Returning to Paris, Lagardère gains access to Gonzague's household by posing as the hunchbacked servant Ésope. Lagardère ultimately marries young Blanche (who has fallen in love with her 'protector') and reunites her with her mother, then reveals Gonzague's treachery before the Regent. When the enraged Gonzague attacks him, Lagardère kills him – poetically, using the secret 'botte de Nevers' manoeuvre learned from his fallen friend.

Féval's novel includes a diegetic ballet titled 'The Daughter of the Mississippi', an allegory for the riches of Louisiana meant to inspire courtiers to invest in the Scottish financier John Law's ill-fated Mississippi Company. Féval offers a vivid description of the scenario, which is rife with stereotypical images of innocent nature-loving 'Indian' maidens, barbaric tomahawk-wielding 'sauvages', and heroic French soldiers. At the start of the ballet, the beautiful 'daughter of the Mississippi' flutters happily among reeds, water lilies, and wild oats, then summons her companions, who arrive bearing garlands of flowers. Frightful 'Indians', 'naked and wearing horns', suddenly emerge from the foliage wielding hatchets and plotting to cannibalise the women. However, French sailors arrive, defeat the male 'Indians' and save the women. A garland dance follows, representing 'the advent of civilisation in these wild lands', while in the finale,

---

70 The New York Public Library catalogue entry for Justamant's choreographic manual credits Alexandre Artus (1821–1911); however, on the basis of the publication of Amédée Artus's 'Quadrille pour *Le Bossu*', we surmise that Alexandre's brother Amédée (1815–92), a prolific composer of incidental music, wrote the music for *Le Bossu*.

the daughter of the Mississippi fills a cup with water from the river and sprinkles it on the Frenchmen as gold coins miraculously shower down upon them.[71] Féval and Anicet-Bourgeois's play placed this ballet in the eighth tableau.[72] As in the novel, the garden of the Palais-Royal is transformed for the fête: attendees enter a large tent richly decorated with velvet draperies, candelabras resembling golden palm trees, and candles burning in crystals shaped like exotic flowers, all meant to transport them to Louisiana, imagined as a type of El Dorado.[73] However, whereas Féval's novel was quite specific in its description of the 'Daughter of the Mississippi' ballet, the libretto for the stage adaptation left much room for interpretation:

> At a sign from the Regent, the tent is removed and reveals the garden transformed into a Louisiana landscape [...] Trees surrounded by lianas, prairies, blue mountains and the golden river of the Mississippi rolling in waves of golden gauze. Groups of young Indian girls, warriors smoking the pipe. But all these Indians are richly costumed.[74]

While the summary of the ballet in the libretto is so brief as to seem almost an afterthought, ballet played an important role in the success of dramatic productions such as Le Bossu and was taken seriously by all involved. The Porte-Saint-Martin, then one of the largest and most celebrated boulevard theatres in Paris, had a reputation for staging magnificent ballets. Although it did not present independent large-scale ballet-pantomimes in the 1860s, almost all of its dramatic productions – comedies, dramas, and *féeries* – included at least one ballet divertissement and sometimes as many as four. Despite being only one element of the spectacle, these divertissements were hugely popular and were sometimes the draw of the show. Reviews often singled them out for having been especially admired or applauded, and critics showered dancers with as much praise as they did the actors or singers – and sometimes more. One

---

71 Paul Féval, *Le Bossu: Aventures de cape et d'épée* (Paris: Bureaux du Siècle, 1858), pp. 312–13.

72 In the 1867 revival, the ballet formed its own distinct tableau. According to a notice in *L'Orchestre*, tableau 8 was 'la tente du Régent' and tableau 9 was 'Un ballet sous la régence': *L'Orchestre*, 1 March 1867, p. 1.

73 'Huitième Tableau: Une fête au Palais-Royal. Une tente richement tendue, ouvrant au fond sur le jardin du Palais-Royal par de larges draperies de velours, baissées quand l'acte commence. – Sous la tente, tables, sièges, riches candélabres. Le tout affectant une forme bizarre. Les candélabres sont des palmiers en or et les bougies brûlent dans des cristaux ayant la forme de fleurs exotiques': Auguste Anicet-Bourgeois and Paul Féval, *Le Bossu* (Paris: Michel Lévy frères, 1862), p. 90.

74 'Sur un signe du Régent la tente s'enlève et laisse voir le jardin transformé en un paysage de la Louisiane [...] Des arbres entourés de lianes, des prairies, des montagnes bleues et le fleuve d'or du Mississipi roulant en effet des flots de gaze d'or. Des groupes de jeunes filles indiennes, des guerriers fumant le calumet. Mais tous ces indiens sont costumés richement': Anicet-Bourgeois and Féval, *Le Bossu*, p. 100.

critic of the 1862 premiere of *Le Bossu*, for instance, declared that 'the audience did not always remember to encourage' the actresses playing the mother and daughter roles of Blanche de Caylus and Blanche de Nevers, 'but in the two divertissements of the fourth and eighth tableaux they heartly applauded the bohemian Mariquitta [*sic*]', while another wrote that audiences had 'especially applauded the *pas sauvage* in the eighth tableau'.[75]

Revivals of older productions in particular relied on the addition of new ballets to attract audiences. Although critics reported that the divertissements choreographed by M. Mabille for the first production of *Le Bossu* had drawn warm applause, announcements of the Porte-Saint-Martin's 1867 reprise singled out the production's two new ballets, choreographed by Justamant and danced by Mlle Mariquita, as a reason to see *Le Bossu* again. As noted above, Ulbach even declared that audiences who had already seen the show would return for the ballets alone.[76] A press announcement published in several newspapers in September 1871 for a Gaîté performance of *Le Bossu* likewise suggested that the ballet, despite being only one element of the five-hour spectacle, helped make each new production distinctive and encouraged audiences to return to a show they had already seen. The fifty-two-word promotional notice, probably sent out by the management of the Théâtre de la Gaîté, announced that 'Anicet Bourgeois and Paul Féval's twelve-tableau production starts at 7 p.m. sharp and features the show's original [Porte-Saint-Martin] star, M. Mélingue, in the principal role of Lagardère. At 10 p.m. is the splendid Indian ballet with the ballerina Mlle Maria Hennecart, who recently made her début at the Gaîté'.[77] The specificity of the timing of the ballet is itself an indication of its importance and suggests that some audience members may have slipped in only to see the ballet.

Performance practices for boulevard-theatre productions ensured that these theatrical spectacles, and their embedded ballets, were seen by a broad swath of the French public, both in Paris and in the provinces. Boulevard theatres presented shows every night, with additional weekend matinées, for as long as they turned a profit, which for a successful show like *Le Bossu* meant a run of several months. The Porte-Saint-Martin's initial 1862 *Le Bossu* production,

---

75 'Mlles Raucourt et Defodon jouent la mère et la fille [...]; elles s'en acquittent avec un zèle que le public [...] oublie parfois d'encourager. En revanche, il applaudit de toutes ses forces dans les deux divertissements du 4ᵉ et du 8ᵉ tableau, une échappée des *Bouffes Parisiens*, la bohémienne Mariquitta' [*sic*]: D. Jouvin, 'Théâtres', *Le Figaro*, 21 Sept. 1862, pp. 1–2, at p. 2. 'On a surtout applaudi dans le huitième tableau un pas sauvage, une espèce de pastorale dont les personnages sont de jeunes peaux-rouges': Nestor Roqueplan, 'Théâtres', *Le Constitutionnel*, 15 Sept. 1862, pp. 1–2, at p. 2.

76 Louis Ulbach, 'Revue Théâtrale', *Le Temps*, 28 Jan. 1867, p. 1.

77 'Au théâtre de la Gaîté, tous les soirs, à sept heures précises, le *Bossu*, drame en douze tableaux, de MM. Anicet Bourgeois et Paul Féval. M. Mélingue dans le rôle de Lagardère. A dix heures, le splendide ballet indien à la fête du Palais-Royal, pour la continuation des débuts de Mlle Maria Hennecart, premier sujet': 'Théâtres – Concerts', *Le Siècle*, 16 Sept. 1871, p. 4. The same announcement ran in *Le Temps*, 16 Sept. 1871, p. 4.

with its 'gypsy' dances and divertissement of 'sauvages' choreographed by M. Mabille, played from early September 1862 through the end of February 1863, for a total of nearly 200 performances (see below). The restaged 1867 production, with new ballets by Justamant, played for a month and returned in 1877, this time with ballets by Mme Mariquita, who also performed the principal danced role. The Porte-Saint-Martin presented *Le Bossu* again in 1878 and in 1882, each time for a month to six weeks.

Choreographers and dancers of Le Bossu, *1862–78*[78]

Premiere: 8 September 1862, Théâtre de la Porte-Saint-Martin
Ballets choreographed by M. Mabille

Act I, 4th tableau: Gypsy Dances
Danced by Mlle Mariquita, with Mmes Rozé, Petit, Laurency, Camille, Fillet, Fenolio, Clauzade, Gayet, Guillemard, and 24 *dames du corps de ballet*

Act III, 8th tableau: 'Pas de Sauvages'
Danced by Mlle Mariquita, with Mmes Vernet, Guimard, Delan, Marchetti, Rozé, Frédérique, Dabbas, Clauzade, Demartini, Bossi 1re, Guillemard, Bossi 2e, Mariaff, Maloubier, Lucy, Guillemin, Riçois, Saticq, and the *corps de ballet*

Reprise: Spring 1864, Théâtre de la Porte-Saint-Martin
(same production as 1862)

Act I, 4th tableau: 'La Posada de Seville'
Danced by Mmes Mariquita, Félicie Delan, Dabbas, de Martini, Mélina, Clauzade, Bossi 1re, Bossi 2e, Guillemard, Sophie, Stephen, Vercruysse, Caban, and Durand

Act III, 8th tableau: 'Un Ballet sous la Régence'
Danced by Vandrysse, Mmes Vernet, Noémi, Brunetti, Frédérique, and the *corps de ballet*

'Les Naturels du Mississippi'
Danced by Mlle Mariquita and Mme Monplaisir

Reprise: 19 January 1867, Théâtre de la Porte-Saint-Martin
Ballets choreographed by Henri Justamant

---

78 The names in this table are drawn from a variety of sources, including programmes, newspaper listings, reviews, and Justamant's notations. Entries vary since casts changed over time and since different sources are more or less detailed.

4th tableau: 'Les Contrebasistas', divertissement
Danced by Mlle Mariquita (*première danseuse de genre*) and the *corps de ballet*

9th tableau: 'Les Filles des Pampas', grand ballet
Danced by Mmes Rozé (*deuxième première danseuse*), Petit, Laurency, Camille, Fillet, Fenolio, and Gayet (*deuxième danseuses*), Clauzade and Guillemard or Buisson (*Coryphées**),[79] and 24 *dames du corps de ballet*

'Le Pas Indien' (called 'Pas Sauvage' in Justamant's manuscript)
Danced by Mlle Mariquita and Mlle Buisseret

Reprise: 16 September 1871, Théâtre de la Gaîté

Ballets choreographed by M. Fuchs with new music by Vizentini

4th tableau: divertissement
Danced by Mlle Buisseret and the *corps de ballet*

9th tableau: 'Grand Ballet Indien'
Danced by Mlles Maria Hennecart (*premier sujet*); Clary and Brunette Wall (*premières danseuses*); Mlles Camille, Clara, Antonia, Dely-David, Buisson, Roch, Testa, and Gardes; and the *corps de ballet*

Reprise: 10 November 1877, Théâtre de la Porte-Saint-Martin

Ballets choreographed by Mme Mariquita

Danced by Mmes Mariquita and Gedda (*premiers sujets, étoiles*); Mmes Rozé, Hennecart, and Léonie (*deuxièmes sujets*); Mmes Gauthier, Figelet, Marchalet, and Laripidie; and 60 *hommes et dames du corps de ballet*

Dramatic spectacles such as *Le Bossu* did not belong to a single theatre but could be staged in any venue that could foot the bill, especially after the 1864 repeal of theatre privileges, which had restricted certain genres to certain theatres. Thus in 1871, the Théâtre de la Gaîté presented *Le Bossu* with a new first-act divertissement and a third-act 'Grand Ballet Indien' choreographed by M. Fuchs to new ballet music by the theatre's conductor, Albert Vizentini. The Gaîté then staged a new opéra-comique adaptation in 1888 with a libretto by Henri Bocage and Armand Liorat, music by Charles Grisart, and choreography by Emile Grédelue. The 1888 Gaîté production did not, however, feature an 'Indian' dance. Instead it seems that Grédelue devised a 'colin-maillard' ballet of shepherds and shepherdesses wearing what several critics described as oddly funereal black costumes piped with silver.[80] It received tepid reviews

---

79 Mme Buisson (*coryphée*) is listed in Justamant's manuscript but not mentioned in cast lists published in the press; Mme Guillemard is listed in the press but not the manuscript.

80 P. G., 'Les Premières Représentations', *Le Petit Parisien*, 21 March 1888, p. 3.

at best. Audiences and critics had by far preferred the rousing caricatures of Indigenous Americans in earlier productions.

Le Bossu could also be seen in several Parisian district theatres as well as in the provinces. The following list, although far from exhaustive, offers a sense of how familiar audiences would have been with this work. *Le Bossu* was performed in Paris at the Théâtre de Belleville (1863 and 1868), the Théâtre des Batignolles (1863), the Théâtre de Montmartre (1866, 1867, and 1893), the Théâtre Belleville (1893), and the Théâtre-Tivoli (1893), and in the provinces at the Théâtre-Français of Bordeaux (1868), the Théâtre Français of Rouen (1868), the Gymnase in Marseille (1871 and 1878), the Théâtre des Variétés in Versailles (1875), the Théâtre de Troyes (1875), the Grand Théâtre in Toulon (1878), the Grand Théâtre in Le Havre (1878), the Grand Théâtre in Nantes (1878), and the Grand Théâtre in Nîmes (1878).[81] All of these productions played for several weeks at a time. Although it is unlikely that all included the 'Indian' ballet, according to one journalist, the authors of *Le Bossu* were apparently reluctant to let theatres stage the show if they could not promise to include a divertissement.[82] Certainly some of the smaller theatres included ballet, performed either by a small in-house troupe or by dancers hired on contract from larger theatres.[83] Advertisements for the March 1893 performances of *Le Bossu* at the Théâtre-Tivoli, for instance, announced a *Divertissement nègre*, choreographed by Mlle Lebreton, a *danseuse-étoile* of the Théâtre de la Gaité and Éden-Théâtre.[84] Although the choreography for the 'Indian' ballet in the many productions of *Le Bossu* varied with each new choreographer, the general contours of the divertissement as outlined by Féval and Anicet-Bourgeois would have remained similar, with the result that *Le Bossu* played an important role in shaping what audiences would have understood to be Indigenous American.

Justamant's Ballet for Le Bossu

The 'Indian' ballets in all Porte-Saint-Martin productions of *Le Bossu* were extended divertissements that combined solo and ensemble dances. On the basis of a compilation of reviews, we can surmise that M. Mabille's 1862 'Indian'

---

81 It was also performed in several Belgian theatres. All of these performance dates are drawn from *L'Orchestre* and *Le Monde artiste*.

82 When the theatre director Raphaël Félix wanted to stage *Le Bossu* in 1869 while waiting for a revival production of *Lucrèce Borgia* to open, the authors declined because they wanted the production to include a ballet and Félix did not want to stage one. *Le Théâtre Illustré*, 2:59 (1869), p. 2.

83 The Théâtre de Montmartre, for instance, listed a 'ballet sous la régence' in press announcements. (In the novel and play, this is the 'Grand Ballet Indien'.) See issues of *L'Orchestre*, Feb. 1866.

84 See announcements in *L'Entr'acte*, 30 March 1893.

ballet included both comic and pastoral dances showcasing Mariquita, along with a final *tableau vivant* that depicted the god of the Mississippi encircled by his naiads. The critic Edmond de Biéville described a 'savage Daphnis and Chloé' courtship *pas de deux* that was in equal parts 'lovely and comical', performed by Mlles Mariquita and Vernet 'with a lot of expression and extraordinary vivacity', and Nestor Roqueplan described a 'pas sauvage' that was 'a kind of pastorale in which the characters are young redskins', with Mariquita as the young girl and Mlle Frédérique as her nimble partner.[85] Roqueplan further noted that this 'pas sauvage' was 'redolent of the forest and freedom'.[86] In 1877, Mariquita reprised her role of 'peau-rouge' in the 'Pas Sauvage' of her own 'Indian' ballet set along the golden Mississippi, which critics described as a mix of 'fastidious noble ballet' and more amusing 'original fantasy'.[87] The 'Pas Sauvage', full of *couleur locale* and apparently highly entertaining for its depictions of 'sauvages' or 'négrillons' swinging their heads and bodies, was by far the preferred segment of the divertissement.[88] This is, however, all we know about the 1862 and 1877 productions of *Le Bossu*, whether of structure, dance type, or choreographic style, and no reviews have turned up that offer insights into the 1864, 1878, or 1884 reprises with M. Mabille's and Mariquita's ballets.

For Justamant's ballet for the 1867 *Le Bossu*, we know more precisely what the 'Grand Ballet Indien' looked like. According to his notations, Justamant's divertissement was structured in five sections: Part One, 'Les Filles des Pampas' ('The Girls of the Grasslands'), and Part Two, 'Les Chasseresses' ('The Huntresses'),

---

85 'Deux danseuses surtout, Mlles Mariquita et Vernet, qui representent un Daphnis et une Chloé sauvages, dansent avec beaucoup d'expression et une vivacité extraordinaire un pas à la fois joli et comique': E. D. de Biéville, 'Revue des théâtres, *Le Siècle*, 15 Sept. 1862, pp. 1–2, at p. 2; 'On a surtout applaudi dans le huitième tableau un pas sauvage, une espèce de pastorale dont les personnages sont de jeunes peaux-rouges. Mlle Mariquita jouait le rôle de la jeune fille. Sa jolie et adroite partenaire est Mlle Frédérique': Roqueplan, 'Théâtres', *Le Constitutionnel*, 15 Sept. 1862, p. 2. These two dances were quite possibly one and the same, with Vernet and Frédérique alternating in the travesty role of an 'homme sauvage', or else one of these critics may have misidentified Mariquita's partner. These vague descriptions do not reflect what took place on stage.

86 'Tout en restant dans le domaine de la chorégraphie, ce pas sent la forêt et la liberté': Roqueplan, 'Théâtres', *Le Constitutionnel*, 15 Sept. 1862, p. 2. Roqueplan's assertion that this *pas* 'stayed within the realm of choreography' suggests that Mabille used the conventional movement vocabulary of classical ballet. In contrast, and possibly referring to a different ballet section, another critic described a 'so-called Indian dance' performed by Mariquita and other dancers as 'a sort of savage pirouette that breaks with choreographic routine and which was highly amusing'. 'Dans un de ces ballets figure un pas soi-disant indien, une sorte de pirouette sauvage qui sort des rangaines habituelles de la chorégraphie et qui a beaucoup amusé. L'une des danseuses de ce pas singulier est Mlle Mariquita': G. de Saint-Valry, 'Revue dramatique, *Le Pays*, 15 Sept. 1862, pp. 1–3, at p. 2.

87 Un Habit Noir, 'La Salle et les coulisses', *Le Petit Parisien*, 12 Nov. 1877, p. 4.

88 Un Habit Noir, 'La Salle et les coulisses', *Le Petit Parisien*, 12 Nov. 1877, p. 4.

introduced two distinct pastoral female communities within the imagined world of the golden Mississippi River. Part Three, 'Groupes des Bouquets et des Arcs' ('Groups of Bouquets and Bows'), brought the two communities together for an *Adagio* of slow, unfolding movements and group poses in various symmetrical shapes, using the props of hunting bows and diamond-encrusted bouquets. (In this allegorical ballet about the riches of Louisiana, the river flows with gold and the flowers are precious gemstones.) Part Four was a 'Pas Sauvage' featuring the two principal 'character' dancers in a comic *pas de deux*; and Part Five, 'Final: Les Filles des Pampas et Les Chasseresses', reunited the rest of the ensemble for an exuberant 'Coda' of solo displays and group formations.

Personnel and Structure of Henri Justamant, 'Ballet du Bossu', *in Divertissements de* La Tour de Nesle *et du* Bossu *(1867), Revival Production, Théâtre de la Porte-Saint-Martin*

Ballet du Bossu par Henri Justamant, musique de M^ssrs Artus et Calendini représenté pour la première fois à Paris sur le Théâtre de la Porte Saint Martin le [blank]

(This transcription edits some, but not all, inconsistencies in Justamant's manuscript.)

Personnel du Ballet

Premier danseur de genre: Mr ᴮertoto
Première danseuse de genre: Mlle Mariquita
Deuxième première danseuse: [Mlle] Rozé
Deuxièmes danseuses: [Mlles] Petit, Camille, Laurency, Fenolio, Fillet, Cayet
Coryphées: [Mlles] Clauzade, Buisson
24 *dames du corps de ballet*

Première Partie: **Les Filles des Pampas**
Musique de Mr Artus

Artistes
Première danseuse: Mlle Rozé
Deuxièmes danseuses: [Mlles] Petit, Camille, Laurency, Fillet, Cayet, Fenolio
12 *dames du corps de ballet*

Première Entrée: '*Les Sauvages*' [32 bars]
Deuxième Entrée: 2 *deuxièmes danseuses* [16 bars]
Troisième Entrée: 4 *deuxièmes danseuses* [16 bars],
Les 6 deuxièmes danseuses et 8 dames du corps de ballet [22 bars]
Quatrième Entrée: la [deuxième] première danseuse (valse) [48 bars],
La première danseuse et les 6 deuxièmes danseuses [25 bars]

Deuxième Partie: **Les Chasseresses**
Musique de Mr Calendini

Artistes
Coryphées: Mlles Clauzade, Dubuisson
12 *dames du corps de ballet*

Entrée des chasseresses [48 bars]
Entrée des deux coryphées [18 bars]

Troisième Partie: **Groupes des Bouquets et des Arcs**
Musique de Mr Artus

Artistes
La deuxième première danseuse [Mlle Rozé]
Les 6 deuxièmes danseuses [Mlles Petit, Camille, Laurency, Fenolio, Fillet, Cayet]
Les 2 coryphées [Mlles Clauzade, Dubuisson]
Les 12 dames aux bouquets (corps de ballet)
Les 12 chasseresses (corps de ballet)

Groupes (Andante) [number of bars not indicated]
Les 2 deuxièmes danseuses [8 bars]
2 autres [*deuxièmes danseuses*] [8 bars]
2 autres [*deuxièmes danseuses*] [8 bars]
Elles enchaînent [21 bars]
Variation de la première danseuse [choreography and number of bars not notated]

Pas Sauvage
Musique de Mr Artus

Artistes
[*Premier danseur de genre*]: Mr Bertoto
[*Première danseuse de genre*]: Mlle Mariquita, Mlle Busserey *en double*

Entrée de la femme [24 bars]
Entrée de l'homme [8 bars]

Final
Musique de Mr Calendini
Les Filles des Pampas et Les Chasseresses (Coda) [32 bars]
Rentrée de la deuxième première danseuse [23 bars]
Entrée des chasseresses [16 bars]
Entrée des deuxièmes danseuses [65 bars]
'*Tous deux*' [60+ bars]

Most of Justamant's choreography for the 'sauvages' of *Le Bossu* uses the standard step vocabulary of ballet. Seen in one way, the use of this vocabulary is appropriate to the divertissement's diegetic function as a luxurious and not particularly realistic or 'authentic' entertainment staged at the Regent's pal-

Justamant's Le Bossu *and Depictions of Indigenous Americans*

ace.[89] And, indeed, one critic described Justamant's ballet as 'combining luxury and grace'.[90] But the more likely explanation is that his divertissement illustrates how 'savage' dances were presented on the nineteenth-century French stage within the familiar language of classical *danse d'école*. From criticism of Mariquita's 1877 version we know that it, too, relied on conventional ballet vocabulary for at least part of the choreography. There are nevertheless some notable divergences – enough to ensure that the audience could see clear markers of difference. These are found mostly in Part One, 'Les Filles des Pampas' (specifically in the first *entrée*, 'Les Sauvages') and in Part Four, the 'Pas Sauvage' devised for the principal dancers Bertotto and Mariquita. The following discussion focuses on these dances but also considers how some of the apparently non-exotic sections of the ballet contributed to its overall aesthetic and highlights intertextualities with other *femmes sauvages* of nineteenth-century ballets that shaped audience expectations of 'Indian' ballets.

Markers of Native American Exoticism

In both its choreography and its costuming, the visual imagery of 'Les Filles des Pampas' derived primarily from the conventions of classical ballet, but with the interpolation of certain key elements signifying Native American exoticism. The opening *entrée* of 'Les Filles des Pampas', 'Les Sauvages', begins with the introduction of twelve *danseuses* in single file, six entering from each side and travelling forward with *petits jetés ordinaires* (small jumps from one foot to the other).[91] They meet in the middle, each dancer falling to her outside knee, and all turn to face the audience holding each other by the waist. None of this is unusual. But next they lean their heads to the right and left, two times to each side, over the course of four bars of music. The twelve *filles des pampas* then repeat their entire opening sequence, including the head tilts. These head movements are the first noticeable choreographic marker of Otherness, sug-

---

89 Within the play, characters sarcastically comment on the décor of this royal *fête* as surprisingly opulent for 'savages' and such a display of extravagance is understood as part of the historical figure John Law's scheme to inveigle aristocratic investors. For example, the character Chaverny remarks, 'Wigwam en velours nacarat... avec crépines d'or... ils se logent bien les sauvages': Anicet-Bourgeois and Féval, *Le Bossu*, p. 91.

90 Charles Monselet, 'Théâtres. Porte Saint-Martin: Reprise du *Bossu*', *Le Monde illustré*, clipping in Henri Justamant, *Divertissements de La Tour de Nesle et du Bossu*, Lincoln Kirstein Collection, The New York Public Library, *MGRN-Res. 73-259, vol. 2.

91 For a more thorough definition of *petit jeté*, see Gail Grant, *Technical Manual and Dictionary of Classical Ballet*, 3rd rev. ed. (New York: Dover, 1982), p. 63. Justamant's notations actually begin with sixteen stick-figures (eight on either side), but this is apparently an error, since his personnel list indicates '12 dames du corps de ballet' and all subsequent illustrations have only twelve stick-figures or shorthand circles.

gesting an asymmetrical, 'off-kilter' alignment of the body perhaps intended to make them look foreign or strange.

Although movements such as head tilts might seem like subtle markers of exoticism today, they were part of a wider gestural vocabulary of Otherness understood by contemporary audiences. For instance, Justamant notated a similar action in his staging of *Giselle* from the 1860s: in Act II, after being summoned by Myrtha their queen, the Wilis tilt their heads from side to side while kneeling, holding each other's waists and looking forwards to the audience.[92] Like the Indigenous river maidens from the ballet described in Féval's novel, the Wilis were a free, all-female community that 'fluttered' about the flowers and foliage of their richly verdant environment. They were also terrifying primeval 'savages', cruel vampiric spirits who mercilessly murdered the men who entered their forest realm.[93] The appearance in both *Giselle* and *Le Bossu* of women moving their heads from side to side while physically connected suggests that this motif was a meaningful signifier of strangeness and even primitivist *sauvagerie*.[94] As noted above, ten years later, when Mariquita

---

92 'Toutes ce [*sic*] tenant par la taille étant baissée [*sic*] un pied à la 4me derrière, elles penche [*sic*] la tête à droite, puis à gauche, et une fois encore de chaque côté': Henri Justamant, *Giselle ou Les Wilis, ballet fantastique en deux actes: Faksimile der Notation von Henri Justamant aus den 1860er Jahren*, ed. Frank-Manuel Peter (Hildesheim: Olms, 2008), p. 144.

93 Furthermore, the composer Adolphe Adam racialised the Wilis' *sauvagerie* by writing their bloodthirsty bacchanale in *alla turca* style, just as Meyerbeer had done with the demonic nuns' bacchanale in *Robert le diable*. Adam's racialisation of the Wilis goes entirely unnoticed by present-day audiences and dance writers. See Helena Kopchick Spencer, 'The *Jardin des Femmes* as Scenic Convention in French Opera and Ballet' (unpublished PhD dissertation, University of Oregon, 2014), pp. 327–9. Ralph Locke has argued that the exotic overtones of various musical devices (reinforced by costumes, makeup, etc., now often unrecoverable) have been lost, and certain works become 'mere' concert pieces and audio recordings, as annotators prefer to avoid 'embarrassing' topics or scholars focus their attention on other aspects of these works: Ralph P. Locke, 'Restoring Lost Meanings in Musical Representations of Exotic "Others"', unpublished paper presented at the American Musicological Society annual meeting, Philadelphia, Nov. 2009.

94 Justamant's *Le Bossu* shared other non-exotic movements and formations with his *Giselle* choreography as well. In 'Groupes des Bouquets et des Arcs', the third-section *Adagio* of Justamant's *Le Bossu* ballet, the *deuxième première danseuse* Mlle Rozé (as a soloist 'sauvage à plume blanche') rises *en pointe* and performs a difficult *entrechat six* (a jump into the air with six rapid crossings of the legs), then turns in place *en piétinant* (with accented movements on her toes) – exactly the same steps performed by Myrtha in a passage from the Wilis' ball. In both ballets, middle-ranking *deuxième danseuses* frame the white-clad solo *danseuse* and perform gliding steps in *arabesque* (supported with one leg, with the other leg extended behind the body). 'La 1re danseuse au milieu relève sur les pointes, et fait un entrechat six. [...] La 1re tourne sur place en piétinant': Justamant, *Le Bossu*, pp. 30–1; 'La reine, sur place monte sur les deux pointes,

choreographed and danced in her own divertissement for *Le Bossu*, one critic commented that 'the *négrillons* were amusing as they rhythmically [*en cadence*] follow Mariquita's movements with a swinging of the head and body'.[95] The second half of Justamant's 'Les Sauvages' *entrée* consists entirely of classical ballet steps, made 'primitive' only by the folk-like gesture of holding hands, as if performing a circle dance.

Much like Justamant's choreography, the costume for the *filles des pampas* is stylised within the familiar realm of traditional ballet, with a few exotic touches (fig. 2.5). The foundation of this 'sauvage' costume was a white tarlatan skirt and bodice, a silver *corsage suissesse* (the diamond-shaped 'Swiss belt' or 'Swiss waist') and light 'flesh-coloured' *maillot* and toe-shoes, making it nearly interchangeable with that of any other non-exotic female ballet character.[96] Yet the abundant red-and-white feathers of the headdress and bodice trim – and perhaps, to a lesser extent, the variegated beaded necklace – served as immediate and distinctive markers of Native American identity.[97] The *deuxième première danseuse* Mlle Rozé – featured as the ballet's most virtuosic 'classical' soloist in the sections 'Les Filles des Pampas', 'Groupes des Bouquets et des Arcs', and 'Final: Les Filles des Pampas et Les Chasseresses' – wore an all-white variation on this 'sauvage' costume. Justamant's costuming notes and a publicity photograph indicate that Rozé wore a white satin skirt and bodice, trimmed in silver embroidery, with a light beige *maillot* and toe-shoes. The only markers of her imagined 'indigeneity' were a white feathered headdress and perhaps the many strands of her white pearl necklace and bracelets (fig. 2.6). Still, within the predominantly classical dance idiom of Justamant's *Le Bossu* divertissement, it would only take a few unconventional gestures or accessories, however subtle, to establish a sense of Otherness.

---

    fait entrechat six, tomber plier et releve en piétinant sur les orteils et en tournant': Justamant, *Giselle*, p. 146. In these cases, *piétiner* technique does not seem to have the same exotic connotations as in the 'Pas Sauvage', discussed below, and it was surely performed in a more delicate style in accordance with the conventional balletic *Adagio*.

95 'Un Habit noir', 'La Salle et les coulisses', *Le Petit Parisien*, 12 Nov. 1877, p. 4.

96 Tarlatan was standard fabric used during this era in the construction of tutus, with the skirts extending slightly below the knee, and the 'maillot de couleur chair' was the standard 'nude' undergarment for light-skinned White European dancers. Felicia McCarren discusses the sexualisation of dancers' clothes, particularly the 'maillot-chair', in *Dance Pathologies: Performance, Poetics, Medicine* (Stanford: Stanford University Press, 1998), p. 82. Non-White characters were often costumed with darker-coloured tights: for example, the eight 'petit Maures' in the Parisian production of Verdi's *Le Trouvère* (1857) – perhaps an anticipation of the Moorish slaves from *Aïda* – wore a 'maillot de couleur chair brûlée': Knud Arne Jürgensen, *The Verdi Ballets* Parma: Istituto Nazionale di Studi Verdiani, 1995), p. 65.

97 Extravagant feathers were part of the 'sauvage américain' costume dating back to mid-seventeenth-century French court spectacles. Meglin, 'Sauvages, Sex Roles, and Semiotics, Part One', p. 92.

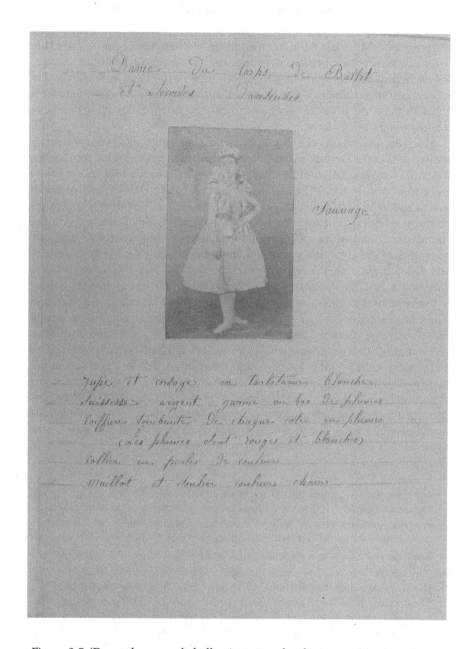

Figure 2.5. 'Dame du corps de ballet / et secondes danseuses / sauvage / Jupe et corsage en tarlatanne blanche / Suissesse argent, garnie au bas de plumes / Coiffure tombante de chaque côté en plumes / (Les plumes sont rouges et blanches) / Collier en perles de couleur/ Maillot et soulier couleur chair'. Publicity photograph and costume description in Justamant, 'Ballet du *Bossu*', in *Divertissements de La Tour de Nesle et du Bossu*(1867), p. 65. The New York Public Library.

Figure 2.6. 'Mademoiselle Rozé – sauvage / Jupe et corsage en satin blanc / Cinture et garnitures en broderie argent / Coiffure tombante de chaque côté en plumes blanches / Collier et bracelets en perles blanches / Maillot et soulier couleur chair'. Publicity photograph and costume description in Justamant, 'Ballet du *Bossu*', in *Divertissements de La Tour de Nesle et du Bossu* (1867), p. 66. The New York Public Library.

Justamant's notations evince much more overt choreographic Otherness in the 'Pas Sauvage', a 'character' showpiece containing the most concentrated distillation of Native American exoticism. However, these notations may not illustrate exactly what was performed on stage, owing to a crucial change in personnel that apparently came late in the pre-production period. According to the manuscript, Justamant originally devised this *pas de deux* for the two leading 'comic' or 'character' dancers at the Porte-Saint-Martin: the *première danseuse de genre* Mariquita and the *premier danseur de genre* Bertotto, who had often partnered Mariquita in previous ballets. Two photographs of Bertotto in costume for *Le Bossu* show the dancer posing proudly with a bow, wearing a 'bronze-coloured' *pantalon* and bodysuit decorated with drawn-on 'tattoos', brown breeches, large earrings, and other elaborate ornaments of multi-coloured feathers and beads (fig. 2.7).[98] Yet it seems that Bertotto's *homme sauvage* never made it to the stage. Some time after the completion of Justamant's notations and the production of publicity photographs showing Bertotto in costume, something unexpected must have happened that prevented this lead performer from dancing as planned. All press coverage of *Le Bossu* indicates that the 'Pas Sauvage' (also called 'Pas Indien' in reviews) was performed instead by Mariquita and Mlle Buisseret, who is credited as an understudy ('en double') in Justamant's manuscript.[99] We do not know exactly how Justamant adapted this dance for Buisseret instead of Bertotto. Nevertheless, Justamant's originally planned choreography is worth examining here because it reveals his ideal vision for the dance and contains the most visible markers of Otherness found in the ballet.

[98] Notably, Bertotto's costume is the only one included in Justamant's manual that attempts to simulate a darker skin tone. Ralph Locke's forthcoming survey of exoticism in nineteenth-century French opera suggests that, even among exotic characters, darker skin tone (achieved through costuming and make-up) was rare, tending to be reserved for ballet ensembles and other supernumerary figures such as servants. Ralph P. Locke, 'The Exotic in Nineteenth-Century French Opera, Part 1: Locales and Peoples', *19th-Century Music*, 54:2 (Fall 2021), 105. See also Locke's discussion of the 'Pas d'esclaves nubiennes' (Dance of Female Nubian Slaves) in Berlioz's *Les Troyens*: Locke, 'The Exotic in Nineteenth-Century French Opera, Part 2: Plots, Characters, and Musical Devices', *19th-Century Music* (forthcoming).

[99] 'Les ballets, dont un nouveau, font honneur à M. Justamant, le maître des cérémonies dansantes de ce théâtre. Nous y avons retrouvé Mme Buisseret, et surtout la fameuse Mariquita, dont le pas indien a soulevé la salle, et qu'on a fait unanimement bisser': E. Adam, 'Théâtres de Paris. Théâtre de la Porte-Saint-Martin. Reprise du BOSSU, drame en douze tableaux de MM. Anicet Bourgeois et Paul Féval', *Le Foyer*, 26 Jan. 1867, pp. 2–3, at p. 3. A notice for *Le Bossu* appearing in *L'Orchestre* read, 'Ballets. Au neuvième tableau, Les Filles des Pampas, grand ballet nouveau de Justamant. Le Pas Indien, pour la rentrée de Mariquitta [*sic*] et les débuts de Mlle Buisseret': *L'Orchestre*, 2 Feb. 1867. The discrepancy between Justamant's manual and the press evidence reminds us that Justamant's preserved notations should not be considered fixed or absolute.

Figure 2.7. 'Monsieur Bertoto. Maillot et pentalon [*sic*] couleur bronze et tatoués / pentalon ringrave l'arge couleur maron / garniture en plumes de toutes couleurs'. Publicity photograph and costume description in Justamant, 'Ballet du *Bossu*', in *Divertissements de La Tour de Nesle et du Bossu* (1867), p. 68. The New York Public Library.

As notated in his staging manual, Justamant's 'Pas Sauvage' is a playful courtship dance in which a woman and a man repeatedly approach each other then come together physically towards the end of the number. Their flirtatious 'stage business' includes a playful movement of their wrists ('en faisant jouer les poignets') while they lean towards each other and back away; a coy face-shielding gesture for the woman;[100] and finally, the man's slight turning away from her and watching her under his arm while she circles him and then points at him with her fingers. After these games of evasion, the *femme sauvage* and *homme sauvage* face each other standing about a foot apart and lean in, putting their heads on each other's shoulders (first one shoulder, then the other). They then 'kiss' by rubbing the tips of their noses together.[101] Nose rubbing as a sign of affection, intimacy, and friendship among Indigenous peoples of the Pacific Islands, Alaska and the Arctic was well known by the mid-nineteenth century, being mentioned in several European accounts (variations of this greeting are known as the *hongi* among the Māori people, *honi* among Native Hawai'ians and *kunik* among the Inuit).[102] Justamant was not the first choreographer to include nose rubbing in his 'character' dances: this gesture also appeared in the 'Eskimo' *pas de deux* from August Bournonville's *Fjernt fra Danmark* ('Far from Denmark', premiered at Det Kongelige Teater, Copenhagen, 1860) as part of the Act II parade-of-nations divertissement staged when sailors attend a costume ball on board a Danish frigate (the divertissement also had an 'Indian' war dance). By the mid-nineteenth century, nose rubbing was so widely recognised a signifier of indigeneity that it could be freely appropriated for an imagined tribe of Native Americans living in Louisiana. The gesture was clearly the highlight of the 'Pas Sauvage' – so much so that it was repeated at the end, along with a closing salutation to the audience.

---

100 Justamant's notations for the 1857 Lyon production of the ballet *Le Corsaire* also include this gesture when the captive Medora resists the amorous advances of the lecherous Pasha: Justamant, *Le Corsaire / Ballet en trois actes et cinq tableaux*, Theaterwissenschaftliche Sammlung der Universität zu Köln, Schloss Wahn, Ms. 70-441, p. 294. This face-shielding gesture also appears in the Act III fairy-tale divertissement from Petipa's *Sleeping Beauty*, as Little Red Riding Hood attempts to fend off the ravenous Wolf.

101 'Tout deux le corps bien en avant croisent la tête appuyée sur l'épaule gauche comme pour s'embrasser puis la relève, et la rebaisse sur l'épaule droite. Ils la relève encore la baisse nez à nez. Remuent la tête de droite à gauche en ce touchant le bout du nez': Justamant, *Le Bossu*, p. 47. Artus's music apparently underscored the tenderness of this moment: Justamant's marginal notes indicate a tempo shift to *Lent* for the climactic four bars when the two *sauvages* finally unite.

102 See, for example, Georges-Bernard Depping, *Aperçu historique sur les mœurs et coutumes des nations* (Paris: Mairet et Fournier, 1842), p. 163; John Lemoinne, 'Le Passage du Nord', *La Revue de Paris*, NS, 1 (Jan. 1854), 1–46, at p. 5; Camille de Roquefeuil, *Journal d'un voyage autour du monde, pendant les années 1816, 1817, 1818 et 1819* (Paris: Ponthieu; Lesage; Gide, 1823), vol. 1, p. 310.

Other examples of unusual gestures denoting exotic Otherness include exaggerated movements performed by the two 'sauvages' designed to make them look primitive. For example, when the man first enters, he makes a 'grotesque gesture of exclamation' upon seeing his partner, followed by a '*soubresaut énorme*' (an 'enormous' jump springing from and landing on both feet) from a platform to the ground, both comical exaggerated movements meant to convey the animalistic athleticism of the *homme sauvage*.[103] As he approaches, the woman adopts a crouching stance ('lowering herself') and watches him from underneath her raised left arm while doing *jetés* (leaps from one leg to the other).[104] Throughout the 'Pas Sauvage', both the man and woman also perform recurring steps such as turning in place while executing two-footed hops (*soubresauts*) or accented movements with their feet (*en piétinant*). The simplistic and often awkward repeated movements seem to have been a meaningful signifier of Otherness and perhaps served to reductively characterise Native American dance as 'stomping'.[105] Finally, certain unusual arm positions served as markers of exotic 'character' movement: both dancers make the gesture of folding one arm across the chest while opening the other arm outwards from the body; and while the man holds his bow above his head with both hands, the woman raises her arms above her head, with the elbows curved but the wrists flopped down and away from the body – an eccentric disruption of the rounded *port de bras* in classical ballet.[106]

The exoticism of Justamant's 'Pas Sauvage' relied not only on unusual movements but also on the skills and reputations of his character dancers, and the enthusiastic reception of the 'Pas' was perhaps due even more to Mariquita's performance than to Justamant's choreography. Mariquita's early association with 'exotic' characters and her foreign persona made her ideally suited to a role such as a *femme sauvage*. Born in Algiers and raised on the stages of the Boule-

---

103 'L'homme parait sur l'estrade en faisant un geste d'exclamation grotesque appercevant sa femme. L'homme fait un soubressau [*sic*] énorme en sautant à terre': Justamant, *Le Bossu*, pp. 44–5. A *soubresaut* may be classified as *grand* in standard ballet terminology, but *énorme* is highly unusual, suggesting an extreme movement beyond even a 'large' jump.

104 'Le femme en se baissant fait des jetés ordinaires et en regardant l'homme sous le bras gauche': Justamant, *Le Bossu*, p. 45.

105 *Piétiner* in the French school of ballet literally means 'to stamp the feet', although this term is defined today as 'accented movements *sur les pointes*' when the dancer is *en pointe*: Grant, *Technical Manual*, p. 83. The technique of *piétiner* is not necessarily associated with 'character' or 'exotic' *pas* (see n. 92 above), but in his notations, Justamant specifies 'sur les orteils' when these accented movements *en piétinant* are to be performed gracefully *en pointe*. Here, it seems that the dancers were meant to stamp their feet more aggressively. On the later use of 'piétinement', 'piétine', and 'piétier' to describe primitivistic 'stamping' or 'stomping' in Nijinsky's choreography for *Le Sacre du printemps*, see Levitz, 'Racism at *The Rite*', pp. 149, 164–5, n. 17.

106 This arm position is not described in Justamant's prose, but is indicated by his drawings; it is unclear whether the palms are facing up or down.

vard du Temple in Paris, Mariquita had since her childhood performed a range of exotic characters, whether from the Middle East, Spain, or Far East, and she had recently returned from dancing for the Royal Theatre of Madrid.[107] Casting Mariquita in the roles of gypsy girl in Act I and 'Indian' woman in Act III would in itself have signalled the promise of alluring exoticism to the Parisian public. While one critic acknowledged the strong contributions of all three leading female soloists, noting that the 1867 *Le Bossu* reprise was 'ornamented by an Indian Ballet in which Mlles Mariquita, Buisseret and Rozé distinguished themselves',[108] many critics focused their praise solely on Mariquita.[109] For instance, in his review of the 1867 revival of *Le Bossu*, Biéville reserved particular acclaim for the '*pas indien* danced by Mlle Mariquita with her characteristic combination of restraint and provocativeness'.[110] And, as Roqueplan wrote in his review of the production, 'Mlle Mariquita dances with the most exquisite originality one of those character dances in which she has never been equalled by anyone else.'[111]

Intertextualities with Other Balletic Femmes Sauvages

Aside from the few exotic markers discussed above, a surface-level analysis of Justamant's ballet shows that the steps, patterns, and poses of the divertissement in *Le Bossu* did not depart significantly from nineteenth-century academic conventions. This suggests that the work's choreographic exoticism was relatively muted and inconsequential. However, a description of the dance vocabulary of *Le Bossu* tells only part of the story. Equally significant are its choreographic connections with other ballets. In the same way that the side-to-side head tilts mentioned earlier signified Otherness in both *Le Bossu* and *Giselle* – and relied on audiences knowing the ballet repertoire for their full impact – so, too, entire scenes in *Le Bossu* recalled older repertoire, creating intertextualities not immediately apparent when the ballet is examined out of

---

107 Mariquita had in 1858 escaped the stifling, sexually exploitative Opéra and had found work in Madrid before returning to Paris to dance at the Porte-Saint-Martin in the early 1860s.

108 'En somme, brillante reprise, ornée d'un ballet indien où se distinguent mesdemoiselles Mariquita, Buisseret et Rozé': Émile L. [Lutz?], 'Théâtres', *Le Figaro*, 24 Jan. 1867, p. 4.

109 For example, one announcement ran, 'Mélingue dans le *Bossu*, deux ballets nouveaux, le pas indien dansé par Mlle Mariquita, mise en scène splendide': 'Bulletin des Théâtres', *Le Siècle*, 26 Jan. 1867, p. 2.

110 'Ajoutez à cette agréable distribution deux ballets pleins d'entrain et un *pas indien* dansé par Mlle Mariquitta [*sic*] avec cette manière à la fois retenue et provocante qui lui est particulière': E. D. de Biéville, 'Revue des Théâtres', *Le Siècle*, 28 Jan. 1867, pp. 1–2, at p. 1.

111 'Mlle Mariquita danse avec la plus exquise originalité un de ces pas de caractère où elle n'a jamais été égalée par personne': Nestor Roqueplan, 'Théâtres', *Le Constitutionnel*, 28 Jan. 1867, pp. 1–2, at p. 1.

context. Once these intertextualities are recognised, they deepen our understanding of how *Le Bossu* might have been understood or interpreted, adding an important layer of meaning.

Most significantly, Justamant's *Le Bossu* divertissement included reworked portions of an earlier mythological ballet, his 'Pas de Diane', a self-borrowing suggesting that stereotypical images of virginal, nature-loving Native American women might be modelled after those of Diana, goddess of chastity, the moon, the forest, and the hunt. And, in fact, this conflation of Diana and the American 'Indian' maiden had a precedent in visual art, as evinced by the early nineteenth-century French painting *Allegory of America* (fig. 2.8). Justamant's 'Pas de Diane' was originally performed in 1862 at the Théâtre de la Monnaie in Brussels, starring Mlle Déléchaux as the goddess Diana and featuring the *deuxième danseuses* Girod and Wesmaël, four *coryphées*, and eight women of the *corps de ballet* as her votary nymphs.[112] Justamant reused his 'Pas de Diane' choreography – along with Calendini's music – in two sections of his *Le Bossu* ballet: Part Two, 'Les Chasseresses', and Part Five, 'Final: Les Filles des Pampas et les Chasseresses'. For 'Les Chasseresses', Justamant repurposed the first two *entrées* of the 'Pas de Diane' – the ensemble *entrée* of twelve nymphs wielding hunting bows, followed by Déléchaux's solo *entrée* – with only minor alterations such as modifying Déléchaux's solo into an *entrée* for two *coryphées* (figs. 2.9 and 2.10). And for the *entrée des chasseresses* in 'Final: Les Filles des Pampas et les Chasseresses', Justamant borrowed the opening sequence of his 'Pas de Diane' Coda ('Les dames ensemble').

Reworking existing choreography – with slight variations or substitutions – is likely to have been a common practice among nineteenth-century choreographers given the considerable amount of choreography they had to produce each year. Adapting his 'Pas de Diane' for the 'Grand Ballet Indien' of *Le Bossu* must have been an obvious choice for Justamant given the parallels between Diana's nocturnal *chasse sauvage* and numerous stereotypical images of Indigenous Americans as hunter-warriors, which Justamant had already worked with in *Jaguarita*. At a basic level, the dancers' accessories of bows, quivers, and arrows allowed for an easy imaginative slippage from Classical nymphs to 'Indian' maidens of the American forests and plains. In both the 'Pas de Diane' and *Le Bossu* divertissement, Justamant's *chasseresses* mime shooting with bows and arrows, triumphantly lift their bows above their heads, and perform numerous 'gliding' steps (*glissades* and other movements performed

---

112 Justamant, '*Pas de Diane, musique de Mr Calandini* [sic], *réglé par Justamant, dansé par Mlle Déléchaux, Girod, Wesmaël, quatre coryphées et huit dames du corps de ballet a Bruxelles (1862)*', in *Grand pas composés par M^r H Justamant représentés à Marseille et Bruxelles*, pp. 45–75, Bibliothèque Nationale de France, Bibliothèque-Musée de l'Opéra, B.217 (24) <gallica.bnf.fr>. Déléchaux's, Girod's, and Wesmaël's ranks appear in Jacques Isnardon, *Le Théâtre de la Monnaie depuis sa fondation jusqu'à nos jours* (Brussels: Schott, 1890), p. 453.

Figure 2.8. America's New World Allegory as a young Indian woman wearing feathers and a bow and arrows. Painting of the French School of the 19th century. La Rochelle, New World Museum. Photo © Photo Josse / Bridgeman Images.

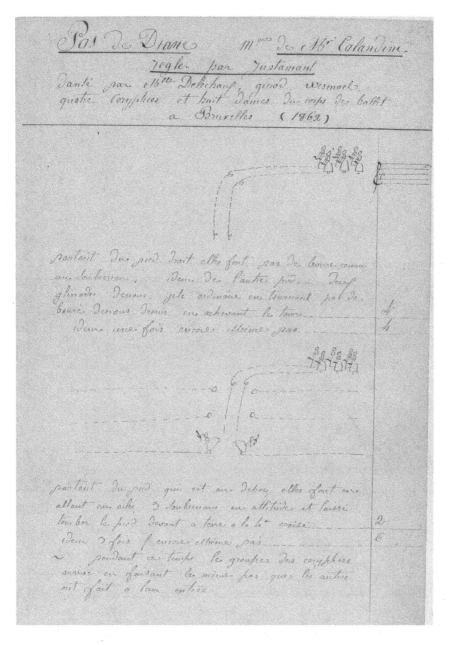

Figure 2.9. Henri Justamant, 'Pas de Diane, musique de Mr Calandini [sic], réglé par Justamant, dansé par Mlle Déléchaux, Girod, Wesmaël, quatre coryphées et huit dames du corps de ballet à Bruxelles (1862)', in *Grands pas composés par Mr H. Justamant representés à Marseille et Bruxelles*, p. 45. Bibliothèque Nationale de France

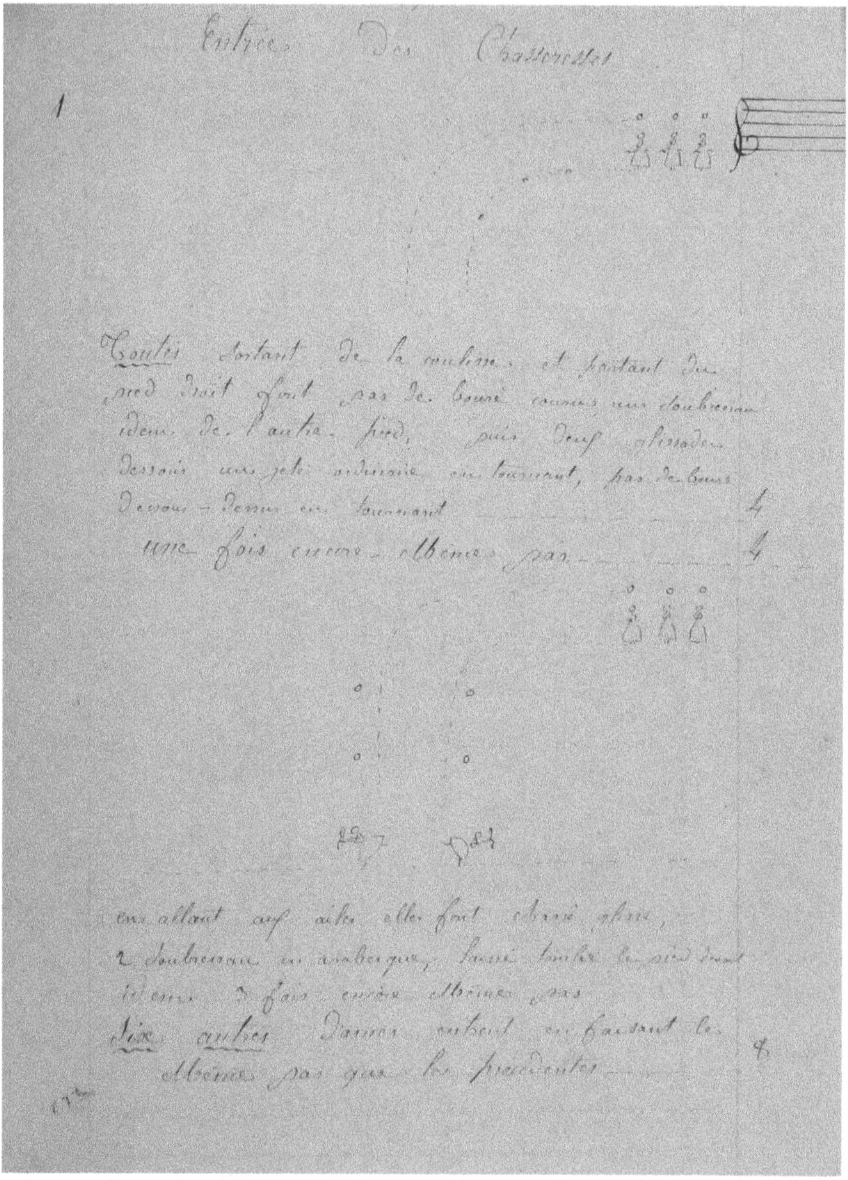

Figure 2.10. Henri Justamant, 'Ballet du *Bossu*', in *Divertissements de La Tour de Nesle et du Bossu* (1867), p. 17, 'Entrée des Chasseresses', opening. The New York Public Library.

glissé), perhaps suggesting the galloping motion of horseback riding or a lithe, slinking movement in pursuit of their target.

Justamant reused several other gestures and formations in his choreographies for *Jaguarita*, the 'Pas de Diane', and *Le Bossu* – suggesting a shared choreographic vocabulary for Native Americans and mythological huntresses in his creative imagination. In all three of these works, his characters mime 'listening in the forest' while wielding hunting bows. Although 'listening in the forest' is a common pantomime gesture in pastoral settings, the women's exotic 'sauvage' costuming in *Jaguarita* and *Le Bossu* likely would have encouraged audiences to interpret their keen listening as a characteristic trait of Indigenous Americans.[113] (See Chapter 7 on Chateaubriand's accounts of Native Americans' seemingly superhuman 'sharpness of the ear' and ability to surveil.) In *Le Bossu*, at the end of 'Les Filles des Pampas', seven 'sauvages' remain on stage for the opening ritournelle of 'Les Chasseresses', leaning to one side and holding their hands to their ears – as if to hear the approach of the *chasseresses* – then run offstage. Later in 'Les Chasseresses', the huntresses themselves form a multi-levelled 'listening-in-the-forest' pose re-created from Justamant's 'Pas de Diane': in a circle, some women lean on their bows with one hand and hold the opposite hand to their ears, while others lower themselves and listen close to the ground; still others stand tall and hold their bows above their heads. All three works also include group poses using the women's bows to form various shapes such as the 'corbeille' (basket), created by a semi-circle of women extending their bows downward into the centre.

Whether it was Justamant's intention or not, the connection between Native American *chasseresses* and Artemisian nymphs reinforced the prevailing myth of the 'noble savage'. In the French imagination, both Indigenous Americans and ancient Greek gods were closely connected to the natural world: both represented ideals of bravery and stoicism, both were eternally unchanging, and both were part of an outdated 'pagan' way of life that was 'vanishing' or already rendered obsolete by the advent of Christianity and modern civilisation. Artemisian and Native American *chasseresses* also reflected fantasies of a feminised landscape and ecomorphic women – that is, women who seem to emerge from and embody the natural world, with their bodies displaying features of hybridity with that environment (e.g. diaphanous insect wings or floral crowns). Diana and her nymphs tended to display attributes of the night sky, wearing crescent-moon tiaras and blue-and-silver-spangled tunics (fig. 2.11), whereas Justamant's *chasseresses sauvages* wore a diadem of red-and-white feathers and jewellery made of animal teeth (fig. 2.12). His *chasseresses sauvages* also wore

---

113 The Wilis of *Giselle* also perform this gesture, albeit without bows, but as a supernatural folkloric type of *femmes sauvages* their listening can likewise be interpreted ominously as a sign of their menacing surveillance of – and lying in wait for – male trespassers Albrecht and Hilarion.

Figure 2.11. Paul Lormier, costume design for Carlotta Grisi as Diane *chasseresse* in *La Jolie Fille de Gand* (1842). Bibliothèque Nationale de France.

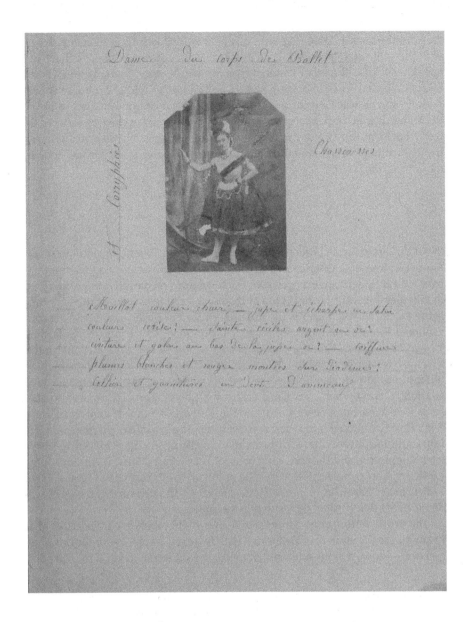

Figure 2.12. 'Dame du corps de Ballet / et Coryphées / Chasseresses / Maillot couleur chair; jupe et écharpe en satin couleur cerise; Sainte Cécile argent ou or; cinture [sic] et galon au bas de la jupe or; coiffure plumes blanches et rouges montées sur diadème; collier et garnitures en dents d'animeaux'. Publicity photograph and costume description in Justamant, 'Ballet du *Bossu*', in *Divertissements de La Tour de Nesle et du Bossu* (1867), p. 67. The New York Public Library.

cerise satin sashes decorated with a jungle animal print, an element shared with the well-established tradition in visual art of adorning Diana with a leopard skin.[114] And, like other balletic *nymphes chasseresses*, Justamant's *chasseresses sauvages* wore light beige-coloured bodysuits that allowed them to appear nude from the waist up, or at least seeming to expose one breast. In short, the stylised 'wild' indigeneity of Justamant's *chasseresses sauvages* was not far removed from the *Diane chasseresse* tradition, suggesting that, in the nineteenth-century French imagination, Indigenous peoples were akin to primeval nature spirits.[115]

Conclusions

What do Justamant's choreographic notations tell us about danced representations of Indigenous Americans, and what broader implications do these findings have for our understanding of how characterisation and narrative were conveyed in nineteenth-century ballet? One of the most striking aspects of the notations is the extent to which they show Justamant's 'Grand Ballet Indien' to be a conventional French ballet and not a comic grotesquery of relentlessly demeaning 'savage' stereotypes. Certainly the divertissement included a few strikingly unusual movements designed to look 'exotic' and even 'primitive', and some of these movements perpetuated Euro-centric racist beliefs. Nose-rubbing might be read as a neutral ethnographic marker, if a geographically inappropriate one for a ballet set in Louisiana, but it also emphasised the 'Otherness' of the Native Americans. Repetitive two-footed jumps and accented stepping in a circle, exaggerated large leaps, and unconventional arm gestures were clearly intended to look anti-balletic, ungraceful, and therefore 'uncivilised'. Yet overt markers of choreographic exoticism were comparatively rare. The principal vocabulary of the 'Grand Ballet Indien' instead drew from *danse d'école*, and it was the steps and gestures of academic ballet that conveyed meaning to the audience.

The exotic setting and costumes of *Le Bossu* did much to contextualise that meaning for the audience. Festooned with feathers, beads – and, for the *chasseresses* – leopard skins and animal teeth, the dancers could be perceived as

114 See Jean-Marc Nattier's various portraits of aristocratic women as Diana: *Madame Adélaïde, fille de Louis XV, en Diane* (1745), *Madame Bouret as Diana* (1745), *Madame Pompadour en Diane* (1746), *Portrait of a Woman as Diana* (1752), *Madame Bergeret de Frouville as Diana* (1756). Leopard skins were used in the costuming of Jules Perrot's 'Pas de Diane chasseresse' (1843), an interpolated dance in his divertissement *Un Bal sous Louis XIV*. See Ivor Guest, *Jules Perrot: Master of the Romantic Ballet* (London: Dance Books, 1984), p. 96.

115 Meglin makes a similar argument that the costuming of the *sauvage américain* in late seventeenth-century and eighteenth-century French opera and ballet was an adaptation of the Classical faun or satyr. See Meglin, '*Sauvages*, Sex Roles, and Semiotics, Part One', pp. 89–92.

Indigenous when viewed through the stereotype-saturated lens of audience expectations for Native American characters, even if performing elegant, traditionally 'European' academic footwork, leaps, and poses. For example, with her graceful and virtuosic choreography, Mlle Rozé, the *sauvage à plume blanche*, may have seemed like a danced reincarnation of Atala, Chateaubriand's idealised virginal 'Indian' maiden. Or, for an older audience member who may have visited George Catlin's Musée de l'Indien in the mid-1840s, the non-exotic circular formations and props of the *chasseresses* and 'filles des Pampas' in the 'Groupes' *Adagio* may have vaguely evoked memories of Catlin's paintings of various Native American round dances with bows, arrows, and spears.

While such connections in the audience's collective memory are ultimately speculative, we do know that narrative meaning and characterisation in Justamant's 'Grand Ballet Indien' were conveyed through choreographic references to or connections with other ballets. Seemingly obscure gestures such as head tilts might have had little meaning on their own, but they would have been understood as markers of difference when seen by audiences who knew the ballet repertoire – which was something choreographers could reasonably expect since ballet was prevalent and popular throughout the nineteenth century. That Justamant could even reuse existing choreography from his 1862 'Pas de Diane' to depict the Native American *chasseresses* of *Le Bossu* demonstrates not only the crucial importance of visual cues such as costuming and set design in establishing a sense of Indigenous American Otherness, but also the persistence and malleability of certain archetypal figures in the French theatrical imagination. Extensive passages of shared material between Justamant's 'Pas de Diane' and *Le Bossu* ballet – as well as certain movements, formations, and gestures that the *femmes sauvages* of *Le Bossu* have in common with the *guerrières sauvages* of *Jaguarita* and the Wilis of *Giselle* – suggest that a more exhaustive examination of Justamant's extant manuscripts will yield additional interchoreologies and intertextualities.

In sum, while perhaps not as overtly demeaning as other late nineteenth-century stage works that presented Indigenous Americans as vicious or bloodthirsty aggressors, Justamant's fanciful, aestheticised images of Native American 'prairie girls' playfully cavorting in an idyllic landscape not only reinforced stereotypes of the naïve 'Indian maiden' with her 'natural' innocence and beauty but also perpetuated narratives of pastoral comfort and serenity that were starkly out of touch with the contemporary realities of Native American life. If Artemisian *nymphes chasseresses* could be readily transformed into *chasseresses sauvages*, this embodied intertextuality reinforced the contemporary tendency to equate Native Americans with mythological deities and nature spirits, a pernicious trope that has long served to marginalise, dehumanise, and exoticise Indigenous peoples in the Western European imagination.

3

Louisiana Imagined:
Gender, Race and Slavery in *Le Planteur* (1839)

Helena Kopchick Spencer[1]

Following major territorial losses in the Seven Years War (1756–63) and the successful Haitian Revolution in Saint-Domingue (1791–1804), France's *Vente de la Louisiane* in 1803 marked the end of the empire's colonial ambitions in the United States.[2] Nevertheless, America remained a prominent locus

---

1 Portions of this chapter were originally presented at the 2020 Annual Meeting of the American Musicological Society. I would like to thank Ralph Locke, Marian Smith, Shaena Weitz, and the volume editors for their helpful feedback on earlier drafts. This essay quotes from historical sources that use racist language. I have attempted to incorporate these quotes judiciously, and have left certain terms untranslated from the original French, in acknowledgement of Toni Morrison's assertion that 'oppressive language does more than represent violence; it is violence': Toni Morrison, Nobel Prize in Literature lecture, 7 Dec. 1993 <https://www.nobelprize.org/prizes/literature/1993/morrison/lecture/>. French colonial slave societies used various technical terms for mixed-race individuals, according to their degree of Blackness and Whiteness: for example, 'mulâtre' (mulatto) referred to the child of a Black parent and a White parent, 'quarteron' (quadroon) referred to the child of a 'mulâtre' parent and White parent, 'octavon' (octoroon) referred to the child of a 'quarteron' parent and a White parent, and so forth. However, I generally avoid these outdated terms unless quoting from a primary source. One notable exception: I use the term 'Tragic Mulatta' to refer to a particular stereotypical figure and narrative trope, since this is the standard designation in literary criticism; otherwise, I use the term 'mixed-race' to describe individuals of Black and White ancestry.

2 Napoléon had regained control of the Louisiana territory from Spain in 1800 as part of a larger effort to reassert France's colonial presence in America and create 'a vast breadbasket to feed the slave societies he hoped to reestablish in the Antilles'. Thomas N. Ingersoll, *Mammon and Manon in Early New Orleans: The First Slave Society in the Deep South, 1718–1819* (Knoxville: University of Tennessee Press, 1999), p. 244. This agenda shifted, though, with the successful Haitian Revolution against French colonial rule and slavery in Saint-Domingue; as the historian Laurent Dubois has argued, the Saint-Domingue Revolution was the most decisive factor leading to the withdrawal of France's colonial presence in America. Laurent Dubois, 'The Haitian Revolution and the Sale of Louisiana; or, Thomas Jefferson's

in the French cultural imagination through widely circulated novels such as Chateaubriand's epic *Les Natchez*, the sociological writings of Alexis de Tocqueville (most notably, *De la Démocratie en Amérique*), and travelogues such as Frances Trollope's *Domestic Manners of the Americans*. American settings and characters also appeared on the nineteenth-century Parisian stage in a variety of theatrical works.[3] One of the most immediately popular – if short-lived – of these was Jules-Henri Vernoy de Saint-Georges and Hippolyte Monpou's *Le Planteur*, premiered at the Opéra-Comique on 1 March 1839. Despite its auspicious premiere, heralded as a great success by several papers,[4] *Le Planteur* did not enter the long-term repertoire at the Comique, closing after a run of forty-six performances in 1839 and two performances in 1840.[5] *Le Planteur's*

(Unpaid) Debt to Jean-Jacques Dessalines', in *Empires of the Imagination: Transatlantic Histories of the Louisiana Purchase*, ed. Peter J. Kastor and François Weil (Charlottesville: University of Virginia Press, 2009), pp. 93–116. On French musico-dramatic works inspired by the Saint-Domingue revolution, see Chapter 1 of this volume.

3 Perhaps the most enduring French stage depiction of America appeared in adaptations of the Abbé Prévost's popular *Histoire du Chevalier des Grieux et de Manon Lescaut* (1731), including Gosse and Propiac's mélodrame (Gaîté, 1820), Scribe and Halévy's ballet-pantomime (Opéra, 1830), Carmouche and de Courcy's drame (Odéon, 1830), Barrière and Fournier's drame (Gymnase, 1851), and Scribe and Auber's opéra comique (Opéra-Comique, 1856). On the operatic adaptations of Prévost's novel, see Vincent Giroud, 'Manon at the Opera: From Prévost's *Manon Lescaut* to Auber's *Manon Lescaut* and Massenet's *Manon*', in *'Music's Obedient Daughter': The Opera Libretto from Source to Score*, ed. Sabine Lichtenstein (New York: Rodopi, 2014), pp. 239–68. In the tradition of Prévost's novel, these *Manon Lescaut* works propagated the image of Louisiana as a penal colony of ill repute and punishing desolation: Manon is deported along with other *filles de joie* (that is, prostitutes) to New Orleans, ultimately dying of exhaustion and exposure in the Louisiana desert – a fictive landscape that functions as a metaphor for the waste and depletion of her own body. This bleak image of a corrupt New World populated by fallen women is a far cry from late eighteenth-century Italian operas such as Haydn's and Paisiello's respective settings of *Il mondo della luna*, which allegorise America as a pastoral lunar utopia and – in the case of Piccinni's *Il regno della luna* – allow women more power and independence. See Pierpaolo Polzonetti, *Italian Opera in the Age of the American Revolution* (Cambridge: Cambridge University Press, 2011), pp. 91–100.

4 As noted in *Le Courrier* on 2 March 1839 (p. 2), the day following its premiere, 'Le Planteur [...] a obtenu ce soir un très grand succès au théâtre de la Bourse.' And in *Le Commerce*, also on 2 March 1839 (p. 4), *Le Planteur* is said to have achieved 'un beau succès à l'Opéra-Comique: succès de paroles, de musique et de chant'.

5 Performance statistics are taken from the 'Tableau des Pièces Représentées à l'Opéra-Comique du 1er Janvier 1825 au 31 Décembre 1893' in Albert Soubies, *Soixante-neuf ans à l'Opéra-comique en deux pages de la première de* La Dame blanche *à la millième de* Mignon, *1825–1894* (Paris: Fischbacher, 1894).

102   *Helena Kopchick Spencer*

impact on Francophone theatrical culture of the late 1830s and early 1840s included numerous productions in the provinces and abroad,[6] but it was not staged in Paris again until its revival at the Théâtre des Fantaisies-Parisiennes in 1867.[7] This essay focuses on the 1839 Comique production.

Le Planteur arrived four years after another popular American-themed opéra comique, *L'Éclair*, a romantic comedy set in the vicinity of Boston.[8] Writing for *La Revue de Paris*, Félix Bonnaire cynically declared:

> Since the great success of *L'Éclair*, the Opéra-Comique is crazy about the New World, not that this rich vegetation inspires it, or that it finds in this atmosphere of sun and fecund vapours the subject of more serious compositions; under the palm trees, they continue to sing the little airs they once crooned so well in their powdery grove of roses. The Opéra-Comique is fond of the New World because the little straw hat of the Creoles goes well with the dark eyes of its female singers and above all because *L'Éclair* has succeeded.[9]

Regardless of the Comique's desire to capitalise on the success of *L'Éclair*, the creation of *Le Planteur* shows how the supposedly 'light' genre of opéra comique could engage – albeit in a limited and stereotypical way – with contemporary themes of American slavery in a former French territory.[10] And

---

6   In France, *Le Planteur* was staged at the provincial theatres of Lyon, Douai, Dijon, Montpellier, and Bordeaux; in Belgium, at the Théâtre de la Monnaie in Brussels, as well as in Anvers and Ghent; and in Switzerland, at the Théâtre de Genève. Barbara T. Cooper, 'Introduction', in Henri de Saint-Georges and Hippolyte Monpou, *Le Planteur*, ed. and intro. Barbara T. Cooper, Collection autrement mêmes, ed. Roger Little (Paris: L'Harmattan, 2015), p. xxv. Cooper adds that this list is probably incomplete, on the basis of a notice in *La France musicale* from October 1843 that *Le Planteur* 'est jouée avec succès sur presque toutes les scènes de la province' (Cooper, 'Introduction', p. xxv).

7   The repertoire of the Fantaisies-Parisiennes is currently the subject of an institutional study by Mark Everist.

8   I wish to thank Diana R. Hallman for bringing this work to my attention. *L'Éclair* and other opéras-comiques of the July Monarchy are the subject of Hallman's forthcoming monograph.

9   'Depuis le grand succès de *l'Éclair*, l'Opéra-Comique raffole du Nouveau-Monde, non que cette riche végétation l'inspire, et qu'il trouve dans cette atmosphère de soleil et de fécondes vapeurs, sujet à des compositions plus sérieuses; il continue à chanter, sous les palmiers, les petits airs qu'il fredonnait si bien autrefois dans son poudreux bosquet de roses: l'Opéra-Comique affectionne le Nouveau-Monde, parce que le petit chapeau de paille des créoles va bien aux yeux noirs de ses cantatrices, et surtout parce que *l'Éclair* y a réussi': F. Bonnaire, 'Théâtres, *La Revue de Paris*, NS, 3 (1839), 70–2, at p. 70.

10   As Ralph Locke notes, scholars have generally neglected lighter genres of French opera, but these genres have much to tell us about contemporary concerns. Nineteenth-century opéra comique and opéra bouffe 'could evoke current events and trends in French society in a manner that was either direct and pointed or indirect but quite transparent': Ralph Locke, 'The Exotic in Nineteenth-Century French Opera, Part 1 Locales and Peoples',

Louisiana Imagined   103

despite Bonnaire's dismissive attitude towards its musical idiom of 'petits airs', opéra comique was widely recognised in nineteenth-century discourse as the 'eminently French genre', emblematic of a 'national spirit', in part because of its distinctive musical aesthetic, which avoided many of the Italianate influences found in grand opéra.[11] Nineteenth-century opéra comique was also considered the 'national' genre because its family-friendly subject matter reflected French bourgeois morality, with plots typically ending in 'the triumph of virtue and innocence, the consolidation of social harmony and a socially appropriate marriage'.[12] Therefore, while there is certainly merit in Bonnaire's argument that the American setting of *Le Planteur* served as a welcome opportunity for the Opéra-Comique to dress up its female stars in appealing 'Creole' costumes, this opéra comique and its critical reception also served as a barometer of French attitudes towards race, gender, and sex – particularly with regard to which characters are deemed marriageable.

Set on a plantation some miles from New Orleans in 1806, the year when American Louisiana's *Code noir* was adopted,[13] *Le Planteur* dramatises the legal and romantic vicissitudes of the young 'Creole' heiress Jenny Makensie. The term 'Creole' has a complicated history of widely varied meanings,[14] but, in

---

19th-Century Music 45:2 (Fall 2021), 116. I would like to thank Prof. Locke for generously sharing his unpublished manuscript with me.

11 Hervé Lacombe, *The Keys to French Opera in the Nineteenth Century*, trans. Edward Schneider (Berkeley: University of California Press, 2001), p. 229; Stephen Huebner, 'Opera and Ballet after the Revolution', in *The Cambridge Companion to French Music*, ed. Simon Tresize (Cambridge: Cambridge University Press, 2015), pp. 221–41, at p. 238.

12 Kimberly White, *Female Singers on the French Stage, 1830–1848* (Cambridge: Cambridge University Press, 2018), p. 103. Here White draws on arguments made in Olivier Bara, *Le Théâtre de l'opéra-comique sous la restauration: Enquête autour d'un genre moyen* (Hildesheim: Olms, 2001). See also Philippe Vendrix, 'L'Opéra comique sans rire', in *Die Opéra comique und ihr Einfluß auf das europäische Musiktheater im 19. Jahrhundert: Bericht über den internationalen Kongreß Frankfurt 1994*, ed. Herbert Schneider and Nicole Wild (Hildesheim: Olms, 1997), pp. 31–41.

13 The French *Code noir* had been introduced in colonial Louisiana in 1724. The year 1806 is not indicated in the libretto, but is specified in the printed full score of *Le Planteur*. 'La scène se passe en 1806 à la Nouvelle Orléans': Hippolyte Monpou *et al.*, *Le Planteur, opéra comique en deux actes, paroles de Mr. H. de St. Georges, musique de Hippolyte Monpou* [full score] (Paris: Richault, n.d. [1839]), n.p. [front matter with list of 'personnages' and the original 'acteurs', followed by the 'catalogue des morceaux'].

14 As the literary scholar Sean X. Goudie summarises, 'colonists of European descent, as well as black and mulatto slaves and freedmen born and raised in the New World, were identified as "creoles" by the British, French and Spanish empires. Yet the term denoted much more than the birth of a colonial subject or slave outside the "borders" of national origin (Europe or Africa). Most significantly, the term "creole" was used to account for admixtures [...] between Old and New World "races" and cultures': Sean X. Goudie, *Creole America: The West Indies and the Formation of Literature and Culture in*

the case of *Le Planteur,* 'Creole' seems to refer to Jenny's mixed racial parentage more than to her birth in America, since the published libretto designates White American characters as simply 'American'.[15] The character of Jenny epitomises the popular mid-century stereotype of the 'Tragic Mulatta': a beautiful, light-skinned woman of mixed race is raised as White in her White father's household, but – usually upon his death and/or financial ruin – her Black ancestry is discovered and she is socially ostracised or, worse, sold into slavery.[16] The narrative typically ends in the heroine's death, often a suicide

---

the New Republic (Philadelphia: University of Pennsylvania Press, 2006), p. 8. Quoted in Kimberly Snyder Manganelli, *Transatlantic Spectacles of Race: The Tragic Mulatta and the Tragic Muse* (Brunswick, NJ: Rutgers University Press, 2012), pp. 192–3.

15   The published libretto identifies Jenny as a 'jeune créole', whereas her White cousin and fiancé Arthur Barcley is a 'jeune Américain', and her White maid Eva is likewise a 'jeune Américaine, au service de miss Makensie'; the White planter Jakson is a 'riche colon de la Louisiane'. Jenny's mixed-race intendant Caton is a 'mulâtre, factotum de miss Makensie', and racial distinctions among the supernumeraries include 'esclaves noirs', 'mulâtresses', and 'domestiques blancs': Hippolyte Monpou *et al.*, *Le Planteur, opéra comique en deux actes, paroles de M. de Saint-Georges; musique de M. H. Monpou. Représenté pour la première fois, à Paris, sur le Théâtre royal de l'Opéra-Comique, le 1er mars 1839* [libretto], *La France dramatique au dix-neuvième siècle, choix de pièces modernes* 7 (Paris: Tresse, 1841), p. 331.

16   In the remainder of this essay, I drop the quotation marks around 'Tragic Mulatta' but retain capitalisation, following the orthographic practice in Manganelli, *Transatlantic Spectacles of Race*. First identified in the early twentieth century by the literary critic and poet Sterling A. Brown, the Tragic Mulatto is a well-educated, 'nearly white' mixed-race character who is the product of an 'illicit union' and ultimately the melancholic 'victim of a divided inheritance', tormented by an internal struggle 'to unite a white intellect with black sensuousness'. Sterling A. Brown, 'Negro Character as Seen by White Authors', *The Journal of Negro Education*, 2:2 (1933), 179–203, at pp. 193–6. See also Brown's discussion of this stereotype ('The Tragic Mulatto Passes for White') in *The Negro in American Fiction* (Washington, DC: Associates in Negro Folk Education, 1937), pp. 142–4. Eve Allegra Raimon argues that Brown's articles and other scholarship – notably, Judith Berzon, *Neither White Nor Black: The Mulatto in American Fiction* (New York: New York University Press, 1978) and Werner Sollors, *Neither Black Nor White Yet Both: Thematic Explorations of Interracial Literature* (Oxford: Oxford University Press, 1997) – have incorrectly gendered this stereotype by using the universalised masculine term 'Tragic Mulatto'. According to Raimon, the doomed mixed-race character is most often female: moreover, 'the very tragedy of the figure's fate depends on her female gender', since 'the sexual vulnerability of a female light-skinned slave is essential to propel the plot forward and to generate the reader's sympathy and outrage'. Eve Allegra Raimon, *The 'Tragic Mulatta' Revisited: Race and Nationalism in Nineteenth-Century Antislavery Fiction* (New Brunswick, NJ: Rutgers University Press, 2004), p. 5. However, Marlene Daut finds that the male version is in fact more common in nineteenth-century Francophone fiction, especially in representations of the Haitian Revolution. See Marlene L. Daut, *Tropics of Haiti: Race and the Literary History of the Haitian Revolution in the Atlantic World, 1789–1865* (Liverpool: Liverpool University

motivated by her shame and self-loathing, or else to escape a fate of sexual servitude to a lecherous master. Most studies of the Tragic Mulatta have focused on her use as a device in American anti-slavery literature; however, this trope was also prominent in nineteenth-century France, not only in novels such as Gustave de Beaumont's *Marie, ou L'Esclavage aux États-Unis* (1835), but also in the theatre, where the startling revelation of hidden or mistaken identities was a favoured dramatic effect.[17] In France, as in America, the Tragic Mulatta trope was fraught with contradictory implications: for, while it was usually intended to foster sympathy for the abolitionist cause by emphasising a 'common humanity' between Black and White people, as well as heightening awareness of slavery's rampant sexual exploitation, the perceived 'injustice' central to the narrative relied on the very invisibility of the heroine's Blackness, thus upholding ideologies now labelled colourism (that is, negative prejudice against members of an ethnic or racial group with darker skin tone and preference for those with lighter skin tone) and White supremacy. Furthermore, as Sterling A. Brown pointed out in his foundational definition of this stereotype, many anti-slavery authors, seeking to temper scenes of abject violence and appease their readers' desire for uplifting narratives, 'at times help[ed] to per-

---

Press, 2015), pp. 330–1. Examples of the (male) Tragic Mulatto in nineteenth-century French literature include Honoré de Balzac and Auguste Le Poitevin de l'Égreville's *Le Mulâtre* (1824, published under the pseudonym 'Aurore Cloteaux'), Anthony Thouret's *Toussaint, Le Mulâtre* (1834), Victor Séjour's *Le Mulâtre* (1837), and Alexandre Dumas *père's Georges* (1843).

17 Examples of the Tragic Mulatta or 'Négresse blanche' in French theatre include the runaway slave Maria ('passing' as the White socialite Lucy Dolsey) in Foucher and Laurencin's drame *Maria* (Gymnase, 1839), set in Guadeloupe; Jenny Laroche in Souvestre's comédie-vaudeville *Le Mousse* (Variétés, 1846), also set in Guadeloupe; and the title character of Jules Barbier's drame *Cora, ou L'Esclavage* (Ambigu-Comique, 1861), set in Paris and Louisiana. Cooper, 'Introduction', pp. xix–xx. Like *Le Planteur, Le Mousse* was based on Souvestre's novel *L'Inventaire du planteur*. See Cooper, 'De *L'Inventaire du planteur* au *Mousse* et au *Cabin boy*: Réorientation et recadrage d'une histoire antiesclavagiste d'É. Souvestre en pièce de théâtre', in 'Études de génétique théâtrale et littéraire', ed. Ana Clara Santos and Natália Amarante, *Carnets*, 2:14 (2018), 1–13 <http://journals.openedition.org/carnets/8649>. See also Cooper, 'Jules Barbier's *Cora, ou L'Esclavage*: A French Anti-Slavery Drama Set against the Backdrop of the American Civil War', *College Language Association Journal*, 45:3 (2002), 360–78. The Tragic Mulatta figure was also known to French readers through the character of Cora, the West Indian-Scottish daughter of Colonel Munro in James Fenimore Cooper's *The Last of the Mohicans* (1826, translated into French that same year by August-Jean-Baptiste Defauconpret and published by Gosselin). Revelations of identity were a stock device of the so-called *pièce bien faite* codified by Eugène Scribe. See the table of plot situations in Scribe's operas in Karin Pendle, *Eugène Scribe and French Opera of the Nineteenth Century* (Ann Arbor: UMI Research Press, 1979), pp. 390–3. These situations were also used in ballet-pantomime; see Marian Smith, *Ballet and Opera in the Age of Giselle* (Princeton: Princeton University Press, 2000), pp. 26–7.

petuate certain pro-slavery stereotypes' such as 'kindly masters' and 'loyal, submissive slaves'.[18] (See earlier representations of the *bon nègre* and *bon maître* in Chapter 1.)

These contradictions are evident in *Le Planteur* and its sources. Saint-Georges's libretto brought to the stage Émile Souvestre's 1838 novella *L'Inventaire du planteur*, originally published serially in *Le National* and based on an anecdote from British sociologist Harriet Martineau's travelogue *Society in America*, published in Paris in 1837 in English and again the following year in a French translation by Benjamin Laroche.[19] As recounted by Martineau, a New Hampshire gentleman went down to Louisiana, where he bought a plantation and entered into a common-law marriage with a 'well-principled, amiable, well-educated woman' of one-quarter Black ancestry who 'had only the slightest possible tinge of colour'.[20] When the planter and his wife died some years later, they left behind three teenage daughters, 'beautiful girls, with no perceptible mulatto tinge'; when the planter's brother arrived to settle the estate, he planned to bring his nieces back up north 'and (as they were to all appearance perfectly White) to introduce them into the society which by education they were fitted for'.[21] Yet the planter's creditors demanded that his mixed-race daughters be sold into slavery, as they were 'a first-rate article' suited for 'other purposes' than the house or field,[22] a cryptic reference to the 'fancy girl' auctions of antebellum New Orleans, where attractive, light-skinned young women were sold at exorbitant prices as sex slaves.[23] Though Martineau intended this anecdote

---

18 Brown, 'Negro Character', p. 193.

19 For a full discussion of the sources of *Le Planteur*, see Cooper, 'Introduction', pp. vii–xxix, especially pp. ix–xix. Cooper's critical edition of the libretto of *Le Planteur* includes the relevant excerpt from Martineau's *Society in America* and the full text of Souvestre's *L'Inventaire du planteur*.

20 Harriet Martineau, *Society in America* (2 vols, Paris: Baudry's European Library, 1837), vol. 2, p. 79. Martineau uses the term 'quadroon', a common label in slave-owning colonial societies that use the principle of hypodescent (commonly known in the American South as the 'one-drop' rule) to legally disenfranchise all people of Black descent. The term *plaçage* originated in the twentieth century to describe the supposed practice of extralegal marriage or concubinage in antebellum New Orleans between White men and Black, Indigenous, or mixed-race women, known as *placées*. Given the absence of nineteenth-century sources using the terms *plaçage* or *placée*, the historian Emily Clark has argued that the '*plaçage* complex' was – like the Tragic Mulatta – a myth 'with a repertoire of standard elements' reproduced in travel accounts and novels. Emily Clark, *The Strange History of the American Quadroon: Free Women of Color in the Revolutionary Atlantic World* (Chapel Hill: University of North Carolina Press, 2013), pp. 148–60.

21 Martineau, *Society in America*, vol. 2, p. 79.

22 Martineau, *Society in America*, vol. 2, pp. 79–80.

23 Manganelli, *Transatlantic Spectacles of Race*, pp. 55–6. As the historian Walter Johnson contends, the excessively high prices paid for these 'fancy girls' were 'a measure not

Louisiana Imagined 107

to inspire anti-slavery sentiment, noting that 'it has excited due horror wherever it is known,'[24] it nevertheless valorised Whiteness: the planter's daughters are worthy of pity because of their light skin and education; in their physical appearance and manners they are, by White colonial standards, 'well bred.'[25]

In his novella, Souvestre streamlined the planter's daughters into a single character, Jenny Makensie; he also invented the character of Jackson, a rich but ugly neighbouring planter who treats his slaves cruelly and lusts after Jenny.[26] After her father's creditors sell her to Jackson, Jenny commits suicide by throwing herself into the river. Saint-Georges's adaptation of this story, in keeping with the conventions of opéra comique, eschewed the tragic ending in favour of a happy one. Jakson, now recast as a man of rough exterior but generous heart (and his name re-spelled, probably to facilitate pronunciation),[27] purchases Jenny only to free her from slavery, and, impressed by his kindness, she decides to marry him. Contemporary reviewers noted obvious parallels with 'Beauty and the Beast' and, indeed, by neatly resolving Jenny's plight, this fairy-tale ending trivialised the real horrors of slavery.[28]

---

only of desire but dominance', symbolising wealthy slave-owners' 'power to purchase what was forbidden and the audacity to show it off': Walter Johnson, *Soul by Soul: Life inside the Antebellum Slave Market* (Cambridge, MA: Harvard University Press, 1999), pp. 113–14. Quoted in Manganelli, *Transatlantic Spectacles of Race*, p. 56.

24 Martineau, *Society in America*, vol. 2, pp. 78–9.

25 Frances Trollope likewise reserved her greatest sympathy for the light-skinned, highly educated mixed-race daughters of White fathers. 'Of all the prejudices I have ever witnessed, this appears to me the most violent and the most inveterate. Quadroon girls, the acknowledged daughters of wealthy American or Creole fathers, educated with all of style and accomplishments which money can procure at New Orleans, and with all the decorum that care and affection can give; exquisitely beautiful, graceful, gentle and amiable, these are not admitted, nay, are not on any terms admissible, into the society of the Creole families of Louisiana': Frances Trollope, *Domestic Manners of the Americans*, 3rd edn (2 vols., London: Whitaker, Treacher, & Co., 1832), vol. 1, pp. 15–16. Within a year, Auguste Defauconpret's French translation of Trollope's travelogue (*Moeurs domestiques des Américains* [Paris, 1833]) was published in two volumes by Gosselin.

26 Souvestre spells this character's name as 'Jackson', whereas Saint-Georges spells the character's name 'Jakson' in his libretto adaptation. Following Barbara Cooper's practice, I have retained the spellings used by each author when discussing their respective works (Jackson for Souvestre's novella, Jakson for Saint-Georges's libretto). See Cooper, 'Introduction', p. xiv, n. 2.

27 Ralph Locke makes this logical suggestion regarding Saint-Georges's spellings of the names Jakson, Barcley, and Makensie: Locke, 'The Exotic in Nineteenth-Century French Opera, Part 1', p. 103, n. 45.

28 'Le nouveau libretto n'est qu'une variante du conte de fées *la Belle et la Bête*, déjà mis en opéra-comique par feu Marmontel sous le titre de *Zémire et Azor*': A.C. [Albert Cler], 'Théâtres. Opéra-Comique. Première représentation du *Planteur*, opéra-comique en 2 actes, paroles de M. de Saint-Georges, musique de M. Monpou', *Le Charivari*,

108 *Helena Kopchick Spencer*

Though *Le Planteur* is no longer in the repertoire, this opéra comique merits attention because it contributed to the contemporary discussion surrounding French colonial slavery. In the mid-1830s the French anti-slavery movement had regained momentum, spurred by Britain's emancipation of its Caribbean colonies and by pressure applied from within the government by Victor de Broglie and Hippolyte Passy, both prominent members of the Société Française pour l'Abolition de l'Esclavage (French Society for the Abolition of Slavery). In 1835, parliamentary bodies debated the slavery question at length for the first time in the July Monarchy,[29] and in February 1838 Passy introduced to the Chamber of Deputies the first bill proposing an end to colonial slavery. Though conservative and gradualist, Passy's bill prompted two parliamentary commissions, both of which recommended general emancipation in the French colonies. By late 1839, abolition seemed imminent: as the historian Lawrence C. Jennings has shown, 'at no time under the July Monarchy would France come closer to legislating the elimination of slavery.'[30] Yet these efforts would soon be stymied by royal pressure, and the combination of a powerful colonial lobby and the government's inertia effectively delayed liberation until the Revolution of 1848.

At the peak of French abolitionism in the late 1830s, however, as anxieties and anticipations ran high, the topicality of *Le Planteur* sparked strong responses among certain critics. Jennings has demonstrated that, in the 1830s, the French press rarely made 'direct comparisons between slavery in the American South and in France's colonies' and that even criticisms of American slavery by French authors such as Tocqueville and Beaumont 'tended to use the American example to incriminate slavery in general rather than to attack directly its existence in the French West Indies.'[31] And, to be sure, few

---

4 March 1839, p. 2. 'Ce libretto, imité du conte de Perrault *la Belle et la Bête*, est assez intéressant': A.C. [Albert Cler], 'Théâtre de l'Opéra-Comique. *Le Planteur*, opéra-comique en 2 actes, paroles de M. de Saint-Georges, musique de M. Hippolyte Monpou', *Le Siècle*, 11 March 1839, p. 3. Other reviews that made this connection include: Alf. D.-S., 'Théâtres. Théâtre de l'Opéra-Comique. *Le Planteur* [...]', *L'Écho français*, 4 March 1839, pp. 1–2; J.T. [Jean-Toussaint Merle], 'Revue dramatique. L'Opéra-Comique. – Première représentation du *Planteur*, opéra-comique en deux actes, de M. de Saint-Georges, musique de M. Monpou', *La Quotidienne*, 4 March 1839, p. 3; A., 'Théâtre de l'Opéra-Comique. *Le Planteur*', *Gazette de France*, 11 March 1839, pp. 1–2.

29 Lawrence C. Jennings, 'French Views on Slavery and Abolitionism in the United States, 1830–1848', *Slavery & Abolition*, 4:1 (1983), 19–40, at p. 19.

30 Jennings, *French Anti-Slavery: The Movement for the Abolition of Slavery in France, 1802–1848* (Cambridge: Cambridge University Press, 2000), p. 134.

31 Jennings, 'French Views', p. 28. Jennings notes that this lack of direct comparisons is surprising, given the establishment of the French Society for the Abolition of Slavery in late 1834 and its influence on French politics, but concludes that such commentary was 'less widespread than has previously been assumed': Jennings, 'French Views', p. 28. Jennings further argues that French interest in American slavery was bound up with its own dip-

Louisiana Imagined   109

reviews of *Le Planteur* explicitly connected its depiction of American slavery to French colonial slavery; as was customary in theatre reviews of this time, many limited the scope of their comments to summarising the plot, then evaluating the music, *mise-en-scène*, and performers.[32] Still, some of these reviews point – even if obliquely – to an awareness of *Le Planteur*'s relevance to current political debates. For one critic, writing in the liberal paper *Le Constitutionnel*, the Louisiana setting of *Le Planteur* was indistinguishable from France's slave-holding colonies: 'Jenny Makensie is an adorable Creole: she lives in Guadeloupe, Martinique or Bourbon, I don't know which. What is certain is that everyone loves her, Blacks, Whites and Quadroons; we love her virtues, we love her appearance, we love her songs, especially when she sings the pretty *chant du Bengali*.'[33] Jenny's diegetic song evoking the *bengali* bird, discussed in greater detail below, was the musical highlight of the opera for critics and the public alike – and, though praised for its *couleur locale*, was part of a long tradition of birdsong arias sung by sopranos in pastoral settings both 'exotic' and European.[34] Moreover, since *bengali* was the nomenclature used by eighteenth-

---

lomatic and domestic crises: journalists were more apt to criticise the United States at the height of the two countries' indemnity claims dispute in 1834–6, or to use American slavery as a metaphor for the July Monarchy's restrictive 'September Laws' of 1835.

32 In her study of French exotic operas of the 1870s–1890s, Karen Henson found 'not a single reference to France's colonial projects and conquests' in contemporary press reviews. Karen Henson, 'Of Men, Women, and Others: Exotic Opera in Late Nineteenth-Century France' (unpublished DPhil thesis, University of Oxford, 1999), p. 19. Quoted in Ralph Locke, 'The Exotic in Nineteenth-Century French Opera, Part 2: Plots, Characters, and Musical Devices', *Nineteenth-Century Music* (forthcoming).

33 'Jenny Mackensie est une adorable créole: elle habite la Guadeloupe, la Martinique ou Bourbon, je ne sais plus lequel; ce qu'il y a de sûr, c'est que tout le monde l'aime, noirs, blancs et quarterons; on aime ses vertus, on aime sa personne, on aime ses chansons, surtout quand elle chante le *Joli chant de Bengali*': A., 'Théâtre de l'Opéra-Comique. *Le Planteur*. Opéra-comique en deux actes, de M. de Saint-Georges, musique de M. Monpou', *Le Constitutionnel*, 8 March 1839, p. 1.

34 'Les couplets du *Bengali*, chantés d'une façon ravissante par madame Jenny Colon, sont un petit chef-d'œuvre de fraîcheur et de couleur locale': Théophile Gautier, *Histoire de l'art dramatique en France depuis vingt-cinq ans* (6 vols, Paris: Hetzel, 1858–9), vol. 1, p. 233. The *chant du Bengali* was beloved by audiences, judging by critics' accounts of 'fanatic' applause. 'Les couplets du *Bengali* ont été applaudis avec *fanatismo*': Alf. D-s, 'Théâtres', *L'Écho français*, 4 March 1839, pp. 1–2. Other examples of birdsong arias include Zémire's 'Air de la Fauvette' in Grétry's *Zémire et Azor* (1771), set in Persia; Philis's aria 'Toi qui nous plaît' in Lebrun's *Le Rossignol* (1816), set in a valley of the Pyrenees Mountains; Marguerite de Valois's 'O beau pays de la Touraine' in Meyerbeer's *Les Huguenots* (1836), sung in the gardens of the Château de Chenonceau in the Loire Valley; and, in later decades, Jeannette's 'Air du rossignol' in Massé's *Les Noces de Jeannette* (1853), set in a rustic French village; and Zora's evocation of the fictitious Brazilian *mysoli* bird, 'Charmant oiseau' in David's *La Perle du Brésil* (1851, rev. 1858). These examples are taken from Locke, 'The Exotic in Nineteenth-Century French Opera,

and nineteenth-century naturalists for various finches native to the East Indies and Africa, the use of this bird suggests a free 'place-mixing' between America and other current French colonial territories.[35] Though the visual and musical exoticism in *Le Planteur* was certainly generic enough to be interchangeable with other New World settings, it seems possible – given the anti-slavery stance of *Le Constitutionnel* – that the reviewer's confusion of place was intentional. For, if the former French colony of Louisiana could serve as a surrogate for France's remaining colonies, then the audience's sympathy for Jenny might translate into concern for the plight of enslaved women in the French East and West Indies.[36]

Indeed, *Le Planteur* struck a nerve with pro-slavery authors, who perceived it as an abolitionist work that promoted the agenda of *les négrophiles*, a derogatory slur used to portray abolitionists as foolish and even degenerate.[37] The

---

Part 1', pp. 104–5, and Mary Ann Smart, 'Roles, Reputations, Shadows: Singers at the Opéra, 1828–1849', in *The Cambridge Companion to Grand Opera*, ed. David Charlton (Cambridge: Cambridge University Press, 2003), p. 111.

35 Hallman makes this argument regarding *Paul et Virginie* (see Chapter 1). On the geographic range of the *bengali* family of birds, the Comte de Buffon's co-author Montbeillard noted in their *Histoire naturelle des oiseaux* that *bengalis* would soon be found in America, too. 'On se tromperoit fort si, d'après les noms de *sénégalis* et de *bengalis*, on se persuadoit que ces oiseaux ne se trouvent qu'au Bengale et au Sénégale: ils sont répandus dans la plus grande partie de l'Asie et de l'Afrique, et même dans plusieurs des îles adjacentes, telles que celles de Madagascar, de Bourbon, de France, de Java, etc. On peut même s'attendre à en voir bientôt arriver d'Amérique': Philippe Guéneau de Montbeillard, 'Les Bengalis et les Sénégalis, etc', in Georges-Louis Leclerc, Comte de Buffon, and Philippe Guéneau de Montbeillard, *Histoire naturelle, générale et particulière, avec la description du Cabinet du Roi: Histoire naturelle des oiseaux* (9 vols, Paris: L'Imprimerie Royale, 1770–83), vol. 4, pp. 88–91, at p. 90. The *bengali vert* in particular was associated with the west coast of Africa in some dictionaries, although the green avadavat or munia bird is endemic to the Indian subcontinent. 'Le Bengali vert, *Fringilla viridis*, se trouve sur la côte occidentale de l'Afrique': *Nouveau Dictionnaire d'histoire naturelle* (36 vols, Paris: Deterville, 1816–19), vol. 12, p. 180.

36 Appealing to 'Christian' sympathy for women and children was a common tactic among abolitionists: in the early to mid-1830s, as part of its gradualist approach to emancipation, the Société de la morale chrétienne 'instituted a program to purchase the freedom of individual young female slaves whose offspring would subsequently be born free. By the mid-1830s the organisation's principal activity concerning slavery was this "redemption of Negresses"': Jennings, *French Anti-Slavery*, p. 19.

37 While many nineteenth-century dictionaries define *négrophile* as synonymous with *ami des noirs*, Duckett's pedagogical dictionary was more transparent about the negative connotation of this word. 'Négrophile, mot formé de deux mots grecs signifiant *noir* et *ami*, et par lequel aux colonies on désigne dérisoirement les amis des noirs, les partisans de l'abolition de l'esclavage. Les *négrophiles* sont nombreux en Angleterre et en France': William Duckett (ed.), *Dictionnaire de conversation à l'usage des dames et des jeunes personnes, ou Complément nécessaire de toute bonne éducation* (10 vols,

most reactionary and frankly racist of these responses appeared in the lengthy exordium of a review published in the *Journal de Paris*:

We complain, with reason, that poetry is going away. Civilisation, as it spreads, bringing nations together, confusing races, impressing its standard on manners and institutions, destroys every day something of these clear nuances, these salient oppositions which gave to the old society such a picturesque aspect, such a poetic character. And it is not only in our old Europe that things are so; the New World itself, which has only really existed for a few centuries, before reaching adulthood, already offers all the signs of decrepitude. Its existence and its prosperity seemed forever guaranteed by the exclusive production of precious foodstuffs that became one of the first needs of modern civilisation, but now that chemistry has just aroused in the beet a terrible enemy of sugar cane, we wait for it to dethrone coffee with the help of some European seed in which it will soon discover hidden virtues. This is not all: by pushing with all their might for the abolition of slavery, the *négrophiles* threaten to completely overturn the foundations of the current constitution of the colonies; the colonists themselves change something of their old habits every day and they have abandoned the white jacket and straw hat to wear the European coat and felt hat. Finally, nature seems to want to contribute to removing the colonies' distinctive physiognomy by erasing, every day, more and more, the differences of race and colour. Soon Blacks will not only no longer be slaves, but they will even have ceased to be black. Before this transformation of the colonies is entirely put into effect, before all the Blacks have become white, before the thoroughbred planter is placed in the class of mythical beings, M. de Saint-Georges wanted to sketch a little picture of American nature and customs. But his play is still an attack on the colonial organisation, a plea in favour of emancipation; indeed, it highlights one of the greatest anomalies of this singular law which, in some cases, gives slave children to a free father.[38]

Paris: Langlois et Leclercq, 1841–2), vol. 8, p. 225. Following the Saint-Domingue Revolution, pro-slavery circles had used this term to denigrate members of the late eighteenth-century abolitionist Société des Amis des Noirs: 'More than a literal synonym of *ami des noirs*, the word *négrophile* referred to those people who had an "unrealistic" appreciation of the natural history of the African as well as a lack of understanding of the realities and advantages of France's colonial empire. Indeed, the term was commonly used to pathologise anti-slavery thinkers, associating them with the horror of Blackness that they supposedly loved. As the anonymous author of *Le danger de la liberté des nègres* (1791) suggested, *négrophilie* was a disease of sorts stemming from a preposterous and quixotic excess of *humanité*': Andrew S. Curran, *The Anatomy of Blackness: Science and Slavery in an Age of Enlightenment* (Baltimore: Johns Hopkins University Press, 2011), pp. 206–7.

38   'On se plaint avec raison que la poésie s'en va. La civilisation, à mesure qu'elle s'étend, en rapprochant les nations, en confondant les races, en promenant son niveau sur

112   *Helena Kopchick Spencer*

Despite the phobia of interracial sex and reproduction embedded in his warning about the erasure of racial differences, this critic also took delight in imagining the American plantation owner's sexual dominance over enslaved women, writing of the star singer who performed the role of Jenny Makensie: 'Madame Jenny Colon is a graceful Creole. In truth, it would be all too pleasant to be a planter if one were to have among his slaves many *négresses* as white as she.'[39]

Other pro-slavery authors took a condescending tone: as the critic Jean-Toussaint Merle noted in the royalist paper *La Quotidienne*, 'This very simple little drama [...] is one of the thousand arguments put forward by *les négrophiles* on the very sophisticated question of emancipation and the abolition of slavery.'[40] Merle's suggestion that the abolitionist case was a naïve response to the pur-

---

les mœurs et les institutions, détruit tous les jours quelque chose de ces nuances tranchées, de ces oppositions saillantes qui donnaient à l'ancienne société un aspect si pittoresque, un caractère si poétique. Et ce n'est pas seulement dans notre vieille Europe que les choses vont de la sorte; le Nouveau Monde lui-même, qui n'existe réellement que depuis quelques siècles, avant d'être arrivé à l'âge viril, offre déjà tous les signes de la décrépitude. Son existence et sa prospérité semblaient à jamais garanties par la production exclusive de ces précieuses denrées qui sont devenues un des premiers besoins de la civilisation moderne, et voilà que la chimie vient de susciter dans la betterave un ennemi terrible à la canne à sucre, en attendant qu'elle détrône le café à l'aide de quelque graine européenne dans laquelle elle découvrira bientôt des vertus cachées. Ce n'est pas tout, en poussant de toutes leurs forces à l'abolition de l'esclavage, les négrophiles menacent de bouleverser de fond en comble les bases de la constitution actuelle des colonies; les colons eux-mêmes modifient tous les jours quelque chose de leurs anciennes habitudes, ils ont abandonné la veste blanche et le chapeau de lantanier pour prendre le frac et le feutre européens. Enfin, la nature semble vouloir contribuer à enlever aux colonies leur physionomie distinctive, en effaçant chaque jour, de plus en plus, les différences de race et de couleur. Bientôt les Noirs non seulement ne seront plus esclaves; mais ils auront même cessé d'être noirs. Avant que cette transformation des colonies soit entièrement opérée, avant que tous les Noirs soient devenus blancs, avant que le planteur pur sang soit rangé dans la classe des êtres fabuleux, M. de Saint-Georges a voulu nous esquisser un petit tableau de la nature et des mœurs américaines. Mais sa pièce est encore une attaque contre l'organisation coloniale, un plaidoyer en faveur de l'émancipation; elle signale en effet une des plus fortes anomalies de cette loi singulière qui, dans certains cas, donne à un père libre des enfants esclaves': A.M., 'Opéra-Comique. *Le Planteur*, opéra-comique en 2 actes [...]', *Journal de Paris*, 4 March 1839, pp. 1–2. Reproduced in *Le Planteur*, ed. Cooper, pp. 151–4, at pp. 151–2.

39   'Mme Jenny Colon est une gracieuse créole. En vérité, il serait trop agréable d'être planteur si l'on devait avoir parmi ses esclaves beaucoup de négresses aussi blanches qu'elle': *Le Planteur*, ed. Cooper, pp. 151–4, at p. 154.

40   'Ce petit drame fort simple dans le récit de miss Martineau, et dont M. Emile Souvestre a fait une nouvelle fort touchante, est un des mille arguments que font valoir les négrophiles, sur la question fort sophistiquée de l'émancipation et de l'abolition de l'esclavage': J.T. [Jean-Toussaint Merle], 'Revue dramatique', *La Quotidienne*, 4 March 1839, p. 3.

ported 'complexities' of slavery was a common strategy used by pro-slavery authors (and even by the gradualist camp of abolitionists) concerned about slavery's essential role in fuelling France's colonial economy. Liberal critics agreed that Saint-Georges's libretto had oversimplified issues of slavery – but to a different end. One, writing for *La Revue et gazette musicale*, commented sarcastically that *Le Planteur* was 'a very touching picture of the happiness and freedom of the slaves in the colonies. In truth, partisans of the abolition of slavery have only to go to see Saint-Georges's play to convince themselves that slavery is a meaningless word and that the slaves (of the Opéra-Comique) are free and happy as much as it is possible to be in this world.'[41]

The Tragic Mulatta as 'Sensational' Spectacle in the Act I Finale

Such mixed responses to *Le Planteur* reflect the work's fundamental paradox: though seemingly abolitionist, it ultimately upheld the status quo. Perhaps the best illustration of this contradiction is the Act I finale, which culminates in the auctioning of Jenny Makensie as a slave. The auction scene was a stock trope, and usually the dramatic crux of the narrative, in Tragic Mulatta literature of the nineteenth century. The public spectacle of a beautiful light-skinned woman's body – reinscribed as Black, trafficked by avaricious slave-traders, and ogled by an audience of potential buyers – was meant to provoke moral outrage on behalf of the sexually imperilled heroine. Yet the inherent voyeurism of this scene was also titillating. As Kimberly Snyder Manganelli has argued, the auction scenes of abolitionist literature are 'sensational' in two regards: 'not only is the body of the mixed-race slave exposed, but both spectators and readers are invited to witness her physical sensations.'[42]

Monpou's musical rendering of Jenny Makensie's physical experience in the auction scene of *Le Planteur* adheres to this same notion of the Tragic Mulatta as 'sensational' spectacle. The Act I finale begins with a rustic chorus of townspeople and slaves heralding Jenny's marriage to her cousin, the Bostonian dandy Arthur Barcley ('La belle fête'). Jenny enters dressed in her wedding attire and singing a decorative cavatine ('Il va venir, doux avenir'), her outbursts of vocal *jouissance* conveying her anticipation of connubial pleasure.[43]

---

41 'C'est, de plus, un tableau bien touchant du bonheur et de la liberté des esclaves des colonies. En vérité, les partisans de l'abolition de l'esclavage n'ont qu'à aller voir la pièce de M. de Saint-Georges pour se convaincre que l'esclavage est un mot vide de sens, et que les esclaves (de l'Opéra-Comique) sont libres et heureux autant qu'il est possible de l'être en ce monde': G****, 'Théâtre Royal de l'Opéra-Comique. *Le Planteur*. Paroles de M. de Saint-Georges, musique de M. Hippolyte Monpou. (Première représentation)', *La Revue et gazette musicale de Paris*, 6:9 (3 March 1839), 70–1, at p. 71.

42 Manganelli, *Transnational Spectacles of Race*, p. 82.

43 This may be a reference to Rachel's Act II romance ('Il va venir') in Halévy's *La Juive*

114 *Helena Kopchick Spencer*

This melismatic singing style also places her in the company of grand opéra's aristocratic female characters who 'express themselves in elaborate coloratura in unabashedly public contexts' as a sign of their '*hauteur* and decadence'.[44] Jenny's cavatine thus signifies both her inheritance of her father's upper-class White privilege and her awareness of her status as an object of desire, particularly in the erotically charged context of her nuptials. Her 'to-be-looked-at-ness' is further reinforced during the agitated instrumental ritournelle that follows, as she approaches her vanity table and adjusts her appearance.[45] This

---

(1835). As Hallman has shown, 'Il va venir' is the first in a series of three numbers in which 'Rachel gradually loses her "innocence" as she reveals her suspicion and subsequently discovers Léopold's Christian identity': Diana R. Hallman, *Opera, Liberalism, and Antisemitism in Nineteenth-Century France: The Politics of Halévy's* La Juive (New York: Cambridge University Press, 2002), pp. 223–4. While 'il va venir' may well be a stock phrase for a female character nervously anticipating her lover's arrival, the added intertextual resonances with *La Juive* – particularly, the revelation of a hidden identity (in the case of *Le Planteur*, Jenny's own identity) and the heroine's subsequent reversal of fortune – are compelling, particularly given the extraordinary success of *La Juive* at the Opéra. I would like to thank Prof. Hallman for this suggestion.

44 Smart, 'Roles, Reputations, Shadows', pp. 110–11. Smart's examples include the princesses Elvire from Auber's *La Muette de Portici* (1828), Isabelle from Meyerbeer's *Robert le diable* (1831), and Eudoxie from Halévy's *La Juive* (1835), and the queen Marguerite de Valois from Meyerbeer's *Les Huguenots* (1836). Jenny's cavatine is most similar in dramatic context to Elvire's wedding cavatine 'Plaisirs du rang suprême'. Florid cadenzas frequently appear in the roles written for Jenny Colon, suggesting that 'her voice lacked nothing in flexibility or suppleness': Eric Jensen, 'Gerard de Nerval and Opéra-Comique' (unpublished PhD dissertation, University of Rochester, 1982), p. 89. At the end of her career, Jenny Colon successfully transitioned into grand opéra repertoire, performing in *Robert le diable*, *Les Huguenots*, and *La Muette de Portici* at the Théâtre de la Monnaie in Brussels: Jensen, 'Gerard de Nerval', p. 82. Jensen's discussion of Colon in 'Gerard de Nerval', pp. 64–92, remains the most thorough treatment of her career, including an attempt to assess her vocal abilities based on the roles written for her. More recently, Kimberly White has also brought attention to Colon's significance within French theatre culture of the July Monarchy. For a synopsis of Colon's career, see White, *Female Singers on the French Stage*, pp. 16–17, 145. On Colon's reception in London during her tours of 1829 and 1834, see Kimberly White, 'Foreign Voices, Performing Frenchness: Jenny Colon and the "French Plays" in London', in *London Voices, 1820–1840: Vocal Performers, Practices, Histories*, ed. Roger Parker and Susan Rutherford (Chicago: University of Chicago Press, 2019), pp. 179–200.

45 'Sur la ritournelle, Jenny s'approche d'une glace, entourée d'Eva et de ses femmes, et rajuste sa toilette': Monpou *et al.*, *Le Planteur* [libretto], p. 341. Louis Palianti's staging manual indicates a 'console sur laquelle est une glace dans un cadre de forme ovale' downstage right: L[ouis] Palianti, *Mise en scène du Planteur, opera-comique en deux actes, paroles de M. de Saint-Georges. Musique de M. H. Monpou. Représenté, pour la première fois, à Paris, sur le Théâtre royal de l'Opéra-Comique, le 1 mars 1839*, Collection de Mises en Scènes rédigées et publiées par M. L. Palianti 77 (Paris: Brière, n.d.), 65. Palianti's manual was originally published as a supplement to the 14 April

act of looking at herself in a mirror, surrounded by an adoring circle of her maid Eva and other female attendants, tacitly permits – even encourages – the audience to similarly admire her beauty.[46] Such a technique further serves to enhance the intended horror of the auction scene, when the heroine's beautiful, nubile body will become a commodified object of prurient intentions.

The *Presto B* major ritournelle choreographs not only Jenny's excited last-minute primping, but also the panicked arrival of her mixed-race 'factotum' Caton, who hurries in with the catastrophic news that the ships carrying cargo pledged to her father's creditors have been lost at sea.[47] Realising that her entire inheritance was mortgaged to secure this enterprise, Jenny shifts to the distant, plaintive key of F minor and mourns her lost inheritance as a ruptured geography, or the alienation of her body from her home: 'Nothing left – all is lost! It is finished! [From now on] misfortune, misery! In this place where I was born, where my heart awaited happiness and love, I am no more than a stranger.'[48] In Monpou's musical setting, the word 'désormais' ('from

---

1839 issue of *La Revue et gazette des théâtres*. Still, as Arnold Jacobshagen has shown, Palianti's *livrets de mise-en-scène* should not be assumed to be 'authentic' or fixed stagings created in conjunction with the original production. See Arnold Jacobshagen, 'Staging at the Opéra-Comique in Nineteenth-Century Paris: Auber's *Fra Diavolo* and the Livrets de Mise en Scène', *Cambridge Opera Journal*, 13:3 (2001), 239–60, and Arnold Jacobshagen, 'Analyzing Mise-en-Scène: Halévy's *La Juive* at the Salle Le Peletier', in *Theater, Music, and Cultural Transfer: Paris, 1830–1914*, ed. Annegret Fauser and Mark Everist (Chicago: University of Chicago Press, 2009), pp. 176–94. The concept of women's 'to-be-looked-at-ness' originates in Mulvey's now-classic essay theorising the male gaze: Laura Mulvey, 'Visual Pleasure and Narrative Cinema', *Screen*, 16:3 (1975), 6–18.

46 As the cultural geographer Gillian Rose writes of the sexualised images of women in visual art (especially in landscape settings), 'perhaps they will be looking in a mirror, allowing the viewer to enjoy them as they apparently enjoy themselves': Gillian Rose, *Feminism and Geography: The Limits of Geographical Knowledge* (Minneapolis: University of Minnesota Press, 1993), pp. 96–7. Mary Ann Smart identifies this same phenomenon of a self-conscious invitation to voyeurism in Act II of *Les Huguenots*, in which Marguerite de Valois sings her elaborate *pastorale* while gazing at herself in a mirror. Mary Ann Smart, *Mimomania: Music and Gesture in Nineteenth-Century Opera* (Berkeley: University of California Press, 2004), p. 104.

47 Jensen describes this passage as 'little more than a pale imitation of Rossini' and evidence of Monpou's occasionally 'awkward and hackneyed' writing: Jensen, 'Gerard de Nerval', pp. 149–50. Still, even if derivative, such Rossinian writing was arguably a way to borrow an easily recognised sonic image of busy stage action and comic energy. (Though Caton brings bad news, he is associated with comic relief in the opera. For a discussion of Caton as racist stereotype of the 'mulâtre fashionable', see Cooper, 'Introduction', pp. xxii–xxiv.)

48 'Tout est perdu! / C'en est fait! désormais le malheur, la misère! / Dans ces lieux où j'ai vu le jour, / Où mon cœur attendait le bonheur et l'amour, / Je ne suis plus qu'une étrangère!': Monpou *et al.*, *Le Planteur* [libretto], p. 341. In Monpou's score, 'vu' becomes 'reçu'.

now on') is omitted and Jenny repeats 'c'en est fait' three times, as if stuck in a state of shock and despair, unable to yet articulate her thoughts.[49] Her impassioned cry reaches its dramatic peaks on the words 'misère' and 'étrangère' with a poignant upward leap of a minor sixth (C_5–Ab_5) followed by 'sighing' stepwise descent to the tonic F_5 (ex. 3.1).[50] While Jenny does not yet realise the full implications of her father's bankruptcy, her anticipation of a painful estrangement from the land of her birth might suggest a deeper awareness of her precarious 'mixed orientation', to borrow a term used by the critical race theorist Sara Ahmed to describe how persons of mixed race experience their place in the world. Drawing on autoethnography and Husserl's phenomenology, Ahmed defines orientation as 'the intimacy of bodies and their dwelling places', noting that 'some intimacies might be experienced as breaking points' when mixed-race bodies are considered 'strangers in places they call home'.[51] Though the enslaved people of the Makensie plantation reassure Jenny of her belonging – and of their belonging to her, in a disturbing affirmation of chattel slavery – a legal revelation from her father's creditors and the local sheriff will wholly fracture her sense of place and identity.

When her father's creditors arrive, singing a sinister D minor repossession chorus ('Cette maison est notre gage'), Jenny relinquishes all of her inherited property, including her mother's jewellery, and vows to exile herself from the land. Marked 'avec une vive sensibilité' ('with a keen sensitivity') in the libretto and 'triste et résignée, avec âme' ('sad and resigned, with soul') in the published score, her *Andante espressivo* soliloquy in B flat major ('Tout est à vous!') uses a placid orchestral texture that David Charlton has identified as the 'expressive medium', normally associated with 'mutual affection or love, untroubled by irony or premonition'.[52] Here, though, the 'untroubled' emotional gesture of

---

49 Monpou *et al.*, *Le Planteur* [piano-vocal score], p. 79 and Monpou *et al.*, *Le Planteur* [full score], p. 125.

50 Jensen cites this passage from Monpou's score as evidence of Jenny Colon's wide-ranging talents: in addition to performing agile roulades, she could also command 'more dramatic and expressive music'. Jensen, 'Gerard de Nerval', p. 91. Jensen also cites the modulation (E sharp to F natural, the new tonic) as an example of the 'startling harmonic transitions' that were hallmarks of Monpou's 'inventiveness', particularly in the relatively conservative musical idiom of opéra comique: Jensen, 'Gerard de Nerval', p. 151.

51 Sara Ahmed, 'Mixed Orientations', *Subjectivity*, 7 (2014), 92–109, at pp. 95–6.

52 As defined by Charlton, the 'expressive medium' consists of 'a slow or moderate tempo; sustained tone, often heard as a pedal point; a rocking or oscillating string figuration; and stable harmony, using either a tonic pedal or steady alternation of tonic and dominant. This configuration acts as the accompaniment to expressive melodies whose nature varies with the general context; if wind instruments are present they either play sustained notes or double the melody': David Charlton, 'Orchestra and Image in the Late Eighteenth Century', *Journal of the Royal Musical Association*, 102 (1975–6), 1–12, at p. 1.

Example 3.1. Hippolyte Monpou, *Le Planteur*, Act I, No. 5: Finale, bb. 164–89 [piano-vocal score]. Paris: Richault, n.d. [1839].

—*(continued)*

Example 3.1—concluded

Jenny's musical idiom reflects her innate nobility and serene acceptance of her fate, at least as she initially understands it.

The creditors quickly reply that Jenny is not free to go and they summon the sheriff; their taunting E flat minor melody is doubled by staccato bassoons (a timbre often associated with the grotesque and the ghastly) and the strings, whose repeated grace-note figures imitate mocking laughter. In response to their intimidation, Jenny confesses in a soft, 'veiled' voice that a dreadful

Louisiana Imagined   119

terror has seized her, making all of the blood in her heart run cold.[53] Her sustained, chromatically descending melody evokes her inner 'sinking' feeling of apprehension and suggests physical enervation, as if her body is beginning to slowly collapse; the string tremolos imitate the fearful quivering of her unstable body and the sudden chill that courses through her veins.[54] Jenny's slaves echo her presentiment, their own dread and deflation reflected in the melodic line's gradual chromatic descent over string tremolos and diminished harmonies (ex. 3.2).

Over the ominous accompaniment of more string tremolos and timpani rolls, the sheriff produces a document and proclaims that since Jenny's mother was never freed from slavery, Jenny is now the legal property of her father's creditors, in accordance with Louisiana's 1806 *Code noir*:

> After research done to guarantee the rights of the creditors of Mr. John Makensie, it appears that the aforementioned Makensie in 1786 married Clara Netty, a young white slave he purchased at a market in Philadelphia; the aforementioned Clara Netty died giving birth to Jenny Makensie, without having been freed by her husband. Now, all the children of slaves being *de jure* slaves like their mother, we, the sheriff of the district of New Orleans, declare Jenny Makensie, the daughter of a slave, a slave like her mother, and belonging *de facto* and *de jure* to her father's creditors.[55]

The sudden shock induced by this decree – sonically illustrated by a loud, rapidly ascending B flat scale marked *Allegro molto, attaquez subito, crescendo molto* – proves too much of a sensory jolt for Jenny's weakened body to endure. With a scream of 'Horreur!' she faints and remains passed out for the rest of the finale.[56] Around Jenny's unconscious body swirls a *Presto feroce* passepied in E

---

53 'O terreur affreuse menace / Dans mon cœur tout mon sang se glace': Monpou *et al.*, *Le Planteur* [piano-vocal score], p. 89. This passage is marked in the score 'à part' and 'avec la voix voilée'. The text here is a slight alteration of the libretto.

54 On musical motion and metaphor theory, see Steve Larson, *Musical Forces: Motion, Metaphor, and Meaning in Music* (Bloomington: Indiana University Press, 2012). My analysis here is inspired in particular by Larson's third chapter, co-authored with Mark Johnson, 'Something in the Way She Moves: The Metaphor of Musical Motion', pp. 61–81.

55 'Après recherches faites pour garantie des droits des créanciers de sir John Makensie, il appert que ledit Makensie épousa en 1786 Clara Netty, jeune esclave blanche achetée lui au marché de Philadelphie; ladite Clara Netty mourut en donnant le jour à Jenny Makensie, sans avoir été affranchie par son époux. Or, tous les enfants d'esclaves étant de droit esclaves comme leur mère, nous, schérif du district de la Nouvelle-Orléans, déclarons Jenny Makensie, fille d'esclave, esclave comme sa mère, et appartenant de fait et de droit aux créanciers de son père': Monpou *et al.*, *Le Planteur* [libretto], p. 342.

56 According to the published libretto and score, Jenny faints into Eva's arms. In Palianti's staging manual, Jenny faints into a chair that one of her slaves pushes forward to catch her: Palianti, *Mise en scène du Planteur*, p. 70. For the final tableau, the libretto

Example 3.2. Hippolyte Monpou, *Le Planteur*, Act I, No. 5: Finale, bb. 371–90 [piano-vocal score]. Paris: Richault, n.d. [1839].

flat major that characterises the villainous creditors as gleefully indifferent to Jenny's suffering, caught up in their heady game of profit.[57]

This intensely gestural music not only invites the audience to witness Jenny's physical sensations, but also encourages them to empathetically partake in the sensual experience of her fear and suffering – a strategy consistent with abolitionist authors' efforts to make White audiences identify with the suffering of enslaved persons. More than embodied musical effects were needed, however, to bring this suffering 'closer' to White audiences: as Saidiya Hartman writes, 'the effort to counteract the commonplace callousness to black suffering requires that the white body be positioned in the place of the black body to make this suffering visible and intelligible.'[58] Furthermore, as Hartman explains, such strategies of 'empathetic identification' rely on 'a racist optics in which black flesh is itself identified as the source of opacity, the denial of black humanity and the effacement of sentience' – all traits necessary for oppressors to justify chattel slavery.'[59] In the auction scene of *Le Planteur*, the White body of Jenny Makensie certainly makes the indignity of her sale (and implied sexual endangerment) more legible to White audiences of the Opéra-Comique than would be the case if she had dark skin colour. After all, post-Revolutionary French representations of Black women tended to fetishise and demonise their bodies as sites of subhuman savagery, hypersexuality, and disease.[60]

The legibility of Jenny's suffering likely also relied on Opéra-Comique audiences' affection for the star performer Jenny Colon (fig. 3.1).[61] As Kim-

---

indicates that Jenny is 'toujours évanouie': Monpou *et al.*, *Le Planteur* [libretto], p. 342. This direction is reproduced in Palianti's staging manual as well.

57 As a musical topic, the passepied has a long-standing association with gaiety and frivolity. See, for example, Wye J. Allanbrook, *Rhythmic Gesture in Mozart:* Le nozze di Figaro *and* Don Giovanni (Chicago: University of Chicago Press, 1983), pp. 39–40.

58 Saidiya V. Hartman, *Scenes of Subjection: Terror, Slavery, and Self-Making in Nineteenth-Century America* (Oxford: Oxford University Press, 1997), p. 19.

59 Hartman, *Scenes of Subjection*, p. 20.

60 Notable examples include Sarah Baartman (1789–1815), the so-called 'Hottentot Venus', whose violated body was displayed and dissected by French naturalists as scientific curiosity; the Senegalese child Ourika (1781?–1799), brought to France as a plaything for aristocrats but reimagined in Gaspard de Pons's poem *Ourika, l'Africaine* (1825) as a vampiric, vengeful femme fatale; and the numerous fictional Black women associated with prostitution in works such as Baudelaire's *La Belle Dorothée*. See Robin Mitchell, *Vénus Noire: Black Women and Colonial Fantasies in Nineteenth-Century France* (Athens, GA: University of Georgia Press, 2020) and T. Denean Sharpley-Whiting, *Black Venus: Sexualized Savages, Primal Fears, and Primitive Narratives in French* (Durham, NC: Duke University Press, 1999).

61 Critics, too, widely praised Colon's performance in *Le Planteur*, attributing the opera's success to her. 'Madame Jenny Colon a beaucoup contribué au succès de la pièce par son jeu fin et spirituel': G****, 'Théâtre Royal de l'Opéra-Comique. *Le Planteur*. Paroles de M. de Saint-Georges, musique de M. Hippolyte Monpou. (Première représentation)',

berly White notes, opéra comique of the 1830s could at times blur 'distinctions between theatre and reality', particularly when 'the cast of performers displayed uncanny resemblances to their counterparts on stage'.[62] Beyond the happy coincidence that Jenny Colon shared a first name with Jenny Makensie, both the singer and the character she portrayed were beautiful, fair-skinned, and blonde.[63] This easy slippage between Jenny Colon the beloved Parisian singer and Jenny Makensie the lovable Louisianian Creole may have generated an added layer of horror – and taboo pleasure – in seeing her passive, vulnerable body displayed as a sexual and racialised spectacle, commodified as the property of ruthless creditors-turned-slave-traders.

Tellingly, the Black characters of *Le Planteur* are never portrayed as deserving pity or liberation: rather, they are the stereotypical 'loyal, submissive slaves' whose constant presence affirms the very institution of slavery. Throughout the finale (and indeed, the entire opera), Jenny's Black slaves lack their own agency, functioning only to comfort and praise their beloved White mistress. When Jenny first learns of her financial ruin and cries that she has become a stranger on her father's plantation (ex. 3.1), her slaves respond incredulously,

---

La Revue et gazette musicale de Paris, 6:9 (3 March 1839): pp. 70–1, at p. 71. This role allowed Colon to showcase both her vocal and dramatic skills, as well as her personal charm, according to the critics Ed. M. [Édouard Monnais], 'Théâtre de l'Opéra-Comique. Première représentation du *Planteur*, opéra-comique en deux actes, paroles de M. Saint-Georges, musique de M. Monpou', *Le Courrier français*, 4 March 1839, pp. 2–3, at p. 3, and Hipp. P. [Hippolyte Prévost], 'Opéra-Comique. *Le Planteur*, opéra en deux actes, paroles de M. de Saint-Georges, musique de M. Hippolyte Maupou [*sic*]', *Le Commerce*, 4 March 1839, pp. 1–2, at p. 2. One critic particularly praised her for using her talents for dramatic effectiveness, not merely for self-display, in *Le Courrier des théâtres*, 3 March 1839, p. 4; see the review reproduced in *Le Planteur*, ed. Cooper, p. 137. In addition to recognising Colon as the standout in the production for her heartfelt interpretation, another noted that her voice had continued to improve: Alf. D.-S., 'Théâtres', *L'Écho français*, 4 March 1839, pp. 1–2, at p. 2.

62 White, *Female Singers on the French Stage*, p. 103. White is referring here specifically to Auber's *L'Ambassadrice*; however, I would argue that the same could easily apply in *Le Planteur*.

63 The character name of Jenny Makensie originated in Souvestre's *Inventaire d'un planteur*, but the close identification – even elision – of Jenny Colon with Makensie's character seems to have been encouraged by Monpou, who dedicated his score to Colon. In Act II Scene 9, Jakson expresses his long-time admiration of Jenny and mentions among her most attractive features her 'pretty, flowing blonde hair' ('jolis cheveux blonds flottants'): Monpou *et al.*, *Le Planteur* [libretto], p. 347. Many anecdotes of Jenny Colon emphasised these same physical attributes. For example, a profile of Colon in the third volume of the *Galerie théâtrale, ou Collection des portraits en pied des principaux acteurs des premiers théâtres de la capitale* (Paris: Bance, 1834) described her as 'a very beautiful and very pleasant singer; her hair is very blonde, her eyes are very beautiful, her skin very white, her figure a bit too full': quoted and translated in Jensen, 'Gerard de Nerval', p. 69.

Figure 3.1. Jenny-Marguerite Colon. Lithograph portrait by Léon Noël. Paris: Lemercier, Benard & Co., 1837. Printed in *L'Artiste*, 14 (1837), 284. Bibliothèque Nationale de France.

'You, a stranger in this place? Never! You command us all; here we are!'[64] In Jenny's distress, they absorb and amplify her pain, making it their own: when Jenny confesses that the creditors' intimidations make her blood run cold, the chorus of slaves reports experiencing the same exact physical sensation (ex. 3.2). Following the sheriff's proclamation, the slaves join in her cry of horror, and during the auction, they softly lament, 'What a terrible blow for us! Ah, what a horrible destiny! O cruel fate!' – apparently not recognising the injustice of their own enslavement.[65] Herein lies an insidious effect of the Tragic Mulatta trope, as articulated by the theatre historian Hazel Waters: the plight of the mixed-race heroine redirects the audience 'towards a consideration of slavery as a personal, internally experienced tragedy and away from slavery as a social, structural issue.'[66] Monpou and Saint-Georges's musico-dramatic images of obsequious slaves as well as the eroticised spectacle of the heroine's light-skinned 'Creole' body are also reinforced in the opera's most overtly exotic numbers, to which we now turn.

Representations of Gender, Race, and Class in Two Exotic Numbers

Le Planteur upheld the status quo not only through its stereotypical auction scene, but also through the familiar exotic imagery of the female ensemble numbers that opened each act. As post-colonialist scholars have noted, the domain of the Other is typically coded – if not directly embodied – as 'feminine', and non-Western European lands have long been metaphorically imagined as mysterious female bodies to be penetrated and explored.[67] It is hardly

---

64 'Vous en ces lieux une étrangère! / Jamais! jamais! nous sommes là! / Commandez-nous tous, nous voilà!': Monpou *et al.*, *Le Planteur* [libretto], p. 341.

65 'Pour nous quel coup terrible/ ah, quel destin horrible/ ô sort cruel': Monpou *et al.*, *Le Planteur* [piano-vocal score], pp. 92–4. The critic Hippolyte Prévost praised the finale's musical contrasts: 'the cruel threats of the creditors, conveyed exclusively by a bass choir, especially produce a great effect in opposition to the testimonies of devotion and affection from the choir of slaves who group themselves around their young and good mistress' ('les menaces cruelles des créanciers traduites exclusivement par une chœur de basses produisent surtout un grand effet en opposition aux témoignages de dévouement et d'affection du chœur des esclaves qui se groupent autour de leur jeune et bonne maîtresse'). Hipp. P., 'Opéra-Comique', *Le Commerce*, 4 March 1839, pp. 1–2.

66 Hazel Waters, *Racism on the Victorian Stage: Representation of Slavery and the Black Character* (Cambridge: Cambridge University Press, 2007), p. 154.

67 As Edward Said has argued, most Western portrayals of the East emphasise not only its 'fecundity', but also its 'sexual promise (and threat), untiring sensuality, unlimited desire' and 'deep generative energies': Edward Said, *Orientalism* (New York: Vintage, 1979), p. 188. Even in non-exotic contexts, 'bounded spatial entities' of human habitation such as countries, regions, cities, and homes have long been conceptualised in terms of the female body: Sue Best, 'Sexualizing Space', in *Sexy Bodies: The Strange Car-*

surprising, then, that critics and audiences perceived the *couleur locale* of Monpou's score as concentrated primarily in musical numbers for the female ensemble.[68] Positioned at the start of each act, these numbers complement the visual imagery of the *mise-en-scène* in depicting a Louisiana setting: Act I opens on the Makensie plantation with a languid afternoon lullaby sung by a chorus of enslaved women, followed by Jenny's performance of the folk-like *chant du Bengali* and another chorus of slaves who sing Jenny's praises (No. 1, 'Introduction et Chant du Bengali'); Act II opens on Jakson's plantation, where Jenny – now a slave herself – performs a *chansonnette créole* to entertain her fellow enslaved women (No. 6, 'Chansonnette et Chœur de Femmes'). In addition to establishing a sense of place, both of these numbers reveal Jenny's *femme créole* identity – here represented stereotypically as White idealised beauty, refinement, and wealth blended with Black languor and sensuality – along with her status as an object of voyeuristic desire and a specially gifted entertainer.[69] Ultimately, however, these numbers show how Jenny's 'Creole' identity amounted to little more than exotic role-play for a White singer, as well as a source of picturesque imagery and tuneful pleasure for White audiences within the safe, conveniently distanced fictional world of opéra comique.

As described in Saint-Georges's libretto and Palianti's staging manual, the opening tableau of *Le Planteur* depicts the hot, humid climate of the American South and establishes Jenny's status as the pampered, privileged mistress of the plantation: in a 'pretty pavilion' lined with window shades to block the blistering sunlight,[70] Jenny takes her midday rest on an elegant sofa enveloped by a gauzy mosquito net; her lady's maid Eva cools her by agitating the folds of the canopy,[71] while a light-skinned slave repels mosquitoes by waving a fan

---

    nalities of Feminism, ed. Elizabeth Grosz and Elspeth Probyn (New York: Routledge, 1995), pp. 181–94, at pp. 181–2.

68 The overture also attracted praise from Gautier for its evocation of a Southern climate. 'La musique de M. Monpou a toutes les qualités qui font les succès populaires. L'ouverture, d'un style chaleureux et ferme, indique tout d'abord le climat où se passe l'action de la pièce: c'est la meilleure qu'ait faite jusqu'ici M. Monpou': Gautier, *Histoire de l'art dramatique*, p. 233.

69 As T. Denean Sharpley-Whiting notes, 'The French conceptualizations of the femme créole and the mulâtresse are virtually interchangeable', in that both are 'white, yet inescapably black, and thus unable to shake the lascivious and ardent stereotypes of black female sexuality'. While the stereotypical *Négresse* was not considered an ideal beauty, the *femme créole* and *mulâtresse* were, by virtue of their light skin: 'The canon of feminine beauty is constructed around whiteness, while voluptuous sexuality is mysterious, dark – black. In a Pygmalion-like fashion, two erotic, exotic and idyllic forms of femininity are created from the Négresse and white femaleness': Sharpley-Whiting, *Black Venus*, pp. 45–6.

70 Palianti, *Mise en scène du Planteur*, p. 65.

71 'Le théâtre représente l'intérieur d'un joli kiosque servant de salon, et entouré de stores de tous côtés. Au fond, un parc; grande porte au milieu; portes latérales; fenêtres à

made of tropical wood and shaped like a peacock's tail.[72] After peeking inside the mosquito net to ensure that Jenny is still sleeping peacefully, Eva leads a chorus of enslaved Black and mixed-race women (indicated in the score as 'négresses et mulâtresses') in singing a tender lullaby. Monpou's music for the women's chorus sonically evoked the Southern climate, at least for the critic Édouard Monnais, who wrote, 'the introduction is distinguished by a pronounced impression of local colour; all of the melodies breathe heat, softness, and sleep.'[73] The orchestral introduction begins with an ostinato 'drumbeat' pattern (staccato quaver Gs played by cellos and basses in open octaves), suggestive of percussion stereotypically associated with non-European cultures and peoples.[74] Above this rhythmic gesture, the first violins – later joined by the oboe – intone a gently swaying G Aeolian melody, jarringly interrupted by accented acciaccatura figures, a familiar marker of the exotic that may also serve here as a symbol of the daytime noise and glaring sunlight from which Jenny seeks her respite.[75] Eva and the other women take up this modal melody, its gently cascading descent metaphorically illustrating their entreaty for 'sweet slumber' to 'close the eyes of our dear mistress'; the women's hushed, soothing voices are doubled by woodwinds, signalling a pastoral *topos* and its connotations of nature and tranquillity (ex. 3.3). This idyll heightens the dramatic irony of Jenny's downfall: as Monnais put it, 'You would think that Jenny Makensie is the happiest Creole who has ever breathed the fragrant breezes of Louisiana, and yet a terrible misfortune hangs over her pretty head.'[76]

---

droite et à gauche. (Au lever du rideau, Jenny entourée de jeunes esclaves mulâtresses, repose sur un canapé; Eva placé près d'elle agite les plis d'un moustiquaire de gaze qui enveloppe Jenny. C'est l'heure de la méridienne.)': Monpou *et al.*, *Le Planteur* [libretto], p. 331.

72 'Une des esclaves blanches de gauche tient un chasse-moustic qu'elle agite de temps en temps': Palianti, *Mise en scène du Planteur*, p. 66. The appendix of 'accessoires' specifies that the mosquito-repellent is 'un éventail au bois des îles, fait en forme de queue de paon, à une esclave de gauche': Palianti, *Mise en scène du Planteur*, p. 73.

73 'L'introduction se distingue par un sentiment prononcé de couleur locale; toutes les mélodies en respirent la chaleur, la mollesse et le sommeil': Ed. M. [Édouard Monnais], 'Théâtre de l'Opéra-Comique', *Le Courrier français*, 4 March 1839, p. 2.

74 'A highly stereotyped drumbeat pattern of four equally spaced beats – LOUD soft soft soft – repeated again and again is still thought by many to represent Native Americans': Ralph P. Locke, *Musical Exoticism: Images and Reflections* (Cambridge: Cambridge University Press, 2009), p. 50.

75 Locke's inventory of exotic style features includes 'quick ornaments used obtrusively' and 'in quick succession', 'presumably intended to be perceived as decorative encrustation – or as dissonant, nerve-jangling annoyance – rather than as organically integrated design': *Musical Exoticism*, pp. 53–4.

76 'Vous croiriez que Jenny Mackensie est la plus heureuse créole qui ait jamais respiré les brises parfumées de la Louisiane, et pourtant un malheur affreux plane sur sa jolie

Example 3.3. Hippolyte Monpou, *Le Planteur*, Act I, No. 1: Introduction, bb. 1–35 [piano-vocal score]. Paris: Richault, n.d. [1839].

—*(continued)*

Example 3.3—*concluded*

Though Monnais and other critics heard this number as rich in 'local colour', the sights and sounds of *Le Planteur*'s opening scene were not by any means exclusively associated with stage representations of Louisiana. With its heady mix of soft perfumed music, gauzy fabrics, a lush background of native trees and flowers,[77] a sultry and languorous atmosphere, and a reclining heroine surrounded by female slaves seated on cushions and engaged in light tasks (weaving wicker baskets, arranging flowers, sewing nets),[78] this sensuous tableau shares similar imagery with numerous other exotic feminine scenes in Parisian music theatre of the 1830s – many of which are set in harems.[79] Orientalist tropes were common in representations of Creole women: as Manganelli notes, late eighteenth-century French, British, and American travel writers attributed Creole women's purported traits of 'intemperance, indolence and sensuality' to the New World's torrid climate, at times drawing parallels to Middle Eastern odalisques.[80] Likewise, in the opening tableau of *Le Planteur*, the conflation of plantation and seraglio characterises Jenny as a sensual exotic woman, an object of fascination and erotic desire. Eva's careful watch over her veiled mistress – reminiscent of the stereotypical harem guardian – further encourages the audience's gaze, inviting them into an intimate feminine space and encouraging heterosexual male spectators' own voyeuristic impulses to spy on the

---

tête': Ed. M. [Édouard Monnais], 'Théâtre de l'Opéra-Comique', *Le Courrier français*, 4 March 1839, p. 2.

77 'Chassis représentant quelques arbres et quelques fleurs du pays': Palianti, *Mise en scène du Planteur*, p. 65.

78 'Sur des coussins semblables à ceux sur lesquels est Eva, sont assises des esclaves blanches travaillant soit à fini un panier en osier, soit à ranger des fleurs dans une corbeille, soit à faire des filets, etc., etc.': Palianti, *Mise en scène du Planteur*, p. 66.

79 On harem scenes in nineteenth-century opéra comique, see Hervé Lacombe, 'The Writing of Exoticism in the Libretti of Opéra-Comique, 1825–1862', trans. Peter Glidden, *Cambridge Opera Journal*, 11:2 (1999), 148–50. This opening tableau also parallels a scenic type that I have identified elsewhere as the '*jardin des femmes* convention', found in opéra comique, grand opéra, and ballet-pantomime. See Helena Kopchick Spencer, 'Eugène Scribe and the *Jardin des Femmes* Convention', in *Meyerbeer and Grand Opéra from the July Monarchy to the Present*, ed. Mark Everist, Speculum Musicae 28 (Turnhout: Brepols, 2016), pp. 287–312; Helena Kopchick Spencer, 'The *Jardin des Femmes* as Scenic Convention in French Opera and Ballet' (unpublished PhD dissertation, University of Oregon, 2014).

80 Manganelli, *Transatlantic Spectacles of Race*, p. 19. Here Manganelli's discussion focuses on descriptions of the Creole women of Saint-Domingue and Jamaica, with 'Creole' women defined as White, Black, and/or mixed-race women born in the West Indies. On the common 'Orientalising' of American mixed-race women and free women of colour as odalisques and houris, see Manganelli, *Transatlantic Spectacles of Race*, pp. 57–64, and Clark, *The Strange History of the American Quadroon*, pp. 138–41.

sleeping heroine.[81] When Jenny awakens from her slumber, she emerges from her canopied sofa accompanied by coyly decorative, chromatically inflected woodwind solos (marked 'delicato' in the published full score) and dressed in a 'very stylish white negligée',[82] thus offering the audience a provocative vision of the heroine in her private bedroom attire. For heterosexual male spectators at the Opéra-Comique, this pleasure would have been further enhanced by the on- and off-stage persona of the attractive Jenny Colon, who was famous for both her 'coquettish' roles and her rumoured romantic affairs.[83]

All this teasing of the audience's visual pleasure is also theatrically effective in focusing attention on the leading lady and heightening anticipation of her cavatine: the diegetic *chant du Bengali*, the most celebrated song in the entire opera. Addressing the enslaved women of her plantation, Jenny explains she could not help but fall asleep, her body succumbing to 'the heat of our colony' and its 'burning effects', adding that she had 'such a sweet dream' during her midday nap.[84] Jenny's blatant display of the leisure that is her White upper-class privilege is compounded by the interjections of Eva and the chorus of enslaved women, who eagerly beg her to tell them her dream. Jenny responds that she dreamt of a song from her childhood, one that her nurse 'sang softly in the evening' to her as she rested in a 'cradle of flowers, floating at the whim of a light zephyr's breezes'.[85] The atmosphere of nostalgia, idyll, and nocturnal mystery in Jenny's fanciful recollection of this cradle song is reinforced by a modulation from E flat major to the distant, luminous key of B major; an accompaniment of undulating strings and sustained horns and bassoons; and a chromatically descending line in the first bassoon and violins on the word 'zephyr', evoking the languid movement of a gently flowing breeze on a Southern summer night. By framing Jenny's *chant du Bengali* as a childhood memory, a lullaby learned

---

81 Heather Hadlock discusses this phenomenon as enacted by the travesty page role of Urbain in Act II of *Les Huguenots*. See Heather Hadlock, 'The Career of Cherubino, or the Trouser Role Grows Up', in *Siren Songs: Representations of Gender and Sexuality in Opera*, ed. Mary Ann Smart (Princeton: Princeton University Press, 2000), pp. 67–92, at p. 73. Because Eva is a lady's maid (not an adolescent male page), her act of looking at her mistress does not break the same taboo as Urbain's forbidden spying on the bathing ladies of Queen Marguerite's court; however, I would argue that *Le Planteur* uses a similar transitive effect, whereby the audience's gaze is directed through watching a character who watches another character (or characters) on stage.

82 'En négligé blanc très-coquet': Palianti, *Mise en scène du Planteur*, p. 73.

83 White, *Female Singers on the French Stage*, p. 103. See also Jensen, 'Gerard de Nerval', p. 70.

84 'Des feux de notre colonie / J'ai senti les brûlants effets, / Et, malgré moi, je me suis endormie; / Mais quel doux rêve je faisais!': Monpou *et al.*, *Le Planteur* [libretto], p. 331.

85 'Dans mon berceau de fleurs qui flottait au caprice / Des brises d'un léger zéphir, / Toute enfant, j'écoutais un air que ma nourrice / Chantait le soir tout bas pour m'endormir': Monpou *et al.*, *Le Planteur* [libretto], p. 331, with slight alterations based on the piano-vocal score.

Louisiana Imagined   131

from her nurse, Saint-Georges and Monpou suggest its diegetic function as an elaborate 'mammy' song meant to emblematise an imagined and highly stereotyped Black American musical culture.[86] Jenny's performance of the *chant du Bengali* therefore exemplifies not only her 'lovability' and 'spectacularity' as she sings for an adoring on-stage audience of obsequious slaves, but also her mobility between White and Black cultures – a privilege afforded by her inheritance of light skin colour.[87]

Jenny's *chant du Bengali* is in a long lineage of bird-themed showpiece arias that align the voice and body of the female lead with the beauty of the natural world, and Saint-Georges's choice of the *bengali* bird is particularly significant as a marker of geographic and racial Otherness – even if, as suggested above, that Otherness was not necessarily place-specific.[88] The *bengali* is a recurring image in French exotic texts, associated with idealised sonic beauty, paradisiacal settings, and love, but also with destruction, devastating loss, and longing. For example, Victor Chauvet's 'Néali, ou La Traite des Noirs', winner of the Académie Française's 1823 poetry competition on the theme of the abolition of the slave trade, includes the *bengali*'s song in a nostalgic evocation of the heroine Néali's lost African home: 'And we, in the soft glow of the rising moon / That revived the caressing breeze of the evening, / Under the flowering ebony tree, to the song of the bengali, / We danced.'[89] The 'Blackness'

---

86 The mammy stereotype was established primarily in American literature of the 1820s, with characters such as Granny Mott in George Tucker's *The Valley of Shenandoah* (1824) and Aunt Chloe in Isabel Drysdale's *Scenes in Georgia* (1827). See Kimberly Wallace-Sanders, *Mammy: A Century of Race, Gender, and Southern Memory* (Ann Arbor: University of Michigan Press, 2008), pp. 16–18. Hints of the stereotype appear in Béraud and de Rosny's *Adonis* of 1798 (see Chapter 1), but it is also evident in French theatrical works of the 1830s, as exemplified by the Black cook Gunima in the ballet-pantomime *La Volière, ou Les Oiseaux de Boccacce* (1838), set on the island of Saint-Domingue. Paul Lormier's costume design features a head scarf, white peasant blouse, yellow-and-red diamond-patterned skirt, and blackface makeup for the dancer Mme Roland (accessible on <gallica.bnf.fr>).

87 As theorised by Sara Ahmed, 'The word inheritance includes two meanings: to receive and to possess. Whiteness becomes a social inheritance; in receiving whiteness as a gift, white bodies, or those bodies that can be recognised as white bodies, come to "possess" whiteness. I am not suggesting here that "whiteness" is an object we can reach or even possess: but that whiteness is an orientation that puts certain things within reach. By objects, we would include not just physical objects, but also styles, capacities, aspirations, techniques, even worlds': Ahmed, 'Mixed Orientations', pp. 99–100.

88 Several decades later, Sélika's lullaby 'Sur mes genoux' in Meyerbeer's *L'Africaine* (1865) includes the *bengali*'s song as part of its exotic imagery.

89 'Et nous, au doux éclat de la lune naissante / Qui ranimait du soir la brise caressante, / Sous l'ébénier en fleurs, au chant de bengali, / Nous dansions': Joseph-Joachim-Victor Chauvin, *Arthur de Bretagne, tragédie en cinq actes, par M. Chauvet. Représenté, pour la première fois, par les comédiens du roi, sur le Théâtre Royal de l'Odéon, le lundi 16 aout 1824. Suivie de Néali, ou La Traite des Nègres, poème qui, au jugement de l'Aca-*

132   *Helena Kopchick Spencer*

of Jenny's *chant du Bengali* is visually reinforced, as well, when Eva fetches a guitar to accompany her.[90] Though plucked string instruments were common in pastoral feminine scenes of the 1830s, suggesting intimate spaces and leisurely music-making,[91] Palianti's staging manual specifies that the guitar rests on a small pedestal table made of ebony wood – a notable detail, given that the room's décor is otherwise dominated by white muslin fabrics that cover the windows and furniture.[92] While, on the one hand, these all-white furnishings are practical for reflecting sunlight and keeping cool in a hot Southern climate, they also project a conspicuously overarching aesthetic of whiteness. Within this (almost) uniformly white interior, the placement of a guitar on a solitary

---

démie Française, a remporté le prix de poésie, décerné dans sa séance du 25 aout 1823 (Paris: Barba, 1824), p. 90. The 'sudden publicity' generated by Duke Victor de Broglie's anti-slavery speech given in the Chamber of Peers on 28 March 1822, along with numerous initiatives sponsored by the slave trade committee of the liberal Société de la morale chrétienne, 'undoubtedly' influenced 'the decision of the then liberal-dominated Académie Française in 1822 to make the question of the abolition of the slave trade the subject of its poetry contest for 1823': Jennings, *French Anti-Slavery*, pp. 12–3. Among many other examples, the *bengali* also appears in Bernardin de Saint-Pierre's influential novel *Paul et Virginie* (1788), set in the French colony then known as the Isle de France (present-day Mauritius; see p. 18) and in Balzac's scandalously salacious Orientalist fantasy 'Voyage de Paris à Java', published in *La Revue de Paris* in 1832. Souvestre, author of *L'Inventaire du planteur*, associated the *bengali* with the Americas in two pastoral poems from his collection *Rêves poétiques* (1830). Souvestre's poem 'Le Concert' features the *bengali*'s song as the soundscape of an American Eden. 'O terre des Incas! dans tes grandes savanes / J'irais chercher un nid au milieu des lianes, / Et, dans l'ombre et les fleurs, là, comme enseveli, / Rêver et m'endormir au chant du bengali': Émile Souvestre, *Rêves poétiques* (Nantes: Mellinet, 1830), pp. 157–62, at p. 161. And Souvestre's 'Le Sauvage' imagines an Indigenous American who entreats the Creole woman he desires with imagery of *bengali* love-birds. 'Comme deux Bengalis, sur quelque hautes branches / Bercés dans un hamac de lianes en fleur, / Tu m'apprendras tout bas cette langue des blanches/ Qui dit si bien les maux du cœur': Souvestre, *Rêves poétiques*, pp. 37–44, at pp. 42–3.

90   'EVA, prenant le guitare': Monpou *et al.*, *Le Planteur* [libretto], p. 331. In Palianti's staging manual, a slave fetches the guitar for Eva: Palianti, *Mise en scène du Planteur*, p. 66.

91   Spencer, 'Eugène Scribe and the *Jardin des Femmes* Convention', p. 291.

92   The staging manual includes a preponderance of white fabrics in the Act I set design, including 'portes vitrées, à deux battans, s'ouvrant sur le théâtre, et garnies de légers rideaux de mousseline blanche', 'croisée à deux battans garnis aussi de mousseline blanche', 'petit sopha très-élégant, entouré d'une moustiquaire en mousseline blanche', 'petit tabouret couvert d'une housse blanche', 'quatre coussins blancs', 'chaises avec des housses blanches' and 'fauteuils garnis de housses blanches': Palianti, *Mise en scène du Planteur*, pp. 65–6. So, too, are light-skinned, nearly White women privileged within Jenny's inner circle, while Black women are positioned in the background of the scene. The staging manual describes the women surrounding Jenny as 'esclaves blanches'; the libretto includes 'domestiques blancs' among its dramatis personae, but mentions only 'jeunes esclaves mulâtresses' in this particular scene: Monpou *et al.*, *Le Planteur* [libretto], p. 331.

Louisiana Imagined   133

black side table is a striking image, perhaps signifying the instrument's Black cultural origins or even suggesting the African American banjo.[93] By extension, if the guitar is a visible artefact of Black culture, it may also symbolise Jenny's marginal Black ancestry, or at least a cultural inheritance that she has peripheralised within her own identity, accessing it at whim only for pleasurable role-playing or token amusement.[94]

The text of Jenny's *chant du Bengali* describes a vaguely exotic environment of a hot savanna and a cedar forest where the green-plumed *bengali* bird foretells both love and danger. Monpou's musical setting emphasises folk-like and pastoral qualities: the strings' ostinato chordal accompaniment figure mimetically represents Eva's guitar strumming, and a duet of flute and clarinet – representing the voice of the *bengali* bird – introduces the lilting melody.[95] Jenny herself imitates the voice of the *bengali* through decorative effects such as frequent grace notes and trills, 'warbling' on sustained notes (marked 'vibrato' in the score) and a concluding melisma (on the vocables 'la la la la') that ascends to a high Bb; these birdsong effects confer on Jenny a special affinity with the

---

93 James Grainger's West Indian Georgic *The Sugar-Cane* (1764) included the following lines in book IV: 'On festal days; or when their work is done; / Permit they slaves to lead the choral dance, / To the wild banshaw's melancholy sound.' In a footnote, Grainger describes the 'banshaw' as 'a sort of rude guitar, invented by the negroes. It produces a wild, pleasing, melancholy sound': James Grainger, *The Sugar-Cane: A Poem* (London: Dodsley, 1764), p. 157. The Abbé Grégoire (1750–1831), an ardent abolitionist, cited this passage, writing, 'Grainger décrit une sorte de guitare inventée par les Nègres, sur laquelle ils jouent des airs qui respirent une mélancolie douce et sentimentale; c'est la musique des cœurs affligés': H. Grégoire, *De la littérature des nègres, ou Recherches sur leurs facultés intellectuelles, leurs qualités morales et leur littérature* (Paris: Maradan, 1808), p. 184. The Dano-French geographer Conrad Malte-Brun (1755–1826) referenced 'various types of guitars and lyres' used in Black African music and dance as part of his racist, condescending description of sub-Saharan Africans as childlike and carefree. 'Ils n'attendent que le coucher du soleil pour se livrer à la danse toute la nuit; les sons rauques de la trompette d'ivoire et les roulemens du tambour continuent à se mêler aux accords de diverses espèces de guitars et de lyres': Conrad Malte-Brun, *Précis de la géographie universelle, ou Description de toutes les parties du monde* (8 vols, Paris: Buisson, 1810–29), vol. 4, p. 665.

94 My analysis here is inspired by Ahmed's suggestion that 'whiteness could also be understood as a gathering of things', as illustrated by her autoethnographic discussion of her childhood home, experienced as a collection of predominantly 'white' English objects and images (for example, white dresses in wedding photos), as opposed to her Pakistani heritage which she experienced in terms of colour (for example, red wedding dresses). Ahmed recalls, 'it was a white home, where its whiteness was shaped by the proximity of certain objects, and how they gathered over time and in space, to create a dwelling': Ahmed, 'Mixed Orientations', pp. 102–3.

95 'Les triolets de flûte qui imitent le chant du bel oiseau exotique se détachent sans affectation et avec beaucoup de charme dans la ritournelle': Hipp. P., 'Opéra-Comique', *Le Commerce*, 4 March 1839, pp. 1–2.

imagined Louisiana landscape as well as a 'natural' sexuality, signalling both her ability to communicate in the esoteric language of this 'prophet bird' and her sonic allure as a passionate siren figure.[96] Monpou also generates exotic 'local colour' through mode mixture, including a foray into the parallel B flat minor (for text describing the *bengali*'s plangent, plaintive cries) and borrowed minor subdominant harmonies in the choral refrain; these chromatic inflections may also foreshadow the metaphorical 'storm' that awaits Jenny.[97]

For now, though, the Makensie sugar plantation is a 'type of Eldorado', in the words of one critic, who added that 'the slaves spend days of joy there, working when they want – that is to say, as little as possible – and singing the praises of the good little mistress all day long'.[98] Indeed, throughout *Le Planteur*, the institution of slavery itself is never criticised: rather, it is constantly idealised through the pro-slavery myth of 'loyal slaves' eager to serve their 'kindly mistress' in an idyllic pastoral setting. As described above, the opening tableau portrays Jenny's enslaved domestics as enjoying comfortable surroundings and only minimal labour; they sing her a gentle lullaby while she slumbers and then join in with the refrain of her *chant du Bengali*. The number concludes with an even more overt display of Jenny's benevolence to the people she enslaves. Immediately following the *chant du Bengali*, Monpou depicts the passage of

---

96 Ralph Locke's list of distinctive musical devices and style features in nineteenth-century French exotic opera includes 'quick ornaments applied to near-excess or over-predictably' (see also n. 75 above and my discussion of the women's slumber chorus, p. 126); wordless melismas that can suggest both 'ritualistic' invocation and 'subtle sexual invitation'; and 'unusual styles of vocal production' such as 'throbbing vibrato', which – along with other effects such as darkened timbre – 'may be understood as indicating seductiveness or passionate intensity': Ralph P. Locke, 'Les Formes de l'exotisme: Intrigues, personnages, styles musicaux', trans. Dennis Collins, in *Histoire de l'Opéra français: Du Consulat aux débuts de la IIIe République*, ed. Hervé Lacombe (Paris: Fayard, 2020), pp. 955–63, at pp. 960–1. Jenny's *chant du Bengali* has much in common with the showpiece aria usually sung by the queen or noblewoman who reigns over a pastoral setting in the scene type I have described as the '*jardin des femmes* convention'; in French grand opéra, this number is usually assigned to the more 'decorative' secondary female role, but here she is the principal female role. Functions of this number include establishing social hierarchy; characterising the 'queen' as superficial, hedonistic, and excessively sexual; and even connoting the religiosity of a quasi-pagan ritual as the 'queen' communes with nature. See Spencer, 'The *Jardin des Femmes* as Scenic Convention in French Opera and Ballet', pp. 49–51.

97 Modal ambiguity, perhaps 'suggesting a society that is not rationally organised', is another exotic style feature of nineteenth-century French opera: Locke, 'Les Formes de l'exotisme', p. 958.

98 'Sir Mackensie, riche colon de la Nouvelle-Orléans, a laissé ses biens à sa fille unique, Jenny, dont l'habitation est une espèce d'Eldorado; les esclaves y filent des jours de joie, travaillant quand bon leur semble, c'est-à-dire, le moins possible, et chantant toute la journée les louanges de la bonne petite maîtresse': Alf. D.-S., 'Théâtres', *L'Écho français*, 4 March 1839, p. 1.

Louisiana Imagined   135

field slaves in the background with a jaunty staccato tune, the sound of pizzicato cellos and basses representing footsteps, the silvery punctuation of triangle hits providing an exotic 'local colour' and the asymmetrical phrase structure subtly suggesting a non-normative primitivism (ex. 3.4).[99] This 'happy slave' music alerts Jenny to their presence and, not wishing her slaves to suffer in the extreme heat, she invites them inside to take a break from their labours. The slaves respond gratefully with a chorus praising their mistress: 'what a pleasure it is to always be near her, to love serving her'.[100]

Regular attendees at the Opéra-Comique may have been reminded of another slave-owning American woman who embodied the myth of the 'kindly mistress': Henriette in Saint-Georges and Halévy's *L'Éclair*. In the opening scene of *L'Éclair*, the American sisters Madame Darbel and Henriette sit together along the sea of Massachusetts Bay, singing of the pleasures of solitude in the countryside.[101] Madame Darbel complains that, as a young and wealthy widow, she has her freedom encumbered by her many suitors: 'they are tyrants who call themselves our slaves'.[102] Henriette replies that she enjoys this region of

99   Locke's list of exotic style features in Western music – especially that of the Classic and Romantic eras – includes 'departures from normative types of continuity' (including asymmetrical phrase structure) and 'foreign musical instruments, or Western ones that are used in ways that make them sound foreign', including unpitched percussion instruments: Locke, *Musical Exoticism*, pp. 51–4. A condensed version of this list also appears in Locke, 'Les Formes de l'exotisme', pp. 960–1. The triangle shows up regularly in exotic and 'feminine' scenes of nineteenth-century French opera – especially harem scenes, where the triangle's long-standing association with the 'alla turca' style lent an imagined geographical authenticity. Jensen points to the asymmetrical phrasing of this passage as evidence of Monpou's subtly innovative opéra comique style. 'By simple elision, he adds variety to what would have been a square and monotonous phrase': Jensen, 'Gerard de Nerval and Opéra-Comique', p. 152. However, applying Locke's approach to analysing musical exoticism, I would argue that the asymmetrical phrase structure works in combination with the 'exotic' triangle timbre to suggest a sonic Otherness associated with the enslaved Black people of the Louisiana plantation setting.

100 'Vive notre maîtresse! / ah! quel bonheur pour nous, ah! quel plaisir / d'être toujours près d'elle pour l'aimer la servir': Monpou *et al.*, *Le Planteur* [piano-vocal score], pp. 31–7. Text is slightly altered from the published libretto.

101 Pierpaolo Polzonetti's observations on the symbolism of seaside settings in eighteenth-century Italian opera buffa are equally applicable to *L'Éclair*. '*L'americano* is set in a non-specified European summer resort by the sea. As in *Così fan tutte*, the open view of the water expanse attunes the audience to a world of adventure and travel, both literal and metaphoric. Both operas involve the vicissitudes of two couples of lovers as their affection and desires are redirected. The erotic turbulence that this potential swapping generates destabilises the regenerative nucleus of the family – the couple': Polzonetti, *Italian Opera in the Age of the American Revolution*, p. 170.

102 'Ce sont des tyrans qui se disent nos esclaves': Fromental Halévy *et al.*, *L'Éclair, opéra-comique en trois actes. Paroles de MM. E. de Planard et H. de Saint-George [sic], musique de M. F. Halevy. Représenté pour la première fois sur le Théâtre royal de*

Example 3.4. Hippolyte Monpou, *Le Planteur*, Act I, No. 1: Introduction, bb. 161–88 [piano-vocal score]. Paris: Richault, n.d. [1839].

—(continued)

Example 3.4—*concluded*

America, where her uncle has entrusted her with control of several plantations: 'I have slaves like you, but these ones really love me; I smile at their labours, and in the evening I take part in their games and amusements.'[103] This brief reference to slavery in *L'Éclair* serves primarily as a marker establishing the work's American setting (even if it is historically inaccurate for nineteenth-century Massachusetts) and the sisters' high socio-economic status, whereas in *Le Planteur* slavery is central to the plot.[104] Still, both works feature images

---

l'Opéra-Comique, le 16 décembre 1835 (Paris, n.d. [1835]), p. 2.

103 'J'ai des esclaves comme toi; mais ceux-là m'aiment véritablement; je souris à leurs travaux, et, le soir arrivé, je partage leurs jeux et leurs délassemens': Halévy et al., *L'Éclair*, p. 2.

104 This brief reference to American slavery in *L'Éclair* is reminiscent of the brief reference to Caribbean slavery in the love duet between Polly and Macheath in *The Beggar's Opera* (1728), first critically discussed by Ralph Locke. As Locke keenly observes, Polly's lines ('Were I sold on [West] Indian soil, / Soon as the burning day was clos'd / I could mock the sultry toil, / When on my charmer's breast repos'd') 'show how nonchalantly slavery was sometimes invoked by Europeans who stood far from its grim daily realities' and 'thus was an urgent subject of current debate trivialised to provide an entertaining night in the commercial theatre': Locke, *Music and the Exotic from the Renaissance to Mozart* (Cambridge: Cambridge University Press, 2015), pp. 272–3.

138   *Helena Kopchick Spencer*

of independent American women who befriend the people they enslave, and are beloved in return.[105] Furthermore, in February 1838, Jenny Colon had successfully performed the role of Henriette in a revival of *L'Éclair*.[106] So when she performed the role of Jenny Makensie the following year, audiences may well have recognised a kind of intertextual resonance between the characters of Henriette and Jenny.

The pro-slavery lie of 'happy slaves' and 'kindly mistresses/masters' returns in Act II of *Le Planteur*, after Jenny has been auctioned as a slave and purchased by Jakson. Despite Jenny's reversal of fortune at the end of Act I, several critics rightly observed that she did not endure any real suffering in her new station. In the anti-slavery paper *Le Siècle*, Albert Cler noted, 'It goes without saying that she is a slave in name only.'[107] In *Le Corsaire*, another critic remarked that Jakson had installed Jenny on his plantation 'not as a slave, but as a queen'.[108] So, too, did François Sauvo of *Le Moniteur universel* comment wryly:

> We next see Miss [Makensie] at the planter's, resigned to her new condition, even cheering up the slave help with gay *chansonnettes*. Do you think Jenny is very unhappy? No. No work, a charming retreat, care, thoughtfulness, deep respect, permission to go out, to come back when she wishes [...][109]

Instead, Jenny's transformation from heiress to slave is a superficial one, relying primarily on her costume: as Caton reports to Jakson in Act II Scene 1, Jenny demands to wear the same clothes worn by the enslaved women of the plantation because 'it is the clothing of her new state' and 'she will now share the work of her companions' (although that work seems to be little more than gathering flowers).[110] Neither the libretto nor Palianti's staging manual provides

---

105 In Act I Scene 3, Jenny asks Eva, 'et mes sujets sont mes amis, n'est-ce pas, Eva?', to which Eva replies, 'Je le crois bien! c'est à qui vous aimera le mieux ici': Monpou *et al.*, *Le Planteur* [libretto], p. 332.

106 Jensen, 'Gerard de Nerval', p. 79.

107 'Il va sans dire qu'elle n'est esclave que de nom. Le digne Jackson l'entoure de soins et d'hommages': A.C. [Albert Cler], 'Théâtre de l'Opéra-Comique', *Le Siècle*, 11 March 1839, p. 3.

108 'Il achète Jenny à un prix fou et l'installe dans son habitation, non pas comme une esclave, mais comme une reine': Unsigned, 'Théâtre de l'Opéra-Comique. *Le Planteur*', *Le Corsaire*, 4 March 1839, p. 2; reproduced in *Le Planteur*, ed. Cooper, p. 145.

109 'Nous revoyons miss chez le planteur, résignée à sa nouvelle condition, égayant même l'assistance esclave de gaies chansonnettes. Croyez-vous Jennie bien malheureuse? Non. Aucun travail, une retraite charmante, des soins, des prévenances, un profond respect, permission de sortir, de rentrer lorsqu'elle le désire, voilà l'unique vengeance de Jakson, que la veille on accablait de dédains': P. [François Sauvo], 'Spectacles. Opéra-Comique. – *Le Planteur*, opéra en trois [*sic*] actes, paroles de M. Saint-Georges, musique de M. Monpou', *Gazette nationale ou le Moniteur universel*, 4 March 1839, p. 4.

110 'Elle dit que c'est l'habit de son nouvel état, qu'elle n'en veut pas d'autres, et qu'elle partagera désormais tous les travaux de ses compagnes': Monpou *et al.*, *Le Planteur* [libretto], p. 343.

specific details of this 'costume en créole',[111] but one critic noted that it included a headwrap made of Madras cotton.[112] For women in antebellum New Orleans, this article of clothing – known as a toque – was the most distinctive marker of mixed-race identity.[113] An illustration of a Creole woman wearing a knotted toque, along with a shoulder scarf and a vibrantly patterned dress, appears on the title page of the sheet music for the 1840 song 'La Créole' (fig. 3.2); this illustration gives us an idea of what Jenny Makensie's 'Creole' costume might have looked like, as well as the flirtatious manner and seductive powers associated with American women of colour.[114]

During Caton and Jakson's dialogue, the orchestra reprises the jaunty 'happy slave' music from Act I (ex. 3.4); in Act II Scene 2, this music signals Jenny's entrance with the other female slaves of Jakson's plantation. The return of this 'happy slave' music recalls Jenny's past status as a 'kindly mistress' who empathises with the enslaved people of her plantation and now enjoys the same camaraderie with the enslaved women of Jakson's plantation; it further suggests that Jakson fosters a similar environment of 'compassionate' ownership – a fallacy promoted by pro-slavery advocates and those who favoured a gradualist approach to abolition. Monpou's cheerful music thus contributes to *Le Planteur's* larger failure to condemn slavery as a social evil, suggesting that enslaved people could be content under the right circumstances.

Performing her new identity, Jenny sings a folk-like *chansonnette créole* to lift the spirits of her fellow enslaved women, who fawn, 'your voice enchants us'.[115] This scene shares several similarities with Jenny's earlier diegetic perfor-

---

111 'Jenny est en costume créole, un petit panier à la main': Monpou *et al.*, *Le Planteur* [libretto], p. 343 Palianti's manual indicates only 'en créole' for Jenny's Act II costume: Palianti, *Mise en scène du Planteur*, p. 73.

112 'Voilà Jenny, devenue esclave, la tête couverte d'un madras et portant un panier à la main': P.M., 'Feuilleton. Théâtre de l'Opéra-Comique. *Le Planteur*', *Le Temps*, 14 March 1839, pp. 1–2; reproduced in *Le Planteur*, ed. Cooper, p. 171.

113 In his 1786 *Bando de buen gobierno*, Louisiana's former Spanish governor Esteban Miró had issued a mandate that all women of colour wear a toque – a brightly coloured, chequered head kerchief made of Madras cotton – in order to visibly signal their non-Whiteness; this dress code reflected anxieties that light-skinned *femmes de couleur libres* might successfully pass for White. Manganelli, *Transatlantic Spectacles of Race*, p. 41; see also pp. 83–4. The racialised use of the toque – or at least its symbolic appearance in literature and visual art – continued well into the nineteenth century. See, for example, mention of the Tragic Mulatta character Aurore's headdress and the definition of the term 'toque' in the appendix of explanatory notes in Thomas Mayne Reid's novel *The Quadroon*, which inspired Dion Boucicault's popular play *The Octoroon*.(1859). Mayne Reid, *The Quadroon; or, A Lover's Adventures in Louisiana* (3 vols, London: Hyde, 1856), vol. 3, pp. 47 and 267.

114 Manganelli, *Transatlantic Spectacles of Race*, pp. 23–4. Here Manganelli refers specifically to French travel writers' accounts of mixed-race women of the West Indies.

115 'Votre voix nous enchante': Monpou *et al.*, *Le Planteur* [piano-vocal score], p. 106. This

Figure 3.2. Ad. Brebant, illustration used for the title page of the song 'La Créole. Chantée par M[r] L[id] Amat. Paroles de A. Bonsergent. Musique d'H[re] Colin'. Paris: Guérin, [1840]. Estampes Scènes CréoleColin (1). Bibliothèque Nationale de France.

mance of the *chant du Bengali* in Act I Scene 1. In both cases, she is the centre of attention, a charismatic performer surrounded by adoring slaves who entreat her to sing a folk song for their pleasure. Jenny takes pleasure in this performance, too, showing off her 'enchanting' vocal beauty and virtuosity with *jouissant* melismas on 'ah!' and doubling the orchestral ritournelle with a jubilant 'la-la la' fanfare gesture whose ostinato rhythm may have suggested a generic Otherness vaguely reminiscent of Spanish flamenco castanets (ex. 3.5).[116] Jenny's *chansonnette* is specifically requested by the enslaved women,[117] and – as in her Act I *chant du Bengali* – they join in the refrain, suggesting the song is well known in the local Black community; Jenny's ability to perform the song likewise confirms her Black inheritance, now unmasked.[118] The text depicts a flirtatious dialogue between 'young Emmy, the flower-girl' and a handsome gentleman admirer who tells her he would rather have the roses of her cheeks and the irises of her blue eyes than the bouquets she's selling; when he urges her to place the flowers near her bosom in order to 'double their value', she replies saucily that she will do so only for her husband.[119] Though not overtly exotic, this mildly erotic text reinforces the stereotypical image of the coquettish, sexually available Creole woman while also suggesting the imagined practice of concubinage or *plaçage* between mixed-race women and wealthy white men, a recurring trope in accounts of antebellum Louisiana.[120] The simple strophic melody in F major, though not imbued with typical generic exotic-style mark-

---

line is not in the published libretto, but was added to the score.

116 In addition to 'floating, timeless' melismas, Locke includes repetitive rhythmic gestures – especially those suggesting ethnic or national dances – as an exotic style feature: Locke, 'Les Formes de l'exotisme', pp. 959–61. In the extended version of this essay, he notes that 'a short ostinato rhythm that begins with a subdivided downbeat seems to have served as an "all-purpose" signifier of the exotic in nineteenth-century French opera': Locke, 'The Exotic in Nineteenth-Century French Opera, Part 2: Plots, Characters, and Musical Devices', *19th-Century Music* (forthcoming).

117 'Ah cédez à notre prière; dites nous la chanson d'Emmy la bouquetière': Monpou *et al.*, *Le Planteur* [piano-vocal score], p. 105. This text is not in the published libretto.

118 Here we might draw a parallel to American musical theatre: in Kern and Hammerstein's *Show Boat* (1927), when the mixed-race character Julie – a later transatlantic example of the Tragic Mulatta archetype – performs 'Can't Help Lovin' Dat Man of Mine', her knowledge of this song reveals her Black identity, even though she is 'passing' as White. See Todd Decker's discussion of this song as variously interpreted in the performance history of *Show Boat*: Todd Decker, *Show Boat: Performing Race in an American Musical* (Oxford: Oxford University Press, 2013), pp. 65–6, 189–90, and 230–5.

119 'Si tu veux placer ces fleurs / Près de ton corsage, / Tu doubleras leurs valeurs / Grace au voisinage. / De ce discours charmant, / Vraiment! / Mon beau monsieur, je ris / Et dis / En fillette bien sage: / Ce bouquet si joli, / Si ma main le place ainsi, / Ce bouquet si joli, / C'est pour mon mari!': Monpou *et al.*, *Le Planteur* [libretto], pp. 343–4.

120 On the myth of *plaçage* and its origins, see Clark, *The Strange History of the American Quadroon*; see n. 20.

Example 3.5. Hippolyte Monpou, *Le Planteur*, Act II, No. 6: Chansonnette, Chœur des Femmes, bb. 98–112 [piano-vocal score]. Paris: Richault, n.d. [1839].

ers like chromaticism, augmented seconds, or modal inflections, nevertheless conveys by virtue of its simplicity and playful dance-like rhythms a sense of Creole women as 'natural', 'unrefined', and in touch with their bodies.[121] Moreover, in keeping with Ralph Locke's 'full-context' paradigm for understanding musical exoticism, the sight of Jenny in her Madras headwrap surrounded by a chorus of 'négresses' in blackface against a background of 'trees and plants of the colonies' and various bamboo furnishings probably encouraged audiences to perceive this song as rich in 'local colour'.[122]

Jenny's performance is also – secretly – observed by Jakson, who admires both her enchanting voice and her exotic attire. The trope of a White male protagonist who desires an alluring 'Other' woman (and watches her sing and dance from a distance) is, of course, a mainstay of nineteenth-century French opera and ballet. What is unusual here is that Jenny and Jakson actually marry in the end, after he frees her from slavery and she discovers that her former fiancé Arthur is an unfaithful cad. Their interracial marriage is particularly significant given the status of opéra comique in promoting bourgeois sociocultural and moral values. In fact, the 'morality' of *Le Planteur* was part of its appeal. Though the critic Félix Bonnaire complained that the opera's American landscape had not inspired a more elevated musical style, he admired its plot, declaring:

> Nothing can be imagined more honest, more virtuous, more moral; from beginning to end, one feels tender, and the eyes burst into tears. This big planter, so common and so ugly, who, in spite of his shaven head, his hearty belly, and his harsh manners, manages by means of care, attentiveness, and loyalty to make himself loved by a young miss who becomes a slave and whom he redeems, is a character who will never fail the sympathies of the subscribers of the Opéra-Comique. Virtue triumphs and vice is rejected.[123]

---

121 Locke, 'Les Formes de l'exotisme', p. 960. Hippolyte Prévost noted that the audience loved this number, but he did not share their appreciation because he found it too banal. 'Au second acte, les couplets que dit Jenny pour payer sa bienvenue au milieu des esclaves de Jakson ont été bissés; nous nous permettrons cette fois de n'être pas de l'avis du public; ces couplets sont faciles, mais communs': Hipp. P., 'Opéra-Comique', *Le Commerce*, 4 March 1839, pp. 1–2.

122 Palianti, *Mise en scène du Planteur*, p. 70. On the full-context paradigm, see Locke, *Musical Exoticism*, pp. 59–64.

123 'On ne peut rien imaginer de plus honnête, de plus vertueux, de plus moral; du commencement à la fin, on se sent attendri, et les yeux fondent en larmes. Ce gros planteur, si commun et si laid, qui, malgré sa tête rase, son ventre copieux et ses rudes manières, parvient, à force de soins, de prévenances et de loyauté, à se faire aimer d'une jeune miss redevenue esclave et qu'il rachète, est un personnage auquel ne manqueront jamais les sympathies des abonnés de l'Opéra-Comique. La vertu triomphe et le vice est éconduit': F. Bonnaire, 'Théâtres, *Revue de Paris*, NS, 3 (1839), 70–2, at p. 70.

That a mixed-race heroine achieves redemption through the domestic role of wife (and potential mother) – and that this union is lauded as virtuous and moral – might seem to suggest an inclusive national vision and a positive anticipation of a harmonious interracial future. Yet the appropriateness of Jenny's marriage to a wealthy White planter is predicated on her ability to pass as White and her eagerness to assimilate. Moreover, the once-independent Jenny escapes slavery and regains her privileged social status only because she is purchased as property by Jakson, a stereotypical 'kindly master'. Manganelli notes this phenomenon in other literary works that feature a Tragic Mulatta 'redeemed' through marriage: a White husband may 'rescue the mixed-race woman', but in these fantasies, the Tragic Mulatta suffers 'a different demise as they lose their independence, individuality and, most notably, their racial identities'.[124] In the end, Manganelli observes, 'the cult of true womanhood remains a realm where only "white" women may tread'.[125] Equally disturbing in *Le Planteur* is the tacit implication that the spouses are well suited to each other because both are somehow 'damaged' or 'defective' – Jakson outwardly so by his unattractive physical appearance, rustic attire, and rough manners; Jenny, less visibly, marred by the hidden 'stain' of her Black ancestry.

To conclude, the conventional expectations of opéra comique – most notably, the 'happily ever after' marriage plot – limited the genre's ability to fully engage with the disturbing subject matter of slavery, sexual violence, and suicide found in the source texts of *Le Planteur*. The reassuring 'redemption' of the heroine undermines any attempt at an abolitionist message in *Le Planteur*, especially because, for all of his purported generosity and benevolence, Jakson does not manumit any of his other slaves, whose lives are idealised as a picturesque pastorale. Moreover, the depiction of these 'loyal, submissive slaves' as eager to serve their 'kindly master and mistress' resonated with the pro-slavery fallacy that the only action needed was to improve slaves' working conditions and their treatment by the planters. Yet all of *Le Planteur*'s limitations actually reveal much about contemporary French attitudes towards race, gender, and sexual politics. This opéra comique underscored French middle-class values while taking a fun armchair tour of an imagined American South, where audiences could hear pleasant music sung by a favourite star, portraying a charming light-skinned 'Creole' girl. Light, popular tunes and a feel-good ending trivialised slavery, allowing White slaveholding characters to appear virtuous, enslaved Black people to seem contented, and the institution of slavery to remain unchallenged.

I would argue further that, with its humanitarian ambitions tarnished by racist stereotypes and a failure to dislodge the deeply entrenched status quo, *Le Planteur* reflects the broader shortcomings of the French anti-slavery movement at the end of the 1830s. It is tempting to speculate, too, that *Le Planteur*'s

---

124 Manganelli, *Transatlantic Spectacles of Race*, p. 147.
125 Manganelli, *Transatlantic Spectacles of Race*, p. 147.

lack of longevity at the Opéra-Comique – ending its run after a total of forty-six performances in 1839 and two in 1840 – was due to a diminished relevance that was bound up with the dissipating energy of the French anti-slavery movement. Poised for a breakthrough in 1839, by mid-1840 this movement was foundering under the weight of the government's callous indifference, colonial plantocrats' obstructionist tactics, and French abolitionists' own tendencies towards cautious gradualism. In the spring of 1839, however, the American tale of *Le Planteur* projected an image in which French critics recognised their own national crisis of conscience. Though Louisiana was no longer subject to French control, as a former French territory still deeply imprinted with French cultural identity, this 'lost colony' could nonetheless serve as a distant mirror for France's debates about the practice of slavery in its remaining colonies and the humanity of the people it enslaved.

PART II

MYTHS OF AMERICA AND INTERSECTING IDENTITIES

4

'Brise du Sud': American Identity and War in the Popular Sheet Music of Francophone New Orleans

Charlotte Bentley

For the Francophone population of nineteenth-century New Orleans, imagining America meant doing so from the inside. It was not simply a matter of escapism, fantasy, or even entertainment: the city's French-speaking residents negotiated their own identity through a process of creating and projecting images of their adoptive homeland. New Orleans's Francophones had been a heterogeneous group from the city's foundation in 1718; the earliest residents were a heady mixture of convicts, nuns, and a few aspiring capitalists.[1] Over the next century, the Francophone population diversified further, coming to comprise people from highly varied economic and racial backgrounds, born on both sides of the Atlantic. Francophone identity in the city, insofar as it can be thought of in the singular, emerged less from a unified sense of heritage than from sets of experiences in the New World shared by French speakers.

By the early nineteenth century, music had come to play an important role in articulating Francophone cultural identity in New Orleans. Francophone theatres in the city produced French-language operas from as early as 1796, and the opening of the Théâtre d'Orléans in 1819 helped to establish transatlantic networks of performers and other connections that would grow over the next forty years.[2] Later, a new French Opera House provided a dedicated home for Francophone opera from 1859 until 1919, when the building burned down.

---

1   On the city's early history, see Emily Clark, *Masterless Mistresses: The New Orleans Ursulines and the Development of a New World Society, 1727 to 1834* (Chapel Hill: University of North Carolina Press, 2007).

2   For more on the history of the theatre and its role in city life, see Henry Kmen, *Music in New Orleans: The Formative Years, 1791–1841* (Baton Rouge: Louisiana State University Press, 1966) and Charlotte Bentley, 'Resituating Transatlantic Opera: The Case of the Théâtre d'Orléans, New Orleans, 1819–1859' (unpublished PhD dissertation, University of Cambridge, 2017).

150   *Charlotte Bentley*

In private and semi-private spaces, too, music helped to create a sense of Francophone identity.[3] Growing piano sales and an emerging sheet music market made the parlour a significant site of musical activity. The *soirée musicale*, where families and invited guests would spend an evening in domestic musical performance and appreciation, was a fundamental part of middle-class social life for French speakers, and music shops around the city proudly published lists of the latest shipments of sheet music and instruments they had received from Paris, knowing that they provided important material for these musical-social gatherings.

My focus in this chapter, however, is not on imported music, but rather on a much smaller but no less significant body of works that were written in New Orleans by Francophone composers. Some of the composers I consider here were Creoles – locally born people of European descent – but had in many cases been educated in Paris.[4] Others had come to New Orleans from France, often initially to work for either the Théâtre d'Orléans or the French Opera House, and some remained in Louisiana for the rest of their lives. Francophone composers of colour – Basile Barès, Edmond Dédé, and Samuel Snaër among others – also worked in New Orleans during this period, and some of them received training or had careers in Europe.[5] While few New Orleans composers achieved any lasting success with operatic compositions (the city's stages remained dominated by major European operas), the local sheet music market welcomed ever-growing numbers of their works.

The songs and piano music these composers wrote, I suggest, both reflected and helped to create a sense of Francophone identity based on experiences of life in America. In particular, I am going to focus in this chapter on pieces composed during or in the aftermath of times of war on United States soil between 1800 and 1880: times at which conceptions of identity could be shattered and remoulded in response to the turmoil of external events. War, I argue, provided the opportunity for Francophone composers working in New Orleans not only to reflect on their relationship with 'Amérique' in real and imagined forms, but

---

3   For more on the musical life of the city beyond the theatre, see John Baron, *Concert Life in Nineteenth-Century New Orleans: A Comprehensive Reference* (Baton Rouge: Louisiana State University Press, 2013).

4   The term 'Creole' was originally used in New Orleans to distinguish people born in the New World from European-born settlers, but it soon came to include people of African descent who had been born on American soil. Its meaning changed frequently: as Carl Brasseaux has shown, at various times in the nineteenth century, it took on racially exclusive meanings. See Carl Brasseaux, *French, Cajun, Creole, Houma: A Primer on Francophone Louisiana* (Baton Rouge: Louisiana State University Press, 2005), pp. 88–98.

5   See Sally McKee, *The Exile's Song: Edmond Dédé and the Unfinished Revolutions of the Atlantic World* (New Haven: Yale University Press, 2017) and Lester Sullivan, 'Composers of Color in Nineteenth-Century New Orleans: The History behind the Music', *Black Music Research Journal*, 8:1 (1988), 51–82.

American Identity and War in Francophone New Orleans   151

also to formulate and express complex personal identities as French, American, and, increasingly, as Louisianian. I do not mean to suggest that there was necessarily a sense of linear development in the way in which Francophones related to their adopted country; instead, the pieces I explore in this chapter are part of a constellation of formulations and expressions of that relationship during various conflicts. Nor do I claim that the compositions and issues explored in this chapter represent a comprehensive Francophone experience: my decision to focus on published musical responses to war in New Orleans resulted in my being unable to unearth comparable pieces by Black composers for discussion, meaning that their struggles to define themselves as French-speaking Americans have not been examined here.[6] Much further work remains to be done on their experiences of Francophone identity.

War and revolution, both directly and indirectly, shaped New Orleans's demographics around the turn of the nineteenth century: the Seven Years' War (and its North American manifestation, the French and Indian War of 1754–63) led to France's forty-year cession of its vast colony of La Louisiane to Spain, following the Treaty of Fontainebleau in 1762.[7] New Orleans's Francophone residents found themselves under Spanish rule, against which they tried – unsuccessfully – to rebel in 1768.[8] The bloody conflict of the Haitian Revolution further altered New Orleans's Francophone community, as thousands of French-speaking refugees – Black and White, free and enslaved – arrived between 1791 and 1810 and, according to Carl Brasseaux, 'literally doubled the size of the Crescent City's population.'[9] Ultimately, Napoléon's failure to suppress the Haitian Revolution and re-establish France's North American empire led to his decision to sell La Louisiane to the United States in the Louisiana Purchase of 1803.[10] The Louisiana Purchase brought increasing numbers of Anglo-American settlers to New Orleans, and by the 1830s, Francophones found themselves numerically in the minority for the first time;[11] although their

---

6   While I have been unable to do so here, Shirley Elizabeth Thompson has written extensively on Black Creoles' struggles to 'become American'. See Shirley Elizabeth Thompson, *Exiles at Home: The Struggle to Become American in Creole New Orleans* (Cambridge, MA: Harvard University Press, 2009).

7   The French and Indian War (1754–63) also displaced French-speaking Acadians from Canada, sending some of them down the Mississippi to rural Louisiana (and smaller numbers to New Orleans), where they re-settled and became known as Cajuns, adding another layer to the Francophone identity of the region.

8   See Junius P. Rodriguez, *The Louisiana Purchase: A Historical and Geographical Encyclopedia* (Santa Barbara: ABC-CLIO, 2002).

9   Brasseaux, *French, Cajun, Creole, Houma*, p. 22.

10   Rodriguez, *The Louisiana Purchase*, p. xxiii.

11   Carl Brasseaux, *The Foreign French: Nineteenth-Century French Immigration into Louisiana*, vol. 1: *1820–1839* (3 vols, Lafayette, LA: Center for Louisiana Studies, University of Southwestern Louisiana, 1990), p. xi.

Charlotte Bentley

influence on the city's cultural life remained important into the second half of the nineteenth century, Francophone hegemony quickly began to wane.[12]

While these wars 'at a distance', to borrow Mary Favret's term,[13] formed part of the fabric of New Orleans's early history, the musical works I discuss in this chapter were responses to war at close quarters, whether in the form of an individual battle or a prolonged occupation. If war at a distance was at least partially responsible for the fragmented nature of Francophone identity in New Orleans, war up close became a means through which Francophones negotiated a sense of group identity based on experience, even if in practice different individuals understood and portrayed that group identity in very different ways.

Francophone-Anglophone Solidarity: The Battle of New Orleans and the Mexican–American War

The earliest conflicts that the people of nineteenth-century New Orleans experienced in close proximity were the Battle of New Orleans (1815) and the Mexican–American War (1846–8). The two were very different in regard to the parties involved, as well as their duration and impact on daily life, but they inspired curiously comparable musical responses from Francophone composers in the city. The Battle of New Orleans took place on 8 January 1815, between the United States army under General Andrew Jackson and the British army.[14] The battle – fought at Chalmette, roughly seven miles downriver from the French Quarter – was a victory for the United States and the final military encounter of the War of 1812: the conflict had been settled in the Treaty of Ghent a few weeks earlier, but this news was yet to reach the United States. Among the American forces deployed from New Orleans were Francophone units of soldiers, comprising both locally born and foreign Frenchmen, who fought on the side of the Americans.[15]

---

12 This inevitably brought tensions between French and English speakers in the city. For more on how this played out in the city's musical life, see Charlotte Bentley, 'The Race for *Robert* and Other Rivalries: Negotiating the Local and (Inter)national in Nineteenth-Century New Orleans', *Cambridge Opera Journal*, 29:1 (2017), 94–112.

13 Mary Favret uses the term 'war at a distance' to describe the 'experience of those living *through* but not *in* a war [my emphasis]' that began to characterise modern warfare in the nineteenth century: contact with war in its mediated, often aestheticised, forms rather than with the bloodshed and upheaval of the battlefield directly. Mary A. Favret, *War at a Distance: Romanticism and the Making of Modern Wartime* (Princeton: Princeton University Press, 2009), p. 9.

14 For more on the Battle of New Orleans, see Robert V. Remini, *The Battle of New Orleans: Andrew Jackson and America's First Military Victory* (London: Pimlico, 1991).

15 Most of the Francophone soldiers belonged to the Battalion d'Orléans under the command of Jean Baptiste Plauché. For more, see Paul D. Gelpi Jr, 'Mr. Jefferson's Creoles:

American Identity and War in Francophone New Orleans   153

Since the Battle of New Orleans lasted all of two hours, musical responses to the conflict were produced after the fact, mainly to coincide with its first anniversary in the winter of 1816. Various musical commemorations of the battle took place in New Orleans's concert venues during January and February 1816, as is evident from Henry Kmen's summary of the months' musical activities.[16] Alongside a set of variations and a march dedicated to General Andrew Jackson by Louis Desforges,[17] the most popular musical commemoration of the conflict was a battle piece, *The Hero of New Orleans: The Battle of the Memorable 8th of January 1815*, by Philippe Laroque (c.1780–c.1838), a Francophone musician born and living in New Orleans, which was performed in an orchestral arrangement and available for purchase as a piece of sheet music for amateur pianists.[18]

Battle pieces – works that retold conflicts in musical form – were an extremely popular way of both translating and aestheticising the horrors of war for an audience that was either geographically or temporally removed from the frontline in this period.[19] As Elizabeth Morgan has shown in the context of the American Civil War, they could even serve as sources of wartime news for women waiting at home (and also allowed female players to imagine themselves at the frontline, as the 'heroic subject' in Morgan's terms).[20] Although the earliest evidence of Laroque's piece comes from a year after the battle, suggest-

---

The Battalion d'Orléans and the Americanization of Creole Louisiana, 1803–1815', *Louisiana History: The Journal of the Louisiana Historical Association*, 48:3 (2007), 295–316. Some units were formed of French-speaking free men of colour, and Charles E. Kinzer has written of their history and their music in 'The Band of Music of the First Battalion of Free Men of Color and the Siege of New Orleans, 1814–1815', *American Music*, 10:3 (1992), 348–69.

16   Kmen, *Music in New Orleans*, p. 224.

17   For biographical information on Desforges, see Baron, *Concert Life in Nineteenth-Century New Orleans*, pp. 141–5.

18   The sheet music is not dated, but Kmen suggests that Laroque 'introduced' the piece to New Orleans on 31 January 1816 (*Music in New Orleans*, p. 224). The piece was entered into copyright and printed in Philadelphia, because there was no facility for music engraving and printing in New Orleans at the time. For more on the history of music publishing in New Orleans, see Peggy C. Boudreaux, 'Music Publishing in New Orleans in the Nineteenth Century' (unpublished MA thesis, Louisiana State University, 1977).

19   Battle pieces remained extremely popular into the second half of the nineteenth century, too, as Gavin Williams shows in 'Gunfire and London's Media Reality', in *Hearing the Crimean War: Wartime Sound and the Unmaking of Sense*, ed. Gavin Williams (Oxford: Oxford University Press, 2019), pp. 59–87.

20   Elizabeth Morgan, 'Combat at the Keys: Women and Battle Pieces for the Piano during the American Civil War', *19th-Century Music*, 40:1 (2016), 7–19; Elizabeth Morgan, 'War on the Home Front: Battle Pieces for the Piano from the American Civil War', *Journal of the Society for American Music*, 9:4 (2015), 381–408. Morgan uses the term 'heroic subject' in 'Combat at the Keys', p. 13.

ing it did not serve a military function, the sheet music nonetheless allowed each performer to re-enact the cooperation between New Orleans's Franco-phone and Anglo-American soldiers during the battle, as it retells the conflict from dawn on the day of the battle to the British forces' request for a truce, all followed by a triumphal march and a rondo finale.[21]

The text narrating the action is printed in both French and English, and the translations do not preserve any distinction between the activities of the Francophone units and their Anglophone counterparts, instead talking simply of 'our' forces. While this might have been a marketing ploy to reach the most consumers possible, on a musical level, too, the piece forges Francophone-An-glophone solidarity through the use of variations on 'Yankee Doodle'. Ini-tially a song sung by British officers to mock their American counterparts in the French–Indian War, and again used as a British insult to the Americans during the Revolutionary War, it became a song of national celebration for the United States.[22] Laroque chose to use the well-known song not at the imagined moment of victory in his piece, but at the height of the battle, as the enemy line begins to crack for the first time (ex. 4.1); it serves almost as a rallying cry for the united American forces – Anglophone and Francophone – to continue the fight as the enemy reforms its lines, and this sense of rallying the troops is underscored by the cries of 'huzza' that overlap with it.

Such opposition of Franco-American and British groups perhaps taps into an older trope (still just about in living memory for some of the older residents of the city) of American–French alliances during the American Revolutionary War.[23] This time, however, in the hands of a Francophone resident in New Orleans, the gesture becomes not just a display of Francophone support for the United States, but a seeming declaration of Francophone identification as American. In Laroque's retelling of the conflict, the presence of an outside 'enemy' united the divergent linguistic factions in New Orleans in a display of American solidarity.

Although the Battle of New Orleans was a very short military engagement, its impact on Francophone identity in New Orleans was a lasting one and con-tinued to be felt more than three decades later in musical responses to the

---

21 Laroque's piece bears close similarities to Franz Kotzwara's immensely popular battle piece *The Battle of Prague*, which had been reprinted across Europe and in the United States following its publication in the late 1780s. For more on the history and reception of Kotzwara's piece, see Jonathan Bellman, 'Expressive and Narrative Strategies in the Descriptive Piano Fantasia', *Journal of Musicological Research*, 34:3 (2015), 182–203.

22 William Gibbons discusses the many uses of 'Yankee Doodle' in American music in '"Yankee Doodle" and Nationalism, 1780–1920', *American Music*, 26:2 (2008), 246–74. He mentions Laroque's piece on p. 255. 'Yankee Doodle' continued to be important in later American conflicts: Robert Walter Johanssen explores its importance during the Mexican War in *To the Halls of the Montezumas: The Mexican War in the American Imagination* (Oxford: Oxford University Press, 1985), pp. 230–40.

23 For more on this relationship, see Norman Desmarais, *America's First Ally: France in the Revolutionary War* (Philadelphia: Casemate, 2019).

Example 4.1. Excerpt from *The Hero of New Orleans: The Battle of the Memorable 8th of January 1815* by Philippe Laroque, p. 6. Philadelphia: G. Willig [1818].

Mexican–American War. While the Battle of New Orleans had formed part of a defence of the United States against the British former colonial power, the Mexican–American War contributed to a growing sense of American nationalism and American expansion.[24] At the root of the conflict was the United States' annexation of Texas, an area previously under Mexican control. Although the fighting was not in close proximity to the city this time, New Orleans served as an important base of operations for the United States forces. Almost all soldiers travelling to the frontline stopped in the city, with many officers being stationed there for weeks or months; the New Orleans press played a vital role

---

24 For more on the Mexican-American War, see Peter Guardino, *The Dead March: A History of the Mexican-American War* (Cambridge, MA: Harvard University Press, 2017).

156   *Charlotte Bentley*

in reporting on the war and in disseminating the latest developments to the rest of the United States.[25]

Eugène Prévost, the French-born *chef-d'orchestre* at the Théâtre d'Orléans, who had lived in New Orleans since 1838, published a song during the war called 'The Departure of the Volunteers: A National Song', dedicated to 'The Army of the Rio Grande'.[26] It was one of numerous songs written in New Orleans in praise of military leaders and their armies during the conflict, doubtless on account of the constant traffic of troops through the city. Indeed, Prévost led a concert on 3 December 1847 at the Théâtre d'Orléans at which General Zachary Taylor (then the much-celebrated chief of the United States forces on the frontline) was guest of honour.[27]

The text of Prévost's 'Departure of the Volunteers' (written by the composer himself) refers back to the Battle of New Orleans, drawing the Mexican–American War into a lineage of conflicts that had shaped the city. Both the French and English texts for the bilingual song play on the idea that the Battle of New Orleans formed part of a shared national heritage for Anglophones and Francophones. The English refers to 'Chalmette's gory clay', thus mentioning the site of the Battle of New Orleans, and then, in order to urge the troops on to victory, states, '[Andrew] Jackson reproaches our delay', thus calling on 'the hero of New Orleans' (who had died in 1845, the year before the outbreak of the war with Mexico) for victory in this new conflict. The French text, meanwhile, also talks of Jackson and alludes to the Battle of New Orleans less directly by mentioning 'the memory of our history' ('le souvenir de notre histoire') and 'arms still red with English blood' ('armes encore [*sic*] rouges de sang anglais'). The earlier Battle of New Orleans, then, provides a shared sense of past and purpose that Prévost applied to the new context of the war with Mexico; the French-born composer evokes a single American 'us', united against Mexico. As in the case of Laroque's earlier piece, there is a strong sense here in which the presence of an external threat led Francophones of both American and foreign birth to join with English speakers and identify fully as American.

---

25 See Johanssen, *To the Halls of the Montezumas*, pp. 16–20.

26 This song is available online through the Lester Levy Sheet Music Collection, Johns Hopkins University, Sheridan Libraries and University Museum. For biographical information on Prévost, see Baron, *Concert Life in Nineteenth-Century New Orleans*, pp. 179–83.

27 The French theatre orchestra, alongside excerpts from François-Adrien Boieldieu's *La Dame blanche* and other French operatic works, played such Anglo-American favourites as 'Yankee Doodle' and 'Hail Columbia!', as well as various patriotic works by Prévost. Juliane Braun mentions General Taylor's visit to the Théâtre d'Orléans in *Creole Drama: Theatre and Society in Nineteenth-Century New Orleans* (Charlottesville: University of Virginia Press, 2019), pp. 135–6. In order to avoid appearing as if he favoured one part of the local population over the other, General Taylor visited the Francophone Théâtre d'Orléans and Anglophone St Charles and American theatres all on the evening of 3 December 1847. See *Daily Picayune*, 4 Dec. 1847.

Nonetheless, the French and English texts to the song do hint that there were differences in the way in which Francophones and Anglophones understood their identity as American. While the English text speaks of Jackson and Taylor and evokes American nationalism in quite a general sense, the French ends with the soldiers bidding adieu to 'darling Louisiana' ('Louisiane Cherie [*sic*]'), suggesting that American identity for Francophones had a more intimate connection with their regional identity as Louisianian. This, as will become evident later in this chapter, was an idea that Francophones developed much more fully in the second half of the nineteenth century.

Southern Breezes in the Civil War

The most major conflict to shape nineteenth-century America, however, had no external enemy against which composers could formulate a unified sense of Franco-American identity. The Civil War divided the United States from within, principally over the issue of slavery. Louisiana seceded from the Union on 26 January 1861, the sixth state to join the Confederacy. Its planter society sought to defend its deeply engrained practices of slave ownership; on the whole, New Orleans's White Creole elite, too, supported the Confederacy and the upholding of slavery. However, although there are numerous scholarly accounts of Creole life in New Orleans in the lead-up to the Civil War, the focus of studies on the Civil War has tended to be along Union–Confederacy lines or, indeed, racial ones, and there has been no dedicated consideration of Francophones' involvement in, or response to, the war.[28]

The Civil War strongly influenced the cultural production as well as the daily lives of Francophones of all backgrounds in New Orleans. The war coincided with a great boom in sheet music publication in nineteenth-century America,[29] and this continued to flourish in the South for much of the war, even if the region's output was by no means as large as that of the Union territories; numerous Civil War-related songs were published in New Orleans during the first half of the 1860s, in both English and French.[30] Most music published under the Confederacy projected a sense of Southern nationalism, whether or not it openly celebrated the Confederate cause. It is unsurprising, therefore, that Francophone composers writing this kind of music were almost

---

28 There has, however, been attention devoted to the impact of the Civil War on Louisiana's rural Francophone population. See Carl A. Brasseaux, *Acadian to Cajun: Transformation of a People, 1803–1877* (Jackson, MS: University Press of Mississippi, 1992).

29 Christian McWhirter, *Battle Hymns: The Power and Popularity of Music in the Civil War* (Chapel Hill: University of North Carolina Press, 2012), p. 1.

30 For more on sheet music production in occupied New Orleans, see Warren K. Kimball, 'Northern Musical Culture in Antebellum New Orleans' (unpublished PhD dissertation, Louisiana State University, 2017), p. 117.

exclusively White; while numerous composers of colour were working in New Orleans at the mid-century and in the Civil War years, I have not been able to find any published works by them that engaged expressly with the war, in either condemnation or support of the Confederacy.

A song called 'Brise du Sud' was published in the city in 1864, while New Orleans was occupied by Union forces.[31] Its text was by Louis Placide Canonge (1823–93) and music by Eugène Chassaignac (1820–78).[32] Chassaignac had come from France in the 1840s and was a music shop owner and composer in New Orleans who sometimes assisted the Théâtre d'Orléans with its recruiting of performers during that decade.[33] Canonge, on the other hand, was born in New Orleans in 1823, but went to Paris for his schooling. After returning to New Orleans in the late 1830s, he established a career as a journalist, poet, playwright, and, eventually, theatre director. Many of his plays received their first performances at the Théâtre d'Orléans.[34]

Chassaignac used a number of Canonge's poems as texts for his songs, and it is likely that, as Francophone men involved with the theatre, the two knew each other personally and potentially worked together. The song was very short: just a single verse, which was printed in both French and English. The text speaks of the southern breeze, bringing news of an absent beloved to the exiled speaker:

Balmy breeze of the South,	Brise qui viens du Sud
Dost thou bear upon thy wing	Portes-tu sur ton aîle [sic]
The ruins and the spoils from the poor exile torn?	Un débris des trésors ravis à l'exilé;
Dost thou waft to my soul	Celle par qui je vis
The sighs of her I loved	Oh! Dis-moi que fait elle;
To cheer this poor sad heart	Sais-tu combien de pleurs de ses yeux ont coulé?
All so long doomed to mourn?	Rends la vie a [sic] mon cœur qui meurt de ton silence;
Come, sweet breeze, come to me!	Au dessus [sic] de ma tête,
Ah, no more be thou silent	O brise, arrête-toi!
Come wave o'er me thy wing	Pour moi, peuple l'instant

---

31 New Orleans was captured by the Union army between 25 April and 1 May 1862, and it remained under Union control until the end of the war.

32 Eugène Chassaignac and Placide Canonge, 'Brise du Sud' (New Orleans: The Bronze Pen Press, 1864). The song's sheet music is held in Special Collections, Howard-Tilton Memorial Library, Tulane University.

33 For biographical information on Chassaignac, see Alfred E. Lemmon, 'Eugène Chassaignac' <https://64parishes.org/entry/eugene-chassaignac> [accessed 1 Jan. 2021].

34 Juliane Braun discusses Canonge's work in Creole Drama and explores his play France et Espagne on pp. 64–71.

American Identity and War in Francophone New Orleans   159

Infancy I would see	Le vide de l'absence;
Loved forms around me cling,	Brise qui viens du Sud, parle-moi! Parle-moi!
Never more to depart	Pour moi peuple l'instant le vide de l'absence;
Balmy breeze of the South, oh	Brise qui viens du Sud, Parle-moi!
speak to me! Speak to me!	Parle-moi![35]

While breezes, exile, and lost love were all popular themes in sentimental songs, the publication of 'Brise du Sud' in 1864 implies a rather more specific context: that the lovers had been separated by the Civil War. Indeed, the absent beloved of the song is perhaps a personification of the South – the speaker's home – rather than a human being.

The speaker's exact location is not clear from the poem, but he views himself as an exile. Many French-born people did indeed leave New Orleans temporarily during the Civil War. Among them were musicians, including Eugène Prévost, the Théâtre d'Orléans's long-term *chef d'orchestre*, who went back to Paris between 1862 and 1867.[36] As Charles Prosper Fauconnet, a French diplomat in New Orleans in the 1860s, noted, the occupying Union troops resolved to treat foreign-born residents of New Orleans as 'neutral' in the conflict only if they could prove that they were in the process of tying up their affairs and preparing to leave the United States.[37] Otherwise, if they refused to swear an oath of allegiance to the Federal government, they were presumed to be active supporters of the Confederacy. This left French-born residents in a life-changing bind: if they failed to make their political position clear, either they had to leave the city and country they had come to think of as home, or they risked conscription into the Confederate army and/or financial ruin.[38] After September 1861, the Confederacy targeted the businesses of foreign nationals living in the seceded states, preventing them from trading with enemies of the Confederacy.[39] A sense of uprootedness in this period, therefore, united Francophones who had been born on both sides of the Atlantic, and it is something that 'Brise du Sud' captures clearly.

Canonge himself – a staunch supporter of the Confederacy – experienced a period of exile during the Civil War: Edward Laroque Tinker claims that the Union general Nathaniel Banks banished him 'beyond the lines' as a result of his refusal to swear allegiance to the Federal government during the Union

---

35 Chassaignac and Canonge, 'Brise de Sud'.

36 Baron, *Concert Life in Nineteenth-Century New Orleans*, p. 181.

37 Charles Prosper Fauconnet, *Ruined by this Miserable War: The Dispatches of Charles Prosper Fauconnet, a French Diplomat in New Orleans, 1863–1868*, ed. Carl Brasseaux and Katherine Carmines Mooney (Knoxville: University of Tennessee Press, 2012), p. 41.

38 Brasseaux and Mooney, 'Introduction' to Fauconnet, *Ruined by the Miserable War*, pp. x–xx.

39 Stève Sainlaude, *France and the American Civil War: A Diplomatic History* (Chapel Hill: University of North Carolina Press, 2019), p. 89.

160   *Charlotte Bentley*

occupation of New Orleans from April 1862.[40] Where Canonge went in the first part of his exile is unclear, but in a letter dated 10 May 1865, Banks himself wrote that Canonge had been living in Mandeville (only thirty-five miles from New Orleans) for the past year, and he gave permission for Canonge to return to New Orleans briefly 'on parole', in order to travel on to Matamoros, Mexico.[41] Canonge's exile did not last long beyond the end of the war in April 1865, however, for on 16 September that year a local newspaper reported that he was offering tutoring in the French language back in New Orleans.[42] Appearing in 1864, then, 'Brise du Sud' was probably published while Canonge was in Mandeville, prevented from entering the city of his birth. Chassaignac registered the song with the clerk's office of the district court of Louisiana that year, but I have not been able to establish whether he, too, was forbidden from entering New Orleans, or whether he had been able to avoid such a punishment.[43]

'Brise du Sud' nonetheless expresses themes of both physical and spiritual exile: it is not simply about geographical absence, but also about a nostalgic longing for times past, for an old South without either the destruction or the social change wrought by the Civil War. Such a sense of nostalgia is particularly evident in the English version of the poem (by no means an exact translation of Canonge's French), where the speaker looks back to his childhood ('Infancy I would see / Loved forms around me cling, / Never more to depart'). Nostalgia pervaded songs written across the United States in the post-Civil War era, and Lee Glazer and Susan Key have shown how Northern and Southern writers, composers, and visual artists alike frequently looked back to an idealised past in their works.[44] As Glazer and Key also demonstrate, a similar sense of longing also marked many earlier artistic efforts, and post-Civil War works frequently 'reiterated both the images and the sense of loss already present in an antebellum classic like Stephen Foster's "Old Folks at Home"'.[45] Such nostalgia reveals less about the place and time recalled than it does about the authors' and composers' desire to remake that past and use it anew in the present.

In exploring themes of exile and isolation, 'Brise du Sud' stands apart from most other songs published in the Confederate South. The majority were mil-

---

40 Edward Larocque Tinker, *Les Écrits de langue française en Louisiane au XIX siècle* (Paris: Librairie Ancienne Honoré Champion, 1932), pp. 67, 73.

41 Letter from General Nathaniel Banks, 10 May 1865, 'Union Provost Marshall's File of Papers Relating to Individual Citizens, compiled 1861–1867', National Archives, Washington, DC.

42 *Daily Picayune*, 16 Sept. 1865.

43 Chassaignac had written the music for at least ten overtly patriotic songs in support of the Confederacy in the first two years of the Civil War, so he was unlikely to have avoided the repercussions under Union occupation.

44 Lee Glazer and Susan Key, 'Carry Me Back: Nostalgia for the Old South in Nineteenth-Century Popular Culture', *Journal of American Studies*, 30:1 (April 1996), 1–24, at p. 1.

45 Glazer and Key, 'Carry Me Back', p. 2.

itary and often triumphant in tone; even those that expressed feelings of separation and loss were often presented as a way of boosting morale on the home front.[46] And yet little about 'Brise du Sud' could be thought of either as presenting a spirit of optimism about the outcome of the conflict or empowering the performers and listeners to resist occupation or exile. Instead, it positions the speaker, exiled either spiritually or physically, as a victim, powerless and forced simply to wait for news and dream of home.

'Brise du Sud' diverges from many other Civil War songs not only in its emphasis on impotence, despair, and interiority rather than community-making power, but also in its generic context. Indeed, the genre designation at the head of this song marks it as belonging to a specifically French musical lineage: 'mélodie'. Whether the designation was added by Chassaignac or Canonge, or whether it was added later by the publisher, it gives us an insight into the way this song's Francophone heritage was positioned for its consumers. The *mélodie* emerged in France from the 1830s (although its fullest flowering did not take place until the final quarter of the century) as a more harmonically complex and often technically demanding form than the ubiquitous *romance*. 'Brise du Sud', however, is largely unsophisticated in its musical realisation, with a simple and predominantly diatonic piano part. Nonetheless, it does bear traces of the *mélodie* genre, particularly in the way the numerous expression and tempo markings in the vocal line lend it something of a declamatory feel, rather than that of a balanced or contrived melody. The designation 'mélodie' in this case, however, had perhaps less to do with the musical substance and more to do with encouraging listeners and performers to perceive a greater sense of artistic ambition in 'Brise du Sud' than in other popular (and largely Anglophone) Civil War songs.[47] It implies a certain sense of the song's being 'art music': it aestheticises the experience of the war exile, rather than actively encouraging listeners to rally behind a particular cause.

Exile was a fairly common theme in both French song and stage works throughout the nineteenth century and, while I have not found any indication of a specific model for 'Brise du Sud', the notion of exile within the song may well have had a broader frame of reference than simply the Civil War conflict. Indeed, the song might speak not simply of exile from the Confederate South, but also of separation from an older French homeland. The song's attitude towards patriotic sentiments is decidedly transnational and deliberately ambivalent, in a way that is particularly evident in its final bars. After the double bar at the end of the verse, Chassaignac appends an extra four bars, unconnected to the previous material. This little four-bar coda contains a two-bar allusion to the *Marseillaise* (ex. 4.2).

---

46 McWhirter, *Battle Hymns*, p. 84.

47 Jacqueline Leary-Warsaw discusses French art song and its composition in New Orleans in 'Nineteenth-Century French Art Song of New Orleans: A Repertoire Study' (unpublished PhD dissertation, Peabody Institute of the Johns Hopkins University, 2000). She mentions 'Brise du Sud' briefly on pp. 159–61.

Example 4.2. Four-bar coda alluding to the *Marseillaise* in 'Brise du Sud' by Eugène Chassaignac. New Orleans: The Bronze Pen Press, 1864.

'Brise du Sud' was certainly not the only piece published in Civil War-era America to make use of this tune: Armard Blackmar (1826–88), a New Orleans publisher, for example, wrote his own words to the tune and named it the 'Southern Marseillaise' (1861).[48] As Lawrence Abel has pointed out, it was the revolutionary associations of the story behind the *Marseillaise* that attracted American attention, with many Southerners drawing comparisons between the French Revolution and the Civil War.[49] Indeed, people from both the Union and the Confederacy related to and appropriated the *Marseillaise* as a reminder of what they saw as the noble cause of the French Revolution during the Civil War. Canonge himself had written new text to the *Marseillaise* melody in 1861.[50]

In 'Brise du Sud', however, the allusion to the *Marseillaise* is not loud or triumphant, but rather, as Chassaignac marks it, an 'echo', in *pp* and *ppp*. Although it is an 'echo', it is not an afterthought, but rather a carefully placed reminder that, behind the calm contemplation of the song, the revolutionary spirit would not be extinguished. Here, Chassaignac's reaching for the French song could be read in multiple ways: as a pragmatic gesture to increase a work's appeal in popular song markets of the time; as an encouraging gesture to the Confederate cause; or, perhaps, as having some personal expressive signifi-

---

48   Lawrence E. Abel, *Singing the New Nation: How Music Shaped the Confederacy, 1861–1865* (Mechanicsburg, PA: Stackpole Books, 2000), pp. 77–8.
49   Abel, *Singing the New Nation*, pp. 77–8. Abel also notes how the song 'Maryland, My Maryland' – a rallying cry to persuade the state of Maryland to join the Confederate cause – came to be nicknamed the 'American Marseillaise' (pp. 67–80). Furthermore, Leary-Warsaw briefly discusses the use of the *Marseillaise* in 'Nineteenth-Century French Art Song of New Orleans', pp. 49–51.
50   Canonge's version was called 'La Louisiane: Chant patriotique sur l'air de la Marseillais [*sic*]' and was published by Sourdes et Chassaignac.

cance. The echo might be a sign of hope for the nostalgic speaker, or it might be one of despair, of hope draining away, as his ideals of liberty and republicanism – which many White Creoles believed the Confederacy represented – are replaced with the individual's sorrow and nostalgia. For Chassaignac, as a Frenchman more recently settled in the United States, the quotation of the *Marseillaise*, a song that had been so closely associated with his birth nation's revolutionary and republican past (and which, at the time of publication of 'Brise du Sud', was actually banned in Napoléon III's France) may well have served more as a reminder of the small but inextinguishable flame of revolutionary potential and the entwined republican histories of France and the United States. His music hints at a larger world beyond the warring Union and Confederacy, in which the spectre of revolution had never quite disappeared.

The spectre of revolution and its transnational manifestations may well have been on a French-born Francophone's mind in 1864. Back in France, attitudes to the Confederacy varied. Although France officially maintained an impartial stance in the conflict, Stève Sainlaude has suggested that Napoléon III's personal inclinations and those of some of his most prominent government officials were towards the independence of the South.[51] Those in favour argued that the Confederacy was not only upholding the right to free trade, but opening the way for Pan-Latin, as opposed to Anglo-Saxon, economic dominance in the Western hemisphere.[52] Francophone cotton merchants on both sides of the Atlantic whose livelihoods were endangered by the Civil War would doubtless have agreed.[53]

The French military intervention in Mexico from 1862 and Napoléon III's installation of Maximilian I as Emperor of Mexico in April 1864 complicated matters further: France, whose earlier republican ideals were reflected in the *Marseillaise*, was now responsible for challenging and attempting to destroy the republican status of Mexico and to bring the country into a quasi-imperial relationship with France. Both Chassaignac and Canonge would probably have been aware that their Francophone identity and the sense of separation and nostalgia expressed in 'Brise du Sud' was shaped transnationally, by global geopolitics as much as by internal conflict in the United States.

---

51 Sainlaude, *France and the American Civil War*, p. 83.

52 Sainlaude, *France and the American Civil War*, p. 83.

53 For the heated discussions in the French press concerning 'the Cotton *Crise*', whereby the Civil War prevented European cotton mills from receiving Confederacy-produced cotton in 1863, see George McCoy Blackburn, *French Newspaper Opinion on the American Civil War* (Westport, CT: Greenwood Press, 1997), pp. 73–90.

La Louisiane and the End of Reconstruction

Confederate defeat in the Civil War was followed by a lengthy period of Reconstruction, which sought to transform the former South through the abolition of slavery and the reintegration of the seceded states into the Union.[54] The economy of the South lay in ruins, and in the ensuing political and social turmoil, New Orleans's Francophones found themselves further marginalised: rules introduced in 1864 stated that all school teaching had to take place in English, and in 1868 the imposed Federal government decreed that all the state's legal and judicial affairs should be conducted and recorded in English only.[55]

Nonetheless, Francophones continued to express themselves in their mother tongue in creative forms. When Reconstruction ended and the final Federal troops withdrew, Francophone poets and composers in the city celebrated. In 1877, Placide Canonge provided the text for a song entitled 'Le Réveil de la Louisiane'.[56] The song's cover stated that it commemorated 24 April of that year: the date of the withdrawal of Federal troops from Louisiana and the beginning of Louisiana's return to self-governance.[57] In terms of race relations and civil rights, the withdrawal would prove to be disastrous, but Louisiana's regained freedom was nevertheless a source of joy for the city's Creoles at the time. The song's first verse reads:

Listen, it is no longer a dream!	Ecoutez, ce n'est plus un rêve!
Listen to these powerful voices	Ecoutez ces puissantes voix!
An immense Hosanna goes up	Un immense hosanna s'élève
From South and North at the same time	Du Sud et du Nord à la fois!
Louisiana, proud queen,	Louisiane, fière reine,
Straighten up your unbeaten brow	Redresse ton front indompté
It is the head, oh my sovereign	C'est la tête, o ma souveraine,
The head of liberty	La tête de ta liberté!
Erect, let the banner wave	Debout! Fais flotter ta bannière
Reinvigorated, reborn at once	Renais à la force, à la foi
And in the torrents of light	Et dans des torrents de lumière

---

54 This process began before the end of the war in 1863, in Union-occupied areas of the South. For more on New Orleans during Reconstruction, see Justin A. Nystrom, *New Orleans after the Civil War: Race, Politics, and a New Birth of Freedom* (Baltimore: Johns Hopkins University Press, 2010).

55 See Jay Gitlin, *The Bourgeois Frontier: French Towns, French Traders, and American Expansion* (New Haven: Yale University Press, 2010), p. 166.

56 Gregorio Curto and Placide Canonge, 'Le Réveil de la Louisiane' (New Orleans: Henri Wehrmann, 1877).

57 Whether the song was actually published on 24 April 1877 is not clear, however. The date itself passed with little special pomp in the local press.

Oh my country, awake Louisiana	O mon pays, réveille-toi Louisiane,
Awake!	Eveille-toi![58]

The song presents the North and South of the United States, so recently divided in the Civil War, coming together at the end of Reconstruction. Louisiana is depicted as regal and a defender of freedom, which has been sleeping since the early 1860s. For Canonge, this was a long-awaited moment, and in the further four verses he goes on to evoke this awakening with a plethora of religious and mythological imagery, apostrophising God, and writing of passing archangels.

Its music was by Gregorio Curto, a Spaniard by birth, who had originally come to New Orleans in the 1830s to sing as a bass in the Théâtre d'Orléans troupe and who was very much an honorary Francophone.[59] Marked 'tempo di marcia' and with fanfare figures in the right hand of the piano, the piece was designed to sound triumphant. As well as the vocal soloist, it also includes a repeated section for three-part chorus, with the option of omitting this section and cutting straight to the final piano coda for solo performances. The inclusion of the chorus parts supports the ideas of unity expressed in the piece: the reunion of the South and the North is symbolised by the move from solo to collective voices.

The desire Canonge expresses in this poem, however, is not simply for a united America, but rather for a specifically Louisianian identity. The state of Louisiana emerges as sovereign in this poem (indeed, the French word Canonge uses is 'pays'), rather than as part of a larger nation, and the state's role in shaping a sense of identity and belonging is emphasised: Louisiana becomes both *pays* and *patrie*. Furthermore, unlike Canonge's earlier 'Brise du Sud', 'Le Réveil de la Louisiane' was written solely in French. Gone is the English-language translation that had shadowed the French text in earlier songs, and it is not hard to imagine that the Louisianian identity Canonge envisaged now that Reconstruction was over was a specifically Francophone one.

This desire for Francophone exclusivity likely stemmed partly from dissatisfaction with the outcome of the Civil War and the hardships of the Reconstruction period, but it had already been in evidence to an extent from the early 1860s. In the literary sphere, local Francophone authors sought to create a sense of Creole nationalism both to distance themselves from the Anglophone North and the ideals of the Union and, later, to attempt to undo some of the ways in which Union occupation and then imposed Federal government had marginalised the French language in Louisiana.[60] Visions of Creole nationalism from the early 1860s were by no means exclusively White: *La Renaissance*

---

58 Curto and Canonge, 'Le Réveil de la Louisiane'. My translation.

59 For biographical information on Curto, see Baron, *Concert Life in Nineteenth-Century New Orleans*, pp. 146–63.

60 Rien Fertel, *Imagining the Creole City: The Rise of Literary Culture in Nineteenth-Century New Orleans* (Baton Rouge: Louisiana State University Press, 2014), pp. 49–70.

Louisianaise, an influential Creole periodical founded in 1861, featured among its original contributors a number of free men of colour, who shared with their White colleagues a Francophone education (often received in France). It offered for a brief moment a glimpse of a pan-racial Creole nationalism built on identification with and birth in Louisiana, but it, like other publications in that decade, quickly became a White-Francophone mouthpiece, often putting forward highly racist viewpoints.[61]

In the aftermath of the Civil War, Creole intellectuals began to wonder if Franco-Louisianian identity might be fundamentally incompatible with a broader sense of belonging to the United States. As Rien Fertel has observed, even during the Civil War, Creole authors began to feel that it was impossible to 'reconcile American citizenship with Louisiana Patriotism'.[62] For Canonge, as for many other Creole authors, the utopian future he imagined in which the French language was no longer marginalised would have to be negotiated carefully so as not to descend into self-indulgent nostalgia either for the antebellum period or for the more distant past and the days of 'la Nouvelle France'. As Fertel has put it, they felt that 'a Southern ascendance [...] would create "a unity and harmony" for Louisiana's Francophones, a place and people unfailingly "set in her traditions, enveloped in her memories [...] almost entirely in her past, a stranger to the progress and the spirit of her times"'.[63]

Other Francophone writers and musicians, however, particularly those born in France rather than in Louisiana, presented rather different hopes and fears for what the future would hold, both for America and for their identity as Francophones within it. Hubert Rolling, who was born in Alsace in 1824 and who moved to New Orleans in 1841,[64] produced a piece called 'Le Réveil' in 1877, which also commemorated the withdrawal of Federal troupes from Louisiana.[65] The words of his song (by Professor E. Berté-St-Ange)[66] do not, unlike Canonge's, celebrate Louisiana and its sovereignty, but rather the 'awakening' of the people of the South at large. In this vision, Louisiana is part of the South as a whole, which the authors see as being firmly part of the United States. The

---

61 Fertel, *Imagining the Creole City*, p. 62.

62 Emile Hiriart, 'La Renaissance Louisianaise', *La Renaissance Louisianaise*, 5 May 1861, pp. 1–2, quoted in Fertel, *Imagining the Creole City*, p. 61.

63 Fertel, *Imagining the Creole City*, p. 60.

64 John Baron includes a brief chapter on Rolling and a list of his compositions in *Concert Life in Nineteenth-Century New Orleans*, pp. 197–204.

65 Hubert Rolling and E. Berté-St-Ange, 'Le Réveil: Chanson patriotique' (New Orleans: F. Charpaux, 1877). The sheet music can be accessed in Tulane University's Digital Library.

66 Berté-St-Ange was born in France and served in the French marines before his arrival in Louisiana. He was an early professor of French at Louisiana State University. Barry C. Cowan, *Louisiana State University* (Charleston, SC: Arcadia Publishing, 2013), p. 49.

American Identity and War in Francophone New Orleans   167

text goes on to situate Louisiana historically, mentioning Washington and then the 'American star', and asks the new president of the United States, Rutherford B. Hayes (inaugurated on 4 March 1877), to guide the South back to prosperity. The text also speaks of 'the continent' and of extending a hand to others: to illustrate the point of a united America, the cover lithograph shows a pair of entwined United States flags and, above them, a small image of two joined hands (fig. 4.1).

This striking cover design was echoed in another publication of the same year: Jules Cartier's 'Les Gardes Lafayette de la Nouvelle-Orléans! Chanson patriotique', which gives out another different message about both its author's ideas of Franco-American identity and the future of Louisiana.[67] The two entwined flags are highly similar to those on the cover of Rolling's piece, but in this instance they are not twin American flags but one American and one French *tricolore* (fig. 4.2).

The text reads:

We are all worthy sons of France	Nous sommes tous dignes fils de la France,
And we follow the glorious flag	Et nous suivons son drapeau glorieux
In upholding this sweet hope	En conservant cette douce espérance
That we will always be victorious	Que nous serons toujours victorieux
We defend also America	Nous défendrons aussi de l'Amérique
Peace, glory, and prosperity	La paix, la gloire, et la prospérité
As the standard of this republic	Car l'étendard de cette république
Already knows our loyalty!	Connait déjà notre fidélité!
You see it, our civic guard	Vous le voyez, notre garde civique
Join the French flag in three colours	Joint le drapeau français aux trois couleurs
To the starred standard of America	A l'étendard étoilé d'Amérique
Encourage your brave defenders.	Encouragez vos braves défenseurs.

---

67 Jules Cartier and Fernand d'Héramberg, 'Les Gardes Lafayette de la Nouvelle-Orléans!' (New Orleans: Henri Wehrmann, n.d. [1877]). The engravers' plate numbers stamped on the sheet music show that this was produced later in the year than both the aforementioned pieces entitled 'Le Réveil'. (The sheet music can be viewed online in Tulane University's Digital Library.) An orchestral version of the chanson was performed at a benefit performance for the 'Gardes Lafayette de la Nouvelle-Orléans' at the French Opera House on 10 November 1877. The 'Gardes Lafayette' were probably a militia group in the city. I have been unable to trace any concrete information about the group, but it could perhaps have been the unit that a local newspaper, the *Daily Picayune*, referred to in English as the 'Lafayette Avenue Guards' whose aim was 'to assist their fellow men in wrenching the State and the city from the hands of tyrants and oppressors'. 'Banner presentations of the Lafayette Avenue Guards', *Daily Picayune*, 3 Sept. 1876. Whoever the members were, their decision to include 'Lafayette' in their name hints at connections back to old Franco-American alliances during the American Revolution.

Figure 4.1. Cover of 'Le Réveil: Chanson patriotique' by Hubert Rolling and E. Berté-St-Ange. New Orleans: F. Charpaux, 1877. William Ransom Hogan Jazz Archive, Howard-Tilton Memorial Library, Tulane University.

Figure 4.2. Cover of 'Les Gardes Lafayette de la Nouvelle-Orléans!' by Jules Cartier and Fernand d'Héramberg. New Orleans: Henri Wehrmann, n.d. [1877]. William Ransom Hogan Jazz Archive, Howard-Tilton Memorial Library, Tulane University.

Oh Louisiana, in conserving glory	O Louisiane, en conservant la gloire
We support the honour of your flag	Nous soutenons l'honneur de ton drapeau
And recall the memorable history of Lafayette and Rochambeau	Et rappelons la mémorable histoire de . Lafayette et du grand Rochambeau
Always in France, they say: nobility obliges	Toujours en France, on dit: Noblesse oblige
We who must follow two standards	Nous qui devons suivre deux étendards
And maintain unceasingly their prestige	Et maintenir sans cesse leur prestige
We will all be real Bayards.	Nous saurons tous être de vrais Bayards.[68]

In keeping with the cover illustration, the relationship between Louisiana and France is key to this song. Calling Louisiana's residents 'worthy sons of France' and invoking the involvement of 'Lafayette and Rochambeau', it draws on a special Franco-American relationship from the eighteenth century to direct its imaginings of the final decades of the nineteenth. For these authors, it was not a developing sense of Creole nationality that would determine the future of both Louisiana and the United States (and, therefore, the role of the Francophone within them), but rather a turning back to an older set of shared ideals of liberty, equality, and brotherhood that had formed an initial connection between France and the United States.

The Francophone composers considered here – Creole and foreign French – used their experiences of conflict in the New World to understand themselves sometimes simultaneously and sometimes by turns as French, American, and Louisianian. While in the early years of the century this negotiation of Francophone identity most often amounted to laying aside local linguistic conflicts and identifying as American in the face of a defined external threat, in the aftermath of the Civil War and Reconstruction Francophones began to question whether they could ever be fully part of the American nation. While some composers continued to attempt to forge a sense of Francophone/Anglo-American unity, the period saw a split between a sign of Franco-American identity based on older ideals of liberty, equality, and brotherhood shared between France and the United States and a newly conceived sense of Creole nationalism, separate from and resistant to incorporation into the United States.

If, as Mary Favret has suggested, wartime 'is a present experience handed down from a past uncertain of its future', these Francophone musical evocations of and responses to war reveal simultaneously a set of possibilities (of varying degrees of optimism) for an imagined future and an unshakeable

---

68 'Cartier and d'Héramberg, 'Les Gardes Lafayette'. My translation. The last line probably refers to Pierre Terrail, seigneur de Bayard (1473–1524), who was a French chevalier frequently described as 'le chevalier sans peur' and 'le chevalier sans reproche'. Guyard de Berville's *Histoire de Bayard* (1760) was reprinted multiple times in the early nineteenth century, reflecting how the noble medieval knight remained an important and popular part of the Francophone cultural imagination.

sense of nostalgia for a utopian Franco-American Republic.[69] Looking at these Francophone poets' and composers' responses to war suggests that their conception of Francophone identity – be it on a local, national, or regional level – remained ultimately transnational, rooted in experiences that crossed national boundaries and extended across generations, linking past, present, and future.

69 Favret, *War at a Distance*, p. 5.

5

'The Most Seductive Creole Indolence':
Louis Moreau Gottschalk in the French Press

Laura Moore Pruett

The American Gottschalk:
Questions of *créolité*, Race and Identity

In its 13 April 1845 issue, *Le Ménestrel* published one of the earliest mentions of Louis Moreau Gottschalk (1829–69) in a French periodical. At the time, he was one month shy of his sixteenth birthday. Misspelling his surname as 'Gottschalb', the journal briefly summarised, 'A pianist of the greatest merit, Mr. Gottschalk, was heard last week at the Salle Pleyel. He played Chopin, Thalberg, and Liszt, so as to merit a first place among our virtuosos'.[1] By March 1849, just under four years later, the journal *La Musique: Gazette de la France musicale* published an extended although unattributed paean to Gottschalk and his composition *Bamboula*. Its author contended,

> You have to be creole, composer and performer, to feel and be able to understand all the originality of *Bamboula*. We have discovered this Creole composer; an American composer, my God! But yes, and a pianist-composer, performing of the highest order, who is still known only in the aristocratic salons of Paris, and whose name soon will have a great impact [...]. His name is Gottschalk.[2]

---

1   'Un pianiste du plus grand mérite, M. Gottschalb [*sic*], s'est fait entendre la semaine dernière chez Pleyel. Il a joué du Chopin, du Thalberg et du Listz [*sic*], de manière à mériter une première place parmi nos virtuoses': *Le Ménestrel: Journal musique, littérature, modes et théâtres*, 582 (13 April 1845), 4. All translations are mine unless otherwise noted.

2   'Il faut être créole, compositeur et exécutant, pour sentir et bien faire comprendre toute l'originalité du *Bamboula*. Ce compositeur créole, nous l'avons découvert; un compositeur américain, bon Dieu! Mais oui, et un pianiste compositeur, exécutant de premier ordre, qui n'est encore connu que dans les salons aristocratiques de Paris, et dont le nom bientôt aura un grand retentissement [...]. Son nom est Gottschakl [*sic*]':

Louis Moreau Gottschalk in the French Press   173

The numerous appearances of the word 'Creole' in this review, considered at length later in this chapter, presage decades of reviews in the French press of Gottschalk's performances and compositions, continuing well after his departure from Paris, in language that both highlighted his Creole heritage and underscored the romantic nature and technical challenges of many of his works.

'Creole' is slippery to define; its meaning is dependent upon the circumstances and contexts of the person or thing to which it is meant to refer. In eighteenth- and nineteenth-century Louisiana, 'Creole' was a loosely defined and wide-ranging term that generally applied to people of any racial heritage – European, African, Native American, or any mixture thereof – who were born in Louisiana.[3] To the French audiences and critics who first encountered Gottschalk and his music in the 1840s, however, the word carried additional implications; not only applicable to Louisiana-born United States citizens, it could also refer to citizens of the French Caribbean, West Indies, or Antilles colonies as well. The French understanding of the concept of 'créole' – in contrast to the Louisianan interpretation of the same term – was further fraught with complex constructions of exoticism and barbarism, spectacle and nostalgia, especially in its connections with Blackness and colonialism.

For many years following the Louisiana Purchase of 1803, French writers continued to mourn the failed prospect of a new French Empire in the Americas, 'la Nouvelle France'. The loss of the gem of the colonial New World islands, the lucrative sugar-producing Saint-Domingue, also figured into this sense of bereavement. Ruth Rosenberg writes about the 'misgivings about the failure of France's colonial ventures in the Americas' experienced by Frenchmen who travelled abroad in the early nineteenth century.[4] 'Reminders of the "lost" new France were omnipresent', she remarks, 'and had taken on a particular, melancholy significance'.[5] (See Chapter 7 on 'sonic memories' of the New World.) The resultant 'sense of historical disorientation and rupture expressed as longing for the past and uncertainty about the future' surely kindled a complicated

---

'Le Bamboula: Un Pianiste américain', *La Musique: Gazette de la France musicale* (11 March 1849), 75–6. Repr. in *La Sylphide: Journal des modes, de littérature, de théâtres et de musique*, 8:15 (30 May 1849), 2–3.

3   The history of the word's etymology and applications in this Louisiana-focused context, including implications of both race and class, has been thoroughly examined. See, for example, Arnold R. Hirsch, *Creole New Orleans: Race and Americanization* (Baton Rouge: Louisiana State University Press, 1992); Andrew Jolivette, *Louisiana Creoles: Cultural Recovery and Mixed-Race Native American Identity* (Lanham, MD: Lexington Books, 2007); Connie Eble, 'Creole in Louisiana', *South Atlantic Review*, 73:2 (Spring 2008), 39–53; and Sybil Kein (ed.), *Creole: The History and Legacy of Louisiana's Free People of Color* (Baton Rouge: Louisiana State University Press, 2000).

4   Ruth E. Rosenberg, 'Among Compatriots and Savages: The Music of France's Lost Empire', *The Musical Quarterly*, 95:1 (Spring 2012), 36–70.

5   Rosenberg, 'Among Compatriots and Savages', p. 37.

perspective and understanding of 'Creole' on the part of French citizens.[6] In particular, it would certainly influence perceptions about Gottschalk, a Creole musician from Louisiana with a heritage intimately tied to the lost sugar plantations of Saint-Domingue.

The New Orleans-born composer and pianist spoke French at home and trained in Paris as a young man. Although Gottschalk departed France in late 1852 to begin touring in the Americas, the French press continued to follow his career. While French critics often focused on the Creole attributes of his compositions, they also celebrated the elegance and grace of his performances, frequently linking him to Chopin, another adopted son. Though both benefited from a warm embrace in Paris, Gottschalk's Creole, French colonial identity perhaps made him a different type of adoptee, one who was less 'foreign' than the Eastern European Chopin. As a composer who consciously embraced a wide range of musical inspirations, from Italian opera arias to Cuban *habanera* rhythms and patriotic hymns to American minstrel songs, Gottschalk had an allure which was the simultaneous presence of the familiar and the Other. This cultural meshing appealed to a cosmopolitan, bourgeois French identity, which was fascinated by the concept of the 'Creole Other' while also subsuming it within a larger concept of 'Frenchness', a complicated notion in and of itself amid national upheaval and revolution in the mid-nineteenth century.

In this chapter, I examine the construction in the French press of a dual identity for Gottschalk: critics highlighted his distinctive Creole heritage in the New World, while also celebrating his connections to the continental French Romantic style – the civilised music of cultivation, at least in the minds of these French reviewers. Drawing upon aspects of Gottschalk's own blended identity as a New Orleans-born Francophone with maternal roots in Saint-Domingue and using musical analysis of piano works frequently mentioned in the reviews, including *Bamboula*, I examine the interplay of Black Creole symbols in this and other works of the 'Louisiana Quartet', juxtaposed with the Francophone or White Creole image of Gottschalk himself as described in the French press. Because of the tensions and contradictions inherent in his heritage as a White French Creole, the negotiations of race palpable in his musical images of Black Creole culture of Louisiana and the Caribbean, and his adaptations of the aesthetics of a Romantic pianist, Gottschalk is an exceptionally complex figure in the French imagination of America.

Gottschalk as *créole* and *français* in New Orleans and Paris

While Creoles of all races and classes inhabited a much wider geographical area, New Orleans remained a central locus for much of the nineteenth century. Musical and artistic culture in the city was largely shaped by the French-speak-

---

6   Rosenberg, 'Among Compatriots and Savages', p. 37.

ing community, including families whose ancestors were immigrants from France as well as those who had come as refugees from the Haitian Revolution (1791–1804).[7] Louis Moreau and his siblings were, in a way, part of both groups. They were undoubtedly Creole by the Louisianan definition of the term, although their parents were not. Louis Moreau's father Edward Gottschalk (1795–1853) was born and raised in London, an Ashkenazi Jewish businessman of German and English origins.[8] His mother Aimée Bruslé (1808–56), on the other hand, was from a French family who had settled as plantation owners in Saint-Domingue (the future Haiti), but was uprooted as a result of the Haitian Revolution; her father fought as a captain in the British army against the uprising led by Toussaint Louverture and other slave leaders. Along with thousands of others from both sides of the conflict, the Bruslé family fled Saint-Domingue in 1793 and, after several years as *émigrés* in Jamaica, resettled in New Orleans with their household slaves in 1804. Edward and Aimée married in 1828; the first of their six children, Louis Moreau, was born the following year.

Gottschalk later recalled learning the troubled tale of his mother's family history in a journal entry dated June 1857. Sailing past Haiti on a boat destined for St Thomas, he

> contemplated the desolate country that opened out before me. [...] Everything, and more especially the name of Santo Domingo [Saint-Domingue], seemed to speak to my imagination by recalling to me the bloody episodes of the insurrection, so closely associated with my childhood memories. When very young, I never tired of hearing my grandmother relate the terrible strife that our family, like all the rest of the colonists, had to sustain at this epoch; the narrative of the massacre at the cape, and the combat fought in the hills by my great-grandfather against the Negroes of Gonaïves.[9]

Recounting his family's near-decimation at the hands of 'the bands of Biassou', he then expressed empathy for the slave revolt, asking,

> Can anyone, however, be astonished at the retaliation exercised by the Negroes on their old masters? What cause, moreover, more legitimate than that of this people, rising in their agony in one grand effort to reconquer their unacknowledged rights and their rank in humanity? [...] From the bosom of this world which crumbles away, rises, sombre and

---

7   See Juliane Braun, *Creole Drama: Theatre and Society in Antebellum New Orleans* (Charlottesville: University of Virginia Press, 2019), especially chapter 1, 'Circum-Atlantic Theatrical Relations: The Emergence of the Francophone Stage in a Spanish City'.

8   Gottschalk's life and ancestry have been well documented in the literature, especially the seminal biography, S. Frederick Starr, *Bamboula! The Life and Times of Louis Moreau Gottschalk* (New York: Oxford University Press, 1995); see pp. 19–21 especially.

9   Louis Moreau Gottschalk, *Notes of a Pianist*, ed. Jeanne Behrend (New York: Knopf, 1964), p. 10. All spellings, capitalisations, and punctuation appear as in original.

imposing, the grand form of Toussaint l'Overture [*sic*], the enthusiastic liberator of a race that nineteen centuries of Christianity had not yet been able to free from the yoke of its miseries.[10]

Gottschalk's ambivalent and multivalent French-American-Creole identity was further complicated by the facts of his father's activities as landowner and slave-owner in New Orleans and keeper of a mistress named Judith Rubio, who was commonly identified as a mulatta, bore several half-siblings to Louis Moreau, and also retained her own slaves (later sold by Edward following his bankruptcy). This identity, partly bound to his family's complex, conflicted racialised past, certainly related to France's own paradoxical relationships to race and slavery in the New World. From this perspective, his lived, private identity actually seems to mirror the multivalent, race-tinged public identity assigned to him by, and traceable in, the French press.

Throughout his life, Moreau tended to reject or at least obscure the English and Jewish parts of his ethnic heritage while embracing the French aspects, perhaps reflecting a desire to absorb the aesthetic and artistic sophistication often associated with Parisian tastes.[11] Life in New Orleans, of course, encouraged his Francophone predilection: though educated at an English-speaking private school, he received individual tutelage in French from a native speaker and spoke mostly French with his mother and siblings, as did many Creoles in the city. Gottschalk continued to write in French throughout his life, using his first language in his private journals, later collected, translated, and published as *Notes of a Pianist*.[12] Many of his compositions were published with French or Francophone-related titles, even when printed in the Americas.

As proved true for many musicians born in the United States, the Gottschalks soon realised that European training would be a necessary component of his musical education. Louis Moreau first travelled to France in May 1841, having just turned twelve. His New Orleans piano instructor Narcisse Letellier had explained to his parents there was no more he could teach the

---

10 Gottschalk, *Notes*, pp. 12–13. On Louverture and Biassou, see Chapter 1.

11 Edward Gottschalk's father, Lazer ben Gottschalk Levi, is believed to have been the son of Anglo-Jewish philosopher Eliakim ben Abraham, also known as Jacob Hart (1756–1814). His mother, Jane Harris, was a German Jewish immigrant to England. Edward was born in London in 1795 and emigrated to New Orleans around 1823 in search of economic advancement. See Bertram W. Korn, *A Note on the Jewish Ancestry of Louis Moreau Gottschalk, American Pianist and Composer* (Philadelphia: Maurice Jacobs, Inc., 1963); repr. from *American Jewish Archives*, 15:2 (Nov. 1963), 117–19. The Gottschalk children were raised in the Catholic faith tradition in New Orleans. See Starr, *Bamboula*, p. 33.

12 Louis Moreau Gottschalk, 'Pocket Diaries, 28 June–31 July 1863, 22 February–1 April 1864 and 20 April–11 May 1864', holographs in pencil, Music Division, The New York Public Library for the Performing Arts.

child, and encouraged them to continue his studies in Paris. And so, after a benefit concert to raise the necessary travel funding, the young man sailed alone on the steamship *Taglioni* and settled in Paris, living and learning at a private boarding school run by the Dussert family.

Gottschalk began lessons in piano with Camille Stamaty and composition with Pierre Maleden after the piano director of the Paris Conservatoire, Pierre Zimmerman, had refused to admit him. In his journal, Louis Moreau recorded Zimmerman's declaration that 'America was only a country of steam engines', an unfavourable prejudgement on all students hailing from the United States.[13] Yet he settled into his new bourgeois milieu with ease, attending masked balls with Madame Dussert and arranging for his portrait to be painted and sent to his family. His mother Aimée joined him in Paris two years later with his six younger siblings, including his sister Clara, who spent her later years collating and publishing her brother's music and diary. Aimée remained in Paris for the rest of her life, except for one return visit to New Orleans in 1846 that produced another son, Gaston.[14]

Gottschalk's first performances were well attended by amateur music-lovers and professional critics alike; reviews from the late 1840s and early 1850s attest to the overwhelmingly positive reception of both his technically challenging yet enchanting compositions and his flashy, virtuosic stage presence. Take, for instance, the rhapsodic review by P.-A. Fiorentino for *Le Corsaire* in March 1851: 'The big surprise and the main attraction of the evening was Gottschalk. To tell you of the enthusiasm he excited [...] would be impossible. [...] I will not allow myself to analyse this talent so original, so poetic, and so marvellous. After Gottschalk, you have to pull the ladder.'[15]

Negotiations of Race in the 'Louisiana Quartet' for Composer and Audiences

When Gottschalk made his Parisian debut with his 'Louisiana Quartet' in 1849, French associations with Creole culture and race in Louisiana and the former French island colonies had taken on new meaning and relevance, just months after the second and final abolition of slavery in the turbulent early

---

13 'l'Amérique n'était qu'un pays de machines à vapeur' (translation by the composer): Gottschalk, *Notes*, p. 52.

14 Biographical details in this paragraph come largely from Starr, *Bamboula*, pp. 44–9.

15 'Mais la grande surprise et le grand attrait de la soirée, c'était Gottschalk. Vous dire l'enthousiasme qu'il a excité [...] serait chose impossible. [...] Je n'essaierai point d'analyser ce talent si original, si poétique et si merveilleux. Après Gottschalk, il faut tirer l'échelle': A.-P. Fiorentino, 'Causeries', *Le Corsaire: Journal des spectacles, de la littérature, des arts, des moeurs et des modes* (16 March 1851), 3.

months of the Deuxième République.[16] Slavery and race were certainly still topical in mid-nineteenth-century France, as illustrated by the adaptations of Harriet Beecher Stowe's novel *Uncle Tom's Cabin* in translations and state productions in France by the time Gottschalk departed for New York in 1853.[17] In some of these adaptations, 'Elisa and her family are portrayed as worthy of French protection due to their perceivable whiteness', despite her mixed-race, mulatto heritage; further, 'education and assimilation into French culture and values were positioned as the "true" indicators of whiteness'.[18] In a similar fashion to Elisa, Gottschalk would be able to inhabit a liminal space in the French imaginary, situated in the nebulous area between civilised and barbaric, native son and Other, White and non-White. He was a cultivated, educated French-speaking White Creole and adopted bourgeois son hailing from France's most important former colony – as well as a grandson and great-grandson of the White planter colonists of the even more economically central island of Saint-Domingue – who through his performances provided opportunities for audiences to consider and navigate their complex emotions about the New World. These included fascination with the concept of the Creole, nostalgia and grief over France's lost colonies of Louisiana and Saint-Domingue, and an uneasy recognition of young America's fraught history and engagement with race, racism, and slavery – which touched on its own problematic history of enslavement as well.

The works Gottschalk performed in his Parisian concerts, in fact, foregrounded the opportunity to explore French constructions of both the American 'exotic' and intersections with tropes of barbarism. Gottschalk's performances of his Creole works incorporated layers of comfort and familiarity for the French audience: here was a White man who spoke French, playing the piano – that most refined of instruments – in a Romantic, virtuosic style, but offering thrilling, syncopated, so-called 'nègre' music to his listeners. He captivated listeners and critics by negotiating the paradoxes of this liminal space. The works in Gottschalk's 'Louisiana Quartet' – *Bamboula, Le Bananier, La Savane*, and *Le Mancenillier* – employed titles referring to colonial island slave culture and Black Creole melodies and rhythms that French audiences would immediately signify as Other and, perhaps further and more specifically, Creole.[19] By incorporating such elements, Gottschalk appealed to French listeners

---

16 See Christopher Guyver, *The Second French Republic 1848–1852: A Political Reinterpretation* (London: Palgrave Macmillan, 2016), p. 77.

17 See Emily Sahakian, 'Eliza's French Fathers: Race, Gender, and Transatlantic Paternalism in French Stage Adaptations of *Uncle Tom's Cabin*, 1853', in *Uncle Tom's Cabins: The Transnational History of America's Most Mutable Book*, ed. Tracy C. Davis and Stefka Mihaylova (Ann Arbor: University of Michigan Press, 2018), pp. 81–115.

18 Sahakian, 'Eliza's French Fathers', pp. 97–8.

19 Starr, *Bamboula*, pp. 70–7. This moniker of 'Louisiana Quartet' is Starr's own invention, although I also find it a useful organisational device for these early compositions.

and critics through commodification of his own Creole heritage and cross-racial connections, whether he did so consciously or not.

Indeed, critics often focused on the Creole connections of Gottschalk's works in their reviews. Following an 1851 dual-pianist event, J. L. Heugel (writing for *Le Ménestrel*) took pains to include the titles of Gottschalk's compositions and explicitly draw attention to their Black Creole connections, yet simply praised the other performer's skills without finding it necessary to name his works:

> Last Saturday, twenty fingers, and more fleeting ones, passed the evening. The first ten had the name Gottschalk and prefer the products of *nègres*: *Le Bananier, Bamboula*, etc.; the other ten, to be hardly of this world and pure Parisian, are none the less skilful. They belong to the young [Francis] Planté, a virtuoso pupil of the Marmontel class.[20]

Just two weeks later, Taxile Delord attended a concert in the 'new hall on the Bonne-Nouvelle boulevard' in which Gottschalk opened with a performance of the *Konzertstück*, Op. 79, by Carl Maria von Weber, a favourite piano-orchestral work at the time. Delord reported in *L'Argus des théâtres* that

> after having paid homage to the masters in his concert, Mr Gottschalk played various pieces of his own composition; *Le Mancenillier*, among others, delighted the audience. Mr Gottschalk understands and expresses with great charm the poetry of the savannas. The success of *Le Bananier* is there to confirm the truth of this assertion.[21]

Delord's use of the term 'savannas' carries implied connections to the island colonies and/or further to Africa; the association between *Le Mancenillier* and the imagined 'savanna' is echoed in several other reviews as well as a later poetic homage to Gottschalk's piano work, discussed below, and of course the title of the third work of the 'Louisiana Quartet'. *La Savane*, further bolsters this imagined vision of island grasslands. According to Delord, and measured by the popularity of his work among French audiences, Gottschalk successfully

---

20 Planté (1839–1934) was a French pianist who made some of the earliest recordings on piano in the early twentieth century. 'Encore samedi dernier vingt doigts, et des plus véloces, défrayaient sa soirée. Les dix premiers avaient nom Gottschalk et se livrent de préférence aux produits nègres: le *Bananier, Bamboula*, etc.; les dix autres, pour être à peine de ce monde et purs parisiens, n'en sont pas moins habiles. Ils appartiennent au jeune Planté, élève virtuose de la classe Marmontel': J. L. Heugel, 'Causeries musicales', *Le Ménestrel*, 16 (16 March 1851), 1.

21 'Après avoir fait les honneurs de son concert aux maîtres, M. Gottschalk a joué divers morceaux de sa composition; le *Mancenillier*, entre autres, a ravi l'auditoire. M. Gottschalk comprend et exprime avec beaucoup de charme la poésie des savanes. Le succès du *Bananier* est là pour constater la vérité de cette assertion': Tacile Delord, 'Concert de Gottschalk', *L'Argus des théâtres: Revue théâtrale et journal des comédiens* (25 March 1851), 1.

180   *Laura Moore Pruett*

translated an understanding, and perhaps even a lived experience, of the Creole way of life into an appreciable and enjoyable musical expression thereof.

Written when he was nineteen years old, Gottschalk's *Bamboula* also explicitly evokes a connection to former French colonies, both Saint-Domingue and Louisiana, in its title and subtitle (fig. 5.1). Bamboula is the name of an African drum that made its way from Saint-Domingue to Louisiana in the eighteenth century; the bamboula was also a dance, as suggested in the work's subtitle, 'Danse des Nègres'.[22] The bamboula drum is often fashioned out of a rum barrel with a skin stretched over one end, and would have accompanied slave dancing in New Orleans's Congo Square by the early nineteenth century (see p. 28).

Published under the title 'Le Bamboula: Un Pianiste américain', the unattributed 11 March 1849 essay on Gottschalk in *La Musique* included a rather extensive musical analysis of *Bamboula*, set within a context of evocative yet clearly hegemonic colonialism. It is worth quoting further and at length (see also p. 172), as the writer waxes rhapsodic on the piece but also draws focus to the persona of the *nègre* and paints an evocative scene for the audience:

> Who does not know Bamboula? Who has not read somewhere the description of this picturesque, provocative dance? Joyful or sad, plaintive, in love, jealous, abandoned, lonely, tired, bored or the heart full of pain, the *nègre* forgets everything if it is Bamboula. Look over there at two women with black complexions, short petticoats, necks and ears adorned with coral, their eyes burning, waving under the banana tree; their whole bodies are in motion; further on, here are groups which excite themselves and indulge in all the excesses of fantasy; two *nègres* roll their nimble fingers on a noisy tambourine, they are accompanied by a languid, lively or passionate song, depending on the attitude of the dancers. *Négrillons*, as in the canvases of Decamps,[23] prance around the fiddlers; it's madness, delirium. The *Bamboula* is complete. [...]
>
> You must have lived under the fiery sky from which the Creole draws his melodies; you have to be immersed in these eccentric songs, which are little dramas in action; in a word, you have to be Creole, composer and performer, to feel and be able to understand all the originality of *Bamboula*. We have discovered this Creole composer; an American composer, my God! But yes, and a pianist-composer, performing of the highest order, who is still known only in the aristocratic salons of Paris, and whose name soon will have a great impact. [...] His name is Gottschalk. [...]

---

22 *Bamboula* was first published by the Bureau Central de Musique in April 1849; two other Creole works, *La Savane* and *Le Bananier*, followed subsequently. All of these pieces (and others) were also published in pirated editions shortly thereafter, evincing their immediate popularity. See Starr, *Bamboula*, pp. 79–82.

23 Alexandre-Gabriel Decamps (1803–60) was a French painter, best known for his Orientalist works. It is unclear to which paintings the critic might be referring; two primate fiddlers, easily read as racist alongside Decamps's frequent use of humour, feature in his *c.*1850s painting *A Monkey Duet*.

On these words: 'Quand patati la cecité, na va mangi li', the Creoles sing a short but poetic and nonchalant motif. Gottschalk took the first four bars of this motif, and on this theme he embroidered all kinds of charming fantasies. The pianist vigorously attacks the Creole melody, then comes a second motif in F sharp [major] with an original and singing rhythm. The accompaniment is very staccato; the primary melody plays languidly, contrasting in a strange way but deliciously poetic with the bass, which always energetically marks the rhythm.

On the third melody in B flat comes a variation with a *fortissimo crescendo*, and immediately after the same pattern in B flat reappears and flees gradually, barely finished, the return is made by a dazzling line that I can only compare to a cascade of pearls; this line very happily brings back the pattern in D flat. Afterwards there are imitations in triplets, made with surprising lightness. The theme in B flat reappears with a *pianissimo* variation whose harmonies are of unparalleled richness. The pianist then falls on the D flat chord, he escapes by an ascending rocket, and he immediately returns to the theme in B flat minor by a descending scale made with prodigious agility. But why continue the analysis of this Bamboula? How to give an idea, even an incomplete idea, with the pen? I would say and repeat a hundred times that there are new variations, patterns in B flat or in D flat, *crescendo, forte, fortissimo*, lines, harp-like arpeggios, etc. etc.; Bamboula is musical poetry that defies analysis, and Gottschalk is a pianist whose name is inscribed on the frontlines of popularity. Here is his horoscope: He will walk next to the stars of the piano, and in the midst of applause and triumphs.[24]

24 'Qui ne connaît le Bamboula? Qui n'a lu quelque part la description de cette danse pittoresque, agaçante? Joyeux ou attristé, plaintif, amoureux, jaloux, abandonné, solitaire, fatigué, ennuyé ou le coeur plein de douleur, le nègre oublie tout s'il s'agit du Bamboula. Regardez là-bas deux femmes au teint noir, au jupon court, le cou et les oreilles ornés de corail; le regard brûlant, s'agitant sous le bananier; tout leur corps est en mouvement; plus loin ce sont des groups qui s'excitent et se livrent à tous les excès de la fantaisie; deux nègres roulent leurs doigts agiles sur un tambourin bruyant, ils s'accompagnent d'un chant langoureux, vif ou passionné, selon la pose des danseurs. Des négrillons à l'image des toiles de Decamps, sautillent autour des ménétriers; c'est de la folie; du délire. Le *Bamboula* est au grand complet. [...] Il faut avoir vécu sous le ciel ardent où le créole puise ses mélodies; il faut s'être imprégné de ces chants excentriques qui sont de petits drames en action, en un mot il faut être créole, compositeur et exécutant, pour sentir et bien faire comprendre toute l'originalité du *Bamboula*. Ce compositeur créole, nous l'avons découvert; un compositeur américain, bon Dieu! Mais oui, et un pianiste compositeur, exécutant de premier ordre, qui n'est encore connu que dans les salons aristocratiques de Paris, et dont le nom bientôt aura un grand retentissement. [...] Son nom est Gottschakl [*sic*]. [...] Sur ces paroles: *Quand patati la cecité, na va mangi li*, les créoles chantent un motif court mais poétique et, nonchalant. Gottschalk a pris les quatre premières mesures de ce motif, et sur ce thème il a brodé toutes sortes de charmantes fantaisies. Le pianiste attaque avec vigueur le chant créole, puis vient un second motif en *fa dièse* d'un rhythme original et chant-

Figure 5.1. L[ouis] M[oreau] Gottschalk, *Bamboula: Danse des Nègres, fantaisie pour piano*, cover and p. 1. Paris: Bureau Central de Musique, n.d. [1849]. Public Domain.

Figure 5.1—*concluded*

The language used in the first paragraph of this review clearly evinces what James Smalls terms the 'desire of Parisian audiences for exotic spectacle, for [...] manifestations of colonialist/imperialist dreams of control and conquest'.[25] The evocative language marks an imagined French vision of Black Creole lived experience. Any emotions the *nègre* might have are swept away by the irresistibility of the dance Bamboula: eyes burn, bodies are in motion, tambourines are played; 'it's madness, delirium'. The critic implies that the dancers are not in control of their responses, coding Blackness as wild, unrestrained, intense.

The reviewer then shifts focus to Gottschalk's breathtaking technical virtuosity, his 'prodigious agility'. Gottschalk is able to harness the uncontrolled passion of the 'eccentric songs', embroidering them into 'all kinds of charming fantasies' and 'cascades of pearls'. Considered as a whole, the review coalesces the two roles the pianist played in the French imagination: the captivating Creole, who ably realised in his music the colonialist imagery of dancing Blacks (rather than the violent realities of the Saint-Domingue uprisings or the ongoing oppressiveness of Louisiana slavery) and the refined Frenchman and virtuoso, who translated that imagined experience into delightful and technically challenging figurations. As Smalls has demonstrated, by the end of the century African American performers in France often served to shift 'racial difference and class distinctiveness into performative and commodified modes of spectacle'.[26] (See Chapter 10 on racialised mediations of the cakewalk.) The Other is thus objectified, a marvel to be enjoyed while the status quo of segregation is

---

ant. L'accompagnement se fait très-*staccato*; le chant du milieu, joué langoureusement, contraste d'une façon étrange, mais délicieusement poétique avec la basse, qui marque toujours énergiquement le rhythme. Sur le troisième chant en *si bémol* vient une variation avec un *crescendo fortissimo*, et aussitôt après le même motif en *si bemol* reparaît et s'enfuit progressivement; à peine fini, la rentrée se fait par un trait éblouissant que je ne saurais comparer qu'à une cascade de perles; ce trait ramène très-heureusement le motif en *ré bémol*. Après se succèdent des invitations en triolets, faits avec une légèreté surprenante. Le theme en *si bémol* reparaît avec une variation *pianissimo* dont les harmonies sont d'une richesse sans égale. Le pianiste retombe ensuite sur l'accord de *ré bemol*, il s'échappe par une fusée ascendante, et il revient aussitôt au thème *si bémol mineur* par une gamme descendante faite avec une agilité prodigieuse. Mais pourquoi continuer l'analyse de ce Bamboula? Comment en donner avec la plume une idée même incomplète? Je dirais et je répéterais cent fois qu'il y a des variations nouvelles, des motifs en *si bémol* ou en *ré bémol*, des *crescendo*, des *forte*, des *fortissimo*, des *traits*, des *harpèges*, etc., etc.; Bamboula est une poésie musicale qui défie l'analyse, et Gottschalk est un pianiste dont le nom est inscrit au front de la popularité. Voilà son horoscope: Il marchera à côté des étoiles du piano, et au milieu des applaudissements et des triomphes': 'Le Bamboula: Un Pianiste américain', *La Musique: Gazette de la France musicale* (11 March 1849), 75–76. Repr. in *La Sylphide: Journal des modes, de littérature, de théâtres et de musique*, 8:15 (30 May 1849), 2–3.

25 James Smalls, '"Race" as Spectacle in Late-Nineteenth-Century French Art and Popular Culture', *French Historical Studies*, 26:2 (Spring 2003), 351–82, at p. 357.

26 Smalls, '"Race" as Spectacle', p. 355.

maintained. In works like *Bamboula*, Gottschalk did the same; however, he did so from within the liminal space of having one foot firmly within the cultural context of the Black Creole, and the other comfortably situated in the bourgeois French world. His authority as a member of both worlds went unquestioned, and thus French audiences could enjoy his works and performances for both their Frenchness and their Blackness.

Beyond the significance of *Bamboula* as the title of his work, Gottschalk's musical treatment is infused both with symbols of Black Creole culture and its connections to his own complex familial identity. He evokes the bass sound of the bamboula drum in the first few bars of his character piece with rhythmic triple-*forte* octaves in the left hand to set the tempo (fig. 5.1). The focus on the dominant–tonic movement in the accompaniment also mirrors the type of tuning that many African membranophones retain when assimilated into Western music. Over this a syncopated, dancing melody teases its way through the introduction before its full realisation in bar 17 (ex. 5.1). This primary melody is based on a Creole song Gottschalk would have heard from his slave nurse Sally, 'Quan' patate la cuite', or 'When potatoes are cooked'.[27] This cross-racial experience from his upbringing is in a way then reflected in the 'creole synthesis' of the work's combination of Black Creole and European elements.[28] Clara Gottschalk Peterson later published this song along with several others her brother had mined for inspiration in a collection after his death, with the title *Creole Songs from New Orleans in the Negro Dialect*, a sort of tribute to and further evidence of the family's cross-racial connections.[29] The rhythmic gesture contained in the melody is based on the *habanera* rhythm, found in the Cuban version of the Spanish *contradanza* as well as in diverse dance genres of Central and South America throughout the nineteenth century; Gottschalk puts it and other syncopated rhythms to good use in this showpiece.

The overall structure of the work, repetitive and almost cyclical, evokes the Afro-Caribbean roots of its inspiration. The first main section in D flat major is 150 bars long, while the second equally long half shifts to the relative key of B flat minor with short diversions back to the major. A final definitive return to the tonic key and two of the related melodies furnishes a grand finale to

---

27 Starr, *Bamboula*, p. 74.

28 In his book *The Creolization of American Culture*, Christopher J. Smith uses the term 'creole synthesis' to describe 'a unique black-white cultural exchange' that existed widely across the antebellum United States and was made audible in the music of blackface minstrelsy. See *The Creolization of American Culture: William Sidney Mount and the Roots of Blackface Minstrelsy* (Urbana: University of Illinois Press, 2013), p. 1. I posit that Gottschalk's 'Louisiana Quartet' pieces accomplished a similar synthesis, even though he was in France at the time of their composition.

29 Clara Gottschalk Peterson (ed.), *Creole Songs from New Orleans in the Negro Dialect* (New Orleans: L. Grunewald, 1902).

Example 5.1. L[ouis] M[oreau] Gottschalk, *Bamboula: Danse des Nègres, fantaisie pour piano*, bb. 16–26. Paris: Bureau Central de Musique, n.d. [1849].

the piece. Overall, the structure reflects the rather simplistic compositional method Gottschalk favoured for works like these throughout the rest of his career; it is sectional in thrust, and he employs several closely related and tuneful melodies in many repetitions throughout the work, often including a short three- or four-bar tag to provide connective tissue and musical variety. In addition, as the piece progresses, certain melodies are given a virtuosic treatment, especially in this case the first melody that we hear in B flat minor. At bar 186, at the second iteration of this melody, the technical difficulty becomes so challenging that the published version included an additional stave marked 'facilité', for pianos with only six and a half octaves and probably intended for amateur parlour players who perhaps were not up to the work's full technical demands.

While the overall structure is indebted to its Black Creole inspirations, these demanding melodic figurations call to mind similarly virtuosic works of Chopin, Liszt, and Thalberg. An elegant section filled with trills and descending arpeggiated chords, high in register, appears around the middle of the second half at bar 213. This interlude resembles the improvisatory function of a cadenza in a piano concerto, though presented here without the contrasting sonorities of an orchestra before and after. Coming as it does about three-quarters of the way through the piece, this moment can be imagined as an opportunity for the young Gottschalk to incorporate either additional virtuosic material or dramatic on-stage gestures and body language – or both – to intensify the audience's delight before returning to the minor-key melody. The technically challenging figurations continue to increase in complexity before culminating in a coda section that returns to the tonic major key and triple-*forte* dynamic to close this crowd-pleaser out with a bang. The synthesis of syncopated rhythms and folk-based melodies with prodigious Romantic virtuosity was a winning combination.

Throughout the late 1840s and early 1850s, French critics continued to draw on racialised language to frame their reviews of Gottschalk's Creole works, and again often brought together the Creole and European elements of the performances. The reviewer for *La Presse* was delighted with the freshness and daring of Gottschalk's concerts as he indulged in fantasies of 'perfumed savannahs', tropical palm trees, and 'savages' dancing to the bamboula in March 1851:

> An originality of good taste and a little eccentricity, without charlatanism, have always appeared to us two eminent qualities in an artist of real talent. We are therefore unreservedly indebted to a feeling of sympathy and admiration for Mr Gottschalk for the first time we have had the pleasure of hearing him. Among our pianists who are in vogue today, there are few who know how to establish an indisputable individuality. [...]
>
> If Mr Gottschalk was able, even when still young, to acquire this individuality that escapes so many others, it is perhaps because, after having formed his talent by solid studies, he let it wander on an adventure in the perfumed savannahs of his country, from which he has brought us perfumes and colours. [...]
>
> Whatever brilliant features and marvellous difficulties are admired in the execution of Mr Gottschalk, the melody is never effaced; sometimes she cradles you nonchalantly as in *La Savane* or *Le Mancenilier*, sometimes her rhythm, accentuated and strange, spins before you a whole round of savages dancing the bamboula, with curtsies, drums, and cymbals.
>
> All these songs of the New World have an originality full of melancholy, energy, and suavity that takes you very far in your fantasies and your dreams, and we believe that their success will be even greater in the intimacy of the living room than in the spotlights of the concert hall.[30]

---

30 'Une originalité de bon gout et un peu d'excentricité sans charlatanisme, nous ont toujours paru deux qualités éminentes chez un artiste de vrai talent; aussi nous sommes-nous laissé aller sans réserve à un sentiment de sympathie et d'admiration pour M. Gottschalk des la première fois que nous avons eu le Plaisir de l'entendre. Parmi nos pianistes en vogue aujourd'hui, il en est peu qui aient su se créer une individualité

Three months later, in July 1851, a writer for *L'Éventail: Écho des coulisses* recorded his impressions of a benefit concert in the Grand Théâtre, explicitly connecting Gottschalk's musical style to both Black Creole and Native American traditions and imagery, envisioning a 'young Indian' singing lullabies over her 'cradle suspended between the palm trees' while '*négresses* in ebony' dance nearby:

> Tonight, an artist still young and already famous in America and Europe, in the new and the old world, eagerly devoted the tribute of his talent to the feet of the holy Charity. The call of the great pianist – playing for the poor – could not fail to make a crowd at the Grand Theatre. [...] We heard Gottschalk with a rare pleasure. [...] We hear the artist confide to his piano, which repeats them with so much feeling, the exotic songs hatched in the warm air of his native country. Listening to the graceful and melancholy expression of American rhythms, the imagination, attentive and charmed, penetrates and immerses itself in the mysterious depths of the virgin forests, so magnificently described by the genius of Chateaubriand. The cradle suspended between the palm trees that the young Indian balances with a liana, singing half-voices the joys of motherhood, – the bouncing dance of *négresses* in ebony, holding in their hands small resounding gourds and whose soft feet make golden circles, – the splendours of the luxuriant nature, – the exuberant life of solitude, – the sweet and sad majesty of the savannahs, – everything suddenly appears to you like in a mirage.[31]

---

incontestable. [...] Si M. Gottschalk a pu, bien jeune encore, acquérir cette individualité qui échappe à tant d'autres, c'est peut-être qu'après avoir formé son talent par des études solides, il l'a laissé errer à l'aventure dans les savanes embaumées de son pays dont il nous a rapporté les parfums et les couleurs. [...] Quels que soient les traits brillans et les difficultés merveilleuses que l'on admire dans l'exécution de M. Gottschalk, la mélodie n'est jamais efface; tantôt elle vous berce nonchalamment comme dans la *Savane* ou le *Mancenilier*, tantôt son rythme accentué et étrange fait tournoyer devant vous tout une rond de sauvages dansant la *bamboula* avec bobbes, tambours, et cymbals. Tous ces chants du Nouveau-Monde ont une originalité pleine de mélancolie, d'énergie et de suavité qui vous entraîne bien loin dans vos fantaisies et dans vos rêves, et nous croyons que leur succès sera plus grand encore dans l'intimité du salon qu'au grand jour de la rampe': 'Concert de Gottschalk', *La Presse* (31 March 1851), 2.

31 'Ce soir là, un artiste tout jeune encore et déjà célèbre en Amérique et en Europe, dans le nouveau et dans l'ancien monde, – vouait avec empressement l'hommage de son talent aux pieds de la sainte Charité. L'appel du grand pianist – jouant pour les pauvres – ne pouvait manquer de faire foule, au Grand-Théâtre. [...] Nous avons entendu Gottschalk avec un rare plaisir. [...] Il faut entendre l'artiste confier à son piano, qui les redit avec tant de sentiment, les chansons exotiques, écloses à l'air chaud de son pays natal. En écoutant l'expression gracieuse et mélancolique du rythme américain, la pensée, attentive, charmée, pénètre et se plonge dans les profondeurs mystérieuses des forêts vierges, si magnifiquement décrites par le génie de Chauteaubriand. Le berceau suspend entre les palmiers que la jeune indienne balance avec une liane, en chantant à demi voix les joies de la maternité; – la danse bondissante des négresses au sein d'ébène,

Without actually naming any particular compositions, the critic invokes an atmosphere of the Other, unfamiliar yet enticing. Again are envisioned 'sweet and sad savannahs', along with an indiscriminate combination of Black and 'Indian' images, a commonplace in French representations of America. The writer then moves on to describe Gottschalk's technical virtuosity, remarking, 'The performance of the pianist is marvelous; of limpid purity. [...] We have seen beautiful eyes fill with tears.'[32] The combination of romantic sensitivities with alluring exoticism invites listeners – and readers, of reviews such as this one – to view Gottschalk through this dual lens of foreign and racialised Other and 'native son' – representative of the civilised, bourgeois musical culture of France.

Even after Gottschalk's departure for New York and his tours in the United States and the Americas more broadly, French writers and newspapers continued to engage with the appeal of his dual identity while alluding to New World images. A striking example appeared in the 9 July 1854 issue of *L'Éventail: Écho des coulisses*: a poem, printed under the title 'La Légende du Mancenilier', explicitly referenced Gottschalk in its subtitle, 'On the motif of Gottschalk'. While no annotation or notes seem to have originally accompanied the poem, it was later republished in the *Almanach des Orphéonistes et des musiciens de l'avenir* in 1868, with an additional prefatory commentary that suggests it was meant to be used as text to be sung to the melody of Gottschalk's Creole work, *Le Mancenillier*.[33] The preface and poem have been translated here; note especially the preface's description of 'this somewhat wild song, imbued with the poetry of oases and savannas':

> The pianist Gottschalk, one of the most delicate and esteemed talents of our time, is of American origin. When he arrived from the New World a few years ago, he brought in strange melodies full of colour. One of them has remained popular and is called *Le Mancenilier*. There have never been any lyrics – until now – on this somewhat wild song, imbued with the poetry of oases and savannas. The legend that we publish is adapted to the main motifs of Gottschalk's work. It will be easy for our readers to adapt it to the music, if they know it, and to specify the deep impressions it gives rise to.

> The Legend of the Mancenilier (On the motif of Gottschalk)

> All sleeps in the distance. On the savanna,
> The bright sun is raining with fire.
> In front of the hut's threshold

---

tenant aux mains de petites gourdes retentissantes et dont les pieds souples sont cerclés d'or; – les splendeurs de la nature luxuriante, – la vie exhubérante des solitudes; – la majesté douce et triste des savanes, – tout vous apparait soudain comme dans un mirage': 'Concert de Gottschalk', *L'Éventail: Écho des coulisses*, 72 (20 July 1851), 1.

32 'L'exécution du pianiste est merveilleuse de pureté limpide. [...] Nous avons vu de beaux yeux se remplir de larmes': 'Concert de Gottschalk', *L'Éventail: Écho des coulisses*, 1.

33 The spelling 'Mancenilier' with one 'l' instead of two is particular to this source.

He rolls and frolics; the child with the blue eyes.
He is looking for a shadow in which
To sleep:
I saw in the air your dark head lift up,
O mancenilier!
Cool marble,
You seduced him.
The child with the blue eyes moves ahead to the foot of the tree,
Or death follows him.
He dozes off.
Already on his stone-cold forehead hovers
The eternal night.
Troubled prayer,
He shivers.
An unknown weight presses down on his eyelids:
He is asleep.[34]

Along with the by-now ubiquitous savannas, the poem's vision of a blue-eyed child, troubled and seeking rest, suggests a metaphor for White vulnerability in a world of Black slaves. Gottschalk's serenade *Le Mancenillier* takes its title from the name of the tropical manchineel tree, which is one of the most toxic trees in the world: the sap contains toxins which can cause blistering, and is present in the tree's bark, leaves, and fruit. 'Mancinella' or 'manzanilla', Spanish for 'little apple', refers to the apple-like appearance of its fruit and leaves.

---

34 'Le pianiste Gottschalk, un des talents les plus délicats et les plus estimés de notre temps, est d'origine américaine. Quand il arriva du Nouveau-Monde, il y a quelques années, il en apporta des melodies étranges et pleines de couleur. L'une d'elles est restée populaire et s'appelle le *Mancenilier*. Il n'a jamais été fait de paroles, – jusqu'à present, – sur ce chant un peu sauvage, empreint de la poésie des oasis et des savanes. La légende que nous publions s'adapte aux motifs principaux de l'oeuvre de Gottschalk. Il sera facile à nos lecteurs de l'adapter à la musique, s'ils la connaissent, et de préciser les impressions profondes qu'elle fait éprouver. La Légende du Mancenilier (Sur le motif de Gottschalk). / Tout dort au loin. Dans la savane, / Le soleil éclatant pleut en jets de feu. / Devant le seuil de la cabane / Il se roule et s'ébat, l'enfant à l'œil bleu. / Il cherche l'ombre / Pour sommeiller: / J'ai vu s'élever dans l'air ta tête sombre, / O mancenilier! / Fraicheur de marbre, / Tu l'as séduit. / L'enfant à l'œil bleu s'avance au pied de l'arbre / Où la mort le suit. / Il s'assoupit. / Déjà plane sur son front d'un froid de pierre / L'éternelle nuit./ Vague prière, / Il a frémi. / Un poids inconnu descend sur sa paupière: / Il est endormi': 'La Légende du Mancenilier', *L'Éventail: Écho des coulisses*, 216 (9 July 1854), 3. I have not been able to determine the poem's author. The language used in the prefatory commentary suggests that it may have accompanied the poem in other publications in 1854, but I have not yet found any other published versions with the commentary from that year or any other. Repr. in *Almanach des Orphéonistes et des musiciens de l'avenir: Avec l'Histoire du concours musical de l'Exposition de 1867* (Paris: Librairie du Petit Journal, 1868), 42.

The poem's central imagery of the 'child with the blue eyes' finding solace under a poisonous tree additionally alludes to the fear of being poisoned by their slaves that White masters often held. A poem by the same name was composed by French poet Charles Millevoye (1782–1816), with whose work Gottschalk was undoubtedly unfamiliar, given both artists also published works with the titles 'La Chute des feuilles' and 'Le Poète mourant'.[35]

While not nearly as syncopated or brash as *Bamboula*, Gottschalk's composition does incorporate a Black Creole melody, 'Ou som souroucou', and a gentle, lulling rhythmic accompaniment in the left hand.[36] Elegant figurations in the right hand and a delightful triplet-rhythm closing section embellish the simple *ABA* structure, making this work another example in which the Creole influences collide with a graceful parlour style, and once again highlighting the confluence of Gottschalk's dual identity in the French imagination.

Connections to Nineteenth-Century French Cultural Identity

When Gottschalk returned to the Americas in 1853, never to return to France, French critics continued to follow his career. Gottschalk indeed retained ties to France, sending money to his mother and siblings who remained there and in effect supporting his entire family with his gruelling schedule of touring and performing throughout the Americas. His abrupt death from yellow fever in Brazil at the age of forty cut short his compositional and performance career all too soon, but posthumous accolades and performances of his works by other pianists continued to appear in the press, both in France and elsewhere. An extended consideration of his legacy appeared in the pages of *Le Ménestrel* in June 1877, eight years after his death. It was the thirteenth entry in an ongoing series by Antoine François Marmontel called 'Les Pianistes célèbres: Silhouettes et médallions', which was published as a complete volume under that name the following year. In addition to summarising Gottschalk's biography and compositional style, Marmontel included an extended comparison between Gottschalk and Chopin, considering both physical and musical similarities:

> Elegant, distinguished and aristocratic, young Gottschalk resembled Chopin: refined and harmonious features, longish and oval face, mild looking, dreamy with a hint of melancholy. His mindset also mirrored Chopin's: extremely impressionable, somewhat sickly, sensitive nature,

---

35 See *Oeuvres complètes de Millevoye, dédiées au roi, et ornés d'un beau portrait* (Paris: Ladvocat, 1822), pp. 153–5. The poisonous manchineel tree intoxicates the slave Sélika to her death in Act V of Meyerbeer's *L'Africaine*; see Gabriela Cruz, *Grand Illusion: Phantasmagoria in Nineteenth-Century Opera* (Oxford: Oxford University Press, 2020), pp. 146–50, 153–9.

36 This melody, too, was included by Clara Gottschalk Peterson in her 1902 publication *Creole Songs from New Orleans*.

and an elite's constitution. Gottschalk received an excellent education, spoke many languages, and had enhanced his initial studies with advanced, conscientious learning. While elevating and broadening the scope of his aspirations, he managed to preserve a pronounced individuality; despite his kinship to Chopin, he drew from many wells. Also let us not see in him a pale imitator of someone inimitable, but rather an original disposition, drawn to an admired master yet resisting the urge to be him. Some details, some melodic contours, some meanderings are reminiscent of Chopin, however the whole retains its own colour. Gottschalk's compositions, inspired by other feelings, born under a different sky, exhibit a brio, a radiance, and a determined allure both individual and local. Gottschalk's harmonies, in their exquisite elegance, seldom represent Chopin's longing, with the latter's tightly woven and heightened drive reaching almost impossible extremes.[37]

Marmontel included connections to other famous virtuosi in his eulogy as well, the same names who had been invoked throughout Gottschalk's time in France and beyond: 'Gottschalk's name will forever live in the memories of his friends. His oeuvre as a composer places him in the footsteps of Chopin; he can take his place with Liszt and Thalberg as a virtuoso.'[38] Chopin was the most common standard with whom to be compared, as in an 1856 review by Gustave Chouquet, published in *La France musicale* three years after Gottschalk's triumphant debut in New York:

37 'Nature élégante, distinguée, tout à fait aristocratique, Gottschalk, jeune, avait une grande analogie avec Chopin: traits fins et réguliers, ovale allongé de la figure, regard doux, rêveur, cachet de mélancolie. Le moral répondait également à celui de Chopin: impressionnabilité extrême, presque maladive, nature de sensitive, organisation d'élite. Gottschalk avait reçu une excellente education, parlait plusieurs langues et avait fortifié ces premières connaissances par des études sérieuses faites avec conscience. Aussi tout en s'élevant et en agrandissant le cadre de ses inspirations, il avait conservé une individualité très-prononcée, et malgré son affinité avec Chopin, il puisait à des sources très-différentes. Aussi ne voyons-nous pas en lui un pâle imitateur d'un style inimitable, mais un tempérament original, participant d'un maître admiré sans tendre à le continuer. Certains détails, certains contours mélodiques, certaines ondulations pourraient faire songer à Chopin, pourtant l'ensemble garde une couleur toute particulière. Inspirées par d'autres sentiments, produites sous un autre ciel, les compositions de Gottschalk on un éclat, un brio, une allure déterminée à la fois individuelle et locale. Les harmonies de Gottschalk, d'une élégance exquise, offrent rarement la recherche précieuse de Chopin, dont le tissue serré, d'une trame très-forte, arrive parfois jusqu'aux limites extrêmes du possible': A. Marmontel, 'Les Pianistes célèbres: Silhouettes et médallions. XIII: Gottschalk', *Le Ménestrel*, 43:28 (10 June 1877), 219–21.

38 'Le nom de Gottschalk vivra toujours dans le souvenir de ses amis. Son oeuvre de compositeur le rapproche de Chopin; comme virtuose il peut prendre place entre Liszt et Thalberg': Marmontel, 'Les Pianistes *célèbres*', p. 221.

In truth, since Chopin, I do not know anyone to place in the same rank as Gottschalk. Like his illustrious predecessor, he is at one and the same time a poet and a scholar in musical matters. [...] He reels off with the most seductive Creole indolence the richest, the most dazzling pearl necklaces; the diamonds run from his fingers, literally. [...] It is claimed that Gottschalk is American by birth; for my part, I do not believe it, and I am eagerly inclined to think that he came to us from the beautiful country of Poetry and Love.[39]

Chouquet's reference to the 'seductive Creole indolence' with which Gottschalk performs his challenging figurations, those exquisite 'pearl necklaces' and 'diamonds', demonstrates yet again the synthesis of bourgeois elegance and Creole features by now ubiquitous in French reviews of his performances, though here the highlighted Creole element is Gottschalk's own languid performance style, not a particular folk song or rhythm. Gottschalk as performer is coded as Creole here, rather than (or in addition to) his compositions.

When considered within the context of French national identity in the mid-nineteenth century, Gottschalk's identity as a Creole composer and performer shaped his reception in a number of ways. He was celebrated for his distinctive heritage and the Creole elements of his compositions, but the composer's work was also considered in relationship to – in fact, as part of – the French Romantic style. France's own colonial past was infused with the history of Black culture and slavery, in both Louisiana and the French island colonies. His intimate personal links to both New Orleans and Saint-Domingue meant that Gottschalk could inhabit a liminal space in the French imaginary, centring on his celebration of Black Creole culture and music, which were sources of strong emotion for the French, but also embedded in a more generalised bourgeois or cosmopolitan French Romantic style. Whereas Chouquet may have believed Gottschalk's birthplace to be a 'beautiful country of Poetry and Love', other writers insisted he was French through and through. In his 1857 book *Three Years in the United States: Study of American Mores and Customs*, the French composer and musicologist Oscar Comettant (1819–98) claimed, 'Among the few musicians that America can, or rather could be proud of, should be placed in the front line [...] the pianist Gottschalk, born in New Orleans. But Gottschalk's only American feature is his birth certificate; he is French in spirit, heart, taste, and habits. It was in Paris that he came as a child

---

39 'En vérité, depuis Chopin, je ne connais personne à placer au même rang que Gottschalk. Semblable à son illustre devancier, il est tout à la fois un poëte et un érudit en matière musicale. [...] Il égrène avec la plus séduisante indolence créole les plus riches, les plus éblouissants colliers de perles: les diamants lui ruissellent des doigts, littéralement. [...] On prétend que Gottschalk est Américain de naissance; pour moi, je n'en crois rien, et j'incline bien plus volontiers à penser qu'il nous est venu du beau pays de la Poésie et de l'Amour': Gustave Chouquet, 'Gottschalk a New-York', *La France musicale*, 20:7 (6 Jan. 1856), 53.

194 *Laura Moore Pruett*

to receive lessons in his art, and it was Paris who braided his first and most precious crowns; he will come back to Paris.'[40]

Conclusions

Gottschalk's exceptional allure in France was the simultaneous presence of the familiar and the Other, the cosmopolitan and the Creole, European virtuosity and Black vitality. In this chapter, I have illustrated how French reviews of the compositions and performances by Louis Moreau Gottschalk reveal the construction of a simultaneous dual identity. His Creole and Francophone heritage, his family connections to New Orleans and Saint-Domingue were all remarked upon and celebrated in the French press, with special focus given to his consequent talents for presenting the fascinating, 'Othered' Black Creole experience within a familiar context of elegant Romantic solo piano works. From the folk songs he learned as a child from his slave nurse Sally to the complex negotiations of race and identity in the resultant 'Louisiana Quartet', Gottschalk's dual identity as an exotic Creole and cosmopolitan Frenchman shaped his reception in the French press, which continued throughout his career after his return to the Americas. His wide-ranging concert tours indeed demonstrate his adaptability to a variety of locales and circumstances, from New Orleans to Paris, from New York City to rural Cuba, from California to Peru.

While he did not reflect at length on his 'Louisiana Quartet' in his journals, he did take time to consider his musical legacy. In a February 1862 entry he recalled receiving a letter from an old friend in Paris in 1853, shortly after his return to the United States, exhorting him to come back to France. 'But I was held back by diffidence', he wrote, 'It was painful to me to return to Paris, first theater of my great success, and confess that I had not succeeded in my own country, America.'[41] The personal and financial struggles he experienced during his American tours apparently paid off, however; less than three years later, he marvelled at the 'rapidity with which the taste for music is developed and is developing in the United States', and at the fact that 'a whole generation of young girls has played my pieces'.[42] Reflecting further on his own vocation, Gottschalk opined, 'We should all, however narrow may be our sphere of action,

---

40 'Au nombre des rares musiciens dont peut, ou plutôt dont pourrait s'enorgueillir l'Amérique, il faut placer en première ligne [...] le pianiste Gottschalk, né à la Nouvelle-Orleans. Mais Gottschalk n'a d'américain que son acte de naissance; il est Français d'esprit, de Coeur, de goût et d'habitudes. C'est à Paris qu'il est venu tout enfant recevoir les leçons de son art, et c'est Paris qui lui a tressé ses premières et ses plus précieuses couronnes; c'est à Paris qu'il reviendra': Oscar Comettant, *Trois ans aux États-Unis: Étude des moeurs et coutumes américaines* (Paris: Pagnerre, 1857), pp. 109–10.

41 Gottschalk, *Notes*, p. 48.

42 Gottschalk, *Notes*, pp. 238–9.

bear our part in the progressive movement of civilization, and I cannot help feeling a pride in having contributed within the modest limits of my powers in extending through our country the knowledge of music.'[43] Though Gottschalk did not see Paris again, his legacy endured there, evinced by the French reviews that appeared throughout his lifetime and beyond. He succeeded in extending 'the knowledge of music' in France early in his career, and continued that trajectory upon his return to his home country. Gottschalk captivated the French imagination with boisterous drums, poisonous trees, and his 'most seductive Creole indolence' in both embodying and embracing France's ambivalent, contradictory views of the Black Creole and its attachment to the country's history of colonialism and enslavement in his compositions and performances.

43 Gottschalk, *Notes*, p. 239.

6

Symphonies from the New World: The Myths and Realities of American Orchestral Music in France

Douglas W. Shadle

Myths about nineteenth-century American orchestral music abound, even in the United States. At one of his Young People's Concerts with the New York Philharmonic, for example, the conductor Leonard Bernstein claimed that 'around the beginning of the twentieth century, American composers were beginning to feel funny about not writing American sounding music. And it took a foreigner to point this out to them – a Czechoslovakian composer named Dvořák.'[1] Of course, American composers had considered the possibility of how to develop a distinctly national style for decades before Dvořák's arrival in 1892. Yet Bernstein's lack of access to their music led him to adopt a myth of German domination saved in successive stages by Dvořák, George Gershwin, and Aaron Copland.

Such is one myth about this repertoire. But even in its own day, musicians outside the United States had little direct contact with American compositions until the end of the nineteenth century. European musicians and music-lovers learned about American orchestral music primarily through overseas press correspondents reporting on concerts in major cities, especially Boston and New York, leaving them to speculate about American musical developments. Even so, certain American composers gained a foothold in the French imagination well before the 1850s when they spent time in France and engaged with significant figures there.

A generation later, the speculation and innuendo following this lack of direct access momentarily subsided when the American conductor Frank Van der Stucken (1858–1929) programmed music by some of the country's most prominent composers for a performance at the 1889 Exposition Universelle in Paris. Although he chose popular works that fitted squarely within European

---

1 Leonard Bernstein, 'What is American Music?', 1 Feb. 1958, television script online at <https://leonardbernstein.com/lectures/television-scripts/young-peoples-concerts/what-is-american-music> [accessed 22 May 2021].

Symphonies from the New World 197

conventions, critics panned the concert with near uniformity, betraying the fact that their imaginations, rooted in a sense of American cultural inferiority, had strongly shaped their expectations. Despite this cool initial reception, the furore surrounding the New York premiere of Dvořák's Ninth Symphony, 'From the New World' (1893), prompted certain French writers to begin viewing American composers as transatlantic partners in ongoing international discourses about the future of classical music, particularly the question of how to construct a national compositional school while confronting the legacies of Beethoven and Wagner.[2] This chapter sketches the fitful transformation of American orchestral music from myth to reality in France during the nineteenth century.

Imagining American Music before the Civil War

The American classical music industry remained in close contact with European musical centres, particularly London, Berlin, Leipzig, Vienna, and Paris, throughout the nineteenth century. The nature of this contact included steady flows of casual travel and immigration *from* these centres to the United States, as well as American travel and relocation *to* these centres. The movement of people was essential for cultural exchange, but the circulation of ideas through the international press was the single most important method by which everyday people learned about activities abroad. Relying on first-hand accounts from potentially biased sources, or in some cases translated reprints from other journals, readers in cities around Europe and the United States developed wildly distorted perceptions about goings-on elsewhere – for example, the Boston critic John Sullivan Dwight's 1853 attempt to woo the favour of the Wagner disciple Richard Pohl (the progressive editor of the *Neue Zeitschrift für Musik*) by sending him press notices of the city's ultra-conservative concert programmes.[3] Although the development of a classical music industry in the United States essentially reflected its European counterparts – with the establishment of diverse performing ensembles, venues, educational institutions, and so on – the Parisian public was nevertheless led to believe that, by the mid-1850s, Americans were money-hungry philistines moved only by extravagant theatrical effects commonly used in outdoor musical venues in London and Paris.

The first four decades of the nineteenth century saw a precipitous rise in classical music activity in the United States, particularly in Boston, Philadel-

---

2 On the emergence of this discourse in France, see Michael Strasser, 'The Société Nationale and its Adversaries: The Musical Politics of *l'invasion germanique* in the 1870s', *19th-Century Music*, 24:3 (Spring 2001), 225–51.

3 See Douglas W. Shadle, 'How Santa Claus Became a Slave Driver: The Work of Print Culture in a Nineteenth-Century Controversy', *Journal of the Society for American Music*, 8:4 (2014), 501–37.

phia, and New York. Although relatively long-standing orchestras had dotted the American landscape in the late eighteenth century, a cluster of new organisations – the Musical Fund Society of Philadelphia, the Boston Academy of Music, and the New York Philharmonic – attracted enough revenue from local memberships and ticket sales to be self-sustaining. Though each had a unique internal structure, the chief goal for these organisations was to cultivate a taste for orchestral music within their communities through the regular presentation of concerts.

These organisations also arose to give opportunities for professional musicians attached to theatre orchestras to gather and perform orchestral repertoire by an emerging canon of symphonic composers that included Haydn and Beethoven. Theatre orchestras, in fact, were the primary employers of professional musicians in larger cities like New York through much of the century.[4] A French musician who had emigrated to the United States in the late 1820s wrote a letter to the *Revue musicale* recounting his experiences working in New York theatres:

> [Theatres here] play comedies, tragedies, grand spectacles, operatic excerpts, and small pieces, but never grand opera. This is because their orchestras are generally extremely bad and incomplete. One rarely finds two clarinets, and there is usually only one bassoon. One never sees oboes, nor trumpets, nor timpani. The oboes are quite unknown in this country, and it is said that in all North America there is only one player on this instrument, who resides in Baltimore.
>
> Haydn's symphonies are performed despite these imperfections. And although the lack of the requisite wind instruments very often produces a void, the orchestra continues to play while barely acknowledging the silence.[5]

Teaching, he added, could be quite lucrative, since 'young music teachers with just mediocre talent [...] might make a fortune and pass for a top-notch artist'

---

4 See John Graziano, 'Invisible Instruments: Theater Orchestras in New York, 1850–1900', in *American Orchestras in the Nineteenth Century*, ed. John Spitzer (Chicago: University of Chicago Press, 2012), pp. 109–29.

5 'On y joue la comédie, la tragédie, des pièces à grand spectacle, des morceaux d'opéra, et de petites pièces, mais jamais de grands opéras: cela tient à ce que leurs orchestres sont en general extrêmement mauvais et incomplets. Rarement il y a deux clarinettes, le plus souvent il n'y en a qu'un avec un basson; on n'y voit jamais ni oboës, ni trompettes, ni timbales. Les oboës sont tout-à-fait inconnus dans ce pays, et il n'y a dans toute l'Amérique septentrionale qu'un jouer de cet instrument, qui demeure, dit-on, à Baltimore. Malgré les imperfections des orchestres, on exécute des symphonies de Haydn, et quoique bien souvent le manque des instrumens à vent obligés produise un vide, ils regardant ce dernier comme un silence, et continuent à jouer': 'Nouvelles étrangères. Lettre d'un musicien parti l'année dernière pour l'Amérique', *Revue musicale*, 5:5 (June 1829), 474–5, at p. 474; all translations are mine unless otherwise noted.

Symphonies from the New World   199

even if they couldn't make a decent living overseas; apparently the most important qualification was the ability to speak English.[6] Despite the easy money, things nevertheless seemed bleak because circus acts, not artistic endeavours, drew the biggest crowds. 'Such is the state of music in New York', he closed. 'I'll see if it's better in Boston, but I doubt it.'[7]

Over the next decade, Boston did in fact become a hub of orchestral music, but Parisian coverage of classical music in the United States naturally drifted towards opera – an area where New York was a clear national leader and, along with New Orleans, became a centre of French-language opera performance.[8] The Parisian press's emphasis on opera in the United States in turn crowded out coverage of orchestral music. Consequently, one of the first significant Parisian reports about New York's orchestras appeared a full five years after the 1842 foundation of the New York Philharmonic. But the correspondent was impressed, noting that in its short life the orchestra had already 'greatly contributed to the advancement of musical art' given that it provided the city with its only opportunities to hear music by composers like Mozart and Beethoven.[9] The virtuoso pianist Henri Herz (1803–88), who was touring the United States at the time, later praised the Philharmonic in similar terms, noting that 'symphonies by the German masters, mainly Beethoven, are performed with love, with intelligence.'[10]

Even with this scanty coverage, an invested Parisian reader who followed musical life in New York might have presumed that the city was making steady progress towards European standards, particularly as musicians educated in

---

6   'Les jeunes professeurs de musique, même avec des talens médiocres, et qui ailleurs gagneraient à peine de quoi vivre, se trouveraient bien ici, et pourraient, avec de l'économie, finir par faire fortune, et passer pour des artistes du premier ordre': *Revue musicale* 5:5 (June 1829), 474–5, at p. 475.

7   'Tel est à New-Yorck l'état de la musique. [...] Je vais voir si elle est meilleure à Boston; mais j'en doute': *La Revue musicale*, 5:5 (June 1829), 474–5, at p. 475.

8   On Boston, see Michael Broyles, *'Music of the Highest Class': Elitism and Populism in Antebellum Boston* (New Haven: Yale University Press, 1992); on opera in New York, see Karen Ahlquist, *Democracy at the Opera: Music, Theater, and Culture in New York City, 1815–60* (Urbana: University of Illinois Press, 1997); and Jennifer C. H. J. Wilson, 'The Impact of French Opera in Nineteenth-Century New York: The New Orleans French Opera Company' (unpublished PhD dissertation, City University of New York, 2015); on New Orleans, see Henry A. Kmen, *Music in New Orleans: The Formative Years, 1791–1841* (Baton Rouge: Louisiana State University Press, 1966).

9   'Elle [la Philharmonic Society] a beaucoup contribué à l'avancement de l'art musical. [...] Ce sont les seuls dans lesquels on ait occasion d'entendre les symphonies de Mozart et de Beethoven': 'Chronique étrangère. New York', *La Revue et gazette musicale de Paris*, 14:14 (4 April 1847), 120.

10 'On y exécute les symphonies des maîtres allemands, et principalement celles de Beethoven, avec amour, avec intelligence': Henri Herz, 'Mes souvenirs de voyage en Amérique', *Le Nouvelliste* (31 Oct. 1851), 1.

200   *Douglas W. Shadle*

European conservatories began to take leading roles in institutions around the city. But they would have had very little if any idea what was happening in the field of composition. In March 1850, for example, the *Revue et Gazette musicale de Paris* reported that a grand musical society in Boston would soon programme a symphony by 'M. Perkins' (Charles Callahan Perkins (1823–86)), which would presumably be 'the first symphony composed by an American' ('la première symphonie composée par un Américain') – a woefully inaccurate remark.[11] The lack of attention to compositional trends in the United States was perhaps unfortunate, because American composers had already developed strong ties to Paris.

During the 1830s and 1840s, Philadelphia became a hub of compositional activity that would have an outsized impact on the rest of the country. At that time, one of the most significant musicians in the city was Francis (or Frank) Johnson, a Black entrepreneurial bandmaster well known for providing accompaniment to balls and other social gatherings. In 1837, Johnson travelled to London, where he encountered 'promenade concerts' – a style of entertainment developed in Paris by the French conductor-composer Philippe Musard (1792–1859) that blended dance music, theatrical effects, and 'light classics'. Just before Johnson and his band arrived in London, the leading music journal described the ambience of a Musard event in Paris:

> The room was very spacious, and elegantly fitted up with looking-glasses, couches, and ottomans: at the end was a café attended by a troop of perfumed waiters ready for operation. In various parts of the room were statues, and fountains surrounded with choice exotics, which being refreshed by the crystal droppings of the water, emitted a delightfully cool fragrance.[12]

A standard programme might include quadrilles, overtures, and even a movement from a symphony or two. Johnson quickly designed his London concerts on this model and returned to the United States the following summer with new ideas in mind.

By winter 1838, Johnson was ready to begin leading concerts in Philadelphia billed as 'à la Musard' – an unmistakable reference to the growing international trend. The city's main newspaper, the *Public Ledger*, often contained advance descriptions of the programs provided by Johnson. His repertoire now included pieces with theatrical effects, such as the 'Sleigh Waltz' series that included the 'cracking of whips, jingling of bells, sound of post horns, & c.' and a 'Railroad Gallop' with 'the getting up of steam, passengers about entering the cars, moving ahead rather slow, then in full speed, bell rings, letting off steam, & c.' These concerts were extraordinarily popular, and a writer for

---

11   'Chronique étrangère. Boston', *La Revue et gazette musicale de Paris*, 17:12 (24 March 1850), 103.

12   'Musard's Concerts at Paris', *The Musical World*, 6:66 (16 June 1837), 5–6, at p. 6.

Symphonies from the New World   201

the *Ledger* remarked after Johnson's death in April 1844 that 'his talents as a musician rendered him famous all over the Union, and in that portion of Europe which he had visited, while his kindness of heart and gentleness of demeanor endeared him to his own people, and caused him to be universally respected in the community'.[13]

Although the music in Johnson's programmes did not always rise to the level of 'high art' as we might understand the term today, it reflected the realities of cultivating an audience for instrumental music when ensembles operated solely on a for-profit basis – that is, without philanthropic subsidy. Touring orchestras like the Germania Musical Society, a group of German emigrés who fled the revolutions of 1848–9, also had to balance competing audience demands to remain solvent. Like Johnson's, their strategy included writing new works evocative of urban themes familiar to local audiences, such as the conductor Carl Lenschow's 'potpourri' *Broadway Panorama*, which was one of the group's most popular staples.[14]

No less important than the financial side of the equation, the aesthetic of these pieces fell within the broad orbit of contemporaneous dramatic European instrumental works that appeared in the wake of Hector Berlioz's *Symphonie fantastique*, especially in France.[15] These works were in a more direct stylistic lineage with symphonies of the Beethoven era than Johnson's or Lenschow's, but they shared the sense of formal and expressive experimentation found in pieces designed to appeal to a broad American public. It is no surprise, then, that another Philadelphia-based composer, Leopold Meignen (1793–1873), also followed in this path in his evocatively titled *Symphonie militaire*, which premiered in 1845.

This two-movement symphony was by no means the first symphony written and performed in the United States but was only one of a handful that received extensive press coverage. The *Public Ledger* provided the following plot:

> A soldier is on guard at midnight: soft music describes the time and scene, the measured tread, the sentinel's challenge, &c. The midnight service of a neighboring church is heard: it reminds the soldier of the scenes of his home; he becomes weary and falls asleep; he dreams of a battle, which is gloriously represented by the confusion of a *double figure* [i.e. fugue], as it is called by musicians; the battle ceases; the retreat bugle sounds; and the dreaming sentinel awakes to the sound of a drum.[16]

---

13   *Public Ledger*, 10 April 1844.

14   See Nancy Newman, *Good Music for a Free People: The Germania Musical Society in Nineteenth-Century America* (Rochester: University of Rochester Press, 2010), p. 130.

15   On this context, see Annegret Fauser, '"Hymns of the Future": Reading Félicien David's *Christophe Colomb* (1847) as a Saint-Simonian Symphony', *Journal of Musicological Research*, 28 (2009), 1–29.

16   'The Musical Fund Society', *Public Ledger*, 17 April 1845.

202 *Douglas W. Shadle*

And the score itself suggests an indebtedness to Johnson's theatrics in special effects like a lengthy recitative for solo clarinet, string players detached from their sections, and a solo bugler sounding a retreat. Although Meignen was himself French – he had served as a regimental bandmaster in Napoléon's army before emigrating to Philadelphia after the fall of the empire – a Parisian public drawn to this type of genre-bending musical spectacle remained unaware of its existence.

That would soon change when one of Meignen's protégés, William Henry Fry (1813–64), travelled to Paris in 1846 as a press correspondent for the *Ledger* and attempted to stage his own crowning work, *Leonora*, an English-language grand opera written in the bel canto tradition. Although Fry was unsuccessful on this front, he remained in Paris as a foreign correspondent until 1852. During this crucial six-year period, which surrounded the revolutions of 1848–9, Fry theorised ways to blend the music he encountered in Philadelphia and in Paris – Johnson's instrumental dances, Meignen's programmatic symphony, Italian bel canto opera, French grand opera, Félicien David's ode-symphonies, and Berlioz's orchestral works – into a radical new form of instrumental music akin to Franz Liszt's symphonic poems. Shortly after Fry returned to the United States in 1852, he hired an orchestra to perform some of his first experiments, which the public adored. But his efforts would experience a significant boost a year later with the arrival of another Parisian: the conductor Louis-Antoine Jullien (1812–60) (fig. 6.1).

Jullien was well known to Parisians as the eccentric, foppish music director at the Jardin Turc who had fled creditors in 1838 and relocated to London. Like his arch-rival Musard, Jullien programmed a wide mixture of repertoire and leaned on theatrical effects and showmanship to create a broadly appealing experience for audiences. By the time of Fry's return to the United States in 1852, Jullien's activities in London were receiving regular reporting in the American musical press (often copied from London newspapers and magazines). After the London press announced that Jullien would tour the United States during the 1853–4 concert season, anticipation ran high. A writer for the *Spirit of the Times* was left nearly speechless:

> Of the residue of his orchestra, we will say nothing – *it must be heard* – for no description of a combination of artistes – each the unrivalled professor of some particular instrument – men culled from every part of the world, for their possession of extraordinary talent – can give any idea of the effect of the *ensemble*. Neither have we alluded to the peculiar style of decoration, and arrangement of space he adopts – but give Jullien's myrmidons a barn, and they will convert it into a scene of fairy splendor – it being the policy of the *maestro* not only to delight the ear, but to gratify the eye.[17]

---

17 'Jullien', *Spirit of the Times*, 30 July 1853, p. 283. This periodical, published weekly in New York City with the subtitle *A Chronicle of the Turf, Agriculture, Field Sports, Literature and the Stage*, was known as the 'American gentleman's newspaper'.

Figure 6.1. Louis Antoine Jullien, *The Fireman's Quadrille* (1854).
The New York Public Library.

Upon his arrival, the prominent critic Richard Storrs Willis added, 'Hail Jullien! We welcome heartily his advent in this country, because we are convinced that his great performances, besides the pleasure they must afford, will also aid materially in refining the taste for music in the community.'[18]

It would be difficult to overstate the importance of Jullien's presence in the United States between September 1853 and his final departure the following summer. The musicologist Katherine Preston has recounted the details of Jullien's American engagements, but, more broadly, has concluded that his orchestra achieved three significant outcomes.[19] First, he produced concerts at the highest artistic level then known to American audiences in cities across the country, thus introducing a wide range of instrumental repertoire to communities that otherwise had very little access. Second, and complementary to the first, his ticket prices were relatively low in comparison to those of membership organisations like the Philharmonic Society of New York. These combined efforts proved to be a 'democratising' force for instrumental music given the enhanced access across social classes as well. Finally, Jullien championed music written by American composers, particularly Fry and his New York compatriot George Frederick Bristow (1825–98), the Philharmonic's concertmaster and a supplementary member of Jullien's orchestra.

Jullien's support of American composers, in fact, became the centrepiece of an extended contretemps between Bristow, Fry, Willis, the Philharmonic, and the Boston critic John Sullivan Dwight, among others. Bristow and Fry accused the Philharmonic of abandoning its duty to programme music by local composers, particularly after the ensemble's German majority seized control of the repertoire after 1850. Willis and Dwight argued that if their music were of higher quality, they would have had more opportunity. Of course, with Jullien by their side, Bristow and Fry had concrete evidence that a top-flight ensemble could present their music to great audience acclaim. Meanwhile, Fry engaged in a corollary discussion about the value of writing programmatic symphonies that were meant to engage audiences with meaningful symbolic narratives.[20] These arguments took place in the pages of American music journals and newspapers over a period of several months in 1854 and received detailed coverage in German-language periodicals.[21] But, if reporting in French music periodicals offers any indication, Parisians

---

18 'Jullien's Concerts', *Musical World and Times*, 3 Sept. 1853, p. 3.

19 Katherine K. Preston, '"A Concentration of Talent on Our Musical Horizon": The 1853–54 Tour by Jullien's Extraordinary Orchestra', in *American Orchestras*, ed. Spitzer, pp. 319–47.

20 Douglas W. Shadle, *Orchestrating the Nation: The Nineteenth-Century American Symphonic Enterprise* (New York: Oxford University Press, 2016), pp. 81–133.

21 See, for example, Dr. F., 'Musikalische Zustände in den Vereinigten Staaten von Nordamerika', *Niederrheinische Musik-Zeitung* (15 April 1854), 113–16.

Symphonies from the New World 205

remained largely oblivious to the centrality of American composers within the broader sweep of Jullien's residency.

Between 1854 and 1855, the *Revue et Gazette musicale de Paris* offered two major reports on instrumental music activity in New York. The first, appearing in September 1854, provided commentary on the musical congress held in June, just before Jullien had returned to England but, more important, just *after* the contretemps had subsided. 'You might think in your European naïveté', the report opens,

> that a musical congress should constitute the general assembly of a country's composers and artists gathered to agree on how to hasten the progress of art, to establish a relief fund, etc. In America, it is quite another thing, as we have recently seen. Jullien, the king of instrumentalists, the inventor of promenade concerts, which he successfully transplanted to the Yankees, and Barnum, king of the entrepreneurs, the ideal of the *impresario*, who made millions with Jenny Lind, have joined forces to organise a musical congress in New York that has resounded throughout the universe.[22]

One gets the sense that a giant 'but' is missing between the two opening sentences, for the rest of the report goes on to explain how the event was so noisy that attendees could not truly listen to the music and that the soloists appeared as 'silent automatons whose gesticulations elicited an irresistible laugh'.[23] And it closes with a sarcastic description of Jullien's most theatrical masterpiece, the *Fireman's Quadrille* (fig. 6.1). Without the context of the preceding few months of serious controversy to guide readers, they were left to believe that Americans cared only about spectacle, not the value of instrumental music for the broader community.

A more accurate, measured account of instrumental music in New York – one that would echo far into the future – appeared in the same journal in June 1855. The piece opens with a brief reflection on the city's rapid physical expansion, hinting at the sense of wide-open opportunity it offers. But, as the author walks around the city, feelings of morose nostalgia for Paris take over:

> If in other things, the people are with the times, in terms of music they betray a quite joyful naïveté. To us, their musical world is new only inso-

---

22 'Peut-être pensiez-vous, dans votre naïveté européene, qu'un congrès musical devrait être l'assemblée générale des compositeurs et des artistes d'un pays, qui viennent s'entendre sur les moyens de hâter le progrès de l'art, de fonder une caisse de secours, etc. En Amérique, c'est tout autre chose, comme on a pu le voir récemment. Jullien, le roi des instrumentistes, l'inventeur des promenades-concerts, et Barnum, le roi des entrepreneurs, l'idéal de l'*impresario*, qui a gagné des millions avec Jenny Lind, se sont associés pour organiser à New-York un congrès musical, dont l'univers a retenti'. D., 'Congrès musical en Amérique', *La Revue et gazette musicale de Paris*, 21:38 (17 Sept. 1854), 304.

23 'Les solistes faisaient l'effet d'automates muets dont les gesticulations provoquaient un rire irrésistible': *La Revue et gazette musicale de Paris*, 21:38 (17 Sep. 1854), 304.

far as it is old in all respects. The classical masters of the last century are greeted with a veneration that has its touching side; with few exceptions, what comes next, is shrouded in the mysteries of the future. America, I've concluded, has not met my expectations. I thought I would find the humbug of grandiose proportions, fabulous concerts, national music, Yankee inspirations – in short, something new. What is it instead? Pale imitations of European musical battles, philharmonic concerts, quartet soirees, opera, classical pretensions. [...] Everything is like home, only it is a hundred times worse.[24]

In a complete reversal of the report on the musical congress, this observer contended that Jullien's residency was the only time the country had gained any forward momentum: 'Unfortunately, it was only a flash of American genius; since then, everything has returned to night. Jullien is gone; of his *Firemen's Quadrille*, only the *Loafers* (firemen) remain.'[25] Where musical culture was supposed to go after his departure was unclear. The remaining commentary focuses on the stodgy Philharmonic Society. Noting the orchestra's democratic governance model, the writer critiqued the fact that too many individuals made decisions behind the scenes whereas not enough players appeared on stage. Meanwhile, at public rehearsals and concerts, 'We ogle pretty women; we invent gossip; we whisper in our ears the latest scandal, the great secret of a small society. [...] We go in, we go out, we get information, and we make a din that covers the orchestra.'[26]

Although the author mentioned the presence of American composers in New York – and added that a full article on their work would be welcome – the crucially missing piece in this overview was the fact that composers like

---

24 'Si pour le reste les gens sont à auteur des temps, sous le rapport de la musique ils trahissent une naïveté tout à fait réjouissante; pour nous autres, leur monde musical n'est nouveau qu'en tant qu'il est vieux à tous égards. Les maîtres classiques du siècle dernier sont accueillies avec une vénération qui a son côté touchant; ce qui vient ensuite est enveloppé, à quelques exceptions près, dans le mystères d'avenir. L'Amérique, je l'avoue, n'a pas répondu à mon attente. Je croyais y trouver le *humbug* sur des proportions grandioses, des concerts fabuleux, une musique nationale, des inspirations d'Yankee; bref, quelque chose nouveau. Au lieu de cela, qu'y a-t-il? De pâles imitations des *musicomachies* européennes, des concerts philharmoniques, des soirées de quatuors, l'opéra, des prétentions classiques. [...] tout y est comme chez nous; seulement c'est cent fois pire': 'La Musique à New-York', *La Revue et gazette musicale de Paris*, 22:24 (17 June 1855), 188–9, at p. 188.

25 'Par malheur, ce ne fut qu'un éclair du génie americain; depuis, tout est rentré dans la nuit. Jullien est parti; de son *Fireman-Quadrille* il n'est resté que les *Loafers* (Pompiers)': *La Revue et gazette musicale de Paris*, 22:24 (17 June 1855), 188–9, at p. 188.

26 'On s'y promène, on lorgne les jolies femmes, on invente les on-dit, on s'y souffle à l'oreille le dernier scandale, le grand secret d'une petite société. [...] On entre, on sort, on s'informe, et l'on fait un vacarme qui couvre celui de l'orchestre': *La Revue et gazette musicale de Paris*, 22:24 (17 June 1855), 188–9.

Symphonies from the New World   207

Fry and Bristow had levelled these same charges against the Philharmonic for years: that it was too reverential towards dead European composers, that the elitist audiences were too disinterested, and that a musical product more akin to Jullien's concerts would move the country forward. Completely missing the point, the author closed the piece by noting, 'I don't need to add that most of the orchestra members are German. Besides, from a musical point of view, these gentlemen have become so amalgamated with the Americans that one can hardly say where one begins and the other ends' – the precise problem that Bristow and Fry had identified in their contretemps a year earlier.[27]

The 1889 Paris World's Fair and Beyond

As communication technology improved, Parisians were able to follow musical events in the United States more quickly and in greater volume. But the twin images of a naïve American public seeking cheap thrills or uncritically worshipping the past would persist in the French imagination over the next several decades, when press coverage tended to focus on opera and touring soloists rather than orchestral music. Meanwhile, American composers continued to critique the truths underlying those stereotypes on the home front.[28]

French audiences finally heard American composers directly in 1889 at the Exposition Universelle, or World's Fair. As the musicologist Douglas Bomberger has shown, a 12 July concert directed by the composer-conductor Frank Van der Stucken marked the first time an all-American programme had appeared in all of Europe (table 6.1).[29] Moreover, the *expectation* that music by American composers would sound a certain way, particularly that it would project a distinct national identity, heavily shaped its reception among critics. Considering all the responses together, it seems clear that expectations of quality were low, whereas expectations of stylistic difference were quite high. The music disappointed on both counts.

The driving force behind critical responses at the fair was the insistent belief that the technological innovations that had fuelled American business success would have an analogue in artistic culture. Writing for *Gil Blas*, for example, Victor Wilder wondered if 'someday, chance will drop the seed of genius into the brain of a Yankee composer and we might see a renewal in the realm of

27 'Je n'ai pas besoin d'ajouter que le plupart des membres de l'orchestre sont allemands: cela s'entend de soi-même. Du reste, sous le rapport musical, ces messieurs se sont tellement amalgamés avec les Américains, qu'on peut à peine dire où les uns commencement et où les autres finissent': 'La Revue et gazette musicale de Paris, 22:24 (17 June 1855), 188–9, at p. 189.

28 See Shadle, *Orchestrating the Nation*, pp. 158–241.

29 E. Douglas Bomberger, 'A Tidal Wave of Encouragement': American Composers' Concerts in the Gilded Age (Westport: Praeger, 2002), pp. 45–64.

Table 6.1. Programme of All-American Composer Concert, Trocadéro, Exposition Universelle, Paris, 12 July 1889, Frank Van der Stucken (conductor)

Overture, *In the Mountains*, Op. 14 (1886)	Arthur Foote (1853–1937)
Piano Concerto No. 2, Op. 23 (1884–6) Edward MacDowell, Piano	Edward MacDowell (1860–1908)
'In Bygone Days', Op. 14, No. 3 (1885)	George Whitefield Chadwick (1854–1931)
'Milkmaid's Song', Op. 10, No. 3 (1885)	Arthur Foote
'Where the Lindens Bloom', Op. 87, No. 1 (1881) Emma Sylvania, soprano	Dudley Buck (1839–1909)
The Tempest, Suite (1883)	Frank Van der Stucken (1858–1929)
Intermission	
Overture, *Melpomene* (1887)	George Whitefield Chadwick
Romanze et polonaise, Op. 11 (1889) Willis Nowell, violin	Henry Holden Huss (1862–1953)
Prelude to *Oedipus Tyrannus*, Op. 35 (1881)	John Knowles Paine (1839–1906)
A Carnival Scene, Op. 5 (1884)	Arthur Bird (1856–1923)
Moonlight' (1887)	Frank Van der Stucken
'Ojalà' (1889)	Margaret Ruthven Lang (1867–1972)
'Early Love' (1886) Maude Starvetta, mezzo-soprano	Frank Van der Stucken
Festival Overture on 'The Star-Spangled Banner'	Dudley Buck

art akin to the miracles of Edison's work in science?'[30] Likewise, Charles Darcours mused in *Le Figaro*, 'In Edison's country, all discoveries are possible, and since everything happens at great speed, one of these days we might expect to see music of the New World arise, formed in one piece, dazzling and original, ready to enchant us on the first attempt.' But, he added, 'it has not found itself.'[31]

---

30 'si, quelque jour, le hasard ait tomber la graine du génie, dans le cerveau d'un compositeur yankee, verrons-nous se renouveler, dans le domaine de l'art, les miracles dont les travaux d'Edison ont été l'éclatante manifestation, dans le domaine scientifique': Victor Wilder, 'La Musique américaine', *Gil Blas*, 16 July 1889, p. 3.

31 'Dans le pays d'Edison, toutes les découvertes sont possibles, et comme tout s'y mène à grand Vitesse, il faut s'attendre à voir un de ces jours la musique du Nouveau-Monde se lever tout d'une pièce, éblouissante, originale, enchanter du premier coup. En attendant, elle ne s'est pas encore trouvée': Charles Darcours, 'Notes de Musique. A L'Exposition', *Le Figaro*, 17 July 1889, p. 6.

Symphonies from the New World 209

This disappointment manifested itself in negative comparisons with contemporary French and German composers, particularly Wagner. Delphin Balleyguier, for example, a writer for *Le Progrès artistique*, found that the music was 'in the manner of Mendelssohn and Weber, which dominates the style of their works, as well as the instrumental groupings. Melodic ideas are less rare [in the United States] than in works of the new French school and, moreover, a frankness emerges from it – a sincerity that bodes well for the future.'[32] Damning with faint praise, he added, 'Perhaps one could desire a greater personality, but at least we don't find any unhealthy eccentricities.'[33] Positioning the music as retrogressive, or at least behind the times, fitted with the picture of American musical life that had emerged in the 1850s – one of unquestioned reverence for classical masters. Such infantilising descriptions overlooked the openly Wagnerian tendencies in George Whitefield Chadwick's *Melpomene* and the prelude to John Knowles Paine's *Oedipus Tyrannus*, leaving readers to assume the music was truly backward.[34]

As Bomberger suggests, critical commentary also drew heavily from beliefs about the nature of nationality, race, and musical expression – a pseudoscientific worldview that critics thought might offer a rational explanation for American backwardness. Wilder remarked,

For the moment, composers of the New World limit themselves to taking models from those of the Old, and this model is almost always something of a composite order, borrowing its elements from Italy, France, and above all Germany. The musical art of the Americans is like their nationality: an amalgam of races, the fusion of which is not sufficiently complete to constitute an irreducible type.[35]

Almost apologetically, Darcours agreed, '[This criticism] is not to say that the United States lacks good musicians, knowing as many notes as in any other country, but that they have not yet discovered the art of amalgamating sounds

---

32 'Ils en sont là-bas à Mendelssohn et à Weber; c'est le style qui domine dans leurs ouvrages, de même, que le groupement des instruments. Les idées mélodiques s'y font moins rares que dans les oeuvres de la nouvelle école francaise; de plus il s'en détache une franchise, une sincérité de bon augure pour l'avenir': Delphin Balleyguier, 'La musique à l'Exposition. Concert américain', *Le Progrès artistique*, 20 July 1889, p. 1.

33 'Peut-être pourrait-on désirer une plus grande personnalité; mais, du moins, nous avons pas y relever des excentricités malsaines': *Le Progrès artistique*, 20 July 1889, p. 1.

34 On Chadwick, see E. Douglas Bomberger, 'Chadwick's *Melpomene* and the Anxiety of Influence', *American Music*, 21:3 (Fall 2003), 319–48.

35 'Pour le moment, les compositeurs du Nouveau-Monde se bornent à prendre modèle sur ceux de l'Ancien, et ce modèle est presque toujours d'ordre composite, empruniant ses éléments à l'Italie, à la France, et surtout à l'Allemagne. L'art musical des Américains est comme leur nationalité, un amalgame de races, dont la fusion n'est pas assez complète pour constituer un type irréductible': *Gil Blas*, 16 July 1889, p. 3.

in a somewhat personal way. America already has its painters, but it still only has everyone else's musicians.'[36] And while these comments at least imagined a better future, one writer, Brument-Colleville, felt the entire project was worthless: 'There is everything in this music, a filet of Mendelssohn with a salmi of Schumann, some hors-d'oeuvres from here, from there, from Wagner or from Brahms, not a few nebulosities and for dessert, boredom and monotony.'[37]

Of course, had these writers been more aware of conversations about music, national identity, and progress taking place in the United States, they would have known that their observations were not new, radical, or particular to the French. Most American composers, in fact, rejected the notion that their music *should* sound any different from the supposedly universal standards set by their European counterparts, and even the degree to which their compositions should conform to contemporary trends such as Wagnerism remained an open question for many. In an essay written for the *American Art Journal* in 1885, for example, the composer William Wallace Gilchrist remarked,

> Let us then, as Americans, strive not to follow this school or that, not for any fixed, deliberate, premeditated character in our work. [...] Let not future generations say: This is good because [it is] American, German, Italian, French. Let them say: This is good because [it is] true; beautiful because it is true.[38]

Taking the opposite view, Calixa Lavallée had argued that Louis Maas's Lisztian programmatic symphony 'On the Prairies' might as well be considered a good start to an American style because it made use of the most progressive elements available.[39]

Still others – a distinct minority – believed that borrowing ideas and gestures from Black or Indigenous folk idioms would pave the way towards developing a uniquely American and thoroughly modern classical style. The Midwestern composers John Broekhoven (1856–1930) and Henry Schoenefeld (1857–1936), for example, invoked Black folk music in suites written in 1884 and 1890, respectively. Both pieces received critical acclaim in the United

---

36 'Ce n'est pas à dire qu'il manque aux Etats-Unis de citoyens bons musiciens, connaissant autant de notes qu'on en sait en tout autre pays, mais ils n'ont pas encore découvert l'art d'amalgamer les sons d'une façon quelques peu personnelle: l'Amérique a déjà ses peintres, elle n'a encore que les musiciens de tout le monde': *Le Figaro*, 17 July 1889, p. 6.

37 Original unavailable; Brument-Colleville, 'Le Concert américain au Trocadéro', *Le Monde musical*, 30 July 1889, p. 7; as quoted and translated in Bomberger, 'A Tidal Wave of Encouragement', p. 54.

38 W.W. Gilchrist, 'Is There to be a Distinctive American School of Music?', *American Art Journal*, 45 (22 Aug. 1885), pp. 277–8 at p. 278.

39 Calixa Lavallée, 'Dr. Louis Maas' Symphony "On the Prairies"', *American Art Journal*, 38 (20 Jan. 1882), 242–3.

Symphonies from the New World   211

States and remained in significant programmes as late as 1892.[40] More importantly, the German-born American conductor Franz Xavier Arens (1856–1932) took the evocative second movement of Schoenefeld's suite on a tour of German-speaking cities in the summer of 1892. Whereas critics responded much as their French counterparts had to the 1889 World's Fair concert (music by many of the same composers appeared in both programmes), Schoenefeld's evocation of Black folk idioms aroused significant positive interest.[41] Relaying this news back to American readers, a music theorist from Chicago named A. J. Goodrich explained,

> Critics were very sparing of their praise until Henry Schoenefeld's characteristic Suite was performed. Ah, they said, here is something new, – something not familiar to European ears. What was it? Nothing more or less than an American plantation melody worked out in various movements. [...] If our American composers at the present time wish to produce works distinctly American they must resuscitate the old slave melodies, or the Indian ghost dances, and make these the motives of their symphonies, suites, and concertos.[42]

Had music like this been in Van der Stucken's programme three years earlier, the critical response would almost certainly have been very different, particularly given the opportunities for guests at the fair to encounter other 'exotic' musical idioms that sparked new creative ideas among French composers.[43]

Parisians were nevertheless able to confront the interwoven issues of colonisation, race, and American national identity when, in May 1893, the Paris edition of the *New York Herald* orchestrated a week-long campaign to publicise statements that Antonín Dvořák had recently made about the possibility of developing a distinctively American style of composition. In September 1892, Dvořák had arrived in New York to take over the directorship of Jeannette Thurber's National Conservatory of Music. During the first few months of his tenure, he had been brought into the ongoing debates about national styles and, in an interview published in the *New York Herald* (US edition) on 21 May 1893, stated, 'I am now satisfied that the future music of this country must be founded upon what are called negro melodies. This must be the real foundation of any serious and original school of composition to be developed in the United States.'[44] The French-speaking press paid little attention to the contro-

---

40 See Douglas W. Shadle, *Antonín Dvořák's New World Symphony* (New York: Oxford University Press, 2021), pp. 80–4.

41 Shadle, *Antonín Dvořák's New World Symphony*, pp. 84–8.

42 A. J. Goodrich, 'Gottschalk as Composer and Pianist', *American Art Journal*, 59 (2 July 1892), 294–6, at p. 295.

43 Annegret Fauser, *Musical Encounters at the 1889 Paris World's Fair* (Rochester: University of Rochester Press, 2005), pp. 139–215.

44 'Real Value of Negro Melodies', *New York Herald*, 21 May 1893.

212   *Douglas W. Shadle*

versy since it originated in English-language sources, but it continued in the United States until the premiere of Dvořák's new symphony, titled 'From the New World', in December.[45]

After the symphony premiered, however, the French press took notice and weighed in as critics evaluated the work's potential impact on Parisian musical life, and European culture more generally. *Le Ménestrel*, for example, reprinted a letter from New York appearing in *Le Temps* on 4 January 1894 that placed the symphony squarely within a Brahmsian lineage despite being inspired by 'mélodies populaires nègres'.[46] At least one commentator found that Dvořák's provocative ideas, allegedly manifested in the symphony, might be portentous. A passage from the *Journal des débats* is worth quoting at length:

> Mr Dvořák, the well-known Czech composer, has just inflicted cruel humiliation on Americans. Called to direct the Conservatory of Boston [*sic*] and wanting to express his gratitude to his hosts, he thought he would be agreeable by giving them something they lacked entirely: national music. Nothing better so far. Unfortunately, conscientious research led him to proclaim that the popular songs of the *nègres* were the only characteristic melodies in the New World and the future American school should be inspired by them. *Indae irae.* The citizens of the United States refuse Mr Dvořák's presents. They cry out that they are White, that, by definition, White people cannot have Black melodies for their national songs, and that, moreover, these are childish melodies, unworthy of any civilised people.[47]

Rather than join most Americans in condemning Dvořák's ideas, this writer took a dramatic leap in the other direction by suggesting that they might have a dramatically positive impact. 'Will Mr Dvořák persist in providing Americans with Negro national music? Is it the New World's music of the future, and will we soon see the birth of a Black Wagner?'[48] Even if this last comment were

---

45   See Shadle, *Antonín Dvořák's New World Symphony*, pp. 98–109.

46   'Nouvelles diverses. Étranger', *Le Ménestrel*, 60:1 (7 Jan. 1894), 6.

47   'M. Dvořák, le compositeur tchèque bien connu, vient d'infliger aux Américains une humiliation cruelle. Appelé à diriger le Conservatoire de Boston [*sic*] et voulant exprimer sa reconnaissance à ses hôtes, il a pensé leur être agréable en leur faisant cadeau d'une chose qui leur manquait entièrement: une musique nationale. Rien de mieux jusqu'ici. Par malheur, des recherches consciencieuses l'ont conduit à proclamer que les chants populaires des nègres étaient les seules mélodies caractéristiques du Nouveau-Monde et que la future école américaine devait s'en inspirer uniquement. *Indae irae.* Les citoyens des Etats-Unis refusent les présents de M. Dvořák. Ils s'écrient qu'ils sont blancs ne peuvent avoir pour chants nationaux des mélodies noires, et que, d'ailleurs, celles-ci sont enfantines, indignes de tout people civilisé': 'Au Jour le jour. M. Dvořák', *Journal des débats*, 15 Jan. 1894, p. 1.

48   'M. Dvořák s'obstinerat-il à deter malgré eux les Américains d'une musique nationale nègre? Est-ce la musique de l'avenir du Nouveau-Monde et verrons-nous bientôt naître

tongue-in-cheek, as if the very idea of a 'Black Wagner' would be ludicrous, it opened the imaginative possibility to international competition with American composers. Although French composers of African ancestry were known to be active (e.g. the American-born composer Edmond Dédé (1827–1901) of Bordeaux; see Chapter 4), and Gottschalk had delighted mid-century Parisians with musical references to slave melodies and the bamboula of Saint-Domingue (see Chapter 5), French commentators deflected the phenomenon of 'Negro melodies' squarely onto the United States, as if a cultural reckoning with the enslavement of Africans would be a purely American undertaking.[49]

Back in the United States, one of Dvořák's former composition pupils, Will Marion Cook (1869–1944), was having similar thoughts. Reflecting on the impact of the symphony, he mused, 'And who knows? Soon perhaps will some native composer, hopeful of the future, take the pen, and inspired by long repressed imagination, paint glowing tone pictures of a radiant dawn – a dawn without a passing – a day without a night.'[50] Of course, segregationist policies at many American conservatories suppressed the ability of Black students to receive musical training equivalent to that of their White peers, though they certainly thrived musically in other ways, often in the fields of commercial or church music, which went on to have significant influence over French musicians for decades to come. Still, Black American musicians like Nora Holt (1884–1974) consistently encouraged others to make what was once a figment in a French imagination become reality: 'If the Negro will seriously study composing as he has medicine, theology, painting, literature, and other sciences and arts, I predict that within the next twenty years the music world will hail a black Wagner and call him master.'[51]

Over the course of the nineteenth century, French perceptions of American concert music shifted fluidly between myth and reality as the press and the public received reports from observers with highly variable motivations and biases. The distinction between the stodgy New York Philharmonic and Louis-Antoine Jullien's spectacular touring orchestra – one of the main French entry points into American concert life at mid-century – carried more than a grain of truth but did little to dispel the stereotype of American cultural inferiority rooted in greed and philistinism. Once Parisians heard a critical mass of American orchestral music for themselves at the 1889 World's Fair, the conductor Frank Van der Stucken's programming choices, designed to illustrate the

---

un Wagner noir?', *Journal des débats*, 15 Jan. 1894, p. 1.

49 On the analogous situation in theatre, see Emily Sahakian, 'Eliza's French Fathers', in *Uncle Tom's Cabins: The Transnational History of America's Most Mutable Book*, ed. Tracy C. Davis and Stefka Mihaylova (Ann Arbor: University of Michigan Press, 2018), pp. 81–115, at p. 88.

50 Will Marion Cook, 'Music of the Negro', *Illinois Record*, 14 May 1898.

51 Lena James [Nora Douglas] Holt, 'The Symphony Concert', *Chicago Defender*, 9 March 1918.

214 *Douglas W. Shadle*

country's adherence to European norms, disappointed listeners who thought they would hear something distinctly national in character – another ill-informed assumption. Myth and reality converged, however, when the American press caused an international furore with its report on Antonín Dvořák's insistence that American composers should in fact try to sound uniquely national by incorporating so-called Negro melodies into classical idioms. But the symphony's contentious reception in the United States seemed to cause no such outrage when it finally premiered before a French-speaking Brussels audience in January 1896. A reviewer for *Le Guide musical* gushed that the symphony would have 'une place d'honneur au Panthéon de l'art' alongside works by Brahms, Strauss, Bruckner, and others but, other than noting that the first movement comprised 'two motives of American origin', failed to mention the work's indebtedness to Black musical expression – an imaginative erasure that placed the French reception of the symphony squarely in line with that of American critics who refused to concede a place for Black music in the American cultural fabric.[52]

---

52   Ed. de H., 'La Haye', *Le Guide musical*, 19 Jan. 1896, p. 53.

PART III

SOUNDSCAPES AND SONIC FANTASIES

7

Historical Acoustemology in the French Romantic Travelogue: Chateaubriand's Sonic Imagining of the New World

Ruth E. Rosenberg

The grave of the writer François-René de Chateaubriand sits dramatically outside the granite walls of the port city of Saint-Malo in Brittany, facing the sea on a nearby island only accessible at low tide. Home to famous explorers such as Jacques Cartier, Saint-Malo is where, as a lonely child, Chateaubriand dreamt of escaping and pursuing life of travel and adventure, inspired by his father's experiences as a sea captain and slave trader. He would eventually become enormously influential in France as a founder of literary Romanticism whose fiction, historical works, and political essays reflected a restless spirit and thirst for novelty. Chateaubriand would become well known for his first-hand accounts of travels in Spain, Italy, Greece, and the Middle East. But his first major voyage was undertaken when he was still a very young man. As the Revolution had begun to upend his country as well as his noble family, Chateaubriand, only twenty-two years old, sailed for North America.

When he embarked on his trip to the New World, Chateaubriand was an unpublished writer with ambitious plans to achieve quick and lasting fame through exploration and the written word. He writes of the circumstances that led to his trip: despite his parents' wishes that he pursue a career either in the Navy or the Church, in 1790 he was an infantry second lieutenant in the royalist Navarre regiment. He writes about the privilege of being able, as a partisan of absolute monarchy, to indulge in this 'voluntary exile' into a republican world which he claimed was a source of great curiosity and admiration for him as a young man. In his memoir he recalls,

> In 1790 I found myself relieved of my duties [...] the revolution was proceeding rapidly: the principles on which it was founded were mine, but I detested the violence that had already dishonoured it. It was joyfully that I set out to see an independence more in conformity with my tastes, more in sympathy with my character.[1]

---

1   'Je me trouvai dégagé de tout lien vers la fin de 1790 [...] la révolution marchoit à

218   *Ruth E. Rosenberg*

Chateaubriand's motivation for travel went well beyond the practical; he imagined the trip might transform him into an explorer, later writing of his plan to discover the Northwest Passage during his journey. The Indigenous people of the continent also held great interest for him as an aspiring novelist looking for inspiration in the exotic and unfamiliar. In July 1791 he arrived in Baltimore, and he then spent several months exploring America east of the Mississippi before returning to France four and a half months later, purportedly when he heard of the king's flight to Varennes.[2] Upon his return, Chateaubriand was wounded while fighting in the Army of the Princes before seeking temporary exile in England. Although the Revolution wreaked personal and financial havoc on him, the sojourn in North America provided the basis for his enduring literary works. As he later wrote, 'Even if I did not find what I was seeking in America, the polar world, I did find a new muse there.'[3] He set his most popular works of fiction, *Atala* (1801), *René* (1802), and *The Natchez* (1826), among the Indigenous people of North America. He also chronicled his experiences in the New World in two memoirs: *Voyage en Amérique* (1827) and *Mémoires d'outre-tombe* (1848–50). Anecdotes and observations of North America – its scenery, its institutions, and its political history and promise – were recycled and retold throughout his oeuvre, mined for what he saw as their historical, political, and aesthetic value.

In his time, Chateaubriand was at the vanguard of a new style of travel writing, one that would become influential on later writers like Alexandre Dumas, George Sand, Gérard de Nerval, and Théophile Gautier. The nineteenth-century literary travelogue is a distinct kind of literature in form and function and proved especially popular with French writers and readers. During the Enlightenment, travel writing had been aimed at the production of knowledge – instructional and empirical in its scientific focus on geographical sites and historical monuments. Chateaubriand's travelogues, by contrast, were full of florid language and richly rendered landscapes, driven by dramatic and emotional (if not always accurate) first-hand narration. He pioneered the figure of the author as restless wanderer, full of sentiment and often nostalgic, personal

---

grands pas: les principes sur lesquels elle se fondoit étoient les miens, mais je détestois les violences qui l'avoient déjà déshonorée: c'étoit avec joie que j'allois chercher une indépendance plus conforme à mes goûts, plus sympathique à mon caractère': François-René Chateaubriand, *Travels in America*, trans. Richard Switzer (Lexington: University of Kentucky Press, 1969), p. 7.

2   Scholars debate the length and extent of Chateaubriand's travels in North America. For detailed discussions see G. D. Painter, *Chateaubriand: A Biography*, vol. 1 (London: Chatto & Windus, 1977); Morris Bishop, 'Chateaubriand in New York State', *PMLA*, 69:4 (1954), 876–88.

3   'En effet, si je ne rencontrai pas en Amérique ce que j'y cherchais, le monde polaire, j'y rencontrai une nouvelle muse': Chateaubriand, *Memoirs from Beyond the Grave 1768–1800*, trans. Alex Andriesse (New York: New York Review Books, 2018), p. 281.

reflection. Following his stylistic lead, authors of travelogues increasingly abandoned the objective lens of the previous era and became more novelistic and autobiographical over the course of the long century. As such, the literary genre of the travelogue became an important expression of Romanticism in France. The characteristic elasticity and sentiment of the Romantic literary travelogue means that these texts go beyond merely pictorial description and embrace the full sensorium in pursuit of an expressive ideal. Thus, Chateaubriand's writings are rich in their portrayals of sonic environments and auditory experiences; in addition, the narratives use references to music, song, and spoken poetry as 'local colour'. Contemporary political events at home in France also shaped such texts, which expressed in lyrical terms the political and social preoccupations of an age of empire and exile.[4]

Despite his lifelong portrayal of himself as an intrepid explorer and keen observer, Chateaubriand's memoirs and fiction are better viewed as works of vision, myth, and confabulation than as scrupulous reportage of America in 1791. The first memoir, *Voyage en Amérique*, was written hurriedly thirty-five years after his actual trip, assembled from notes that intermingled his first-hand experience with the writings of others who travelled before and after him. Informed by wide reading on the subject, he also liberally embellished his story with fabrications from his imagination; his account was further blurred by the distance of decades between his own travels and the publication of his work. After an exhaustive review of Chateaubriand's travels in New York State that turned up many inconsistencies, the historian Morris Bishop has written of the American memoir, 'His story seems like a hallucinated version of other travellers' tales'.[5] Of the purported events described by the traveller, Bishop concludes simply that, in many cases, 'He could not have seen what he says he saw'.[6]

In what follows, I examine some of the often overlooked sonic traces, musical elements, and observations on listening found in Chateaubriand's memoirs of his American journey for the way in which they illuminate his works' major themes and images of America. In approaching sonic phenomena in Chateaubriand's writing about America, I would offer Bishop's same caution by extension: as readers, we should not assume that Chateaubriand necessarily heard what he said he heard. However, because of the popularity and influence of his writings, it is indisputable that Chateaubriand's accounts of America hold value as reflections of how the French perceived America and the New World during the nineteenth century. *Atala* alone was reprinted in six editions in the first year it was published, captivating French readers and soon appearing in English and German translations.[7] His writings about North America contain

---

4   C. W. Thompson, *French Romantic Travel Writing: Chateaubriand to Nerval* (Oxford: Oxford University Press, 2012), pp. 22–3.

5   Bishop, 'Chateaubriand in New York', p. 885.

6   Bishop, 'Chateaubriand in New York', p. 885.

7   François-René Chateaubriand, *Atala, ou Les Amours de deux sauvages dans le désert*

220   *Ruth E. Rosenberg*

several common themes expressed in musical moments and anecdotes about sound and listening. These themes, which I will consider in turn, include the comparative experience of revolution and republicanism in France and America, the experience of exile and recent loss of formerly French-held territories in North America, the virtues of 'primitive society', and the 'divine revelation of nature's sublime', which was part of Chateaubriand's literary embrace of Christianity in the wake of the French Revolution and given its full expression in his *Génie du christianisme*, published in 1802.[8]

A Traveller's Soundtrack

The main narrative of Chateaubriand's travels in North America was conveyed in two publications: *Voyage en Amérique* (1827) and the *Mémoires d'outre-tombe* (1849, 1850).[9] Significant episodes were also recounted in his *Essai historique, politique, et moral sur les révolutions anciennes et modernes* and *Génie du christianisme*.[10] All reflect events along the author's purported itinerary from Baltimore, up through Philadelphia and into parts of New York State via the Hudson River. At Niagara Falls, Chateaubriand suffered a fall and paused to recuperate, before, he claims, travelling down the Mississippi to visit the Natchez and even as far as Florida.

When they are approached from the perspective of music and sound, a convenient place to begin is with an analysis of these narratives' overt references to songs and music-making. The incorporation of such material itself is not a surprising gesture. Stylistically, this reflects the way in which the late eighteenth and nineteenth-century French travelogue emphasised the picturesque; artefacts of oral tradition and snippets of dialogue were elements of the toolkit with which writers conveyed their explorations of exotic places and their own identity. In Chateaubriand's case, the inclusion of songs creates opportunities for reflection on at least two major themes of his early work: the trauma of revolution and the experience of exile.

The first instance of the interpolation of song into Chateaubriand's American tale comes when he recounts his experience travelling up the Hudson River towards Albany, New York. From aboard a ship ferrying a large, friendly

---

(Paris: Migneret, 1801). For more on the popularity of the work see Ter Ellingson, *The Myth of the Noble Savage* (Berkeley: University of California Press, 2001), pp. 196–7.

8   Thompson, *French Romantic Travel Writing*, p. 24; François-René Chateaubriand, *Génie du christianisme* (5 vols, Paris: Migneret, 1802).

9   François-René Chateaubriand, *Voyage en Amérique* (2 vols, Paris: Librairie Marcel Didier, 1964); François-René Chateaubriand, *Mémoires d'outre-tombe* (2 vols, Paris: Gallimard, 1997).

10 François-René Chateaubriand, *Essai historique, politique, et moral sur les révolutions anciennes et modernes* (London: J. Deboffe, 1797).

Chateaubriand's Sonic Imagining of the New World 221

group of American officers and women, Chateaubriand took in the stunning landscape. The natural scenery was so beautiful, he notes, that the crowd fell unwittingly into awed silence. All of a sudden, a passenger cried out, pointing to a spot on the shore where the British major John André had been executed for espionage during the American Revolution after colluding with Benedict Arnold. Chateaubriand describes how, at the urging of the ship's passengers, a young Quaker girl on board intoned a well-known ballad about the event:[11]

> She began to sing in a shy voice, full of voluptuousness and emotion. The sun set and we were sailing between high mountains [...] between the clouds we could see rocky summits and the hairy tops of pine trees, which looked like they could be small islands floating in the air. [...] We stayed profoundly silent; as for me, I hardly dared to breathe. Nothing interrupted the plaintive song of the young passenger, apart from the insensible sound that the ship, pushed by a light breeze, made as it glided on the waves. At times the voice rang out as we grazed closer to the shore; in two or three places it was repeated by a faint echo.[12]

This unlikely moment for a song in Chateaubriand's narrative evokes a sort of soundtrack to supplement his lushly described scenery. It heightens the aesthetic beauty of the scene he paints by adding a sonic dimension to the page. But, more importantly, it makes space for political commentary and reflection, because it allows him to report the unspoken sentiments of the American officers around him. He imagines they are recalling their recent experiences of revolution and violence as they listen to the ballad:

> The American officers and I had tears in our eyes; me, by the effect of the delicious meditation in which I was immersed; them, no doubt, by the memory of the past troubles of the fatherland, which heightened the sense of calm of the present moment. They could not contemplate without out a kind of ecstasy of heart, these places, recently laden with sparkling battalions and resounding with the noise of weaponry, now buried in profound peace [...] animated by the soft whistling of the cardinals and

---

11 A version of 'The Ballad of Major André' collected in 1822 can be found in John Anthony Scott, *The Ballad of America* (New York: Grosset & Dunlap, 1967). Chateaubriand did not cite any lyrics.

12 'Elle commença faire entendre une voix timide, pleine de volupté et d'émotion. Le soleil se couchoit; nous étions alors entre de hautes montagnes [...] on découvroit la cime des rochers et les sommets chevelus des sapins, on eût cru voir de petites îles flottantes dans les airs. [...] Nous gardions un profond silence; pour moi j'osois à peine respirer. Rien n'interrompoit le chant plaintif de la jeune Passagère, hors le bruit insensible que le vaisseau poussé par une légère brise, faisoit en glissant sur l'onde. Quelquefois la voix se renfloit un peu davantage lorsque nous rasions de plus près la rive; dans deux ou trois endroits elle fut répétée par un faible écho': Chateaubriand, *Essai historique, politique, et moral sur les révolutions anciennes et modernes*, vol. 1 (London: J. Deboffe, 1797), pp. 524–5.

222   *Ruth E. Rosenberg*

the cooing of the wild woodpeckers, and whose simple inhabitants, seated on the point of a rock, at some distance from their cottages, watched quietly as our vessel passed through the river below them.[13]

Here, the author infers that the sonic incongruity of the moment was what caused the officers' tears. He compares their memories of the 'bruit des armes' with the peaceful soundscape at the current scene: the 'mélodie touchante' sung by the girl, the echo off the mountains (which he imagines is the soul of the ill-fated André responding to her), a chorus of birdsongs, a group of silent onlookers ashore, and the subtle sound of the ship cutting its course through water.

The song is significant because it allows Chateaubriand to evoke the spectre of the American Revolution by contrasting the peaceful tableau with the revolutionary tumult that America had recently seen and from which he was escaping in France. Interestingly, Chateaubriand later incorporated a version of the same story in *Mémoires d'outre-tombe* in a way that references the French Revolution more directly. In this later version, he identifies the ballad's subject as the British captain Charles Asgill, who was a prisoner of war during the American Revolution. Sentenced to death during an event known as the 'Asgill Affair' (1782), he was ultimately spared in part because of pressure put on Washington by King Louis XVI and Queen Marie Antoinette of France.

As in the initial version of the story, the memory of the American Revolution is evoked sonically in this later telling, with the song and the natural soundscape symbolising the peace of democracy in post-Revolutionary America. The second version, however, adds an additional layer of meaning. Because in this version he claims that the subject of the song is Asgill, the author goes beyond speculating on the thoughts of the American servicemen and reports his subjective experience of hearing the ballad. He writes that it prompted him to recall the 'generous intervention of [his] doomed queen' Marie Antoinette, just before the ascent of Napoléon.[14] With this alteration, Chateaubriand evokes his own nostalgia for monarchy and misgivings about the revolution that prompted his flight from France. Thus, the song facilitates a commentary on the triumph of one revolution and the unfulfilled promises of another. This point is made more directly elsewhere in the book, in particular when he com-

---

13 'Les officiers Américains et moi nous avions les larmes aux yeux; moi, par l'effet du recueillement délicieux où j'etois plongé; eux, sans doute, par le souvenir des troubles passé de la patrie, qui redoubloit le calme du moment présent. Ils ne pouvoient contemplar sans une sorte d'extase de cœur, ces lieux, naguères chargés de bataillons étincelants et retentissants du bruit des armes, maintenant ensevelis dans une paix profonde [...] animés du doux sifflement des Cardinaux et du roucoulement des Ramiers sauvages, et dont les simples habitans, assis sur la pointe d'un roc, à quelque distance de leurs chaumières, regardoient tranquillement notre vaisseau passer sur le fleuve au-dessous d'eux': Chateaubriand, *Essai historique, politique, et moral*, p. 525.

14 Chateaubriand, *Memoirs*, p. 282.

Chateaubriand's Sonic Imagining of the New World 223

pares George Washington with Bonaparte.[15] But it is a striking and nuanced example of how Chateaubriand introduced the sensory into the staid genre of travel writing to make it a vehicle of subjective political commentary. In both tellings, the passenger's song serves as a 'soundtrack' to the journey, overlaid by Chateaubriand to add poignancy to, embellish, and sustain the author's observations about revolutions in France and the New World.

In addition to evoking this contrast between the American and French experience of revolution, the Quaker girl's song disrupts the temporality of the travel account. This is a key aspect of Chateaubriand's literary style – how he stretched the limits of the genre to suit his own purposes. With it, Chateaubriand opens a space for recollection and commentary that ruptures the travel narrative, thus 'kinking and breaking lines of time', a gesture he used throughout his literary career, according to Peter Fritzsche.[16] In this case, the temporal rupture is achieved by dredging up and reworking a sonic souvenir of the past to contrast with the narrative present.

The ballad heard on the boat in Albany is not the only example of Chateaubriand inserting a song into his American travel writing. In *Mémoires d'outre-tombe*, Chateaubriand describes how, later in the trip, after arriving at Niagara Falls, he broke his arm and was nursed back to health in a nearby 'Indian village'. In this brief chapter, the author laments the 'dégradation' of traditions he observes among the Indigenous Americans, describing how their displacement and conflict with European settlers would eventually lead to their extinction and erasure from history. He wishes to observe 'reenactments of their old customs, for these customs had already ceased to exist', and in particular requests to hear the singing of his hosts.[17] An 'Indian' girl named Mila sang something for him. He goes on to quote the verse: 'Adder, stay; stay, adder, that my sister may, by the pattern of thy many-coloured coat, fashion and work a rich ribbon [...] so may thy beauty and thy ornament be forever preferred above all other serpents.'[18]

Once again, the inclusion of a song ruptures the temporality of the travel narrative and opens the moment to the author's commentary on his imagined America. For after quoting the song, Chateaubriand here tells the reader that Mila's song is the same one recorded by Montaigne in his 1580 essay 'Of Can-

---

15 Chateaubriand, *Travels*, pp. 18–9.

16 Peter Fritzsche, 'Chateaubriand's Ruins: Loss and Memory after the French Revolution', *History and Memory*, 10 (1998), 102–17, at p. 103.

17 'Je m'enquis de leurs coutumes; j'obtins pour de petits présents des représentations de leurs anciennes mœurs, car ces mœurs elles-mêmes n'existent plus': Chateaubriand, *Memoirs*, p. 301.

18 'Couleuvre, arreste-toy; arreste-toy, couleuvre, à fin que ma sœur tire sur le patron de ta peinture la façon et l'ouvrage d'un riche cordon [...] ainsi, soit en tout temps ta beauté et ta disposition préférée à tous les autres serpents': Chateaubriand, *Memoirs*, p. 302.

nibals'.[19] This confabulation serves to link together the two European writers in their inscription of indigenous customs of the New World, something significant for Chateaubriand because he views these songs as some of the last remnants of a noble, disappearing civilisation. He comments of his hosts, 'Their traditional songs fade with the last memory that retains them and vanish with the last voice that repeats them.'[20] This is one of many places in his work where Chateaubriand expresses the trope of the 'vanishing Indian', which he perpetuated in works such as *Atala*.[21]

What he perceived as the 'degradation' and eventual destruction of the Indigenous population in North America is a consistent preoccupation for Chateaubriand in *Voyage en Amérique*. In his writing, Chateaubriand employed the figure of the 'vanishing Indian' with sympathy and also with a sense of kinship, reflecting his own anxieties about the political and social fate of the French aristocracy during the Revolutionary period. The historian Henry Liebersohn argues persuasively that Chateaubriand and other writers created an image of' Indians' as a native nobility with many similarities to European aristocracy.[22] Writing in a historical moment when 'nobility in France itself was under a physical and intellectual threat of execution', Chateaubriand, as Liebersohn observes, portrayed 'Indian' society as a possible site for the 'reinventing [of] noble values'.[23]

This imagined kinship between the Indigenous inhabitants of America and the threatened aristocrats of France is made more poignant by Chateaubriand's constant evocation of the New World as a 'lost empire' of France. His regrets over his country's former colonial possessions in North America are expressed in several places. For example, in *Mémoires d'outre-tombe* Chateau-

---

19 Chateaubriand, *Memoirs*, p. 302. In his 1580 essay 'Of Cannibals', the French philosopher Montaigne mounted a challenge to the European view of the 'barbarians' of the New World. Taking information collected first-hand by Frenchmen who had travelled to the Bay of Rio a decade earlier, Montaigne presents a utopian picture of the Tupinambá of Brazil, dwelling especially on the practices of cannibalism and polygamy. His essay ultimately judges Tupinambá society superior to his own European one. See Michel de Montaigne, *The Complete Essays of Montaigne*, trans. Donald M. Frame (Stanford: Stanford University Press, 1965).

20 'Leurs chansons traditionnelles périssent avec la dernière mémoire qui les retient, s'évanouissent avec la dernière voix qui les répète': Chateaubriand, *Memoirs*, p. 302.

21 On the 'vanishing Indian' in Chateaubriand, see Philippe Roger, *The American Enemy: The History of French Anti-Americanism*, trans. Sharon Bowman (Chicago: University of Chicago Press, 2005), p. 48.

22 Henry Liebersohn, *Aristocratic Encounters: European Travelers and North American Indians* (New York: Cambridge University Press, 2001), p. 58.

23 Liebersohn, *Aristocratic Encounters*, p. 59. The 'ennobling' of 'Indians' in Chateaubriand is not a straightforward reiteration of Rousseau's 'noble savage' idea, as has often been claimed. It is complicated by Chateaubriand's commentary use of 'savage' figures to comment on his own experience of revolutionary chaos, exile, and religion. For more, see Ellingson, *The Myth of the Noble Savage*, pp. 196–209.

briand writes, 'Thinking of Canada and Louisiana, looking over the old maps of the former French colonies in America, I must ask myself how my country's government could have let go of these colonies, which would today be an inexhaustible source of prosperity.'[24] Likening the former empire to a phantom that haunts him, he continues bitterly, 'Once we possessed vast lands overseas: they offered asylum to the surplus of our population, a market for our commerce, and nourishment for our navy. We are now excluded from the new universe, where the human race is starting over again.'[25] Fritzsche has noted that Chateaubriand's temporary political exile on former French territory sparked a nostalgic identification with Indigenous societies, which he saw being stripped of their territory and traditions. He depicted both the French and 'Indians' as belonging to what he called a '"different race"': 'exiles who had become strangers in their own time and read contemporary history as dispossession.'[26]

Upon hearing Mila's song, and claiming to recognise it, Chateaubriand renders it simultaneously foreign and familiar, a remnant from the French literary past in the narrative present that links the exiled Frenchman in his 'lost empire' with the 'vanishing Indians' who are rapidly being displaced from their homeland. His nostalgia for France's former empire leads him to symbolically restore relations to the New World through Mila's song – making it a kind of *lieu de mémoire* of the former empire, where physical monuments to France are difficult for him to find.[27] Elsewhere he depicts an idealised kinship between the French and the Indigenous population in a more direct way, such as when he meets an elder of the Onondaga tribe and reports how he complained of the Americans robbing them of their land, and assured him that 'the Savages never stopped missing the French.'[28]

Noble Silence

Songs such as the two I have just discussed are a significant sonic element of Chateaubriand's writing on America; the ways in which he depicts sonic

24 'En parlant du Canada et de la Louisiane, en regardant sur les vieilles cartes l'étendue des anciennes colonies françaises en Amérique, je me demandais comment le gouvernement de mon pays avait pu laisser périr ces colonies': Chateaubriand, *Memoirs*, p. 306.

25 'Nous possédions outre-mer de vastes contrées: elles offraient un asile à l'excédent de notre population, un marché à notre commerce, un aliment à notre marine': Nous sommes exclus du nouvel univers, où le genre humain recommence': Chateaubriand, *Memoirs*, p. 307.

26 Peter Fritzsche, 'Specters of History: On Nostalgia, Exile, and Modernity', *The American Historical Review*, 106:5 (2001), 1587–1618, at p. 1588.

27 For more on this, see Ruth E. Rosenberg, 'Among Compatriots and Savages: The Music of France's Lost Empire', *The Musical Quarterly*, 95:1 (Spring 2012), 38–70, at pp. 38–52.

28 'Il m'assura que les Sauvages ne cessoient de regretter les François': Chateaubriand, *Travels*, p. 28.

landscapes and sonic phenomena also deserve attention. Chateaubriand uses the symbolism of sound to draw out a key theme of his travel writing, which was the conflict between civilised and savage virtues he observed in America.[29] One consistent trope is the 'Indian' as a figure free and uncorrupted, in a primitive state of nature, but threatened by the contamination of settler society and industry. In many instances, noise in Chateaubriand is negatively associated with the intrusion of European settlers and encroaching civilisation, while silence is used as part of his characterisation of Indigenous inhabitants as stoic and virtuous, as well as disempowered.

A few examples from *Voyage en Amérique* illustrate this device. During his stay at the 'Indian village' near Niagara Falls, Chateaubriand notes: 'At a distance, young boys were playing; but in the course of their games, jumping, running, throwing balls, they spoke not a word. There were not to be heard the deafening cries of European children; these young Savages bounded like bucks, and they were as mute as bucks are.'[30] He remarks, 'The Indian children do not quarrel, do not fight. They are neither noisy, annoying, nor surly; they have in their appearance something serious, like happiness, something noble, like independence.'[31] The observation associates silence with profundity, peacefulness, and a primitive sense of freedom.

In addition to silence, Chateaubriand attributes to Indigenous Americans the related virtue of especially acute powers of listening. For example, in the wilderness, he recounts a meeting with a party of 'Indians' who had anticipated his arrival for days before they met:

> There are Indians who hear the footfall of another Indian four or five hours away if they put their ears to the ground [...] Our guests have informed us that they had been hearing us for two days; they knew we were palefaces, since the noise that we made walking was greater than the noise made by the redskins. I asked them the cause of this difference; they answered me that it came from the manner of breaking branches and clearing a trail. The white man also reveals his race by the weight of his step; the noise he produces does not increase regularly. The European goes in circles; the Indian walks in a straight line.[32]

---

29 Robert F. Berkhofer, *The White Man's Indian* (New York: Vintage Books, 1978), p. 80.

30 'A quelque distance, de jeunes garçons s'ébattoient; mais au milieu de leurs jeux, en sautant, en courant, en laçant des balles, ils ne prononçoient pas un mot. On n'entendoit point l'étourdissante criaillerie des enfants européens; ces jeunes Sauvages bondissoient comme des chevreuils, et ils étoient muets comme eux': Chateaubriand, *Travels*, pp. 31–2.

31 'Les enfants indiens ne se querellent point, ne se battent point: ils ne sont ni bruyants, ni tracassiers, ni hargneux; ils ont dans l'air je ne sais quoi de sérieux comme le bonheur, de noble comme l'indépendance': Chateaubriand, *Travels*, p. 33.

32 'Il y a tel Indien qui entend les pas d'un autre Indien à quatre et cinq heures de distance, en mettant l'oreille à terre [...] Nos hôtes nous ont appris qu'ils nous entendoient

The characterisation is that Europeans are less adept, less effective, and even careless in the wilderness, with noise symbolic of their intrusion into the primitive world where 'Indians' are at home. He describes their 'sharpness of the ear' as 'prodigious' and suggests that their 'savage cries' are as much a part of the primitive world of nature they inhabit as the calls of the wild animals.[33] Their ability to covertly 'eavesdrop' and surveil seems almost superhuman, and Chateaubriand purports to admire this as a tactical advantage over Europeans.

Noise is specifically associated with the negative influence of European settlers and civilisation in another anecdote from *Voyage en Amérique*. While hiking near Lake Onondaga in New York, Chateaubriand recounts stopping for a peaceful moment of rest near an 'Indian hut'. He describes how his reverie was interrupted by loud voices as three Europeans and their fat cows entered the scene. He writes that their intrusion into so 'solitary a place [...] was extremely disagreeable; their violence made them even more annoying'.[34] An Indigenous woman whom he calls 'miserable' and 'indigent' emerges from the nearby hut; he describes how the Europeans 'bursting with laughter, chas[ed] the poor animal through the rocks, making it run the risk of it breaking its legs'.[35] In response, he writes, the woman speaks softly to the cow, which responds with a 'little moo of joy' ('avec un petit mugissement de joie').[36] Where the settlers are noisy, lively, intrusive, the Indigenous woman and her cow are nearly mute. The sonic characterisation continues when he visits a group of Onondagas in a nearby village the next day; he finds that they are 'enclaved in the whites' clearings and have taken on European manners and possessions'.[37] Unlike the solitary women in the woods, he remarks, 'They made much noise and seemed very happy' ('Ils faisoient grand bruit et avoient l'air fort joyeux'), continuing this association of noise with the influence of settlers and the changing fates of the Indigenous people.[38]

---

depuis deux jours; qu'ils savoient que nous étions des *chairs blanches,* le bruit que nous faisons en marchant étant plus considérable que le bruit fait par les chairs rouges. J'ai demandé la cause de cette différence; on m'a répondu que cela tenoit à la manière de rompre les branches et de se frayer un chemin. Le blanc révèle aussi sa race à la pesanteur de son pas; le bruit qu'il produit n'augmente pas progressivement: l'Européen tourne dans le bois; l'Indien marche en ligne droite': Chateaubriand, *Travels*, pp. 46–7.

33 Chateaubriand, *Travels*, p. 29.

34 'L'apparition de ces Européens dans un lieu si désert me fut extrêmement désagréable; leur violence me les rendit encore plus importuns': Chateaubriand, *Travels*, p. 25.

35 'Ils chassoient la pauvre bête parmi les roches, en riant aux éclats, et en l'exposant à se rompre les jambes': Chateaubriand, *Travels*, p. 25.

36 Chateaubriand, *Travels*, p. 25.

37 'Enclavées dans les défrichements des blancs, ont pris quelque chose de nos mœurs': Chateaubriand, *Travels*, p. 27.

38 Chateaubriand, *Travels*, p. 27.

The Haudenosaunee (whom Chateaubriand calls 'Iroquois') held special fascination for the author. To him, they represented the natural leaders of the continent, whose position of dominance was usurped by European aggression and expansion. He writes, 'The explorers of the North American interior found, among the various savage nations, every form of government known to civilised man. The Iroquois belonged to a race that seemed destined to conquer other Indian races, if outsiders had not come to drain his blood and quash his spirit'.[39] Chateaubriand identifies 'the Onondaga's Lake' as a site of a former empire within the new American republic – its Indigenous inhabitants 'the last remnant of one of the six Iroquois nations' ('reste d'une des six nations iroquoises').[40] (Indeed, Chateaubriand was at the sacred site of what the Onondaga consider the first representative democracy in the West – the Haudenosaunee Confederacy.) The author's portrayal of the 'Iroquois' as the 'natural nobility' of the American wilderness includes this vivid picture of them as warriors against encroachers: 'His head adorned with feathers, his ears slit [...] his arms tattooed and dyed with blood, this New World champion became as daunting to see as he was to fight on the shores he defended, foot by foot, against the invaders'.[41] Alongside his fearsome look, Chateaubriand also imagined the silent stoicism of this figure: 'These intrepid men were not awed by firearms when they were first used against him. They stood tall while bullets whistled and cannons boomed, as if they had heard these things all their lives: they appeared to pay them no more mind than they would a thunderstorm'.[42] Here, Chateaubriand depicts the Indigenous of North America as invulnerable to the sonic intrusion of foreign arms. This portrayal reinforces the stereotype of 'Indians' as a part of the natural landscape of the New World, and also indicates their bravery in the face of certain tragedy.

39 'Quand on parcourut l'intérieur de l'Amérique septentrionale, on trouva dans l'état de nature, parmi les diverses nations sauvages, les différentes formes de gouvernement connues des peuplas civilisés. L'iroquois appartenait à une race qui semblait destinée à conquérir les races indiennes, si des étrangers n'étaient venus épuiser ses veines et arrêter son génie': Chateaubriand, *Memoirs*, p. 290.

40 Chateaubriand, *Memoirs*, p. 287.

41 'La tête ornée de panaches, les oreilles découpées [...] les bras tatoués et pleins de sang, ce champion du Nouveau Monde devint aussi redoutable à voir qu'à combattre, sur le rivage qu'il défendit pied à pied contre les envahisseurs': Chateaubriand, *Memoirs*, p. 291.

42 'Cet homme intrépide ne fut point étonné des armes à feu, lorsque pour la première fois on en usa contre lui; il tint ferme au sifflement des balles et au bruit du canon, comme s'il les eût entendus toute sa vie; il n'eut pas l'air d'y faire plus d'attention qu'à un orage': Chateaubriand, *Memoirs*, p. 290.

Night Sounds

The two previous sections have established how Chateaubriand employed song and sound symbolism to inject historical and political commentary into his North American travel narratives, promulgating what would become enduring and problematic stereotypes in some cases. In this final section I turn to more personal sonic experiences that Chateaubriand claimed to have had in the wilderness of America. In some of the more remarkable portions of *Voyage en Amérique*, Chateaubriand displays his inward gaze and vulnerability as an artist, traveller, and exile through moments of close listening and sonic sensitivity. These traits, not coincidentally, connect him with what he sees as some of the admirable qualities of the 'Indians' and his ideal of 'primitive man': for him, both are prodigious listeners, stoic, and at one with nature.

Travelling is an experience of observation and spectacle, and Chateaubriand's memoirs are full of richly rendered landscapes. By the light of day, a traveller like Chateaubriand is able to visually apprehend his environment, focusing a careful eye on everything from its broad vistas to the smallest petal on a wildflower, contemplate the way a blue sky peeks through the green of the forest canopy, and make notes on the wildlife he identifies. Navigation, hunting and foraging, sketching: the daily activities that Chateaubriand engages in as he travels are dependent on the eye, whether it is passively gazing or intensely *looking out for*. The portion of his travelogue entitled 'Diary without Dates' opens with a point-of-view, highly pictorial description of a majestic landscape that gives a sense of this emphasis on visual spectacle:

> The sky is pure over my head, the water limpid under my boat, which is flying before a light breeze. On my left are some hills rising like cliffs and flanked with rocks from which hang the morning glory with white and blue blossoms, festoons of begonias, long grasses, rock plants of all colours; to my right reign vast prairies. As the boat advances new scenes and new views open up: at times solitary and laughing valleys, at times bare hills; here the sombre porticoes of a cypress forest, there the sun playing in a light maple forest as if shining through a piece of lace.[43]

In Chateaubriand's account of his travels, all that is essential and all that is gratuitous in nature are offered up to his eye and conveyed for the readers' benefit. At least while the sun is out. In the wilderness, night-time belongs to the ear. Inescapable sounds, like an enveloping din of insects, might torment the

---

43 'Le ciel est pur sur ma tête, l'onde limpide sous mon canot, qui fuit devant une légère brise. A ma gauche sont des collines taillées à pic et flanquées de rochers d'où pendent des convolvulus à fleurs blanches et bleues, des festons de bignonias, de longs graminées, des plantes saxatiles de toutes les couleurs; à ma droite régnent de vastes prairies. A mesure que le canot avance s'ouvrent de nouvelles scènes et de nouveaux points de vue: tantôt ce sont des vallées solitaires et riantes, tantôt des collines nues; ici c'est une forêt de cyprès dont on aperçoit les portiques sombres; là c'est un bois léger d'érables, où le soleil se joue comme à travers une dentelle': Chateaubriand, *Travels*, p. 42.

230   *Ruth E. Rosenberg*

traveller. Darkness creates audience, sharpening the sense so that the traveller might detect an approaching footstep. Historians of aurality often highlight the particularly immersive, intrusive, even transgressive character of sound. The 'Diary without Dates' is a section of Chateaubriand's journey in which he creates an hourly record of his experience of the forest overnight, where sound is indeed an overwhelming force. Here are the night-time entries of Chateaubriand's 'diary' from *Voyage en Amérique*:

Midnight

The fire is beginning to go out, the circle of its light, diminishing. I listen. A formidable calm weighs upon these forests; one would say that silences follow upon silences. I seek vainly to hear in a universal tomb some noise betraying life. Whence comes that sigh? From one of my companions. He is complaining, although asleep. Thou livest; therefore thou sufferest: such is man.

Half Past Midnight

The repose continues, but the decrepit tree cracks and falls. The forests bellow; a thousand voices are raised. Soon the noises weaken and die in almost imaginary distance. Silence once again invades the wilderness.

One o'Clock in the Morning

Here is the wind: it is rushing over the tops of the trees, shaking them as it passes over my head. Now it is like the waves of the ocean breaking sadly on the shore.

The sounds have awakened sounds. The forest is all harmony. Do I hear the deep sounds of the organ, while lighter sounds wander through the vaults of verdure? A short silence follows: the aerial music begins anew; everywhere sweet complaints, murmurs that contain within them other murmurs; every leaf speaks a different language, each blade of grass gives off its own note.

An extraordinary voice resounds: it is that frog who imitates the bellowing of the bull. From all sides of the forest, the bats hanging from the leaves raise their monotonous song. It seems like a continual tolling, the funeral sounding of a bell. Everything brings us back to some idea of death because that idea is at the base of life.[44]

---

44   'Minuit. Le feu commence à s'éteindre, le cercle de sa lumière se rétrécit. J'écoute: un calme formidable pèse sur ces forêts; on diroit que des silences succèdent à des silences. Je cherche vainement à entendre dans un tombeau universel quelque bruit qui décèle la vie. D'où vient ce soupir? D'un de mes compagnons: il se plaint, bien qu'il sommeille. Tu vis, donc tu souffres: voilà l'homme. Minuit et demi. Le repos continue; mais l'arbre décrépit se rompt: il tombe. Les forêts mugissent; mille voix s'élèvent. Bientôt les bruits s'affoiblissent; ils meurent dans des lointains presque imaginaires: le silence envahit de nouveau le désert. Une heure du matin. Voici le vent; il court sur la

Chateaubriand's Sonic Imagining of the New World   231

These entries, which stand out in the book as a strangely decontextualised dispatch from an unnamed location, are dedicated to the activity of listening and the pictorialising of the wilderness through sound. The darkness having robbed him of anything else to describe, Chateaubriand gradually reveals a dramatic and purely audible landscape. The initial silence at midnight reminds him of a tomb. At first, he hears only the human complaint of his travelling companion. Slowly, human concerns recede as the natural soundscape becomes dominant, moving from silence to 'bellowing' to silence again. Soon, he describes sounds multiplying sympathetically into a kind of instrumental harmony of leaves, grass, and finally animal voices. These he compares to a funeral bell tolling, and he contemplates, circling back to the first entry, how in the night the sounds he sought to indicate the presence of life around him still unavoidably remind him of mortality.

Although he enumerates them one by one, the overall effect is still uncanny and fanciful (certainly he was not actually hearing the ultrasonic cries of bats). The metaphor of the organ and the bell evoke the sacred. The experience of the night sounds makes nature ascendent and shrinks the figure of the rootless Romantic writer-traveller down to size. With his recording of this cacophony of the New World, Chateaubriand shows how his initial vulnerability to sound and his own intent listening (which allies him with 'primitive men') open him to an experience that is beyond the Old World and New, outside past and present. In a similar episode, recorded in *Mémoires d'outre-tombe*, the would-be silent forest offers unexpected sonic intrusions against the backdrop of Niagara Falls.

> The moon rose above the treetops [...] everything would have been silence and stillness but for the fall of a few leaves, the passage of a sudden wind, the whoop of an owl; in the distance, you could hear the muted roar of Niagara prolonged, in the calm night, from wilderness to wilderness, slowly fading through the lonely forests. It was in these nights that an unfamiliar muse appeared to me. I gathered some of her accents, and I marked them down in my book, by starlight, as a common musician might transcribe the notes dictated to him by some great master of harmonies.[45]

---

cime des arbres; il les secoue en passant sur ma tête. Maintenant c'est comme le flot de la mer qui se brise tristement sur le rivage. Les bruits ont réveillé les bruits. La forêt est toute harmonie. Est-ce les sons graves de l'orgue que j'entends, tandis que des sons plus légers errent dans les voutes de verdure? Un court silence succède; la musique aérienne recommence; partout de douces plaintes, des murmures qui renferment en eux-mêmes d'autres murmures; chaque feuille parle un différent langage, chaque brin d'herbe rend une note particulière. Une voix extraordinaire retentit: c'est celle de cette grenouille qui imite les mugissements du taureau. De toutes les parties de la forêt, les chauves-souris accrochées aux feuilles élèvent leurs chants monotones: on croit ouïr des glas continues, ou le tintement funèbre d'une cloche. Tout nos ramène à quelque idée de la mort, parce que cette idée est au fond de la vie': Chateaubriand, *Travels*, pp. 45–6.

45   'La lune se montrait à la cime des arbres [...] tout aurait été silence et repos, sans la

The dramatic spectacle of the cataract is here transmuted into an unseen roar that fills the boundless wilderness. Chateaubriand again places himself in the silent role of the primitive man, humbled in the cathedral of nature, surrounded by otherworldly sounds and the mystery of the Divine.

Conclusion: The Traveller as Listener

Evocations of sound and music like those I have discussed here show how the Romantic literary travelogue opened new possibilities for French writers imagining the New World during the nineteenth century. For Chateaubriand, the lost French territories in the New World sparked a sense of nationalistic regret and nostalgia that he expressed both directly and indirectly. Serendipitous encounters with songs facilitated imaginative connections which the writer used to compare his views of the French and American Revolutions and reflect on alternative outcomes of empire through imagined soundscapes. His romanticised characterisations of 'Indians', inflected by his subjective experience of exile, influenced later French writers who built upon the idea of a mythic kinship between America's Indigenous inhabitants and the French. When aural phenomena are centred in an analysis of his travel narratives, it becomes apparent how Chateaubriand used sound in his characterisation of the social complexities of the American frontier. He used sound and acts of listening to represent 'Indians' as natural citizens of an Edenic landscape, degraded by the chaotic noise of European settlers. With such accounts he created depictions at once ennobling and dehumanising.

Among his other contributions, in these narratives Chateaubriand established the literary device of the traveller as listener – a construction very different from the Enlightenment's traveller as surveyor, whose 'imperial eyes' laid claim to everything in sight.[46] His multi-sensory apprehension of America served his political and social commentary as evidenced by some of the examples analysed above. His poetic flights occasioned by the nocturnal sounds of the forest demonstrate what was for Chateaubriand the endpoint of any journey: the discovery of new worlds within and without oneself, and a muse available to any traveller's rapt ear.

---

chute de quelques feuilles, le passage d'un vent subit, le gémissement de la hulotte; au loin, on entendait les sourds mugissements de la cataracte de Niagara, qui, dans le calme de la nuit, se prolongeaient de désert en désert, et expiraient à travers les forêts solitaires. C'est dans ces nuits que m'apparut une muse inconnue; je recueillis quelques-uns de ses accents; je les marquai sur mon livre, à la clarté des étoiles, comme un musicien vulgaire écrirait les notes que lui dicterait quelque grand maître des harmonies': Chateaubriand, *Memoirs*, pp. 295–6.

46 Mary Louis Pratt, *Imperial Eyes: Travel Writing and Transculturation* (London: Routledge, 1992), p. 7.

8

La Liberté éclairant le monde: Transatlantic Soundscapes for the Statue of Liberty

Annegret Fauser

On 25 April 1876, the Union Franco-Américaine held a well-publicised fundraiser in Paris at the newly opened Palais Garnier for a monument that would become the Statue of Liberty. This massive sculpture was a transatlantic civic project that had been in the works since the end of the American Civil War in 1865, intended to celebrate political freedom, and in particular the abolition of slavery, while also reaffirming Franco-American friendship, an alliance famously forged in the crucible of the American Revolutionary War. Taking place in a theatre decorated with American and French flags, with a backdrop painted by Jean-Baptiste Lavastre that showed the projected statue in New York Harbor, the gala event attracted a veritable who's-who of Franco-American grandeur – from Lafayette's grandson, Oscar de Lafayette, to the United States Minister to France, Elihu B. Washburne.[1] For its musical portion, the celebration featured a cantata written for the occasion by Charles Gounod, *La Liberté éclairant le monde*, as well as several other musical items, including the American anthem 'Hail, Columbia'. Yet despite all of these efforts, the fundraiser turned out to be but a lukewarm accomplishment, both financially and artistically, simultaneously competing for attention with such major theatrical events as Giuseppe Verdi's *Aida*, which had its premiere three days earlier, on 22 April, and continued to draw the public and critics into the Théâtre-Italien.

Despite its modest impact, however, the 1876 fundraiser counts among the better-known musical events in the transatlantic story of the Statue of Liberty.[2] The saga of this monument began in the early summer of 1865 around a

---

1 Following the gala, Lavastre's backdrop depicting the monument was shipped to New York for the 4 July celebrations in 1876 and hung from a building at the north-west corner of Madison Square Park. See Yasmin Sabina Khan, *Enlightening the World: The Creation of the Statue of Liberty* (Ithaca: Cornell University Press, 2010), p. 132.

2 The fundraiser is generally mentioned in the literature dedicated to the history of the Statue of Liberty. See, for example, Khan, *Enlightening the World*, p. 125; Edward Berenson, *The Statue of Liberty: A Transatlantic Story* (New Haven: Yale University Press, 2012), p. 47; Elizabeth Mitchell, *Liberty's Torch: The Great Adventure to Build*

234 *Annegret Fauser*

dinner table at the home of the French legal scholar and abolitionist Edouard de Laboulaye (1811–83).[3] Among the guests were not only Lafayette's grandson Oscar and Alexis de Tocqueville's brother Hippolyte, but also a young sculptor, Frédéric-Auguste Bartholdi (1834–1904). Given that Napoléon III had backed the Confederacy, this group of liberal supporters of the North and admirers of Lincoln resolved then and there to find a way tangibly to show French loyalty to the reasserted ideals of the victorious American republic.[4] It would take until 1871, however, for the project and Bartholdi's design to crystallise into the idea of a colossal female statue for New York Harbor, and a few more years to bring on board the somewhat reluctant Americans who considered the gift something of an imposition. In 1875, Laboulaye and Bartholdi formed the Union Franco-Américaine to raise the necessary funds. Rather optimistically, they expected to have the statue ready to be sent to the United States for the centenary of the American Revolution, in 1876. Instead, it took a good five years just to collect the money through subscriptions and fundraising events on both sides of the Atlantic, including the evening at the Palais Garnier. It was not until 28 October 1886 that the statue would finally be unveiled on Bedloe Island.[5]

In the eleven years between the founding of the Union Franco-Américaine and the unveiling of the statue, well-publicised fundraising events and political spectacles on both sides of the Atlantic kept the monument in the public eye as it shifted its status from an idiosyncratic pipedream fashioned by a group of liberal assenters to a major public-private enterprise that carried the imprimatur of presidents and statesmen in France and the United States. Whether gala dinners or public processions, these occasions drew on well-established forms both of civic celebrations and of semi-public banquets and the like that often put transatlantic political and social elites on carefully curated display. In this framework, musical performances and shared sound practices – from community singing to cannon salvos – formed 'sonic vernaculars' that relied for their effect on the emblematic characteristics of the expected and the unre-

---

the Statue of Liberty (New York: Atlantic Monthly Press, 2014), p. 113; Francesca Lidia Viano, *Sentinel: The Unlikely Origins of the Statue of Liberty* (Cambridge, MA: Harvard University Press, 2018), pp. 422–27.

3   Berenson, *The Statue of Liberty*, p. 8.

4   Berenson (*The Statue of Liberty*, pp. 10–11) questions the commonly held assumption that the project of a female statue was decided during the dinner party. Rather he locates the specific development of the monument in the following years.

5   Berenson (*The Statue of Liberty*, p. 30) makes the point that the gestation period of the Statue of Liberty was, in effect, not unusually long for major American monuments: 'For comparison's sake, it's important to keep in mind that the Washington Monument, designed by an American architect to honor perhaps the most widely admired figure in U.S. history, took thirty-six years (1848–85) to build. The Lincoln Memorial took fifty-five years (1867–1922) from conception to realisation, and the Roosevelt Memorial twenty-three (1974–97).'

markable.[6] Much of the music heard on these occasions was familiar: marches, anthems, hymns, and songs: even Gounod's specially composed *La Liberté éclairant le monde* was nothing if not predictable.[7] In effect, the work's very ordinariness presented a crucial aspect within the transatlantic soundscapes enveloping the statue, a parallel to the aesthetic qualities of the monument itself, which Edward Berenson has summarised as 'abstractness, artistic banality, and colossal size'.[8] Bartholdi himself declared at the time of its unveiling that the monument 'cannot be considered as a very great work of art. It is an ordinary statue enlarged and placed on a pedestal.'[9] Only a handful of incongruous moments and unexpected sonic events stand out, giving this musical story its unique touches. Long overshadowed by the spectacular monumentality of the statue and its accumulated meanings shaped both by visual representation and by verbal mediation, the sonic receded both from memory and in actual practice.[10] It is telling, for instance, that only one song connected to the statue – Irving Berlin's setting of 'Give Me Your Tired, Your Poor' (1949) – has retained any presence in performance over the years.

Given the mutedness of the sonic in the history of the Statue of Liberty, information about the music performed and shared during the events connected to its genesis and inauguration remains scarce and fragmentary. This often unrecorded practice leads to questions about the historiography of such soundscapes and their roles – both receptive and generative – in the framing of the monument. It opens up a challenge on how to address the sonic vernaculars of these events in a manner that does not ignore the music in favour of a sociocultural discussion, exploring both the sonic experience and the meaning and impact of a music that was indeed banal, whether because of its familiar-

---

6 Benjamin Tausig, 'Sound and Movement: Vernaculars of Sonic Dissent', *Social Text*, 36:3 (2018), 25–45. Tausig defines 'sonic vernaculars' as being 'composed of locally trenchant sonic and aural practices and the symbolic meanings that they transduce and mediate' (p. 26).

7 The problems posed by predictability and banality are not dissimilar to the ones that Alexander Rehding addresses in his monograph *Music and Monumentality: Commemoration and Wonderment in Nineteenth-Century Germany* (New York: Oxford University Press, 2009). As he points out, 'the very self-evidence of monumentality constitutes a hurdle to academic reflection' (p. 4).

8 Berenson, *Statue of Liberty*, p. 3.

9 'M. Bartholdi Interviewed', *The World*, 20 Oct. 1886, quoted in Albert Boime, *Hollow Icons: The Politics of Sculpture in Nineteenth-Century France* (Kent, OH: Kent State University Press, 1987), p. 113.

10 In recent literature, historians and art historians have debated how the statue acquired its symbolic aura and whether its meaning depended on – as Albert Boime put it in 1987 – a quality of emblematic 'hollowness'. Boime, *Hollow Icons*, 113. For a critique of Boime's concept, see Viano, *Sentinel*, p. 11. Berenson, *The Statue of Liberty* (pp. 103–25 and pp. 140–65), dedicates two chapters to the accumulated layers of the statue's significations.

ity or its subservient ritualised function, and therefore warranted barely any specific discussion and at most a reference to its presence.[11] The history of the statue presents a stark contrast between the material permanence and apparent immutability of the monument and the ephemerality of its sonic vernaculars that has left few traces in the documents from the past. But recent scholarship has drawn attention to absences in archives such as these and has proposed critical frameworks through which to recuperate vanished soundscapes.[12]

Most of the sources for the transatlantic soundscapes connected to the statue consist of paper (whether or not now in digital form), and some include compositions and evidence of their performance.[13] All these traces share their ontological condition as mediated and mediating discourse networks (*Aufschreibesysteme*) interceding between past and present and reflecting the values that such mediators attributed to their various subjects.[14] The performance-studies scholar Diana Taylor has set up a dialectic relationship between the archive as mediating discourse networks and embodied experiences of the past by pointing out that 'insofar as it constitutes materials that seem to endure, the archive exceeds the live', while – at the same time – 'embodied memory, because it is live, exceeds the archive's ability to capture it'.[15] Drawing

11 How to address such music and its practice has formed the topic of several publications. On music in urban processions, often identified by its function, see Tim Carter, 'The Sound of Silence: Models for an Urban Musicology', *Urban History*, 29 (2002), 8–18. In communist Poland, community singing served as a routine form of protest, especially in 'small gatherings around patriotic monuments to commemorate anniversaries'. See Andrea F. Bohlman, *Musical Solidarities: Political Action and Music in Late Twentieth-Century Poland* (New York: Oxford University Press, 2020), p. 236.

12 In a different context, Chérie Rivers Ndaliko addresses archival ephemerality, absence, and reconstitution in 'The Accidental Archivist: Memory, Resonance, and Decay in Kivu', in *Performing Commemoration: Musical Reenactment and the Politics of Trauma*, ed. Annegret Fauser and Michael A. Figueroa (Ann Arbor: University of Michigan Press, 2020), pp. 240–62.

13 On the concept of 'paper' and the function of documents, see Lisa Gitelman, *Paper Knowledge: Toward a Media History of Documents* (Durham, NC: Duke University Press, 2014). This paragraph is based on, and expands, my reflections in Annegret Fauser, 'Sound, Music, War and Violence: Listening from the Archive', *Transposition: Musique et sciences sociales*, hors série 2 (2020), 'Sound, Music and Violence' <https://journals.openedition.org/transposition/4310>.

14 Friedrich Kittler's notion of the *Aufschreibesystem* still offers a valuable hermeneutic concept to address the material conditions of mediation. Unfortunately, the English term 'discourse network' misses some of its specificity; a more literal translation would be 'notation systems'. It matters how something is written down, both actually and epistemologically. See Friedrich A. Kittler, *Aufschreibesysteme 1800 / 1900* (Munich: Fink, 1985); in English as *Discourse Networks 1800 / 1900*, trans. Michael Metteer with Chris Cullens (Stanford: Stanford University Press, 1990).

15 Diana Taylor, *The Archive and the Repertoire: Performing Cultural Memory in the*

Transatlantic Soundscapes for the Statue of Liberty 237

on Taylor's observation, I consider the Statue of Liberty itself becoming part of the archive, yet failing to 'capture' its sonic vernaculars entirely. This dialectical tension may be resolved, in Ana María Ochoa Gautier's words, through 'an acoustically tuned exploration of the written archive', an approach that reveals the entangled history of aural and documentary practices.[16] Such tuning into the sonic vernaculars surrounding the genesis and inauguration of the statue means, on the one hand, recovering the particulars of events deploying music and sound – whether in banquets or parades – and on the other, exploring their sonic agency in both musical and symbolic terms.

Given the purpose of the statue, the framework for these events was explicitly transnational, even though their specific iterations were anchored within the local socio-political contexts of Paris and New York, respectively.[17] Moreover, despite the ostentatious bilateralism of these Franco-American transactions, the story of the monument also included a phantom actor in the form of the German Empire, given its entanglement with the United States both during the American Civil War (1861–5) – when Prussia supported the Union – and the recent events of the Franco-Prussian War (1870), when the United States favoured the Germans.[18] This triangulation played out on both sides of the Atlantic, explicitly in newspaper articles reminding their readers about American sympathies for Germany, and symbolically in some of the musical choices, even in such a transnational contact zone as the Exposition Universelle of 1878.

Paris

A number of Parisian events were notable for their inclusion of music and sound, especially early on, between 1875 and 1879. Obviously, the launching of the fundraising enterprise in the autumn of 1875 needed to be marked by one

---

Americas (Durham, NC: Duke University Press, 2003), pp. 19–20.

16 Ana María Ochoa Gautier, *Aurality: Listening and Knowledge in Nineteenth-Century Colombia* (Durham, NC: Duke University Press, 2014), p. 3.

17 The enmeshment of transnational scope and local practice has been discussed across theoretical writings. For an early introduction into the issues, see Patricia Clavin, 'Defining Transnationalism', *Contemporary European History*, 14:4 (2005), 421–39, at p. 437.

18 On American support of Prussia, see Berenson, *The Statue of Liberty*, pp. 24, 32–3, 45. Berenson (p. 40) connects the lackluster response of French donors to the Franco-Prussian War: 'After all, the French people were being asked to donate money for a gigantic, expensive statue to be given to a foreign country whose leaders and opinion makers had mostly favored France's enemy in the recent Franco-Prussian war.' For a foundational study presenting the complex and, at times, acrimonious history between the United States and France, see Jean-Baptiste Duroselle, *France and the United States: From the Beginnings to the Present*, trans. Derek Coltman (Chicago: University of Chicago Press, 1978).

such occasion: a Franco-American celebration on 19 November at the Palais de l'Industrie during the Exposition Internationale des Industries Maritimes et Fluviales which followed on the heels of a banquet organised in the main gallery of the Louvre on 6 November.[19] The *New York Times* reported that it was 'a grand and successful fête', emphasising that not one but two musical programmes were given that afternoon, the first by the beloved band of the Garde Républicaine, and the second a vocal concert featuring 'The Star-Spangled Banner', which 'was sung amid great cheering'.[20] By contrast, the few French press reports simply acknowledged the brilliance of the event, especially the display of a model of the statue, without much reference to its sonic side.[21] An exception was a brief report in *La Liberté* that identified the musicians for the second concert as the chorus and orchestra of the Opéra and placed the model on the platform with the orchestra.[22] Behind – across the nave of the Palais de l'Industrie – Lavastre's backdrop presented for the first time a vision of how the statue might look in New York Harbor.[23] What mattered most at the beginning of the campaign for the French press, however, was the meaning of the project in general for the fledgling Third Republic and its complicated relationship to the United States. In an article about the fundraising campaign in *Le Petit Journal*, Thomas Grimm, for instance, emphasised two of the leitmotifs of the unfolding French discourse surrounding the statue: on the one hand, its role in repairing Franco-American relations strained throughout the previous decade by the Second Empire's support of the Confederacy and America's siding with the Prussians in 1870; and on the other, the spectacular quality of the monument, not least in terms of surpassing by a good twenty metres in height the German *Arminius* memorial (the *Hermannsdenkmal* in Nordrhein-Westfalen) completed in July that year, an achievement cast as a symbolic win.[24] Clearly – with the fundraising focused on the statue as material object – the visual magnificence of the monument and its potential transatlantic impact were front and centre at the start of the launch.

19 Berenson, *The Statue of Liberty*, p. 46; on the banquet, see the description (including a transcript of the speeches by Washburn and Laboulaye) in *Journal des débats*, 8 Nov. 1875.

20 'The Franco-American Monument', *New York Times*, 20 Nov. 1875.

21 See, for example, 'Faits divers', *Le Temps*, 21 Nov. 1875.

22 'On avait exposé sur l'estrade de l'orchestre un dessin représentant une réduction demi-naturelle de la statue en bronze de la Liberté qui doit être placée à l'entrée du port de New-York': 'Echos de partout', *La Liberté*, 21 Nov. 1875.

23 None of the newspaper articles identify the backdrop specifically, but – during the lead-up to the 1876 gala event – the unnamed critic for *La Gazette* (12 April 1876) makes the connection: 'Quant à l'immense toile, représentant l'œuvre de M. Bartholdi, nous l'avons vu cet automne au palais de l'Industrie'.

24 Thomas Grimm, 'La Statue de la Liberté', *Le Petit Journal*, 28 Sept. 1875.

By contrast, the gala event six months later, in April 1876, was billed as a musical event *per se*: a 'grande solennité musicale'. It built on the trope of reaffirming mutual political and historical entanglements between the American and French republics while celebrating the unique magnificence of the proposed statue. The advertising flyer underscored that the premiere of Gounod's specially composed work, performed by 800 *orphéonistes* and conducted by the composer, would be the musical highlight of the evening. In a promotional letter to *Le Petit Journal*, Édouard Philippe stressed that the event was also to be cast as a 'fête des orphéons', for it was the first time – he pointed out – that the stage of the Opéra was going to be opened to the singers of the Orphéon Français, performers who formed 'the élite of the Orphéon societies from the *Département de la Seine*'.[25] Moreover, the director of the Opéra, Olivier Halanzier, had offered the in-kind contribution of the house and its orchestra as well as two of its ensemble members, Rosine Bloch and Eugène Caron. Francesca Viano also highlights one crucial connection, given that 'most of the supporters of the Opéra were in one way or another connected to the Union Franco-Américaine'.[26]

The programme combined speeches, poetic recitations, and musical performances (table 8.1). It touched on predictable parameters for such a politically and culturally framed event. From the two overtures with their Republican echoes to the choruses exhorting military sacrifice to the religious evocations in Jean-Baptiste Faure's 'Les Rameaux' and Gounod's 'Ave Maria', the musical selection was tailored to the commemoration of Franco-American military martyrdom in the service of independence and United States statehood.[27] Liberty herself took to the stage in the persona of Rosélia Rousseil from the Comédie Française, splendid – as Gédéon Nazim reveals in *Le Tintamarre* – 'in a white peplum, matte golden tiara, the American flag in her arms'.[28] The poem she recited was written specifically for the event by the dramatist and librettist Edouard Blau, exalting the sacrifice of French blood in the American War

25 'Pour la première fois, l'*Orphéon français* aura l'honneur de chanter sur notre grande scène lyrique [...] 800 hommes, formant l'élite des sociétés orphéoniques du département de la Seine, chanteront trois chœurs sous la directions des auteurs': Édouard Philippe, 'La Fête des Orphéons', *Le Petit Journal*, 13 April 1876.

26 Viana, *Sentinel*, p. 423.

27 Antoine Elwart (*Le National*, 27 April 1876) characterised the two overtures as follows: 'Deux ouvertures, républicaines par essence, celle de la *Muette* d'Auber, et celle de *Guillaume Tell* de Rossini, ont été enlevées par l'excellent orchestre d'Ernest Deldevèze'. The only author to address the selection of overtures, Viana (*Sentinel*, p. 425) over-interprets their connotations for Parisian audiences in 1876, clearly unaware of their respective performance histories.

28 'Mlle Rousseil, superbe dans son costume de Liberté, peplum blanc, diadème d'or mat, le drapeau américain dans les bras, a dit admirablement des vers qui lui doivent beaucoup': Gédéon Nazim, 'Opera: Solennité franco-américaine', *Le Tintamarre*, 30 April 1876.

Table 8.1 Programme, *Grande Solennité Musicale*, Palais Garnier, 25 April 1876

First Part

1. Daniel François Esprit Auber, Overture to *La Muette de Portici* (Orchestra of the Opéra)
2. Speech by Edouard de Laboulaye
3. Jean-Baptiste Faure, 'Les Ramaux', text by Jean Noté (Eugène Caron, baritone, and the orchestra of the Opéra)
4. Laurent de Rillé, 'Les Martyres aux arènes', text by the composer (Orphéon Français, conducted by the composer)
5. Charles Gounod, 'Ave Maria' for voice, violin, organ, and harp (Rosine Bloch, mezzo-soprano, accompanied by members of the Orchestra of the Opéra)
6. Edouard Blau, 'Après cent ans' (poem recited by Rosélia Rousseil)

Second Part

7. Gioachino Rossini, Overture to *Guillaume Tell* (Orchestra of the Opéra)
8. Gioachino Rossini, *Sémiramis*, cavatina of Arsace: 'Ah, quel giorno ognor rammento' (Rosine Bloch, mezzo-soprano, and the Orchestra of the Opéra)
9. Armand Saintis, 'Sur les remparts', text by the composer (Orphéon Français, conducted by the composer)
10. R. Cottier, 'Le Soldat', text by Paul Déroulède (Eugène Caron, baritone, and the Orchestra of the Opéra)
11. Charles Gounod, *La Liberté éclairant le monde*, text by Émile Guiard (Orphéon Français and the orchestra of the Opéra, conducted by the composer)
12. Philip Phile, 'Hail Columbia', text by Joseph Hopkinson, orchestrated by Victor Pons (Orchestra of the Opéra)

Source: Based on a copy of the programme that is preserved in one of Bartholdi's scrapbooks, Paris, Archives du Conservatoire National des Arts et Métiers, Fonds Bartholdi, box 1 FB 1.

of Independence and bestowing the Continent's blessings on its allies.[29] More than one commentator felt that they attended a Republican festival of old, with additional echoes of theatrical representations and musical performances during the siege of Paris and the Commune, especially with the presence of such a sizeable male choir. Indeed, the two choruses – Laurent de Rillé's 'Les Martyres aux arènes' and Armand Saintis's 'Sur les remparts' – were familiar works of the Orphéon repertoire, and were received as such.

The piece that was promoted as the musical highlight of the evening was Gounod's cantata for four-part male chorus and orchestra, *La Liberté éclairant le monde*, on a poem by the fledgling playwright, Émile Guiard. Originally, the text was to have been written by Victor Hugo, whom the composer had approached in flattering terms.[30] After Hugo declined because of health reasons, the text was entrusted to Guiard. Cast in the tradition of Revolutionary hymns, his verses exalted freedom as drenched in the blood of transatlantic patriotic sacrifice; predictably, the two heroic defenders of Liberty were named as Washington and Lafayette, before whom all were forced to kneel: 'Washington, Lafayette/ Sont mes sauveurs qu'on bénit à genoux.'[31] The text was as much a memorial of the dead as it was a celebration of transatlantic connections.

Gounod's musical setting starts with an expansive orchestral introduction, followed by the martial melody of a hymn with its contour and rhythm clearly inspired by the *Marseillaise* (ex. 8.1). The homophonic four-part texture reflects that of countless Orphéon choruses, a genre with which Gounod was highly familiar given that he led successfully, between 1852 and 1859, the Orphéon de Paris.[32] Even after Gounod stepped down from this position, he remained connected to the institution, both through guest appearances and through his compositions, not least the Ophéonic idiom of the soldiers' chorus from Act IV

---

29 The poem ends with an evocation of eternal friendship written in blood. See Edouard Blau, *Après cent ans* (Paris: Typographie Lahure, 1876), pp. 12–13: 'Les ancêtres couchés sous la terre natale / Aux ancêtres venus pour mourir avec eux / Diront tout bas: "Voyez! de nos jours belliqueux / Voilà qu'on se souvient de ce jour pacifique; / Votre France est encore sœur de notre Amérique!" / Et refermant les yeux et reposant leur front, / Avec un fier sourire ils se rendormiront.'

30 Charles Gounod, letter to Victor Hugo, 1 March 1876, Archives du Musée d'Orsay, Paris, Bartholdi file, cited in English translation in Mitchell, *Liberty's Torch*, p. 113.

31 The text for *La Liberté éclairant le monde* is reproduced on the evening's programme; a copy is kept in Paris, Archives du Conservatoire National des Arts et Métiers, Fonds Bartholdi, box 1 FB 1 (henceforth, FB 1).

32 Clair Rowden, 'Choral Music and Music-Making in France', in *Nineteenth-Century Choral Music*, ed. Donna M. Di Grazia (New York: Routledge, 2013), pp. 205–12, at p. 208. Jann Pasler addresses Gounod's connection to the Orphéon societies in *Composing the Citizen: Music as Public Utility in Third Republic France* (Berkeley: University of California Press, 2009), p. 167. On Gounod's tenure as director of the Orphéon de Paris, see also Donna M. Di Grazia, 'Concert Societies in Paris and their Choral Repertoires c.1828–1880' (unpublished PhD dissertation, Washington University, 1993), vol. 1, pp. 128–49.

Example 8.1. Charles Gounod, *La Liberté éclairant le monde*, text by Émile Guiard, bb. 51–64. Paris: Imp. Arouy, Fouquet, 1876.

—*(continued)*

Example 8.1—*concluded*

of *Faust* (1859) that had, in turn, become an Orphéon staple.[33] In his autobiography, Gounod credited his experience leading the Orphéon de Paris for his ability 'to utilize large masses of vocal sound so as to develop the maximum of sonority under very simple methods of treatment'.[34] A note on the autograph score for *La Liberté éclairant le monde* reveals that Gounod's orchestration had clearly taken into account the large choral group: 'it was scored with an eye towards a considerable vocal mass; it is thus necessary that the chorus is rather large so as to avoid any sonic disproportion between the orchestra and the voices'.[35] Moreover, the choice of Gounod as the creator and conductor of the evening's musical highpoint also made sense in the Franco-American scope of the event: Gounod – as the critic for the daily newspaper *L'Evénement* pointed out – had been asked just the previous year to move to the United States to direct an unspecified new conservatory and thus held credentials uniquely apt for this particular context.[36]

---

33 Rowden, 'Choral Music and Music-Making in France', p. 211, n. 21.
34 Charles Gounod, *Autobiographical Reminiscences*, cited in Pasler, *Composing the Citizen*, p. 187, n. 96.
35 'Ce morceau est instrumenté en vue d'une masse vocale considérable ; il est donc essentiel que les chœurs soient nombreux pour éviter la disproportion de sonorité entre l'orchestra et les voix. ' : Charles Gounod, 'La Liberté éclairant le monde', autograph manuscript, cited in Gérard Condé, *Charles Gounod* (Paris : Fayard, 2009), p. 841.
36 'Au mois de juillet dernier on lui avait proposé la direction d'un conservatoire en Amérique': Tabarin, 'La Solennité franco-américaine à l'Opéra', *L'Evénement*, 27 April 1876. Tabarin quotes at length a letter by Gounod from 1 Aug. 1875, in which the composer explains why he was to refuse the honour of 'becoming the Atlas of this New World' ('devenir l'Atlas de ce Nouveau-Monde').

The audience, it seems, was enthusiastic – but the press, less so. Those newspapers that supported the enterprise often decided to ignore the musical side of the evening, simply mentioning Gounod's cantata as a prestige object and instead celebrating Laboulaye's impressive speech. Tabarin, writing in *L'Evénement*, passed quickly over the musical and dramatic part of the event, for – in his words – 'it was just the *hors d'œuvre* of this beautiful evening'.[37] Charles de la Rounat considered Gounod's hymn 'magnificent' and applauded his decision to conduct the work himself, but he said nothing about the rest of the musical performance.[38] By contrast some journalists – especially 'Un Monsieur de l'Orchestre' in *Le Figaro* – were less sanguine and took pleasure in panning the entire evening as an incoherent amalgamation of incongruous elements.[39] What was particularly hurtful among the negative reviews was the destructive response of journalists to the Orphéon singers on the opera-house stage, caricaturising their performance as provincial and boring, with one particular wit suggesting that Offenbach, who was visiting New York at the time, ought to recast the title of his famous operetta (1858) as *Orphéon aux enfers* to suit the peculiar American taste.[40] While one defender of the choral movement accused the mainstream press of habitually using Orphéons as easy targets, the damage was done.[41] This attack was all the more poignant given the careful preparation, with weeks of rehearsals in the Orphéon circles. The leading

---

37 'Nous passerons rapidement sur la partie musicale et dramatique qui, cette fois, c'était que le hors-d'œuvre de cette belle soirée' : Tabarin, 'La Solennité franco-américaine à l'Opéra', *L'Evénement*, 27 April 1876.

38 'Je n'insisterai donc pas sur la partie purement artistique de cette soirée, qui n'avait, à ce point de vie, rien de particulièrement attractif, sauf un magnifique chœur de Gounod, chanté par sept cent orphéonistes que l'illustre compositeur dirigeait lui-même' : Charles de la Rounat [Aimé-Nicolas-Charles Rouvenat], 'Causerie dramatique', *Le XIXe Siècle*, 2 May 1876.

39 'Quelle étrange soirée ! Et pourquoi diable a-t-on invité la presse à venir juger ces déclamations grotesques et toutes ces manifestations puériles ? A-t-on vraiment cru qu'on prendrait au sérieux cet assemblage étonnant d'orphéonistes, de musiciens, de conférenciers et de poètes qui nous a permis d'admirer l'ouverture de la *Muette*, Laboulaye, les *Martyres aux arènes* de Laurent de Rillé et Mlle Rousseil en statue de la Liberté, se drapant dans les plis du drapeau des Etats-Unis !' : Un Monsieur de l'Orchestre, 'La Soirée théâtrale : Le Festival franco-américain', *Le Figaro*, 26 April 1876.

40 'Il a préféré s'en tenir à ses orphéons, ce qui pourrait faire croire que l'Amérique a une prédilection particulière pour ce genre de divertissement. Si bien qu'en arrivant à New York, Offenbach va se croire évidemment forcé de modifier le titre d'une de ses pièces et de l'intituler désormais : *Orphéon aux enfers*' : *La Gazette*, 26 April 1876.

41 'Les grands journaux avaient été invité à cette soirée ; les organisateurs n'auront pas à la remercier de leur bienveillance, car ils se sont presque tous livrés à un éreintement en règle ; c'est leur habitude, du reste, et les orphéonistes sont pour eux des têtes de Turcs sur lesquelles ils ne se lassent jamais de frapper' : 'Nouvelles des sociétés', *Echo des feuilletons*, 27 April 1876.

article for that week's *L'Orphéon* connected the history and the very fabric of the institution to the gala appearance at the Opéra, ending with the assessment that, 'guided by a generous thought of fraternity and union', the Orphéon 'sings for the fatherland'.[42]

The inclusion of the Orphéon singers in the 1876 musical fundraiser at the Opéra points to two issues that relate, on the one hand, to the construction of the sonic vernacular of such an event and, on the other, to Parisian views of American cultural practice. The diametrically opposed responses to the same performance by an openly excited audience and by a caustically critical Parisian press begs the question of how different expectations shaped what each group heard and saw during that evening.[43] The audiences – a mix of journalists from France and the United States, the who's who of the American colony in Paris, and a cross-section of French supporters of the statue – encountered a visual and sonic programme that delivered the anticipated elements of gala events resounding with patriotic affirmation.[44] The stage was set with the medieval hall of Elsevier from Ambroise Thomas's opera *Hamlet*, complemented by Lavastre's splendid backdrop of Liberty in front of New York Harbor and a line-up of American and French flags. What the audiences and American critics saw was a visual feast worthy of this grand cause; by contrast, the eyes of the Parisian critics perceived a tasteless amalgamation of unrelated visual elements.[45] Similarly, the musical and oratorical line-up hit all the marks that would be expected in such a socio-political framework: rousing instrumental music, a passionate speech by Laboulaye, dramatic recitation, vocal display in arias, choral and national hymns, and a newly composed work by a transatlantic master. Yet for the ears of the critics, the sonic patchwork could not be reconciled with the institutional framework of the national stage of the Opéra. Georges Boyer suggested that the more modest Salle Favart (the Opéra-Comi-

---

42 'Guidé par une généreuse pensée de fraternité et d'union [...] il chante pour la patrie' : Henri-Abel Simon, untitled leading article, *L'Orphéon*, 25 April 1876. Earlier in the text, Simon made a point to emphasise that the singers were honoured by performing with the orchestra of the Opéra : 'Ce soir l'Orphéon français remporte une nouvelle victoire, il a l'honneur de venir joindre ses chants sur la première scène du monde aux accents de l'orchestre de l'Opéra, c'est-à-dire à ceux de l'élite de nos artistes musiciens.'

43 The evening was reported in the American daily press, but the text is clearly a wire-shared piece between major news services, as the story printed, for example, in the *New York Times, New York Observer, Philadelphia Inquirer*, and *Pittsburgh Gazette* (in their respective 26 April 1876 editions) was almost word-for-word identical.

44 In one of the few positive reviews, Antoine Elwart (*Le National*, 27 April 1876) wrote : 'Jamais, depuis la fondation de l'Opéra, la scène de ce théâtre n'avait retenti d'accents aussi patriotiques que mardi soir.'

45 Not all critics explained in detail where the various stage elements were sourced, but those who did identified the various elements. See, for example, Un Monsieur de l'Orchestre, 'La Soirée théâtrale : Le Festival franco-américain', *Le Figaro*, 26 April 1876, and Tabarin, 'La Solennité franco-américaine à l'Opéra', *L'Evénement*, 27 April 1876.

246 *Annegret Fauser*

que) would have been more appropriate. Both he and several others took great delight in contrasting the habitual splendour of operatic costumes with the sombre, ostentatiously egalitarian suits of the choir members.[46] Hearing such choruses and seeing a large group of men clad in black suits in the Elsevier décor was considered jarring. Moreover, one critic claimed, it was a waste to involve the Opéra's orchestra 'in this mess.'[47] Here, classist concepts of opera stood crosswise to the evening's performative choices. Putting the amateur singers of the Orphéon with their working-class aura on the premier stage of the nation was perceived as a lowering of taste that critics laid right at the feet of the American contingent among the members of the Union Franco-Américaine. A particularly nasty piece in the royalist *Gazette* fantasised about how one might have made the event even more 'American'; one suggestion was to replace the audience every half hour in order performatively to generate a 'New World' while simultaneously packing the four corners of the hall with 'young dancers and pretty female marchers charged to explain the American gaze to the public.'[48] Other commentators, too, considered the programme and its use of the Orphéon choirs as reflecting poor American judgement. Even the audience's attire was judged as mirroring 'an entirely American simplicity.'[49] For the critical and cultural élite of Paris, the idea of Americanisation carried associations simultaneously of bad taste and austerity, a spectre that would haunt the following events organised by the Union Franco-Américaine as well. Nonetheless, after the gala performance, the tide began to turn, and the project started to generate momentum and support.

In effect, the next Parisian event garnered significant visibility in the press, as it was closely connected to the visit to France in October and November 1877 by one of the statue's most prominent American supporters, the former United States president General Ulysses Grant. His image was splashed all

46 'Pourquoi aussi choisir l'Opéra? La salle Favart eût été bien mieux en situation, et le public d'hier y eût tenu bien à l'aise. Rien d'assommant, d'ailleurs, comme cette soirée, avec les 700 orphéonistes groupés dans le décor d'*Hamlet*. Curieux à voir quand ils sont en scène, mais bien ennuyeux dès qu'ils chantent': Georges Boyer, 'De Huit Heures à minuit', *Paris Journal*, 27 April 1876. 'Sur la scène de l'Opéra, habituée à la somptueuse mise en scène et aux costumes éclatants, on a vu s'avancer, ou plutôt rester immobiles, six cents messieurs en noir, ornés de cravates blanches et de gants blancs': unsigned and untitled article, *La Gazette*, 26 April 1876.

47 'Nous avons regretté vivement de voir se fourvoyer dans cette galère, d'abord l'excellent orchestre de l'Opéra, puis M. Caron, qui a chanté les *Rameaux*': Georges Boyer, 'De Huit Heures à minuit', *Paris Journal*, 27 April 1876.

48 'J'aurais placé dans tous les coins de la salle de jeunes danseuses et des jolies marcheuses, chargées d'expliquer au public ce que c'est que l'œil américain. Enfin, j'aurais renouvelé les spectateurs toutes les demi-heures, afin d'avoir constamment du *Nouveau-Monde*': *La Gazette*, 26 April 1876.

49 'Peu de toilettes: une simplicité toute américaine': Un Monsieur de l'Orchestre, 'La Soirée théâtrale: le festival franco-américain', *Le Figaro*, 26 April 1876.

over the French illustrated press, and journalists followed his steps everywhere, including to an evening at the Opéra on 31 October, where the victorious Union general attended a gala performance in his honour of Fromental Halévy's *La Reine de Chypre*. As befitted a visiting statesman, his entrance was marked by the American national anthem – at that time 'Hail Columbia'.[50] A few days later, the American community in Paris organised a gala banquet at the Grand Hotel at the cost of thirty francs per person to raise further funds for the statue. A Second Empire luxury establishment with splendid reception rooms, the hotel provided a sumptuous framework for the festivities. That there should be music at such an event was not a surprise as and for itself. As expected, for example, Grant's formal entrance was honoured by 'Hail Columbia', and the guests proceeded to dinner, with waltzes and polkas by such popular composers as Johann Strauss the younger performed in the background. What was unusual, however, was the request halfway through the meal by the American host, General Edward Noyes, now to pay attention to a musical interlude: 'The Star-Spangled Banner', followed by an aria from Gaetano Donizetti's *Lucrezia Borgia* and other pieces.[51] The guests were asked not to make noise with their cutlery – a request considered in the French press to show a somewhat American attitude – as music followed toast, and so on.[52] As a long and detailed article published in the *American Register* revealed, the sequence of toasts and musical performances was carefully choreographed to convey the symbolic entanglement of Franco-American civic and military history all the way back to the American Revolution while reaffirming current and future friendship, including a toast to the American military. Nothing was left to chance, and a committee was charged with the preparation.[53] As with the gala

50   'Le général Grant a assisté avant-hier à la représentation de gala donnée en son honneur à l'Opéra; on donnait la *Reine de Chypre*. A son entré dans la salle, le général Grant a été salué par l'hymne national américain': *Le National*, 3 Nov. 1877.

51   An unsigned note inserted in the 'Carnet de la journée', *La France*, 8 Nov. 1877, pointed out that 'The Star-Spangled Banner' garnered excessive applause ('applaudi à outrance').

52   'A sept heures et demie, l'excellent orchestre de M. Desgrange saluait l'entrée du général Grant par un *Hail Columbia*! exécuté avec brio [...] Au beau milieu du diner, on nous fit la surprise toute américaine d'introduire deux chanteuses et deux chanteurs, qui prirent place sur une estrade en face de la table d'honneur. Les valses et les polkas de Strauss cessèrent, et le général Noyes se leva encore une fois. Restant un instant silencieux, il finit par s'écrier d'une voix tonitruante: "Mesdames et messieurs, nous allons entendre ces jeunes personnes; elles vont nous chanter des airs connus par leurs beautés. Je vais vous prier de ne pas faire de bruit avec vos fourchettes et vos couteaux; le bruit, il est inutile de vous dire, nuit à l'inspiration de l'art"': Spectator, 'Un banquet américain', *Le Gaulois*, 8 Nov. 1877.

53   'The American Banquet Tendered to General U. S. Grant, Ex-President of the United States, at the Grand Hotel, November 6th, 1877', *American Register*, 10 Nov. 1877. The committee appointed the following subcommittees: Dinner Committee; Committee of

concert at the Opéra the previous year, the uniquely American twist – in this case the insertion of musical performances in the middle of a dinner – to an otherwise unremarkable social ritual was what was made the evening's entertainment newsworthy. Both Parisian galas, in 1876 and 1877, were considered to offer American cultural practices to Parisians so that even entirely ordinary musical elements such as national anthems, familiar aria selections, and male choirs took on a symbolic quality in establishing the transatlantic meaning of the monument. But by the end of 1877, the statue had also begun to capture the popular imagination to the point that it found its way into the end-of-year review, 'Les Menus Plaisirs de l'année'.[54]

The subsequent year, 1878, shifted the symbolic associations with the Statue of Liberty, connecting it more firmly with French values and ideas. By the time the Exposition Universelle had opened its doors, the head of the monument was in the process of being completed, and Bartholdi organised its display right between the Champ de Mars and the Trocadéro (fig. 8.1). On 27 June 1878, in the evening, a large carriage pulled by sixteen horses made its way slowly down the Champs-Elysées towards the exhibition grounds, transporting the statue's enormous head, which journalists claimed weighed eight tons.[55] A crowd of about 1,500 people followed, waving, baring their heads, shouting 'Vive la République', and singing the *Marseillaise*.[56] For the crowds, the statue embodied the Republic, and it became audible in the resounding sonic markers of French Republicanism in what seems to have been a mixture of orchestrated and spontaneous manifestations as the procession made its way from the Arc de Triomphe to the Champ de Mars. Until that point, the Statue of Liberty had not been associated with the French national anthem. But what might have been a case of mistaken identity of the monument during the head's transport through the streets of Paris turned into a sonic ritual thereafter. Now shouts of

---

Invitation; Committee for Toasts; Committee on Music (the article lists three members, Mr J. Ryan, Col. Evelyn, Dr W. E. Johnston); and Committee on Printing.

54 Charles Clairville, *Les Menus-Plaisirs de l'année. Revue à spectacle en 3 actes et 17 tableaux* (Paris: A. Allourad, 1877). A copy of the libretto dedicated by the author to Bartholdi is kept in FB 1.

55 *Le Rappel*, 30 June 1878; *Le Républicain*, 2 July 1878. Both are snippets preserved in one of Bartholdi's scrapbooks, FB 1.

56 'Depuis le point de départ, quinze cent personnes suivaient le chariot en chantant la *Marseillaise*': *La France*, 29 June 1878. 'Jeudi, vers huit heures du soir, nous avons été témoin, aux Champs-Elysées, d'un spectacle aussi saisissant qu'inattendu. Comme nous suivions au petit trot d'un cheval de fiacre les courbes du rond point, une tête colossale, fantastique, se profile tout à coup dans l'ouverture de l'arc de triomphe, tandis que des cris de: *Vive la République!* retentissent en puissantes salves dans les lointains de l'avenue [...] Sur le passage du char, malgré soi, on portait la main au chapeau pour lui rendre sa politesse. La foule suivait en chantant la *Marseillaise*': *La République*, 1 July 1878. Bartholdi's scrapbooks, FB 1.

Figure 8.1. Albert Fénique, head of the Statue of Liberty, Exposition Universelle, Paris, 1878. Black-and-white photograph. The Library of Congress.

'Vive la République' and the singing of the *Marseillaise* were not out of place in French civil ceremonies connected to the statue.

Indeed, just three days later, on 30 June, at the Exposition Universelle, French Republicanism became reaffirmed as part of the statue's transatlantic soundscape. Liberty's head faced another monumental statue, that of *La République* by Auguste Clésinger, which was unveiled that day with ministerial speeches and music provided by the band of the Garde Républicaine. A large crowd had gathered for this widely advertised event of national significance. Yet the dedication took an unexpected turn: after the speeches and music for the dedication of *La République* had ended, Clésinger suggested that the assembled dignitaries should visit another monument, created by his fellow artist, Bartholdi, and so they processed ceremoniously across the *grande allée*, followed by the band and the crowd and led by Senator Krantz, the Commissioner-General of the Exposition Universelle. In front of the Statue of Liberty, where Bartholdi had placed a model of the entire monument next to the finished head, the band performed three pieces: first 'Hail Columbia', then an arrangement of the duet from Daniel Auber's *La Muette de Portici* – a musical favourite that shared its textual incipit, 'Amour sacré de la patrie', with the sixth strophe of the *Marseillaise* – and, by popular demand, once more the French national anthem, the audience joining in to sing with great enthusiasm. Here, too, shouts of 'Vive la République' punctuated the 'frenetic applause' of the audience.[57] If the transatlantic connection was previously made visually through the pairing of flags, and verbally in speeches and writing, now it had also found its explicit sonic equivalency by pairing musical emblems of nationhood. In 1876, the sonic connection had remained subterranean in Gounod's musical allusions to the *Marseillaise*. With this next step, however, Liberty – though destined for New York Harbor – had taken on a distinctly French identity.

The statue was again on display the following year, on 11 May 1879, this time in a cavalcade themed as 'Les cinq parties du monde' and organised for the benefit of the poor by the Société Reconstituée des Fêtes de Versailles.[58]

---

57 'la musique a fait entendre l'air national américain, un morceau de la Muette, et la Marseillaise': *Le XIXe Siècle*, 3 July 1878. 'Pendant qu'on examine cette tête ainsi qu'une réduction de la statue complète, placée non loin, la garde républicaine joue l'air national américain, le célèbre duo de *la Muette*: "Amour sacré de la Patrie", et sur la demande de plusieurs conseillers municipaux, *la Marseillaise*. Le public applaudit avec frénésie': *Le Gaulois*, 2 July 1878. 'L'air national retentit de nouveau, et cette fois le public se mêle de la partie et entonne le refrain du chant national. Les cris de: *Vive la République!* se font entendre à plusieurs reprises, répétés avec enthousiasme par la foule des assistants': *Le Petit Républicain*, 1 July 1878. 'La musique de la garde républicaine s'est alors de nouveau fait entendre; elle a exécuté le duo de la *Muette*, *Amour sacré de la patrie*, puis, après de nombreuses acclamations, le cortège s'est séparé, et la foule s'est dispersé dans toutes les parties du Champ de Mars': *Le Figaro*, 1 July 1878. All these extracts are in Bartholdi's scrapbooks, FB 1.

58 A flyer for the event is preserved in FB 1.

Cavalcades had become a much-loved form of fundraising for charities, and this one competed with several others taking place in and around Paris at the same time. It was clearly inspired by the displays of the Exposition Universelle the previous year, and presented Liberty on its own chariot as simultaneously French and universal on top of a globe (fig. 8.2). The music was provided by the French military bands that helped stage the event, which relied on a great many theatre props and costumes, including a number provided by the Théâtre de la Gaîté.[59] The newspaper *La Liberté* announced that four musical groups would represent different nations in addition to numerous military bands, a musical prop that was probably rendered by local Western musicians.[60] A short description in *Le Temps* puts the enthusiastic audience at 40,000, many of whom had crowded the trains from Paris to make it to Versailles in time for the start of the parade.[61] In the 'multi-national' musical festivities, cheered on by onlookers lining the streets and hanging out of windows, the sonic vernacular expanded the transatlantic to an imagined global sounding at the feet of a statue whose height – even in its reduced size on top of the 'grand chariot of the world' ('le grand chariot du Monde') – dominated the event.

If the 1879 event framed the statue in global terms through a soundscape of fake world music, the last major ceremony on French soil – organised by Bartholdi and the Union Franco-Américaine on 4 July 1884 to mark the monument's completion – returned to the binational symbolism of American and French emblems, including the familiar sonic markers of their respective national anthems.[62] The music for the occasion was provided by the Harmo-

---

59 Given the limited descriptions in the press and the announcements in the flyer that mention specific musical groups, it seems that the cavalcade represented other nations and ethnicities in costumes and makeup rather than the integration of musicians and peoples from abroad. See, for example, the announcement in 'Départements', *La Lanterne*, 12 April 1879: 'Cette cavalcade aura un caractère tout à fait actuel. Les sujets qui la composeront se rapportent tous à la réunion des nations au grand concours international de l'an dernier: ce sera comme l'apothéose de l'Exposition universelle [...] Plusieurs musiques militaires [...] prêteront leur concours à cette cavalcade.' The theatrical resources are identified in 'Nouvelles du jour', *Le Temps*, 13 May 1879.

60 'Elle comprendra, outre les tambours, clairons, fifres et trompes de chasses, quatre corps de musique de diverses nations.' Two weeks later, *La Petite Presse* published a preview ('La Cavalcade de Versailles', 8 May 1879) that promised that 'Les cinq parties du monde seront représentées au point de vue ethnographique et pittoresque' and detailed what music was to be heard, including 'un corps de musique indienne à cheval' and Mexicans on horseback 'avec tambours, fifres et clairons': 'La Fête de bienfaisance de Versailles', *La Liberté*, 24 April 1879.

61 'Nouvelles du jour', *Le Temps*, 13 May 1879.

62 Khan (*Enlightening the World*, pp. 164–5) offers a description of this event, including the presence of a band that 'played the national anthems of the United States and France'. A few weeks earlier, the American ambassador, Levi P. Morton, had given a dinner for the Franco-American Union in honour of the statue's completion. See 'A travers Paris', *Le Figaro*, 12 June 1884.

Figure 8.2. 'Versailles. – Grande Cavalcade des cinq parties du monde, le dimanche, 17 mai', *L'Univers illustré*, 22 (1879), 312. Bibliothèque Nationale de France.

nie des Batignolles, a local group from the part of Paris in which the statue had been built.[63] Attended by the American ambassador to France, now Levi P. Morton, the solemn transferral of the statue to the Americans took place on a hot summer's day, though without the promised presence of the French president, Jules Ferry, who had been taken ill the day before. Instead, Ferdinand de Lesseps gave the French dedication speech, followed by 'Hail Columbia'. As the French press noted pointedly, Morton then gave his speech in English. He had barely finished when the band launched into the *Marseillaise*.[64] Several French newspapers connected Morton's speech in English with the immediacy of the French musicians' performance, though without further comment.[65] But it was not difficult to read between the lines. Clearly, the actual sequence of speeches and anthems had been decided in advance; yet for the French journalists, Morton's choice of language probably seemed a breach of protocol or at least a sign of arrogance, for it was singled out in every single newspaper article.[66]

With this ceremony, the Parisian side of the transatlantic story ended, though many a French admirer of the statue wondered at that point whether Liberty should not better remain in Paris, where her towering presence had become a fixture near the Parc Monceau. One journalist mused that instead of being shipped across the Atlantic, the statue could be moved to the Franco-German border as a French and Republican answer to the newly built *Germania* (the *Niederwalddenkmal*), in honour of German unification following the Franco-Prussian War, that overlooked the Rhine since 1883.[67]

New York

In comparison to Paris, relatively few events took place in New York and elsewhere on the East Coast in the lead-up to the 1886 inauguration of the statue.

---

63 'La Société musicale "l'Harmonie des Batignolles" prêtait son concours à cette solennité': 'La Statue de la Liberté', *Le XIXe Siècle*, 6 July 1884. The article published in *La Liberté* identified the band as one of the best of Paris: 'L'Harmonie des Batignolles, une des meilleures musiques de Paris, prêtait son concours à la cérémonie': 'La Statue de la Liberté éclairant le monde', *La Liberté*, 5 July 1884.

64 'A peine M. Morton s'était-il rassis que la musique a joué la *Marseillaise*': 'La Statue de la Liberté', *Le Temps*, 5 July 1884.

65 Besides the article in *Le Temps* (see n. 65), see, for example, 'Le Plat du jour', *Le Radical*, 6 July 1884, and 'La Statue de la Liberté', *Le Rappel*, 6 July 1884.

66 American newspapers published the same short summary of events that had made its way across the Atlantic by wire. A search in Proquest Historical Newspapers nets a large number of publications, from the *San Francisco Chronicle* to the *Baltimore Sun*, which published the exact same text.

67 Berenson, *Statue of Liberty*, pp. 67–8.

254   *Annegret Fauser*

The monument's first ambassador to the United States was its creator, Bartholdi. He had travelled across the Atlantic already in 1871, not only to promote the project for the Statue of Liberty but also potentially to emigrate to the United States. As Edward Berenson points out, Bartholdi at that time felt doubly alienated: as a French Alsatian, had seen his birthplace lost to Germany in the wake of the Franco-Prussian War, and as a moderate Republican, he felt in exile from the Commune in Paris.[68] Already during his second day in New York, he identified Bedloe Island as the place where his colossal statue could make the highest visual impact, an idea he pursued over the coming years. During his almost six months abroad, Bartholdi consolidated the concept of the statue and started garnering American support.

When Bartholdi returned to the United States in 1876, not only was he better known as a sculptor, but his ideas for the Statue of Liberty also began to take hold in the American popular imagination, not least because of his excellent salesmanship. The backdrop that Lavastre had painted in 1875 was in Bartholdi's luggage in 1876 and was displayed in Madison Square, in front of the New York Club, for the big centennial parade on 4 July. Beneath the picture, the lines from Guiard's poem for Gounod's chorus were displayed in both French and English.[69] To make the image more visible during the evening parade, it was illuminated by a spotlight placed at the World Monument across the street.[70] If this first exposure to Bartholdi's Liberty began to intrigue the American public, it was a different monument that would trigger major support for this project: a statue of the Marquis de Lafayette commissioned by the French government that Bartholdi created for Union Square Park in New York and that was inaugurated – with a markedly sonic event – on 6 September 1876.[71] The *New York Times* led its article about the occasion with the sentence 'Yesterday saw something of the amenities of two great republics', setting the tone for the response to the proceedings as rebooting amicable Franco-American relations.

Before the dedication itself, which was scheduled for 3:30pm but started half an hour later, a large procession of military regiments and their bands, as

---

68   "'At the end of the war," Bartholdi wrote, "I couldn't go to my home province, since the Germans had excluded me, while in Paris, the commune was in full force, and civil war at hand." A political exile in his own country, the sculptor resolved to head for the United States': Berenson, *Statue of Liberty*, p. 26.

69   'The Statue of Liberty', *New York Herald*, 6 July 1876. The article attributes the poem to Guiard's uncle, Émile Augier, and reprints the first strophe in both French and English.

70   'The Statue of Liberty', *New York Herald*, 6 July 1876.

71   The monument had been commissioned by the French government to express its gratitude for United States support during the Franco-Prussian War, a gesture which seems to have been more apposite for anticipating future relations than reflecting actual support during the conflict. See Khan, *Enlightening the World*, 133. The inscription on the south side of the statue reads: 'To the City of New York, / France, / in remembrance of sympathy / in times of trial / 1870-71'. See <https://www.nycgovparks.org/parks/union-square-park/monuments/884>.

Transatlantic Soundscapes for the Statue of Liberty   255

well as New York fire brigades and civic societies – including those representing the French citizens of the region all the way up to Canada – assembled just after 1:00pm and marched from Madison Square to Union Square. The military line-up even included – as a brief article in the *Cincinnati Enquirer* emphasised – 'a battalion of German riflemen'.[72] French and American flags were everywhere, and according to the *Evening Post*, 'every regiment and society in the procession was preceded by a military band'.[73] One entire section of the line-up, its fifth, was reserved for French–American music societies.[74] The French-language New York newspaper *Le Messager franco-américain*, took great pains to list them all.[75] One in the fifth division, possibly the Société Patriotique Alsace-Lorraine, was 'conspicuous for a flag on which was inscribed "Alsace et Lorraine", the top of the flag-staff being surmounted with a bunch of black crepe'.[76]

Those who waited in Union Square witnessed the arrival of the procession, 'and the previously indistinct murmur of its music burst full upon the ears of the multitude'.[77] Once the procession had stopped, the dedication ceremony proper began. Predictably, its programme alternated speeches and musical works, and was punctuated by a military salute. The music included not only 'Hail Columbia' and the *Marseillaise*, but also Laurent de Rillé's chorus for male voices 'France', one of the best-known pieces of the Francophone Orphéon repertoire. Whereas the *Marseillaise* was sung by all choirs present, accompanied by the full band contingent, 'France' was performed by a Francophone Alsatian choral society, L'Espérance, a choice that did not go unnoticed. There was more music on the schedule afterwards, but the press in general simply wrote 'music' to describe it; *Le Messager franco-américain* identified it as French and American in origin.[78] The detailed description in the *New York Times* of the dedication put its sonic focus on the *Marseillaise*, reporting that 'when the "Marseillaise" was rendered, after its magic fashion, making the blood flow warmer and the

---

72 'Lafayette', *Cincinnati Enquirer*, 6 Sept. 1876.

73 'The Statue of Lafayette', *Evening Post*, 6 Sept. 1876.

74 'The Lafayette Statue: Unveiling and Presentation of the Memorial', *New York Tribune*, 7 Sept. 1876.

75 'La cinquième division est peu nombreuse mais très française; elle était précédée de la fanfare de l'Association musicale. A la suite des membres de cette association, des sociétés chorales l'Espérance et l'Orphéon, et du Cercle Lyrique Fraternel, nous voyons la Société patriotique Alsace-Lorraine, avec le drapeau de l'option, président V. Fortwengler; puis l'Union Alsacienne, l'Alsace Lorraine et l'Union Alsace-Lorraine de Williamsburg': 'La Statue de Lafayette', *Le Messager franco-américain*, 7 Sept. 1876.

76 'Sights in Gotham', *Courier-Journal*, 12 Sept. 1876.

77 'Lafayette's Statue', *New York Times*, 7 Sept. 1876.

78 'The Statue of Lafayette. France's Gift to the City of New York', *New York Times*, 6 Sept. 1876. *Le Messager franco-américain*, 6 Sept. 1876, specified that the *Marseillaise* was 'exécutée par les musiques réunies et les chœurs', whereas Rillé's 'chœur patriotique' used only the members of the choral society, L'Espérance.

256   *Annegret Fauser*

pulse beat quicker, the boom of cannon came in like a battle-blast to the aid of Rouget de Lisle's famous *chanson*.[79]

Given the entanglement of the Lafayette statue's dedication with the complicated transnational history of the Franco-Prussian War, on the one hand, and the centenary of the American Revolutionary War, on the other, the identity politics displayed and ensounded during this event was unsurprising. The prominence of French immigrants from Alsace-Lorraine and their ostentatious display of allegiance to France was noticeable, and all the more given the presence of German-American riflemen. As the telling of the *Marseillaise*'s overwhelming sonic dominance indicates, this celebration of Lafayette in America was about French pride and honour. And in New York, at least, Alsace-Lorraine was still part of France, whatever the geopolitical realities might be in Europe. That the Alsatian choral society had chosen to perform De Rillé's 'France' was as clear a signal as the choice of the Alsatian choral society over any other Francophone one. On the surface, the dedication's musical programme consisting of the two national anthems, De Rillé's Orphéonic chorus, and a selection of Franco-American tunes seems as commonplace as the musical selection, six months earlier, for the gala event in Paris at the Palais Garnier. Yet in this particular framework, it took on a surprisingly provocative character in political terms that were not lost on either Francophile or Germanophile journalists in the United States.

A short postlude reinforces the impression of a deliberately political musical programme for the dedication of the Lafayette statue. The night before Bartholdi's return to France at the end of January 1877, the Alsatian choir, L'Espérance, serenaded the sculptor with a number of French choruses, including – once more – De Rillé's 'France'. Not only did the reporter for *Le Messager franco-américain* make it clear that this was an honour bestowed on their fellow Alsatian, but Bartholdi – in an improvised and 'most political' speech – afterwards greeted his 'double-compatriots' as both French and Alsatian.[80] As conventional as the specific musical pieces may have been, their context created a symbolic matrix that imbued them with meanings beyond those they had carried in Paris.

The decade between 1876 and the inauguration of the statue in 1886 was spent by the American supporters of the monument in the service of fundraising for the statue's massive pedestal. Although music – including Gounod's

---

79 'Lafayette's Statue', *New York Times*, 7 Sept. 1876.

80 'Nous avons annoncé le départ de M. Bartholdi pour Le Havre sur le paquebot la *France*. Dans la soirée de vendredi, les Alsaciens de New-York ont voulu faire les adieux à l'éminent sculpteur sous la forme d'une sérénade donnée par la Société chorale alsacienne, l'Espérance. Les membres de cette société se sont rendus au n⁰ 9 Livingston place, où était descendu M. Bartholdi, et ils ont exécuté, sous la direction de M. Dupin, plusieurs morceaux parmi lesquels nous citons le *Départ du Régiment*, *France*, le *Bal champêtre* et *les Buveurs*. A la suite de cette sérénade, M. Bartholdi a voulu serrer la main aux sociétaires qui sont doublement ses compatriotes, comme Français et comme Alsaciens. Il a aussi improvisé un petit discours dans lequel il a exprimé les sentiments les plus patriotiques': 'Chronique', *Messager franco-américain*, 28 Jan. 1877.

Liberté éclairant le monde – sometimes was pressed into service through charity concerts and as a sonic background for other fundraising ceremonies, few journalists mentioned any specifics. By the time of the 1886 inauguration, the monument had become a familiar feature in the American imagination without, however, acquiring any broader musical signature – despite a small but growing body of sheet music decorated with images either of Liberty or, in the case of Giovanni E. Conterno's *Bartholdi March*, of the sculptor.[81] A copy of James M. Stewart's new 'national hymn', titled 'Fair America: "Liberty Enlightening the World"' and dedicated 'To the Memory of Washington', was placed in the cornerstone of the pedestal on 5 August 1884. Both poetically and in its melodic contour and rhythm, the piece follows closely 'The Star-Spangled Banner', if in a more singable form.[82] This hymn, beginning 'Fair America rose in the pride of her youth, / With the wisdom of age in her noble endeavor', forms part of the emerging story of the current American national anthem as 'Hail Columbia' slowly became displaced by 'The Star-Spangled Banner' – a subplot in this statue's history but not an entirely irrelevant one (see Chapter 9). The laying of the cornerstone brought with it another civic ceremony when some five to seven hundred guests stood in pouring rain as the 'Governor's Island Band played several national airs, including the *Marseillaise*'.[83] The press found it worth noting the presence of a large number of women, while the *New York Times* also emphasised that 'nearly one-half of the gathering was made up of Frenchmen'.[84] As in the case of the dedication of the Lafayette monument in 1876, French New Yorkers turned out in droves to highlight their presence as an integral part of the American population. Moreover, what marked this event as unusual was that it foregrounded the participation of the Masonic lodges of New York. As the Deputy Grand Master of the Grand Lodge of the State of New York pointed out in his speech: 'Never since the building of the Temple of Solomon have Masons participated in a work more exalted than this'.[85] A twenty-one-gun salute accompanied the laying of the stone, followed by the band playing 'Praise God from Whom All Blessings Flow', a seventeenth-cen-

---

81 Giovanni E. Conterno, *Bartholdi March: The New Two Step* (New York: Carl Fischer, 1893).

82 James M. Stewart, 'Fair America: "Liberty Enlightening the World"' (New York: C. H. Ditson & Co., 1884).

83 'New York: Laying the Corner-Stone of the Pedestal of the Bartholdi Statue', *Detroit Free Press*, 6 Aug. 1884. This text was clearly a syndicated report of a newsworthy event, for it reappears in other American newspapers, including the *Courier-Journal*, the *Daily American*, the *Philadelphia Inquirer*, and the *Washington Post*, all on 6 Aug. 1884. The New York newspapers offered a more in-depth account and estimated the number of guests closer to seven hundred.

84 'Liberty's Place of Rest', *New York Times*, 6 Aug. 1884.

85 'New York: Laying the Corner-Stone of the Pedestal of the Bartholdi Statue', *Detroit Free Press*, 6 Aug. 1884.

tury Anglican hymn by Thomas Ken often paired with the Calvinist melody of 'Old Hundredth' and commonly treated as a Protestant doxology.[86] The next two pieces were 'Hail Columbia' and – once more – the *Marseillaise*, which was followed by a speech of the French consul general, Albert Lefaivre. After the ceremony, the musicians returned to the city and performed the French national anthem in front of the nation's consulate.

The 1884 ceremony reflected a subtle shift in the sonic vernaculars associated with the Statue of Liberty by integrating prayer and religious song within a civic ritual. This American inclusion of Christian emblems had been entirely absent from the programmes in Republican Paris and contributed to the move that was beginning towards the Americanisation of the statue's meanings.[87] It is significant in this context that the copper box buried under the cornerstone contained only American artefacts – from copies of the Constitution and the Declaration of Independence to Stewart's newly composed 'Fair America' – with the box itself inscribed with the words by a Union general, John Adams Dix: 'If any man attempts to haul down the American flag, shoot him on the spot.'[88] This move towards American civic rituals meant that the French national anthem became a marker of the statue's entry into an immigration narrative rather than a musical symbol of American transatlantic entanglement.

The festivities for the grand inauguration of the statue two years later, on 28 October 1886, proved to be 'entirely American', at least for the French delegation and the newspaper readers back in Paris.[89] The reporter for the conservative and ultramontane newspaper *L'Univers* clarified with an envious eye one 'peculiarity' that made it American in his eyes, for 'the ceremony began with a prayer, as the Protestants themselves felt, with reason, that all national manifestation must have a religious character.'[90] Indeed, religious ritual was no less firmly enshrined in the events that October day than military parades

---

86 For in-depth information about the hymn and its history, see Victoria Schwarz and Wilson Pruitt, 'History of Hymns: "Praise God, from Whom All Blessings Flow"' <https://www.umcdiscipleship.org/articles/history-of-hymns-praise-god-from-whom-all-blessings-flow>.

87 That French Republicanism was not entirely divorced from Christian ritual is discussed in Jennifer Walker, *Sacred Sounds, Secular Spaces: Transformations of Catholicism in the Music of Third-Republic Paris* (New York: Oxford University Press, 2021). However, in the deliberately secular celebrations of Liberty in France, religious music and prayer had no explicit place. The closest a Parisian event came to including religious content was the jointly organised 1876 gala at the Opéra with the programming of Gounod's 'Ave Maria'.

88 'Liberty's Place of Rest', *New York Times*, 6 Aug. 1884.

89 'tout-à-fait américaine': 'Chronique', *L'Univers*, 31 Oct. 1886.

90 'Une particularité dont ne parlent pas non plus les journaux révolutionnaires; c'est que la cérémonie a commencé par une prière, les protestants eux-mêmes trouvant avec raison que toute manifestation nationale doit avoir un caractère religieux': 'Chronique', *L'Univers*, 31 Oct. 1886.

and civic pageants. By now – thanks to the sustained fundraising campaign by the newspaper editor Joseph Pulitzer, especially in his paper *New York World* – the statue had become a strong presence in the American imaginary.[91] Consequently, the statue's inauguration turned into a major national ceremony in which the American president, Grover Cleveland, played a leading role.

Preparations for the event were reported in newspapers as far away as the *San Francisco Chronicle*, and also in those with a predominantly local readership. The *Hartford Daily Courant* (Connecticut) made a point of emphasising that the unveiling would be sonically marked by a salvo from '500 guns. It will be the biggest salute ever given in this country.'[92] Following a naval parade, the waters of New York Harbor were to be filled with steamers and other vessels decorated with flags from all over the world, their whistles adding to the soundscape of the event. Whether or not the *Boston Daily Globe* was correct in its estimate that 'a full million people will be looking on' as the colossal statue was unveiled, it was a noisy holiday in New York, and the city was packed with locals and visitors despite the dreary weather.[93] During the military and civic parade, the crowds hailed not only the regiments and carriages but also the sculptor after they recognised him, 'until the heavy air was shaken with a roar of cheering that must have gladdened the heart of the Alsatian.'[94] There were bands galore during the parade, so many that the *New York Times* wondered whether it had 'rained brass bands during the night'. Whether they included a 'tooting Teuton' or a player from Buffalo with 'a dropsical tuba', regionally and ethnically marked brass bands reigned the day.[95] Yet all of them – one newspaper reveals – played the *Marseillaise* at one point or other that morning, though the performance of the Twenty-Second Regiment's band, led by Patrick Sarsfield Gilmore, 'best caught the inspiration of the day' by playing 'a few bars of the French national anthem, then a few bars of "Yankee Doodle", and so mixed melody fraternally. It vastly pleased the President and visitors.'[96] So

91 Berenson, *The Statue of Liberty*, p. 6.

92 'The Bartholdi Statue: Details of the Arrangements for Thursday', *Hartford Daily Courant*, 27 Oct. 1886. The article goes into great detail about how the 'simultaneous firing of so many guns will be accomplished'.

93 'Liberty and Love', *The Boston Daily Globe*, 28 Oct. 1886. This article sums up 'the four memorable events' of the day as 'the grand military and civic parade at the forenoon, the naval parade early in the afternoon, the ceremonies of unveiling, occupying the remainder of the afternoon, and the display at night'. The latter were fireworks over the Statue of Liberty. The number of 'a million patriotic citizens' was repeated in 'Unveiled!', *St. Louis Post*, 28 Oct. 1886.

94 'Unveiled!', *St Louis Post*, 28 Oct. 1886. The full passage of this incident traces how the sound travelled from one group to the next until it enveloped most of the parade route.

95 'France's Gift Accepted', *New York Times*, 29 Oct. 1886. The article offers a detailed if not delirious account of the sight and sounds provided by the bands. It ends with the sentence quoted at the end of the next paragraph.

96 'Enshrined', *Cincinnati Enquirer*, 29 Oct. 1886.

sonorous were the events of 28 October that journalists spent large segments of their reports trying to capture what made the soundscape of the statue's inauguration so unique.

The unveiling ceremony in the afternoon followed the familiar script of alternating musical and spoken performances (table 8.2). A raised platform had been built for the speakers, with a stand 'for the use of musicians above it'.[97] But before the ceremony could even begin, sound echoed over the harbour: salutes answered by the guns on the warships and 'every steam whistle in the fleet'.[98] It sounded to the ears of one journalist like 'a jungle full of wild elephants on a spree', while another praised the fact that it 'made a volume of glorious greeting such as was never heard on this continent'.[99] Following the predictable rendering of the *Marseillaise*, the event unrolled from opening prayer to the final benediction. For the *Boston Daily Globe*, however, it was neither the music and the cannon salute nor the prayers and speeches that stood out during the dedication of the statue, 'but rather the homely doxology played by the band, sung by the assembly, echoed by the people and carried by the press through all the land'.[100] As in 1884, the hymn 'Praise God from Whom All Blessings Flow' marked a solemn moment, strengthened this time by inviting the participation of all present in a communal rendering. Yet for most observers, it was the massive sound wave in response to the unveiling – starting with the pre-choreographed five-hundred-gun salute after the flag was dropped from the statue's face – that provided a thirty-minute sonic climax to the day. As the journalist for the *New York Times* reported:

> thunder upon thunder shook cloud and sea, the brazen voice of steam lifted its utmost clamors, colors dipped, men cheered and women applauded, the sounds from the sea were hurled back from the land, bell spoke to bell and cannon to cannon, till all men of the thousands gathered in her honour knew that Liberty had been given and received.[101]

By contrast, a reader of the Parisian press would have had a different impression. The wire dispatch from New York which the majority of newspapers printed, generally on their front pages, barely referenced the unbridled soundscape of the parades or the harbour: it simply reported enthusiastic cheers of the crowd, band music, and cannon salutes.[102] The report merely went through

---

97 'Liberty's Great Statue', *New York Times*, 28 Oct. 1886.

98 'All Aglow. Liberty's Torch Unveiled', *Boston Daily Globe*, 29 Oct. 1886.

99 'All Aglow. Liberty's Torch Unveiled', *Boston Daily Globe*, 29 Oct. 1886; 'Emblem of Liberty', *Detroit Free Press*, 29 Oct. 1886.

100 'All Aglow. Liberty's Torch Unveiled', *Boston Daily Globe*, 29 Oct. 1886.

101 'France's Gift Accepted', *New York Times*, 29 Oct. 1886.

102 'Les voiles qui couvraient la colossale statue sont tombés et celle-ci est apparue saluée d'une explosion de cris enthousiastes: les musiques se sont mises à jouer; les forts et les vaisseaux de guerre ont tiré des salves de coups de canon': 'Inauguration de la statue de la liberté', *Gil*

Transatlantic Soundscapes for the Statue of Liberty 261

Table 8.2. Programme, dedication ceremony of the Statue of Liberty,
Bedloe Island, 28 October 1886

All musical works were performed by the Twenty-Second Regiment's band,
led by Patrick Sarsfield Gilmore.

1. Music during the landing and seating of the assembly.
2. Signal gun.
3. Prayer by the Rev. Richard R. Storrs, D.D.
4. Count Ferdinand de Lesseps, on behalf of Franco-American Union.
5. Presentation Address, the Hon. William M. Evarts.
6. Unveiling.
7. Salute. A salvo from all the guns in the harbor.
8. Music.
9. Acceptance of the statue by the President.
10. Representative on behalf of the republic of France, Le Ministre Plénipo-
    tentiaire et Délégué Extraordinaire, A. Lefaivre.
11. Music.
12. Commemorative Address, the Honorable Chauncey M. Depew.
13. Music. Doxology – tune "Old Hundred"; in which the assembly is invited
    to join.
14. Benediction. Right Rev. Henry C. Potter, D.D. The assembly upon the is-
    land will be dismissed and will re-embark upon the steamers, which will
    return to their piers in the city, joining with the batteries in the general
    salute.
15. National salute. To be fired simultaneously from all the batteries in the
    harbor, ashore and afloat.

Source: Transcribed from 'Liberty's Great Statue', *New York Times*, 28 Oct. 1886.
The programme's final item (No. 16) specified fireworks later in the evening that
were, however, delayed a few days because of bad weather.

the sequence of events, highlighting the speeches of Ferdinand de Lesseps and
the American president. Perhaps a syndicated wire with its limited word count

---

Blas, 31 Oct. 1886. The same article was published in (among others) *Le Gaulois, Le Journal
des débats, La Justice, Le Petit Journal, Le Petit Parisien, Le Rappel, Le Temps,* and *Le XIXe
Siècle,* on either 30 or 31 October. The editors for *La Petite Presse* clearly used the same wire
text but rewrote the report to the taste of its penny-press readership.

was not the place to render through fulsome description how sonically unique the statue's inauguration seems to have been.[103] Yet the French newspapers focused more on the honours bestowed by the Americans – their president included – on Bartholdi and the French delegation than on the events of the inauguration itself. Nonetheless, Germany remained a phantom actor in this context, too. Writing for *Le Figaro*, Salvador gauged American enthusiasm for its old ally by the fact that even those whose sympathies lay with Germany rendered homage to France's gift.[104]

The shifting transatlantic soundscapes that were associated with the Statue of Liberty between 1875 and 1886 revealed and enshrined the subtle entanglements and differences between musical and civic practice in France and the United States. On both sides of the Atlantic, prejudice and cultural stereotyping were as much part of this story as were genuine attempts at (re-)establishing mutual respect and a shared cultural experience. Even if – as the clearly Germanophile writer for the *Chicago Daily Tribune* put it – 'no two peoples are more unlike than the French and the American', the carefully orchestrated events surrounding the genesis and inauguration of the statue worked at establishing the performance of common ground. For such an enterprise to succeed, the musical artefact needed to be familiar, simple, and – in symbolic terms – both legible and malleable. Here the aesthetic tenets of both statue and music blended in their emphasis on the banal and expected. But as the statue grew in size, so did the sonic vernaculars associated with it, each entering the realm of the monumental that also raises important questions about the nature of musical monumentalism and its links to prosaic banality. As the soundscape of the inauguration made audible, only a prodigious sonic event could frame a colossal statue, a sonic apotheosis that was remarkable not only for its sheer volume but also for the musical orchestration of gun volleys and steam whistles. The developments in those eleven years were not only in terms of sonic expansion, however, but also in the way music became instrumentalised for its symbolic meanings. At first, the works selected for the gala events and other celebrations were many and varied, and in particular, the French national anthem remained in the background. As the statue entered the public imagination, however, the *Marseillaise*, rather than any other piece, became the work associated with the statue, both in France and in the United States. Only once the American identity of the statue was fully affirmed in an inauguration ceremony moulded entirely on United States dedication rituals did Liberté change into Liberty.

103 'The Bartholdi Statue Dedication', *Chicago Daily Tribune*, 29 Oct. 1886.

104 'Les Américains – même ceux qui ne dissimulent pas leur sympathie pour l'Allemagne – rendent hommage au don de la France et à son auteur': Salvador, 'Figaro en Amérique', *Le Figaro*, 9 Nov. 1886.

PART IV

AMERICA, COMMODIFICATION AND RACE AT THE *FIN DE SIÈCLE*

9

Buffalo Bill and the Sound of America during the 1889 World's Fair

Mark A. Pottinger

The 1889 Exposition Universelle was one of the most famous global expositions of culture ever witnessed, made more so by the iconic Eiffel Tower, which stands today as a reminder of French aspirations at the end of an extremely turbulent century. The French colonial empire, which had grown to enormous proportions by 1880, was a central theme of the fair.[1] From May until November, representatives of nations and tourists from around the globe came to Paris to witness what was claimed by one writer for *Le Figaro* as 'a gigantic encyclopedia [...] it shows everything and explains all'.[2] In the same piece, the writer continues in his discussion of the importance of the fair with a business analogy:

> Following the example of the industrialist who does his inventory to the last penny in order to work out his profits and his future revenue, one could argue that the whole of humanity has come, in 1889, to do its stocktake in Paris, between the Esplanade des Invalides and the Trocadéro.[3]

1 Since 1830 and the conquest of Algiers, France had expanded its colonial empire into Africa, Asia, and Oceana throughout the nineteenth century. Justified by a policy of civilising 'inferior races' with Christian faith and French language and culture, the French colonial reach by the late nineteenth century was massive, being rivalled only by England. For more information about the French colonial empire in the nineteenth century, see Tony Chafer and Amanda Sackur (eds), *Promoting the Colonial Idea: Propaganda and Visions of Empire in France* (New York: Palgrave, 2002); Robert Aldrich, *Greater France: A History of the French Overseas Expansion* (Basingstoke: Macmillan Press, 1996); Alice Conklin, *A Mission to Civilize: The Republican Idea of Empire in France and West Africa, 1895–1930* (Stanford: Stanford University Press, 1997); and Pascal Blanchard, Sandrine Lemaire, Nicolas Bancel, and Dominic Richard David Thomas (eds), *Colonial Culture in France since the Revolution* (Bloomington: Indiana University Press, 2014).

2 'L'Exposition de 1889 réunit donc les éléments d'une encyclopédie gigantesque [...] Elle montre et elle explique tout': Émile Berr *et al.*, *Exposition de 1889: Guide bleu du 'Figaro' et du 'Petit Journal'* (Paris: Le Figaro, 1889), p. 12. This and other translations of French are mine, unless otherwise noted.

3 'A l'exemple des industriels qui font leur inventaire chaque année afin d'évaluer à un sou

Published in a guidebook for attendants at the fair, the above remark highlights the goal of the 1889 Exposition Universelle, which in large part was for the French 'to take stock' literally of their possessions in various parts of the globe but also to see how France compared with other nations in culture, science, and industry. Thus attendants at the fair were able to stroll past simple dwellings inhabited by native peoples from the colonies of Martinique, Guadeloupe, Tunisia, Algeria, Madagascar, Senegal, Loango (Congo), Pahouin (Central Africa), French Guinea, Tonkin and Annam (North and Central Vietnam), Cochinchina (South Vietnam), and Kanak (Malaysia) in order to eventually arrive at the Eiffel Tower, a symbol of French progress and industrial strength. Like the ancient Tower of Babel, the Eiffel Tower became a rallying point throughout the fair to showcase the racial hybridity of the world and the supremacy of the French nation.[4]

Such a comparative stance taken by the French in relationship to other nations, codified by the fair itself, is key to our understanding of America in the eyes and ears of the French at the end of the nineteenth century. In its display of cultural supremacy, the 1889 World's Fair may also be viewed as a joint celebration of France's 'sister republic', which after the turmoil of the Civil War had found itself emerging on the global stage.[5] This transformation of America was defined throughout the fair in the live-action scenes performed by Buffalo Bill and the Wild West Company. Although not part of the official proceedings of the fair, Buffalo Bill's Wild West Company exhibited a similar array of foreign people and objects that made *l'ouest sauvage* a fitting counterpart to the series

---

près leurs bénéfices d'hier et leurs ressources de demain, on peut dire que l'humanité tout entière est venue, en 1889, faire son inventaire à Paris, entre l'esplanade des Invalides et le Trocadéro': Berr *et al.*, *Exposition de 1889*, p. 12.

4   For a discussion of how race and French nationalism played a role in the 1889 Exposition Universelle, see Pascal Blanchard, Gilles Boetsch, and Nanette Jacomijn Snoep, *Human Zoos: The Invention of the Savage* (Paris: Musée de Quai Branly, 2011); Jann Pasler, 'Listening to Race and Nation: Music at the Exposition Universelle de 1889', *Musique, images, instruments: Revue française d'organologie et d'iconographie musicale*, 13 (2012), 52–74; and Michael Adcock, 'The 1889 Paris Exposition: Mapping the Colonial Mind', *Context*, 22 (Spring 2001), 31–40.

5   Following the establishment of the Monroe Doctrine in 1823, America ardently defended its right to expand into other territories within North and South America as well as around the world. By the start of the twentieth century, America had acquired all of the western frontier of what is now the United States, as well as Alaska, the annexation of Hawaii, parts of Samoa, Puerto Rico, Guam, and the islands of the Philippines. For more information on American colonialism in the late nineteenth century, see Charles S. Maier, *Among Empires: America's Ascendancy and its Predecessors* (Cambridge, MA: Harvard University Press, 2007), pp. 143–285; Daniel Immerwahr, *How to Hide an Empire: A History of the Greater United States* (New York: Farrar, Straus and Giroux, 2019); and David Brody, *Visualizing American Empire: Orientalism and Imperialism in the Philippines* (Chicago: University of Chicago Press, 2010).

of human villages displayed under the Eiffel Tower on the Champ de Mars, the so-called *Village Nègre*. Through the show's multi-cultural spectacle of Native Americans, White Americans, African Americans, Mexicans, and Canadians, French audiences perceived that America had indeed grown to define a 'New World' made up of many races and cultures within and beyond its own borders, held together with the simple populist notion central to the ideology of both nations that 'all men were created equal'.[6] As we shall see, the ideas and symbols of American populism, be they in the universalising merits of technology (e.g. the Edison phonograph and incandescent light bulb) or the pluralistic racial mix of America, were heard in the 'sound of America'. For the French *c.*1889, this sound had become the sound of mass entertainment and the duplicity of commercialism – in short, the new modern.[7]

America at the Fair

In the days following the opening of the fair, Robert McLane (1815–98), the former American ambassador to France, hosted a ceremonial banquet at the Hôtel Continental in Paris to honour the leading organisers. In his speech, McLane brought clarity on what the 1889 Exposition Universelle meant to the two republics:

> At this great international feast, you have invited all people, thus giving them an opportunity to show the way they have travelled on the various avenues of human activity [...] the republicans of America are happy to celebrate here with you the centenary, these grand competitions of art and industry, which have contributed so much to the bringing together

6   This vision of America was articulated by Alexis de Tocqueville (1805–59), whose two-volume *De la Démocratie en Amérique* (Paris: Ch. Gosselin, 1835–40) reaffirmed for the French that America's definition of equality (albeit fraught with hypocrisy) was worthy of emulation. On this much researched topic, see Alexis de Tocqueville, *Tocqueville on America after 1840: Letters and Other Writings*, ed. Aurelian Craiutu and Jeremy Jennings (Cambridge: Cambridge University Press, 2009); Jeremy Jennings, 'French Visions of America: From Tocqueville to the Civil War', in *America through European Eyes: British and French Reflections on the New World from the Eighteenth Century to the Present*, ed. Aurelian Craiutu and Jeffrey C. Isaac (University Park: Pennsylvania State University Press, 2009), pp. 161–86.

7   For more information on the image of America as a modernising force for Europe, see Jürgen Osterhammel, *The Transformation of the World: A Global History of the Nineteenth Century* (Princeton: Princeton University Press, 2014); Emily C. Burns, 'Taming a "Savage" Paris: The Masculine Visual Culture of Buffalo Bill's Wild West and France as a New American Frontier', in *Popular Frontier: Buffalo Bill's Wild West and Transnational Mass Culture*, ed. Frank Christianson (Norman: University of Oklahoma Press, 2017), pp. 129–54; and Vanessa Schwartz, *Spectacular Realities: Early Mass Culture in Fin-de-Siècle Paris* (Berkeley: University of California Press, 1998).

of all people. It was only right for France to open the one we see here today, because its own art, civilising genius, artistic taste, generous aspiration [...] a position that allows France to be an example to other nations. The 1889 exhibition will bear fruit; it will have the effect of stimulating the industrial activity of all people, and of engaging them more strongly in those relations of commerce and of individual interest that are the surest guarantee of peace in the world.[8]

The special relationship between France and the United States would be further acknowledged on 4 July 1889 with a public ceremony on the banks of the Seine, where the current American ambassador to France, Whitelaw Reid (1837–1912), and a large group of American expatriates presented to the people of France a copy of Bartholdi's Statue of Liberty. This 11.5-metre bronze version of the original was in acknowledgement of France's own gift of the same presented to the United States a few years earlier in 1884, which cemented the bond between the two countries and their similar struggle for independence.[9] (See Chapter 8 on transatlantic soundscapes of Bartoldi's project.) The 1889 ceremony was held in front of 4,000 invited guests, including the French president, Sadi Carnot, several government ministers, as well as Buffalo Bill and Chief Red Shirt of the Lakota tribe, who were to serve as honoured representatives of America.[10] The statue remains in Paris today on the

8   'A cette grande fête internationale, vous avez convié tous les peuples, leur fournissant ainsi l'occasion de montrer le chemin parcouru dans les différentes avenues de l'activité humaine [...] les républicains d'Amérique sont heureux de célébrer ici avec vous le centenaire, ces concours grandioses de l'art et de l'industrie qui ont tant contribué au rapprochement des peuples. C'était le droit de la France d'ouvrir celui auquel nous assistons aujourd'hui, car son art, son génie civilisateur, son goût artistique, ses aspirations généreuses [...] L'Exposition de 1889 portera ses fruits; elle aura pour effet de stimuler l'activité industrielle des peuples, et de les engager plus fortement dans ces relations de commerce et d'intérêts individuels qui sont les plus sûrs garants de la paix du monde': 'Chronique de l'Exposition', Le Temps, 20 May 1889, p. 2.

9   In the arms of the statue, a stone plaque reads '4 Juillet 1776 = 14 Juillet 1789', which equates America's Declaration of Independence from Britain with France's own struggle for a republic. For more information on the connection between France and the United States as symbolised by the Statue of Liberty, see Joseph Klaits and Michael Haltzel, Liberty/liberté: The American and French Experiences (Baltimore: Johns Hopkins University Press, 1991); also see Chapter 8, n. 2.

10   Charles Chincholle, 'Les Fêtes d'hier', Le Figaro, 5 July 1889, pp. 1–2. Chief Red Shirt (1847–1925) was an Oglala Lakota chief of the Pine Ridge Reservation (founded in 1878 in the southwestern region of South Dakota). Before joining William Cody (Buffalo Bill) and the Wild West Company in 1887, Red Shirt served as a United States army Native Scout with the 4th Calvary Regiment in the Great Sioux War of 1876–7. Throughout his nearly thirty years with the Wild West Company, Red Shirt presented choreographed performances in front of White audiences both in the United States and abroad. When he arrived in France in May 1889, Red Shirt was well known from several favourable reports of the Wild West Company's earlier trip to England in May

Buffalo Bill and the Sound of America   269

southern tip of the Île aux Cygnes, facing west towards the United States and the New York Harbor.

This homage to a prominent visual symbol of French-American alliances and the elaborate dinner hosted by a chief American diplomat were obvious attempts by America to distinguish itself as a modern nation in the eyes of the French. The 1889 Exposition Universelle was certainly not the first time American representatives had attended a World's Fair, but never before had the nation assembled such an impressive array of artists, musicians, inventors, and businessmen.[11] Chief among the American participants at the fair was Thomas Alva Edison, who in the view of one French journalist was 'the king of the elements [...] the sage of Llewellyn [New Jersey]'.[12] Literally banking on Edison's appeal with the French, American organisers gave Edison's inventions a prominent place in the allotted area for all American industrial products in the Palais

---

1887. For more information on Chief Red Shirt and other Native American performers of the Wild West Company, see Jason A. Heppler and Douglas Seefeldt, 'Buffalo Bill's Wild West and the Progressive Image of American Indians', in *Buffalo Bill Project* <buffalobillproject.unl.edu/research/showindians/> [accessed 2 Jan. 2020]; Linda McNenly, *Native Performers in Wild West Shows: From Buffalo Bill to Euro Disney* (Norman: University of Oklahoma Press, 2012); and Deanne Stillman, *Blood Brothers: The Story of the Strange Friendship between Sitting Bull and Buffalo Bill* (New York: Simon & Schuster, 2017).

11 Following the 6 April 1887 invitation from the French government and the 10 May 1888 joint resolution by Congress to accept the invitation, the governor of each US state and territory was tasked with assembling a delegation of artists, performers, scientists, machinists, industrialists, educators, and inventors to be sent to Paris. The US government set aside the modest sum of $250,000 to ensure the construction of pavilions, the shipping of exhibition items, and the round-trip travel of each participant. For detailed information on the actions of the US government to fulfil France's request to participate in the fair, see *Reports of the United States Commissioners to the Universal Exposition of 1889 at Paris* (4 vols, Washington, DC: US Government Printing Office, 1890–1). For more on the American presence at the fair, from politicians to entertainers, see, for example, Kathleen Adler *et al.*, *Americans in Paris: 1860–1900* (London: National Gallery, 2006); Nancy Green, *The Other Americans in Paris: Businessmen, Countesses, Wayward Youth, 1880–1941* (Chicago: University of Chicago Press, 2014); Andrew R. Valint, 'Fighting for Recognition: The Role African-Americans Played in World Fairs' (unpublished MA thesis, Buffalo State College, State University of New York, 2011); Emily C. Burns, *Transnational Frontiers: The American West in France* (Norman: University of Oklahoma Press, 2018); Jill Jonnes, *Eiffel's Tower: And the World's Fair where Buffalo Bill Beguiled Paris, the Artists Quarreled, and Thomas Edison Became a Count* (New York: Viking Press, 2009); and David McCullough, *The Greater Journey: Americans in Paris* (New York: Simon & Schuster, 2011), pp. 414–21.

12 Georges Robert, 'Sa Majesté Edison', *Le Figaro*, 8 Aug. 1889, p. 1. On the reception of Edison's inventions at the World's Fair, especially the phonograph, see Annegret Fauser, *Musical Encounters at the 1889 Paris World's Fair* (Rochester: University of Rochester Press, 2005), pp. 297–312.

des Machines, the iron pavilion built to house 'all the marvels of human activity' ('toutes les merveilles de l'activité humaine') (fig. 9.1).[13]

In keeping with the image of America as a modern republic of human technical advancement that could literally share the stage with any country in Europe, the American-born conductor Frank Van der Stucken (1858–1929) organised a concert of American symphonic music on 12 July 1889 at the Palais du Trocadéro, a large, echo-filled auditorium opposite the Eiffel Tower.[14] The pieces were all performed by French musicians from the Théâtre de l'Opéra-Comique and conducted by Van der Stucken, who also had a number of his own pieces in the programme. Advertised to the French as 'a grand American concert' that would be worthy of 'the *grande salle des fêtes* of the *Trocadéro*', the event was well attended by nearly 3,000 people, including many from the French musical world as well as a number of American visitors to the fair.[15]

The French press was not kind in its reception of the American concert, as Douglas Shadle further discusses (see Chapter 6). In fact, words such as 'derivative', 'unoriginal', and 'devoid' were commonly found in the French reviews. The predominantly negative perspective that the Parisian critic circle had of the American concert was due in large part to a preconceived notion of America by the French as a nation lacking a musical history similar to its own, where one can trace musical elements from ancient origins all the way to the present day. Although, by the 1850s, Parisian correspondents had occasionally written about American concert works performed in the United States and Gottschalk had performed his piano music in Paris (see Chapters 5 and 6), American music as heard and published in France was primarily vernacular music, from African American spirituals and Native American lullabies to New England Protestant hymns and outdoor parade music, all music that reflected a separate people with a separate American experience, and one that was populist and immediate in character. The fact that America did not have a cohesive sound that spoke to a single national origin was further cause for the French to dismiss the art music at the concert as not reflective of a 'true' American sound, for that singular perspective of American music did not exist.[16] To be fair, America was still attempting to come to terms with its own musical voice for the concert hall, which prompted the exporting of the American symphonic concert in the first place. The tension between the perpetuation of the music inheritance from Europe and the desire to create uniquely 'American music' persisted alongside

---

13 *Exposition de 1889: Guide bleu du 'Figaro' et du 'Petit Journal'*, p. 118.

14 E. Douglas Bomberger, '*A Tidal Wave of Encouragement': American Composers' Concerts in the Gilded Age* (Westport: Praeger, 2002), p. 46. For a discussion of the Trocadéro as a suitable space in which to hear music, see Fauser, *Musical Encounters*, pp. 16–18.

15 Bomberger, '*A Tidal Wave of Encouragement*', pp. 49–50.

16 As Fauser argues in her study, 'notions of racial purity were strongly linked with concepts of originality'; see Fauser, *Musical Encounters*, pp. 52–4.

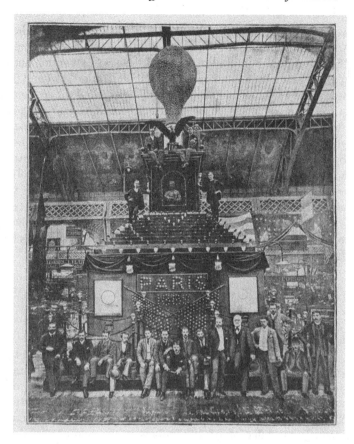

Figure 9.1. 'Mammoth Edison Lamp', in *The Universal Exhibition of Paris: The United States of America, 1889*, p. 130. New York, London, and Paris: American Commission, 1889. Yale University Library, Digital Collections, CC BY 4.0.

the founding of philharmonic societies across the country and the creation of the National Conservatory of Music in 1885 (see pp. 197–8; 210–11).[17]

The negative reviews by the French were also shared by many American critics who were not fully convinced of America's own unique artistic voice given the large immigrant population in the country.[18] Would the art music of America be based on European models? Or, as Dvořák would argue a few years later in 1893

---

17 For information about the emergence of an American cultural voice in the nineteenth century that could compete with the high-art tradition of Europe, see Lawrence W. Levine, *Highbrow/Lowbrow: The Emergence of Cultural Hierarchy in America* (Cambridge, MA: Harvard University Press, 1988); John Spitzer (ed.), *American Orchestras in the Nineteenth Century* (Chicago: University of Chicago Press, 2012); and David Nicholls (ed.), *The Cambridge History of American Music* (Cambridge: Cambridge University Press, 1998), part 1.
18 Bomberger, 'A Tidal Wave of Encouragement', pp. 50–61.

272   *Mark A. Pottinger*

(as pointed out by Shadle and many music historians), would the sound of a collective America be based on the music of Native Americans and former African slaves?[19] Such a question of national identity in music was a vexing one and one that would not be adequately addressed until after World War I and the rise of modernism in the 1920s, when Europe became enamoured with the quintessential American sound of jazz and its ability to connect with larger intellectual currents at the time.[20] Whatever it could be, however, the sound of America and the people who defined it had to be based on its founding, as a nation of both Indigenous people and immigrants, in which the ethnic diversity of Native Americans, former Europeans, and former African slaves and their descendants all defined a collective identity. At least, this was the narrative put forth by Colonel William F. Cody and his western caravan, the Wild West Company, which gave the French not only a strong historical narrative to define the American republic but also helped to satisfy the unease that the French had concerning America's European borrowings in relation to an 'authentic' national voice.[21]

Buffalo Bill's America

From the arrival of the pilgrims in 1620 to the opening of the West after the Mexican–American War in 1848, the story of America was defined by expansion from eastern regions of the United States to the West. Nowhere was this more on display than in the image and historical narrative that accompanied Cody and his Wild West Company, who were installed a few kilometres northwest of the fairgrounds in the Neuilly district of Paris in a 55,000-square-metre hippodrome. The installation of '250 Indians, scouts and cowboys, pioneers, Mexican vaqueros, riflemen, markswomen, Canadian patriots, etc. [...] 200 horses and ponies, 20 buffalo and wild bulls' did not go unnoticed in France.[22] In fact, the arrival of Cody and the Wild West Company in France was so well

---

19 For a critical discussion of the article as well as American responses to Dvořák's pronouncement, see Michael Beckerman, 'The Real Value of Yellow Journalism: James Creelman and Antonín Dvořák', *The Musical Quarterly*, 77:4 (Winter 1993), 749–68.

20 See Carol J. Oja, *Making Music Modern: New York in the 1920s* (Oxford: Oxford University Press, 2000); Richard H. Pells, *Modernist America: Art, Music, Movies and the Globalization of American Culture* (New Haven: Yale University Press, 2011); and Robert Crunden, *Body & Soul: The Making of American Modernism* (New York: Basic Books, 2000).

21 For information about the American school of composers in the late nineteenth century, see Nicholas E. Tawa, *The Coming Age of American Art Music: New England's Classical Romanticists* (Westport: Greenwood Press, 1991).

22 '250 Indiens, Scouts et Cow Boys [*sic*], pionniers, chasseurs mexicains, rifflemen [*sic*], mark's women [*sic*], patriotes canadiens, etc. ..., ayant tous pris part à la dernière guerre. 200 chevaux et poneys, 20 buffles et taureaux sauvages, etc.': *Le Petit Journal*, 21 May 1889, p. 4.

Buffalo Bill and the Sound of America 273

advertised by the press that many came out to see the company's arrival in Le Havre on 10 May and to witness the entire Wild West Company disembark from a steamship onto trains bound for Paris.[23] And thanks to John M. Burke (1842–1917), the mastermind behind the advertising campaign of the Wild West Company, posters depicting the likeness of Cody on horseback, hunting buffalo, or a simple portrait of the man in a wide-brimmed hat were plastered all over Paris to such a degree that many Parisians felt invaded by this American form of mass marketing and overt commercialism.[24] As one member of the press remarked:

> Paris will have learned everything from this exhibition, even American advertising, considered the *most* ingenious and the *most* daring in the world. Have we had enough eyes on this Buffalo Bill for a fortnight?! Eyes cannot be open without them being flung to a poster plastered to his glory. Here, he is seen in a bust, with his hair in the back, looking inspired, with a physiognomy reminiscent of that of the poet [Frédéric] Mistral. There, he is on horseback, rifle in hand. Sometimes he stood on a point of a rock, probing the horizon with his gaze; at one time he is in full gallop in charge of a troop of Indians engaged in stealing from a stagecoach. It is a profusion of images all concentrated in order to give the impression of a very handsome hero, intrepid and the bearer of many romantic adventures.[25]

---

23 Georges Grison, 'Buffalo-Bill à Paris', *Le Figaro*, 12 May 1889, p. 2.

24 'Arizona' John Burke first met William Cody in 1866, when Cody was serving as a scout for the US army in the Montana Territory. In Montana, Burke, as Cody's personal attendant, recorded all of Cody's exploits in helping to settle the territory for the US government. When Cody began the Wild West Company in 1883, Burke served as the chief press agent and publicist; in 1893, he published *Buffalo Bill: From Prairie to Palace* (Chicago: Rand McNally & Co., 1893), which highlights Cody's meteoric rise to Buffalo Bill. Burke was a pioneer in 'guerilla marketing', initiating direct forms of marketing that included press kits sent to local newspapers, travelling billboards, the plastering of life-sized posters, and celebrity endorsements. On Burke's life as well as his advertising prowess, see Joe Dobrow, *Pioneers of Promotion: How Press Agents for Buffalo Bill, P. T. Barnum, and the World's Columbian Exposition Created Modern Marketing* (Norman: University of Oklahoma Press, 2018).

25 'Parle aura tout connu pendant l'Exposition, même la réclame américaine, réputée la plus ingénieuse et la plus audacieuse du monde. Avons-nous eu les yeux assez occupés de ce Buffalo-Bill depuis quinze jours? On ne pouvait plus les ouvrir sans qu'ils tomassent sur une affiche placardée à sa gloire. Ici, il était vu en buste, les cheveux dans le dos, l'air inspiré avec une physionomie rappelant à s'y méprendre celle du poète Mistral. Là, il était à cheval, le rifle au poing. Tantôt il se dressait sur une pointe de rocher, sondant l'horizon du regard; tantôt il chargeait au grand galop une troupe d'Indiens occupés à dépouiller une diligence. C'était une profusion d'images toutes concertées dans le but de donner l'impression d'un héros très beau, intrépide et ayant eu beaucoup de romanesques aventures': 'Au jour le jour: La bande des Buffalo Bill', *Le Temps*, 20 May 1889, p. 2.

274 *Mark A. Pottinger*

Here the author makes an interesting reference to Frédéric Mistral (1830–1914), a French poet who sought to raise the status of the Provençal language throughout France. Mistral was often seen in public wearing a wide-brimmed hat from the southern region of France as well as a prominent moustache and a goatee, styled in a similar fashion to that of Buffalo Bill. Although Mistral's appearance was defined before the arrival of Buffalo Bill in France, the two men and their work were often compared in the press. As Buffalo Bill was attempting to salvage America's past in the face of the modern present, Mistral was doing the same for the Provençal language and culture to develop a collective national identity.[26]

To return to the critique of the advertising of Buffalo Bill in Paris, the writer continues in the same article to insist that the posters 'contained as much truth as one can demand from an advertisement, and the Company of Buffalo Bill is a sight to behold. It is a living illustration of all that will be able to remain in the memory from the stories of Cooper and Gustave Aymard.'[27] Indeed, owing to the success of the Wild West Company in London in May 1887 to celebrate Queen Victoria's Golden Jubilee, as well as the proliferation of western-frontier novels in France, the French became increasingly interested in this *grand campement pittoresque* assembled by Colonel Cody (Buffalo Bill) and his business partner Nate Salsbury.[28] And, reflective of the educational goals of the 1889 World's Fair, the real-life exotic participants of the Wild West Company, from the Native Americans to the multi-racial cast of cowboys, were viewed by many French critics as authentic interpreters of America's past. Despite the overt commercialism of Buffalo Bill's marketing, the company played into the idea of authenticity by denouncing any mention of 'show' or 'entertainment'

26 See Robert Zaretsky, 'Playing Cowboys and Indians in the French Camargue', *Historical Reflections/Réflexions historiques*, 30:2 (Summer 2004), 151–77.

27 'Eh bien, tout cela contenait autant de vérité qu'on en peut exiger d'une réclame, et cette bande de Buffalo Bill est un spectacle à voir. C'est une illustration vivante de tout ce qui pourra vous rester dans la mémoire des récits de Cooper et de Gustave Aymard': 'Au jour le jour', *Le Temps*, 20 May 1889, p. 2. James Fenimore Cooper (1789–1851) lived in France from 1826 to 1833, when he continued to publish stories on Nathaniel 'Natty' Bumppo, a fictional White pioneer raised by Native Americans, who makes his first appearance in *The Leatherstocking Tales*, a series of five novels that included *The Last of the Mohicans* (1826) and *The Deerslayer* (1841). Gustave A[i]ymard (1818–83) was a French novelist, who, after living in America and then returning to France, wrote several western-themed novels, including *Les Pirates des prairies* (1858), *Les Trappeurs de l'Arkansas* (1858) and *Les Rôdeurs de frontières* (1861).

28 For information on the business relationship between Cody and Salsbury, see Sarah J. Blackstone, *Buckskins, Bullets, and Business: A History of Buffalo Bill's Wild West* (New York: Greenwood Press, 1986); John M. Burke, *Buffalo Bill: From Prairie to Palace*, ed. Chris Dixon (Lincoln: University of Nebraska Press, 2012); and Venita Datta, 'Buffalo Bill Goes to France: French–American Encounters at the Wild West Show, 1889–1905', *French Historical Studies*, 41:3 (Aug. 2018), 528–35.

Buffalo Bill and the Sound of America 275

in the advertising posters or souvenir booklet, preferring the label of the more serious-minded genre *faits historiques* (fig. 9.2).[29]

In the pages of the official souvenir programme for the Wild West Company – a 47-page booklet in which the exploits of Buffalo Bill and some of the famous individuals in the show, including the Texas cowboy Buck Taylor (William Levi Taylor), the sharp-shooter Annie Oakley (Phoebe Ann Mosey), and even Buffalo Bill's horse, 'Vieux Charlie', receive prominent mention – the racialised history of America was made clear:

> In the development of its contemporary history, North America does not offer more thrilling pictures of interest than the gradual and rapid expansion of its western frontier. The expansive force of the White race, proven by the movement of [European] emigrants, and the extension of our railroad [network], together with that of the military power of the central government, have, to a certain extent, broken down the barriers behind which *le Peau Rouge* [the Red Skin] fought against the progress of [White] civilisation. Nevertheless, the 'Far-West' still exists for the man in the wild, a refuge where the law is supported only with a revolver, and where the buccaneer and the White nomad are as formidable as *le Peau Rouge*. With regard to the existence of [White] man in the Rocky Mountain region and the neighbouring plains, the history of our country has only been half told, and the [writings in romance novels] have remained far from reality [...] Could a man now living have stood on the shore of the Red Sea and witnessed the passage of the children of Israel and the struggle of Pharaoh [...] what a sight he would have seen [...] How interesting would be the story of a man, if he were now living, that had witnessed the landing of Christopher Columbus on the shores of the New World; or the story of one of the hardy English Puritans who took passage on the *Mayflower*, and landed on the rock-bound coast of New England [...] A few years more and the great struggle for possession will be ended, and generations will settle down to enjoy the homes their fathers constructed for them. Then will come the painter. He who, with pen, pencil and panel can tell the story as he understands it [...] These are the thoughts that come to us as Buffalo Bill unrolls before our eyes the great living painting of his Far Wild West [*sic*]. In the whole world, every man, woman, and child should be able to contemplate this materialisation of authentic historical facts.[30]

29 Richard Slotkin, *Gunfighter Nation: The Myth of the Frontier in Twentieth-Century America* (Norman: University of Oklahoma Press, 1998), p. 67.

30 'Dans le développement de son histoire contemporaine, l'Amérique du Nord n'offre pas de tableaux plus palpitants d'intérêt que celui de l'extension progressive et rapide de sa frontière de l'Ouest. La force d'expansion de la race blanche, prouvée par le mouvement des émigrants, et l'extension de nos voies ferrées, conjointement à celle de la puissance militaire du gouvernement central ont brisé, jusqu'à un certain point, les barrières à l'abri desquelles le Peau Rouge luttait contre les progrès de la civilisation.

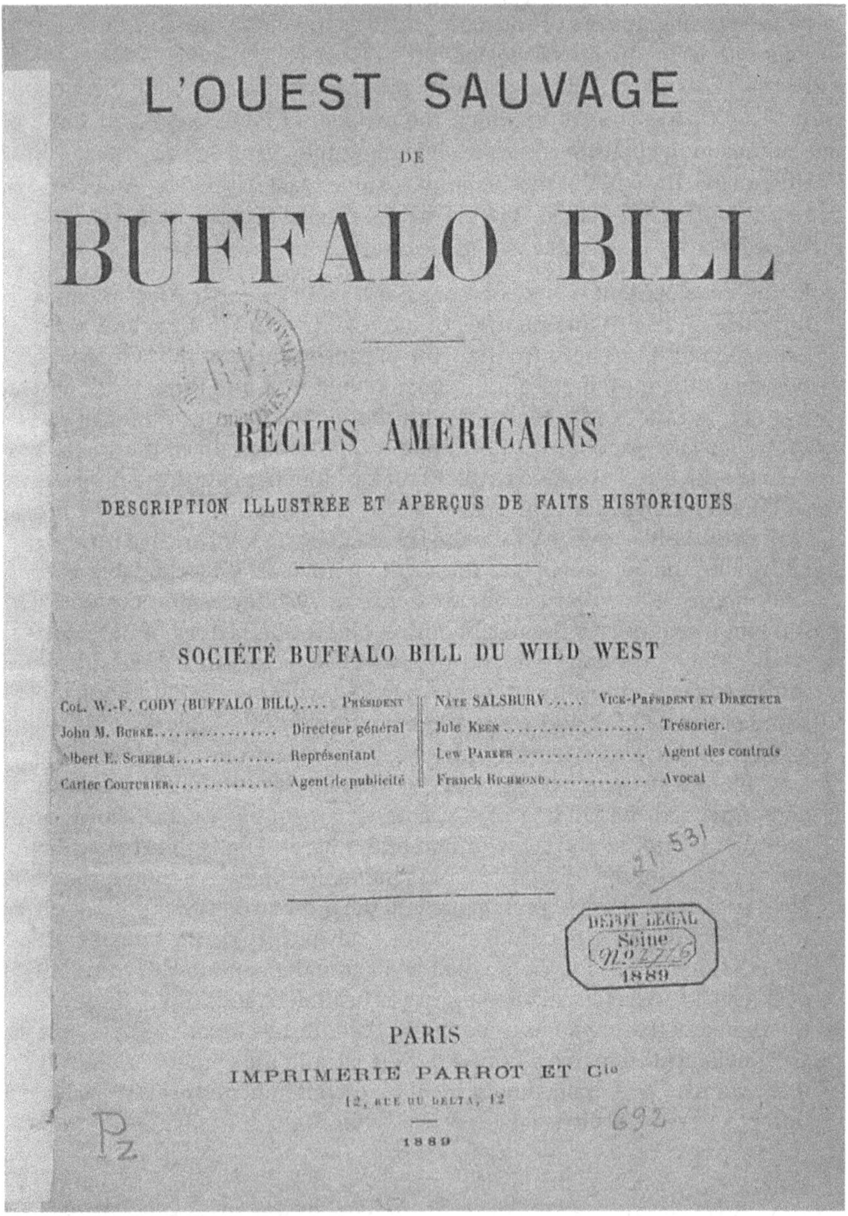

L'OUEST SAUVAGE

DE

BUFFALO BILL

RÉCITS AMÉRICAINS

DESCRIPTION ILLUSTRÉE ET APERÇUS DE FAITS HISTORIQUES

SOCIÉTÉ BUFFALO BILL DU WILD WEST

Col. W.-F. CODY (BUFFALO BILL)....	Président	Nate SALSBURY.....	Vice-Président et Directeur
John M. Burke.................	Directeur général	Jule Keen.....................	Trésorier.
Albert E. Scheible...............	Représentant	Lew Parker....................	Agent des contrats
Carter Couturier...............	Agent de publicité	Franck Richmond...............	Avocat

---

PARIS

IMPRIMERIE PARROT ET Cⁱᵉ

12, RUE DU DELTA, 12

1889

Figure 9.2. Cover page of the Wild West Company's French-language
souvenir booklet *L'Ouest Sauvage de Buffalo Bill*. Paris: Parrot et Cⁱᵉ, 1889.
Bibliothèque Nationale de France.

Buffalo Bill and the Sound of America   277

Complete with witness accounts and quotations from leading military figures, the Paris souvenir programme was translated from the English-language version produced for the London tour in 1887. Nonetheless, thanks perhaps to careful planning or simple happenstance by advertising itself as a *fait historique*, the Wild West Company emphasised the verisimilitude of historical representation in a way not too dissimilar from the display of history in the late eighteenth-century *fait historique* and French grand opéra of the July Monarchy, two French theatrical genres that use historic individuals to unfold their 'human story' in a set of imagined dramatic pictures in authentic dress and appearance.[31] In fact, throughout the nineteenth century, the French seemed to have a propensity for the display of the past through not only opera but also in the more spectacle-filled genres of the panorama, diorama, and the wax museum.[32]

More than its connection to French theatrical genres of historical representation, which encouraged the French to think of the Wild West Company as presenters of authentic history, the racial language of the programme further highlighted the 'civilising project' and colonialist ideals shared by America and France in the late nineteenth century. As previously mentioned, one of the main

---

Néanmoins le "Far-West" est encore sur plusieurs points, pour l'homme à l'état sauvage un refuge où l'action de la loi n'est soutenue que par le revolver, et où le flibustier et la blanc nomade sont aussi redoutables que le Peau-Rouge. En ce qui touche à l'existence de l'homme dans les montagnes rocheuses et dans les plaines voisines, l'histoire de notre pays n'a été révélée qu'à demi, et le roman lui-même est resté bien loin de la réalité [...]. S'il existait encore un témoin du passage de la mer Rouge par les Israélites, des efforts du Pharaon et de son armée innombrable, avec quel intérêt, on écouterait le récit de ce fait historique! [...] Qu'il serait intéressant d'entendre un témoin de l'arrivée de Christophe Colomb sur une plage du Nouveau-Monde, où un contemporain des rudes puritains anglais qui prirent passage sur la "Mayflower" et débarquèrent sur la côte de la Nouvelle-Angleterre, si hérissée d'écueil et de rochers! [...] Encore quelques années et la grande lutte pour la possession de la terre sera terminée; des générations nouvelles s'établiront pour jouir paisiblement des habitations construites par leurs pères. Alors viendra la peintre: celui qui avec la plume, le crayon où la palette saura raconter l'histoire de la conquête telle qu'il la comprendra [...] Telles sont les pensées qui nous viennent en voyant Buffalo Bill dérouler devant nos yeux la grande peinture vivante de son Far West sauvage': Buffalo Bill (Col. W.-F. Cody), *L'Ouest Sauvage de Buffalo Bill: Récits américaines; Description illustrée et aperçus de faits historiques* (Paris: Parrot et Cie, 1889), pp. 2, 9–10.

31 See Mark A. Pottinger, *Staging of History in France: Characterizations of Historical Figures in French Grand Opéra during the Reign of Louis Philippe* (Saarbrücken, Germany: VDM Verlag, 2009).

32 There is much research on the French desire for dramatic stage sets (i.e. *tableaux vivants*) as well as visual authenticity in spectacle entertainment throughout the nineteenth century; see, for example, Sarah Hibberd and Richard Wrigley (eds), *Art, Theatre and Opera in Paris, 1750–1850: Exchanges and Tensions* (Abingdon: Routledge, 2016); Stephen Pinson, *Speculating Daguerre: Art and Enterprise in the Work of L. J. M. Daguerre* (Chicago: University of Chicago Press, 2012); and Schwartz, *Spectacular Realities*.

278   Mark A. Pottinger

desires of the 1889 Exposition Universelle was to present the global expanse of the French colonial empire. The organiser of the fair's decision to showcase French colonised nations was not for display alone (as with wild game trophies) but to demonstrate the superiority of the White race, which the Eiffel Tower dramatically materialised as the climax of human achievement. In the shadow of the tower, non-White peoples were presented at the fair as members of static cultures that lacked technical know-how and scientific advancement. These same individuals, 'over four hundred Indigenous peoples from various French colonies', ate, slept, danced, created artwork, and, in general, served as living specimens for researchers in the prevailing science of 'race biology', a form of Social Darwinism to show 'the congenital inferiority of races with depressed or squeezed skulls'.[33] Following this interpretation, a stark separation of the races was presented even in the mere layout of the fair, including its display of industry and accompanying 'march of progress', and shared by the Wild West Company's own White supremacist narrative.[34]

The live-action presentation of Buffalo Bill's America was supported by music throughout the two-and-a-half-hour programme. Each performance of the Wild West Company, one at 3:00pm and one at 8:30pm, Monday to Sunday, was accompanied by a sixteen-member wind ensemble, the Buffalo Bill Wild West Cowboy Band. The band included a D flat piccolo, three B flat clarinets, one E flat clarinet, three B flat cornets, two E flat alto horns, two trombones, a baritone, tuba, snare drum, and bass drum (see fig. 9.3).[35] The leader of the

33   Lauren Cross, Lauren Seitz, and Shannon Walter, 'The First of its Kind: A Cultural History of the Village Nègre', *Digital Literature Review*, 3 (2016), 21, 23. The *Village Nègre* 'displayed Arabs, Kanaks (who are the Indigenous Melanesian people of New Caledonia in the Southwest Pacific), the Gabonese, Congolese, Javanese (from Java, Indonesia), and Senegalese, all of whom were from areas that had been colonized by France' (p. 22).

34   See n. 4. For more information on the connection between Buffalo Bill's Wild West Company and the fears and tensions of White America at the end of the nineteenth century, see Louis S. Warren, *Buffalo Bill's America: William Cody and the Wild West Show* (New York: Alfred A. Knopf, 2005); Robert W. Rydell, 'Buffalo Bill's *Wild West*: The Racialization of the Cosmopolitan Imagination', in *Colonial Advertising & Commodity Racism*, ed. Wulf Hund, Michael Pickering, and Anandi Ramamurthy (Zürich: Lit Verlag, 2013), pp. 97–118; Richard Slotkin, 'Buffalo Bill's *Wild West* and the Mythologization of the American Empire', in *Cultures of United States Imperialism*, ed. Amy Kaplan and Donald E. Pease (Durham, NC: Duke University Press, 1993), pp. 164–84; Dan Moos, *Outside America: Race, Ethnicity, and the Role of the American West in National Belonging* (Hanover: Dartmouth College Press, 2005), pp. 146–207; and Barbara McCloskey, 'From the *Frontier* to the Wild West: German Artists, American Indians, and the Spectacle of Race and Nation in the Nineteenth and Early Twentieth Centuries', in *I Like America: Fictions of the Wild West*, ed. Pamela Kort and Max Hollein (New York: Prestel, 2006), pp. 298–321.

35   Michael L. Masterson, 'Sounds of the Frontier: Music in Buffalo Bill's Wild West' (unpublished PhD dissertation, University of New Mexico, 1990), pp. 119–22.

Figure 9.3. Buffalo Bill's Wild West Cowboy Band, 1887. Photograph, Buffalo Bill Center of the West.

band was William F. Sweeney (1858–1917), a cornet player who joined Cody in 1882, when the Wild West Company was still in its infancy. The musicians, who mostly came from East Coast music schools, were dressed as American cowboys throughout the show, thus showcasing for the French the appearance of an 'authentic' Wild West identity in image and sound.[36]

Before the actual presentation, while members of the audience were finding their seats in the arena, the Cowboy Band would play a musical selection of popular songs and melodies of the day, including 'all kinds of dance music from the waltz to the ragtime cakewalk'.[37] Although a detailed list of the songs played by the Cowboy Band at the 1889 World's Fair does not exist, the 1897 publi-

---

36 Masterson, 'Sounds of the Frontier', p. 123. Masterson makes the comment in his study of the Cowboy Band that having the members of the ensemble dressed in cowboy uniforms helped to 'visually maintain the [band's] anonymity while providing support for the performers' (p. 125). Such uniformity allowed for the Wild West Company to maintain the illusion of authenticity, thus keeping with the late nineteenth-century theatrical desire to remove the mechanisation of stage production in order to create a natural, realistic presentation.

37 Masterson, 'Sounds of the Frontier', p. 126.

cation *Buffalo Bill Wild West Songster* contains twenty-five songs performed by the Wild West Cowboy Band during shows throughout the 1890s. Many of the songs are referred to as 'coon songs', such as the popular song 'My Gal is a High-Born Lady' (1896) with words and music by Barney Fagan (1850–1937), a famous dancer and composer of blackface minstrelsy (see fig. 9.4 and ex. 9.1).[38] Musical works similar to 'My Gal' were probably performed at the fair among a medley of military marches and arranged popular songs. Even if the French did not know them, the songs created a festive atmosphere for the event and thus presented to the French a populist soundscape to engage in the visual retelling of America's past, one that was filled with music of diverse peoples, including music that parodied former African slaves and descendants of slaves living in America. In fact, the explicit use of racially charged music would become a staple of the Wild West Company in the decades after the fair.[39] In 1895, when James Bailey (of Barnum & Bailey Circus) joined the Wild West Company, it began to incorporate side shows that featured Black and White minstrelsy and various circus acts. This inclusion of the side show would have certainly watered down the educational aspects of the Wild West Company's 'historic' presentation of America that was so heavily marketed in Paris.[40]

The show officially opened with a playing of Sweeney's arrangement of 'The Star-Spangled Banner', which offered a sonic emblem of America well before

38 For a detailed analysis of the lyrics and musical structure of 'My Gal is a High-Born Lady', see Masterson, 'Sounds of the Frontier', pp. 212–21. Although dating from the 1820s, 'coon songs' were extremely popular in the United States from the time of post-Reconstruction to the start of World War I; see Brandi A. Neal, 'Coon Song', *Grove Music Online* (2013), <https://doi-org.ezproxy.uky.edu/10.1093/gmo/9781561592630.article.A2249084> [accessed 10 Jan. 2020]. For more information on the use of coon songs in American circus music and on how they were defined in American society in general, see Micah Childress, '*Examine the Contents*: Clowning and Songsters in American Circuses, 1850–1900', *Popular Entertainment Studies*, 1:2 (2010), 26–43; James H. Dormon, 'Shaping the Popular Image of Post-Reconstruction American Blacks: The "Coon Song" Phenomenon of the Gilded Age', *American Quarterly*, 40:4 (Dec. 1988), 450–71; Anne-Marie Bean, James V. Hatch, and Brooks McNamara (eds), *Inside the Minstrel Mask: Readings in Nineteenth-Century Blackface Minstrelsy* (Hanover: Wesleyan University Press, 1996); and Matthew D. Morrison, 'Race, Blacksound, and the (Re)Making of Musicological Discourse', *Journal of the American Musicological Society*, 72:3 (Fall 2019), 781–823.

39 Note in ex. 9.1 the racially charged text throughout the first verse of two. Following the verse, the chorus (not shown here) continues the overtly racist language: 'My gal is a high born lady, She's black, but not too shady. Feathered like a peacock, just as gay. She is not colored, she was born that way. I'm proud of my black Venus. No coon can come between us. Long the line they can't out shine, this high born gal of mine!'

40 For further information on the collaboration between Bailey and Cody in the Wild West Company, see Henry Blackman Sell and Victor Weybright, *Buffalo Bill and the Wild West* (New York: Oxford University Press, 1955) and Masterson, 'Sounds of the Frontier', p. 190.

Figure 9.4. Front cover of 'My Gal is a High-Born Lady' by Barney Fagan. New York: M. Witmark & Sons, 1896. The New York Public Library Digital Collections.

Example 9.1. Melody of 'My Gal is a High-Born Lady' by Barney Fagan, bb. 1–17. New York: M. Witmark & Sons, 1896. (Transcription is my own.)

the song would become America's national anthem in 1931 (see Chapter 8).[41] Eighteen different live-action scenes followed (fig. 9.5) – all introduced by an English-speaking narrator in the centre of the ring, much to the amusement (and confusion) of the French, to the extent that one commentator noted that 'his intentions were good, but his accent was deplorable; in spite of his thundering voice, the *pioublic* [sic] did not understand his explanations'.[42] The music and the souvenir programme, therefore, helped to clarify for the French audience how best to interpret the action in the ring. The Cowboy Band provided melodies and rhythmic accompaniment to all the scenes in the show, including

41 The playing of 'The Star-Spangled Banner' throughout the Wild West Show's thirty-year run in both Europe and the United States contributed to the song's ascendancy and to the show's enduring impact on America; see Masterson, 'Sounds of the Frontier', p. 124. An orchestral arrangement of 'The Star-Spangled Banner' was also included in the programme of the American Composers' Concert on 12 July 1889 at the Trocadéro, which further highlighted for the French the populist sound of American concert music.
42 'Il annonçait les différents morceaux du spectacle et nommait les acteurs. Son intention était bonne, mais son accent était déplorable; en dépit de sa voix tonnante, le "pioublic" ne comprenait rien à ses explications': 'Théâtres et Concerts', *Journal des débats*, 19 May 1889, p. 2.

the quieter moments between the scenes, when the band played familiar selections from the French boulevard theatre, including selections from Jacques Offenbach.[43] Offenbach in fact visited the United States in 1876 in order to participate in (or better yet, profit from) the first international World's Fair held in the United States, the so-called Centennial Exhibition in Philadelphia, from 10 May to 10 November 1876, when Offenbach's music was often characterised as representative of the frivolity and excess of the Second Empire.[44]

As the show reached its climax, the Deadwood Stage (representing the famous multiple-horse stage coach that transported gold from the Black Hills of South Dakota) entered the arena at breakneck speed, pursued by 'whooping Indians'. Driven off by Cody and the cowboys (made up of Mexicans, African Americans, White Americans, and Canadians), the Native Americans returned to demonstrate bareback racing and tribal dances. Following presentations of sharp-shooting, bronco riding, and buffalo hunting by Cody, the grand finale was an Indian attack on a European settler's cabin. Once again, the Native Americans were driven off by the show's star and 'Le Roi des Hommes de la Frontière', William Cody, who was often introduced with a wind arrangement of Handel's 'See, the Conquering Hero Comes', which supported the highly marketed image of Buffalo Bill as a true 'hero of the plains'.[45]

Little is mentioned in the French press about the critical reception of the music performed during the Wild West Company's performances. The reception that does remain is rather telling, nonetheless, especially regarding the French perception of America. One consistent comment by critics in the French press refers to their surprise on seeing American attendants stand to their feet upon hearing 'The Star-Spangled Banner' (often confused by the French with 'Yankee Doodle Dandy', a more well-known patriotic tune) performed by the Cowboy Band, leading one writer in *Le Petit Journal* to remark, 'this is a curious observation', which was made even more astonishing by the fact that the French did not stand for the playing of the *Marseillaise* that immediately followed.[46] The display

---

43 Masterson, 'Sounds of the Frontier', p. 126. According to the CD liner notes written by Masterson for *Wild West Music of Buffalo Bill's Cowboy Band* (Buffalo Bill Historical Center, 1996), the Offenbach selections were taken from E. Boettger, *Offenbachiana: Selections from Offenbach's Operas* (New York: Carl Fischer, 1884), a set of wind-band arrangements of selections from *Barbe-Bleue, La Périchole, La Belle Hélène, Geneviève de Brabant, La Jolie Parfumeuse, La Grande-Duchesse de Gérolstein*, and *Orphée aux enfers*.

44 Buffalo Bill's reception in France appears somewhat analogous to Offenbach's reception in America: both men were seen as representatives of their age and nation while abroad, while simultaneously often struggling for serious respect by the critics back at home. On the composer's descriptions of his American trip, see Jacques Offenbach, *Offenbach en Amérique: Notes d'un musicien en voyage* (Paris: C. Lévy, 1877); on Offenbach's reception, see Laurence Senelick, *Jacques Offenbach and the Making of Modern Culture* (Cambridge: Cambridge University Press, 2017), pp. 122–42.

45 Masterson, CD liner notes, *Wild West Music*, p. 4.

46 'Quand il s'est avancé, porté par un des plus beaux hommes de la troupe, la musique

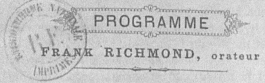

Figure 9.5. Programme of the Wild West Show in Paris, inset, in Buffalo Bill (Col. W.-F. Cody), *L'Ouest Sauvage de Buffalo Bill: Récits américains, description illustrée et aperçus de faits historiques.* Paris: Parrot et Cie, 1889. Bibliothèque Nationale de France.

Buffalo Bill and the Sound of America   285

and sound of American patriotism shocked the French critics, while at the same time reaffirmed the pageantry of American identity.

Other comments by the French press about the music performed by the Wild West Company were made in comparison to the music heard on the fairgrounds near the Eiffel Tower, especially music performed in the *Village Nègre*. One example comes from an article by Julien Tiersot (1857–1936), the French musicologist and author of *Histoire de la chanson populaire en France* (Paris, 1889), who observed that the heavy use of drums played during the 'Danses des Indiens' in the Wild West Company's programme was similar to that performed by other 'primitive' peoples throughout the fair:

> But of all the instruments, the one which, incontestably, has the preferences of all the Negroes, is the drum. Almost all Negro dances are accompanied exclusively by these instruments, using a generally isochronous rhythm [...] The same goes for the North American *Peau-Rouges*, actors in the amusing buffoonery of Buffalo-Bill. One of the program numbers of this show consists of Sioux, Apache and other heroes revived from Fenimore Cooper: the Warrior Dance, which could be compared to the Arab Sword Dance and similar traditions [...] Again, the footsteps of the dancers were punctuated by the drums, beaten, in a moderate tempo, in equal note [lengths]: the cries that were interspersed at times, not being subject to any cadence, were for the sole purpose of exciting the dancers, and no melodic instrument came to mingle with these cries and these drums.[47]

---

de Buffalo-Bill a jouée le *Yankee Doodle* [*sic*] et tous les Américains se sont levés, en s'étonnant, du reste, que nous n'en ayons pas fait tous autant lorsque la même musique avait joué *La Marseillaise*. C'est la une observation curieuse, dont nous voulons d'ailleurs reparler ces jours-ci': *Le Petit Journal*, 20 May 1889, p. 2. Two days later, in the 22 May edition of the same newspaper, the following article appears: '*Le Marseillaise: Debout ou assis?*' Apparently, the French critique of America's overt patriotism forced the French to question sitting or standing for their own display of national unity; see Pasler, 'Listening to Race and Nation', pp. 55–7.

47   'Mais, de tous les instruments, celui qui, incontestablement, a les préférences de tous les nègres, c'est la tambour. Presque toutes les danse des nègres sont accompagnées exclusivement par quelqu'un de ces instruments, sur un rythme généralement isochrone. [...] Même chose encore pour les Peaux-Rouges de l'Amérique du Nord, acteurs de l'amusante clownerie de Buffalo-Bill. Un des numéros du programme de ce spectacle se compose de danses des Sioux, Apaches, et autres héros renouvelés de Fenimore Cooper: danse guerrières, que l'on pourrait rapprocher encore des danses de l'épée arabes et des traditions analogues dont il a été question dans le chapitre précédent. Là encore, les pas des danseurs étaient seulement rythmés par les tambours, battus, dans un mouvement modéré, par notes égales: les cris qui s'y mêlaient par moments, n'étant soumis à aucune cadence, avaient pour seul but d'exciter les danseurs, et nul instrument mélodique ne venait se mêler à ces cris et à ces tambours': Julien Tiersot, 'Promenades Musicales à l'Exposition', *Le Ménestrel*, 55:40 (6 Oct. 1889), 315. The popularity in France of Fenimore Cooper's literary depiction of the western frontier had both a positive and negative effect on the critical reception of the Wild West Company, which further high-

286   *Mark A. Pottinger*

The lack of serious attention that a French music scholar affords the dance music of Native Americans, which was heard more as befitting the accompaniment of circus clowns or a work of fiction than as 'authentic' dance music, further highlights the critique of the American sound as spectacle entertainment at best and 'primitive' noise at worst.

The noise of American music was even the subject of a long editorial that appeared in *Gil Blas*, in which the French playwright and essayist Émile Bergerat directs his ire at Buffalo Bill for destroying the quietness of his street, which was near the camp grounds of the Wild West Company:

> I am disarmed, in this same century of Richard Wagner, against rogues who murder me via the ear. At whose feet must I throw myself to receive justice? [...] I beg you, have my cruel prosecutors guillotined [...] I am this frightful phenomenon: A Frenchman who has a good ear! Yes, this rare occurrence, I embody it and embrace it here on an isolated street in a discreet district, where until the arrival of Buffalo Bill, there was no sound of any noise except that of the wind [...] These organs of barbary have become organs of ferocity. No one plays well, not even a little; it is to make the teeth fall out and whiten the hair to hear this concert of dissonance to which my poor soul is prey [...] I pay my taxes, I have the right to enjoy the silence of my street. I cannot speak for Buffalo Bill [...] [but] these noises do not represent music.[48]

In spite of the mixed reception of the music of the Wild West Company, from overtly patriotic to noise-like, primitive sounds, in the end, the music performed by Sweeney and the Cowboy Band provided a succinct order to the presentation, which at times must have seemed chaotic as buffalo, horses, and dogs ran in and out of the arena, carriages moved at thunderous speed, and the percussive sounds of rifle shots and long bows rang out. Similar to what would be experienced in the 'Western'-genre films in the early twentieth century, the

---

lights the intimacy between entertainment and live-action drama, fiction, and history in the late nineteenth century. For more about Tiersot's writings on the music of the 1889 Exposition Universelle, see Fauser, *Musical Encounters at the 1889 Paris World's Fair* and Jean-Paul Montagnier, 'Julien Tiersot: Ethnomusicologue à l'Exposition Universelle de 1889. Contribution à une histoire française de la ethnomusicologie', *International Review of the Aesthetics and Sociology of Music*, 21:1 (1990), 91–100.

48 'Je suis désarme, en plein siècle de Richard Wagner, contre des coquins qui me tuent par l'oreille. Aux pieds de qui me jeter pour obtenir justice? [...] Je t'en supplie, fais guillotiner mes cruels persécuteurs [...] Je suis cet affreux phénomène: un Français qui a l'oreille juste! Oui, ce monstre rare, je l'incarne, et je l'incarne dans une rue isolée d'un quartier lointain, où, jusqu'à l'arrivée de Buffalo-Bill, il ne broyait d'autre bruit que celui du vent [...] ces orgues de Barbarie sont devenues des orgues de Férocité. Pas un ne joue juste, même approximativement, et c'est à faire tomber les dents et blanchir les cheveux que d'ouïr le concert de discordance auquel ma pauvre âme est en proie [...] Je paie mes impositions, j'ai droit à jouir du silence de ma rue. Je ne dis rien pour Buffalo-Bill [...] ces bruits ne se donnent pas pour musicaux': Émile Bergerat, 'Accordes les orgues', *Gil Blas*, 16 June 1889, 1.

music allowed the constant noise-filled, dynamic energy of the show to be controlled, ordered, and placed at a certain voyeuristic distance to assure the audience that this was only a presentation and there was nothing to fear. And, in the reverse, whatever the original association of the music – be it French (Offenbach), British (Handel), or pseudo-Native American – the action of the arena created new associations for the music that allied it with America's expansionist narrative. Like the use of Rossini's *William Tell* Overture to accompany the heroic exploits of the Lone Ranger in the 1930s American radio (and later television) serial of the same name, the music performed by the Cowboy Band helped the French not only to digest the violent history of America's founding as one that is both heroic and immediately accessible, but also, more importantly, to directly connect the images and 'sound' of America to the dramatic music of the theatre and spectacle entertainment, thus convincing the audience to see one thing that was 'real' and to hear another thing that was not.

This association of America with mass entertainment and its ability to represent dual and often competing realities is further revealed through a French popular song, 'Ainsi soit-il, Buffalo Bill!' ('So be it, Buffalo Bill!'), written and performed during the time of the 1889 World's Fair. It is among a handful of French popular works, located in the Département de la Musique of the Bibliothèque Nationale de France, that were written during the fair and that bear either 'Américaine' or 'Buffalo Bill' in the title. These works include Hilaire Leleu, *'Buffalo Bill' Galop pour piano*, Op. 39 (Paris: A. André, 1889), Paul Fauchey, *Buffalo Bill's Polka-Marche, après les motifs américaines exécuté à Buffalo, pour piano* (Paris: J. Hiéliard, 1889), and Henri de Gruytters, *La Joyeusse: Danse américaine, pour piano* (Versailles: Vernède, 1889), the last of which appears to define the rhythmic signature of the cakewalk. All three French piano works include quick *vivace* tempos, constantly changing dynamics, piano flourishes in both the right and left hands, and percussive accents on the off-beats of the bar. It is significant to note that all three works define the 'sound' of America as dance music – albeit of Polish and French origins, in addition to African American (i.e. polka, galop, cakewalk) – and not music depicting the picturesque landscape or the dramatic literature of America, which were the main subject matter for the pieces included on the American symphonic concert at the Trocadéro. As we shall see, the melody and text of 'Ainsi soit-il, Buffalo Bill!' not only highlight a familiar genre of the Belle-Époque period in France but also bear witness to the cultural position that America held for the French at the end of the nineteenth century, which was one primarily defined by the duplicitous nature of performance – even that of historical spectacle – and its 'Americanised' marketing.

'Ainsi soit-il, Buffalo Bill!'

A stone's throw away from the Exposition Universelle fairgrounds, attendants at the fair could enjoy food, drink, and light entertainment at several café-concerts along the Champs-Élysées. Since the 1860s, the café-concert had become not merely a space for incidental entertainment with drinking and dancing, but a performance genre in its own right that curated bawdy songs, ballads, patriotic tunes, and comic melodies filled with wit and political satire.[49] One of the oldest and most famous café-concert venues on the Champs-Élysées was the Cafés des Ambassadeurs.[50] Situated at the entrance of the grand boulevard, directly opposite the Place de la Concorde, the Ambassadeurs hosted famous singers and actors, including the singer, writer, and comedic actor Éloi Ouvrard (1855–1938), who would firmly establish himself as one of the top performers at the café-concert in the latter part of the nineteenth century.[51]

Among the over 800 songs composed by Ouvrard, 'Ainsi soit-il, Buffalo Bill!' was performed by him at the Ambassadeurs throughout the month of August during the Exposition Universelle; in fact the *chansonnette* served as the opening number of the evening show.[52] One critic proclaimed that Ouvrard was 'hilarious' ('désopilant') in his rendition of the song.[53] Like most songs of Ouvrard, it features a mostly conjunct vocal melody with few intervallic leaps, syllabically set in a fairly straightforward conversational style and structured in a simple song form of *AABA*, not too distant from the characteristics of American minstrelsy performed by the Wild West Company as described earlier (fig. 9.6).[54]

---

49   Patrick O'Connor, 'Café-concert', *Grove Music Online* (2001) <https://doi-org.ezproxy. uky.edu/10.1093/gmo/9781561592630.article.49068> [accessed 4 Aug. 2019]. Other famous singers were Yvette Guilbert (1865–1944) and Aristide Bruant (1851–1925), who both would come to establish the politically charged venue of the cabaret in the Montmartre district in the 1880s.

50   Chantal Brunschwig, Louis-Jean Calvet, and Jean-Claude Klein, *Cent Ans de chanson française* (Paris: Seuil, 1981), pp. 18–19.

51   Le Chat Noir is considered to have been one of the first cabaret venues in Paris. Established in 1881 in bohemian Montmartre, the club (and its genre of cabaret) soon distinguished itself from the more genteel café-concert venues in central Paris. On the establishment of cabaret and the fortunes of the café-concert in the nineteenth century, see Jean-Claude Klein, *La Chanson à l'affiche: Histoire de la chanson française du café-concert à nos jours* (Paris: Du May, 1991).

52   Other songs written and performed by Ouvrard helped to create the genre of *comique troupier*, in which a singer, dressed in uniform, presented comedic songs and monologues from the supposed life of a soldier. The heightened militarism of the Third Republic made such comedic display popular during the 1870s, bringing a sense of levity and a bit of satire to the rise of General Boulanger and the revenge politics of the 1880s. In his 1894 book *La Vie au café-concert: Mémoires et études de moeurs* (Paris: Paul Schmidt, 1894), Ouvrard recounts the song styles, main performers, venues, and directors, as well as the fortunes of the genre after nearly twenty years of singing and performing in Paris. Ouvrard retired from the stage in 1911 (Brunschwig, Calvet, and Klein, *Cent Ans de chanson française*, p. 293).

53   'Les Théâtres', *Le Petit Journal* (19 Août 1889), p. 2.

54   Along with 'Ainsi soit-il, Buffalo Bill!', I examined nearly thirty songs by Ouvrard

Figure 9.6. É. Ouvrard, 'Ainsi soit-il, Buffalo Bill!' Paris: E. Benoit, 1889, p. 1. Bibliothèque Nationale de France.

As can be gleaned from the title, the song makes reference to Buffalo Bill, who, as we have seen, achieved celebrity status in France during the fair. Curiously, the words 'Ainsi soit-il' ('So be it') offer particular insight into his French reception, if one understands them as the literal translation of the Hebrew word 'Amen' common to both Jewish and Christian liturgy. This phrase becomes the refrain in all six verses, in which each verse presents a situation in which one is given one thing and receives something else. Although it is unknown whether

written between 1881 and 1892 and housed in the Département de la Musique, Bibliothèque Nationale de France.

the song was performed as a kind of responsory, with the audience joining Ouvrard in the refrain, such call-and-response between leader and chorus was common in both American minstrel shows and the French café-concert. Thus, by ending each verse with the phrase 'so be it, Buffalo Bill', the refrain presents a kind of mock-sacred praise over a false reality shared by all, an 'Amen' that highlights the duplicitous reality of Buffalo Bill, as both a performer and an authentic interpreter of the past. (The original words of all six verses and their translation are included in table 9.1.)[55] Looking at the lyrics in more detail, we see Ouvrard's heavy use of bawdy, often sexist humour (for example, in verses 3, 4, and 5) with a number of *double-entendres*. This is not uncommon in other songs of the Belle-Époque café-concert, in which women were often objectified to highlight the weaknesses of men.[56] Beyond the sexist language, however, the quasi-sanctimonious tone of the recurring 'Ainsi soit-il' more importantly suggests the constant presence of Buffalo Bill in Paris, where (as previously mentioned) advertising posters of his Wild West Show were viewed as so overt and numerous that they often received more mockery than praise.[57] Such derision can be gleaned from verse 2, where the lyrics speak of Ouvrard's previous success with a pair of songs as 'Huge posters' ('affiches énormes') or well-advertised 'hits' that 'Created new forms'. With allusions to Buffalo Bill's show and promotion, the lyrics continue with 'What else is new?', as if to comment upon how such advertised success (i.e. *HUGE* posters), which promise the spectacle of the new, is a tired marketing trope made more so by this American entertainer. This same satirical stance continues throughout the rest of the song, which culminates in verse 6 with the playful use of the Aramaic word for God, namely 'Eloi' – a word that carries a dual reference to Ouvrard's first name and, in foreswearing any falsehood, to the very truth of what he speaks, namely the dual reality of what one sees and what one actually gets. The song thus concludes on a delightful ironic twist that asks the audience to applaud quickly in order to *prove* the song's artistic worth, a mockery of the very *truth* that the song is attempting to make clear with its suggestion that the *appearance* of truth is all that matters in the end. The use of 'Eloi' here once again highlights the fraudulent reality of both the person and image of the American frontiersman William Cody/Buffalo Bill, who, according to Ouvrard, was the ultimate 'poster boy' of public deception.

The song's satirical nature and the mischievous use of language are further emphasised by the illustrated cover page of the published sheet music, which

---

55 I am grateful to Samira Hassa, Associate Professor of French Linguistics at Manhattan College, for her assistance with the translation.

56 On the low-brow culture of Paris as reflected in songs and art of the period, see Catherine Authier, *Femmes d'exception, femmes d'influence: Une Histoire des courtisanes au XIXe siècle* (Paris: Armand Colin, 2015) and Pierre-Robert Leclercq, *Soixante-dix ans de café-concert, 1848–1918* (Paris: Les Belles Lettres, 2014).

57 See *Le Temps*, 20 May 1889, p. 2.

Table 9.1. Text and translation of 'Ainsi soit-il, Buffalo Bill!' by Éloi Ouvrard. Paris: E. Benoit, 1889.

'So be it, Buffalo Bill!'	'Ainsi soit-il, Buffalo Bill!'
I ask for your indulgence	Je demande l'indulgence
Because I'm going to sing	Car je vais chanter
A little romance	Une petit romance
That I just made.	Que j'viens de fabriquer.
It's a cheerful tune	Comme elle est guillerette
That makes the heart happy,	Elle met le coeur en fête
The title is very simple:	Le titre est très gentil,
So be it, Buffalo Bill!	Ainsi soit-il, Buffalo Bill!
I'll start my story	Je commence mon histoire
Without further ado,	Sans plus de boniment,
It's not C'est ta poire [qu'il nous faut!]	C'est pas C'est ta poire,
Nor Le Bi [du Bout] du Banc,*	Ni le Bi du banc,
Huge posters [that]**	Des affiches énormes
Created new forms	Cré'ut de nouvelles formes
What else is new?	Le nouveau quell est-il? ..
So be it, Buffalo Bill!	Ainsi soit-il Buffalo Bill!
I would like the darlings	Je voudrais que les cocottes,
To stop stuffing their bras	Ne se rembourrent plus
And wearing boots	Qu'elles ne mettent plus de bottes
And fake _____.	Ni même de faux c ... ots.
And everything on their face	Et sur leur figure
To be natural,	Que tout soit nature,
Their eyes, their eyebrows,	Les yeux, les sourcils,
So be it, Buffalo Bill!	Ainsi soit-il Buffalo Bill!
With my cousin	Avec ma cousine
I went out the other day	Je partis l'autre jour
To pick [in the] hawthorn bush	Cueillir l'aubépine
And chat about love,	Et causer d'amour
She fell to the ground	Elle tomba par terre

—(continued)

Table 9.1—*concluded*

I saw her garter	Je vis sa jarretière
Made of cotton	Qui était en coutil
So be it, Buffalo Bill!	Ainsi soit-il Buffalo Bill!
Feeling uncomfortable,	Me sentant mal à l'aise
I go to the doctor	Je vas chez le docteur
Who says to me: 'My goodness,	Qui me dit: nom d'une fraise
No need to be afraid'.	Faut pas avoir peur,
Then he shows me	Puis il me présente
In a charming way	D'une façon charmante
His little utensil	Son petit ustensile
So be it, Buffalo Bill!	Ainsi soit-il Buffalo Bill!
This new saw	Cette nouvelle scie
I tell you, upon Eloi***	Je vous le dis foi d'Eloi
I certify it	Met je le certifie
My heart in turmoil	Mon coeur en émoi
For its success	Pour sa réussite
Applaud quickly,	Applaudissez vite,
Because I'm on the grill [in hell],	Car je suis sur le gril,
So be it, Buffalo Bill!	Ainsi soit-il Buffalo Bill!

* Two popular songs by Ouvrard.

** Probably a reference to Buffalo Bill posters throughout Paris.

*** 'Eloi' (in the Gospel of Mark 15:34) is the ancient name for 'God' as spoken by Jesus on the cross. As used here, it is also a reference to Ouvrard's first name.

Source: Bibliothèque Nationale de France.

Buffalo Bill and his Wild West Company.[58] The two individuals are depicted in full merriment, with Ouvrard (on the right) winking at the viewer while pointing his thumb at the marketing poster of Buffalo Bill and members of his company (fig. 9.7).

The harmonic underlay of each verse of the strophic setting, which presents a kind of plagal ('Amen') cadence between the subdominant and tonic in F major, reinforces the religious allusions in the song. Established in the first two bars, the F major tonic moves to the subdominant of B flat major in the third bar, which appears to cadence in the fourth bar on the tonic; this movement is repeated in the second set of four bars. A dominant–tonic cadence does appear in the final passage following bars of melodic and harmonic contrast (bb. 9–12), but, because of the lack of an E or G of the dominant in the simple scalar melody, the tonic chord is the more apparent harmony heard in the last bars of each verse (ex. 9.2).

Once again, the simplicity in the musical language – the folkish melody, the square rhythm and four-measure phrasing, the major harmony – all emphasise a simple naïve quality and, coupled with the sardonic, parodistic text, serve as ironic commentary of the overly commercial reality of Buffalo Bill's god-like image and the 'American history' that his show conveys: that you never get what you pay for, or, what you see (or hear) may not be true. In addition, one notes that with this song about Buffalo Bill, the musical setting and rhythm are not unlike those of the minstrel song 'My Gal is a High-Born Lady' (discussed above), which also sets a highly satirical text to a scalar melody in a tight four-bar phrase structure in the major. Such musical simplicity, which is common to many popular songs of both America and France during this period, enhances the witty banter of Ouvrard's *chansonnette*, which serves as an unorthodox example of the critical reception of Buffalo Bill's America as heard by the French.

Conclusion

Although the American symphonic concert in Paris in 1889 was meant to show to the French that America is similar to Europe in its cultural aspirations, this symphonic 'sound of America' was understood as inauthentic, lacking a singular reducible 'America' that the French could embrace and define as unique and separate from other nations. The 'cosmopolitanism' of America that the French of the *fin de siècle* found so exhilarating and engaging about the 'New World' was not an urban, Euro-centric cosmopolitanism but one reflected in the exotic, 'frontier' character of Buffalo Bill and the multi-cultural members

---

58 Paul Bourgès (1840–1901) performed café-concerts at the nearby L'Horloge, a popular café-restaurant in the gardens of the Champs-Élysées; see Jean-Claude Calvet, *Cent ans de chanson française* (Paris: Archipel, 2008).

Figure 9.7. É. Ouvrard, 'Ainsi Soit-il, Buffalo Bill!', cover page. Paris: E. Benoit, 1889. Bibliothèque Nationale de France.

Example 9.2. Melody and basic harmonic movement of 'Ainsi soit-il, Buffalo Bill!' by Éloi Ouvrard, bb. 1–16. Paris: E. Benoit. (Transcription is my own.)

and images of the Wild West Company. For the French, the history of America was the Wild West, a fictional space created by both French and American novelists to be sure, but realised nonetheless via real-life diverse individuals who performed in Paris twice a day, Monday to Sunday, from mid-May to early November. Interestingly, this same commercial form of spectacle entertainment was embraced as the idealistic presentation not only of the 1889 World's Fair but also of the Belle Époque, a period in France that saw renewed interest in global expansionism and technological advances, as well as mass marketing and the ubiquity of spectacle entertainment and popular culture in modern society. Furthermore, the cultural definition of the era was one that portrayed a heightened commercialism, a form of populist entertainment in which the genres of vaudeville, strip tease, physical dance, and the satirical song all mingled together to create a culture for a republic that desired a collective unity across an increasingly diverse Francophone world. In Buffalo Bill's America, the 'lowbrow' spectacle of roping cattle, shooting buffalo, and the attempted rape and murder of White European immigrants by Native Americans, all accompanied by wind-band arrangements of the popular songs of the day, made America a product of this modern populist moment in nineteenth-century French society. This point is evidenced by the fact that when America is referred to in the title or dedication of a French work here in the late nineteenth century, the genre invariably is of light entertainment, which became a part of the celebrated café-concert houses of the day. We witnessed this association in Ouvrard's song 'Ainsi soit-il, Buffalo Bill!', which uses the popular and tokenistic image of Buffalo Bill in order to characterise all things experienced in the public realm as duplicitous and false, a mockery of popular culture with popular culture. Thus, when the popular emerges as the voice of the modern epic of the late nineteenth century through the spectacle of Buffalo Bill's Wild West Company, the 'sound of America' becomes the paradigm of this modern moment in France.

10

Cakewalking in Paris: New Representations and Contexts of African American Culture

César A. Leal

Most narratives of the cakewalk assert that, during its early life in antebellum America, this genre perhaps represented one of the very few safe ways in which Black slaves could respond to the cultural and social practices of their oppressors. Enslaved Americans observed social dances and developed the cakewalk as a parody of their masters' dance movements. In such a parody, full of exaggerated gestures, the ultimate goal was to win the 'cake', an award given to the couple with the best moves. As slave-owners became aware of the origin of the slaves' burlesque, they deemed such renditions of their dances non-threatening but, instead, entertaining. Since the cakewalk was not a challenge to their authority or a stern criticism of their own cultural and social values, slave-owners observed the slaves' imitation as an aspirational activity – an attempt to emulate their sophisticated rituals. Seeing the cakewalk as a homage rather than a subversive practice, slave-owners developed a taste for the dance and incorporated its steps as created by enslaved Americans into their own repertoire of dances. Jayna Brown emphasises this racial and class inversion, pointing out the 'satirical meanings hidden in full view of the masters' and the 'delightful twisting irony' of the masters' 'mimesis'.[1] After the Civil War, American minstrelsy not only would put African Americans and non-Black performers on the same stage, but would bring genres like the cakewalk to nearly every corner of the United States. The popularity of minstrel shows among audiences in northern urban centres such as New York during the early nineteenth century attracted the attention of impresarios and agents, who organised international tours and brought minstrel shows to European cultural capitals like London and Paris. By the early 1900s, African American music had become a strong cultural agent in such centres. However, the ways in which American-based racialised interactions, as well as transatlantic transformations of African American music, affected the European reception of genres like the cakewalk from the early nineteenth to the early twentieth century are

---

1 Jayna Brown, *Babylon Girls: Black Women Performers and the Shaping of the Modern* (Durham, NC: Duke University Press, 2008), p. 130.

Cakewalking in Paris 297

still under consideration, and comprehensive narratives of this complex subject are still under construction.

In studies of the history of Black American music in France, the cakewalk and other American vernacular genres, such as ragtime and the foxtrot, are often presented as insubstantial precursors to the advent of jazz in the 1920s.[2] During the first decade of the twentieth century, however, the African American genres that whetted the curiosity of Parisian audiences also stimulated French impresarios and artists to explore new enterprises and artistic exchanges with these particularly American expressions. Central to such exchanges was the cakewalk (see p. 287), which rapidly grew in popularity after the first documented performances by John Philip Sousa's band during the 1900 Exposition Universelle. Despite Sousa's renderings (and possibly earlier representations of the cakewalk), some existing literature as well as press reports of the time have declared the premiere of the American pantomime *Joyeux Nègres* at the Nouveau-Cirque on 20 October 1902 as the more impactful point of departure, consolidation, and popularisation of the cakewalk in France. Although *Joyeux Nègres* had several different acts, including a sketch by the recognised Parisian comedic duo Footit and Chocolat, what caught the attention of viewers and critics were the various cakewalks danced by an American dance troupe that featured both White and Black performers.[3] At the forefront of the racially mixed troupe of *Joyeux Nègres* were the spouses Monsieur and Madame Elk (Les Elks), allegedly White dancers from the United States. In addition to Les Elks, the troupe included Les Enfants Nègres (also identified in some documents as Les Négrillons), two African American siblings, Ruth Walker (1891–?) and Frederick Walker (1893–1977), also known as Rudy and Fredy Walker,

2 See Andy Fry, *Paris Blues: African American Music and French Popular Culture, 1920–1960* (Chicago: University of Chicago Press, 2014), p. 6. Although the cakewalk lies outside the chronological scope of his study, Fry offers a thorough analysis of African American music culture in Paris, including this basic description: 'The familiar narrative goes something like this: African American entertainers first came to France as minstrels in the nineteenth century and cakewalkers around the turn of the century (witness Debussy's popular piano pieces "Golliwogg's Cake-Walk" and "The Little Nigar")'. See also Fionnghuala Sweeney and Kate Marsh (eds), *Afromodernisms: Paris, Harlem and the Avant-Garde* (Edinburgh: Edinburgh University Press, 2013), p. 47, which states: 'In Europe the cakewalk acted as a precursor to jazz, which became an essential element of popular culture in the 1920s'.

3 The White English clown George Footit (1864–1921) and the Black Cuban clown Rafael 'Chocolat' Padilla (1868?–1917) were recognised entertainers in Paris and the stars of the Nouveau-Cirque. Their popularity is reflected not only in recent scholarship but also in posters and drawings by well-known artists of the time. See, e.g., Adrienne L. Childs and Susan H. Libby (eds), *Blacks and Blackness in European Art of the Long Nineteenth Century* (London: Routledge, 2017). See also Henri de Toulouse-Lautrec, 'Nib (Supplément de La Revue Blanche)', Accueil (Bibliothèque de l'Institut National d'Histoire de l'Art, collections Jacques Doucet, 1 Jan. 1894).

298   *César A. Leal*

whose caricaturised performances were amply showcased in posters and other publicity (fig. 10.1).[4] Other artists commonly associated with *Joyeux Nègres* included Les Soeurs Pérès, Jeanne (dates unknown) and Nina (dates unknown), and Les Nègres, two African American dancers, whose performances often included cross-dressing and gender impersonation.[5] As other authors have noted, *Joyeux Nègres* at the Nouveau-Cirque was unmistakably a turning point in the cakewalk's importation into French culture. Within two months, the overwhelming success of *Joyeux Nègres* catapulted the cakewalk into the salons, the theatres, and a plethora of public and private events in Paris.[6]

4   Documents such as the *Code noir* (1685) describe the French colonial empire's usage of terms such as 'nègre' and 'négresse' to generalise the identities of Black male and female slaves. Such painful categorisations also included 'négrillon', a word used to describe pre-pubescent child-slaves. Notwithstanding its evident colour and age codes, 'négrillon' often served to reinforce colonial stereotypes of Black adults – infantilising and portraying them as uneducated, unrefined, and naïve. Barbara T. Cooper has indicated that such terminology might now be read as a 'sign of [Whites'] inability to deconstruct their inbred notions of racial "otherness"'. See Cooper's article 'Performing Race Relations in a French Children's Drama: Subjugation and Control of the Body in Vanderburch's Séliko, ou Le Petit Nègre', *CLA Journal*, 60:3 (March 2017), 363–76, at p. 364. In private communications, Jody Blake shared further thoughts on her influential work *Le Tumulte noir: Modernist Art and Popular Entertainment in Jazz-Age Paris, 1900–1930* (University Park, PA: Pennsylvania State University Press, 1999). Blake proposed reinterpretations of African American dance movements as well as common depictions of Blacks as children in Modernist art in Paris. She elaborated on the infantilising implications of Debussy's inclusion of 'Golliwogg's Cake-Walk' in his *Children's Corner* suite (1906–8), and in paintings such as Pablo Picasso's *Petite Danse barbare* (1905) and Jacques Villon's *Cakewalk des petits filles* (1904).

5   No available information about the chronology or background of Les Soeurs Pérès can be found in the documents related to *Joyeux Nègres*. Existing images reveal two young adult women with dark hair and pale complexion. Their last name might suggest a French transliteration of the Sephardic Portuguese surname Peres or its Spanish variant, *Pérez*. Comparatively, rosters of Spanish people connected with the Nouveau-Cirque since its 1886 opening are extensive. At the top of such a roster is Joseph Oller (1839–1922), the Catalan entrepreneur who owned the Cirque. See Ferran Cayamares, *José Oller y su epoca: El hombre del Moulin Rouge* (Barcelona: Plaza & Janes, 1963). Unsurprisingly, information about Les Nègres is even less specific. Available documents consist of postcards with a couple of artists posing in costume. For the postcards featuring Les Nègres, Les Elkes [*sic*], Les Négrillons, and other artists from *Joyeux Nègres*, see 'Le Cake-Walk au Nouveau Cirque (1903) by Louis Lumière, Five Short Films of Cakewalk Dance Teams Performing, including Rudy and Fredy Walker', in *Songbook* <https://songbook1.wordpress.com/fx/si/african-american-musical-theater-1896-1926/rudy-and-fredy-walker/le-cake-walk-au-nouveau-cirque-1903-louis-lumiere-five-short-films/> [accessed 29 May 2019].

6   'Le Cake Walk au Nouveau Cirque', *Paris qui chante*, 31 Jan. 1903, pp. 4–7. The front cover of this weekly revue featured M. et. Mme Elks, 'créateurs et danseurs du "cakewalk", au Nouveau-Cirque'. This publication included an article devoted to the cake-

Allegedly, Parisians' attraction to the cakewalk stemmed not from an interaction with the music and dance alone, but rather from one with the spectacle of the genre when presented, in this case, as a pantomime.[7] During the nineteenth century the term 'pantomime', which initially defined muted action with or without musical accompaniment, acquired a variety of new meanings. It had long been associated with ballet in France (sometimes joined in the collective noun 'ballet-pantomime'); in nineteenth-century and early twentieth-century popular theatre, it was also used broadly to include short theatrical works in which music accompanied the artists' sometimes exaggerated gestures. Thanks to the rather general scope and flexible format of the genre, pantomimes such as *Joyeux Nègres* were granted easy access into a wide variety of theatres and performing spaces such as the circuses (which at the time were also considered theatres).[8]

Around the time of the performances of *Joyeux Nègres*, many cakewalks were created and published in France; however, they did not seem to have a direct or clear connection with African American culture. They were often

---

walk, which showcased the piano score of *Le Célebre Cake Walk* [*sic*] by Onin Arober (dates unknown) as well as a two-page illustrated description of the dance. A photograph of the troupe of cakewalk performers at the Nouveau-Cirque prefaced the score of *Le Célebre Cake Walk*: *Les Elks* and Ruth and Frederick Walker (Les Négrillons) are at the front of the parade. Following in the depicted parade are Les Soeurs Pérès (Jeanne and Nina) and the African American duo Les Nègres. See James Deaville, 'Debussy's Cakewalk, Race, Modernism and Music in Early Twentieth-Century Paris', *Revue musicale OICRM*, 2:1 (2014), 20–39. Deaville provides a concise survey of the cakewalk in the French cultural context. Additionally, although tentatively, he suggests that Onin Arober was a 'retrograde of Italian composer Nino Robera' (p. 29).

7   See, for instance, Matthew F. Jordan, *Le Jazz: Jazz and French Cultural Identity* (Urbana: University of Illinois Press, 2010), p. 20. Jordan indicates that 'when *Les joyeux nègres* (the Happy Negroes) opened at the Nouveau-Cirque on 20 October 1902, their act created an immediate stir that unleashed a wave of cultural anxiety in the press'. See also Sweeney and Marsh (eds), *Afromodernisms*: 'It was in 1902–03 when the cakewalk first arrived in Europe, following the use by the Nouveau Cirque [*sic*] in Paris or dance and ragtime as part of a pantomime called *Les Joyeux Nègres*' (p. 46).

8   For an analysis of the history of the circus and its role in French culture during the nineteenth century, see Patric Désile, '"Cet opéra de l'oeil": Les Pantomimes des cirques parisiens au XIXe siècle', in *Histoires de cirque aux XIXe et XXe siècles* (2011), 2–14. In this work, the author emphasises that, throughout the nineteenth century, most Parisian circuses functioned as theatres. In 1806–7, legislation assigned particular dramatic genres to specific theatres; in 1811, the legislation was modified to include venues such as the Cirque Olympique, which received authorisation to perform pantomimes. Circus pantomimes, according to Désile, 'may not involve any dialogue, but they are, very often, partially or entirely dialogued' ('peuvent, certes, ne comporter aucun dialogue, mais elles sont, très souvent, partiellement ou entièrement dialoguées') (p. 4). Certainly, danced cakewalk acts such as *Joyeux Nègres* would fit into the open concept of the pantomime.

transformed to reflect French tastes and values in ways that may be seen as a 'de-Americanisation' of the cakewalk, as well as a further 'whitening' of the genre beyond that of Sousa's band renditions or the Elks' performances. National or localised adaptations were particularly evident in thematised cakewalk acts, which often offered political and/or social commentary and echoed colonial France's attitudes towards race, class, and gender. Through recontextualised performances of the Black, or non-White, body (and, at times, replacement of the non-White body), the cakewalk became a meta-representation of Otherness, exoticism, and foreignness rather than a venerating simulation of African American culture. In many of these adaptations, images of the African American and the African are dissolved into a single (French) representation of Blackness. Such cakewalks, often with textual allusions to the African continent, clearly illustrate France's linkage of African American and African colonial cultures, seemingly on the basis of skin colour and essentialist characteristics – at times with implications of barbarity or low class status that were contrasted with ideals of the 'civilised' bourgeoisie. This linkage, as well as the fact that the rapid popularisation of the cakewalk took place amid the accelerated French colonial expansion in Africa of the *fin de siècle*, points to possible connections to France's colonial past and present and its colonialist discourse.[9] Despite such adaptations and racial constructs, African American elements did not disappear from this repertoire and, although existing in a detached or 'ghostly' manner, traits linked to its African American origins remain. The African American basis of the genre and the vestiges of African American culture that survived in French cakewalks – along with the merging of African American and African characters and symbols – made it a socially provocative and even subversive genre, despite the fact that it was 'Frenchified' or 'whitened'. This chapter will explore France's reimagining of the genre through the transforming processes of appropriation and recontextualisation at the *fin de siècle* and will re-examine the impact of these processes on the French cultural landscape and on the genre itself. In particular, it will interrogate ways in which France exploited this unique form of Black American culture within diverse theatrical genres and venues, as new manifestations of cross-racial, cross-class interplay in the adaptations of the cakewalk and as a means for conveying and wrestling with its racialised, colonialist views and values.

Among scholars who have considered the cultural significance of the cakewalk, James Deaville and Davinia Caddy have explored ideas of race and identity as reflected by the genre's popularity in *fin de siècle* Paris. Deaville reopens the discussion about the multiple dynamics that affect our idea of 'Modernism' and addresses the relationship between Debussy and the set of racialised identities represented in 'cakewalk traditions' – one defined by the complex

---

9   In 1900, France's established colonies were located mainly in the north of Africa (Algeria) as well as in Congo and Senegal. By 1914, France had colonised most of the northern, central, and western parts of the continent.

Figure 10.1. *Nouveau Cirque: Le Cake-Walk* (1903), poster by Maurice Mahul (1879–1929). Bibliothèque Nationale de France.

colonial mindset of the time. Contrastingly, in her work on Parisian cakewalks, Davinia Caddy contemplates issues beyond the musical dimension of the genre. By focusing on the cakewalk as a dance and a 'system of gestural signification', Caddy connects various sonic manifestations and images of the cakewalk such as Debussy's 'Golliwogg's Cake-Walk', the performances at the Nouveau-Cirque by Les Elks, and Georges Méliès's film *Le Cake Walk infernal*. The present study elaborates and expands on Caddy's idea of looking at signifiers found in extra-musical representations of the cakewalk to strengthen our understanding of the genre. In response to Caddy's work, which establishes the importance of 'placing due emphasis' on the various agents of 'social mediation and reception', I argue that widening the scope to include various literary genres of the time as well as other visual materials offers alternative ways of categorising and interpreting this repertoire.[10]

A variety of cakewalk types and practices emerged in France around 1900, as reflected in French musical editions, newspaper accounts, iconography, and occasional films. A survey of the various French musical editions of cakewalks reveals different paths and practices through which the genre entered local

---

10 Davinia Caddy, 'Parisian Cakewalks', *19th-Century Music*, 30:3 (2007), 288–317, at p. 317; Deaville, 'Debussy's Cakewalk'.

culture. In this chapter, works belonging to such repertoire will be divided into three categories: cakewalk-chansons, danced cakewalks, and staged cakewalks. Although these categories would inevitably intersect, particularly danced and staged cakewalks, and although all retain the genre's main musical characteristics of a fast pace, duple metre, and abundant syncopation, each shows distinctive attributes in regard to form, length, and instrumentation. Cakewalk-chansons are cakewalks with lyrics commonly in French or a combination of French and English. The presence of dialect, particularly in French, is rather common. The music of danced cakewalks, as found in published editions, is instrumental and reflective of the formal structure of the dance: scores include clearly marked sections that can be repeated, with written dance instructions for each section, suggesting that they were probably used to meet the needs of social dances, dance instructors, or performers in social settings. Staged cakewalks make reference to works in theatrical settings that contributed to the popularisation of the genre as a public spectacle; there are two main subcategories: thematised cakewalk acts and danced cakewalk acts. Danced cakewalk acts (which obviously overlap with the category of danced cakewalks) were choreography-focused shows which drew paying customers and included professional dancers/entertainers who were often recognised for their performing expertise (e.g. *Joyeux Nègres*). However, the cakewalk's popularity also precipitated its inclusion in other theatrical popular genres such as vaudevilles, *comédies*, short-story collections, and the visual arts (e.g. caricature and film). Some literary and theatrical works presented the cakewalk as a medium or prop that facilitated the delivery of a plot or social commentary. Although silent films such as *Le Cakewalk infernal* (1903) by Georges Méliès (1861–1938) did not offer diegetic representations of the cakewalk, they did include cakewalk choreographies.[11] Unlike their choreography-focused counterparts, thematised cakewalk acts did not always include danced performances of the cakewalk. Instead, they interpolated, for the most part, music and dialogue in theatrical settings. In thematised cakewalk acts, the cakewalk functioned as an unseen character, which contributed to the articulation of the plot and influ-

---

11 *Le Cake-Walk infernal*, directed by Georges Méliès, France: Cinéma Muet, 1903. This work is unique within Méliès's output for it is the only one inspired by this genre. In this short film (about 5'20"), Méliès establishes a connection between the underworld (where all the action takes place) and the silent bodies embodying the cakewalk. See Jacques Malthête and Laurent Mannoni, *Méliès: Magie et cinéma: Espace EDF Electra, 26 Avril–1er Septembre 2002* (Paris: Paris Musées, 2002). See also Christophe Wall-Romana, *Cinepoetry: Imaginary Cinemas in French Poetry* (New York: Fordham University Press, 2015). Although Wall-Romana explores the question of the transformation of French poetry into cinema, his text highlights the connection between the Parisian cultural landscape and the visual arts: 'eighteen months after the commercial debut of cinema in Paris, the poet [Stéphane Mallarmé] wrote a short, clearly theoretical note anticipating the changes the "cinématographe" would bring to the relationship between images and text' (p. 2).

enced the action of the play. In this way, thematised cakewalk acts presented the genre (or the idea of it) within a theatrical context, in which the presence of the dance became less relevant for the structural cohesiveness of the piece. Dancing did not necessarily play a central role in thematised cakewalk acts. Instead of explicit instructions for cakewalk performances, the texts for some of these theatrical works suggest the presence of undetermined cakewalk melodies performed off stage. In other words, although dancing and musical performances of actual cakewalks may not have been a significant part of theatrical works in this category, the cakewalk's role as an unseen or disembodied character nonetheless reflects its importance in the structure and meaning of thematised cakewalk acts.

By 1903, the cakewalk had had a remarkable on-stage career in Paris. Echoing the success of cakewalks as chansons and the proliferation of musical editions of this genre, increasing numbers of literary and/or theatrical works featured the cakewalk. In some staged and non-staged works, such as the one-act (in twelve scenes) vaudeville *Le Sacré Cake-Walk* (1902) by Georges Rose Fils (1873–1946) and F. Bouveret (dates unknown), the cakewalk serves as a pillar upon which their plots relied.[12] For instance, although the text of *Le Sacré Cake-Walk* does not include (or represent) Black characters on stage, references to specific repertoire, or any choreographic demonstrations resembling the life of the genre in the theatre or ballroom, general references to the existence of the cakewalk in Paris and the simultaneous desire and resistance to dance it become the source of tension between the central characters. In other theatrical works, such as *Rococo et Modern Style* (1903) by Rodolphe Berger (1865–1916) and Surtac (1864–1938), the cakewalk shared the stage with dances of the French cultural past such as waltzes, gavottes, and minuets. Although some works did include sung cakewalks, it is the interaction between the cakewalk and other dances that occupies our attention.[13]

In *Le Sacré Cake-Walk* ('The Sacred Cakewalk'), the cakewalk operates as the heart of the plot and represents the main conflict upon which the storyline develops. This work articulates tensions between the ideas of (French) civilisation, the 'enlightened'/bourgeois gentility, and savagery/barbarity/low-classness. Unsurprisingly, alleged uncivilised practices were linked to ideas of

---

12 See G. Rose Fils and F. Bouveret, *Le Sacré Cake-Walk* (Paris: C. Joubert, 1903). Other examples of such works are the one-act comédie *Isidore-Frelon danse le Cake-Walk* (Paris: Éditions du 'Nouveau Journal', 1905) by Jacques Férol (dates unknown), and the illustrated short story *Les Petits Cake-Walk* (1905) by R. de La Nézière (1865–1953) and Rodolphe Bringer (1871–1943).

13 Rodolphe Berger and Surtac, *Rococo et Modern Style* (Paris: Enoch & Cie., 1903). Berger, also known as the King of the Waltz, was a prominent composer of popular genres and works that were widely performed throughout France and Europe. Surtac, on the other hand, was the pseudonym of the leading French impresario Gabriel Astruc. See Georges d'Heylli, *Dictionnaire des pseudonyms*, new edn (Paris: Dentu, 1887), p. II.

African American (or African), foreign, Black sounds (street cakewalk music), and Black movements (cakewalk dance steps). The opening of *Le Sacré Cake-Walk* introduces Pharamond, a mathematics professor, working diligently at his home office on solving a mathematical problem. His concentration is abruptly broken by a barrel organ loudly playing a cakewalk on the street, just outside his office. [14] 'The cake-walk again. Always this dance', Pharamond grumbles. 'In what century do we live, so that a population that thinks of itself as enlightened ... the population of the city of lights ... seems, at this point, interested in a dance of savages.'[15] Pharamond's unequivocal rejection of the street (off-stage) cakewalk music has various implications. First, the professor, who represents values associated with intelligence, sophistication, knowledge, and favourable socioeconomic status, is presented in direct opposition to the cakewalk, which he characterises with eloquence. In regards to class, in addition to the informality of street performances, the distinction is made through the use of the barrel organ, a symbol of the popular, urban, folk-like, and uncultured world. Rather than being played in the traditional sense, this instrument is simply manipulated to produce sound, with actions that do not require musical training. From the vaudeville's very beginning, such associations show the audience a diametrically opposed set of values, in particular those of class and race, between the professor as the gatekeeper of French bourgeois tradition and the threatening practice of the cakewalk.

Pharamond seems unable to escape the cakewalk. Even his own family – including his nephew, Philéas – has been bitten by the foreign 'bug'. Philéas, a young unemployed medical doctor, has begged his uncle for a loan of 500 francs to purchase fifty seats at the Olympia Theatre to support Canillette, a dancer at that theatre and the object of his desire, in her debut dancing the cakewalk. Pharamond refuses to provide Philéas with the funds and encourages the young doctor to earn the money through his own work; his reluctance, however, may have been affected as much by his disapproval of the dance and those who performed it as by his concern for his nephew's independence.

Pharamond's frustrations increase throughout the play when his work and interactions are constantly interrupted by the cakewalk. Although interruptions are caused mostly by off-stage music (always suggesting music in the street as opposed to bourgeois venues), conversations related to the cakewalk seem to have a similar effect on the irritable mathematician. After learning that there would be a cakewalk competition at the Nouveau-Cirque, Pharamond loses his temper. 'I cannot stand it', he complains even more vehemently, 'I go out ... I go anywhere ... at the Tuileries ... on the quays ... I want to pull my hair out ... This is a cakewalk epidemic ... And what do our great doctors do? They

---

14 G. Rose Fils and F. Bouveret, *Le Sacré Cake-Walk* (Paris: C. Joubert, 1903).

15 'Encore le Cake-Walk. Toujours cette danse. En quel siècle vivons-nous, pour qu'une population qui se prétend éclairée ... la population de la ville lumière ... puise s'intéresser à ce point à une danse de sauvages': Fils and Bouveret, *Le Sacré Cake-Walk*, p. 3.

Cakewalking in Paris   305

do not manage to stop the sickness.'[16] Pharamond's reference to the presence of the cakewalk at the Tuileries, once royal gardens, reflects the clash between social classes as well as the tensions between the aforementioned ideas around which the character defined 'Frenchness' vis-à-vis the Other.

During Scene 6 (at the midpoint of the vaudeville), Philéas convinces Canillette, the debutante dancer, Augustine, a maid at Pharamond's home, and Polydore, a machinist at the Olympia Theatre who also works as the professor's chimney sweeper, to pretend they suffer from a so-called 'cakewalk disease', whose main (and only) symptom is the inability to stop dancing the cakewalk. They are to exhibit such symptoms in the presence of Pharamond, whose tolerance of the cakewalk has exceeded his limit. After observing his employees as well as Canillette displaying the aforementioned symptoms, the terribly distressed Pharamond reverses his earlier decision and offers Philéas the 500 francs, but only if or when he is able to cure them. The outcome is predictable. Philéas not only cures Augustine, Polydore, and Canillette but also Pharamond, who, at some point, has developed the same symptoms. Relieved that he and others have been saved from the dancing disease and greatly impressed by the medical prowess of the young doctor and nephew, Pharamond not only doubles the prize initially offered (1,000 francs) but also gives one of his properties to Philéas for him to create a research institute.

The social and cultural messages encoded in the cakewalk representations and meta-representations of this light, humorous vaudeville stand out starkly. As Jennifer Treni emphasises, the vaudeville offered an immediate gauge of urban trends and 'consumer' tastes of the Parisian public: 'vaudeville representations provided a vivid mirror of the social dynamics of consumption then coming into play. As consumer culture began to take root in Paris, the performative dimensions of social exchange, status competition, and identity creation were increasingly foregrounded.'[17] Notably, in the eyes of Pharamond, as a member of the educated, 'enlightened' upper-middle class and the most intellectual and sophisticated character of the play, the cakewalk is a 'terrible disease' ('maladie aussi terrible'), 'a dance of savages' made 'to seduce uneducated brains' ('séduire les cerveaux incultes') – which he actively, yet unsuccessfully, tries to avoid.[18] Pharamond, and the elite Parisian public that he symbolises, probably sensed certain musical aspects of the cakewalk, such as its rapid tempos and movement-inducing syncopated rhythms, as part of its

---

16   Je n'y puis tenir. je sors ... je vais n'importe où ... aux Tuileries ... sur le quais ... j'ai envie de mordre ... C'est une épidémie de cake-walk ... que font donc nos grands médecins? Ils ne parviennent donc pas à enrayer le mal': Fils and Bouveret, *Le Sacré Cake-Walk*, p. 7. For idiomatic purposes, I have translated 'j'ai envie de mordre' ('I want to bite') as 'I want to pull my hair out'.

17   See Jennifer L. Terni. 'A Genre for Early Mass Culture: French Vaudeville and the City, 1830–1848', *Theatre Journal*, 58:2 (2006), 221–48, at p. 226.

18   Fils and Bouveret, *Le Sacré Cake-Walk*, pp. 4, 11.

'contagious' attributes. However, Pharamond's rejection of the cakewalk is not based on its possible damaging effect on the idea of true 'Frenchness' he represented and defended but, instead, on the reality of its ubiquity. When Pharamond describes the genre and its practitioners with adjectives such as 'sauvage' and 'incultes', he is reacting to its negative impact on French culture. He is also suggesting a cakewalk invasion on French territory of considerable proportions. As the intruder, the cakewalk occupied spaces of great significance such as the Tuileries, a former symbol of the French monarchy and, during Pharamond's time, an icon of French culture and source of entertainment in the heart of Paris. It also invaded the Olympia Theatre, perhaps suggesting not only the degeneration of a sacred mythological site but also the intrusion into venues with public access in which the middle class would lower their ambitions, lose all trace of civilisation, and forgo French virtues. Additionally, by invading the *quais* (river banks and train platforms), the cakewalk occupied public spaces, imposing itself on nearly every pedestrian. Lastly, it intruded in Pharamond's own home and, as he claimed, there was no place to hide. The pervasiveness and uncontrollable dissemination of this genre has been echoed by scholars such as Matthew Jordan, who has suggested that 'the un-French forces represented by the cakewalk threatened the imaginary true French culture'.[19] Thus the alleged invasion of the cakewalk occurred through its occupation of public spaces with strong ties to French traditions and, like a disease, infected French bodies.

The cakewalk's invasion of French spaces and bodies might have implications beyond the aforementioned tensions between the 'civilised' and the 'savage' as well as between the elite and low-class. As an invader of French spaces, the sound or even the imagining of the cakewalk acquired a physical dimension, a moving body, whose attributes are defined by its Black origins and the bodies that created it. Additionally, though it is not particularly evident in this vaudeville, pairing the cakewalk with a 'contagious disease' may also be viewed through the lens of its musical content. To the anti-cakewalk elite, the idea of willingly learning and dancing the cakewalk seemed unnatural and inexplicable. The particular debate about the supposedly uncontrollable desire to dance cakewalks emerged, for the most part, when the genre occupied yet another sacred French space: the salon (which I address below). The cakewalk's syncopated rhythm, its improvisatory nature, and its comparatively exaggerated dance steps opposed the elegance and sophistication of salon dances such as the waltz, which based their entire repertoire of movements on the balance of a strong first beat and less accented subsequent beats. The tacit association between the cakewalk and Blackness (despite the absence of designated Black characters in this vaudeville) would have been easily understood by French audiences of the time.

---

19 Jordan, *Le Jazz*, p. 36.

As seen in other light, the cakewalk becomes a 'pseudo spiritual' ritual, to be seized or caught by listeners in rapture, yet it holds on to the implications of 'disease' as suggested above. The cakewalk's ubiquity as well as the characters' intense attraction and uncontrollable desire to dance the cakewalk render their initial efforts to resist it useless. With the characters unable to recognise or restrain internal feelings of desire, their feelings are thus depicted as a sickness. In its antagonist role, the cakewalk is objectified as an agent that needs to be controlled, stopped, and 'cured'. Through such objectification, works like *Le Sacré Cake-Walk* may have helped to emphasise the physical dimension of the cakewalk, which provided the French with an illusion in which they could manipulate and control the genre and, by proxy, its Blackness.

The French construction of Blackness, which in the case of the cakewalk merged the concepts of African American and African into a single idea, also appears in genres like the vaudeville. In most cases, not only were the different African identities blended into a single identity, but non-White characters were commonly modelled on long-standing archetypes. Black characters were practically stock characters, and writers continued to use identifiers like 'nègre' or 'négresse' instead of proper names, as can be found in eighteenth- and nineteenth-century theatrical and literary works (see Chapter 1). In her article on French vaudeville, Lisa Schreier points out that, during the mid-nineteenth century, 'black characters were an integral component of the vaudeville'; however, she also suggests 'that the genre, for all of its predictability, presented them in ways that often transcended racial difference'.[20] Schreier identifies two significant ways in which writers of vaudevilles featuring leading Black roles developed the stock (Black) character. Additionally, she includes yet another layer commonly found in these works: the sexualised non-White character who is attracted and desired by his/her White counterpart.

> First, they [vaudevilles] define the characters by their skin tone and identify them by use of such words as 'nègre', 'négresse', 'noir', or 'noire'. The plays provide no other information about their background or ethnicity, and geography at best. When characters of color are portrayed outside of metropolitan France, they reside in various places [...], but their surroundings are described in such generic ways that they could just as well be living anywhere. Second, vaudeville plays including dark-skinned protagonists feature cross-racial desire.[21]

As in many cakewalks, the titles of the mid-nineteenth-century vaudevilles that Schreier analysed include the same racial identifiers (e.g. 'nègre', 'négresse', 'noir', or 'noire') prevalent in titles of other genres of the eighteenth and early

---

20 Lisa Schreier, 'Reading Race in Nineteenth-Century French Vaudeville', in *French Cultural Studies for the Twenty-First Century*, ed. Masha Belenky, Kathryn Kleppinger, and Anne O'Neil-Henry (Lanham: University of Delaware Press, 2017), pp. 41–71, at p. 45.

21 Schreier, 'Reading Race', p. 46.

308   *César A. Leal*

nineteenth centuries.[22] In the early twentieth century (or towards the end of the long nineteenth century), however, these identifiers of colour are somewhat less frequent in the titles or dramatic texts of the theatrical or literary works in question, such as the vaudeville *Le Sacré Cake-Walk* (1902) or the short illustrated story *Les Petits Cake-Walk* (1905). Instead, race is connoted through the term 'cake-walk' itself, along with the colour-coded and age-coded 'négrillon', though in significantly different ways. While the title of the former sheathes the genre in a pseudo-spiritual tone, *Les Petits Cake-Walk* uses 'cake-walk' and 'négrillons' interchangeably to refer to the story's two non-White protagonists.

The story narrates *Les Petits Cake-Walk*'s journey back to the fictional African region of Oubanghi after reaching financial success performing the cake-walk in Paris at the Cirque Moderne. At the beginning of the story, the *petits* enthusiastically declare, 'We rich! we want see Oubangui again' ('Nous riches! nous vouloir revoir Oubanghi!'). The treatment of the geographical and ethnic backgrounds of the protagonists of *Les Petits Cake-Walk* follows the characteristics explained by Schreier. Instead of being African American, the two *petits négrillons* who, according to the story, 'created the cakewalk' are from Oubanghi in central Africa. The journey is treacherous but, along the way, they receive the help of various European (White) characters. They bring with them an assortment of objects, including clothing and machinery, with the intention of 'civilising' their own community. Once they are in the distant and exoticised Oubanghi – their national anthem is titled 'The Crocodile and the Giraffe' – anthropomorphised animals and locals share not only the same spaces but also similar sociocultural values. The relationship between the locals and the apes is presented as particularly strong. Fitting all possible stereotypes, the protagonists are portrayed as physically able, infantilised, and good-hearted individuals. They are also referred as 'short-haired anthropoids' ('anthropoïdes à poil ras') and 'monkeys' or 'apes' ('singes') and portrayed as intellectually dependent, unsophisticated, and unaware (on one occasion, visiting Europeans are unable to distinguish clothed apes from non-White locals).[23] Towards the 'happy' ending, after the eventful (and even violent civilising process), *les petits* become king and queen of Oubanghi and start the 'dynastie Cake-Walkienne' in their newly civilised home.[24]

As mentioned above, another significant point in Schreier's argument is the concept of cross-racial desire. The popularity of pantomimes such as *La Noce de Chocolat* ('The Wedding of Chocolat'), which premiered in 1889 at the Nouveau-Cirque (where the 1902 premiere of *Joyeux Nègres* also took place), suggests that the French were somewhat comfortable, at least within the enter-

---

22   For instance, *Le Célèbre Cake Walk* (1903) by Onin Arober, *You You Cake-Walk* (1903) by Teresa Dal-Mutto and Laurent Halet, and *Petite Americaine: Cake-Walk chanté* (1903) by Surtac and Berger.

23   See n. 4.

24   G. Rose Fils and F. Bouveret, *Le Sacré Cake-Walk* (Paris: C. Joubert, 1903), pp. 7, 27.

tainment industry, with the idea of biracial couples. Possibly, too, certain theatres exploited the allure, provocation, or subversiveness of cross-racial images or stories. A *pantomime nautique, La Noce de Chocolat* included a forty-piece orchestra conducted by M. L. Grillet (dates unknown) and featured Chocolat, one of the star entertainers of the cirque life of the time.[25] *La Noce de Chocolat* narrates the adventures of the clown's bride who, on the couple's wedding day, is kidnapped by a group of students and endures all sorts of comedic situations in which the actors display various types of physical prowess. At the end, wedding guests rush to assist the bride, who, while in a state of panic, jumps into a river (probably the pool of the theatre), possibly enacting an escape from this 'improper' alliance. Of particular interest is the fact that, unlike the dark-skinned groom, the bride is White (fig. 10.2). The poster of the popular pantomime shows the couple in their wedding attires, smiling and seemingly dancing. While the bride's wedding dress follows social conventions (a white, discreet dress, complemented by a veil and a flower bouquet), Chocolat's light bluish suit, his light-coloured hat, and especially his red socks visually reinforce the cultural differences between them. An illustration of strikingly similar characteristics appears on the cover of an edition of *Black and White* (1903), a cakewalk for piano by F. Volpatti (fig. 10.3). The title makes pointed reference to the Black man and his White female dancing partner. In addition to the inclusion of a simplified dance method, which provides a pass to salon repertoire and places this work in the category of cakewalks in social settings, the image of this cover remarkably resembles the poster of *La Noce de Chocolat.* While the prominence of the female character in Volpatti's cakewalk is clear, in the poster of *La Noce de Chocolat* poster and the cover of *Black and White,* both of the couples appear dancing in close proximity or arm in arm.

The staged marriage between Chocolat and his wife might retain an artificial quality. Possibly, the French saw staged relationships like this as a way to safely channel and mediate a culturally and socially unaccepted interracial desire. In other words, the stage may have served to mediate, channel, accommodate, and/or contain feelings of desire of a truly curious French audience. Regardless of the dynamics between the audience of the Nouveau-Cirque and the interracial marriage featured in *La Noce de Chocolat,* a similar interaction displayed on the cover of *Black and White* is likely to have posed a new set of challenges to the French upper class. The relationship of the couple of *Black and White's* cakewalk takes place in the salon, a hallowed space of the French elite. Although cross-racial desire seemed widely present in popular culture of the time, experiencing it within the reality of the salon probably threatened the preservation of 'Frenchness' and its ideals of 'civilised' culture. Presumably, the presence of interracial interactions in the salon filled the French elite with anxiety and added another layer to the aforementioned tensions: the possibility not

25 See n. 3.

Figure 10.2. Poster of *La Noce de Chocolat* (1900). Bibliothèque Nationale de France.

Figure 10.3. F. Volpatti, *Black and White: Américan Cake Walk*. Paris: E. Gaudet, 1903. Bibliothèque Nationale de France.

only of co-existing daily with the 'savage' and 'uncivilised' but of being 'infected' in exclusive spaces with what they considered a disease.

Another example of cross-racial imagery is found in the sheet music cover for *Les Nègres blancs* (1903) by the French composer Louis Balleron (1869–1916), which features a Black couple dancing a 'true cakewalk', but it does not offer any apparent reason for the oxymoronic title (fig. 10.4).[26]

The 'whitening' of Blacks was a central preoccupation of the civilising mission of colonial France. The racial and sociocultural implications associated with the necessity of normalising an attraction to Blackness were apparent in French modifications to the repertoire. French culture of the time sought a set of qualities that could neutralise, according to its own colonial mindset, the negative attributes they assigned the Black body. If there were a set of qualities which could provide a Black person with the ability to exist also as a White person, any non-White individual could negate and abandon their Blackness. Furthermore, the same set of qualities could be useful to neutralise the (White) discomfort of experiencing cross-racial desire. Colonisers may have felt that any cross-racial interactions were exclusively with 'whitened' Blacks. The answer to this task was rather simple: they separated a Black body from its 'Black soul'. Associating Blackness with something spiritual and invisible like one's soul made it, in the eyes of the French, susceptible to transformation. Remarkably, distinguishing the Black body from its Black soul gave the French the opportunity to whiten the Black body figuratively, while acknowledging the impossibility of whitening its skin. A Black man or woman with a 'White soul' was a colonial fabrication that allowed the French to rationalise their attraction to the Black body. This seemingly arbitrary dichotomy between a Black body and its White soul has been identified by scholars such as Brett A. Berliner, who states that 'like good citizens of the Third Republic, many women felt that the civilising mission could perfect the black. [...] In the French woman's imagination in 1920 the reception of the *nègre* was determined by his level of civilization and the color of his soul (determined by the French) as much as by his appearance.'[27] In sum, colonial France managed to justify its attraction to and desire for the Black body by removing its soul and giving it a new racial dimension.

France's conflicted views towards the cakewalk as a proxy for the Black body, which included dealing with the genre's race and class signifiers and the distinct desires it stimulated, transpired in other works created during this period. Such conflicted views and emotions, for instance, can be observed in *Rococo et Modern Style: 'Danses de jadis et d'à present'* (1903), a one-act theatrical work by Berger and Surtac, written for and performed by the Mante

---

26 Louis Balleron, *Les Nègres blancs: Véritable Cakewalk* (Paris: Fatout & Girard, 1903).

27 Brett A. Berliner, *Ambivalent Desire: The Exotic Black Other in Jazz-Age France* (Amherst: University of Massachusetts Press, 2002), p. 54.

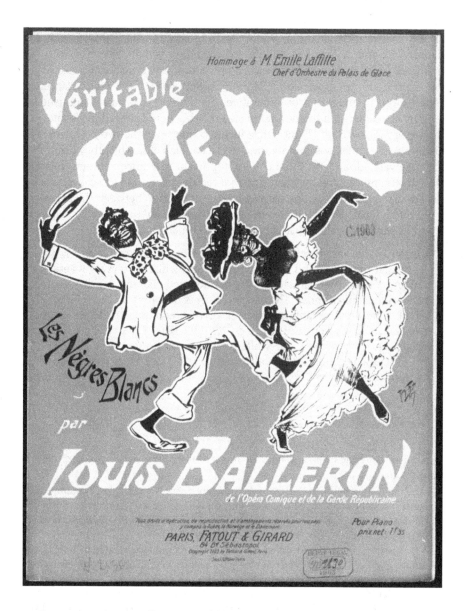

Figure 10.4: Louis Balleron, *Les Nègres blancs: Véritable Cakewalk*. Paris: Fatout & Girard, 1903. Bibliothèque Nationale de France.

314   *César A. Leal*

sisters (Louise and Blanche) and Lyse Berty.[28] *Rococo et Modern Style* included pantomime and dialogue as well as singing and dancing. Advertisements for this work in journals such as *Le Figaro* reveal that it was performed as part of larger programmes of *variétés*.[29] The April 1903 issue of *Les Modes*, 'an illustrated monthly magazine of decorative arts applied to women', published a lengthy article written by the Mante sisters, who were featured performers of *Rococo et Modern Style*.[30] The article includes images of the two performers in elaborate costumes, possibly alluding to the Parisian elite while they exemplify the cakewalk, along with three dances important to France's cultural history: the gavotte, minuet, and waltz.[31] The Mantes' description of the cakewalk evidences not only the tensions created by the interaction between the cakewalk and French local genres but also the idea of 'whitening' the genre by civilising it and imposing the alleged superior ways of French culture:

> Certainly, this very fanciful dance is not admissible in a soirée as it is performed at the circus and or in a concert. But, while preserving its essential and distinctive characters, it can be adapted, like the Pas de Quatre, to worldly conventions. [The cakewalk] thus becomes, in the middle of a ball, a picturesque fantasy, cheerful, correct, and amusing by its eccentricity. [...] That's what we tried to do. It's not a Black Cake-Walk [*sic*] that we dance, it's a White Cake-Walk. [...] We take the steps of Cake-Walk without exaggerating them and trying to put grace in lieu of its usual burlesque intentions [...][32]

---

28 For another sisters' act, see n. 5.

29 See 'Courrier des Théâtres', *Le Figaro*, 14 March 1903.

30 Louise Mante and Blanche Mante, 'Rococo et Modern Style', *Les Modes*, April 1903, p. 19.

31 The interaction between the cakewalks and other genres in a single programme suggests a juxtaposition of the coloniser and colonised. See also A. Holzmann, 'Smoky Mokes. Célébre "Cake-Walk", ou danse nouvelle américaine', in *Album Musica*, ed. Pierre Lafitte (Paris), Dec. 1902, pp. 70–1. *Album Musica* was a musical supplement to *Musica*, the prominent illustrated magazine devoted to music created in 1902 by the impresario Gabriel Astruc and the well-known editor Pierre Lafitte. Holzmann's cakewalk shares the edition with pieces by composers such as Saint-Saëns and Leroux. Of particular interest is that the score of *Smoky Mokes* directs the reader to see the cakewalk's dance theory in the magazine *Fémina*, 15 Nov. 1902, a magazine popular mostly among upper-middle-class French women. Juxtaposing musical styles and genres in a single programme is widely discussed by Jann Pasler; see her book *Composing the Citizen: Music as Public Utility in Third Republic France* (Berkeley: University of California Press, 2009).

32 'Certes, cette danse très fantaisiste n'est pas admissible dans une soirée telle qu'on l'exécute au cirque et ou concert. Mais on peut, en lui conservant ses caractères essentiels et distinctifs, l'adapter, comme le Pas de Quatre, aux convenances mondaines. Il devient ainsi, au milieu d'un bal, une fantaisie pittoresque, gaie, correcte et amusante par son excentricité. [...] C'est que nous avons essayé de faire. Ce n'est pas un Cake-Walk [*sic*]

In this work, Surtac and Berger present the taming force of French tastes as necessary for the cakewalk and, to a lesser degree, the waltz. A process of 'sophistication' would render non-French cultural expressions worthy of interacting with refined dance genres such as the minuet and gavotte, the iconic French court dances of the seventeenth and eighteenth centuries. At the beginning of Scene 4, the narrator comments on the slow waltz that has just ended and introduces the cakewalk. By expressing, through the narrator's voice, a sense of pride in the 'Frenchness' of their 'slow waltz', the authors emphasise French refinement through the de-Othering of Eastern European elements in this dance that had become associated with both Parisian and Viennese high society in the nineteenth century. In the case of the cakewalk, they promise a somewhat equivalent 're-classing' of the dance, while hinting at a de-Americanising and de-racialising process:

> Thus is the slow waltz, which remained truly French despite the Romanian, Gypsy and Moldavian influences. It kept its local flavor [...] I can see from here the terror reflected on your faces! Do not worry, there's Cake-Walk and there's Cake-Walk! Pile of rude gestures and coarse swaying movements! Our dance is a selective Cake-Walk and banishes the triviality of the Music Hall.[33]

The libretto of *Rococo et Modern Style* alludes to the existence of two different cakewalks. Berger and Surtac are probably comparing cakewalks as performed at venues such as the Nouveau-Cirque with their own rendition. As stated in the text, the association of a 'black cakewalk' with 'rude gestures' and 'rough movements' is quite explicit. This was a body language that challenged sociocultural and racial conventions of French ballrooms and traditional ballet in the theatre. Berger, Surtac, and the performing artists and choreographer probably felt that they were able (and entitled) to appropriate and override the original choreography in order to dance a 'whitened' cakewalk. By using their own bodies for such purpose, dancers and choreographer exercised power over the non-White body and the codes of expression associated with the African American origins of the cakewalk. Surtac, as the creator of the work, exerted domination over the non-White body and the non-White creative authority by replacing both with the White body and White-defined movements. Such attempts at racial and cultural domination can also be observed in musical editions of danced cakewalks.

---

nègre que nous dansons, c'est un Cake-Walk blanc. [...] Nous faisons les pas du Cake-Walk sans les exagérer et en tâchant de mettre de la grâce où l'on met ordinairement des intentions burlesques': Mante and Mante, 'Rococo et Modern Style', p. 26.

33 'Telle est la valse lente, restée bien française malgré les influences roumaines, tziganes et moldo-valaques. Elle a gardé son parfum de terroir [...] Je vois d'ici la terreur se peindre sur vos visages! Rassurez-vous, il y a Cake-Walk et Cake-Walk! Foin des gestes grossiers et des déhanchements canailles! Notre danse est un Cake-Walk de choix et bannit la trivialité du Music-Hall': Berger and Surtac, *Rococo et Modern Style*.

316   *César A. Leal*

After the success of *Joyeux Nègres* at the Nouveau-Cirque, the cake-walk underwent a fast transitional process from the stages into the salons. A glimpse into some French cakewalks for the social dance scene offers further ideas about the ways in which French culture may have reconciled its approach to Blackness and the presence of a Black genre such as the cakewalk in the salon. The popularity of the dance and the possibility of its becoming a part of salon culture faced resistance. An anxious press frequently reminded the French about the alleged *sauvage* nature of the cakewalk. The *Revue univer-selle*, corresponding to reactions in other periodicals, insisted that this 'violent, sometimes barbaric' dance, though 'relieved by a hint of *sauvage* voluptuous-ness', was 'condemned to never be a salon dance, as some have thought'.[34] Some papers like *Le Figaro* described it as a 'fight for the cake, Darwinism in action, the ferocious and colossal *danse macabre* that has led the human race for cen-turies'.[35] Here, the writer suggests that competing for a cake was a representa-tion of survival practices linked to evolution. These narratives that connected Darwinism with Blackness were widely used by the French in reference to the African territories they occupied. The usage of such narratives in the context of the cakewalk, a proxy for Blackness, fuses African American and African iden-tities. Rae Beth Gordon emphasises that 'the way that black American enter-tainers were perceived at the height of the French colonisation of sub-Saharan Africa during the Third Republic, was colored by attitudes, fears, and myths surrounding Africans'.[36] The fearful, stereotypical perceptions of Black Amer-ican entertainers are made especially evident through the editorial processes of published danced cakewalks that increasingly emphasised the cakewalk as representation of crude but fascinating African American expression as well as a meta-representative vehicle of Otherness.

Cakewalks in Social Settings and the New Codes

Editors of ballroom dance methods who included the cakewalk in their publi-cations echoed the scepticism and concerns with the crudity of 'Black' move-ments expressed in *Rococo et Modern Style*. The cover of an early edition of the

---

34   'Violente, parfois barbare, relevée d'une pointe de volupté un peu sauvage, telle est cette danse de que son caractère même condamne à n'être jamais une danse de salon, comme l'ont pensé quelques-uns': Georges Moreau (ed.), 'La Vie et l'image', in *Revue. universelle: Recueil documentaire universel et illustré* (Paris: Librairie Larousse, 1903), p. 101.

35   'la lutte pour le gâteau, le darwinisme in action, la féroce et colossale danse macabre qui mène l'espèce humaine depuis des siècles': Jules Claretie, 'Le Cake-Walk', *Le Figaro*, 13 Feb. 1903, p. 1.

36   Rae Beth Gordon, *Dances with Darwin and Vernacular Modernity 1875–1910* (Alder-shot: Ashgate, 2007), p. 151.

Traité de danse (c.1900) by Lussan-Borel announces descriptions of 'all ballroom dances' ('tout les danses de salon') and includes an appendix with a 'new theory for the waltz and [B]oston cotillion and cake-walk' ('théorie nouvelle de valse et boston du cotillon et du cake-walk'). The instructions for the cakewalk were prefaced by a disclaimer, which contained the editors' hesitations about including the cakewalk in a ballroom method. The authors conclude that even though 'this *nègre* dance [...] seems out of place in the salon' ('cette danse nègre [...] ne nous semble pas à sa place dans un salon'); in order for the cakewalk to fit in their publication, they 'adjusted and pruned its exaggerations' ('réglée et émondée de ses exagérations').[37]

Many aspects of the *Traité* were designed to prevent the alienation of the upper-middle-class consumer. It is likely that editors found it *risqué* to include the cakewalk in their ballroom method. An image on its first page featuring an elegantly dressed couple of White cakewalkers (perhaps representing upper-middle-class dance enthusiasts) reinforced existing social, cultural, and racial cues associated with the French ballroom scene and beyond. Additionally, the usage of ballet terminology to adapt and translate the cakewalk provided members of social dance communities with a relatable and safe context in which to practice the dance.

The successful efforts to modify the originally African American cakewalk, combined with an audience eager to learn the heavily advertised 'French' version of the dance, led to the proliferation of cakewalk methods. Although sharing many of the core ideas of the dance, most descriptions of the French cakewalk were, indeed, different from each other. However, all available methods included comparable traits such as describing similar positions for each gender, figures, and number of bars per each step.[38]

Musical Codifications and the Cakewalk

As seen in the aforementioned published cakewalks (i.e. Volpatti's *Black and White* and Balleron's *Les Nègres blancs*), the presence of the cakewalk in the French salon scene increased the ongoing tensions between the local and the foreign and the refined/sophisticated and the uncivilised. The proliferation of

---

37 Lussan-Borel, *Traité de danse avec musique* (Paris: Flammarion, n.d.), pp. 236–7. Unfortunately, several editions of this dance method that include the cakewalk do not contain a publication date. The first available dated edition of this document, also published by E. Flammarion, is from 1904. However, between 1900 and 1906, editors such as Labrousse also published editions of this same method, which included the cakewalk.

38 See, for instance, F. Volpatti, *Black and White: Américan Cake Walk* (Paris: E. Gaudet, 1903). A preface containing the *Théorie de danses simplifiée pour les salons* by H. de Soria appears in this musical edition.

318   *César A. Leal*

new French cakewalks, many of which included new dance methods and 'whitened' imagery, contributed to the codification of the genre. Many illustrated editions of cakewalks that feature Black characters also contain clearly identifiable racial stereotypes. In 1899, Enoch & Cie published an edition of *Whistling Rufus*, a cakewalk for piano composed in 1899 by the American composer Kerry Mills (1869–1948) (fig. 10.5). On the cover of the American version, an African American character (presumably Rufus) is shown seated, wearing a colourful tuxedo and performing the guitar while five well-dressed African American couples dance in the background. Rufus is depicted as slightly overweight, with palm-like fronds behind him and with disproportionately large lips. Curiously, the tropical imagery behind Rufus suggests southern as well as Caribbean environments. An inscription at the top of the first page, above the title, states:

> No cakewalk given in the Black Belt District in Alabama was considered worthwhile attending unless 'whistling Rufus' was engaged to furnish the music. Unlike other musicians, Rufus always performed alone, playing an accompaniment to his whistling on an old guitar, and it was with great pride that he called himself the 'one-man-band'.[39]

In the French edition of *Whistling Rufus*, the title was translated as *Le Nègre siffleur* and the opening quotation was removed. The musical content is identical. However, in the French version there are no repetition signs: all repetitions are written out in the music. The most striking difference is in the cover illustration (fig. 10.6). Unlike the American version, *Le Nègre siffleur* introduces the French Rufus as a tall, well-dressed, slender Black character, who is standing with his shiny shoes pointing towards the floor, rather than sitting, and, instead of a guitar, he is shown holding a cane. The attire and attitude of the French Rufus, particularly the cane replacing the guitar, might place him as a participant in a bourgeois promenade at a salon. Nonetheless, similar physical stereotypes, such as bright red oversized lips, are still present. There are no African American couples or botanical allusions to coastal plantation life. While the American representation of Rufus depicts a Black character performing locally for an African American audience in what seems to be a social setting, Rufus's French representation shows, instead of a musician, a sophisticated Black cakewalk dancer/entertainer or even a partaker in a ballroom dance event. However, a German edition of the same cakewalk by the Berlin-based publisher C. M. Roehr, *Rufus das Pfeifgigerl* ('Rufus the Whistler'), includes the same artwork, with no discernable difference between the American and German representations of Rufus (fig. 10.7). Most of the text, including the title, is translated into German, but it retains the English inscription at the top of the page. Furthermore, in this edition the score remains the same. The unaltered imagery of the German edition might

---

39 Kerry Mills, *Whistling Rufus* (New York: F. A. Mills, 1899), p. 3.

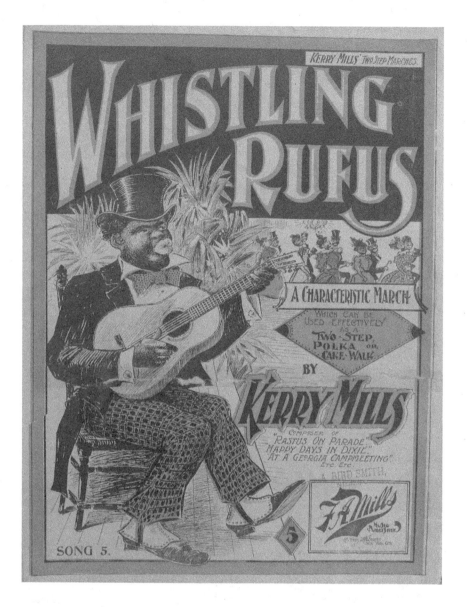

Figure 10.5. Kerry Mills, *Whistling Rufus*. New York: F. A. Mills, 1899. The New York Public Library.

Figure 10.6. Kerry Mills, *Le Nègre siffleur/Whistling Rufus.* Paris: Enoch & Cie, 1899. The New York Public Library.

Figure 10.7. Kerry Mills, *Rufus das Pfeifgigerl*. Berlin: C. M. Roehr, *c*.1900. The New York Public Library.

suggest that, in the eyes of local consumers of this repertoire, the presence of an 'uncultivated' Black American cakewalk did not pose the same threat to German culture as it did to French culture.

The musical content of French cakewalks was also modified to fit market needs. Editions of danced cakewalks, as stated at the beginning of this chapter, proliferated during the cakewalk craze. *Cake Walk de salon* (1903), a cakewalk for piano by Roger de Beaumercy (18??–1943), is representative of this category.[40] The cover of this musical edition features an upper-middle-class White couple dancing a cakewalk in a ballroom while being observed by a large crowd of their peers. The image in the upper-left corner suggests a distant image of romanticised plantation life or, perhaps, the past of the new, 'civilised' version of the dance. The gestures and the outfits make the White version more refined and 'suitable for the Ballroom'. The cover also advertises the 'Théorie', or dance methods, by the dance instructor E. Giraudet (fig. 10.8).

Although Beaumercy's *Cake Walk de salon* follows all musical conventions of the genre, the piano score does not contain the traditional formal indications commonly found in other instrumental scores of cakewalks (e.g. sections like the 'trio'). Instead, the form of the piece is articulated by the names of the steps, which appear above the first bar of the section in which such steps should be performed. As in most dance methods, cakewalk patterns are either eight or sixteen bars long. *Cake Walk de salon* includes 'Introduction' (four bars in G major), 'Entrée' (sixteen bars), 'Promenade' (sixteen bars), 'Balancé' (eight bars in C major), 'Two-Step' (eight bars), 'Promenade' (sixteen bars, back to G major), 'Tourniquet' (eight bars in D major), 'Two-Step' (eight bars), 'Promenade' (sixteen bars, back to G major), 'Balancé' (eight bars in C major), 'Two-Step' (eight bars), and 'Sortie' (sixteen bars in G major). Unlike cakewalk-chansons or staged cakewalks, danced cakewalks followed the tradition of the French salon and adapted its formal structure accordingly.

In this particular case, the cover juxtaposes existing representations of Black culture, plantation life, and the Black body, which includes the 'coarse' way it moves, with the meta-representation in French culture. This graphic depiction of a recontextualised cakewalk emphasises the aforementioned tensions of class and race as represented by images of White and Black bodies. Similarly, the musical content juxtaposes the sonic image – linked to the cakewalking of Black bodies – with the modified musical structure that matches cakewalking White bodies.

Conclusions

In France, the spectacularised rendition of the cakewalk not only decontextualised the genre from its American origins, but also provided it with a prominent place on theatre stages and in salons, two important spaces for the consoli-

---

40 Roger de Beaumercy, *Cake Walk de salon* (Paris: E. Gallet, 1903).

Figure 10.8. Roger de Beaumercy, *Cake Walk de salon*, cover, 'Introduction', and 'Promenade'. Paris: E. Gallet, 1903. Bibliothèque Nationale de France.

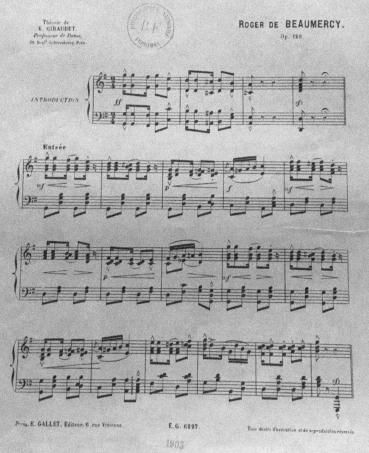

Figure 10.8—*continued*

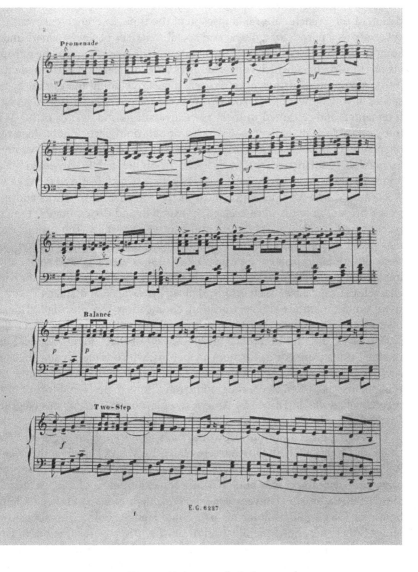

Figure 10.8—*concluded*

326   *César A. Leal*

dation of the French cultural landscape of the time. In French cakewalks, the cakewalk as a parody of cultural and social practices of slave-owners and the complicated histories of slavery and plantation life seemed erased by European visions of Blackness, which converted African American and African identities into a single one. Furthermore, French stages, including the circus, became spaces in which the identities of African American performers were, yet again, fragmented and reframed to meet the expectations and desires of the White (often elite) French audiences and salon or ballroom participants. As a result of such recontextualisation, and in order to adapt to the needs and desires of French local audiences of the *fin de siècle*, the French public witnessed the creation of a plethora of works, in a variety of genres, which featured the cakewalk. According to the ways in which most of the representative works addressed in the present chapter were created, consumed, and disseminated, they may be classified as cakewalk-chansons and danced cakewalks. The various examples presented in this chapter show the mechanisms through which *fin de siècle* France appropriated the cakewalk as well as the racial and sociocultural implications of such processes. To such end, and although retaining individual characteristics, cakewalk-chansons, danced cakewalks, and staged cakewalks share similar methods of objectification, codification, recontextualisation, and meta-representation to assert control over Black culture and the Black body. Nonetheless, despite the French generalisation of Black identities, cakewalks retained traits from African American identity, which is identifiable in aspects such as the presence of English lyrics (sometimes in dialect) in some cakewalk-chansons as well as choreographic renditions in performances of instrumental cakewalks in France by American entertainers such as Les Négrillons (Rudy and Fredy Walker) or Les Nègres.[41]

Observing other non-musical works such as *Journal d'un nègre à la Exposition de 1900* (1901), an illustrated book by the White French author Gaston Bergeret (1840–1921), may provide new insights into this process of appropriation and adaptation. This book narrates the experiences of a Black character at the 1900 Exposition Universelle and offers illustrations by François Clément Sommier (1844–1907) under his pen-name Henry Somm. The art historian James Smalls describes the illustration on the title page of this book, which 'depicts a black man in profile bedecked with all the accoutrements that mark him as a dandy and/or bourgeois gentleman of leisure. He is dressed in a frock coat with flowered lapels, high stiff collar, white gloves, and top hat. In his right hand he carries a cane.'[42] Almost immediately, the meta-representation of Rufus, the African American character in the aforementioned cover illustration to the French edition of *Whistling Rufus* (published as *Le Nègre siffleur*), comes to mind. Smalls's description of the character on the cover of *Journal*

---

41 See n. 5 and fig. 10.1.

42 James Smalls, '"Race" as Spectacle in Late-Nineteenth-Century French Art and Popular Culture', *French Historical Studies*, 26:2 (Spring 2003), 351–82, at p. 352.

d'un nègre à la Exposition de 1900 corresponds with the image of Rufus on the cover of *Le Nègre siffleur*.[43]

The paradox of comparing these two characters in the context of race and class relations helps to illuminate colonial France's vision of Blackness. Rufus *circa* 1900 and the *nègre* at the 1900 World's Fair are both the same character and, at the same time, they are no one. However, both characters resonate with the ideas and goals that accompanied the process of appropriation of cultural phenomena like the cakewalk. By creating (and owning) the personal experiences of a Black man at the 1900 World's Fair, White characters like Henry Somm imposed himself on the character. In other words, Somm and the editors of *Le Nègre siffleur* managed to whiten not only the experience and expression of the Black individual but also his body.

Similarly, the codification of the idea of cakewalking by French dance instructors and composers such as Beaumercy in his *Cake Walk de salon* was a way of whitening the genre and, by extension, whitening the Black body that originally expressed it. As in the examples of thematised cakewalks reviewed in this article, White French dancers, composers, journalists, and entrepreneurs insisted on differentiating White cakewalks from Black cakewalks. The codification of the genre through new lyrics, dancing instructions following the French ballroom tradition, and structural modification of the music to fit different performance practices (including performance through social dance) provided *fin de siècle* France with the tools to recontextualise and meta-represent African American culture.

Imposing a White voice on an African American genre, pathologising such a genre by describing it as a 'maladie terrible',[44] and constructing visual representations of Blackness were effective ways to reinforce the colonial civilising mission, within France as well as within its own colonies beyond France. Similarly, tailoring the cakewalk's musical structures to fit local social conventions of the French salon and, furthermore, to facilitate its interaction with 'classical' dances associated with the elite (such as minuets and waltzes) reinforced colonial structures of power and its impact on race and class. By creating new 'whitened' representations of the cakewalk, France was able to exercise cultural power over the genre and, consequently, the Black body that served as an emblem of the subjugated 'savage' of both the American and French colonial past and present.

---

43 The French Rufus seems to bear some affinity with Zip Coon, the urban dandy stereotype of American blackface minstrelsy.

44 In *Le Sacré Cake-Walk*, the main character refers to the cakewalk as a 'maladie aussi terrible' and a 'danse des sauvages' (see n. 18).

Bibliography

Primary Sources (Archival)

Justamant, Henri. *Ballets dans les Parisiens à Londres*, Lincoln Kirstein Collection, The New York Public Library, *MGRN-Res. 73-259 v.1.

——. 'Ballet du *Bossu* par Henri Justamant, musique de M^ssrs Artus et Calendini, represente pour la première fois sur le théâtre de la Porte Saint Martin le [...]', in *Divertissements de La Tour de Nesle et du Bossu drames avec les gravures des costumes*, pp. 1–69, Lincoln Kirstein Collection, New York Public Library, *MGRN-Res. 73-259 vol. 2.

——. *Le Corsaire, ballet en trois actes et cinq tableaux par Messieurs de St George et Mazillier, musique de Mr A. Adam, représenté pour la première fois sur le grand théâtre à Lyon le 17 fevrier 1857, mise en scène par Mr H. Justamant, direction de Mr Halanzier Dufrenoi*, Theaterwissenschaftliche Sammlung der Universität zu Köln, Schloss Wahn, Ms. 70-441.

——. *Divertissements de Faust réglés par Mr Justamant, représentés pour la première fois à L'Académie Impériale de Musique, le 3 Mars 1869*, Theaterwissenschaftliche Sammlung der Universität zu Köln, Schloss Wahn, Ms. 70-454.

——. 'Divertissements de *Juagarita* [sic], réglés par Mr H. Justamant, représentés pour la première fois à Lyon sur le Grand Théâtre 1856 à 1857, direction de Mr Halanzier', in Henri Justamant, *Divertissements d'opéras comiques avec coryphées et dames du corps de ballet*, pp. 3–21, Bibliothèque Nationale de France, B.217 (19).

——. *Grand pas composés par Mr H. Justamant, représentés à Marseille et Bruxelles*, Bibliothèque Nationale de France, Bibliothèque-Musée de l'Opéra, B.217 (24) <gallica.bnf>.

——. *Monsieur de Pourceaugnac, intermèdes de danses réglés par Mr Justamant, musique de Lulli [sic], représentés à Paris pour la première fois sur le Théâtre de la Gaîté (nouveau Lyrique) le 2 avril 1876, direction de Mr Albert Vizentini*, Lincoln Kirstein Collection, The New York Public Library, *MGRN-Res. 73-259 vol. 8.

Bibliography

Primary Sources (Printed)

Adam, Adolphe, *et al. La Jolie Fille de Gand, ballet-pantomime en trois actes et neuf tableaux, par MM. de Saint-Georges et Albert, musique de M. Adolphe Adam, décorations de MM. Cicéri, Philastre et Cambon, représenté pour la première fois sur le Théâtre de l'Académie Royale de Musique, le mercredi 22 juin 1842,* 2nd edn (Paris: Jonas, 1842).

——. *Les Mohicans, ballet-pantomime en deux actes, de M. Guerra, musique de M. Adolphe Adam, décors de MM. Devoir et Pourchet, représenté pour la première fois sur le Théâtre de l'Académie Royale de Musique, le mercredi 5 juillet 1837* (Paris: Thomassin, 1837).

Almanach des Orphéonistes et des musiciens de l'avenir: Avec l'Histoire du concours musical de l'Exposition de 1867 (Paris: Librairie du Petit Journal, 1868).

Anicet-Bourgeois, Auguste, and Paul Féval. *Le Bossu, drame en cinq actes et douze tableaux* (Paris: Michel Lévy frères, 1862).

Anicet-Bourgeois, Auguste, Clairville, and Laurent. *Les Quatre Parties du monde* (Paris: Michel Lévy frères, 1851).

Arober, Onin. *Le Célèbre Cake Walk* (Paris: Impr. P. Dupont, 1903).

Balleron, Louis. *Les Nègres blancs: Véritable Cakewalk* (Paris: Fatout & Girard, 1903).

Beaumercy, Roger de. *Cake Walk de salon* (Paris: E. Gallet, 1903).

Beaumont, Gustave de. *Marie, ou L'Esclavage aux États-Unis: Tableau de mœurs américaines,* 2nd edn (2 vols, Paris: Gosselin, 1835).

Béraud, Louis-François-Guillaume, and Joseph de Rosny. *Adonis, ou Le Bon Nègre, mélodrame, en quatre actes, avec danses, chansons, décors et costumes Créoles, par les Citoyens Béraud de la Rochelle et Joseph Rosny, ballets du Cit. Milon, artiste du Théâtre des Arts, représentée, pour la première fois, sur le théâtre de l'Ambigu-Comique, en fructidor de l'an 6ᵉ de la République* (Paris: Chez Glisau, Pigoreau, Pan, 1798).

Berger, Rodolphe, and Surtac. *Petite Américaine: Cake-Walk chanté* (Paris: Enoch & Cⁱᵉ, 1903).

——. *Rococo et Modern Style* (Paris: Enoch & Cⁱᵉ, 1903).

Berr, Émile, *et al. Exposition de 1889: Guide bleu du 'Figaro' et du 'Petit Journal'* (Paris: Le Figaro, 1889).

Billardon de Sauvigny, Edme-Louis. *Vashington, ou La Liberté du Nouveau Monde, tragédie en quatre actes, par M. de Sauvigny, représentée pour la première fois le 13 juillet 1791, sur le Théâtre de la Nation* (Paris: Maillard d'Orivelle, 1791).

Blau, Edouard. *Après cent ans* (Paris: Typographie Lahure, 1876).

Bringer, Rodolphe, and R. de La Nézière. *Les Petits Cake-Walk* (Paris: F. Juven, 1905).

Brissot (Warville), J. P. *Nouveau Voyage dans les États-Unis de l'Amérique septentrionale, fait en 1788* (3 vols, Paris: Buisson, 1791).

Bibliography 331

Buffalo Bill (Col. W.-F. Cody). *L'Ouest sauvage de Buffalo Bill: Récits américains, description illustrée et aperçus de faits historiques* (Paris: Parrot et Cie, 1889).

Burke, John M. *Buffalo Bill: From Prairie to Palace*, ed. Chris Dixon (Lincoln: University of Nebraska Press, 2012).

Le Cake-Walk infernal, film, directed by Georges Méliès (Paris: Cinéma Muet, 1903).

Cartier, Jules, and Fernand d'Héramberg. 'Les Gardes Lafayette de la Nouvelle-Orléans!' (New Orleans: Henri Wehrmann, n.d. [1877]).

Chassaignac, Eugène, and Placide Canonge. 'Brise du Sud' (New Orleans: The Bronze Pen Press, 1864).

Chateaubriand, François-René. *Atala, ou Les Amours de deux sauvages dans le désert* (Paris: Migneret et Dupont, 1801).

——. *Essai historique, politique, et moral sur les révolutions anciennes et modernes* (London: Boosey, 1797).

——. *Génie du christianisme* (5 vols, Paris: Migneret, 1802).

——. *Mémoires d'outre-tombe* (2 vols, Paris: Gallimard, 1997).

——. *Memoirs from Beyond the Grave 1768–1800*, trans. Alex Andriesse (New York: New York Review Books, 2018).

——. *Travels in America*, trans. Richard Switzer (Lexington: University of Kentucky Press, 1969).

——. *Voyage en Amérique* (2 vols, Paris: Librairie Marcel Didier, 1964).

Chauvin, Joseph-Joachim-Victor. *Arthur de Bretagne, tragédie en cinq actes, par M. Chauvet. Représenté, pour la première fois, par les comédiens du roi, sur le Théâtre Royal de l'Odéon, le lundi 16 aout 1824. Suivie de Néali, ou La Traite des nègres, poème qui, au jugement de l'Académie Française, a remporté le prix de poésie, décerné dans sa séance du 25 aout 1823* (Paris: Barba, 1824).

Clairville (Louis-François Nicolaïe) and Jules Cordier. *L'Alchimiste, ou Le Train de plaisir pour la Californie* (Paris: Tress, 1850).

Clairville, Charles. *Les Menus-Plaisirs de l'année. Revue à spectacle en 3 actes et 17 tableaux* (Paris: A. Allourad, 1877).

Comettant, Oscar. *Trois ans aux États-Unis: Étude des moeurs et coutumes américaines* (Paris: Pagnerre, 1857).

Conterno, Giovanni E. *Bartholdi March: The New Two Step* (New York: Carl Fischer, 1893).

Curto, Gregorio, and Placide Canonge. 'Le Réveil de la Louisiane' (New Orleans: Henri Wehrmann, 1877).

Dalayrac, Nicolas, and Benoît-Joseph Marsollier des Vivetières. *Arnill, ou Le Prisonnier américain, comédie en prose, en un acte, paroles de Marsolier, musique de Dalayrac, représentée sur le Théâtre de la rue Favart* (Paris: Barba, 1797).

Dal-Mutto, Teresa, and Laurent Halet. *You You Cake-Walk* (Paris: Blanc, 1903).

332   Bibliography

David, Félicien. *La Perle du Brésil, drame lyrique en trois actes par MM. J. Gabriel et Sylvain Saint-Étienne, musique de M. Félicien David, représenté pour la première fois, a Paris, sur le Théâtre de l'Opéra-National, le 22 novembre 1851 et sur le Théâtre-Lriyque [sic], le 10 mars 1858* (Paris: Lévy, 1858).

——. *La Perle du Brésil, opéra comique, en trois actes, pour piano et chant, paroles / de MM. J. Gabriel et Sylvain St.-Étienne. Musique de Félicien David* (Paris: Launer, n.d.).

d'Ennery, Adolphe. *La Prière des naufragés* (Paris: Michel Lévy frères, 1853).

Depping, Georges-Bernard. *Aperçu historique sur les moeurs et coutumes des nations* (Paris: Mairet et Fournier, 1842).

Duckett, William, ed. *Dictionnaire de conversation à l'usage des dames et des jeunes personnes, ou Complément nécessaire de toute bonne éducation* (10 vols, Paris: Langlois et Leclercq, 1841–2), vol. 8.

Étienne, Charles-Guillaume, and Alphonse Martainville. *Histoire du théâtre français depuis le commencement de la révolution jusqu'à la réunion générale* (Paris: Barba, 1802).

Fagan, Barney, 'My Gal is a High-Born Lady'. New York: M. Witmark & Sons, 1896.

Fauconnet, Charles Prosper. *Ruined by this Miserable War: The Dispatches of Charles Prosper Fauconnet, a French Diplomat in New Orleans, 1863–1868*, ed. Carl Brasseaux and Katherine Carmines Mooney (Knoxville: University of Tennessee Press, 2013).

Favières, Edmond de. *Paul et Virginie, comédie en trois actes, en prose melée d'ariettes, représenté par les comédiens italiens* (Paris: J. L. de Boubers, 1794).

——. *Paul et Virginie, comédie en trois actes et en prose, mêlée d'ariettes, représentée par les comédiens italiens, le 15 janvier 1791* (Avignon: Jacques Garrigan, 1792).

Férol, Jacques. *Isidore-Frelon danse le Cake-Walk* (Paris: Éditions du 'Nouveau Journal', 1905).

Féval, Paul, *Le Bossu: Aventures de cape et d'épée* (Paris: Bureaux du Siècle, 1858).

Fils, G. Rose, and F. Bouveret. *Le Sacré Cake-walk* (Paris: C. Joubert, 1903).

Fleury, Victor. 'Beaux-Arts. La Tentation, ballet-opéra en cinq actes, par MM. *** et Coraly, musique de MM. Halévy et Gide', *L'Artiste* S1, 3 (1832), 241–5.

Galerie théâtrale, ou Collection des portraits en pied des principaux acteurs des premiers théâtres de la capitale (Paris: Bance, 1834).

Gallenberg, W. Robert (comte de). *Brezila ou La Tribu des femmes, ballet en un acte, par M. Taglioni, musique de M. le Comte de Gallenberg; représenté pour la première fois sur le Théâtre de l'Académie Royale de Musique, le 8 avril 1835* (Paris: Librairie Centrale, 1835).

Gardel, Pierre-Gabriel. *Paul et Virginie, ballet-pantomime en trois actes par M. Gardel, maître des ballets de sa majesté, chef de la danse de L'Académie* royale de musique, et membre de la Société philotechnique, musique de M. Kreutzer, premier violon de la Chapelle de Sa Majesté, représenté sur le théâtre de l'Académie de musique le mardi 24 du mois de juin 1806 (Paris: Chez Roullet, 1815).

Gautier, Théophile. *Gautier on Dance*, ed. and trans. Ivor Guest (London: Dance Books, 1986).

——. *Histoire de l'art dramatique en France depuis vingt-cinq ans* (6 vols, Paris: Hetzel, 1858–59), vol. 1.

——. 'Theatres. Les Indiens Ioways', *La Presse*, 19 May 1845, pp. 1–2.

Gide, Casimir, *et al. Ozaï, ballet en deux actes et six tableaux par M. J. Coralli, musique de M. Casimir Gide, décors de M. Cicéri, représenté pour la première fois sur le Théâtre de l'Académie Royale de Musique, le 26 avril 1847* (Paris: Jonas, 1847).

Gossec, François. *Le Triomphe de la République ou Le Camp de Grand Pré, divertissement lyrique en un acte, représenté à l'Opéra le 27 Janvier l'an 2ème de la République Française une et indivisible, paroles du Citoyen Chenier, la musique du Citoyen Gossec, les ballets du Citoyen Gardel* (Paris: Mozin, H. Naderman, n.d.).

Gottschalk, Louis Moreau. *Bamboula: Danse des Nègres, fantaisie pour piano* (Paris: Bureau Central de Musique, n.d. [1849]).

——. *Notes of a Pianist*, ed. Jeanne Behrend (New York: Knopf, 1964).

Gounod, Charles. *La Liberté éclairant le monde*, text by Emile Guiard (Paris: Imp. Arouy, Fouquet, 1876).

Grainger, James. *The Sugar-Cane: A Poem* (London: Dodsley, 1764).

Grégoire, H[enri]. *De la Littérature des nègres, ou Recherches sur leurs facultés intellectuelles, leurs qualités morales et leur littérature* (Paris: Maradan, 1808).

Halévy, Fromental, and Eugène Scribe. *Manon Lescaut, ballet-pantomime en trois actes, par M. Scribe. Musique composée par M. Halévy, décors de M. Cicéri, représenté pour la première fois, sur le Théâtre de l'Académie Royale de Musique, le 30 Avril 1830* (Paris: Bezou, 1830).

Halévy, Fromental, *et al. L'Éclair, opéra comique en trois actes. Paroles de MM. E. de Planard et H. de Saint-George [sic], musique de M. F. Halévy. Représenté pour la première fois sur le Théâtre royal de l'Opéra-Comique, le 16 décembre 1835* (Paris: Boulé, n.d. [1853]).

——. *Jaguarita l'Indienne, opéra comique en trois actes, par MM. de Saint-Georges et de Leuven musique de M. F. Halévy de l'Institut. Décorations de MM. Cambon, Thierry, Chéret et Lechevalier. Divertissements de M. Clair Bénié. Représenté pour la première fois à Paris, sur le Théâtre-Lyrique, le 14 mai 1855* (Paris: Lévy, 1855).

——. *Jaguarita l'Indienne, opéra comique en trois actes, poëme de MM. de St. Georges et de Leuven, musique de F. Halévy, membre de l'Institut. Partition Piano et Chant par L. Croharé* (Paris: Jules Heinz, n.d.).

Hugo, Victor, *Bug-Jargal* (Paris: Urbain Canel, 1826).

——. *Bug-Jargal*, ed. Roger Borderie (Paris: Gallimard, 1970).

334   Bibliography

Justamant, Henri. *Giselle ou Les Wilis, ballet fantastique en deux actes: Faksimile der Notation von Henri Justamant aus den 1860er Jahren*, ed. Frank-Manuel Peter (Hildesheim: Olms, 2008).

Kreutzer, Rodolphe. *Paul et Virginie. Ballet-pantomime en 3 actes. Musique de Kreutzer. Représenté pour la première fois le jeudi 12 juin 1806* [Musique manuscrite].

——. *Paul et Virginie, comédie en prose et en trois actes, paroles de M **** [Edmond de Favières], *representée pour la 1re fois par les comédiens italiens le samedy 15 janvier 1791* (Paris: Auteur, n.d.).

Holzmann, A. 'Smoky Mokes. Célébre "Cake-Walk", ou danse nouvelle américaine', in *Album Musica*, ed. Pierre Lafitte (Paris), Dec. 1902, pp. 70–1.

LaJarte, Théodore. *Bibliothèque musicale du Théâtre de l'Opéra: Catalogue historique, chronologique, anecdotique* (2 vols, Paris: Librairie des Bibliophiles, 1876), vol. 2.

Laroque, Philippe. *The Hero of New Orleans: The Battle of the Memorable 8th of January 1815* (Philadelphia: G. Willig, 1818).

Leclerc, Georges-Louis, Comte de Buffon, and Philippe Guéneau de Montbeillard. *Histoire naturelle, générale et particulière, avec la description du Cabinet du Roi: Histoire naturelle des oiseaux* (9 vols, Paris: L'Imprimerie Royale, 1770–83), vol. 4.

Lemoinne, John. 'Le Passage du Nord', *La Revue de Paris*, NS, 1 (Jan. 1854), 1–46.

Le Sueur, François. *Paul et Virginie (ou Le Triomphe et la vertu), drame lyrique en trois actes, représentée sur le Théâtre Faydeau [sic], paroles de l'auteur d'Iphigénie en Tauride de Piccinni* [Alphonse Dubreuil], *musique de Lesueur* (Paris: J. H. Naderman, n.d.).

Lussan-Borel. *Traité de danse avec musique* (Paris: Flammarion, n.d.).

Mahul, Maurice. *Nouveau Cirque: Le Cake-Walk*, poster, 1903.

Malte-Brun, Conrad. *Précis de la géographie universelle, ou Description de toutes les parties du monde* (8 vols, Paris: Buisson, 1810–29), vol. 4.

Martineau, Harriet. *Society in America* (2 vols, Paris: Baudry's European Library, 1837), vol. 2.

Millevoye, Charles. *Oeuvres complètes de Millevoye, dédies au roi, et ornés d'un beau portrait* (Paris: Ladvocat, 1822).

Mills, Kerry. *Le Nègre siffleur* (Paris: Enoch & Cie, 1899).

——. *Rufus das Pfeifgigerl* (Berlin: C. M. Boher, c.1900).

——. *Whistling Rufus* (New York: F. A. Mills, 1899).

Ministère de l'Instruction Publique et des Beaux-Arts. *Catalogue général des livres imprimés de la Bibliothèque nationale: Auteurs*, vol. 31, Colombi–Corbiot (Paris: Imprimerie Nationale, 1907).

Monpou, Hippolyte, *et al*. *Le Planteur, opéra comique en deux actes, paroles de M. de Saint-Georges; musique de M. H. Monpou. Représenté pour la première fois, à Paris, sur le théâtre royal de l'Opéra-Comique, le 1er mars 1839* [libretto], *La France dramatique au dix-neuvième siècle, choix de pièces modernes 7* (Paris: Tresse, 1841), pp. 331–53.

Bibliography   335

——. *Le Planteur, opéra comique en deux actes, paroles de M*r*. H. de St. Georges, musique de Hippolyte Monpou* [full score] (Paris: Richault, n.d. [1839]).

——. *Le Planteur, opéra comique en deux actes, paroles de M*r*. H. de St. Georges, musique de Hippolyte Monpou* [piano-vocal score] (Paris: Richault, n.d. [1839]).

Montagne, Édouard, and Alfred Reneaume. *Dans une île déserte* (Paris: Charlieu, 1857).

Montaigne, Michel. *The Complete Essays of Montaigne*, trans. Donald M. Frame (Stanford: Stanford University Press, 1965).

Montépin, Xavier de, and Jules Dornay. *Bas-de-Cuir* (Paris: Lacour, 1866).

Montulé, Edouard de. *A Voyage to North America and the West Indies in 1817* (London: Sir Richard Phillips & Co., 1821).

Moreau de Saint-Méry, Médéric-Louis-Élie. *De la danse* (Parma: Bodoni, 1801).

——. *Description topographique, physique, civile, politique et historique de la partie française de l'isle Saint-Domingue [...] à l'époque du 18 octobre 1789 et d'une nouvelle carte* (2 vols, Paris: Dupont, 1797).

——. *Voyage aux États-Unis d'Amérique, 1793–1798*, ed. Stewart L. Mims (New Haven: Yale University Press, 1913).

Nouveau dictionnaire d'histoire naturelle (36 vols, Paris: Deterville, 1816–19), vol. 12.

Offenbach, Jacques. *Offenbach en Amérique: Notes d'un musicien en voyage* (Paris: C. Lévy, 1877).

Ouvrard, Éloi. 'Ainsi soit-il, Buffalo Bill' (Paris: E. Benoit, 1889).

——. *La Vie au café-concert: Mémoires et études de moeurs* (Paris: Paul Schmidt, 1894).

Palianti, L[ouis]. *Mise en scène du Planteur, opéra comique en deux actes, paroles de M. de Saint-Georges. Musique de M. H. Monpou. Représenté, pour la première fois, à Paris, sur le Théâtre royal de l'Opéra-Comique, le 1 mars 1839*, Collection de mises en scènes rédigées et publiées par M. L. Palianti 77 (Paris: Brière, n.d. [1839]), pp. 65–73.

Peterson, Clara Gottschalk (ed.). *Creole Songs from New Orleans in the Negro Dialect* (New Orleans: L. Grunewald, 1902).

Picquenard, J. B. *Adonis, ou Le Bon Nègre, anecdote colonial* (Paris: Didot jeune, 1798).

Pigault-Lebrun. *Le Blanc et le noir, drame en quatre actes et en prose, représenté et tombé sur le Théâtre de la Cité le 14 Brumaire de l'an IV* (Paris: Mayeur, Libraire et Commissionnaire; Barba, Libraire, 1795).

Pillet, Fabien. *Indicateur dramatique ou Almanach des théâtres* (Paris: chez Lefort; Malherbes, 1798).

Planard, Eugène de, and Henri de Saint-Georges. *L'Éclair* (Paris: Dubuisson, [1835]).

Prévost, Eugène. 'The Departure of the Volunteers: A National Song' (New Orleans, n.d. [1846]).

336   Bibliography

Prosper (Auguste Lepoitevin de L'Égreville) and Auguste Anicet-Bourgeois. *Les Massacres de Saint-Domingue, ou L'Expédition du général Leclerc, pièce inédite, présentation de Barbara T. Cooper* (Paris: L'Harmattan, 2019).

Raynal, Guillaume Thomas. *Histoire philosophique et politique des établissements et du commerce des Européens dans les deux Indes* (3 vols, Geneva: Librairies Associés, 1775).

——. *La Revolution de l'Amérique* (London: Locker Davis, 1781).

Reid, Mayne. *The Quadroon; or, A Lover's Adventures in Louisiana* (3 vols, London: Hyde, 1856), vol. 3.

Reports of the United States Commissioners to the Universal Exposition of 1889 at Paris (5 vols, Washington, DC: US Government Printing Office, 1890–1).

Robinson Crusoé. Programme, Théâtre du Châtelet, Oct. 1899, Bibliothèque Nationale de France, WNA-25.

Rochefoucauld, Frédéric-Alexandre de la, duc de Liancourt. *Journal de voyage en Amérique et d'un séjour à Philadelphie, 1 octobre 1794–18 avril 1795, avec des lettres et des notes sur la conspiration de Pichegru* (Baltimore: Johns Hopkins University Press, 1940).

Rolling, Hubert, and E. Berté-St-Ange. 'Le Réveil: Chanson patriotique' (New Orleans: F. Charpaux, 1877).

Roquefeuil, Camille de. *Journal d'un voyage autour du monde, pendant les années 1816, 1817, 1818 et 1819* (Paris: Ponthieu; Lesage; Gide, 1823), vol. 1.

Rosny, Joseph de, Claude-François-Xavier Mercier de Compiègne, and François-Félix Nogaret. *Le Tribunal d'Apollon, ou Jugement en dernier ressort de tous les auteurs vivans*, vol. 2 (Paris: Marchand, 1799).

Rousseau, Jean-Jacques. *Du Contrat social; ou Principes du droit politique*. Amsterdam: Chez Marc Michel Rey, 1762.

Sabin, Joseph. *A Dictionary of Books Relating to America, from its Discovery to the Present Time*, vol. 4 (New York: Sabin, 1871).

Saint-Georges, Henri de, and Hippolyte Monpou. *Le Planteur, opéra comique en deux actes, précédé d'un extrait du Voyage aux États-Unis ou Tableau de la Société Américaine de Harriet Martineau et de L'Inventaire du Planteur d'Émile Souvestre et suivi de nombreux documents inédits*, ed. and intro. Barbara T. Cooper, Collection autrement mêmes, ed. Roger Little (Paris: L'Harmattan, 2015).

Saint-Pierre, Jacques-Bernardin-Henri de. *Paul et Virginie* (Lausanne: Chez J. Mourer, 1788).

Sand, George. 'Les Sauvages de Paris', in *Les Maîtres Mosaïstes* (Paris: Hetzel, 1856), pp. 41–8.

Soubies, Albert. *Soixante-neuf ans à l'Opéra-Comique en deux pages de la première de* La Dame blanche *à la millième de* Mignon, *1825–1894* (Paris: Fischbacher, 1894).

Souvestre, Émile. *Rêves poétiques* (Nantes: Mellinet, 1830).

Bibliography 337

Spontini, Gaspare. *Fernand Cortez, ou La Conquête du Mexique, opéra en trois actes, représenté, pour la première fois, le 28 novembre 1809, et remis, avec des changements, sur le Théâtre de l'Académie Royale de Musique, le lundi 26 mai 1817* (Paris: Roulet, 1817).

Stewart, James M. 'Fair America: "Liberty Enlightening the World"' (New York: C. H. Ditson & Co., 1884).

Trollope, Frances. *Domestic Manners of the Americans*, 3rd edn (2 vols, London: Whitaker, Treacher, & Co., 1832), vol. 1.

Volpatti, F. *Black and White: Américan Cake Walk* (Paris: E. Gaudet, 1903).

Newspapers and Periodicals

American Art Journal
L'Argus des théâtres
L'Artiste
Le Charivari
Chicago Defender
Le Commerce
Le Constitutionnel
Le Corsaire
Le Courrier
Le Courrier français
Le Courrier des théâtres
Daily Picayune
L'Écho français
L'Entr'acte
L'Europe
L'Éventail: Écho des coulisses
Fémina
Le Figaro
Le Foyer
La France musicale
Le Gaulois
Gazette de France
Gazette nationale ou Le Moniteur universel
Gil Blas
Le Guide musical (Brussels)
Illinois Record
Indicateur dramatique ou Almanach des théâtres
Journal de Paris
Journal des artistes
Journal des débats
Le Ménestrel

338 *Bibliography*

Mercure de France
Les Modes
Le Monde artiste
Le Monde illustré
Le Monde musical
Musica and Album Musica
The Musical World (London)
Musical World and Times
La Musique
New York Herald
Niederrheinische Musik-Zeitung
Le Nouvelliste
L'Orchestre
Paris qui chante
Le Petit Journal
Le Petit Parisien
La Petite Presse
La Presse
Le Progrès artistique
Public Ledger (Philadelphia)
La Quotidienne
La Revue blanche
La Revue de Paris
La Revue et gazette musicale de Paris
La Revue musicale
Le Siècle
Spirit of the Times (New York)
La Sylphide
Le Temps
Le Théâtre illustré
La Vigilante

Secondary Sources

Abel, Lawrence E. *Singing the New Nation: How Music Shaped the Confederacy, 1861–1865* (Mechanicsburg: Stackpole Books, 2000).

Adcock, Michael. 'The 1889 Paris Exposition: Mapping the Colonial Mind', *Context*, 22 (Spring 2001), 31–40.

Adler, Kathleen, *et al. Americans in Paris: 1860–1900* (London: National Gallery, 2006).

Ahlquist, Karen. *Democracy at the Opera: Music, Theater, and Culture in New York City, 1815–60* (Urbana: University of Illinois Press, 1997).

Ahmed, Sara. 'Mixed Orientations', *Subjectivity*, 7 (2014), 92–109.

Bibliography 339

Aldrich, Robert. *Greater France: A History of the French Overseas Expansion* (Basingstoke: Macmillan Press, 1996).

Allanbrook, Wye J. *Rhythmic Gesture in Mozart:* Le nozze di Figaro *and* Don Giovanni (Chicago: Chicago University Press, 1983).

André, Naomi. *Black Opera: History, Power, Engagement* (Urbana, Illinois: University of Illinois Press, 2018).

—— Karen M. Bryan, and Eric Saylor (eds). *Blackness in Opera* (Urbana, Illinois: University of Illinois Press, 2012).

Authier, Catherine. *Femmes d'exception, femmes d'influence: Une Histoire des courtisanes au XIXe siècle* (Paris: Armand Colin, 2015).

Bara, Olivier. *Le Théâtre de l'Opéra-Comique sous la restauration: Enquête autour d'un genre moyen* (Hildesheim: Olms, 2001).

Baron, John. *Concert Life in Nineteenth-Century New Orleans: A Comprehensive Reference* (Baton Rouge: Louisiana State University Press, 2013).

Bartlet, M. Elizabeth C. 'The New Repertory at the Opéra during the Reign of Terror: Revolutionary Rhetoric and Operatic Consequences', in *Music and the French Revolution*, ed. Malcolm Boyd (Cambridge: Cambridge University Press, 1992), pp. 107–56.

Bean, Anne-Marie, James V. Hatch and Brooks McNamara (eds). *Inside the Minstrel Mask: Readings in Nineteenth-Century Blackface Minstrelsy* (Hanover: Wesleyan University Press, 1996).

Beckerman, Michael. 'The Real Value of Yellow Journalism: James Creelman and Antonín Dvořák', *The Musical Quarterly*, 77:4 (Winter 1993), 749–68.

Bellman, Jonathan. 'Expressive and Narrative Strategies in the Descriptive Piano Fantasia', *Journal of Musicological Research*, 34:3 (2015), 182–203.

Bentley, Charlotte. 'The Race for *Robert* and Other Rivalries: Negotiating the Local and (Inter)national in Nineteenth-Century New Orleans', *Cambridge Opera Journal*, 29:1 (2017), 94–112.

Berenson, Edward. *The Statue of Liberty: A Transatlantic Story* (New Haven: Yale University Press, 2012).

Berkhofer, Robert F. *The White Man's Indian* (New York: Vintage Books, 1978).

Berliner, Brett A. *Ambivalent Desire: The Exotic Black Other in Jazz-Age France* (Amherst: University of Massachusetts Press, 2002).

Berthier, Patrick. *Le Théâtre en France de 1791 à 1828, le sourd et la muette* (Paris: Honoré Champion, 2014).

Berzon, Judith. *Neither White Nor Black: The Mulatto in American Fiction* (New York: New York University Press, 1978).

Best, Sue. 'Sexualizing Space', in *Sexy Bodies: The Strange Carnalities of Feminism*, ed. Elizabeth Grosz and Elspeth Probyn (New York: Routledge, 1995), pp. 181–94.

Betzwieser, Thomas. *Exotismus und 'Türkenoper' in der französischen Musik des Ancien Régime: Studien zu einem ästhetischen Phänomen* (Laaber: Laaber, 1993).

Bibliography

Bishop, Morris. 'Chateaubriand in New York State', *PMLA*, 69:4 (1954), 876–86.

Blackburn, George McCoy. *French Newspaper Opinion on the American Civil War* (Westport, CT: Greenwood Press, 1997).

Blackstone, Sarah J. *Buckskins, Bullets, and Business: A History of Buffalo Bill's Wild West* (New York: Greenwood Press, 1986).

Blake, Jody. *Le Tumulte noir: Modernist Art and Popular Entertainment in Jazz-Age Paris, 1900–1930* (University Park, PA: Pennsylvania State University Press, 1999).

Blanchard, Pascal, Gilles Boetsch, and Nanette Jacomijn Snoep. *Human Zoos: The Invention of the Savage* (Paris: Musée de Quai Branly, 2011).

Blanchard, Pascal, Sandrine Lemaire, Nicolas Bancel, and Dominic Richard David Thomas (eds). *Colonial Culture in France since the Revolution* (Bloomington, IN: Indiana University Press, 2014).

Bloechl, Olivia. *Native American Song at the Frontiers of Early Modern Music* (Cambridge: Cambridge University Press, 2008).

Bohlman, Andrea F. *Musical Solidarities: Political Action and Music in Late Twentieth-Century Poland* (New York: Oxford University Press, 2020).

Boime, Albert. *Hollow Icons: The Politics of Sculpture in Nineteenth-Century France* (Kent, OH: The Kent State University Press, 1987).

Bomberger, E. Douglas. 'Chadwick's *Melpomene* and the Anxiety of Influence', *American Music*, 21:3 (Fall 2003), 319–48.

——. *'A Tidal Wave of Encouragement': American Composers' Concerts in the Gilded Age* (Westport: Praeger, 2002).

Bonin, Kathrine M. 'Signs of Origin: Victor Hugo's *Bug-Jargal*', *Nineteenth-Century French Studies*, 36:3–4 (Spring–Summer 2008), 193–204.

Bourdin, Philippe. *Aux Origines du théâtre patriotique* (Paris: CNRS, 2017).

Brasseaux, Carl. *Acadian to Cajun: Transformation of a People, 1803–1877* (Jackson: University Press of Mississippi, 1992).

——. *The Foreign French: Nineteenth-Century French Immigration into Louisiana*, vol. 1: *1820–1839* (Lafayette: Center for Louisiana Studies, University of Southwestern Louisiana, 1990).

——. *French, Cajun, Creole, Houma: A Primer on Francophone Louisiana* (Baton Rouge: Louisiana State University Press, 2005).

—— and Katherine Carmines Mooney. 'Introduction' to *Ruined by this Miserable War: The Dispatches of Charles Prosper Fauconnet, A French Diplomat in New Orleans, 1863–1868* (Knoxville: University of Tennessee Press, 2013), pp. x–xx.

Braun, Juliane. *Creole Drama: Theatre and Society in Nineteenth-Century New Orleans* (Charlottesville: University of Virginia Press, 2019).

Brody, David. *Visualizing American Empire: Orientalism and Imperialism in the Philippines* (Chicago: University of Chicago Press, 2010).

Brown, Jayna. *Babylon Girls: Black Women Performers and the Shaping of the Modern* (Durham, NC: Duke University Press, 2008).

Bibliography 341

Brown, Sterling A. 'Negro Character as Seen by White Authors', *The Journal of Negro Education*, 2:2 (1933), 179–203.

——. *The Negro in American Fiction* (Washington, DC: Associates in Negro Folk Education, 1937).

Broyles, Michael. *'Music of the Highest Class': Elitism and Populism in Antebellum Boston* (New Haven: Yale University Press, 1992).

Brunschwig, Chantal, Louis-Jean Calvet, and Jean-Claude Klein. *Cent Ans de chanson française* (Paris: Seuil, 1981).

Burns, Emily C. 'Taming a "Savage" Paris: The Masculine Visual Culture of Buffalo Bill's Wild West and France as a New American Frontier', in *Popular Frontier: Buffalo Bill's Wild West and Transnational Mass Culture*, ed. Frank Christianson (Norman: University of Oklahoma Press, 2017), pp. 129–54.

——. *Transnational Frontiers: The American West in France* (Norman: University of Oklahoma Press, 2018).

Burns, Michael. *Rural Society and French Politics, Boulangism and the Dreyfus Affair, 1886–1900* (Princeton: Princeton University Press, 1984).

Caddy, Davinia. 'Parisian Cakewalks', *19th-Century Music*, 30:3 (2007), 288–317.

Calvet, Jean-Claude. *Cent Ans de chanson française* (Paris: Archipel, 2008).

Carlson, Marvin. *The Theater of the French Revolution* (Ithaca: Cornell University Press, 1966).

Carter, Tim. 'The Sound of Silence: Models for an Urban Musicology', *Urban History*, 29 (2002), 8–18.

Cayamares, Ferran. *José Oller y su epoca: El hombre del Moulin Rouge* (Barcelona: Plaza & Janes, 1963).

Chafer, Tony, and Amanda Sackur (eds). *Promoting the Colonial Idea: Propaganda and Visions of Empire in France* (New York: Palgrave, 2002).

Chapman, John V. 'Jules Janin: Romantic Critic', in *Rethinking the Sylph: New Perspectives on the Romantic Ballet*, ed. Lynn Garafola (Hanover, NH: Wesleyan University Press, 1997), 197–241.

Charlton, David. 'Orchestra and Image in the Late Eighteenth Century', *Journal of the Royal Musical Association*, 102 (1975–6), 1–12.

Chew, William L. (ed.). *National Stereotypes in Perspective: Americans in France, Frenchmen in America* (Amsterdam: Rodopi, 2001).

Childress, Micah. *'Examine the Contents*: Clowning and Songsters in American Circuses, 1850–1900', *Popular Entertainment Studies*, 1:2 (2010), 26–43.

Childs, Adrienne L., and Susan H. Libby (eds). *Blacks and Blackness in European Art of the Long Nineteenth Century* (London: Routledge, 2017).

Clark, Emily. *Masterless Mistresses: The New Orleans Ursulines and the Development of a New World Society, 1727 to 1834* (Chapel Hill: University of North Carolina Press, 2007).

Bibliography

——. *The Strange History of the American Quadroon: Free Women of Color in the Revolutionary Atlantic World* (Chapel Hill: University of North Carolina Press, 2013).

Clavin, Patricia. 'Defining Transnationalism', *Contemporary European History*, 14:4 (2005), 421–39.

Colombo, Laura. 'Le Pas de la Déesse: Enquête sur les Transformations de la figure de Diane dans les livrets de ballet français', in *'La cruelle douceur d'Artémis': Il mito di Artemide-Diana nelle lettere francesi, Gargnano del Garda, 13–16 giugno 2001*, ed. Liana Nissim (Milan: Cisalpino, 2002), pp. 343–60.

Condé, Gérard. *Charles Gounod* (Paris: Fayard, 2009).

Conklin, Alice. *A Mission to Civilize: The Republican Idea of Empire in France and West Africa, 1895–1930* (Stanford: Stanford University Press, 1997).

Cooper, Barbara T. 'Introduction', in Henri de Saint-Georges and Hippolyte Monpou, *Le Planteur*, ed. and intro. Barbara T. Cooper, Collection autrement mêmes, ed. Roger Little (Paris: L'Harmattan, 2015), pp. vii–xxix.

——. 'Jules Barbier's *Cora, ou L'Esclavage*: A French Anti-Slavery Drama Set against the Backdrop of the American Civil War', *College Language Association Journal*, 45:3 (2002), 360–78.

——. 'Performing Race Relations in a French Children's Drama: Subjugation and Control of the Body in Vanderburch's Séliko, ou Le Petit Nègre', *CLA Journal*, 60:3 (March 2017), 363–76.

Cowan, Barry C. *Louisiana State University* (Charleston, SC: Arcadia Publishing, 2013).

Craiutu, Aurelian, and Jeffrey C. Isaac (eds). *America through European Eyes: British and French Reflections on the New World from the Eighteenth Century to the Present* (University Park: Pennsylvania State University Press, 2009).

Cross, Lauren, Lauren Seitz, and Shannon Walter. 'The First of its Kind: A Cultural History of the Village Nègre', *Digital Literature Review*, 3 (2016), 21–31.

Crunden, Robert. *Body & Soul: The Making of American Modernism* (New York: Basic Books, 2000).

Cruz, Gabriela. *Grand Illusion: Phantasmagoria in Nineteenth-Century Opera* (Oxford: Oxford University Press, 2020).

Curran, Andrew S. *The Anatomy of Blackness: Science and Slavery in an Age of Enlightenment* (Baltimore: Johns Hopkins University Press, 2011).

Darlow, Mark. *Staging the French Revolution: Cultural Politics and the Paris Opéra, 1789–1794* (New York: Oxford University Press, 2012).

Datta, Venita. 'Buffalo Bill Goes to France: French–American Encounters at the Wild West Show, 1889–1905', *French Historical Studies*, 41:3 (Aug. 2018), 528–35.

Daut, Marlene L. *Tropics of Haiti: Race and the Literary History of the Haitian Revolution in the Atlantic World, 1789–1865* (Liverpool: Liverpool University Press, 2015).

Davis, Tracy C., and Stefka Mihavlova (eds). *Uncle Tom's Cabins: The Transnational History of America's Most Mutable Book* (Ann Arbor: University of Michigan Press, 2018).

Deaville, James. 'Debussy's Cakewalk, Race, Modernism and Music in Early Twentieth-Century Paris', *Revue musicale OICRM*, 2:1 (2014), 20–39.

Decker, Todd. *Show Boat: Performing Race in an American Musical* (Oxford: Oxford University Press, 2013).

Desan, Suzanne. 'Transatlantic Spaces of Revolution: The French Revolution, *Sciotomanie*, and American Lands', *Journal of Early Modern History*, 12 (2008), 467–505.

Désile, Patric. '"Cet opéra de l'oeil": Les Pantomimes des cirques parisiens au XIXe siècle', in *Histoires de cirque aux XIXe et XXe siècles* (2011), pp. 2–14.

Desmarais, Norman. *America's First Ally: France in the Revolutionary War* (Philadelphia: Casemate, 2019).

Dickason, Olive Patricia. *The Myth of the Savage and the Beginnings of French Colonialism in the Americas* (Edmonton: University of Alberta Press, 1997).

Dobrow, Joe. *Pioneers of Promotion: How Press Agents for Buffalo Bill, P. T. Barnum, and the World's Columbian Exposition Created Modern Marketing* (Norman: University of Oklahoma Press, 2018).

Dormon, James H. 'Shaping the Popular Image of Post-Reconstruction American Blacks: The "Coon Song" Phenomenon of the Gilded Age', *American Quarterly*, 40:4 (Dec. 1988), 450–71.

Dubois, Laurent. *A Colony of Citizens: Revolution & Slave Emancipation in the French Caribbean, 1787–1804* (Chapel Hill: University of North Carolina Press, 2004).

——. 'The Haitian Revolution and the Sale of Louisiana; or, Thomas Jefferson's (Unpaid) Debt to Jean-Jacques Dessalines', in *Empires of the Imagination: Transatlantic Histories of the Louisiana Purchase*, ed. Peter J. Kastor and François Weil (Charlottesville: University of Virginia Press, 2009), pp. 93–116.

—— and John D. Garrigus (eds). *Slave Revolution in the Caribbean, 1789–1804: A Brief History with Documents* (Boston: Bedford/St. Martin's, 2016).

Duroselle, Jean-Baptiste. *France and the United States: From the Beginnings to the Present*, trans. Derek Coltman (Chicago: University of Chicago Press, 1978).

Eble, Connie. 'Creole in Louisiana', *South Atlantic Review*, 73:2 (Spring 2008), 39–53.

Ellingson, Ter. *The Myth of the Noble Savage* (Berkeley: University of California Press, 2001).

Ellis, Katharine. 'Olivier Halanzier and the Operatic Museum in Late Nineteenth-Century France', *Music and Letters*, 96:3 (2015), 390–417.

Étienne, Servais, *Les Sources de 'Bug-Jargal'* (Brussels: L'Académie Royale de Langue et de Littérature Françaises, 1923).

Fairchild, Sharon L. 'George Sand and George Catlin – Masking Indian Realities', *Nineteenth-Century French Studies*, 22:3–4 (Spring–Summer 1994), 439–49.

Fauser, Annegret. '"Hymns of the Future": Reading Félicien David's *Christophe Colomb* (1847) as a Saint-Simonian Symphony', *Journal of Musicological Research*, 28 (2009), 1–29.

——. *Musical Encounters at the 1889 Paris World's Fair* (Rochester: University of Rochester Press, 2005).

——. '*Le Sacre du printemps*: A Ballet for Paris', in *The Rite at 100*, ed. Severine Neff, Maureen Carr, and Gretchen Horlacher (Bloomington: Indiana University Press, 2017), pp. 83–97.

Favret, Mary A. *War at a Distance: Romanticism and the Making of Modern Wartime* (Princeton: Princeton University Press, 2009).

Ferrer, Ada. 'Talk about Haiti: The Archive and the Atlantic's Haitian Revolution', in *Tree of Liberty: Cultural Legacies of the Haitian Revolution*, ed. Doris L. Garraway (Charlottesville: University of Virginia Press, 2008), pp. 21–40.

Fertel, Rien. *Imagining the Creole City: The Rise of Literary Culture in Nineteenth-Century New Orleans* (Baton Rouge: Louisiana State University Press, 2014).

Fritzsche, Peter. 'Chateaubriand's Ruins: Loss and Memory after the French Revolution', *History and Memory*, 10 (1998), 102–17.

——. 'Specters of History: On Nostalgia, Exile, and Modernity', *The American Historical Review*, 106:5 (2001), 1587–1618.

Fry, Andy. *Paris Blues: African American Music and French Popular Culture, 1920–1960* (Chicago: University of Chicago Press, 2014).

Gaffield, Julia (ed.). *The Haitian Declaration of Independence: Creation, Context, and Legacy* (Charlottesville: University of Virginia Press, 2016).

Gaitet, Pascale. 'Hybrid Creatures, Hybrid Politics, in Hugo's "Bug-Jargal" and "Le Dernier Jour d'un condamné"', *Nineteenth-Century French Studies*, 25:3–4 (Spring–Summer 1997), 251–65.

Gautier, Ana María Ochoa. *Aurality: Listening and Knowledge in Nineteenth-Century Colombia* (Durham, NC: Duke University Press, 2014).

Gelpi, Paul D., Jr. 'Mr. Jefferson's Creoles: The Battalion d'Orléans and the Americanization of Creole Louisiana, 1803–1815', *Louisiana History: The Journal of the Louisiana Historical Association*, 48:3 (2007), 295–316.

Ghachem, Malick W. *The Old Regime and the Haitian Revolution* (Cambridge: Cambridge University Press, 2012).

Gibbons, William. '"Yankee Doodle" and Nationalism, 1780–1920', *American Music*, 26:2 (2008), 246–74.

Girard, Philippe R. 'The Haitian Revolution, History's New Frontier: State of the Scholarship and Archival Sources', *Slavery & Abolition* 34:3 (Sept. 2013), 485–507.

Bibliography   345

——. *The Slaves Who Defeated Napoléon: Toussaint Louverture and the Haitian War of Independence, 1801–1804* (Tuscaloosa: University of Alabama Press, 2011).

Giroud, Vincent. 'Manon at the Opera: From Prévost's *Manon Lescaut* to Auber's *Manon Lescaut* and Massenet's *Manon*', in *'Music's Obedient Daughter': The Opera Libretto from Source to Score*, ed. Sabine Lichtenstein (New York: Rodopi, 2014), pp. 239–68.

Gitelman, Lisa. *Paper Knowledge: Toward a Media History of Documents* (Durham, NC: Duke University Press, 2014).

Gitlin, Jay. *The Bourgeois Frontier: French Towns, French Traders, and American Expansion* (New Haven: Yale University Press, 2010).

Glazer, Lee, and Susan Key. 'Carry Me Back: Nostalgia for the Old South in Nineteenth-Century Popular Culture', *Journal of American Studies*, 30:1 (1996), 1–24.

Gordon, Rae Beth. *Dances with Darwin and Vernacular Modernity 1875–1910* (Aldershot: Ashgate, 2007).

Goudie, Sean X. *Creole America: The West Indies and the Formation of Literature and Culture in the New Republic* (Philadelphia: University of Pennsylvania Press, 2006).

Grant, Gail. *Technical Manual and Dictionary of Classical Ballet*, 3rd rev. ed. (New York: Dover, 1982).

Graziano, John. 'Invisible Instruments: Theater Orchestras in New York, 1850–1900', in *American Orchestras in the Nineteenth Century*, ed. John Spitzer (Chicago: University of Chicago Press, 2012), pp. 109–29.

Green, Nancy. *The Other Americans in Paris: Businessmen, Countesses, Wayward Youth, 1880–1941* (Chicago: University of Chicago Press, 2014).

Grondeux, Jérôme. *La France contemporaine: La France entre en République, 1870–1893* (Paris: Librairie générale française, 2000).

Guardino, Peter. *The Dead March: A History of the Mexican-American War* (Cambridge, MA: Harvard University Press, 2017).

Guest, Ivor. *Jules Perrot: Master of the Romantic Ballet* (London: Dance Books, 1984).

——. *The Romantic Ballet in Paris* (Alton, Hampshire: Dance Books, 2008).

Gutsche-Miller, Sarah. 'Liberated Women and Travesty Fetishes: Conflicting Representations of Gender in Parisian Fin-de-Siècle Music-Hall Ballet', *Dance Research*, 35:2 (2017), 187–208.

——. *Parisian Music-Hall Ballet, 1871–1913*, Eastman Studies in Music (Rochester: University of Rochester Press, 2015).

Guyver, Christopher. *The Second French Republic 1848–1852: A Political Reinterpretation* (London: Palgrave Macmillan, 2016).

Hadlock, Heather. 'The Career of Cherubino, or the Trouser Role Grows Up', in *Siren Songs: Representations of Gender and Sexuality in Opera*, ed. Mary Ann Smart (Princeton: Princeton University Press, 2000), pp. 67–92.

346 *Bibliography*

Hallman, Diana R., *Opera, Liberalism, and Antisemitism in Nineteenth-Century France: The Politics of Halévy's* La Juive (New York and Cambridge: Cambridge University Press, 2002).

Halpern, Jean-Claude. 'L'Esclavage sur la scène révolutionnaire', *Annales historiques de la Révolution française*, 293–4 (1993), 409–20.

Harsanti, Doina Pasca. *Lessons from America: Liberal French Nobles in Exile, 1793–1798* (University Park, Pennsylvania: Pennsylvania State University Press, 2010).

Hartman, Saidiya V. *Scenes of Subjection: Terror, Slavery, and Self-Making in Nineteenth-Century America* (Oxford: Oxford University Press, 1997).

Heat-Moon, William Least, and James K. Wallace (eds). *An Osage Journey to Europe, 1827–1830: Three French Accounts* (Norman: University of Oklahoma Press, 2013).

Herring, Joseph B. 'Selling the "Noble Savage" Myth: George Catlin and the Iowa Indians in Europe, 1843–1845', *Kansas History*, 29 (2006–7), 226–45.

D'Heylli, Georges. *Dictionnaire des pseudonyms*, new edn (Paris: Dentu, 1887).

Hibberd, Sarah, and Richard Wrigley (eds). *Art, Theatre and Opera in Paris, 1750–1850: Exchanges and Tensions* (Abingdon: Routledge, 2016).

Hirsch, Arnold R. *Creole New Orleans: Race and Americanization* (Baton Rouge: Louisiana State University Press, 1992).

Hoffmann, Léon-François. *Le Nègre romantique: Personnage littéraire et obsession collective* (Paris: Payot, 1973).

——. 'Victor Hugo, les Noirs et l'esclavage', *Francofonia*, 31 (Autumn 1996), 47–60.

Huebner, Stephen. 'Opera and Ballet after the Revolution', in *The Cambridge Companion to French Music*, ed. Simon Trezise (Cambridge: Cambridge University Press, 2015), pp. 221–41.

Immerwahr, Daniel. *How to Hide an Empire: A History of the Greater United States* (New York: Farrar, Straus and Giroux, 2019).

Ingersoll, Thomas N. *Mammon and Manon in Early New Orleans: The First Slave Society in the Deep South, 1718–1819* (Knoxville: University of Tennessee Press, 1999).

Irvine, William D. *The Boulanger Affair Reconsidered: Royalism, Boulangism, and the Origins of the Radical Right in France* (Oxford: Oxford University Press, 1989).

Isnardon, Jacques. *Le Théâtre de la Monnaie depuis sa fondation jusqu'à nos jours* (Brussels: Schott, 1890).

Jacobshagen, Arnold. 'Analyzing Mise-en-Scène: Halévy's *La Juive* at the Salle Le Peletier', in *Theater, Music, and Cultural Transfer: Paris, 1830–1914*, ed. Annegret Fauser and Mark Everist (Chicago: University of Chicago Press, 2009), pp. 176–94.

——. 'Staging at the Opéra-Comique in Nineteenth-Century Paris: Auber's *Fra Diavolo* and the Livrets de Mise en Scène', *Cambridge Opera Journal*, 13:3 (2001), 239–60.

Jennings, Jeremy. 'French Visions of America: From Tocqueville to the Civil War', in *America through European Eyes: British and French Reflections on the New World from the Eighteenth Century to the Present*, ed. Aurelian Craiutu and Jeffrey C. Isaac (University Park: Pennsylvania State University Press, 2009), pp. 161–86.

Jennings, Lawrence C. *French Anti-Slavery: The Movement for the Abolition of Slavery in France, 1802–1848* (Cambridge: Cambridge University Press, 2000).

——. 'French Views on Slavery and Abolitionism in the United States, 1830–1848', *Slavery & Abolition*, 4:1 (1983), 19–40.

Jeschke, Claudia, and Robert Atwood. 'Expanding Horizons: Techniques of Choreo-Graphy in Nineteenth-Century Dance', *Dance Chronicle*, 29:2 (2006), 195–214.

Jeune. Simon. *De F. T. Graindorge à A. O. Barnabooth: Les Types américains dans le roman et le théâtre français (1861–1917)* (Paris: Librairie Marcel Didier, 1963).

Johannsen, Robert Walter. *To the Halls of the Montezumas: The Mexican War in the American Imagination* (Oxford: Oxford University Press, 1985).

Johnson, Walter. *Soul by Soul: Life inside the Antebellum Slave Market* (Cambridge, MA: Harvard University Press, 1999).

Jolivette, Andrew. *Louisiana Creoles: Cultural Recovery and Mixed-Race Native American Identity* (New York: Lexington Books, 2007).

Jonnes, Jill. *Eiffel's Tower: And the World's Fair where Buffalo Bill Beguiled Paris, the Artists Quarreled, and Thomas Edison Became a Count* (New York: Viking Press, 2009).

Jordan, Matthew F. *Le Jazz: Jazz and French Cultural Identity* (Urbana: University of Illinois Press, 2010).

Jordan, Ruth. *Fromental Halévy: His Life and Music, 1799–1862* (New York: Limelight, 1996).

Jullien, Dominique. 'Bug-Jargal: la Révolution et ses doubles', *Littérature*, 139 (Sept. 2005), 78–92.

Jürgensen, Knud Arne. *The Verdi Ballets* (Parma: Istituto Nazionale di Studi Verdiani, 1995).

Kein, Sybil (ed.). *Creole: The History and Legacy of Louisiana's Free People of Color* (Baton Rouge: Louisiana State University Press, 2000).

Kelly, Deirdre. *Ballerina: Sex, Scandal, and Suffering Behind the Symbol of Perfection* (Vancouver: Greystone Books, 2012).

Khan, Yasmin Sabina. *Enlightening the World: The Creation of the Statue of Liberty* (Ithaca: Cornell University Press, 2010).

Kinzer, Charles E. 'The Band of Music of the First Battalion of Free Men of Color and the Siege of New Orleans, 1814–1815', *American Music*, 10:3 (1992), 348–69.

Kittler, Friedrich A. *Aufschreibesysteme 1800 / 1900* (Munich: Fink, 1985); in English as *Discourse Networks 1800 / 1900*, trans. Michael Metteer with Chris Cullens (Stanford: Stanford University Press, 1990).

348   Bibliography

Klaits, Joseph and Michael Haltzel. *Liberty/liberté: The American and French Experiences* (Baltimore: Johns Hopkins University Press, 1991).

Klein, Jean-Claude. *La Chanson à l'affiche: Histoire de la chanson française du café-concert à nos jours* (Paris: Du May, 1991).

Kmen, Henry. *Music in New Orleans: The Formative Years, 1791–1841* (Baton Rouge: Louisiana State University Press, 1966).

Korn, Bertram W. *A Note on the Jewish Ancestry of Louis Moreau Gottschalk, American Pianist and Composer* (Philadelphia: Maurice Jacobs, Inc., 1963); repr. from *American Jewish Archives*, 15:2 (Nov. 1963), 117–19.

Körner, Axel. *America in Italy: The United States in the Political Thought and Imagination of the Risorgimento, 1763–1865* (Princeton: Princeton University Press, 2017).

Labbé, Dolores Egger (ed.), *The Louisiana Purchase and its Aftermath, 1800–1830* (Lafayette: Center for Louisiana Studies, University of Southwestern Louisiana, 1998).

Lacombe, Hervé. *The Keys to French Opera in the Nineteenth Century*, trans. Edward Schneider (Berkeley: University of California Press, 2001).

——. 'The Writing of Exoticism in the Libretti of Opéra-Comique, 1825–1862', trans. Peter Glidden, *Cambridge Opera Journal*, 11:2 (1999), 135–58.

Larson, Steve. *Musical Forces: Motion, Metaphor, and Meaning in Music* (Bloomington: Indiana University Press, 2012).

Leavelle, Tracy N. 'The Osage in Europe: Romanticism, the Vanishing Indian, and French Civilization during the Restoration', in *National Stereotypes in Perspective: Americans in France, Frenchmen in America*, ed. William L. Chew, III. Studia Imagologica: Amsterdam Studies on Cultural Identity 9 (Amsterdam: Rodopi, 2001), pp. 89–112.

Leclercq, Pierre-Robert. *Soixante-dix ans de café-concert, 1848–1918* (Paris: Les Belles Lettres, 2014).

Lehning, James R. *To be a Citizen: The Political Culture of the Early French Third Republic* (Ithaca: Cornell University Press, 2001).

Leith, James A. 'Le Culte de Franklin en France avant et pendant la Revolution Française', *Annales historiques de la Révolution française*, 48:226 (1976), 543–71.

Levine, Lawrence W. *Highbrow/Lowbrow: The Emergence of Cultural Hierarchy in America* (Cambridge, MA: Harvard University Press, 1988).

Levitz, Tamara. 'Racism at *The Rite*', in The Rite of Spring *at 100*, ed. Severine Neff, Maureen Carr, and Gretchen Horlacher, with John Reef (Bloomington: Indiana University Press, 2017), pp. 146–78.

Liebersohn, Harry. *Aristocratic Encounters: European Travelers and North American Indians* (New York: Cambridge University Press, 2001).

Locke, Ralph P. 'Exotisme et colonialisme', trans. Dennis Collins, in *Histoire de l'opéra français: Du Consulat aux débuts de la IIIe République*, ed. Hervé Lacombe (Paris: Fayard, 2020), pp. 963–8.

——. 'Les Formes de l'exotisme: Intrigues, personnages, styles musicaux', trans. Dennis Collins, in *Histoire de l'opéra français: Du Consulat aux débuts de la IIIe République*, ed. Hervé Lacombe (Paris: Fayard, 2020), pp. 955–63.

——. *Musical Exoticism: Images and Reflections* (Cambridge: Cambridge University Press, 2009).

——. *Music and the Exotic from the Renaissance to Mozart* (Cambridge: Cambridge University Press, 2015).

——. 'The Exotic in Nineteenth-Century French Opera, Part 1: Locales and Peoples', *19th-Century Music*, 54:2 (Fall 2021), 93–118.

——. 'The Exotic in Nineteenth-Century French Opera, Part 2: Plots, Characters, and Musical Devices', *19th-Century Music* (forthcoming).

——. 'Restoring Lost Meanings in Musical Representations of Exotic "Others"', unpublished paper presented at the annual meeting of the American Musicological Society, Philadelphia, Nov. 2009.

——. 'Les Territoires de l'exotisme', trans. Dennis Collins, in *Histoire de l'opéra français: Du Consulat aux débuts de la IIIe République*, ed. Hervé Lacombe (Paris: Fayard, 2020), pp. 949–55.

Maier, Charles S. *Among Empires: America's Ascendancy and its Predecessors* (Cambridge, MA: Harvard University Press, 2007).

Malthête, Jacques and Laurent Mannoni. *Méliès: Magie et cinéma: Espace EDF electra, 26 Avril–1er Septembre 2002* (Paris: Paris Musées, 2002).

Manganelli, Kimberly Snyder. *Transatlantic Spectacles of Race: The Tragic Mulatta and the Tragic Muse* (Brunswick, NJ: Rutgers University Press, 2012).

Maslan, Susan. *Revolutionary Acts: Theater, Democracy and the French Revolution* (Baltimore: John Hopkins University Press, 2005).

McCarren, Felicia. *Dance Pathologies: Performance, Poetics, Medicine* (Stanford: Stanford University Press, 1998).

McCloskey, Barbara. 'From the *Frontier* to the Wild West: German Artists, American Indians, and the Spectacle of Race and Nation in the Nineteenth and Early Twentieth Centuries', in *I Like America: Fictions of the Wild West*, ed. Pamela Kort and Max Hollein (New York: Prestel, 2006), pp. 298–321.

McCullough, David. *The Greater Journey: Americans in Paris* (New York: Simon & Schuster, 2011).

McKee, Sally. *The Exile's Song: Edmond Dédé and the Unfinished Revolutions of the Atlantic World* (New Haven: Yale University Press, 2017).

McMillen, Margot Ford, and Heather Robeson. *Into the Spotlight: Four Missouri Women* (Columbia: University of Missouri Press, 2004).

McNenly, Linda. *Native Performers in Wild West Shows: From Buffalo Bill to Euro Disney* (Norman: University of Oklahoma Press, 2012).

McWhirter, Christian. *Battle Hymns: The Power and Popularity of Music in the Civil War* (Chapel Hill: University of North Carolina Press, 2012).

Meglin, Joellen A. '*Sauvages*, Sex Roles, and Semiotics: Representations of Native Americans in the French Ballet, 1736–1837, Part One: The Eighteenth Century', *Dance Chronicle*, 23:2 (2000), 87–132.

350   *Bibliography*

———. '*Sauvages*, Sex Roles, and Semiotics: Representations of Native Americans in the French Ballet, 1736–1837, Part Two: The Nineteenth Century', *Dance Chronicle*, 23:3 (2000), 275–320.

Miller, Christopher L. *Blank Darkness: Africanist Discourse in French* (Chicago: University of Chicago Press, 1985).

Mitchell, Elizabeth. *Liberty's Torch: The Great Adventure to Build the Statue of Liberty* (New York: Atlantic Monthly Press, 2014).

Mitchell, Robin. *Vénus Noire: Black Women and Colonial Fantasies in Nineteenth-Century France* (Athens, GA: University of Georgia Press, 2020).

Montagnier, Jean-Paul. 'Julien Tiersot: Ethnomusicologue à l'Exposition Universelle de 1889. Contribution à une histoire française de la ethnomusicologie', *International Review of the Aesthetics and Sociology of Music*, 21:1 (1990), 91–100.

Moore, Fabienne. *Prose Poems of the French Enlightenment: Delimiting Genre* (Burlington, VT: Ashgate, 2009).

Moos, Dan. *Outside America: Race, Ethnicity, and the Role of the American West in National Belonging* (Hanover: Dartmouth College Press, 2005).

Moreau, François. 'Des Guerres d'Amérique à la Révolution française: Le Théâtre de Billardon de Sauvigny', *Revue de la Société d'histoire du théâtre*, 41:3 (June 1989), 271–84.

Moreau, Georges, ed. *Revue universelle: Recueil documentaire universel et illustré* (Paris: Librairie Larousse, 1903).

Morgan, Elizabeth. 'Combat at the Keys: Women and Battle Pieces for the Piano during the American Civil War', *19th-Century Music*, 40:1 (2016), 7–19.

———. 'War on the Home Front: Battle Pieces for the Piano from the American Civil War', *Journal of the Society for American Music*, 9:4 (2015), 381–408.

Morrison, Matthew D. 'Race, Blacksound, and the (Re)Making of Musicological Discourse', *Journal of the American Musicological Society*, 72:3 (Fall 2019), 781–823.

Mulvey, Laura. 'Visual Pleasure and Narrative Cinema', *Screen*, 16:3 (1975), 6–18.

Ndaliko, Chérie Rivers. 'The Accidental Archivist: Memory, Resonance, and Decay in Kivu', in *Performing Commemoration: Musical Reenactment and the Politics of Trauma*, ed. Annegret Fauser and Michael A. Figueroa (Ann Arbor: University of Michigan Press, 2020), pp. 240–62.

Ndiaye, Pap, and Louise Madinier. *Le Modèle noir de Géricault à Matisse: La Chronologie* (Paris, Musée d'Orsay: Flammarion, 2019).

Newman, Nancy. *Good Music for a Free People: The Germania Musical Society in Nineteenth-Century America* (Rochester: University of Rochester Press, 2010).

Nicholls, David (ed.). *The Cambridge History of American Music* (Cambridge: Cambridge University Press, 1998).

Nystrom, Justin A. *New Orleans after the Civil War: Race, Politics, and a New Birth of Freedom* (Baltimore: Johns Hopkins University Press, 2010).

Bibliography 351

Oja, Carol J. *Making Music Modern: New York in the 1920s* (Oxford: Oxford University Press, 2000).

Osterhammel, Jürgen. *The Transformation of the World: A Global History of the Nineteenth Century* (Princeton: Princeton University Press, 2014).

Painter, George D. *Chateaubriand: A Biography*, vol. 1 (London: Chatto & Windus, 1977).

Parakilas, James. 'The Soldier and the Exotic: Operatic Variations on a Theme of Racial Encounter, Part I', *The Opera Quarterly*, 10:2 (1993), 33–56.

Pasler, Jann. *Composing the Citizen: Music as Public Utility in Third Republic France* (Berkeley: University of California Press, 2009).

——. 'Listening to Race and Nation: Music at the Exposition Universelle de 1889', *Musique, images, instruments: Revue française d'organologie et d'iconographie musicale*, 13 (2012), 52–74.

Pells, Richard H. *Modernist America: Art, Music, Movies and the Globalization of American Culture* (New Haven: Yale University Press, 2011).

Pendle, Karin. 'The Boulevard Theaters and Continuity in French Opera of the 19th Century', in *Music in Paris in the Eighteen-Thirties*, ed. Peter Bloom (Stuyvesant, NY: Pendragon, 1987), pp. 509–35.

——. *Eugène Scribe and French Opera of the Nineteenth Century* (Ann Arbor: UMI Research Press, 1979).

Philips, Edith. *The Good Quaker in French Legend* (Philadelphia: University of Pennsylvania Press, 1932).

Pinson, Stephen. *Speculating Daguerre: Art and Enterprise in the Work of L. J. M. Daguerre* (Chicago: University of Chicago Press, 2012).

Pisani, Michael V. *Imagining Native America in Music* (New Haven: Yale University Press, 2005).

——. '"I'm an Indian Too": Creating Native American Identities in Nineteenth- and Twentieth-Century Music', in *The Exotic in Western Music*, ed. Jonathan Bellman (Boston: Northeastern University Press, 1998), pp. 218–57.

Polzonetti, Pierpaolo. *Italian Opera in the Age of the American Revolution* (Cambridge: Cambridge University Press, 2011).

Popkin, Jeremy D. *Facing Racial Revolution: Eyewitness Accounts of the Haitian Insurrection* (Chicago: University of Chicago Press, 2007).

——. *You Are All Free: The Haitian Revolution and the Abolition of Slavery* (Cambridge: Cambridge University Press, 2010).

Porter, Laurence M. 'Consciousness of the Exotic and Exotic Consciousness in Chateaubriand', *Nineteenth-Century French Studies*, 38:3–4 (Spring–Summer 2010), 159–71.

Portes, Jacques. *Fascination and Misgivings: The United States in French Opinion, 1870–1914*, trans. Elborg Forster (Cambridge: Cambridge University Press, 2009).

Pottinger, Mark A. *Staging of History in France: Characterizations of Historical Figures in French Grand Opéra during the Reign of Louis Philippe* (Saarbrücken, Germany: VDM Verlag, 2009).

Bibliography

Powers, David M. *From Plantation to Paradise: Cultural Politics and Musical Theatre in French Slave Colonies, 1764–1789* (East Lansing, MI: Michigan State University Press, 2014).

Prasad, Pratima. *Colonialism, Race, and the French Romantic Imagination* (New York: Routledge, 2009).

Pratt, Mary Louise. *Imperial Eyes: Travel Writing and Transculturation* (London: Routledge, 1992).

Prest, Julia T. 'The Familiar Other: Blackface Performance in Creole Works from 1780s Saint-Domingue', in *Colonialism and Slavery in Performance: Theatre and the Eighteenth-Century French Caribbean*, ed. J. Leichman and K. Bénac-Girous (Liverpool: Liverpool University Press, 2021), pp. 41–63.

——. 'Pale Imitations: White Performances of Slave Dance in the Public Theatres of Pre-Revolutionary Saint-Domingue', *Atlantic Studies*, 16:4 (2019), 502–20 <https://doi.org/10.1080/14788810.2018.1469352>.

Preston, Katherine K. '"A Concentration of Talent on Our Musical Horizon": The 1853–54 Tour by Jullien's Extraordinary Orchestra', in *American Orchestras in the Nineteenth Century*, ed. John Spitzer (Chicago: University of Chicago Press, 2012), pp. 319–47.

Pritchard, Jane. 'Divertissement Only: The Establishment, Development and Decline of the Music Hall Ballet in London' (unpublished manuscript, 2005).

Raimon, Eve Allegra. *The 'Tragic Mulatta' Revisited: Race and Nationalism in Nineteenth-Century Antislavery Fiction* (New Brunswick, NJ: Rutgers University Press, 2004).

Remini, Robert V. *The Battle of New Orleans: Andrew Jackson and America's First Military Victory* (London: Pimlico, 1991).

Rehding, Alexander. *Music and Monumentality: Commemoration and Wonderment in Nineteenth-Century Germany* (New York: Oxford University Press, 2009).

Rémond, René. *Les États-Unis devant l'opinion française (1852–1952)* (2 vols, Paris: Armand Colin, 1962).

Revel, Jean-François. *Anti-Americanism*, trans. Diarmid Cammell (San Francisco: Encounter Books, 2003).

Rodriguez, Junius P. *The Louisiana Purchase: A Historical and Geographical Encyclopedia* (Santa Barbara: ABC-CLIO, 2002).

Roger, Philippe. *The American Enemy: The History of French Anti-Americanism*, trans. Sharon Bowman (Chicago: University of Chicago Press, 2005).

Roos, Jane M. 'Courbet, Catlin, and the Exploitation of Native Americans', in 'Call and Answer: Dialoguing the American West', *Transatlantica* (2017), no. 2 <https://doi.org/10.4000/transatlantica.11062>.

Rose, Gillian. *Feminism and Geography: The Limits of Geographical Knowledge* (Minneapolis: University of Minnesota Press, 1993).

Rosenberg, Ruth E. 'Among Compatriots and Savages: The Music of France's Lost Empire', *The Musical Quarterly*, 95:1 (Spring 2012), 36–70.

Bibliography 353

——. *Music, Travel, and Imperial Encounter in 19th-Century France: Musical Apprehensions* (New York and London: Routledge, 2014).

Rowden, Clair. 'Choral Music and Music-Making in France', in *Nineteenth-Century Choral Music*, ed. Donna M. Di Grazia (New York: Routledge, 2013), pp. 205–12.

Rydell, Robert W. 'Buffalo Bill's *Wild West*: The Racialisation of the Cosmopolitan Imagination', in *Colonial Advertising & Commodity Racism*, ed. Wulf Hund, Michael Pickering, and Anandi Ramamurthy, (Zürich: Lit, 2013), pp. 97–118.

Sahakian, Emily. 'Eliza's French Fathers: Race, Gender, and Transatlantic Paternalism in French Stage Adaptations of *Uncle Tom's Cabin*, 1853', in *Uncle Tom's Cabins: The Transnational History of America's Most Mutable Book*, ed. Tracy C. Davis and Stefka Mihavlova (Ann Arbor: University of Michigan Press, 2018), pp. 81–115.

Said, Edward. *Orientalism* (New York: Vintage, 1979).

Sainlaude, Stève. *France and the American Civil War: A Diplomatic History* (Chapel Hill: University of North Carolina Press, 2019).

Savage, Roger. 'Rameau's American Dancers', *Early Music*, 11:4 (1983), 441–52.

Schreier, Lisa. 'Reading Race in Nineteenth-Century French Vaudeville', in *French Cultural Studies for the Twenty-First Century*, ed. Masha Belenky, Kathryn Kleppinger, and Anne O'Neil-Henry (Lanham: University of Delaware Press, 2017), pp. 41–71.

Schwartz, Vanessa. *Spectacular Realities: Early Mass Culture in Fin-de-Siècle Paris* (Berkeley: University of California Press, 1998).

Scott, John Anthony. *The Ballad of America* (New York: Grosset & Dunlap, 1967).

Sell, Henry Blackman, and Victor Weybright. *Buffalo Bill and the Wild West* (New York: Oxford University Press, 1955).

Senelick, Laurence. *Jacques Offenbach and the Making of Modern Culture* (Cambridge: Cambridge University Press, 2017).

Shadle, Douglas W. *Antonín Dvořák's New World Symphony* (New York: Oxford University Press, 2021).

——. 'How Santa Claus Became a Slave Driver: The Work of Print Culture in a Nineteenth-Century Controversy', *Journal of the Society for American Music*, 8:4 (2014), 501–37.

——. *Orchestrating the Nation: The Nineteenth-Century American Symphonic Enterprise* (New York: Oxford University Press, 2016).

Sharpley-Whiting, T. Denean. *Black Venus: Sexualized Savages, Primal Fears, and Primitive Narratives in French* (Durham, NC: Duke University Press, 1999).

Shulman, Peter A. *Coal and Empire: The Birth of Energy Security in Industrial America* (Baltimore: John Hopkins University Press, 2015).

Slotkin, Richard. 'Buffalo Bill's *Wild West* and the Mythologization of the American Empire', in *Cultures of United States Imperialism*, ed. Amy

354 *Bibliography*

Kaplan and Donald E. Pease (Durham, NC: Duke University Press, 1993), pp. 164–84.

——. *Gunfighter Nation: The Myth of the Frontier in Twentieth-Century America* (Norman: University of Oklahoma Press, 1998).

Smalls, James. "'Race" as Spectacle in Late-Nineteenth-Century French Art and Popular Culture,' *French Historical Studies*, 26:2 (Spring 2003), 351–82.

Smart, Mary Ann. *Mimomania* (Berkeley: University of California Press, 2004).

——. 'Roles, Reputations, Shadows: Singers at the Opéra, 1828–1849,' in *The Cambridge Companion to Grand Opera*, ed. David Charlton (Cambridge: Cambridge University Press, 2003), pp. 108–30.

Smethurst, Colin. *Chateaubriand: Atala and René* (London: Grant and Cutler, 1995).

Smith, Christopher J. *The Creolization of American Culture: William Sidney Mount and the Roots of Blackface Minstrelsy* (Urbana: University of Illinois Press, 2013).

Smith, Marian. *Ballet and Opera in the Age of* Giselle (Princeton: Princeton University Press, 2000).

——. 'The Disappearing Danseur', *Cambridge Opera Journal*, 19:1 (2007), 33–57.

—— and Doug Fullington. *Five Ballets from Paris and St Petersburg:* Giselle, Paquita, Le Corsaire, La Bayadère, *and* Raymonda (Oxford: Oxford University Press, forthcoming).

Sollors, Werner. *Neither Black Nor White Yet Both: Thematic Explorations of Interracial Literature* (Oxford: Oxford University Press, 1997).

Sowell, Debra Hickenlooper. 'Romantic Landscapes for Dance: Ballet Narratives and Edmund Burke's Theory of the Sublime,' *Dance Chronicle*, 34:2 (2011), 183–216.

Spencer, Helena Kopchick. 'Eugène Scribe and the *Jardin des Femmes* Convention,' in *Meyerbeer and Grand Opéra from the July Monarchy to the Present*, ed. Mark Everist, Speculum Musicae 28 (Turnhout: Brepols, 2016), pp. 287–312.

Spitzer, John (ed.). *American Orchestras in the Nineteenth Century* (Chicago: University of Chicago Press, 2012).

Spohr, Arne. "'Mohr und Trompeter": Blackness and Social Status in Early Modern Germany,' in 'Music, Race, and Ethnicity,' special issue of *Journal of the American Musicological Society*, 72:3 (Fall 2019), 613–64.

Starr, S. Frederick. *Bamboula! The Life and Times of Louis Moreau Gottschalk* (New York: Oxford University Press, 1995).

Stillman, Deanne. *Blood Brothers: The Story of the Strange Friendship between Sitting Bull and Buffalo Bill* (New York: Simon & Schuster, 2017).

Stoever, Jennifer Lynn. *The Sonic Color Line: Race and the Cultural Politics of Listening* (New York: New York University Press, 2016).

Bibliography   355

Strasser, Michael. 'The Société Nationale and its Adversaries: The Musical Politics of *l'invasion germanique* in the 1870s', *19th-Century Music*, 24 (2001), 225–51.

Street, Susan Castillo. 'Writing Race and Slavery in the Francophone Atlantic: Transatlantic Connections and Contradictions in Claire de Duras's *Ourika* and Victor Hugo's *Bug-Jargal*', in *The Edinburgh Companion to Atlantic Literary Studies*, ed. Leslie Elizabeth Eckel and Clare Frances Elliott (Edinburgh: Edinburgh University Press, 2016), pp. 119–30.

Strohm, Reinhard. '*Les Sauvages*, Music in Utopia, and the Decline of the Courtly Pastoral', *Il saggiatore musicale*, 11:1 (2004), 21–50.

Sullivan, Lester. 'Composers of Color in Nineteenth-Century New Orleans: The History behind the Music', *Black Music Research Journal*, 8:1 (1988), 51–82.

Sweeney, Fionnghuala, and Kate Marsh (eds). *Afromodernisms: Paris, Harlem and the Avant-Garde* (Edinburgh: Edinburgh University Press, 2013).

Tausig, Benjamin. 'Sound and Movement: Vernaculars of Sonic Dissent', *Social Text*, 36:3 (2018), 25–45.

Tawa, Nicholas E. *The Coming Age of American Art Music: New England's Classical Romanticists* (Westport: Greenwood Press, 1991).

Taylor, Diana. *The Archive and the Repertoire: Performing Cultural Memory in the Americas* (Durham, NC: Duke University Press, 2003).

Terni, Jennifer L. 'A Genre for Early Mass Culture: French Vaudeville and the City, 1830–1848', *Theatre Journal*, 58:2 (2006), 221–48.

Thompson, C. W. *French Romantic Travel Writing: Chateaubriand to Nerval* (Oxford: Oxford University Press, 2012).

Thompson, Shirley Elizabeth. *Exiles at Home: The Struggle to Become American in Creole New Orleans* (Cambridge, MA: Harvard University Press, 2009).

Tinker, Edward Larocque. *Les Écrits de langue française en Louisiane au XIX siècle* (Paris: Librairie Ancienne Honoré Champion, 1932).

Tocqueville, Alexis de. *Tocqueville on America after 1840: Letters and Other Writings*, ed. Aurelian Craiutu and Jeremy Jennings (Cambridge: Cambridge University Press, 2009).

Toinet, Paul. *Paul et Virginie: Répertoire bibliographique et iconographique* (Paris: G.-P. Maisonneuve et Larose, 1963).

Trouillot, Michel-Rolph. *Silencing the Past: Power and the Production of History* (Boston: Beacon, 1995).

Turo, Heather. '"Bug-Jargal" and Victor Hugo's Linguistic Commentary on Haitian Creole', *The Journal of the Midwest Modern Language Association*, 43:2 (Fall 2010), 169–85.

Vendrix, Philippe. 'L'Opéra comique sans rire', in *Die Opéra comique und ihr Einfluß auf das europäische Musiktheater im 19. Jahrhundert: Bericht über den internationalen Kongreß Frankfurt 1994*, ed. Herbert Schneider and Nicole Wild (Hildesheim: Olms, 1997), pp. 31–41.

Bibliography

Verhoeven, Tim. 'Shadow and Light: Louis-Xavier Eyma (1816–1876) and French Opinion of the United States during the Second Empire', *The International History Review*, 35:1 (2013), 143–61.

Vettermann, Gabi. 'In Search of Dance Creators' Biographies: The Life and Work of Henri Justamant', in *Les Choses Espagnoles: Research into the Hispanomania of Nineteenth-Century Dance*, ed. Claudia Jeschke, Gabi Vettermann, and Nicole Haitzinger (Munich: E-Podium, 2009), pp. 124–32.

Viano, Francesca Lidia. *Sentinel: The Unlikely Origins of the Statue of Liberty* (Cambridge, MA: Harvard University Press, 2018).

Wakefield, David. 'Chateaubriand's *Atala* as a Source of Inspiration in Nineteenth-Century Art', *The Burlington Magazine*, 120:898 (1978), 13–24.

Walker, Jennifer. *Sacred Sounds, Secular Spaces: Transformations of Catholicism in the Music of Third-Republic Paris* (New York: Oxford University Press, 2021).

Wallace-Sanders, Kimberly. *Mammy: A Century of Race, Gender, and Southern Memory* (Ann Arbor: University of Michigan Press, 2008).

Wall-Romana, Christophe. *Cinepoetry: Imaginary Cinemas in French Poetry* (New York: Fordham University Press, 2015).

Warren, Louis S. *Buffalo Bill's America: William Cody and the Wild West Show* (New York: Alfred A. Knopf, 2005).

Waters, Hazel. *Racism on the Victorian Stage: Representation of Slavery and the Black Character* (Cambridge: Cambridge University Press, 2007).

White, Kimberly. *Female Singers on the French Stage, 1830–1848* (Cambridge: Cambridge University Press, 2018).

——. 'Foreign Voices, Performing Frenchness: Jenny Colon and the 'French Plays' in London', in *London Voices, 1820–1840: Vocal Performers, Practices, Histories*, ed. Roger Parker and Susan Rutherford (Chicago: University of Chicago Press, 2019), pp. 179–200.

Williams, Gavin. 'Gunfire and London's Media Reality' in *Hearing the Crimean War: Wartime Sound and the Unmaking of Sense*, ed. Gavin Williams (Oxford: Oxford University Press, 2019), pp. 59–87.

Yee, Jennifer. *The Colonial Comedy: Imperialism in the French Realist Novel* (Oxford: Oxford University Press, 2016).

——. *Exotic Subversions in Nineteenth-Century French Fiction* (New York: Routledge, 2008).

Zaretsky, Robert. 'Playing Cowboys and Indians in the French Camargue', *Historical Reflections/Réflexions historiques*, 30:2 (Summer 2004), 151–77.

Unpublished Theses

Bentley, Charlotte. 'Resituating Transatlantic Opera: The Case of the Théâtre d'Orléans, New Orleans, 1819–1859' (unpublished PhD dissertation, University of Cambridge, 2017).

Bonin, Kathrine M. 'Reading the Literary Island: Colonial Narratives of France 1762–1832' (unpublished PhD dissertation, University of California, Berkeley, 2003).

Boudreaux, Peggy C. 'Music Publishing in New Orleans in the Nineteenth Century' (unpublished MA thesis, Louisiana State University, 1977).

Delne, Claudy. 'Le Bâillonnement de la Révolution Haïtienne dans l'imaginaire occidental à travers des textes fictionnels des dix-neuvième et vingtième siècles' (unpublished PhD dissertation, The City University of New York, 2013).

Di Grazia, Donna M. 'Concert Societies in Paris and their Choral Repertoires c.1828–1880' (unpublished PhD dissertation, Washington University, 1993).

Henson, Karen, 'Of Men, Women, and Others: Exotic Opera in Late Nineteenth-Century France' (unpublished DPhil thesis, University of Oxford, 1999).

Jensen, Eric. 'Gerard de Nerval and Opéra-Comique' (unpublished PhD dissertation, University of Rochester, 1982).

Kimball, Warren K. 'Northern Musical Culture in Antebellum New Orleans' (unpublished PhD dissertation, Louisiana State University, 2017).

Leary-Warsaw, Jacqueline. 'Nineteenth-Century French Art Song of New Orleans: A Repertoire Study' (unpublished PhD dissertation, Peabody Institute of the Johns Hopkins University, 2000).

Masterson, Michael L. 'Sounds of the Frontier: Music in Buffalo Bill's Wild West' (unpublished PhD dissertation, University of New Mexico, 1990).

McClellan, Michael. 'Battling over the Lyric Muse: Expressions of Revolution and Counterrevolution at the Théâtre Feydeau, 1789–1801' (2 vols, unpublished PhD dissertation, University of North Carolina at Chapel Hill, 1994).

Sabbatini, Tommaso. 'Music, the Market, and the Marvelous: Parisian Féerie and the Emergence of Mass Culture, 1864–1900' (unpublished PhD dissertation, University of Chicago, 2020).

Spencer, Helena Kopchick. 'The *Jardin des Femmes* as Scenic Convention in French Opera and Ballet' (unpublished PhD dissertation, University of Oregon, 2014).

Valint, Andrew R. 'Fighting for Recognition: The Role African-Americans Played in World Fairs' (unpublished MA thesis, Buffalo State College, State University of New York, 2011).

Wilson, Jennifer C. H. J. 'The Impact of French Opera in Nineteenth-Century New York: The New Orleans French Opera Company' (unpublished PhD dissertation, The City University of New York, 2015).

Web-Based Sources

Bernstein, Leonard. 'What is American Music?', 1 Feb. 1958. Television script published online at <https://leonardbernstein.com/lectures/television-scripts/young-peoples-concerts/what-is-american-music> [accessed 22 May 2021].

'Le Cake-Walk au Nouveau Cirque (1903) by Louis Lumière, Five Short Films of Cakewalk Dance Teams Performing, Including Rudy and Fredy Walker', *Songbook* <https://songbook1.wordpress.com/fx/si/african-american-musical-theater-1896-1926/rudy-and-fredy-walker/le-cake-walk-au-nouveau-cirque-1903-louis-lumiere-five-short-films/> [accessed 29 May 2019].

Cooper, Barbara T. 'De *L'Inventaire du planteur au Mousse* et *au Cabin boy*: Réorientation et recadrage d'une histoire antiesclavagiste d'É. Souvestre en pièce de théâtre', in 'Études de génétique théâtrale et littéraire', ed. Clara Santos and Natália Amarante, *Carnets*, 2:14 (2018), 1–13 <http://journals.openedition.org/carnets/8649>.

Fauser, Annegret. 'Sound, Music, War and Violence: Listening from the Archive', *Transposition: Musique et sciences sociales*, hors série 2 (2020), 'Sound, Music and Violence' <https://journals.openedition.org/transposition/4310>.

Heppler, Jason A., and Douglas Seefeldt. 'Buffalo Bill's Wild West and the Progressive Image of American Indians', in *Buffalo Bill Project* <buffalobillproject.unl.edu/research/showindians/> [accessed 2 Jan. 2020].

Lemmon, Alfred E. 'Eugène Chassaignac' <https://64parishes.org/entry/eugene-chassaignac> [accessed 1 Jan. 2021].

Morrison, Toni, Nobel Prize in Literature lecture, 7 Dec. 1993 <https://www.nobelprize.org/prizes/literature/1993/morrison/lecture/>.

Schwarz, Victoria, and Wilson Pruitt. 'History of Hymns: "Praise God, from Whom All Blessings Flow"' <https://www.umcdiscipleship.org/articles/history-of-hymns-praise-god-from-whom-all-blessings-flow>.

Index

Page numbers in bold type refer to illustrations, music examples, and their captions.

abolitionism/antislavery advocacy
  abolition of slavery 3, 16, 24, 33,
    108, 111–13, 131–2, 164, 177–8,
    233
  abolitionist authors, ideals, and
    works 3, 7, 15–21, 23, 24, 32,
    33, 40, 44–5, 49, 105, 108, 110,
    111–13, 121, 131–2, 133 n.93,
    144–5, 234
  gradualism 45, 108, 112–13, 139
  in France 19–21, 23–4, 27, 105, 108,
    111–13, 121, 124, 144–5, 234
    opposition to 23–4, 33, 44–5,
      111, 121, 139
  in the Anglosphere 105, 106–7,
    108, 121
  See also slavery – manumission,
    Société des Amis des Noirs,
    terms--*négrophile*
Académie Française 131
Acadia 151 n.7
Adam, Adolphe 57, 62, 63, 66, 82
Adonis, ou Le Bon Nègre (Béraud and
  de Rosny) 17–18, 23–33, 34
  n.65, 35, 44, 45, 47, 48,49
  Adonis 24, 25, 28, 29, 30, 32
  Biassou *see* Biassou, Georges
  Madame d'Hérouville 24, 29, 30, 32
  Monsieur d'Hérouville 24, 25, 29,
    30, 31, 32, 45
  Marinette 25, 28, 29
  Simon 25, 28, 29
  Zerbine 39, 32, 34 n.65

Adonis, ou Le Bon Nègre (Pique-
  nard) 17, 44
advertising 76, 239, 273–5, 287,
  290, 298
'Ah, quell giorno ognor rammen-
  to' 240
Aida 233
'Ainsi soit-il, Buffalo Bill!' 287–93,
  289, **294**, 295
Alabama 318
Albany, New York 220, 223
Alboize de Pujol, Jules-Édouard 166
*Alchimiste, ou Le Train de Plaisir
  pour la Californie, L'* 67
Algeria (Algiers) 89, 265 n.1, 266,
  300 n.9. *See also* Mlle/Mme
  Mariquita
*Almanach des Orphéonistes et des
  musiciens de l'avenir* 189
Alsace–Lorraine 166, 254–6, 259.
  See also Franco–Prussian War,
  Frédéric-Auguste Bartholdi
Apache 285
amateur performers
  audiences including 177
  instrumental 186. *See also* band
    music
  organizations for 255
  vocal 221–2, 234, 251–3. *See
    also* Harmonie des Batignolles,
    Orphéon de Paris
  See also dance – cakewalk – as
    social dance

360   *Index*

American Art Journal   210
American Register   247
American Revolution   1–3, 6, 7, 10, 15, 17, 21
  and France   21, 220, 222, 233, 239–41, 254–6
  depicted   17, 39–40, 49, 55
  remembered or commemorated   154, 221–3, 239–41, 247, 254–6, 268
Amérique, concept of   17, 18, 68 n.63, 150–1. *See also* colonies of France, Nouvelle France
André, John   221, 222
Anicet-Bourgeois, Auguste   18, 47–8, 72–3, 77, 81
Annam   266
Anvers   102 n.6
Arens, Franz Xavier   211
Argus des théâtres, L'   179
Arminius   238
Army of the Princes   218
Arnold, Benedict   221
  depicted   55
art, visual   200, 210, 245, 246–7, 254, 273, 302, 326–27
  as marker of class   117, 229, 314
  depicting Black subjects   24 n.32, 180, 298, 301,309
  depicting Indigenous subjects   2, 4, 52–3, 56, 57, 58, 91, **92**, 98, 277
  sheet music illustrations   139, 160, 167, 290–4, 309, 312, 318
  See also Statue of Liberty
art song   157–61, 165, 164–70, 208, 240
Artus, Amédée   53 n.8, 72, 79, 80, 88 n.101
Asia as exotic setting   56, 89, 217
Asgill, Charles   222
Astruc, Gabriel ("Surtac")   303, 312, 315
Atala   4, 99

Atala, ou Les Amours de deux sauvages dans le désert   4, 53 n.9, 54, 98, 218, 219, 224
Atala au tombeau   4, 53
Auber, Daniel-François-Esprit   62, 240, 250
Aubin, Alexandrine (Mlle)   **43**
'Ave Maria' (Gounod)   239, 240, 258 n.87
Aymard, Gustave   274
Aztecs, depicted   58–9

Bailey, James   280
Balleron, Louis   312–17
Ballet *see under* dance
Balleyguier, Delphin   209
Baltimore, Maryland   16 n.3, 198, 218, 220
Bamboula *see under* dances – bamboula, instruments – bamboula
Bamboula (Gottschalk)   172–3, 174, 180–7
Bananier, Le   179
band music
  American bands performing in France   270, 278–9, 282–3, 295, 297. *See also* John Philip Sousa, Wild West Company
  as 'ethnic' genre   250, 259, 261
  in France   200, 202, 238, 250, 251, 253
  in United States   152–3 n.15, 200–1, 254–5, 257, 259, 261. *See also* Francis or Frank Johnson
Barès, Basile   150
Barnum & Bailey Circus   280. *See also* James Bailey, P.T. Barnum
Barnum, P.T.   56, 205
Bartholdi, Frédéric-Auguste   234–5, 248, 250–1, 254, 256–7, 259, 262, 268
'Bartholdi March'   257
Bas-de-Cuir   54–5, 68, 69, 71

battle pieces 153–4. *See also symphonie militaire*
Baudelaire, Charles 56
Beaumercy, Roger de 322
Beaumont, Gustave de 105
Bedloe Island, New York 234, 254, 261. *See also* Statue of Liberty
Beethoven, Ludwig van 198, 197, 199, 201
Belgium 2 n.9, 77 n.81, 102 n.6
Belley, Jean-Baptiste 24 n.32
benefit concerts 63, 176, 188, 239–41, 247–8, 250–1
Bénie, Clair 60
Béraud, Louis-François-Guillaume 17, 24 n.31, 30
Berenson, Edward 235, 254
Berger, Rodolphe 303, 312, 315
Bergerat, Émile 286
Bergeret, Gaston 326
Berlin 197
Berlin, Irving 235
Berliner, Brett A. 312
Berlioz, Hector 201, 202
Bernstein, Leonard 196
Berté-St-Ange, E. 166–7
Berthier, J.-B.-C. 44
Berton, Henri-Montan 47
Berty, Lyse 314
Biassou, Georges 24, 175
    depicted 24, 25, **26**, 28, 30, 31, 32, 44, 46, 47, 48, 49
Biéville, Edmond de 78
Billardon de Sauvigny, Edme 17, 20, 21
Bird, Arthur 208
birdsong arias 109–10, 131–8
Bishop, Morris 219
"Black and White" 309, 317
blackface 8, 11, 18, 25, 62 n. 42, 131 n. 86, 143
    dancers' costumes 84 n.98
blackface minstrelsy 8, 11, 185 n.28, 280, 288, 290, 296, 318–19, 327 n. 43

Blackness and Black representation 33, 47, 48, 105, 121, 213, 307
Black dialect 26
Black musical style 174, 187 210, 211, 214, 285, 306, 308. *See also* dances – cakewalk
Black physicality 105, 121, 184, 277, 308, 312
Black savagery/*sauvagerie* 17, 28, 47
Black women and hypersexuality 121
    pathologization of Black/non-White culture 110–11 n.37, 121, 191, 277, 305–7, 309–12, 316, 327. *See also* sexuality
    See also stereotypes and stereotypical characters, *bon nègre, bonne négresse*, Creole – Black Creole, *créolité*, Tragic Mulatta, slavery
Black people 33, 46
Black leaders 16, 24, 25, 30, 32, 44, 46, 175. *See also* Georges Biassou, Dutty Boukman, Toussaint Louverture
Black musicians 150, 200–1, 212–13
Black slaves 17, 20, 25, 35, 42, 49
    See also nationalism in music, stereotypes, stereotypical characters
Blackmar, Armand 161
Blanc et le noir, Le 24
Blau, Edouard 239, 240
Bloch, Rosine 239, 240
Bocage, Henri 76
Bomberger, Douglas 207, 209
bon maître (stereotype) 17, 25, 30–2, 34–5, 49, 105–6, 138–9, 144
    in *Adonis, ou Le Bon Nègre* 30–2
    in *Le Planteur* 138–9, 144
    in *Paul et Virginie* 34–5

362   Index

bon nègre (stereotype)   7, 17, 25, 29–30, 34–5, 44, 46, 48, 49, 106, 307
  in *Adonis, ou Le Bon Nègre*   25, 27, 29–30
  in *Bug-Jargal*   44, 46
  in *Le Planteur*   122–4, 134, 138
  in *Paul et Virginie*   34–5
bonne maitresse (stereotype)   28–30, 32, **43**, 119, 134–5, 139
  in *Adonis, ou Le Bon Nègre*   28–30, 32
  in *Le Planteur*   138–9, 144
  in *Paul et Virginie*   34–5, **43**
bonne négresse (stereotype)   28–9, 34 n. 65, 44
  in *Zoflora*   34 n. 65, 44
Bonnaire, Félix   102, 103, 143
Bordeaux   77, 102 n.6, 213
Bossu, Le   50–3, 60, 68, 72–99
  as boulevard theatre   68, 71–2
  ballet in   50–3, 72–99, **84, 85, 87, 94, 97**
  exoticism in   81–99
  influences, literary   50, 53, 68, 72–3, 77 n.83. 82
  influences, operatic/balletic   56–65, 90–5
  revivals   50–3, 72–7
Boston, Massachusetts
  and French critical press   196, 212
  as musical center   197, 199, 200, 204
  dance style   317
  depicted   42, 102, 113
Boston Academy of Music   198
Boston Daily Globe   259, 260
Bougainville, Louis-Antoine de   62
Boukman, Dutty, depicted   43
Boulevard theatre   66–72, 283. See also *Le Bossu*
Bourgès, Paul   293
Bournonville, August   88
Bouveret, F.   303

Boyer, Georges   245
Brahms, Johannes   210, 212, 214
Brasseaux, Carl   151
Brazil   191, 224 n.19
  depicted   59, 63
Brézila, ou La Tribu des femmes   63
'Brise du Sud'   158–62, 165
Brissot, Jacques-Pierre   20, 21, 22, 49
Bristow, George Frederick   204, 207
Brittany   217
Broadway Panorama   201
Broekhoven, John   210–11
Broglie, Victor de   108
Brown, Jayna   296
Brown, Sterling A.   105
Bruckner, Anton   214
Brument-Colleville   210
Bruslé, Aimée *see* Aimée (Bruslé) Gottschalk
Brussels   91, 102 n.6, 214
Buck, Dudley   208
Buffalo Bill *see* William Frederick Cody
'Buffalo Bill Galop'   287
Buffalo Bill Wild West Cowboy Band
  function   286–7
  members and instrumentation   278–9
  reception   285–6
  repertoire   279–283
  See also Wild West Company
Buffalo Bill Wild West Songster   280
'Buffalo Bill's Polka–Marche'   287
Buffalo, New York   259
Bug-Jargal   4, 18, 44–7, 48
Burke, John M.   273
Burlesque   296, 314. *See also* dance – cakewalk

Café des Ambassadeurs   288
Café-concerts   288–9, 290, 295
Cajuns   151 n.7, 157 n.28
cakewalk *see under* dance
Cake Walk infernal, Le   301, 302

Cake Walk de salon 322
Calendini 90
California 194
  depicted 71
Canada 218
  Canadians in the Wild West Company 267, 272, 283
  Canadians depicted 67
  significance as former French colony 151 n.7, 225, 255
cannibalism depicted 63, 66, 71, 72. *See also Of Cannibals*
Canonge, Louis Placide 158, 159–60, 161–6
Carnival Scene, A 208
Carnot, Sadi 268
Caron, Eugène 239, 240
Cartier, Jacques 217
Cartier, Jules 167
Catlin, George 56, 58, 59 n.36, 99, cavalcades 250–1, 252
celebrity
  of Jenny Colon 112, 121–2, **123**, 130
  of Louis Moreau Gottschalk 177
  of Mlle/Mme Mariquita 50, 74, 75, 78, 90
censorship 16, 23–4, 46, 47 n.94, 164
Centennial Exhibition (1876) 283
Chadwick, George Whitefield 208, 209
Chalmette, Louisiana 152, 156
chansonette 34, 125, 138, 139, 288, 293
Charleston, South Carolina 16 n.3, 20
Chassaignac, Eugène 157–8, 161, 163, 164
Chateaubriand, François-René de 2, 4, 6, 53–4, 66, 69 n.64, 95, 99, 101, 188, 217–32
  in the wilderness 229–32
  on Indigenous people 223–9, 232

on memory of American Revolution 220–3
on nature and civilization 225–8
travels and travelogues 217–19, 232
Chauvet, Victor 131
Chenier, Marie-Joseph 22
Chicago, Illinois 211
Chicago Daily Tribune 262
Chocolat (Rafael Padilla) 297, 309
Chopin, Frédéric 172, 174, 186, 191–3
choral music 238
  Orphéonic societies 239–43, 245–6, 251–3, 255
  of Gounod 233, 235, 240–4, 256–7
  typical of public celebrations in United States 165, 255, 257–8, 261
chorus, role in opera 113, 116, 124–6, 130, 134–5, 143
Chouquet, Gustave 192, 193
'Chute des feuilles, La' 191
Cincinnati Enquirer 255
Cinq parties du mond, Les 250
circus
  in France 280, 286, 299, 314, 326
  in United States 199, 280
  See also Nouveau-Cirque, Wild West Company
Civil War (United States) 237, 258, 266, 296
  French attitudes toward 163, 233, 238
  French-speaking Americans during 157–64
class 114, 136–7, 184, 189, 193, 247
  and musical institutions
    in the United States 150, 198
    opera attendance 103, 144, 246
    Orphéon de Paris 246
    salons and soirées musicales 150, 309–12

364   *Index*

class (*cont'd*)
  in career of Louis Moreau
    Gottschalk   174, 177, 178, 184–5
  in the cakewalk   296, 300, 303–4,
    326
  shaped by print culture   197, 317,
    322
Cler, Albert   138
Clésinger, Auguste   250
Cleveland, Grover   259, 261, 262
clowning   286, 297. *See also* circus
Club Massiac   23, 33, 45
Cochinchina   266
Code noir, Le   7, 17, 103, 119, 298 n.4
Cody, William Frederick 'Buffalo
    Bill'   266, 268, 272, 278, 283
  depicted   272–5, 287–93, 295
Colon, Jenny   112, 121, 122, 130, 138
colonies of France   2, 3, 5, 7, 9, 11,
    16, 18, 34, 57, 108, 109, 110, 145,
    151, 173, 177, 178, 179, 193, 265,
    278, 327
  African   18, 46, 56, 89, 131 n.89,
    109, 110 n.35, 121 n.60, 179,
    266, 278 n.33, 300, 308, 312
  Asian   18, 34 n.65, 110, 266, 278
    n.33
  Caribbean   3, 5, 9, 11, 100 n.2, 105
    n.17, 108, 109, 173, 177, 178,
    179, 193, 266. *See also* Haiti
    (Saint-Domingue), Haitian
    Revolution (Saint-Domingue
    Revolution)
  compared to other empires   228,
    266 n.5. *See also* slavery
  musically depicted or evoked   25–
    9, 34–5, **36–7, 38–40,** 56, 179,
    180, 300–1, 308
  withdrawal from North Ameri-
    ca   100, 102, 145, 173–4, 178,
    220, 224–5. *See also* Amérique,
    East Indies, Louisiana, Mauritius,
    Nouvelle France, memory of
    former colonies, West Indies,
    Whiteness – and colonial projects

colonialism   3, 24, 59 n.35, 265
  colonial bonds of France and the
    United States   2, 6, 23
  colonialist exhibitions   5, 56, 184,
    265–6, 268
  colonialist narratives   4, 17, 18, 23,
    25, 33, 34, 53 n.9, 54, 59 n.35
  colonialist systems and
    codes   6–7, 15–17, 44–5, 48.
    See also slavery
colonists, French   26, 31 n.51, 33,
  depicted   35, 44, 45, 48 n. 98
  during and after Haitian Revolu-
    tion   18, 23, 25, 26, 31, 32, 33,
    45, 175, 178
Columbus, Christopher   275
Congo (Luongo)   266, 278 n.33, 300
    n.9
coon songs   280. *See also* blackface
    minstrelsy
comédie (theatrical genre)   302
Comédie Française   23, 239
Comettant, Oscar   193
Commune, Paris   241, 254
concert tours   207
  of conductors and orchestras   201,
    202, 204, 211
  of minstrel troupes   296
  of pianists   189, 191, 199
Congo, French   266, 278 n.33, 300
    n.9
Congo Square   28 n.40, 180
Constitution (United States)   258
Constitutionel, Le   108–9
Conterno, Giovanni E.   257
Cook, Will Marion   213
Cooper, James Fenimore   54–5, 57,
    63, 68, 69 n.63, 105 n. 17, 274,
    285. *See also Les Mohicans*
Copenhagen   88
Copland, Aaron   196
Cornu, Francis   40
Corsaire, Le   138, 177
Cortés, Hernán, depicted   58
costume   139 n.113, 246

Index 365

as element of spectacle 246, 251, 293, 314
for Black characters 103, 326–7
for Indigenous characters 62, **64**, **65**, 69, 73, 83, **84**, **85**, 86, **87**, 88, **92**, 95, **97**, 98
for White characters 130, 132, 138–9
Cottier, R. 240
cotton industry 163
couleur locale (local colour) 28, 47, 60, 67, 78, 109, 125, 126, 129, 134, 135, 143, 219
Courcy, Frédéric de 40
Creole (Créole) 2, 6, 7, 45, 103–4, 150, 157, 164, 166, 172, 173–4, 175, 176, 177, 178, 184, 194
 Black Creole (*le noir créole*) 2, 46, 112, 122, 124, 125, 126, 151 n.6, 174, 178, 179, 184, 185, 186, 188, 191, 193, 195
 Creole authors 166
 Creole composers 150, 164, 170, 180, 193. *See also* Louis Moreau Gottschalk
 Creole costume 25, 102, 103, 139
 Creole dialect 25–6, 46
 Creole, meaning of 7, 103–4, 150 n.4, 173–4
 Creole music 125, 139, 150, 157–8, 166, 180–81, 186–9, 191, 193, 194. *See also* Louis Moreau Gottschalk
 Creole nationalism 6 , 166, 170, 171
 Creole woman or girl (*femme créole*) 125 n. 69, 129, 131–2 n. 89, 139, 141, 143, 144
 créolité, depicted or musically evoked 25–7, 34–5, 60, 63 n.48, 102–9, 112, 122, 124, 125, 139–43, **140**, 178–9, 185
 perception within racial systems 'Blackness' of White Creoles 34, 125, 131, 178, 179, 188, 193

 self-identity in United States 157, 163, 165–6, 171, 172–3, 175–6
 White Creole 29, 34, 107 n. 25, 157, 163, 174, 178
Creole Songs from New Orleans in the Negro Dialect 185, 191
Creoles, Les 47
criticism 204, 210–11, 212–13, 244–6
 of ballet 57–8 n. 28, 73–4, 76–7, 89
 of Louis Moreau Gottschalk's performances in France 172–95
 of opera 101, 102, 109, 111–13, 126, 134, 138
 of U.S. music performed in France 209–10, 270–2
 of U.S. musical institutions 199, 200, 205, 207–8, 260–2
 See also names of news networks, productions, journals, and critics
Cuba 174, 185, 194, 297
Curto, Gregorio 165

dance
 ballet 33, 50–99
 ballet-pantomime 41, 73, 101 n.3, 105 n.17, 129 n.79, 131 n.86, 299
 Le Bossu 50–3, 72–99
 Danse d'école 28, 66, 81, 98
 exoticism in *danse d'école* 28, 68, 90, 95–9
 pas de deux 74, 79, 86, 88
 'Pas de Diane' 91, **93**, 95, 98 n. 114, 99
 pas de quatre 314
 pas sauvage (*pas Indien*) 74, 75, 78, 80, 81, 82–3, 86, 88–90
 role in theatre 22, 65, 72–3
 teaching and notating choreography 28, 50–2, 317

366   *Index*

dance (*cont'd*)
  bamboula   34 n.64, 180, 184,
    187, 213. *See also Bamboula*
    (Gottschalk), instruments –
    bamboula
  cakewalk
    as social dance in France   316–
      22
    civilizing project   308, 312–16
    cross-racial desire in   308–312
    history and historiogra-
      phy   296–7
    introduction to France   297–301
    pathologized   303–7
    subtypes of   301–3
  chica   47
  contradanza   185
  corporeality of dance   285, 287,
    300–1, 306, 309, 315
  cotillion   317
  exoticism in choreography   81–2,
    84, 88–9, 97–8
  foxtrot   297
  galop   68, 287
  gavotte   303, 314, 315
  Indigenous dances performed in
    France   277, 283
  minuet   303, 314
  polka   247, 287
  polonaise   208
  social dance   177, 200, 247, 296,
    302, 316–17, 322
  waltz   200, 279, 303, 306, 315, 317
  See also divertissements
dancing/entertaining slave (stereotype)   17, 28, 135, 296. *See also*
  dance – cakewalk
Darcours, Charles   208, 209–10
Darwinism   277, 316
David, Félicien   59, 109 n. 34, 202
De la démocratie en Amérique   1, 4,
  101, 267 n. 8
Debussy, Claude   300–1
Decamps, Alexandre-Gabriel   180

*Déclaration des droits de l'homme et
  du citoyen*   15
Declaration of Independence   15,
  258, 268 n.9
Dédé, Edmond   150, 213
Delacroix, Eugène   54, 56
Delan, Félicie   75
Delaunay, David   55, 56
Delord, Taxile   179
'Departure of the Volunteers,
  The'   156
Depew, Chauncey M.   261
Déroulède, Paul   240
Desforges, Louis   153
Deux Indes   18, 35. *See also* Indies,
  French
dialect, racialized   18, 25–6, 29, 34,
  46, 185
  in cakewalk lyrics   300, 302, 326
  in theater   25–6, 29, 34, 46
  See also language, blackface min-
    strelsy
Diana (Diane)
  depictions of Indigenous wom-
    en   91, 95, 98, 99
  'Pas de Diane'   91, **93**, 95, 98 n.114,
    99
Dijon   102 n.6
diplomacy and international relations   238
  between France and United
    States   233, 246–7, 253, 258,
    267–8
  role of art in   234, 254, 262, 269
    n.11
divertissement   22, 23 n. 27
  in ballet   50–99
  in *féeries*   73
Dix, John Adams   258
*Domestic Manners of the Ameri-
  cans*   101
domestic music   149–71, 187, 194,
  287
Donizetti, Gaetano   247

Douai 102
dress *see* costume
Du Contrat social 19–20
Dvořák, Antonín 196, 197, 211–14
Dwight, John Sullivan 197, 204

'Early Love' 208
East Indies *see under* Indies, French
Éclair, L' 102, 135
Eden-Théâtre 77
Edison, Thomas 208, 267, 269
Eiffel Tower 265, 266, 270, 277
Elks, Les 297, 300
England 176, 218. *See also* London
Enlightenment, legacy of 18–22, 24, 45, 217, 232
Ennery, Adolphe d' 67, 69
esclavage
as concept in Francophone discourse 15, 17, 19–23, 32–3, 40, 45–9
depiction in the theater and literature 17–18, 19–49
See also slavery
Esclavage des noirs, ou L'Heureux Naufrage 23–4
Espérance, L' 255–6
Espion, L' 39
Essai historique, politique, et moral sur les révolutions anciennes et modernes 220
Europe, L' 48
Evarts, William M. 261
Evenément, L' 243, 244
Evening Post 255
Éventail, L' 188, 189
exoticism 98, 187, 188–9, 293–5, 300
dramatic 18, 24, 25, 28, 34, 49, 50–2, 54, 57–60, 62–3, 67, 81–90, 95–99
literary 47, 218, 219, 220
markers, gestural 80–3, 86, 88–9, 91, 95, 98–9
markers, sonic 124–43, 178–91

typified as feminine 124–5, 188
Exposition Internationale des Industries Maritimes et Fluviales 238
Exposition Universelle (1878) 237, 248, 250, 251
Exposition Universelle (1889) 196–7, 207–9, 213–14, 267–70, 288
Exposition Universelle (1900) 297, 326–7

Fagan, Barney 280
'Fair America' 257, 258
faits historiques 275, 277
Fauchey, Paul 287
Fauconnet, Charles Prosper 159
Faure, Jean-Baptiste 239, 240
Faust (Gounod) 243
Favret, Mary 152, 170–1
féeries 66, 67, 73
Félix et Éléonore, ou Les Colons malheureux 44
femme sauvage (stereotype) **65,** 88–9, 90–9
Fernand Cortez, ou La Conquête du Mexique 58–9
Ferry, Jules 253
Fertel, Rien 166
'Festival Overture on the Star-Spangled Banner' 208
Féval, Paul 50, 68, 72, 73, 74, 77, 82
Figaro, Le 47, 208, 244, 262, 265, 314, 316
film 286, 301, 302
Fiorentino, P.-A. 177
'Fireman's Quadrille' 205, 206
Fjernt fra Danmark 88
Florida 220
folie-vaudeville 67
Foote, Arthur 208
Footit, George 297
Foster, Stephen 160
Foucher, Paul 39
Fourth of July celebrations
in France 251, 267–9
in United States 254

368   Index

France (de Rille)   255, 256
France musicale, La   192
Franco–Mexican War, Second   163
Franco–Prussian War   253, 254
    Siege of Paris commemorat-
        ed   241
    United States during   237, 238,
        254–6
*Franklin à Passy ou le bonhomme
    Richard*   39
Franklin, Benjamin   21–2, 22–3
    depicted   22, 40
French and Indian War *see* Seven
    Years' War
French Opera House (New
    Orleans)   149, 150
French Revolution   1, 3, 6, 22
    and François-René Chateaubri-
        and   217, 219, 220–5
    and American Revolution   1, 3, 6,
        49, 220, 268
    and U.S. Civil War   161–2
French-speakers in the United
    States   149–71, 255
    citizenship and self-identity   151,
        152, 154
    Louis Moreau Gottschalk as   174,
        176
    migration/exile   150, 159, 161
Fritzsche, Peter   223, 225
Fry, William Henry   202, 204, 207
Fuchs, M.   76

Gabon   278 n.33
Gallenberg, W. Robert   63
Garde Républicaine   238, 250
Gardel, Maximilien   22
Gardes Lafayette de la Nouvel-
    le-Orléans   167–70
Gautier, Théophile   56, 57–8, 218
Gazette, La   246
Génie du christianisme   220
Germania Musical Society   201
German-speaking world   199, 201,
    204, 211, 219, 253, 318, 322

impact on U.S. music   196, 201,
    204, 207, 209, 211, 255, 259
music in   211, 219, 318
political relationship with
    France   237, 238, 253, 262
Gershwin, George   196
Ghent   102 n.6
Gil Blas   207
Gilchrist, William Wallace   210
Gilmore, Patrick S.   259, 261
Giraudet, E.   322
Girodet, Anne-Louis   4, 54
Girondin   20
Giselle   82–3, 90, 95 n.113, 99
'Give Me Your Tired, Your Poor'
    (Berlin)   235
Glazer, Lee   160
'Golliwogg's Cake-Walk'   301
Gonaïves   175
Goodrich, A.J.   211
Gordon, Rae Beth   316
Gossec, François-Joseph   22
Gottschalk, Aimée (Bruslé)   175–6,
    177, 191
Gottschalk, Clara   177, 185, 191
Gottschalk, Edward   175
Gottschalk, Gaston   177
Gottschalk, Louis Moreau
    as Creole and as French   174–7,
        193–5
    in French press   172–95, 213, 270
    musical influences   174, 176–7
    poem about   189–90
Gouges, Olympe de   23, 25 n.36, 35
Gounod, Charles   233, 235, 239, 240,
    241, 244, 250, 254, 256–7
Governor's Island Band   257
Grand Hotel   247
grand opera   103, 114, 198, 202, 240,
    250, 277
Grand Théâtre (Le Havre)   76
Grand Théâtre (Nantes)   76
Grand Théâtre (Nimes)   76
Grand Théâtre (Paris)   188
Grand Théâtre (Toulon)   76

Grant, Ulysses S. 246
Grédelue, Émile 71,n. 66, 76
Greece 217
Greece, Ancient 22
  iconography and symbolism 91,
    92, 93, 95, **96**, 99, 165, 306
Grillet, M.L. 309
Grimm, Thomas 238
griot 47
Grisart, Charles 76
Gruytters, Henri de 287
Guadeloupe 105 n.17, 109, 266
Guerra, Antonio 57
Guerre de l'independence, ou L'Amérique en 1780, La 39, 55
Guiana, Dutch, depicted 59
Guiard, Émile 240, 251, 254
Guide musical, Le 214
Guillaume Tell 240, 287
Guinea, French 266
Gustave III, ou Le Bal masqué 62
Gymnase (Marseille) 77
gypsy, depicted 50, 75, 90, 315. *See also* Romani

'Hail, Columbia' 233, 240, 247, 250, 253, 255, 257, 258
Haiti (Saint-Domingue) 7, 16, 34, 173–4, 180
  Black culture of 25–8, 180
  depictions 4, 24–5, **26, 27**, 28–32, 34, 44–9, 131 n.86, 213
  emigrants to United States 109, 151
  Louis Moreau Gottschalk's ties to 151, 174, 175, 178, 184, 193, 194, 213
Haitian Revolution (Saint-Domingue Revolution) 3, 15–19, 44, 48, 49, 100, 184
  compared to French and American revolutions 15–16, 44, 47, 48, 49, 175
  first-hand accounts fictionalized 25, 31, 32–3, 45, 46

subsequent migration 151, 175–6
Halanzier, Olivier 239
Halévy, Fromental 41–2, 43, 59, 135, 247
Halévy, Léon 39, 57
Hamilton, Alexander, depicted 55
Hamlet (Ambrose) 245
Handel, George Frederick 283, 287
Harmonie des Batignolles 251–3
Harsanti, Doina Pasca 33
Hartford Daily Courant 259
Hartman, Saidiya 121
Haudenosaunee Confederacy 228
Haudenosaunee people 228
Hawai'ians 88
Haydn, Franz Joseph 198
Hayes, Rutherford B. 167
Helvétie 22. *See also* Liberté anthropomorphized
Hennecart, Maria 74, 76
Hermannsdenkmal 238
'Hero of New Orleans, The' 153–4
Herz, Henri 199
Heugel, J.L. 179
Histoire de la chanson populaire en France 285
Histoire philosophique et politique des établissements et du commerce des Européens dans les deux Indes, L' 18
Holt, Nora 213
Hopkinson, Joseph 240
Hotel Continental 267
Hudson River 220
Hugo, Victor 4, 18, 44–7, 56, 241
hunting, depicted 50, 52, 56, 60, 78–9, 91, 95
Hurons 68–9
Huss, Henry Holden 208
Husserl, Edmund 116

iconography *see* visual art
Île Bourbon 109, 110 n.35
'In Bygone Days' 208
'In the Mountains' 208

370   *Index*

Incendie du Cap, L' 44
Indianist music   211, 272. *See also*
  Antonín Dvořák, nationalism in
  music
Indies, French   18, 110
  East   15, 35, 110 n.35, 266, 278
    n.33
  West   15, 28, 33, 108, 110, 173. *See*
    also Haiti (Saint-Domingue)
Indigenous people   50 n.4, 51, 53,
  54, 56–9, 63, 88, 98–9, 228
  as metaphor for France   53, 56,
    224–5, 228, 232
  depicted   20 n.17, 49, 50 n.5, 52,
    56–71, 77, 80, 87–9, 98–9
    iconography   56, 58, **64, 65**, 69,
      70, 82–6, **84, 85, 87**, 90, **92**,
      94–5, **97**, 98
  Indigenous Americans/Native
    Americans   50 n.4, 53, 55, 57,
    58, 60, 66, 69, 71, 77, 95, 98
  Indigenous characters   54, 60, 62
    n.42, 63
  Indigenous physicality   84, 88, 94,
    226–7 228
  multiple groups conflated   87, 98,
    188–9
  music and dance of   58 n.30, 211,
    223, 270–2
    'Indian' dances and representa-
      tion in ballet   50–99; War
      dances   51 n.5, 56, 69, 88
    performed in France   55, 98, 283
  stereotypes about   52–7, 58–9, 65,
    66–9, 84, 88, 94, 226–7, 228
  treatment by U.S. government crit-
    icized by French   33, 57, 218,
    223–5, 227
  visiting France   55–6, 251 n.60,
    267, 272, 274, 277, 283
  See also costume – for Indigenous
    characters, names of individual
    Indigenous groups
instruments signifying racial or class
  difference   69, 135 n.99

Balafo/balafon   47
banjo   25, 133
bamboula   28, 180, 185. *See also*
  Bamboula (Gottschalk), dance
  – bamboula
barrel organ   304
calebasses   28
cymbals   187
guitar   47, 131–2
marimba   47
percussion generally   126, 187,
  285
tambour   47
tambourine   180, 184
tam-tam   47
Inuit   88
Inventaire du planteur, L'   106
Iowa people   56–7
Iroquois *see* Haudenosaunee Confederacy, Haudenosaunee people
Isle de France   18, 131–2 n.89
Italy   217
  musical influence of   103, 174,
    202, 209

Jackson, Andrew   152, 153, 156–7
Jaguarita, l'indienne   59–60, 95
Jamaica   175
Jardin Turc   202
Jazz   272, 297
Jennings, Lawrence C.   108
Jerusalem délivrée, La   28
Johnson, Francis (or Frank)   200–2
Jolie Fille de Gand, La   62, **96**
Jordan, Matthew   306
Journal d'un nègre à la Exposi-
  tion   326–7
Journal de Paris   111
Journal de voyage en Amérique   33
Journal des débats   212
Jouy, Étienne de   58
'Joyeusse, La'   287
Joyeux Nègres   297–9, 302, 308, 316
Jullien, Louis-Antoine   202–5, 206,
  207, 213

Justamant, Henri 50–53
  Le Bossu 60, 71, 72, 74, 75, 77–81,
    84, 85, 86, **87**, 88–90, 91, 95,
    97, 98–9. *See also under* dance
    – *pas sauvage*
  Giselle 82
  Jaguarita 59–60, **61**, 95
  'Pas de Diane' *see under* dance

Kanak 266, 278 n.33
Kansas River, depicted 67
Kearney, Nebraska, depicted 69
Ken, Thomas 258
Key, Susan 160
Kmen, Henry 153
Kongelige Teater, Det 88
Konzertstück, Op. 79 (von We-
    ber) 179
Kranz, Sen. 250
Kreutzer, Rodolphe 18, 33–42
  Paul et Virginie 18, 35, **36**–7,
    38–42, **43**

Laboulaye, Edouarde de 233–4,
    240, 244, 245
Lafayette, Gilbert du Motier, Mar-
    quis de
  and Franco-American identity 1,
    167, 170, 233, 254, 257
  commemorated 241, 254, 257
  depicted 21, 39, 49
Lafayette, Oscar de 233, 234
Lakota people 268
Lami, Eugène 62
Lang, Margaret Ruthven 208
language
  availability of literature in transla-
    tion 106, 178, 197, 219
  multilingualism 154, 156, 158,
    192, 199, 254, 255, 302, 318
  non-White languages conflated
    with one another 179, 187,
    189–90, 274
  politics of language in France 211,
    245, 253, 283, 290, 326

Provençal 274
  See also Blackness–Black dia-
    lect, Creole – Creole dialect,
    French-speakers in the United
    States, racialized terms
Laroche, Benjamin 106
Laroque, Philippe 153, 154, 156
Laurens, Henry, depicted 20, 21
Laurens, John, depicted 20
Laurent 50
Lavallée, Calixa 210
Lavastre, Jean-Baptiste 233, 245,
    254
Law, John 71
Le Havre 77, 276
Leatherstocking Tales 54, 68, 274
    n.27
Leclerc, Charles 47
Ledger (Philadelphia) 202
Lefaivre, Albert 258, 261
'Légende du Mancenilier, La' 189
Legrand, Augustin 38
Leipzig 197
Leleu, Hilaire 287
Lenschow, Carl 201
Leonora 202
Lesseps, Ferdinand de 253, 261
Letellier, Narcisse 176
Liberté
  anthropomorphized 22, 239,
    251, 262. *See also* Statue of
    Liberty
  as concept in Francophone dis-
    course 17, 18, 19–23, 36–48
  as concept related to America 1,
    3–4, 6, 15, 21–3, 233, 262
Liberté éclairant le monde, La (canta-
    ta) 233, 235, 240–4, 256–7
Liberté éclairant le monde, La
    (statue) *see* Statue of Liberty
Liberté, La 238, 251
Liebersohn, Henry 224
Lincoln, Abraham 234
Lincoln, Benjamin, depicted 20
Lind, Jenny 205

372 *Index*

Liorat, Armand 76
Lisle, Claude Joseph Rouget de 256.
　See also 'La Marseillaise'
Liszt, Franz 172, 186, 192, 202, 210
Llewellyn, New Jersey 269
Loango 266. *See also* Congo,
　French
local colour *see couleur locale*
*Loiz et constitutions des colonies
　françaises de l'Amérique sous le
　vent* 33
London 175, 197, 202
　U.S. music in 200, 274, 296
Lone Ranger, The 287
Lormier, Paul 62, **64, 65, 96**
Louis XVI 218, 222
Louisiana
　as French colony 7, 57, 110, 145,
　　151, 178, 180, 193, 225
　cultural identity 145, 151, 156,
　　165–6, 180, 225
　depicted 44, 72–3, 79, 88, 98,
　　100–45
　landscape and climate 129, 132,
　　133–4, 143, 158, 187
　political history 151, 157, 164
Louisiana Purchase 100, 151, 173
'Louisiana Quartet' 177–91. *See
　also Bamboula* (Gottschalk), *Le
　Bananier, Le Mancenillier, La
　Savane*
Louverture, Toussaint 1, 15, 24, **27**,
　44, 47, 175
　depicted 24, 44, 47, 48, 49
　White reactions to 44, 47, 48,
　　175–6
Lucrezia Borgia 247
Lussan-Borel 317
Lyon 102 n.6

Maas, Louis 210
Mabille, M. 74, 75, 77, 78
MacDowell, Edward 208
Madagascar 47, 110 n.35, 266
Madison Square 254

Madrid 90
Malaysia 266, 278 n.33
Maleden, Pierre 177
mammy (stereotype) 17, 131 n.86
　Black nannies in French drama 29–
　　30, 125–6, 130–1
　Sally, nurse in Gottschalk house-
　　hold 185, 194
Mancenellier, Le 179, 187, 189, 190–1
Mandeville, Louisiana 159, 160
Manon Lescaut (1830) 41, 62
Manon Lescaut (1856) 62, 101 n.3
Mante, Blanche 312–14
Mante, Louise 312–14
Māori 88
march 60, 153–4, 235, 257, 280,
　287
Marie Antoinette 222
*Marie, ou L'Esclavage aux États-
　Unis* 105
Mariquita, Mlle/Mme 50, 69 n.65,
　71, 74, 75–6, 78–81, 82–3, 86,
　89–90
Marmontel, Antoine Francois 179,
　191
'Marseillaise, La' 162 n.49, 255–6, 283
　association with Statue of
　　Liberty 240–50, 253, 257–60,
　　262
　quoted, imitated, and paro-
　　died 161–2, 163, 241, 242–3,
　　250
Marseille 77
Martineau, Harriet 106–7
Martinique 109, 266
Martyres aux arènes, Les 240, 241
Masonry 257
Massachusetts, depicted 102, 113,
　135
*Massacres de Saint-Domingue,
　Les* 18, 47
Matamoros 159
Mauritius (Isle de France) 18,
　131–2 n.89
Maximilian I of Mexico 163

McLane, Robert 267
Meignen, Leopold 201–2
Méliès, Georges 301–2
Mélingue, M. 50, 74
mélodie 161
melodrama 17, 24, 32, 47–8
Melpomene 208, 209
Mémoires d'outre-tombe 218, 220,
   222, 223–4, 224–5, 231
memory
  and construction of knowl-
     edge 99, 178, 223–4, 236
  and migration/exile 161, 205
  of former colonies 173–4, 219,
     220, 224–5
  wars and revolutions 153, 154,
     156, 160, 167–70, 221–4, 247
Mendelssohn, Felix 209, 210
Ménestrel, Le 59, 172, 179, 191–2,
   212
Menus-Plaisirs de l'année 248
Mercure de France 22
Merle, Jean-Toussaint 112
Messager franco-américain, Le 255,
   256
Mexico 156, 163
  depicted 67
  Mexicans in the Wild West Com-
     pany 267, 272, 283
  See also Second Franco–Mexican
     War, U.S.–Mexican War
Middle East 217, 278 n.33, 285
  depicted 57, 67, 90
Midwest region 210–11
migration 200–1, 243, 258, 275
  exile 218, 220, 225, 232, 254, 256
  French musicians abroad 198,
     202–4, 257
  role in U.S. music industry 197,
     204, 201, 210–11
  U.S. émigrés in Paris 211, 245,
     283
  See also French-speakers in the
     United States
'Milkmaid's Song' 208

Millevoye, Charles 191
Mills, Kerry 318
Milon, Louis 28
miscegenation 54, 116, 141, 176
  feared 46, 111–12, 176
  fetishised 125, 307
  positive depictions 59, 143–4,
     178, 308–9
  See also mûlatre fashionable
     (stereotype), Tragic Mulatta
     (stereotype), sexuality
Mississippi Company 72
Mississippi River 220
  depicted 50, 72–3, 75, 78, 79
Missouri River, depicted 67
Missouria, depicted 56, 67
Mistral, Frédéric 273–4
Moctezuma II, depicted 58
Modes, Les 314
Mohicans, Les 54, 55, 57–8, 63, **65**,
   66
Moldova 315
Moniteur universel, Le 23, 138
Monnais, Edouard 48, 126
Monpou, Hippolyte 44, 101, 113,
   115, 124–5, 133, 139
Montaigne, Michel de 223
Montpellier 102 n.6
'Moonlight' 208
Moreau de Saint-Méry, Médéric-
   Louis-Élie 7, 33
Moreau, François 20
Morgan, Elizabeth 153
Morton, Levi P. 253
Mosey, Phoebe Ann 275
Mozart, Wolfgang Amadeus 199
Müller, Hedwig 50 n.1
Muette de Portici, La 240, 250
mûlatre fashionable (stereo-
   type) 115 n.47, 318, 326–7
Musard, Philippe 200, 202
Musée de l'Indien 55, 57, 98
museums 55, 56, 58, 266–7, 277.
   See also Expositions Universelles,
   Wild West Company

374　*Index*

music education
　France a destination for　166, 177,
　　199–200, 202, 243
　of U.S. musicians　166, 176, 198–9,
　　212, 213, 243, 271, 279
Musical Fund Society of
　Philadelphia　198
*Musique, La: Gazette de la France
　musicale*　172–3, 180–1, 184–5
'My Gal Is a High-Born Lady'　280,
　293

Nantes　77
Napoléon I　24, 40, 202, 222
　and the Americas　16, 47, 48,
　　222–3
Napoléon III　163, 234
Natchez, Les　101, 220
Natchez people　220
　depicted　54, 218, 220
National Conservatory of Music
　(New York)　211, 213, 271
National, Le　106
nationalism in music
　Black and Indigenous music in U.S.
　　art music　210–13
　in France　207, 209–10, 270–1,
　　293–5
　in United States　210–11, 271–2
Native Americans *see* Indigenous
　people, names of individual
　groups
Navarre Regiment　218
Nazim, Gédéon　239
'Néali, ou La Traite des Noirs'　131
nègre généreux (stereotype)　29 n.45.
　See also bon nègre
'Nègre siffleur, Le'　318–19, 326–7
'Nègre blancs, Les'　312, 317
Nerval, Gerard de　218
Neue Zeitschrift für Musik　197
New England　275
New Hampshire　106
New Orleans, Louisiana　103,
　149–71

cultural influences on　28 n.40,
　151, 165, 166, 157–6, 178
depicted　41, 62
musical life of　28 n.40, 150, 158,
　180, 199
　Congo Square　28 n.40, 180
　French-born musicians in　155,
　　157–8
　Louis Moreau Gottschalk　174,
　　193, 194
　wars affecting　151–4, 155, 156,
　　157
New York　219, 220, 227
New York City　16 n.3, 211
　French musicians on and in　178,
　　189, 194, 196, 205, 244
　musical life of　198, 199, 204,
　　205–8, 296. *See also* New York
　　Philharmonic Society
New York Club　254
New York Herald　211
New York Philharmonic Socie-
　ty　196, 198–9, 204, 206, 213
New York Times　238, 255, 257, 259
New York World　259
news networks
　domestic　153, 166, 196, 199, 211,
　　246–7
　international　16, 163–4, 196–7
　　France–Germany　237
　　France–United States　202,
　　　204–5, 207, 238, 245, 258
　　United States–Germany　204,
　　　211, 237, 256
　　United States–United King-
　　　dom　202
　methods
　　correspondents　196, 198–9,
　　　202, 211, 245
　　wire reporting　202, 245 n.43,
　　　253 n.66, 260 n.102
　See also censorship, criticism, lan-
　　guage, publishers of music
Niagara Falls　220, 223, 226
Niederwalddenkmal　253

Index 375

Nimes 76
noble savage (stereotype) 2, 4, 5, 53, 95, 188
in Chateaubriand's writing 220, 224–8, 229–31
origins 2, 224 n.23
Noce de Chocolat, La 308
Nordrhein-Westfalen 238
Northwest Passage 218
nostalgia *see* memory
Noté, Jean 240
Notes of a Pianist 175–6, 177, 194–5
Nouveau Voyage dans les États-Unis 20, 21
Nouveau-Cirque 297, 301, 304, 308, 315, 316
Nouvelle France 4, 5, 6, 166, 173. *See also* Amérique, colonies of France, memory of former colonies
Nowell, Willis 208
Noyes, Edward 247

Oakley, Annie 275
Ochoa Gaultier, Ana Maria 237
ode-symphonie 202
Oedipus Tyrannus 208, 209
Of Cannibals 223–4
Offenbach, Jacques 244, 283, 287
Oglala 268
Ógle Šá 268
Ohio 255
'Ojalà' 208
Ojibwe 56
Old Hundredth (Old Hundred) 257–8, 261
Olympia Theatre 304, 306
Omaha, Nebraska 69
On the Prairies 210
Onondaga people 225, 227
Onondaga, Lake 227–8
opera *see* grand opera, opéra comique, names of productions and theatres

Opéra, Paris 28, 57–8, 66, 67, 247, 248
as national institution 238–9, 244–5
premieres at 22, 41, 44, 57, 62, 63
opéra comique 18, 33, 42, 43, 47, 62, 76, 102–3, 107, 122, 125, 143. *See also Le Planteur*, Théâtre de l'Opera-Comique
Opéra-National 59, 66
oratory 239–40, 244–5, 250, 253, 255, 256–8, 267–8, 282
orchestral music 179, 239
aesthetics of 200–2, 209–14, 239 n.27, 245
at Expositions Universelles 207–9, 270, 293
ensembles 197–207, 238, 270. *See also* names of individual orchestras
See also programmatic music
Orientalism 129, 180 n.23
Orphée aux enfers 244
Orphéon de Paris 241–3, 245–6, 255
Orphéon Français 239–41, 251–3
Orphéon, L' 245
Osage people 55–6
'Ou som souroucou' 191
Ouvrard, Eloi 288, 290, 292
Ozaï 62

Padilla, Rafael "Chocolat" 297, 309
Pahouin 266
Paine, John Knowles 208, 209
Palais du Trocadéro 270
Palais Garnier 233–4, 256. *See also* Opéra, Paris
Palianti, Louis 125, 138
pantomime 28, 35, 46, 69, 297, 299, 309, 314. *See also* dance – *ballet-pantomimes*

376   *Index*

Paris
 audiences and tastes in   55–6,
  66–8, 73–4, 179, 200, 251
 locations
  Arc de Triomphe   248
  Batignolles   251–3
  Bonne-Nouvelle   179
  Boulevard du Temple   89–90
  Champ de Mars   248, 267
  Champs-Elysées   289
  Esplanade des Invalides   265
  Île aux Cygnes   269
  Louvre   238
  Neuilly district   272
  Palais de l'Industrie   238
  Palais des Machines   269–70
  Palais Royal, depicted   73. *See*
   also Théâtre du Palais-Royal
  Parc Monceau   253
  Place de la Concorde   288
  Seine River   268
  Trocadéro   248, 265, 270
  Tuileries   304–5
  U.S. musicians in   150, 176–7, 194,
   196–7, 202, 273, 296
  See also names of performance
   venues
Paris Conservatoire   177
Passy, Hippolyte   108
patriotic songs
 'Maryland, My Maryland'   162
  n.49
 'Yankee Doodle'   154, 259, 283
 See also 'Hail, Columbia', 'La Mar-
  seillaise', 'The Star-Spangled
  Banner'
Paul et Virginie (Kreutzer)   18,
  33–41, **36–7, 38–41**, 45, 49
 Zabi   34 n.65, 35, **36–7, 38, 43**
Paul et Virginie (Le Sueur)   18
Paul et Virginie (Saint-Pierre)   18,
  33, 131–2 n.89
Pawnee people, depicted   69, 71
Pays de l'or, Le   71
peaux-rouges   74 n.75, 78, 275, 285

Pérès, Jeanne   298
Pérès, Nina   298
Perin, René   44
Perkins, Charles Callahan   200
Peru   194
 Peruvians depicted   67
Peterson, Clara Gottschalk   177,
  185, 191
Petit Journal, Le   238, 239, 283
petit-nègre see Blackness – Black
 dialect
Petits Cake-Walk, Les   308
Philadelphia, Pennsylvania   16 n.3,
  220
 depicted   119
 musical life of   200–1, 283
Phile, Philip   240. *See also* "Hail,
 Columbia"
Philippe, Edouard   239
Pianistes celebres, Les   191
piano music
 concert music   172, 177–91, 208,
  270. *See also* names of pianists
 domestic and popular con-
  texts   150, 178, 194, 287, 309,
  318–19, 322
Picquenard, J.B.   17, 34 n.65, 44
Pigault-Lebrun   24
Planté, Francis   179
Planteur, Le   43, 100–45
 and antislavery movement   108–
  13
 background and descrip-
  tion   100–8
 exoticism in   124–44
 revivals of   101–2
 tragic Mulatta trope in   113–24
'Poète mourant, Le'   191
Pohl, Richard   197
Poland   174, 287
Pons, Victor   240
Potter, Henry C.   261
Presse, La   48, 56, 187
Preston, Katherine   204
Prévost, Eugène   156, 159

Prière des naufragés, La 67
programs of concerts, reproduced 208, 240, 261, 284
programmatic music 201–2, 208,
  210
  merits debated 204
Progrès artistique, Le 209
promenade concerts 200–1, 205
Prosper (Auguste Lepoitevin de
  l'Égreville) 18, 47
provincial France, music in 74, 76,
  102, 239, 244
Prussia 237. *See also* Franco–Prussian War
Public Ledger, The 200, 201, 202
publishers of music
  in France 150, 270, 301–2, 318
  in the United States 150, 153 n.18,
    157, 161
  importation and piracy of 150,
    180 n.22, 270
  of cakewalks 301–2, 318
Pulitzer, Joseph 259

Quaker 4, 10, 21 n.19, 221, 223
'Quan' patate la cuite' 185
Quatre Parties du monde, Les 67
Quotidienne, La 112–3

race *see* Black people, Blackness,
  Creole, Indigenous people,
  racialized terms, stereotypes,
  Whiteness
racialized terms, discussed and
  defined 17 n.7, 34–5, 45, 49 n.4,
  100 n.1, 275, 298 n.4
  griffe 45
  mulâtre fashionable 115 n.47,
    318, 326–7
  nègre/négresse 17, 76, 23, 61,
    178–9, 307
  'Nègres *congos*, les' 46
  nègre généreux 29 n. 45
  négrillon 180, 297, 308
  négrophile 110–12

peaux-rouges 74 n.75, 78, 275,
  285
quadroon 106 n.20
sacatra 45
See also bon nègre, bonne négresse,
  Creole–Black Creole, White
  Creole, *créolité*, Tragic Mulatta
racism 32–3
radio 284
ragtime 279, 297, 299 n.7
Rameaux, Les 239, 240
Raynal, Guillaume Thomas 1, 18,
  24, 49
Reconstruction era (U.S.) 164–70,
  266
Red Shirt, Chief 268
Reid, Whitelaw 268
Reine de Chypre, La 247
religion 201, 217, 258
  and national identity 20, 239,
    257–61
  Jewish assimilation 175–6
  meanings of Christianity 68,
    95, 110 n.36, 176, 220, 230–2,
    275
  non-White 46, 57, 211
  paganism onstage 59, 63, 66,
    68, 78
  Quakers as models for France 21
    n.19, 221, 223
  religious ideas in secular mu-
    sic 113 n.43, 165, 289, 290,
    292–3, 307
  See also sacred music
Renaissance Louisianaise, La 165–
  6
René 218
Republique, La 250
reunion (réunion) of regions, na-
  tions 165, 251 n.59
'Reveil de la Louisiane, Le' 164–7
Revolutions *see* American Revolu-
  tion, Haitian Revolution, French
  Revolution
Revolutions of 1848 108, 201, 202

378   *Index*

Revolutionary Catechism   19
Revue de Paris, La   102
Revue et Gazette musicale de Paris   113, 200, 205–7
Revue musicale   198
Revue universelle   316
Rhine River   253
Rille, Laurent de   240, 241, 255, 256
Robinson Crusoé   71
Rochambeau, Jean Baptiste Donatien de Vimeur, comte de   21, 170
   depicted   39, 49
Rochefoucauld, Frédéric-Alexandre de la, duc de Liancourt   33
Rocky Mountains   275
Rococo et Modern Style   303, 312–15, 316
Roehr, C.M.   318
Rolling, Hubert   166
Roman Republic   22, 238
Romania   315
Romani   50 n.4, 315. *See also* gypsy
Romanze et polonaise, Op. 11 (Huss)   208
Roqueplan, Nestor   78, 90
Rose *fils*, George   303
Rosny, Joseph de   17
Rossini, Gioachino   240, 287
Rouen   77
Rounat, Charles de la   244
Rousseau, Jean-Jacques   2, 10, 19–20, 24, 49
Rousseil, Roselia   239, 240
Royal Theatre (Madrid)   90
Rubio, Judith   176
'Rufus das Pfeifgigerl'   318–19, 326–7

Sacre Cake-Walk, Le   303–6, 307, 308
sacred music   233, 239, 244, 270
   hymnody   235, 258, 260–1, 270
   of Black people   211, 213, 270
   See also religious ideas in secular music

Saint-Aubin, Alexandrine (Mlle)   **43**
Saint-Domingue *see* Haiti
Saint-Domingue Revolution *see* Haitian Revolution
Saint-Georges, Henri de   42, 101, 106–7, 111, 113, 124–5, 131, 135
Saint-Malo   217
Saint-Pierre, Jacques-Bernardin de   18, 33
Saintis, Armand   240, 241
Salle Favart   245
salons and soirées   150, 206
   and Louis Moreau Gottschalk   172, 180
   and the cakewalk   298, 306, 309–12, 316–18, 322 326
Salsbury, Nate   274
Salvador   262
San Francisco Chronicle   259
Sand, George   56, 218
sauvagerie   2, 5, 6, 17, 18, 46–7, 52–3, 56, 57 n.28, 61, 77–8, 88, 95–6, 118, 121
   in dramatic genres   52–3, 56–7, 60, 67–9, 72, 78, 95, 98
      Le Bossu   52, 72, 74, 78, 81–2, 84, 86, 88–9
   in instrumental music   180, 187
   in the cakewalk   303–4, 316
   literary   225
   See also noble savage
Sauvigny, Billardon de   17, 20
Sauvo, Francois   138
Savane, La   179, 187
scenery and décor of theatres   63 n.50, 132, 197, 200, 202, 245–6, 251, 277 n.32
Schoenefeld, Henry   210–11
Schumann, Robert   210
Scribe, Eugène   41–2, 60, 62, 105 n.17
'See, the Conquering Hero Comes'   283
Seine, Departement de la   239
Sémiramis   240

Senegal   121 n.60, 266, 278 n.33, 300 n.9
Seven Years' War   100, 151, 154
sexuality   91
hypersexualization
of Black women   47, 121, 129, 134, 141
of Indigenous people   59, 67, 82, 91, 95
plaçage   106 n.20, 141, 176
sexual violence
and slavery   105, 106, 107, 112, 114, 121, 129
as thrill and spectacle   112, 114, 121, 129
feared from Indigenous people   63, 68, 72, 295
feared from Black people   46, 47, 105
tropes in diverse musical genres   103, 288, 290, 298
See also miscegenation
sheet music   149–71, 257, 287, 290, 309, 312
iconography of   139, 160, 167, 290–4, 309, 312, 318
Siècle, Le   72, 138
Sioux   67, 285
Six Nations (Haudenosaunee)   67, 228
slavery   108, 217
and the cakewalk   269, 280, 322, 326
and Gottschalk family   175, 176
in French colonial territories   28, 31, 184, 190–1
depictions   15, 18, 23, 40–4
in United States, French attitudes towards   15, 19, 32–3, 40, 108–9, 213, 272
depictions   40–4, 102, 113–44
manumission   18, 33, 35, 38, 44, 45, 107, 119, 144
See also abolitionism, *esclavage*
Snaër, Samuel   150

Société des Amis des Noirs   18, 20, 110–11 n.37. *See also* racialized terms – *négrophile*
Société Française pour l'Abolition de l'Esclavage   108
Société Patriotique Alcase–Lorraine   255
Société Reconstituée des Fêtes de Versailles   250
Society in America   106–7
Soirées musicales *see* salons and soirées
'Soldat, Le'   240
Sommier, Francois Clément ('Henry Somm')   326–7
Soulié, Frédéric   47
soundscapes   235–7
noise as intrusion   225–8, 232, 286, 304
noisy concerts and music as noise   205, 207, 247, 286, 304
role in constructing ideas about foreign places   219–20, 223, 229–32, 234–5, 259–60
Sousa, John Philip   297, 300
South Dakota, depicted   283
'Southern Marseillaise'   162
Souvestre, Émile   106, 107
Spain   217
as exotic location in French theatre   67, 72, 90, 141
musical life of   90, 165, 298
spectacle   55, 184, 229, 277 n.32, 229
costume as aspect of   246, 251, 293, 314
exemplified in or with music   66–8, 69, 113–24, 200, 202, 267, 287, 295, 322–6
in United States   197–8, 205. *See also* scenery and theatrical decor
Spirit of the Times   202
Spontini, Gaspare   58
St. Thomas   175

Index

Stamaty, Camille 177
'Star-Spangled Banner, The' 257
  and 'La Marseillaise' 283
  performed in France 208, 238, 247, 257, 280–1, 283
Starvetta, Maude 208
Statue of Liberty
  and Lafayette memorial 254–6
  and other monumental art 234 n.5, 238, 250, 253, 254
  background of 233–7
  completion celebrated in Paris 251–3
  copy presented to France 268–9
  displayed at 1878 Exposition Universelle 248–50
  displayed at 'Les cinq parties du monde' 250–51
  Franco-American celebration (1875) 237–8
  inauguration 258–62
  Palais Garnier fundraiser (1876) 233, 239–46
  pedestal, fundraising for 256–8
  visit of Pres. Grant (1877) 246–7
stereotypes and stereotypical characters 33, 184, 212, 308. *See also bon maître, bon nègre*, dancing/entertaining slave, *femme sauvage*, mammy, *nègre genereux*, noble savage, *mûlatre fashionable*, Tragic Mulatta, vanishing Indian
Stewart, James M. 257, 258
Storrs, Richard R. 261
Stowe, Harriet Beecher 178
Strauss, Johann 247
Strauss, Richard 214
Stucken, Frank Van der 196, 207–8, 211, 213–14, 270
sublimity 220–1, 230–2
sugar industry 16, 111, 134, 173–4
'Sur les remparts' 240, 241
Surtac (Gabriel Astruc) 303, 312, 315

Sweeney, William F. 278, 281, 286
Switzerland 102 n.6
  as republican model 22, 240
Sylvania, Emma 208
Symphonie fantastique 201
Symphonie militaire 201–2
Symphony No. 9 (Dvořák) 197, 212–14

Tabarin 244
Taglioni, Filippo 63
Taglioni, Marie 57–8, n. 28, 62 n.42, 63
Tahiti 62
Taylor, Diana 236
Taylor, William Levi "Buck" 275
Taylor, Zachary 156–7
technology 266
  as civilizing force 225–6, 266, 267, 269, 308
  French associate with United States 177, 207–8, 225–6, 267, 275
  of communication 153 n.18, 267
  of travel 69, 259, 260, 262, 275
  See also news networks – methods
television 287
Tell, Guillaume 22, 240. *See also Guillaume Tell* (opera)
Tempest, The 208
Temps, Le 50, 212, 251
Texas 155, 275
Thalberg, Sigismond 172, 186, 192
Théâtre Belleville 77
Théâtre d'Orléans 149, 150, 156, 158, 159, 165
Théâtre de Genève 102 n.6
Théâtre de l'Ambigu-Comique 23, 25, 67
Théâtre de l'Odéon 39
Théâtre de l'Opéra-Comique 18, 35, 42, 47, 57, 62, 66, 67, 101, 143, 145, 245–6, 270
Théâtre de la Gaîté 39, 55, 66, 68, 69, 71, 74, 76, 77, 251

Théâtre de la Monnaie 90, 102 n.6
Théâtre de la Nation 20
Théâtre de la Porte-Saint-Martin 50,
  51, 52, 60, 66, 68, 69, 71, 72, 73,
  74, 77, 79, 86
Théâtre de Montmartre 77
Théâtre de Troyes 77
Théâtre des Batignolles 77
Théâtre des Fantaisies-Parisi-
  ennes 102
Théâtre des Variétés (Versailles) 65,
  66, 77
Théâtre du Châtelet 66, 71
Théâtre du Cirque Olympique 467
Théâtre du Palais Royal 40
Théâtre Français (Bordeaux) 77
Théâtre Français (Rouen) 77
Théâtre-Italien 233
Théâtre Lyrique 59, 66
Théâtre National 67
Théâtre-Tivoli 77
Thomas, Ambrose 245
Three Years in the United States 193
Thurber, Jeannette 211
Tiersot, Julien 285
Tinker, Edward Laroque 159
Tintamarre, Le 239
Tocqueville, Alexis de 101, 234
Toqueville, Hippolyte de 234
Tonkin 266
topic theory 82 n.93, 116–21
  hunt topics 50, 52–3, 60, 78,
    91–8, **92, 93, 96, 97**
  pastoral topics 52–3, 78, 79, 95,
    99, 109, 132
Toulon 77
Tour du monde en 80 jours 69, **70,**
  71
tragédie lyrique 22
Tragic Mulatta (stereotype) 7, 11,
  100 n.1, 104–6, 113–24, 139 n.
  113, 141 n. 118, 144
Traité de danse 317
travelogues 2, 3–4, 193, 218, 220

as source for fiction 106–7
depictions of race and slavery 2,
  19 n.11, 32–3, 53–4, 129. *See
  also Voyage en Amérique*
genre history 101, 218–19, 223,
  232
Treaty of Fontainebleau 151
Treaty of Ghent 152
Treni, Jennifer 305
*Triomphe de la République ou Le
  Camp de Grand Pré, Le* 22
Trollope, Frances 101
Troyes 77
Tupinambá people 224 n.19

U.S.–Mexican War 152, 154–6, 272
Ulbach, Louis 50, 74
Ultramontanism 258
Uncle Tom's Cabin 10, 178
Union Franco–Américaine 233,
  234, 239, 246, 251, 261
Union Square Park 254, 255
Univers illustré, L' 258

Valley Forge, Pennsylvania, depict-
  ed 21
vanishing Indian trope 54, 56 n.22,
  224–5
Vannoy 50
Varennes 218
*Vashington, ou La Liberté du Nou-
  veau Monde* 17, 20–2
vaudeville, 67, 295, 302, 303–8
  comédie-vaudeville 105 n.17
  folie-vaudeville 67
  vaudeville anecdotique 40
Verdi, Giuseppe 233
Verne, Jules 69, 71
Versailles 77, 250–1
Viano, Francesca 239
Victoria, Queen 274
Vienna 197, 315
Vietnam 266
Vieux Charlie 275

382   *Index*

virtuosity 59, 114, 192, 199, 245
  of Jenny Colon 109–10, 116 n.50,
    131–8
  of Louis Moreau Gottschalk 177,
    178, 181, 184–5, 186–7
  of Mlle Rozé, 98. *See also* celebrity
Vizentini, Albert 76
Volpatti, F. 309, 317
Voltaire 1, 19 n.13
Voyage en Amérique 218, 219,
  220–4, 5 226–31

Wagner, Richard 197, 209, 210,
  212–13
Walker, Frederick ('Freddy') 297–8,
  326
Walker, Ruth ('Rudy') 297–8, 329
Wall, Brunette 76
war 21, 47, 150–2, 202, 217–18,
  221, 247, 254, 255, 256, 277
  music of
    battle pieces 153–4, 201–2
    comique troupier 288 n.25
    cannon salvoes during musical
      events 234, 256, 259, 260, 262
    See also band music
  See also Civil War (United States),
    Franco–Prussian War, Second
    Franco–Mexican War, Seven
    Years' War, War of 1812
War of 1812 152–4, 156
Washburn, Elihu B. 233
Washington, George 167, 222–3,
  241, 257
  depicted 20–1, 39, 49, 55
Waters, Hazel 124

Weber, Carl Maria von 179, 209
West Indies *see* Indies, French
'Where the Lindens Bloom' 208
'Whistling Rufus' 318–19, 326–7
Whiteness 174
  and colonial projects 178, 212,
    275, 277, 312
  supported or threatened by mu-
    sical genres 102–3, 191–4,
    245–6, 280, 299–300, 306
  See also Blackness, Creole –
    créolité
Wild West Company 266, 272,
  277–8, 285, 293, 295
  musical repertoire of 278, 288
  reception in France 265–7,
    272–7, 283, 287–93
Wilder, Victor 207, 209
Willis, Richard Storrs 204
World Monument 254
World War I 272
world's fairs *see* Centennial Exhibition (1876), Exposition Internationale des Industries Maritimes
  et Fluviales, Exposition Universelle (1878, 1889, 1900)
Wyandot people *see* Hurons

Yorktown, Virginia 21

Zimmerman, Pierre 177
Zip Coon *see mûlatre fashionable*
  (stereotype)
Zoflora ou La Bonne Négresse 43
zoos, human 55–6, 121 n.60, 277,
  278 n.33

Music in Society and Culture
Volumes already published

History in Mighty Sounds:
Musical Constructions of German National Identity, 1848–1914
Barbara Eichner

Music and Ultra-Modernism in France: A Fragile Consensus, 1913–1939
Barbara L. Kelly

The Idea of Art Music in a Commercial World, 1800–1930
Edited by Christina Bashford and Roberta Montemorra Marvin

Nation and Classical Music: From Handel to Copland
Matthew Riley and Anthony D. Smith

Musical Debate and Political Culture in France, 1700–1830
R. J. Arnold

Performing Propaganda:
Musical Life and Culture in Paris during the First World War
Rachel Moore

Musical Journeys:
Performing Migration in Twentieth-Century Music
Florian Scheding

Béla Bartók in Italy:
The Politics of Myth-Making
Nicolò Palazzetti

The Creative Labor of Music Patronage in Interwar France
Louis K. Epstein